# GEORGETTE HEYER:
## A Critical Retrospective

# GEORGETTE HEYER:
## A Critical Retrospective

Mary Fahnestock-Thomas

PrinnyWorld Press

**Publisher's Cataloging-in-Publication**
*(Provided by Quality Books, Inc.)*


Fahnestock-Thomas, Mary.
   Georgette Heyer: a critical retrospective / Mary Fahnestock-
Thomas -- 1st ed.
      p. cm.
   Includes bibliographical references and index.
   LCCN: 00-110370
   ISBN: 0-9668005-3-2

   1. Heyer, Georgette, 1902-1974—Criticism and interpretation.
2. English fiction—20th century—Book reviews.  I. Title.

PR6015.E795F34 2001                    823'.912
                                        QBI00-1084


First printing, 2001.
For information on this or other PrinnyWorld Press titles, contact:

PrinnyWorld Press
P. O. Box 248
Saraland, AL 36571
http://www.prinnyworld.com

For my parents,
Jeanne Winter Van Pelt Fahnestock (1920-1989),
who introduced me to Georgette Heyer,
and
George Reeder Fahnestock (1914-1988),
who never really understood Heyer,
but certainly understood laughter.

## PUBLISHER'S NOTE

Except for the Hagemann article, which was originally annotated parenthetically within the text, all footnotes have been reprinted from the original sources and renumbered for clarity and continuity. Ms. Fahnestock-Thomas's annotations are designated by brackets.

Every effort has been made to obtain permission to use copyrighted material—no small feat in a work of this sort, where many of the publications cited are long out of print and the authors deceased. However, should any contributor find his or her work included here without consent, the publisher would welcome the opportunity to rectify the omission.

# *Table of Contents*

ix

xi

# Acknowledgements

*Arabella* book review by John Hay © Commonweal Foundation.

Mary Shen Barnidge's review of Lifeline Theatre's adaptation of *Cotillion* previously published in *Windy City Times*. Reprinted with permission.

Mary Shen Barnidge's review of Lifeline Theatre's adaptation of *The Talisman Ring* previously published in *The Chicago Reader*. Reprinted with permission.

*Becoming a Heroine*, by Rachel Brownstein. Copyright © 1982 by Rachel M. Brownstein. Used by permission of Viking Penguin, a division of Penguin Putnam Inc.

*Behold, Here's Poison* audio review from *Wilson Library Bulletin*. Copyright © 1993. Reprinted with permission of The H. W. Wilson Company.

All *Best Sellers* materials © *Best Sellers*, University of Scranton.

*A Book of Prefaces to 50 Classics of Crime Fiction, 1900-1950.* © 1976 by Jacques Barzun and Wendell Hertig. Reproduced by permission of Taylor & Francis, Inc./Routledge, Inc., http://www.routledge-ny.com.

*A Catalogue of Crime*, by Jacques Barzun and Wendell Hertig Taylor. Copyright © 1971 by Jacques Barzun and Wendell Hertig Taylor. Reprinted by permission of HarperCollins Publishers, Inc.

Cover photo used by permission of Sir Richard Rougier.

"Cross-Dressing in Wartime: Georgette Heyer's *The Corinthian* in Its 1940 Context," in *War and Culture: Social Change and Changing Experience in World War Two*, Pat Kirkham and David Thoms, eds., © Lawrence and Wishart, London 1995.

# *Introduction*

My mother was a voracious and omnivorous reader of both fiction and non-, to the extent that she not infrequently astonished my more scientific and systematic father with her unsuspected knowledge in fields he tacitly regarded as his own.  But she always returned to Georgette Heyer, whose novels she often shared with my younger sisters, calling them—with a twinkle in her eye—"high-class trash."  I, however, was In Literature and did not read trash, lowering myself no nearer, in fact, than Dorothy L. Sayers's murder mysteries, which challenged my ability to recognize literary quotations and even required that I resurrect my high-school Latin.  Politely inspecting a well-thumbed paperback displaying a very 1950s-looking girl in a long pink dress on a lavender dustjacket, I asked what kind of novels Georgette Heyer (pronounced "higher?" "hayer?" "hair?") wrote.  "Oh, mostly Regency romances," was the reply, and I winced inwardly at the vision of my perhaps somewhat eccentric, but certainly bright, discriminating, even feminist mom betraying herself at the drugstore checkout counter.

Then came yet another New Year's Eve when my dissertation on Jane Austen in German-speaking Europe *still* was not finished and even *Pride and Prejudice* had lost its ability to give me pleasure.  As I retired early and only too gladly to my bed, I picked up *The Nonesuch* with no expectation of reading beyond the first page or two. . .

By breakfast I had learned two things about myself:  first, that even I could stay up all night reading a book—something that had never happened to me before; and second, that, after all, I still had the capacity to laugh out loud at the printed word.

That was almost twenty years ago, and Georgette Heyer has continued to rescue me periodically from a flagging sense of humor and perspective; and I now know that I am far from alone.  More than one

1

person included in this collection remarks that since Jane Austen wrote only six novels, one must eventually turn elsewhere for a similar experience in reading, and Georgette Heyer comes closest to filling the bill. She in turn, however, wrote only fifty-six novels (and one volume of stories), and although their wealth of detail and conversational nuance makes them eminently re-readable, one begins to wish she could have lived and written forever.

This collection is my attempt to extend my experience of Georgette Heyer, and to express my deep gratitude for the very real role her books play in my life. The collecting has brought me much pleasure, not least because almost every piece raises my blood pressure a little, eliciting a surprisingly strong positive or negative reaction. In the process, I have been reminded that, while we are not all alike and do not all love the same things, each of us gains strength and clarity from what we do love, and the strength and clarity bring us together after all in the long run. So I do not propose to talk much about the material included here beyond establishing what, where, why, and how; let the reader read and revel in his or her own reactions and responses.

This collection is not intended as a scholarly effort. Indeed, some maintain that Georgette Heyer does not merit scholarly attention. The material here shows that she has nevertheless received it more than once, and with varying conclusions; but my intention is simply to present what I have found for those who, like myself, enjoy Georgette Heyer and believe that the pure pleasure her works have given us is worth far more than any scholarly seal of approval.

*Mary Fahnestock-Thomas*

# *I. Her short published pieces*

Georgette Heyer has always been best known for her 56 novels, but she did have a few other publications as well, namely three separate stories, in 1922, 1936, and 1939; a 1929 article on her acquaintance with rhinos in Africa; two articles on literary topics in 1954; and a volume of stories in 1960.

"A Proposal to Cicely" (1922) appeared in *The Happy Magazine* between her first and second novels. It has a contemporary setting, like her twelve mysteries and the four novels she later suppressed, and is reminiscent of Oscar Wilde or Noel Coward. In some elements it also presages some of the sixteen novels mentioned, perhaps most notably in the presence of a bull terrier named Bill.

"Runaway Match" first appeared in *Woman's Journal* in April 1936, but was more recently chosen for reprinting in *The Oxford Book of Historical Stories* in 1994 with a descriptive blurb acknowledging that, while Georgette Heyer's name was primarily associated with the "forsooth and furbelows" of historical romance, she was nevertheless "a deliberately, and seriously, comic novelist."

"Pursuit" (1939) appeared in the same year as Georgette Heyer's twenty-sixth novel, hence almost halfway through her publishing career, and, like most of her novels, is set in Regency England. It reappeared in a considerably altered version as "A Clandestine Affair" in 1960 in her volume *Pistols for Two and Other Stories*, but it was first included in—and perhaps written expressly for—*The Queen's Book of the Red Cross*. Among the other contributors are A. E. W. Mason with a story, John Masefield and T. S. Eliot with poems, A. A. Milne with a "duologue," E. M. Delafield and Daphne du Maurier with stories, C. Day Lewis with a new translation from Virgil, Mary Thomas with a practical essay on knitting for and in the army, and Edmund Dulac and Rex

Whistler. It also contains a message from the Queen, printed on Buckingham Palace letterhead and in her own script. The publisher, Hodder and Stoughton, expresses gratitude "to the authors and artists whose kindness and ready co-operation in many matters of detail have alone made possible the production of [this book] within two months of its conception."

The one piece Georgette Heyer published which has nothing at all to do with literature was "The Horned Beast of Africa," which appeared in *The Sphere* in 1929. It was apparently occasioned by the fact that during Ronald Rougier's two years in Tanganyika as a mining engineer, he shot a rhinoceros with a horn unique in both size and placement. I am unaware of any other reference in Georgette Heyer's writing to her experience in Africa or Macedonia with her husband during the late 1920s, though she was obviously writing novels all the while. This extended absence from England may account for the one or two inaccuracies in detail detected in those novels.

Her two other essays, "Books About the Brontës" and "How to Be a Literary Critic" (1954), appeared in *Punch.* I personally find them surprisingly inferior in style and wit to her novels and stories, almost as if she felt constrained outside the realm created by her imagination, where she could express herself freely but covertly in the guise of so many different characters and leave the reader to "sort her out." This impression seems consistent with her determination to remain a "very private person," and suggests that she was, indeed, most comfortable in the "private world" she created.

## A Proposal to Cicely

(short story published in *The Happy Magazine*,
4 September 1922, pp. 341-46)

Cicely hurled a cushion across the room.

"*That's* how I feel!" she said, and glared at her first-cousin once removed, Richard Spalding.

"Good Lord!" he remarked, with a proper amount of sympathy in his lazy voice.

"And you sit there—idling about in my room—laughing at me! I quite hate you, Richard!"

"Oh, I say!" he expostulated, "I wasn't laughing—honour bright!"

Cicely looked scornful.

"I'm absolutely sick of it all. Dead sick of it." Cicely nodded so vigorously that her brown, bobbed curls seemed to jump. "I never want to go to another dance as long as I live."

"That's bad," said Spalding respectfully. "What's brought on this sense of repletion?"

"Everything. I've been trotted round till I want to scream! I feel like doing something desperate."

At that Spalding dragged himself upright and threw away his half-smoked cigarette.

"Oh, splended, Cis! I hoped that if I waited long enough you'd melt. When shall it be? Be a sport, now, and—"

Cicely covered her ears with her hands.

"No, no, no! I don't want to do anything as desperate as that!"

Richard sank back again.

"Thought it was too good to be true." He pulled a leather diary from his waistcoat pocket and proceeded, gloomily, to make an entry.

"What's that?" asked Cicely.

"Diary."

"But what are you writing?"

" 'Friday. Proposed to Cicely. Refused.' "

In spite of herself Cicely giggled.

"Dicky, you *are* idiotic! When will you give it up?"

5

"When we're married."

"We're not going to be!" Cicely's chin went up defiantly.

"You can't possibly tell. You never know what you may come to," said Spalding cheerfully.

"I'll never come to that! And now we've got on to that subject I may as well tell you, Richard, that that's another of the things I am fed up with. You ask me to marry you every day of the week, and I'm—"

"No, I don't!" Spalding was righteously indignant. "I've only asked you three times this week and three and a half last week. It's down in the book, if you want to verify it."

"Can't you be serious for one moment? That's one of the things I hate about you. You're too beastly flippant! You don't *do* anything. My husband'll have to be a worker!"

"He will be," murmured Richard.

Cicely disregarded him.

"I know you think you do a lot—standing for Parliament, and—and all that sort of thing—but you're just—flabby!"

Richard, an athlete and an amateur boxer, blew another cloud of smoke.

"Have you ever done a day's work—hard, manual work—in your life?" demanded Cicely.

"The complete park-orator. Four years in the trenches, that's all."

Cicely was slightly mollified.

"I don't count that," she said.

"No, I didn't think you would. What next ?"

"You're too civilised. Too drawing-roomified. I'd want to feel that I could rely on my husband—not just that he'd be a great success at any party I took him to. All you think about is clothes and racing and whether your tie's on straight. It's not good enough for me."

"In five minutes' time I think I shall propose to you again," he said. "I'm sorry you're so sick of everything."

"I've found a remedy," said Cicely. "I am going into seclusion."

"What? Into a convent?"

"No, silly. I am going into the country. I've taken a cottage."

"Cottage? You? D'you mean to say Uncle Jim's mad enough to let you go off on your own?"

"Daddy knows that I am perfectly capable of looking after myself, thank you."

"Where is he?" demanded Richard, preparing to get up.

"He's out. Besides, it's nothing to do with you. As a matter of fact, I'm not going by myself."

Spalding looked slightly relieved.

"I'm going with a great friend of mine, Maisie Duncannon."

"What, that fat, stolid girl who's been hanging round here lately?"

"Y—es. That's one way of describing her. Are you satisfied?"

"No, I'm not."

Cicely reached out her hand to stroke her diminutive Pekinese. "Chu-Chu-San is going, of course."

"That puts quite a different complexion on it," he said. "He'll look nice in the country. Stir the villagers up a bit."

"He's a lot pluckier than your rotten bull-terrier!" said Cicely fiercely.

Spalding brightened.

"I say, will you take Bill? Do, Cis! I'd feel a lot happier about you if you'd got a decent sort of guard!"

"Chu-Chu *is* a good guard!"

"Oh, rather!" said Richard hastily. "But you must admit, he's a bit small, what? Take old Bill—please! I've been wanting to get him out of town for some time."

Cicely hesitated. She knew that the last statement was entirely without truth, but she reflected that Bill would bring with him a certain sense of security.

"He'd miss you," she said, uncertainly.

"Not a bit of it. Besides—" Richard checked himself. "Do take him, old girl!"

"It's awfully nice of you," Cicely thanked him. "If you think it 'ud do him good—"

"I do, most decidedly. By the way, where is this cottage?"

"Bly—I'm not going to tell you! No one's going to know 'cept Daddy, and he's promised not to tell a soul."

7

"Bly. I'll remember that."

"You'll never find it!"

Richard recognised the challenging note.

"Like to have a bet on it? An even bob?"

"I don't mind. *My* money's safe."

Richard smiled, and made a note in his pocket-book.

"Don't you count your chickens before they're hatched," he said.

The pony trotted down the village street in a leisurely, abstracted way, paying no heed to his mistress's voice. The excited barking of Chu-Chu-San he took to be an encouragement to him to proceed. He ambled on.

"Whoa!" said Cicely, sharply. She tugged at the reins. "Whoa!" she repeated, more as a request. The pony still ambled on. "Oh, please, whoa!" begged Cicely. "Timothy *dear!*"

Timothy waggled one ear to show that he was attending to her. Chu-Chu-San yapped again and he waggled the other, accelerating his pace.

"Shut up, Chu-Chu! Whoa, you! *Stop!*"

Farther down the street a man stood, watching the pony advance. He was dressed in rough tweeds and riding-breeches with stout leather gaiters, and he carried a short riding-crop. He observed Cicely's struggles without a smile. When the trap drew alongside he stepped forward and caught the rein. Timothy halted obediently and looked round.

"Oh, thank you!" sighed Cicely. "I don't know what I should have done if you hadn't stopped him. He's frightfully pig-headed. It takes ages to make him start, and when once he's got going he simply won't stop—oh, no, Bill, *don't* go and fight that dog, *please!*" She dropped the reins and hauled the departing bull-terrier back into the seat.

Her rescuer half-raised his cap.

"Glad to be of use. Dan Brown's pony, I think?"

"Yes," nodded Cicely. "But I'd no idea how tiresome he was, or I'd never have hired him." She smiled, and ran her eyes over him appraisingly.

He was fairly tall, and thick-set, with very broad shoulders and a

8

tanned face. Quite good-looking, she decided, and with a wonderfully square chin. Dogged and purposeful. And a grim mouth, too. Blue eyes that looked straight at you—almost steely. Cicely felt quite thrilled.

Under her frank scrutiny the man had flushed a little, but his eyes held hers unwaveringly. Cicely was unabashed.

"Well, thanks very much," she said. "And if you wouldn't mind turning us round I might get Timothy to walk back to the butcher's."

For the first time a hint of a smile crossed his face.

"I'll lead him to the butcher's if you like."

"Thanks awfully," she said.

For a few minutes they proceeded in silence, while Cicely studied the back of the man's head. Then he looked over his shoulder.

"I reckon you're the girl who's taken Miss Fletcher's cottage?" he said.

Cicely nodded. "Yes. Do you live near?"

"Mortby Farm."

"Do you really? Why, that's just at the back of our cottage! Do come in and see us some time! And, oh, I should like to go over your farm. George—that's the gardener, you know—says you've got the sweetest little pigs. Are you Mr. Talbot?"

"Fred Talbot. You're Miss Duncannon, I daresay?"

"No, that's my friend. I'm Cicely Carruthers."

"Oh!" said Talbot, and relapsed into silence. He spoke no more until they came to the butcher's shop. Then he released the pony's rein, and again touched his cap.

"You'll be all right now. Mean what you said about my coming in to see you?"

"Oh, rather!" said Cicely. She descended gingerly from the trap. Talbot made no effort to help her, but watched her with an amused air. "Come in to tea this afternoon. We're fearfully bored. An' then you can take us over your farm."

She received a shock.

"Can't manage it this afternoon, I'm afraid. I'm busy. Can I drop in to-morrow if I have time?"

"Oh, certainly," said Cicely, not too pleased at this cavalier treatment.

9

"Whenever you like. And thanks so much for helping me with Timothy. Good-bye!" She extended a slim, gauntleted hand. It was crushed in a grip that made her wince.

"Not at all," said Talbot. "Pleasure. Good-bye."

Half-an-hour later Cicely walked into the living-room of her cottage, and nodded briskly at Maisie Duncannon, who was flipping over the pages of a novel.

"You missed something by not coming with me, Maisie," she announced.

"Mr. Spalding hasn't turned up, has he?" inquired Maisie, a sudden gleam of interest in her eye.

Cicely blushed ever so faintly.

" 'Course not. He won't either, thank goodness! I've been talking to an aborigine."

"Oh!" yawned Maisie, and returned to her book.

Cicely rather wondered whether Talbot would come at all, but he did, and stayed for over an hour. Maisie objected strongly to him, but then, Cicely reflected, Maisie was in the mood to object to anything. She was already "bored stiff" with the country. So was Cicely, but she would not admit it.

For a fortnight it had been glorious. They had gloated over the quaint old village and told one another that they could live here content for months. At the end of the next week the simple life had begun to pall on them. There was no tennis and no society. The atmosphere began to be rather tense between the girls.

So Cicely welcomed the diversion in the shape of Fred Talbot. Maisie complained that he brought mud into the house. Cicely told her that she needn't speak of Talbot as though he were a dog. Maisie retorted that that was just what he was—a shaggy, uncouth, sheepdog.

As Talbot came more and more frequently to Rose Cottage, Maisie, to show her disgust, retired either to her room or to the neighbouring woods.

So engrossed was Cicely in Talbot's farm that it never occurred to her that she was encouraging Talbot to fall in love with her. She was not at all flirtatious, and not one of her numerous adorers would have taken her frank, unaffected friendliness for anything other than it was meant to be.

But Talbot was not a society man; neither was he used to the ways of a Cicely Carruthers. The girls he knew belonged to the village of Blythe, or its environs, and were fifty years or so behind the times. This was his first experience of the modern girl. At first he was a little shocked at the free and easy way in which she wandered into his place, or invited him into hers; then he was no longer shocked, but thought he understood. He came still more frequently to Rose Cottage.

Another fortnight slipped by. Maisie had sunk into a sort of sullen apathy, but Cicely, tanned by the sun, and pulsing with energy, was on the road to becoming the complete farmer. She had come to associate Talbot merely with his farm. Had he but known it, she was treating him as her inferior in that she still called him Mr. Talbot, and confined her conversation to farming.

She had a rude awakening. She came into the cottage one afternoon, her hair dishevelled by the wind, and her shoes caked in mud, and collapsed into a chair.

"Oo! I *am* tired!" she remarked.

Maisie raised her eyes from the inevitable novel.

"I don't wonder at it if you will go mucking about a dirty farm," she said.

Cicely was roused to wrath.

"It is not a dirty farm! It's a beautiful farm! You don't know what you're talking about!"

"All right." Maisie shrugged her shoulders and went on reading. After a short pause Cicely continued:

"The last incubator lot are hatching themselves. Isn't it wonderful? And Mr. Talbot's coming here to-day, and afterwards he's going to take me to see the chicks coming out of the eggs. You've no idea how interesting it is, Maisie! It's simply—"

"Is that man coming here to tea?" demanded Maisie.

"Yes, he is. And I do think you might be civil. He's not at all a bad sort—underneath his extraordinary manners."

"Then I'm going over to see the Frasers," said Maisie, disregarding

11

her.

The Frasers were friends of hers, living some three miles away.

"All right, you can," answered Cicely. "I don't care."

She waited until Maisie had left the room and then added: "And I hope Timothy runs away with you."

Talbot tramped in at a few minutes past four. "Hullo!" said Cicely. "Sit down and I'll make the tea."

Talbot lowered himself into a chair. It did not occur to him that he might help his hostess. It did occur to Cicely, and she sighed. With all his faults, Richard— She set the kettle down smartly, and came to the tea-table.

Talbot seemed rather thoughtful. Tea over, she lit a cigarette and saw that he was frowning.

"I don't like to see a girl smoking," he said heavily.

"Really?"

"I'd not allow my wife to smoke."

"Really?" said Cicely again. "But I am not your wife."

He looked full into her eyes in that bold, dogged way that had first intrigued her.

"Seems to me, my girl, we'd best come to an understanding," he said.

Indignation robbed Cicely of words. Fred Talbot to address her as "my girl"! With an effort she controlled herself.

"I don't know what you mean," she said icily. "Will you have a cigarette?"

"No." He brushed it aside. "Reckon you know all right. I want you to marry me."

"What?" Cicely gasped. "To—" Again she controlled herself. "Thanks very much," she said lightly, "I'm afraid not. I'm sorry you should think—think—"

"Reckon I think what I'm meant to. I don't pretend to understand you town-girls, but I know what I want, and I get what I want."

Cicely drew herself up.

"Mr. Talbot, you forget yourself. Please don't say any more! I had no idea you were—you had—you wanted to marry me, or I shouldn't

12

have—well, anyhow, don't let's talk about it. It's a pity to spoil a very pleasant friendship, isn't it?"

He smiled rather grimly.

"Suppose you cut out the fine talk, my girl, and come to grips? I don't know why you should pretend you'd no idea I wanted to marry you. You've been in and out of my place for weeks. I'm not a fool, my girl, and I know what to make of that."

"Don't call me that!" exploded Cicely. "I'm not your girl, and I won't have such an—such an impertinence! I came to your farm because I was interested! We were just friends, as you very well know! I've never given you the right to talk to me like this!"

"Think so?" He rose and stood over her. "You were just playing, were you?—leading me on?"

Cicely pushed back her chair and sprang up.

"How dare you?" she cried. "How dare you say such a thing to me? Please—go! I am exceedingly sorry you should have made such a dreadful mistake—but to blame me—? Why, I've never been anything but friends with you!"

He came nearer.

"Reckon a girl's not friends with a man unless there is something more," he drawled.

Cicely backed to the wall.

"Mr. Talbot, will you please go? If I were not alone here, you would not dare to speak to me in this way. I tell you, once and for all, I am not going to marry you. If you really care for me, you'll go now."

"I'm not going. You've had your fun with me, and now you'll pay for it." He strode forward as he spoke, and gripped her by the shoulders.

Panic seized Cicely, at the mercy of this dreadful person.

"Bill!" she shrieked. "Bill, Bill, Bill!"

From the garden came the sound of yelping barks. Bill showed no signs of coming to the rescue. Only he barked and barked in wild excitement.

Talbot crushed Cicely against him. She could not even struggle under his iron hold. She was kissed roughly on her panting mouth, and then—

Someone pushed open the cottage door.

"You owe me a bob," said a lazy, pleasant voice. "Get down, Bill!"

"Richard!" sobbed Cicely. "Oh, Richard!"

Still holding her with one arm, Talbot wheeled about. Cicely never quite knew what happened next. All that she remembered was that she was suddenly whisked from the farmer's hold and deposited on the sofa. And Richard's voice, dangerously sweet, was inviting Talbot to come outside. Then the two men seemed to disappear, shutting Bill into the cottage.

Cicely crouched on the sofa, shivering still, and Bill snuffed and whined at the door with suppressed excitement.

Then, after what seemed to Cicely countless ages, the door opened and Richard strolled in, calm and imperturbed. He passed the palm of his left hand across his knuckles and looked at his flushed cousin.

"Has—has he—gone?" asked Cicely, in a very small voice.

"Oh, yes!" said Richard.

"Did—did—you—hurt him much?"

"I hope so," said Richard, and there was a short, uncomfortable pause.

"How—how did you—find me?" she inquired, with would-be carelessness.

"Process of deduction. What was that poisonous blighter doing in your cottage?"

"Ha—having—tea," said Cicely, nervously.

"Where's that fat fool—Maisie?"

"Gone to—to see some friends."

"What does she mean by leaving you with a man like that?"

"She—she doesn't like him."

"Shows her good taste. Don't you know better than to ask a brute like that to tea with you alone?"

Cicely blinked away a tear.

"I—I didn't kn—know—he—he'd—I always *d—do* ask my friends to tea!"

"Your father's house is rather different, isn't it?"

A muffled sob came from the sofa. Cicely was staring down at her

14

hands, biting her lips. Richard went to her and sat down with his arm about her shoulders. "Poor little kid! I won't rag you any more. Don't cry, Cis."

Cicely shed a few tears into his coat pocket, and sat up. She mopped her eyes with a diminutive handkerchief.

"I—I am glad you came," she sighed. "I n—never thought you would."

There was another pause.

"Are—are you staying at the inn?"

"I am."

"Are—are you going to stay for long?"

"Looks as though I'd better," said Richard drily.

"Oh!" Cicely digested this. Then she spoke again. "P'raps you'll be able to manage Timothy," she said hopefully. There was no answer.

Cicely looked at him sideways. She sat for a moment, twisting a cushion-tassel. Richard said nothing at all, but watched her with that curious look in his eyes.

A tiny smile came, shyly. And Cicely came to him and dived her hand into his waistcoat pocket.

"What do you want, Cis?"

"Diary," said Cicely briefly.

It was handed to her. She hesitated for a moment, not looking at him. Then she opened the book, and sucked the pencil. She scribbled diligently, and shut the book with a snap. Richard was watching her half-smiling, half-anxious. Cicely held out the book.

"There you are! I've finished with it."

Richard took it. He slipped his arm round her once more. Cicely subsided meekly, and buried her face in his coat.

Richard dropped a kiss on to the fluffy head.

"Am I allowed to read what's written here?" he asked.

"If you—like," said a muffled voice.

He opened the book. The last entry was written in a round, sprawling hand. It was quite short.

"Tuesday. Proposed to Cicely. Accepted."

# The Horned Beast of Africa

**The Primitive Trail-breaker of Tanganyika, the Rhinoceros, is one of the Most Unpleasant of Beasts to Encounter.**

("The Accompanying Article Tells of Rhino Adventures and Rhino Habits," essay in *The Sphere*, 22 June 1929, p. 656)

Karagwe, the northernmost corner of Tanganyika, lies west of Lake Victoria and east of Ruanda, the Mandated Belgian territory. I have lived for a year in a mining camp in this district, and I can truthfully assert that one of the most common beasts found there is the black rhinoceros. On account of them it was never safe to go more than a mile from the camp in any direction without a heavy rifle, and upon the march one has always to be on the look-out for a chance rhino. It is not nice to come suddenly upon one.

But they have their uses. They make paths that are flat and broad, with the tall grass trampled down, and in a country where there are no roads these are invaluable. I have walked for miles down rhino tracks, and I have been more fortunate than some in that I never once walked into the real owner of the path. My marching was done by day, of course, when the animal life is sleeping; I should not care to venture down one of these tracks at about four in the afternoon, when the rhinos are out for a constitutional.

The first time I saw one of these grotesque beasts I felt considerably scared, but as time went on I became a little *blasé* about them. Familiarity breeds contempt.

But it is not wise to despise the rhino. One never knows what he will do. Perhaps four times out of five he will make off, but there is always the fifth time, when he will charge like a swift tank, crashing through the undergrowth as though it were paper. Our car was several times chased by one, and we paced him by our speedometer and found that he was doing thirty-three to thirty-four miles an hour apparently without effort. Once under way—and it is surprising how quickly he can take off—there is nothing to stop him, for he weighs two tons.

16

Once, at six o'clock one morning, a rhino wandered right into our camp and was seen through the lifting mist not twenty yards from one of the houses. Panic seized the natives, who stampeded into the nearest compound; my husband came flying back to our house for his rifle, and awakened me with a shout of "Quick! There's a rhino in the camp!"

This was so thrilling a piece of news that I jumped out of bed, caught up a coat over my pyjamas and hurried out after him.

We found that the rhino had moved off slowly through the camp, followed by Mr. J. V. Oates, the first man on the scene, who presently shot it. My Sealyham terrier hastened up to the spot, full of importance, sniffed at the huge corpse rather scornfully and turned away with the air of saying, "Dead, I see. Nothing for me to do here." When told to get on the rhino's back he did so without the slightest hesitation

The hide of this rhino was made into whips. The horn of a rhino is not real horn at all, but is actually congealed hair. When it is freshly sawn off stubbly strands can be seen at the root, while round the base the hair is still growing, rather like a short wire brush. As the horn tapers it becomes smooth and polished, and one would scarcely believe that it could be made of hair.

The rhino with the rear horn longer than the front, seen in the third photograph, was an old cow shot on the Niergongo plain, miles from anywhere. The length of the rear horn is somewhat freakish, and only occurs in some of the old cows.

The young rhinos seem to stay with their mothers until they reach quite a mature age. Upon one occasion my husband was motoring down a rough road when he chanced to see some partridges ahead on the edge of a large clump of thorns. He stopped the car, got out with his shot-gun, and fired. Immediately there was a sudden tremendous commotion in the thorn-clump—a snorting and trampling and crashing. Three rhinos broke from the clump at full speed. They were a family of mother and father and well-grown son, and they came charging out, enraged by the sudden noise. Fortunately, they were too startled to make sure of their direction, and hurtled off, one through a bush, another across country, and the third over the road within a few feet of my husband.

The trio lived in that thorn-clump for several weeks, and waged a sort of guerilla warfare on our cars. After that first time they had no doubts as to the way they should charge, and when any car or lorry passed they would burst forth and charge after it full tilt. None of the trio had good horns, so we were loth to shoot them, but the situation was becoming really dangerous, and we were afraid we should have to blot them out. But as though they guessed our intention they suddenly elected to change their abode, and removed to some quieter spot much to our relief.

The last rhino shot by my husband in the country was a freak, clearly heaven-sent, for the front horn is in a fair way to being the record for Tanganyika. The rear horn is insignificant, but thick and heavy. The front horn measures 33½ in. from base to tip, and grew in the extraordinary fashion seen in the photographs. Instead of curving upwards, more or less at right angles to the head, it grew outwards, almost on a line with the snout.

My husband was returning to headquarters after a *safari* of several days and stopped at a village on the slopes of a hill above a dense valley. At a point below the village the valley was crossed by a small flay overgrown with coarse grass, some ant-hills, and some scrubby bushes. My husband was out after buffalo, but had no luck, and was just returning to the village when his gun-boy suddenly whispered "Look, B'wana! Rhino!"

About 200 yards off my husband could just see in the grass a rhino evidently feeding, for his head was down. In this position, owing to its curious growth, the enormous front horn was not visible, since it lay almost along the ground. My husband got out his Zeiss glasses, but could distinguish only the rear horn, which he took to be the front one. He was unimpressed, and decided not to shoot but to take a photograph.

There was no wind, so he slung his gun over his shoulder and crept cautiously up to within forty or fifty yards. But no sooner had he levelled the camera than a little breeze sprang up straight from him to the unconscious rhino. Up came the great head, sniffing at the air; there was a gasp from the gun-boy, and a startled whisper of: "B'wana, look at the horn!"

My husband took one look, saw this colossal horn above the grass, flung his camera to the boy, and grabbed his rifle. Just as the rhino, who happened to be in a bad temper, was about to start his charge my husband fired. The rhino checked, spun round in a half-circle—sure sign of a good shot—and dashed behind a bush.

The huntsman quickly ejected the cartridge, and the rifle jammed. This meant that the second cartridge had to be ejected also, leaving only three in the magazine. This wasted a few seconds, then my husband ran forward, expecting either to see the rhino down or making off. Instead of this it came charging out from the other side of the bush with that great front-horn pointing straight at my husband's solar plexus!

My husband fired again at a range of thirty yards and got in a good neck shot. But even as he ejected again he saw that the mad rush was not checked. On came the rhino, pouring blood at nose and mouth but seemingly undaunted. My husband fired a third time, and turned and ran!

He caught his foot in a tangle of undergrowth, fell, sprang up again, and turned to see the rhino standing still at the spot where he had last fired at it. He reloaded and gave the brute a fourth shot to finish him. Then at last the rhino went over, slowly at the first, like a felled tree, and then with a crash.

Upon inspection every shot was found to be a killer. The rhino was a very old bull and correspondingly tough. He was the only one my husband had ever had trouble with in this way, since usually we have found that they go over at one good heart shot. As far as I know the horn is unique both in its size and its growth

# Runaway Match

(short story in *Woman's Journal*, April 1936;
reprinted in *The Oxford Book of Historical Stories*, eds. Michael Fox &
Jack Adrian [Oxford: Oxford University Press, 1994], pp. 341-52, 439)

As the post-chaise and four entered the town of Stamford, young Mr.
Morley, who had spent an uncomfortable night being jolted over the
road, remorselessly prodded his companion.

"We have reached Stamford," he announced. "We change horses
here, and whatever you may choose to do, *I* shall bespeak breakfast."

Miss Paradise, snugly ensconced in her corner of the chaise, opened a
pair of dark eyes, blinked once or twice, yawned behind her feather muff,
and sat up.

"Oh!" said Miss Paradise, surveying the spring morning with
enthusiasm. "It is quite daylight! I have had the most delightful sleep."

Mr. Morley repeated his observation, not without a hint of pugnacity
in his voice.

Since the start of the elopement, rather more than nine hours before,
Miss Paradise, who was just eighteen, had been a trifle difficult to
manage. She had begun by taking strong exception to the ladder he had
brought for her escape from her bedroom window. Her remarks,
delivered in an indignant undertone as she had prepared to descend the
ladder, might have been thought to augur ill for the success of the
runaway match; but Mr. Morley, who was also just eighteen, had
quarrelled with Miss Paradise from the cradle, and thought her behaviour
the most natural in the world. The disposition she showed to take the
management of the flight into her own hands led to further wrangles,
because, however much she might have been in the habit of taking the
lead in their past scrapes an elopement was a very different matter, and
called for a display of male initiative. But when he had tried to point this
out to Miss Paradise she had merely retorted, "Stuff! It was I who made
the plan to elope. Now, Rupert, you know it was!"

This rejoinder was unanswerable, and Mr. Morley, who had been
arguing in favour of putting up for the night at a respectable posting-

house, had allowed himself to be overruled. They had travelled swiftly northwards by moonlight (a circumstance which had filled the romantic Miss Paradise with rapture) with the result that a good deal of Mr. Morley's zest for the adventure had worn off by the time he made his announcement at eight o'clock.

He was prepared to encounter opposition, but Miss Paradise, engaged in the task of tidying her tumbled curls, assented light-heartedly.

"To be sure, I am excessively hungry," she said.

She picked up a chip hat from the seat and tied it on her head by its green gauze ribbons.

"I dare say I must look a positive fright," she remarked; "but you can have no notion how much I am enjoying myself."

This buoyancy had the effect of making Mr. Morley slightly morose.

"I can't imagine what there is to enjoy in being bumped about all night," he said.

Miss Paradise turned her enchanting little face towards him, and exclaimed with considerable chagrin:

"Are you not enjoying it at all, Rupert? I must say I do think you need not get into a miff merely because of being bumped a trifle."

"I am not in a miff!" said Mr. Morley, "but—"

"Oh, Rupert!" cried Miss Paradise, letting her muff fall.   "Don't, don't say that you do not want to elope with me, after all!"

"No, of course I do," responded Mr. Morley. "The fact is, I didn't contrive to sleep above an hour or two.   I shall be in better cue after breakfast."

"Yes, I expect that's it," nodded Miss Paradise, relieved. "Only, I don't think we should waste very much time, you know, because when papa discovers our flight he is bound to pursue us."

"I don't see that," objected Mr. Morley. "He can't know where you have gone."

"Yes, he can," said Miss Paradise. "I left a note on my pillow for him."

"What!" ejaculated Mr. Morley. "Good heavens, Bab, why?"

"But he would be in a dreadful rout if I hadn't told him," explained Miss Paradise. "And even though he has behaved shockingly to me I

21

don't want him to be anxious about me."

Mr. Morley retorted: "If you think to have put an end to his anxiety by telling him you have eloped with me you very much mistake the matter."

"No, but at least he will be sure that I am safe," said Miss Paradise. "You know that he likes you extremely, Rupert, even though he does not wish me to marry you. *That* is only because he says you are too young; and because he has this stupid notion that I must make a good match, of course," she added candidly.

"Well, I think you must be mad," said Mr. Morley. "I'll lay you a button he rides over immediately to tell my father. Then we shall have the pair of them at our heels, and a pretty pucker there will be."

"I hadn't thought of that," confessed Miss Paradise. "But I dare say we shall have reached Gretna Green long before they come up with us."

The chaise had arrived at the George Inn by this time, and had turned in under the archway to the courtyard. The steps were let down and the travellers alighted. Mr. Morley felt stiff, but Miss Paradise gave her tiffany skirts a shake and tripped into the inn for all the world as though she had enjoyed a perfect night's rest.

There was not much sign of activity in the George at this early hour, but the landlord came out and led the way to a private parlour overlooking the street, and promised to serve breakfast in the shortest possible time. He betrayed no extraordinary curiosity, the extremely youthful appearance of his guests leading him to suppose them to be brother and sister.

Miss Paradise, realizing this, was disappointed, and commented on it to Mr. Morley with considerable dissatisfaction.

"Well, thank Heaven for it," said Mr. Morley.

"Sometimes, Rupert," said Miss Paradise, "I think you are not romantic in the very least."

"I never said that I was," replied Mr. Morley.

"You may not have said it, but you did say that you would rescue me from that odious Sir Roland, and if that is not—"

"Well, I *am* rescuing you," interrupted Mr. Morley, "and I don't object to being romantic in reason. But when it comes to you wanting a rope-ladder to escape by," he continued, last night's quarrel taking possession of his mind again, "I call it the outside of enough."

"Who ever heard of any other kind of ladder for an elopement?" demanded Miss Paradise scathingly.

"I don't know, but how was I to find such a thing? And now I come to think of it," pursued Mr. Morley, "why the devil did you want a ladder at all? Your father and your aunt were both gone out, and you told me yourself the servants were all in bed."

A disarming dimple peeped in Miss Paradise's cheek.

"Well, to tell you the truth, it wasn't *very* necessary," she confessed. "Only it seemed so much more exciting."

The entrance of a serving-man with a tray prevented Mr. Morley from uttering the indignant retort that sprang to his lips, and by the time the table was laid and the covers set on it the mingled aromas of coffee and broiled ham and ale had put all other thought than that of breakfast out of his head. He handed Miss Paradise to a chair, drew out one for himself, and was soon engaged in assuaging the first pangs of his hunger.

Miss Paradise, pursuing thoughts of her own, presently said:

"I dare say they won't have found my note yet."

"I wish to Heaven you hadn't written it, Bab!"

"Well, so do I now," admitted Miss Paradise. "Because although I made certain that Aunt Albinia would not think of going to my room when she came home last night, it has all at once occurred to me that perhaps she might."

Mr. Morley, who was carving the cold sirloin, gave a groan.

"Why? If she never does—"

"Yes, but you see, I said I had the headache, and she might go to my room to see how I did. I had to say I had the headache, Rupert, because they would have forced me to go with them to the dinner-party if I hadn't." Her brow darkened. "To meet that odious old man," she added broodingly.

"Sale?" enquired Mr. Morley.

"Yes, of course."

"He isn't as old as that, Bab. Hang it, he can't be much above thirty. And you don't know that he's odious after all."

"Oh, yes, I do," retorted Miss Paradise with strong feeling. "He wrote to papa that he was perfectly willing to fulfil his obligations and marry me. I never heard of anything so odious in my life. He must be the most horrid creature imaginable, and as for papa, I am sorry to be obliged to say it, but he is very little better; in fact, I think, *worse*, because it was he who made this abominable plan to marry me to an Eligible Person with whom I am not even acquainted. And Sir Joseph Sale, too, of course, detestable old man that he was."

"Gad, he was!" agreed Mr. Morley. "Do you remember—"

"No," said Miss Paradise. "At least, I'm not going to, because one should never speak ill of the dead. But you may depend upon it his nephew is just like him, and if papa thinks I am going to marry to oblige him he very much mistakes the matter. As though you and I had not said years and years ago that we would marry each other."

"Parents are all alike," said Mr. Morley gloomily. "However, this should show my father that I am not to be treated like a child any longer."

"Yes," said Miss Paradise, pouring out another cup of coffee. "And if they don't like it on account of your being too young, I shall tell papa that it is all his fault, because if he hadn't made an arrangement for me to marry a man I've never clapped eyes on we shouldn't have thought of being married for a long time, should we?"

"No," said Mr. Morley. "Not until I had come down from Oxford, at all events, and after that, I believe, there was a scheme for me to make the Grand Tour, which I must say I should have liked. I dare say we shouldn't have thought of being married for four or five years."

Miss Paradise paused in the act of drinking her coffee and lowered the cup.

"Four or five years!" she repeated. "But I should be twenty-two or three years old."

"Well, so should I," Mr. Morley pointed out.

"But that is not at all the same thing," said Miss Paradise indignantly.

"Oh, well, there's no sense in arguing about it," replied Mr. Morley, finishing his ale, and getting up. "They have compelled us to elope, and there's an end to it. I had best tell them to have the horses put to at once,

I think. We have no time to lose."

Miss Paradise agreed to it, and engaged to be in readiness to resume the journey by the time Mr. Morley had paid the reckoning and seen a fresh team harnessed to the chaise. He went out, and she was left to drink the last of her coffee, to tie on her becoming hat once more, and to straighten her tucker. This did not take long; she was ready before her swain, and was about to sally forth into the yard when the sound of a carriage being driven fast down the street made her run to the window.

It was not, however, a post-chaise, and no such dreaded sight as Sir John Paradise's face met her alarmed gaze. Instead, she saw a curricle and four driven by a gentleman in a very modish dress of dark blue with gold buttons. He wore a gold-laced tricorne on his own unpowdered hair, and a fringed cravat thrust through a gold buttonhole. A surtout with four laps on each side hung negligently open over his dress, and on his feet he had a pair of very highly polished top-boots. He was looking straight ahead, and so did not see Miss Paradise peeping at him over the short blind. She had a glimpse of a straight, rather haughty profile as the curricle passed the window; then the horses were checked, and the equipage swung round under the archway into the courtyard.

"Bab!" gasped Mr. Morley, who had entered the room behind her. "We are overtaken!"

Miss Paradise gave a shriek and dropped her muff.

"Mercy on me! Not papa?"

"No, I don't know who it can be, but a man has this instant driven into the yard—"

"Yes, yes, I saw him. But what in the world can he have to do with us?"

"I tell you I don't know, but he asked the landlord if he had seen anything of a young lady and gentleman. I did not wait for more, as you may imagine. What are we to do? Who in thunder can he be?"

A premonition had seized Miss Paradise. She took a step back, clasping her hands together in great agitation.

"Good heavens, Rupert! Could it be—Sir Roland?" Mr. Morley stared at her.

"Sale? It can't be! How should he know of our elopement?"

"Papa must have brought him back with him last night. Oh, this is dreadful! I declare I am ready to sink!"

Mr. Morley squared his shoulders.

"Well, if he is Sale, he shan't take you back, Bab. He has to reckon with me now."

"But he is not in the least like Sir Joseph!" said Miss Paradise numbly. "He is quite handsome!"

"What in the world has that to do with it?" demanded Mr. Morley.

Miss Paradise turned scarlet.

"Nothing at all!" she replied. "Whoever he is like he is odious. *Willing to fulfil—* But I never dreamed that *he* would follow us!"

At this moment the door was opened again, and a pleasant, slightly drawling voice said:

"So I have caught you, my children? I thought I might," and the gentleman in the modish surtout walked into the room.

He paused on the threshold and raised his quizzing-glass. Miss Paradise, who had retreated to Mr. Morley's side, blushed, and gave him back stare for stare.

"But I must humbly beg my apologies," said the newcomer, a faintly quizzical smile in his grey eyes. "I seem to have intruded. Madam—"

"Yes," said Miss Paradise. "You have intruded, Sir Roland!"

The quizzical smile lingered; one eyebrow went up.

"Now, I wonder how you knew me?" murmured the gentleman.

"I am well aware that you must be Sir Roland Sale," said Miss Paradise, "but I do *not* know you, and I do not desire to know you!"

Sir Roland laughed suddenly and shut the door.

"But are you not being a trifle hasty?" he enquired. "Why don't you desire to know me?"

"I imagine you must know very well!" said Miss Paradise.

"Indeed I don't!" said Sir Roland. He came further into the room, and laid his hat and his elegant fringed gloves down on the table. He looked thoughtfully from one flushed countenance to the other, and said in a tone of amusement: "Is it possible that you are running away from me?"

"Certainly not!" said Miss Paradise. "But I think it only proper to tell you, sir, that this is the gentleman I am going to marry."

Mr. Morley tried to think of something dignified to add to this pronouncement, but under that ironic, not unkindly gaze, only succeeded in clearing his throat and turning redder than ever.

Sir Roland slid one hand into his pocket and drew out a snuff-box. "But how romantic!" he remarked. "Do, pray, present me!"

Mr. Morley took a step forward.

"You must have guessed, sir, that my name is Morley. Miss Paradise has been promised to me these dozen years."

Sir Roland bowed and offered his snuff-box.

"I felicitate you," he said. "But what part do I play in this charming—er—idyll?"

"None!" replied Miss Paradise.

Sir Roland, his snuff having been waved aside by Mr. Morley, took a pinch and held it to one nostril. Then he fobbed his box with an expert flick of the finger and put it away again.

"I hesitate to contradict you, Miss Paradise," he said, "but I cannot allow myself to be thrust into the role of a mere onlooker."

Miss Paradise replied, not quite so belligerently:

"I dare say you think you have a right to interfere, but you need not think that I will go back with you, for I won't!"

Mr. Morley, feeling himself elbowed out of the discussion, said with some asperity:

"I wish you will leave this to me, Bab! Pray, do be quiet a moment!"

"Why should I be quiet?" demanded Miss Paradise. "It is quite my own affair!"

"You always think you can manage everything," said Mr. Morley. "But this is between men!"

"What nonsense!" said Miss Paradise scornfully. "Pray, whom does he want to marry, you or me?"

"Lord, Bab, if you're going to talk like a fool I shall be sorry I ever said I'd elope with you!"

"Well, I'm sorry now!" said Miss Paradise instantly.

Mr. Morley cast her a withering glance and turned once more to Sir Roland.

27

"Sir, no doubt you are armed with Sir John Paradise's authority, but—"

"Let me set your mind at rest at once," interposed Sir Roland. "I am here quite on my own authority."

"Well, sir! Well, in that case—"

Miss Paradise entered into the conversation again.

"You can't pretend that you cared as much as that!" she said impetuously. "You could not have wanted to marry me so very much when you had never so much as set eyes on me!"

"Of course not," agreed Sir Roland. "Until I set eyes on you I had not the least desire to marry you."

"Then why did you write that odious letter to papa?" asked Miss Paradise reasonably.

"I never write odious letters," replied Sir Roland calmly.

"I dare say you may think it was very civil and obliging of you," said Miss Paradise; "but for my part I have a very poor notion of a man allowing his marriage to be arranged for him, and when it comes to writing that you are willing to fulfil your—your *obligations*—"

A muscle quivered at the corner of Sir Roland's mouth.

"Did I write that?" he asked.

"You must know you did!"

"I am quite sure I wrote no such thing," he said.

"Well, what did you write?" she demanded.

He walked forward till he stood quite close to her and held out his hand. He said, looking down at her:

"Does it signify what I wrote? After all, I had not seen you then. Now that we are acquainted I promise you I will not write or say anything to give you a disgust of me."

She looked at him uncertainly. Even though his fine mouth was perfectly grave his eyes held a smile which one could hardly withstand. A little colour stole into her cheeks; the dimple peeped again; she put her hand shyly into his, and said:

"Well, perhaps it does not signify so *very* much. But I am going to marry Mr. Morley, you know. That was all arranged between us years ago."

Sir Roland still kept her hand clasped in his. "Do you never change your mind, Miss Paradise?" he asked.

Mr. Morley, who had begun in the presence of this polished gentleman to feel himself a mere schoolboy, interrupted at this moment and said hotly: "Sir, I deny any right in you to interfere in Miss Paradise's affairs! She is under my protection, and will shortly be my wife. Bab, come with me! We should press on at once!"

"I suppose we should," agreed Miss Paradise rather forlornly.

Mr. Morley strode up to her and caught her wrist. Until the arrival of Sir Roland he had been regarding his approaching nuptials with mixed feelings, but to submit to a stranger's intervention, and to see his prospective bride in danger of being swayed by the undeniable charm of a man older, and far more at his ease than he was himself, was a little too much for him to stomach. There was a somewhat fiery light in his eyes as he said: "Bab, you are promised to me! You know you are!"

Miss Paradise raised her eyes to Sir Roland's face. "It is quite true," she said with a faint sigh. "I am promised to him, and one must keep one's word, you know."

"Bab!" said Mr. Morley sternly, "you wanted to elope with me! It was your notion! Good heavens, you could not turn back now and go meekly home!"

"No, of course I couldn't," said Miss Paradise, roused by this speech. "I never heard of anything so flat!"

"I knew you would never fail!" said Mr. Morley, casting a triumphant look at Sir Roland. "Let us be on our way immediately."

Sir Roland flicked a grain of snuff from his wide cuff. "Not so fast, Mr. Morley," he said. "I warned you, did I not, that I could not allow myself to be thrust into the role of mere onlooker?"

Mr. Morley's eyes flashed. "You have no right to interfere, sir!"

"My dear young man," said Sir Roland, "anyone has the right to do what he can to prevent two—er—young people from committing an act of the most unconscionable folly. You will not take Miss Paradise to Gretna today—or, in fact, any other day."

There was a note of steel in the drawling voice. Miss Paradise, realizing that the adventure was becoming even more romantic than she

29

had bargained for, clasped her hands in her muff and waited breathlessly.

Mr. Morley laid a hand on his sword-hilt. "Oh?" he said. "Indeed, sir?"

Sir Roland, observing the gesture, raised his brows in some amusement.

Mr. Morley said through his teeth: "We shall do better to continue our discussion outside, sir, I believe."

Miss Paradise caught her muff up to her chin, and over it looked imploringly at Sir Roland. He was not attending to her; he seemed to be considering Mr. Morley. After a moment he said slowly: "You are a little impetuous, are you not?"

"Sir," said Mr. Morley dramatically, "if you want Bab you must fight for her!"

Miss Paradise's mouth formed an "O" of mingled alarm and admiration.

There was a slight pause. Then Sir Roland smiled and said: "Well, you have plenty of courage, at all events. I am perfectly prepared to fight for her."

"Then follow me, sir, if you please!" said Mr. Morley, striding to the door.

Miss Paradise gave a cry and sprang after him. "Oh, Rupert, no!"

She was intercepted by Sir Roland, who laid a detaining hand on her arm. "Don't be alarmed, Miss Paradise," he said.

Miss Paradise said in an urgent undervoice: "Oh, please don't! He can't fight you! He is only a boy, Sir Roland!"

Mr. Morley, who was plainly enjoying himself at last, shut the door upon Miss Paradise, and demanded to know whether Sir Roland preferred swords or pistols. When Sir Roland unhesitatingly chose swords he bowed, and said that he believed there was a garden behind the inn which would serve their purpose.

He was right; there was a garden, with a small shrubbery screening part of it from the house. Sir Roland followed Mr. Morley there and took off his coat and tossed it on to a wooden seat. "This is damned irregular, you know," he remarked, sitting down on the bench to pull off his boots. "Are you very set on fighting me?"

"Yes, I am," declared Mr. Morley, removing his sword-belt. "A pretty fellow I should be if I gave Bab—Miss Paradise—up to you for the mere asking!"

Sir Roland drew his sword from its sheath and bent the slender blade between his hands. "You would be a still prettier fellow if you carried her off to Gretna," he said dryly.

Mr. Morley coloured. "Well, I never wanted to elope," he said defensively. "It was all your doing that we were forced to!"

Sir Roland got up from the bench in his leisurely way, and stood waiting with his sword-point lightly resting on the ground. Mr. Morley rolled up his sleeves, picked up his weapon, and announced that he was ready.

He had, of course, been taught to fence, and was by no means a dull pupil; but within ten seconds of engaging he was brought to a realization of the vast difference that lay between a friendly bout with foils and a duel with naked blades. He tried hard to remember all he had been taught, but the pace Sir Roland set was alarmingly swift, and made him feel singularly helpless and clumsy. It was all he could do to parry that flickering sword-point; several times he knew he had been too slow, and almost shut his eyes in the expectation of being run through. But, somehow, he always did seem to succeed in parrying the fatal lunge just in time, and once he managed to press Sir Roland hard with an attack in a high line. He was very soon dripping with sweat and quite out of breath, fighting gamely but with thudding pulses, and with a paralysing sensation of being pretty much at his opponent's mercy. And then, just as he had miraculously parried thrust in *seconde*, Sir Roland executed a totally unexpected *volte*, and the next instant Mr. Morley's sword was torn from his grasp and he had flung up his hands instinctively to guard his face.

"Mr. Morley," said Sir Roland, breathing a little fast, "do you acknowledge yourself worsted?"

Mr. Morley, sobbing for breath, could only nod.

"Then let us rejoin Miss Paradise," said Sir Roland, giving him back his sword.

He moved towards the bench and began to pull on his boots again.

31

Mr. Morley presently followed his example, crestfallen and very much out of countenance.

"I suppose," said Mr. Morley disconsolately, "you could have killed me if you had chosen?"

"Yes, certainly I could; but then, you see, I am a very good swordsman," said Sir Roland, smiling. "Don't look so downcast. I think, one day, you may be a very good swordsman, too."

Considerably cheered, Mr. Morley followed him back to the inn parlour. Miss Paradise, who was looking pale and frightened, sprang up at their entrance and gave a gasp of relief.

"Oh, you haven't killed each other!" she cried thankfully.

"No; it was much too fine a morning for anything of that nature," said Sir Roland. "Instead, we have decided that it will be best if I take you back to your papa, Miss Paradise. These Gretna marriages are not quite the thing, you know."

Miss Paradise seemed undecided, and looked towards Mr. Morley for support.

"We shall have to give it up, Bab," he said gloomily.

Miss Paradise sighed.

"I suppose we shall, though it does seem horridly flat to go home without any adventure at all."

"Well, I've fought my first duel," pointed out Mr. Morley.

"Yes, but I haven't done anything!" objected Miss Paradise.

"On the contrary," put in Sir Roland tactfully, "you were the whole cause of the duel."

"So I was!" said Miss Paradise, brightening. She gave Sir Roland one of her frank smiles. "You are not at all what I thought you would be," she confided. "I didn't suppose you were the sort of person who would come after us so—so romantically!"

Sir Roland looked down at her with a rueful twinkle in his eyes.

"Miss Paradise, I must make a confession. I did not come after you."

"You did not? But—but what did you come for, then?" she asked, considerably astonished.

"I came to meet my sister and my young brother," said Sir Roland.

"Sister! Brother!" echoed Miss Paradise. "I did not know you had

32

any. How can this be? Did you not see my father last night? There must be some mistake!"

"I have never met your father in my life," said Sir Roland.

Light broke in on Mr. Morley. He cried out:

"Oh, good heavens! *Are* you Sir Roland Sale?"

"No," said the other. "I am only one Philip Devereux, who got up early to meet his sister on the last stage of her return from Scotland, and stumbled upon an adventure."

Miss Paradise gave a choked cry.

"Oh, how *could* you?" she said, in a suffocating voice.

Mr. Morley, quite pale with excitement, waved her aside.

"Not—not *the* Devereux?" he faltered. "Not—oh, not *Viscount* Devereux of Frensham?"

"Well, yes, I am afraid so," replied his lordship apologetically.

"Bab!" ejaculated Mr. Morley. "Do you hear that? I have actually crossed swords with one of the first swordsmen in Europe! Only think of it!"

Miss Paradise showed no desire to think of it. She turned her head away.

The viscount said: "Do you think you could go and see what has been done with your chaise and my curricle, Mr. Morley?"

"Oh, yes, certainly!" said Mr. Morley. "I'll go now, shall I?"

"If you please," said his lordship, his eyes on Miss Paradise's profile. He waited until the door was shut behind Mr. Morley, and then said gently: "Forgive me, Miss Paradise!"

"You let me say—you let me believe you were the man papa says is going to marry me, and I—"

She stopped, for he had taken her hands and was looking down at her in a way that made her heart beat suddenly fast.

"I haven't the least idea what papa will say, but I can assure you that I am the man who is going to marry you," said his lordship, with complete composure.

33

# *Pursuit*

(short story published in *The Queen's Book of the Red Cross. With a Message from Her Majesty the Queen and Contributions by Fifty British Authors and Artists. In Aid of The Lord Mayor of London's Fund for the Red Cross and the Order of St. John of Jerusalem.* London: Hodder and Stoughton, 1939, pp. 203-13)

The curricle, which was built on sporting lines, was drawn by a team of four magnificent greys, and the ribbons were being handled by one of the most noted whips of his day: a member of the Four Horse Club, of the Bensington, the winner of above a dozen races—in short, by the Earl of Shane, as anyone but the most complete country bumpkin, catching only the most fleeting glimpse of his handsome profile, with its bar of black brow, and masterful, aquiline nose, would have known immediately. Happily, however, for his companion's peace of mind, the only persons encountered on the road were country bumpkins, the curricle having passed the Islington toll-gate, and entered upon the long, lonely stretch of road leading to the village of Highgate.

The Earl's companion was a governess, a lady, moreover, who would very soon have attained her thirtieth year, and who was seated bolt-upright beside him, dressed in a sober round gown of French cambric under a green pelisse, and a bonnet of moss-straw tied over her smooth brown ringlets. Her hands, in serviceable gloves of York tan, were clasped on the crook of a plaid parasol, and she appeared to be suffering from a strong sense of injury. Her eyes, which were a fine grey, and generally held a good deal of humour, stared stonily at the road ahead, and her mouth (too generous for beauty) was firmly compressed. For several miles she had seemed to be totally oblivious of the Earl's presence, and except for shuddering in a marked fashion whenever he sprang his horses, she paid not the smallest heed to the really remarkable driving skill he was displaying. Though he feather-edged his corners to perfection, put his horses beautifully together, cleared all obstacles, including a huge accommodation-coach which took up nearly all the road, in the most nonchalant style, and handled his long whip with the veriest flick of the wrist, he might as well, for all the admiration he evoked, have been a stage-coachman.

To do him justice, he had neither the expectation nor the desire of being admired. The excellence of his driving was a matter of course; he was, besides, in a very bad temper. He had been interrupted in the middle of his breakfast by the arrival on his doorstep of his ward's governess, who had travelled up to London from his house in Sussex to inform him, in the coolest fashion, that her charge had eloped with a lieutenant of a line regiment. He considered her attitude to have been little short of brazen. Instead of evincing the contrition proper in a lady who had so grossly failed in the execution of her duty, she had said in her calm way that it served him right for not having given his consent to the marriage six months before. You would have thought from her manner that she had positively sped the young couple on their way to the Border (though that she swore she had not); and she had actually had the effrontery to advise him to make the best of it.

But the Earl, who had enjoyed his own way ever since he could remember, was not one who acquiesced readily in the oversetting of his will, and instead of accepting Miss Fairfax's advice he had ordered out his curricle and greys, had commanded Miss Fairfax to mount up on to the seat beside him, turning a deaf ear to her protests, and had driven off at a spanking rate, with the express intention of overtaking the runaways, and of bringing the recalcitrant Miss Gellibrand back to town under the escort of her governess.

Since he was driving an unrivalled team over the first stage of the journey, and could afford to change horses as often as he chose, Miss Fairfax could place little dependence on the eloping couple's contriving to outstrip pursuit. They had, indeed, several hours' law, but she guessed that Mr. Edmund Monksley, living upon his pay, would have to be content to travel with a pair of horses only harnessed to his post-chaise. The hire of post-horses was heavy, the journey to Gretna Green long, and the Earl's method of driving too swift for any job-chaise and pair to outdistance.

The bare expanse of Finchley Common being reached, a faint hope of being held up by highwaymen sustained Miss Fairfax's spirits for some way, but when the equipage arrived at the Whetstone gate without incident, she relapsed again into melancholy.

Her silence seemed to irritate the Earl. He said in a sardonic voice, "We have a good many miles to cover, I dare say, so you may as well come out of your sulks, ma'am. I should be interested to learn what right you imagine *you* have to indulge in this air of outraged virtue!"

"I have told you, sir, until I am quite tired of it, that I had nothing to do with Lucilla's flight," said Miss Fairfax coldly.

"No! You merely encouraged the fellow to visit my ward whenever he chose, and in spite of my prohibition—which you were perfectly well aware of!"

"I didn't encourage him at all. He never set foot inside your house, sir."

"Then where the devil did they meet?" demanded his lordship.

"In the orchard," replied Miss Fairfax.

"Very romantic!" said the Earl, with a snort of disgust. "And pray what were you about, ma'am?"

"Looking the other way," said Miss Fairfax unblushingly.

"I wonder you dare to sit there and tell me so! It only remains for you to say that this damnable elopement has your approval!"

"Well, it has not," she replied. "I should have preferred a pretty wedding for them, but since you were so extremely disagreeable, and Mr. Monksley's regiment has been ordered to the Peninsula, I really do not know what else they could have done, poor things!"

"Do you realise, ma'am," demanded the Earl, "that you have helped my ward to throw herself away, at the age of seventeen, upon a penniless nobody, wholly dependent for his advancement upon the hazards of war?—since I am very certain he will never be able to afford to buy his promotion!"

"No, I fear not," she agreed. "I do not know, of course, the extent of Lucilla's fortune."

"Negligible!"

"Then I expect you will be obliged to purchase a company for him," said Miss Fairfax.

"I?" he ejaculated, looking thunderstruck.

"You are so wealthy a few hundred pounds can't signify to you, after all."

"Upon my word, ma'am! I shall do nothing of the kind!"

"Very well," said Miss Fairfax, "if you are determined on being disobliging, I dare say Lucilla won't care a button. She is a soldier's daughter, and not in the least likely to turn into a fashionable young lady. I feel sure she and Mr. Monksley will deal extremely together."

"Are you aware, ma'am, that it is my intention to marry Lucilla myself?"

There was a slight pause. Miss Fairfax said rather carefully, "I was aware of it, sir, but I have always been at a loss to know why. You must be quite sixteen years her senior, nor have you, during the three years I have been in charge of Lucilla, shown the least partiality for her society. In fact, you have kept her secluded in the country, and have only visited her at the most infrequent intervals."

"If you mean that I am not in love with her, no, certainly I am not!" responded the Earl stiffly. "The match was the wish of both our fathers."

"How elevating it is to encounter such filial piety in these days!" observed Miss Fairfax soulfully.

The Earl dropped his hands, and let his team shoot, nearly unseating Miss Fairfax.

Silence reigned once more. At Barnet, which marked the end of the first stage, the greys were still going well, a circumstance which induced the Earl to sweep past the Red Lion, with its yellow-jacketed postboys and its twenty-six pairs of good horses, and press on for another nine miles to Hatfield. Miss Fairfax, who had never driven so fast in her life, began to fear that at any moment they must overtake the fugitives. She ventured presently to ask the Earl when he expected to catch up with them.

"I have no means of knowing. Before nightfall, I trust."

"Indeed, I trust so too!" said Miss Fairfax, with a good deal of feeling. "But if you do not?"

"Then, ma'am, we shall put up at an inn for the night, and continue our journey in the morning."

Miss Fairfax appeared to struggle with herself, saying presently in a voice of strong emotion, "I shall pass over the impropriety of such a scheme, my lord, but I desire to point out to you that all the baggage I have with me is this reticule!"

He shrugged his shoulders. "I regret the inconvenience, but it can't be helped."

This was too much for her. "Let me tell you, sir, that it can be helped very easily, by your abandoning this chase, and returning, like a sensible man, to London!"

"I shall return when I have caught my ward, and not before."

"Well," said Miss Fairfax, controlling herself with an obvious effort, "it all goes to show how mistaken one may be in a person's character. I was used to think you, sir, for all your faults, perfectly amiable and gentlemanly."

"For all my faults!" he repeated, surprised into looking round at her. "And pray what are these faults of mine?"

"Temper, pride, reserve, obstinacy, stupidity, and the most overbearing manners!" she replied, without hesitation.

There was just the suggestion of a quiver at the corners of his mouth. "You are frank, ma'am! I, on the other hand, thought you, until this morning, the perfect governess."

Miss Fairfax did not appear to derive any extraordinary degree of gratification from this tribute, but turned a little pale, and said unsteadily, "I beg your pardon. I should not have spoken so. I am aware that in your eyes I have acted wrongly."

He glanced quickly down at her, a softer expression on his face, but he said nothing for a few minutes, being fully engaged in quartering the road, to avoid a succession of deep pits in it. After a time, however, he said in a gentler tone, "Come! We gain nothing by bickering, after all. I never thought to find myself quarrelling with you, Mary Fairfax!"

"Didn't you, sir?"

"Why, no!" he said, slightly smiling. "You have always seemed to me the most restful of women, ma'am."

"I suppose you mean unobtrusive," said Miss Fairfax crossly.

It was many hours later, and the last grey light was fading from the sky, when the curricle entered Grantham, a distance of over a hundred miles from London. Miss Fairfax, by this time resigned to her fate, was enveloped in his lordship's many-caped driving-coat of drab cloth, and his lordship himself was in a mood of dangerous exasperation.

All had gone smoothly during the first part of the journey. The greys had held up until Hatfield was reached, and there the Earl had been fortunate enough to secure a team of strengthy, quick-actioned beasts to carry him to the next stage. But a little beyond Biggleswade they had encountered a whisky, driven by a very down-the-road-looking man, who came sweeping round a bend on the wrong side, and collided with the curricle. Thanks to the Earl's presence of mind in swerving aside almost into the ditch, there was not much damage done, but a necessary repair to one of the off-side wheels had to be effected at the next town they came to. This meant a delay of nearly an hour, but the Earl's temper was not seriously impaired until much later, when, crossing Witham Common, one of the wheelers of the team put-to at Stamford went dead lame. To be reduced at the end of a long day to running pick-axe set the seal to his lordship's exasperation. There was nothing for it but to drive slowly on to the next posting-house. The Earl, mounting the box again, after an inspection of the wheeler's leg, told Miss Fairfax bitterly that the whole business, from start to finish, might be laid at her door, an accusation which she received in weary silence.

Conversation thereafter was of a desultory nature. In Grantham, the Angel and Royal showed welcoming lights glowing in its oriel windows; and as the curricle passed under the Gothic stone arch into the courtyard, Miss Fairfax was conscious, not of any desire to return to London, but of a profound inclination towards dinner, and a well-aired bed.

The Earl handed her down from the curricle. She was so stiff that to move was quite painful, but she managed to discard the voluminous driving-coat, to straighten her bonnet, and to walk with a very fair assumption of dignity into the inn. She fancied that the maidservant who escorted her to a bedchamber looked at her curiously, but she felt too tired to enter upon any extempore explanation of her baggage-less condition.

The Earl had engaged a private parlour, and, although it was early summer, had caused a fire to be kindled in the grate. He looked to be in a better humour when Miss Fairfax presently entered the room. He was engaged in snuffing one of the candles in a branch on the table, and said in his abrupt way: "I hope you are hungry. The cooking is good here."

"I am hungry," she replied. "But mostly I am quite in a worry to know how to account to the chambermaid for my lack of baggage. It must present the oddest appearance!"

"You need not regard it. I am known here."

This careless response did not seem to Miss Fairfax to offer the least explanation of her plight, but she refrained from pointing this out to his lordship. As she moved towards the fire, he said, "When we changed horses at Stilton, I made certain enquiries. From what I was able to ascertain, we should by now have caught up with the runaways, had it not been for those unfortunate mishaps. They certainly stopped at Stilton, not many hours before we did. They are travelling with a single pair of post-horses. Since there is no moon, I fancy they will be putting up at Newark, or thereabouts, for the night."

A suspicion that the couple might be in Grantham crossed Miss Fairfax's mind. As though he had read her thought, the Earl said, "I cannot discover that they stopped in this town. Nothing has been seen of them here, or at the George. It seems odd, but it is possible, of course, that they changed horses at Greetham. I wish now that I had enquired for them there. However, they will scarcely go beyond Newark tonight. I shall drive there when we have dined."

"Nothing," said Miss Fairfax, with resolution, "would induce me to travel another mile this day!"

"It will be quite unnecessary for you to do so. I shall bring Lucilla back with me."

"If you would only let them be married!" sighed Miss Fairfax.

He ignored this remark, and, upon a servant's coming in to lay the covers, merely invited Miss Fairfax to sit down at the table. She obeyed him, but although she had fancied herself to have been hungry, and was now confronted with a very handsome dinner, she found that she was too tired to partake of anything but the lightest of repasts. The Earl pressed her in vain to salmon, lamb, green goose, and apricot tartlets: she would take nothing but some soup and a glass of wine. "To tell you the truth," she said candidly, "I feel a trifle sick."

"This, I collect, is a reproach to me for having obliged you to come with me!" said his lordship, in a goaded voice.

"Oh, no!" she murmured.

He went on eating his dinner, a heavy frown on his face. Miss Fairfax was wondering whether she would be permitted to go to bed before the Earl's return from Newark, with (or without) his ward, when one of the servants came into the room with the intelligence that a lady and gentleman had that instant arrived at the inn, and were demanding to see his lordship.

"A lady and gentleman?" repeated the Earl. "Demanding to see *me*?" He looked towards Miss Fairfax in the liveliest astonishment. "This is certainly unexpected!" he said. "Can it be that Lucilla has thought better of her rashness?"

Miss Fairfax, who had risen from the table and gone back to the fireside, did not feel equal to hazarding any conjecture. She agreed that it was indeed unexpected.

It turned out to be more unexpected than the Earl had bargained for. Instead of Miss Gellibrand and her swain, a matron with a face not unlike a parrot's sailed into the parlour, closely followed by an insipid-looking gentleman in a sad-coloured redingote.

The Earl stood staring, his napkin still grasped in one hand, the other lightly holding the back of his chair. The matron, having paused on the threshold, tottered forward, all the plumes in her beehive-bonnet nodding in sympathy with her evident agitation, and pronounced in thrilling accents, "We are in time!"

"What in the name of heaven does this mean?" demanded the Earl, looking as black as thunder.

Miss Fairfax, who had recognised the newcomers as the Earl's aunt-in-law and her son, his cousin and heir, blinked at them in considerable surprise.

Lady Wilfrid Drayton paid no heed to her, but said, addressing her nephew, "It means, Charles, that I am in time to stop your doing what you will regret all your life!"

"Upon my word, ma'am, someone seems to have been busy! What

the—what do you know of the matter, pray?"

"I know all!" said the lady comprehensively.

"The devil you do! Perhaps you will be so obliging as to tell me, ma'am, to which of my servants you are indebted for your information?"

"It does not signify talking!" she said, sweeping this home-question aside. "Most solemnly I warn you, Charles, that you are making a terrible mistake!"

Her son, who had been engaged in sucking the knob of his cane, removed it from his mouth to say, "Knowing it to be a matter closely concerning us—"

"I know nothing of the sort," interrupted the Earl, looking at him with cold contempt. "In fact, I cannot conceive what the devil you mean by thrusting yourself into my affairs!"

"Your actions are the concern of all your family," announced Lady Wilfrid. "When I learned how you had set off with this woman, and with what disastrous purpose, I saw my duty plain before me!"

A slight flush rose to the Earl's cheeks. "Be good enough, if you please, to speak of Miss Fairfax with civility, ma'am!"

"I shall never believe that the whole affair has not been her doing!"

"That, ma'am, is not a question for you to decide!"

"You may say what you please, but I know better. I knew her for a designing female the instant I clapped eyes on her, though never did I dream she would have gone to these lengths!"

"Miss Fairfax's conduct," said the Earl surprisingly, "has throughout been unimpeachable!"

"My poor Charles, you have been sadly deceived! As a mother, as your aunt, I most earnestly implore you to give up this project, and return with us to London! Do not allow your own good judgment to be overcome by the wiles of an unprincipled woman!"

"You are labouring under a misapprehension, ma'am," said the Earl, meticulously polite, but with a dangerous sparkle in his eyes. "So far from my having acted upon Miss Fairfax's instigation, she is here wholly against her will!"

The effect of this pronouncement was hardly what he had expected. Lady Wilfrid uttered a shriek, and exclaimed, "Merciful heavens!" while her son turned a pair of goggling eyes upon Miss Fairfax, saying, "Good Gad! You don't say so, cousin! Well, if this does not beat all! 'Pon my soul, I would not have thought it of you, no, damme, I would not!"

"I don't believe it!" said Lady Wilfrid, recovering from her stupefaction. "She meant to entrap you from the start!"

"Oh!" cried Miss Fairfax, raising her hand to a suddenly burning cheek.

The Earl, glancing swiftly from one to the other of his relatives, said, "We are, I believe, at cross-purposes, ma'am. Oblige me by telling me in more precise terms, if you please, why you have followed me to this place."

His aunt bent a look of deep reproach upon him. "Attempt to pass that unprincipled female off with what degree of credit you may, you will not deceive me! Can you deny that you are on your way to Gretna Green?"

"So that's it, is it?" said the Earl. His frown had vanished, but the smile which took its place caused his cousin to remove himself thoughtfully to the other side of the table. "No, my dear Aunt Almeria, I do not deny it!"

The afflicted lady gave a gasp. "A nobody!" she said. "You, a confirmed bachelor (for I don't consider for a moment that nonsensical notion you had once of marrying your ward!), to fall under the sway of a wretched little dab of a governess! You cannot mean it!"

Miss Fairfax, who felt ready to sink, made a movement of protest, but the Earl spoke before she had time to forestall him.

"I never meant anything more in my life," he said deliberately. "You have had your journey for nothing, ma'am: my determination to wed Miss Fairfax is fixed. As for your dismay, I am well aware that my marriage must come as a sad blow to my cousin there, but I have more than once warned him that it is ill waiting for dead men's shoes. I have the honour, ma'am, to wish you a very good evening!"

He strode to the door, and wrenched it open. Before anyone could move, however, his effect was spoiled by the tempestuous entrance of a young lady in a travelling cloak whose hood had fallen back from a head of bright, tumbled curls. Without appearing to notice the other occupants

43

of the room, this damsel cast herself upon his lordship's chest, exclaiming, "Oh, my dear guardian, I'm so thankful you are here! The most dreadful thing! You must come at once!"

The bemused silence which had greeted Miss Gellibrand's dramatic entrance was broken by the voice of Lady Wilfrid, stridently demanding to be told what Lucilla was doing in Grantham. No one enlightened her. The Earl, disengaging the lapels of his coat from his ward's grasp, said, "What has happened? What has that fellow been doing to you?"

"Oh, nothing, nothing, you stupid thing!" said Miss Gellibrand, stamping her foot. "He is in a deep swoon, and I am quite distracted!"

"In a deep swoon!" exclaimed the Earl, in tones of considerable surprise. "In God's name, why?"

"I think his shoulder is broken," said Miss Gellibrand tragically.

"What in the world has he been doing to get his shoulder broken? And how do you come to be here? I thought you at Newark!"

"So we should have been, only that that odious chaise lost a wheel, just as we had passed the Ram Jam, and we were pitched into the ditch. And Edmund, in attempting to save me, was thrown heavily on to the side of the chaise, all amongst the breaking glass!"

"Oh, my poor child, were you hurt?" cried Miss Fairfax, moving towards her.

"Oh, is that you, Mary? No, only the tiniest scratch. And at first I had no notion that Edmund had sustained any serious injury, for he never said anything, and in the scramble I didn't notice that he was not using his left arm. We thought only of proceeding on our journey, knowing that Shane, and very likely you too, would be hard on our heels. Then the thing was, how to come by another chaise? We thought we should have been able to have hired one at Stretton, and we got on to a cart that was going there, while the postboy rode on to get a wheelwright to fetch the chaise away. Only when we reached Stretton there was no chaise to be had, no suitable conveyance of any sort. There was nothing for it but to come on by the stage to Grantham. And I must say," added Miss Gellibrand buoyantly, "had it not been for my beginning to be in a pucker over Edmund, I should have enjoyed it above all things! Only fancy, dear sir, we had to sit four a side, and a horrid old man was chewing green onions all the way! And such an uproar as was made over our not being on the way-bill! Edmund had actually to bribe the coachman before he would take us up. He said if it was discovered he had *shouldered* us he would very likely be dismissed! However, that doesn't signify. Though we had lost so much time, we were not unhopeful of out-stripping pursuit, and my spirits at least were mounting when they were utterly overpowered by the sight of you, sir, driving past the stage! I thought all was lost, not knowing then how glad I should be to see you! For when we reached this town, we were set down at the most vulgar-looking inn, and I discovered that Edmund was suffering the greatest anguish, hardly able to stand! There was no staying at that horrid tavern, so we came to the Angel, Edmund leaning upon my arm, and myself, as you may suppose, in the greatest alarm imaginable. And then, to crown all, they tried to turn us away from here, saying it was a posting-house, and they could not admit stage-passengers! I do not know what would have become of us had not Edmund sunk suddenly into a swoon! Everything was bustle and confusion then, but I caught sight of your curricle being wheeled into a coachhouse, my dear sir, and staying only to see my sainted Edmund carried into the house, I ran upstairs to find you. Please, please come to Edmund at once, and explain everything to that odious landlord!"

Lady Wilfrid, who had listened to this tumultuous recital in astonished silence, turned towards Miss Fairfax, as the Earl left the room in the wake of his volatile ward, and said in a stunned voice, "It is Lucilla who is eloping?"

"Yes," said Miss Fairfax.

Lady Wilfrid eyed her suspiciously. "Am I to understand, then, that you are not about to marry my nephew?"

"No, indeed," said Miss Fairfax, rather forlornly. "I accompanied Lord Shane merely to take Lucilla home again."

"Well, I don't understand!" suddenly announced Mr. Drayton. "He said he was about to be married to you!"

"I think," said Miss Fairfax diffidently, "that you made him lose his temper, and he said it to make you angry."

"He was always a disagreeable creature," said Lady Wilfrid. "I

45

collect that he has set his face against Lucilla's marriage, I dare say for no other reasons than pride and self-will."

"Indeed, ma'am, I believe Mr. Edmund Monksley to be a most unexceptionable young man," replied Miss Fairfax, perceiving that in Lady Wildrid Lucilla would find an eager ally. "The only objections are Lucilla's youth and Mr. Monksley's lack of fortune."

Lady Wilfrid fixed her with a singularly calculating gaze. "My nephew had never the least disposition to sympathise with the Pangs of Love," she uttered. "With me, it is otherwise. I have the tender heart of a parent, and such vulgar considerations as poverty, or inequality of birth, weigh with me not at all. Nothing could be more affecting than Lucilla's story! But then I am all sensibility, quite unlike Shane, who has a heart of stone! I shall tell him that he has no right to forbid this marriage."

The Honourable Frederick, who had apparently been pondering the situation, once more ceased sucking the knob of his cane to say in a tone of great relief, "Well, this is famous! If he does not wed the governess, and we can prevail upon him to consent to Lucilla's marriage to this swooning-fellow, I do not at all despair of a happy issue."

"Excuse me," said Miss Fairfax, conscious of her reddening cheeks. "I think I should go downstairs to assist in restoring Mr. Monksley."

By the time Miss Fairfax reached his side, Mr. Monksley, a fresh-faced young man, with very blue eyes and a decided chin, had recovered consciousness. Finding himself looking straight up into the countenance of his Lucilla's guardian, he at once embarked on a speech, which would no doubt have become extremely impassioned had not the Earl cut it short by saying, "Yes, you may tell me all that later, but you had better be still now until the surgeon has attended to your shoulder."

Tenderly clasping one of Mr. Monksley's hands, Miss Gellibrand said in resolute accents, "Nothing you can say, Shane, will prevent my going to Gretna as soon as Edmund is well enough!"

"Nonsense!" said his lordship. "These Gretna weddings are not at all the thing, and you had better put such romantic fustian out of your head at once."

"Believe me, my lord," said Mr. Monksley faintly, "nothing but the sternest necessity could have prevailed upon me to propose so clandestine a union to one for whom I entertain feelings of the deepest respect!"

"I wish you will not talk to me like a play-actor!" said his lordship irritably. "If you must marry my ward, let it at least be in a respectable fashion!"

"Angel!" cried Miss Gellibrand, lifting a glowing face.

His lordship regarded her with the utmost disfavour. "If it is angelic to be more than willing to rid myself of a most tiresome charge, I am certainly an angel," he said witheringly.

The arrival of a surgeon, carrying an ominous black bag, created a timely diversion. Mr. Monksley's broken shoulder was set and securely bound; two of the serving-men carried him upstairs to a bedchamber; and it was not until he had been comfortably disposed between sheets, and was being fed with spoonfuls of broth by his adoring Lucilla, that Miss Fairfax had leisure to go in search of her employer. She found him in the parlour belowstairs, giving some directions to the landlord. When he saw her, he smiled, and held out his hand, a gesture which made her feel very much inclined to burst into tears. The landlord having bowed himself out of the room, she said, however, in as prosaic a tone as she was able to command, "Mr. Monksley is feeling much easier now. You have been so very kind, sir!"

"Oh, the devil take Monksley, and Lucilla too!" said his lordship. "We have more important things to consider. What in thunder are we to do, Mary Fairfax? I told that abominable old woman that we were going to be married at Gretna Green. But no consideration on earth would prevail upon me to behave in such a preposterous fashion! Besides, I cannot possibly take you to Gretna without another rag to your back than what you stand up in."

"My dear sir, there is no need for you to trouble your head about it," said Miss Fairfax, trying to smile. "I told Lady Wilfrid there was no question of our going to Gretna."

"You did, did you?" said the Earl, looking at her rather keenly.

"Yes, of course, sir. Where—where is Lady Wilfrid?"

"Gone to put up at the George, where I heartily hope she may find the

GEORGETTE HEYER:

sheets damp!"

"But—but why?" stammered Miss Fairfax.

"Because," said the Earl, "*I* told her that we were going to be married just as soon as I can procure a license!"

Miss Fairfax had the oddest sensation of turning first hot and then cold. "You are being absurd!" she said, in a voice which did not seem to belong to her.

"Mary," said his lordship, taking her hands in his, and holding them fast, "have those shocking faults of mine given you a disgust of me?"

"No," said Miss Fairfax weakly. "Oh, no!"

"I don't know how I came to be such a fool (but you said I was stupid), yet—would you believe it?—it was not until my aunt accused me of it that I knew I have been in love with you for years!"

Miss Fairfax trembled. "But you can't! Marry to disoblige your family? Oh, no, no!"

"My family be damned!" said the Earl. "I wish you will look at me, Mary!"

"Well, I won't," said Miss Fairfax, making a feeble attempt to free her hands. "I did think that you regarded me sometimes with—with a certain partiality, but I know, if you do not, how shocking such a match would be, and I won't marry you. I shall look for another eligible situation."

"No one will employ you without a testimonial, and I shan't give you one."

"I think you are extremely disagreeable, besides being mad!" said Miss Fairfax, in a scolding tone.

"Yes," said the Earl, taking her in his arms. "And I have also the most overbearing manners, so you may as well stop arguing with me, and kiss me instead."

Miss Fairfax, apparently much struck by this advice, abandoned her half-hearted struggles, said, "Oh, my dearest!" in a wavering voice, and subsided meekly into his embrace.

## Books About the Brontës

(essay published in *Punch*, 31 March 1954, p. 414)

A certain author, being engaged at the time in research into the life of Shakespeare, once remarked to me that there seemed to be something about Shakespeare which sends people slightly mad. The appearance of yet another Book about the Brontës has set me wondering whether the same observation might not apply equally well to this family. There is no end to the books about them, no end to the theories about them, and no end to the readers of the books. I will confess at once that I read them myself, although (and I tremble with terror as I write these words) the only member of the family whose work I really admire is Emily.

I find Anne's books unreadable; and while I appreciate the rich melodrama of *Jane Eyre*, I cannot away with *The Professor*, or *Shirley*, and find *Villette* not quite my cup of tea. I admire Charlotte for having written a splendid best-seller, but when I am asked to place her alongside the Olympians I can't do it. Nor do I find her, as she reveals herself in her correspondence, sympathetic. Only one of her biographers succeeded in diminishing my dislike of her, and he did this by making me see how funny she was. Which is heresy.

I have no interest in Branwell, or in Patrick; my appreciation of Emily's work doesn't imbue me with a desire to discover whether she really was any of the things various biographers have decided she must have been; and as for Sweet Little Anne, who could find nothing better to do than to use her own brother as a model for a book designed to warn young men of the evils of drink, drugs, and falling in love with other men's wives, I can only say that her particular brand of piety makes me feel unwell.

So why do I still read Books about the Brontës? Obviously, because they had more compelling personalities than even their most ardent worshippers realize.

I have read so many books about them that if only I had a New Theory to advance I could write one myself. I know the rules, and I have been made familiar with the facts.

The rule for the Charlotte-biographer is that whatever she wrote or said must be taken to be strictly true, and not a self-dramatization, or the truth merely as her imagination saw it. Not even when she states that she and Emily and Anne walked the parlour floor night after night, discussing the books each was writing, must her accuracy be doubted. And, indeed, I don't doubt that this is what she thought they did; and to suggest that neither Emily nor Anne ever got a word in edgeways, or that no novelist, writing with the passionate absorption of Charlotte and Emily, ever took more than a perfunctory interest in the books other people happened to be writing, will not do at all. Only when Charlotte's words seem to contradict one's own theory must they be in any way impugned. When this occurs they can be *reinterpreted.*

Emily's biographer can dismiss Charlotte's testimony by explaining that although she wrote in good faith she was ignorant of certain circumstances, and so is not to be believed. Of course, if she said anything that supports the New Theory, that *is* to be believed. In fact, for Emily's biographer no holds are barred, and there are infinite opportunities for the free exercise of one's imagination. Almost anything can be read into her poems.

When I write *my* Book about the Brontës it will be a book to Clear Up All Doubts, so that no one need write another. I shall start by discussing in a very temperate way every previous biography; but before I have progressed far those mysterious, dead personalities will have acquired a grip on me. Rage will begin to possess my soul, and with far more fervour than temperateness I shall expose the errors of my predecessors. I shall deprecate the tendency of others to idealize, or to read too much into stray lines; and I shall laugh at those who have invested the Brontës with extraordinary characteristics. I shall be quite sincere about this, but the Brontës will get me into their thrall, and when I have flattened out all previous biographers I shall urge with passion and conviction a new and even more fantastic theory.

And then someone will be moved by the spirit to write another Book about the Brontës, utterly demolishing mine, and so it will go on. And if, wheresoever they may be, the Brontës have developed senses of humour, what fun they must be having! Who can doubt, in face of all the wildly conflicting theories they have put into our heads, that they are having fun? And who would grudge it to them?


## *How to be a Literary Critic*
(essay published in "Booking Office,"
*Punch*, 28 April 1954, pp. 520-21)

The first step towards this goal is to write a book, or even, if you are very industrious, two or three books, and to get these published. Failing a book, a few articles will do. They need not be profound, or beautifully written, and the book need not be successful, the whole point of this admittedly laborious start to your chosen profession being that by getting into print you will subsequently be able to appear as a critic in the guise of a Well-known Author. The publication of an article will turn you into an author; and editorial or B.B.C. propaganda will very soon make you well known.

The next step is to rid yourself of diffidence. If, when you are first handed the latest work of one whom you suspect to be your literary superior, you feel that it would be effrontery for you to criticize it, do not decline to do so. Remember that no qualifications are necessary for a Literary Critic, and that this is the Day of the Little Man, when the more insignificant you are, and the more valueless your opinions, the greater will be your chance of obtaining a hearing. Moreover, if you stick to the job you will soon cease to feel such qualms. There is nothing like sitting in judgment on other people's work for increasing your self-esteem.

There are four kinds of Literary Criticism, but it will only be necessary to discuss three of these, since the first kind is a fast-vanishing one, and is in the hands of a few survivors from the Bad Old Days. These persons hold obstinately to the belief that a Literary Critic should not only be himself a distinguished man of letters but should also be (if not an expert on the subject of the book he is to review) at least a man of wide culture and critical ability. This belief is obviously too out-worn to be worthy of consideration, so we will pass on to the three more important kinds of Literary Criticism. The first of these is the Descriptive. For this you write a précis of the plot of the book—which doesn't, of course mean that you have to read the whole book. All you have to do is to skim the first half and write an outline of the plot up to the point where you left off. You then say that to divulge how the story ends would spoil it for the author's countless admirers, adding (to spike the guns of carping persons who might otherwise object that you hadn't criticized the book at all) that it is an excellent story, or a very indifferent story.

The second and the third kinds are for the more advanced critics, who have gained enough assurance to deal with any book, from the latest novel to a definitive work on Ancient Greek Civilization. The second kind is the Hagiological, and the third the Abusive. Much the same rules apply to each, except that the second kind should be practised with less discrimination than the third. In neither should you allow yourself to be deterred by ignorance, and never should you waste your time verifying either the author's statements or your own, possibly erroneous, convictions. If you are a Hagiologist, the author will be gratified by your praise (always supposing that he reads your review), and the people you are writing for won't know any better than you do. If you are an Abuser, it is rather more difficult, for in the case of the book which deals with a specialized subject you must take care to condemn it only on general grounds, such as saying that it is dull, or has too many footnotes, or hasn't convinced *you*. In neither case is it necessary to go into detail. Do not, for instance—supposing you should recognize them—say anything about the style or technique. These are very unimportant matters, and won't interest Mr. and Mrs. Littleman in the least.

The book dealing with Ideas can be regarded by the Critic as a piece of cake. If the ideas happen to coincide with your own, and the author is not a political opponent of the organ which employs you, you can spread yourself in encomiums, though this won't be such fun as when the author's ideas aren't yours, and the policy of your organ is to suppress him. You can then work off any personal spite you may have against him by writing slightingly of his mental capacity and hinting that he is on the verge of senility; or, if you merely disagree with his opinions, you can just condemn his book without reserve.  After all, if he's only writing about Ideas, no one can say that you're wrong when you state that these are childish, trashy, laughable, or so boring that they sent you to sleep; and as you won't be called upon to pit your wits against his in public argument, your readers, or hearers, won't have the chance to compare your respective mental powers, and will very likely assume that you must be pretty brainy yourself to have been given the book to review at all.

But this last form of Literary Criticism should not be attempted by the novice who has not entirely shaken off his modesty.  Let but a doubt of your competence to criticize the work of a possibly distinguished author creep into your mind and you will find yourself demurring at his conclusions only in terms verging on the polite, or even the respectful. Don't be afraid of making a fool of yourself!  Reflect that you could have written the book much better yourself, if only you had had the time and the inclination for the task; and that the literate won't be listening, if you're speaking on the air, or doing more than glance at your review, if it appears in print; and go right ahead!  There will be no reprisals.  If the author is young and struggling, he won't dare to expose your pretensions; and if he is well established he won't think it worth while to do so.

## II. Reviews of her books

Over 400 reviews—more than half of which are included here. That averages out to about seven reviews per book, but, of course, that is not how it was in fact. While each book has been reviewed at least once—*The Convenient Marriage* (1934), *Regency Buck* (1935), and *The Nonesuch* (1962) indeed *only* once—the most reviews received by any one book—*Arabella* (1949)—has been fifteen. The number has apparently depended less on how enjoyable the book is than on the circumstances under which it was published. *These Old Shades* (1926), for example, with which her writing career is said by some to have really gotten under way, and which is still a favorite with many fans, has been reviewed only twice, and then in the trade journal *Publishers Weekly*, while *My Lord John* (1975), which equally many fans find virtually unreadable, but which was her last book and published posthumously, was reviewed fourteen times immediately after its publication, including reviews in *The Wall Street Journal* and *The Atlantic Monthly*.

The length of the individual reviews is just as unpredictable in hindsight, and seems to depend simply on the reviewer, the nature of the reviewing publication, and the space available. *Simon the Coldheart* (1925) and *Barren Corn* (1930), though comparatively unpopular and even suppressed by Georgette Heyer herself, both received well over 1000 words in the *Boston Evening Transcript* shortly after their initial publication. Meanwhile, reviews in *The New Yorker* and *Time* have rarely been much over 50 words, however positive (or negative). From the standpoint of general and literary readership, as well as breadth of audience, the two most significant and consistent reviewing organs have been the *Times Literary Supplement* (London) and the *New York Times Book Review*, which over the years have published 27 and 34 Georgette

Heyer reviews respectively. It is interesting that the American periodical has reviewed over half of her books, while the English one has reviewed fewer than half, but I will not attempt to speculate as to the reason for this.

For the most part, the reviewers' names are unfamiliar, at least to me. Literary critic V. S. Pritchett wrote a short review of *Barren Corn* for *The Spectator* in 1930, damning the novel as dull and quite unworthy of the novelist's "pretty talent." American humorist Will Cuppy reviewed several of the mysteries for *The New York Herald Tribune*, five of which are included here, as is a review of *The Grand Sophy* by historical novelist Elswyth Thane. In 1963 feminist novelist Brigid Brophy greeted *False Colours* in *New Statesman* as "a piece of childish let's-pretend but blessedly unpretentious" and "nimble to the point of wit in copying period detail." And in 1970 another well-known English writer, Marghanita Laski, wrote a longish article for *The Times* (London) ostensibly in response to the publication of *Charity Girl*; however, since it really had almost nothing to do with the novel and almost everything to do with Laski's dubious response to Georgette Heyer in general, it is included not in section II with the reviews, but in section V with "other books and articles" on the novelist.

The reviews in general are fun to read, some more so than others, but they also give an idea of both Georgette Heyer's publishing history and her presumed audience. I had originally intended that this book include a complete record of all the editions of Georgette Heyer's novels published anywhere or in any language, but the task rapidly became so monumental as to lose its meaning. Suffice it to say on the basis of her reviews that her books have been continuously in print since she was first published in the 1920s, reaching their height of popularity in the late 1960s, which is also when she was first referred to in a review as Mrs. Rougier. Since the mid-'70s there have been fewer reviews simply because her reputation was by then established. Even the four contemporary novels she published early on and subsequently suppressed have been available in unauthorized American reprints since the 1970s, when their international copyright expired. One or more of Georgette Heyer's novels have also been translated into at least seventeen different languages, including

Chinese, Finnish, Turkish, Greek, Czech, and Portuguese. There have been more German translations than anything else—all but the suppressed novels, in fact—but Russia is rapidly catching up. Her Austrian/German publishers kindly sent me a representative collection of reviews in German, but they are so similar to the reviews in English (in both general content and entertaining little mistakes) that I have not included them here.

When I first began to read Georgette Heyer and mentioned the fact to friends with similar backgrounds and, I thought, tastes, the frequent reply, especially from those in the UK, was, "Oh yes, I read her in my teens," the implication being that we should all be beyond that now. Many reviews, especially in such periodicals as *Library Journal* and *Horn Book*, do recommend her novels for teenage girls or "young adults," and when it was first published, *Simon the Coldheart* (1925), more adventure and history than romance, was suggested even for "older boys, as well as lovers of romance." In general, however, the library journals seem to recommend acquisition of her novels for the general collection, and my experience suggests that, indeed, most if not all public libraries of any size at least in the United States have a few of her books and perhaps even an audiotape or two.

Much more could be deduced or extrapolated from so many reviews, but I leave that to the taste and interest of the individual reader and add only as food for thought a favorite quotation, taken from Martin Levin's review for *The New York Times*: "What Edgar Rice Burroughs was to the African jungle, Georgette Heyer is to Regency England." So wrong, and yet so right!

## 1921

**1. "New Books and Reprints,"** *The Times Literary Supplement*, **22 September 1921, p. 614:**

*The Black Moth*. A Romance of the Eighteenth Century. By Georgette Heyer. 334 pp. Constable. 7s.6d.n.

This stages the eighteenth century with the usual stage business and scenery—highwaymen, duelling, gaming; and high society in London, Bath, and Sussex (Horace Walpole crosses the stage for a moment). The peg on which the plot hangs is a dramatic moment when Richard Carstares, son of Lord Wyncham, cheats at cards, and his elder brother Jack, heir to the title, takes the blame, quits society, and takes to the road. Jack's easy-going smiling quixotry is almost excessive; but he makes a fascinating hero of romance; and it is a well-filled story which keeps the reader pleased.

**2. *The Saturday Review* (London) 132, 5 November 1921, p.542:**

*The Black Moth*, by Georgette Heyer (Constable, 7s. net), is a romance of the eighteenth century, with wicked Duke, self-sacrificing elder brother, weak younger brother, highwayman, gambling, abduction, and rescue all complete. The hero takes care to appear in appropriate costume on each occasion we meet him; his horse and his fencing are of the best. Seriously, the author has made quite a respectable story of these old properties, far more life-like than could have been expected.

**3. I. W. L. in "The Christmas Bookstalls," *Boston Evening Transcript*, 23 November 1921, pt. 4, p. 6:**

*The Black Moth*. A Romantic Story of Eighteenth Century England. By Georgette Heyer, Boston: Houghton Mifflin Company.
The Black Moth, man! Have ye never heard of Devil Belmanoir? 'Tis evident ye were not raised in London, then, in the days of the Hanover Princess, no, nor yet mixed with the gallant and fair at Bath, when Beau Nash ruled the Pump Room. Tracy, Duke of Andover, was his birthright, and many another name beside, but Devil Belmanoir men called him, for the twinkling light that dwelt in those black and long-lashed eyes. Devil Belmanoir, when men waxed hot in their cups, Devil Belmanoir when stakes at cards ran high, and Devil Belmanoir, God help

us all, at the swish of a perfumed petticoat. As many paramours as the French Louis had Tracy, Duke of Andover, and a handsomer calf, and a far better hand at the sword hilt, and as handsome a leg could he make at a duchess's rout as any gallant of them all. Yet did he not flee happiness, Tracy of Belmanoir, and he took defeat, black heart though he had, like a gentleman.

For the Black Moth is not the hero, only, in joyous olden fashion, the villain. The title role is reserved for that prince of good fellows, that peerless highwayman, Jack Carstares, Duke of Wyncham. Highwayman, say you, and yet a duke? Aye, faith, and for no good reason, merely to chase away ennui in a gentleman forced from his home. For Jack has a younger brother, Dick, who cheated at cards on a distant night, when both loved a pretty lady, and Jack, the elder, went forth with all men's scorn, and the younger married a wife. But, tare an 'ouns, he could not have done it, our Jack o' the laughter-lit eyes, who holds up a coach so gallantly, who succors a lady so valiantly. What then? Have ye guessed it?

They crossed each other's paths from the first, Devil Belmanoir, with that look in his eye of race and breeding and a good breed gone bad, and Jack, Duke of Wyncham, whose brother Dick has married the lady of Belmanoir, Tracy's sister, the lovely Lady Lavinia, crossed it from the night when Tracy, far-seeing, picked up a scratched card and laughed, and then, with a look, crossed the room. Yet who would have thought, on that black night, when the devil held up Diana's coach, that it was highwayman Jack who lurked in the shadows, who fought, with a hole in his shoulder, and saved the lady, only to faint in her arms! What can highwayman Jack do with a lady, Jack with a blackened name? Naught, says he, between his teeth, and rides away. But Devil Belmanoir is not used to failure. This time there is no highwayman in the offing. To cover he rides with his captive and kisses her in the great hall of Andover. "By God, it is too late," he swears. "Nought can avail you now!"

"You delude yourself, Belmanoir," says a voice from the recessed window. And Carstares turns to meet his Grace. A pretty fight is it, then, though one man has ridden half the night on his small mare Jenny, and the old wound in his shoulder needs but a touch to break into life. Riposte and quinte, quartre and riposte, such a fight as one seldom sees between a day and a night. Then Tracy lunges the length of his arm and a deep, red splash stains the whiteness of my Lord's sleeve. Well fought, oh, Jack, the highwayman, well fought, but the end is near.

A tale of love and adventure is this, and withal, a tale of personages well met in the old streets of London, of character work of a clearness and charm, and an originality to delight a delver in men's thoughts, yet, tare an 'ouns, a tale to stir one's blood. Those nights on the open road— we sympathize with Jim, Jack's faithful servant, because, glad though he is that my lord, again my lord, still wants a rude fellow like him he pulls, on a sudden, a long face, in the middle of tying the bow to his master's wig. "What's amiss now? And what have you done with my patches?"

"In that little box, sir—yes—that one. I was just thinking—here's the haresfoot, sir—that I shall never be able to see ye hold up a coach now." And my lord laughs, as that good friend across the hall, O'Hara, has not heard him laugh, no not for many a day. What days are these, God help us all, that we see such highwaymen no more. But at least we may take to the ribbon of road in the moonlight, for a brief space, with Jack and with Black Moth.

## 4. *The Springfield Sunday Republican*, 25 December 1921, p. 11a:

*The Black Moth.* England in the picturesque 18th-century era of the Spectator, Henry Esmond, the stage coach and horse pistols, is made the basis of an interesting historical romance by Georgette Heyer in *The Black Moth.* In workmanship and interest it is an agreeable specimen of the historical type of novel. Outstanding among the scenes portrayed in the vigorous action are the ball masque, the Pump Room at Bath, and other historical sites. Belles in crinolines and beaux in powdered wigs and silk stockings furnish a picturesqueness to the various scenes. Action is centered about "The Black Moth," a sinister figure, who wears his hair unpowdered, has other as characteristic differences from the general run, and only once meets his match with the sword. There is a winsome heroine who is also the center of lively action.

## 1923

**5. F. B. in the** *Boston Evening Transcript,* **23 June 1923, Book Section, p. 5:**

*The Great Roxhythe.* An Historical Romance of the Days of Charles II. By Georgette Heyer. Boston: Small, Maynard & Company.

An unusual historical romance is this, considering that while the period is the reign of Charles II, the actors of the drama it unfolds are, in a large majority, men. The four women who do appear are Lady Castlemaine, the Duchess of Portsmouth, la belle Stuart, Katherine the Griselda-like Queen of England, and "Madame," that sister of the English King married to the Duc d'Orléans, brother of the King of France. With the exception of the last named, who is one of the chief political intriguers in the earlier scenes of the drama, these women play but transient parts. To lovers of historical romance, especially when it is that of the epochal events which write the history of nations, this freedom from the detail of the "affaires" of the Stuart King brings a sense of relief. And although at times one wearies a trifle at the exaggeration of "the great Roxhythe's" irresistibleness—he being portrayed somewhat after the fashion of the "elegant, imperturbable," fascinatingly wicked hero of *Under Two Flags,* and those of other of Ouida's novels—we follow with an increasing interest to its logical end the story of the else unrecorded part played by My Lord the Marquis of Roxhythe in those political plots of the day.

The portrait of Charles II, as detail after detail is painted in through nearly four hundred pages, is one whose verisimilitude history has proved. Utterly without moral scruples, and in spite of a certain careless kindness of heart, never forgetting the days when, with Roxhythe and a few other loyal friends, he had been hunted from one corner of Europe to another, and deep down in his Stuart heart never forgiving the English

Parliament which exiled him, he stands out rather more clearly drawn than is usual, against the background of a period when France, striving for the hegemony of Europe, was endeavoring to make a cat's paw of England in her schemes against Spain and Holland. The personality of his chief favorite, Roxhythe, faithful unto death with a loyalty worthy a better cause, is evidently modelled upon that of the Duke of Buckingham, who was, historically, his royal master's go-between in those long-drawn-out secret negotiations, through which a king of England became the pensioner of a French king. To the character of Roxhythe, however, is given an element of loyalty to at least one object the great Buckingham "conspicuously lacked."

The story begins in the year 1670, when the Government of England had allied itself with Holland and Sweden in that Triple Alliance so popular with the English. A secret treaty was signed this same year between the kings of France and of England, by which Charles II engaged to make a public profession of the Roman Catholic religion, to assist Louis XIV in subjugating Holland, and to uphold his claims to the throne of Spain. In return, Louis agreed to pay Charles three million livres a year, and to help subdue the English people, should they learn of this secret treaty and rebel against the Crown. In these negotiations, Roxhythe is the English King's agent. Both the king of England and of France strive, of course secretly, to win to their support the young Prince of Orange, afterward William III of England. But as incorruptible as his great ancestor, "the Silent," is this prince. He is, indeed, the one figure in the book—young Christopher Dart, the great Roxhythe's secretary, excepted—who through all the political plots of the last decade of the reign of Charles II proves incapable of being bribed. The present story covers these ten years. Wars followed by wars on the Continent, the rulers of the three dominant European nations continually plotting to attain their ends: Louis of France for the hegemony of Europe; William of Orange for his inherited rights and for the political integrity of Holland; Charles of England for the money to pay his never-ceasing pleasures. Charles distrusted by Louis; Louis distrusted by Charles; both distrusted by the English, and the Prince of Orange feared by both kings.

This, the historical maze through which the players of the drama wind, some blindly, all save a very few in pursuit of personal aggrandizement. Until, one February day in 1685, Roxhythe kisses for the last time the fast-chilling hands of that most amiable and engaging of men, his "little master," Charles II, and with the hushed works of the king's physician, "Gentlemen, the King is dead," leaves Whitehall, to himself meet death as insouciantly as becomes "the great Roxhythe."

### 6. "Latest Works of Fiction," *The New York Times Book Review*, 24 June 1923, p. 17:

*The Great Roxhythe.* By Georgette Heyer. Boston: Small, Maynard & Co. $2.

That colorful period of the English Restoration, brilliant, witty cynical, amusing and immoral, taking its tone from the witty, cynical and charming King who stands in its forefront, has always possessed a fascination for writers of romances. And a good deal of fascination, too, for the reader, who gets the thrill of the so-called Popish plot, of the intrigues and the perils, the turmoil over the Exclusion bill, vicariously, and without any of the dangers which beset the men and women of the time. But if the men of the time make an interesting group, a group composed for the most part of strongly contrasted and no less strongly emphasized individualities, it is the women gathered about the King, from the unhappy Queen herself to that frolicsome baggage Nell Gwynn, on whom the attention of the romancers are usually fixed.

It is here that Georgette Heyer's novel breaks sharply with tradition. For, though the beautiful Henriette d'Angleterre, Duchesse d'Orléans, appears several times, though the Duchess of Portsmouth, Lady Castlemaine and the Duchess of Cleveland form part of the story's background, it is principally a tale of men and of the deep love and friendship of men for one another. The strongest emotion in the life of Christopher Dart, the young, ingenuous, idealistic patriot who became secretary to the Most Noble the Marquis of Roxhythe, was his adoring love for the man who was his lord and master, the man he trusted absolutely, against whom he was warned more than once, but of whom he would believe no evil, until, and to his lasting grief, that evil was proved, and proved up to the hilt.  And as the strongest emotion in Christopher's life was his affection for Roxhythe so the motive power in Roxhythe's life, the feeling to which he sacrificed everything and every one, Christopher included, was the bond which held him to the King.  As his cousin and friend, Lady Fanny Montgomery, once told him, he had sacrificed "truth, honour, patriotism for man"; for the King's sake he had lied and intrigued and betrayed until no one else trusted him.

Beginning in 1668, when Charles had been on the throne for only a few years, the novel closes not long after the accession of the stupid and ill-fated James.  And while it gives an interesting picture of the life of the time as seen and lived by one who was the favorite and constant companion of Charles II, it suffers somewhat from having too large a canvas, and from a certain monotony in the telling.  My lord's exploit in Holland, his very interesting interview with that Prince of Orange who was one day to become King of England, form one episode.  Then comes the Treaty of Dover, when Charles sold his country to France, followed by the intrigues regarding the succession, and the plot to exclude James from the throne, Charles's triumph and his death.  The effect of climax, of an accumulative building up is lacking, and this lack injures the drama of it all.  Then, too, the book is very much too long; there is a great deal of repetition, many incidents and conversations which do little to deveop character, while of story there is almost none.  For the book is primarily the study of a single, complex character, the character of "The Great Roxhythe."

To the men and women surrounding him he was an enigma; even the "little master" he loved so dearly did not always understand him, although the clue lay in his devotion to that same master. Brilliantly clever, extremely able, cynical, graceful and gracious, kindly and cruel, cool, self-possessed at all times, courageous, daring, clear-sighted and clear-headed, the reader is made to feel more than a little of the fascination to which young Christopher so utterly succumbed. There are in the book a number of clever sketches of men and women; most notable, perhaps, the portrait of the Prince of Orange.  A colorful and interesting account of a colorful and interesting period is this which Georgette Heyer presents to us under the name of the man who to a very great extent personifies it, the man who is here represented as the power behind the throne, David, Marquis of Roxhythe, whose one aim and desire in life was to do the King's pleasure.

## 7. *The Open Shelf*, September 1923, p. 68:

Heyer, Georgette. *The Great Roxhythe.*
An historical romance of the court of King Charles II, in which the hero is His Majesty's faithful favorite, the Marquis of Roxhythe, and the emphasis is upon political intrigue, although several beautiful duchesses and other fair ladies flit through the pages.

## 8. "The World of Books," *Springfield Republican*, 3 October 1923, p. 8:

*The Great Roxhythe.* A Strong Political Romance of the Reign of Charles II.
Georgette Heyer, who has previously dared the field of historical fiction, comes forward with another story, *The Great Roxhythe*, (Small, Maynard & Co, Boston; $2), which is a character study of the closest political friend of Charles II of England, the Marquis of Roxhythe, "who did the king his will." The Restoration reign has many landmarks on the pages of history, but the author has chosen to stick closely to the political field, involving plots and counterplots, French alliance, Dutch alliance and the problem of the succession, whether Catholic James, the king's brother, or Protestant Monmouth, the king's illegitimate son, or William of Orange, the king's nephew and husband of Princess Mary, should follow the merry monarch upon the English throne.
In the kaleidoscope of personal ambitions and genuine patriotisms, there was one man who never swerved from his creed. Roxhythe was the

king's man; his loyalty was to Charles and not to land or party. An exquisite, a courtier, a diplomat, one cannot help admiring his steadfast devotion to the king, no matter what opinion one may hold of his morals and his political finesse. Regarded by some as too lackadaisical to exert himself in intrigue, suspected by others who saw in him an emissary of Charles in local and international plots, and feared by all who knew him as the king's favorite, this remarkable man pulled wires at the courts of England, France and Holland for the personal advantage of his spendthrift master.

That Roxhythe was a lovable man is shown in the delineation of Christopher Dart, his young secretary, who worshiped him and who, blind to his diplomatic immoralities for nine years, continued to love him after resigning from a service whose duplicity he finally sensed. William of Orange is one of the minor characters in the story, a man incapable of being moved by cajolery, straightforward politically, yet hardly more able than an iceberg to evoke enthusiasm from the average statesman. It is a sorry picture on the whole of schemes and plots as history attests and as the author of this romance sets forth with careful detail of local color and broad grasp of essential facts.

**9. "New Books and Reprints. Fiction,"** *Times Literary Supplement*, **29 November 1923, p. 838:**

*Instead of the Thorn.* By Georgette Heyer. 318 pp. Hutchinson. 7s.6d.n.

The author's theme is the old tangle created by the marriage of a man, all aflame with the rights of manhood but altogether ignorant of the consideration and co-partnership which matrimony demands, to a maid all affectionate but totally without understanding. The setting is, however, altogether Georgian. Elizabeth's coming out was into a world of dance clubs. It was at one such that she met and was promptly fascinated by Stephen. Dancing and motoring made up the courtship. Relations and friends are presented, foolishly candid about what does not matter, hopelessly reticent where real things are concerned. This same middle-class throng, just those whom you will meet at the Wisley Hut or at Burford Bridge any fine Sunday in the year, makes up the men and women of the story, and it is to the author's credit that she has made such good use of such plaster-of-paris material.

**1924**

**10. *The New York Times Book Review*, 13 April 1924, pp. 17 & 19:**

*Instead of the Thorn.* By Georgette Heyer. 345 pp. Boston: Small, Maynard & Co. $2.

Georgette Heyer has produced, in *Instead of the Thorn*, a sugar-coated handbook to married life which purports to illustrate how husband and wife may be happy though married. The receipt appears to be that couples should understand one another and make judicious allowances for one another's idiosyncrasies. This is not at all unusual and, indeed, is quite often the case. It is to be doubted, however, that feminists will approve of the culmination of this particular theme, for there is far less adjustment on the husband's side than there is on the wife's. She must go a mile to meet him in this mutual adjustment, while he takes but a desultory step or two toward her. Of course, he is a genius, a writer of novels, and she is but a romantic and reticent child suffering from a Victorian upbringing. Right here the author has produced an extra-ordinary couple, in fact so out of the usual run that it is difficult to perceive how any general rules for married behavior may be drawn from them.

Elizabeth Arden, essentially a prude, educated in the most antiquated way, entirely ignorant of men, is, as her father proudly puts it, "a modest violet in the dell." Stephen Ramsay, a successful young novelist, a light-hearted bohemian, wise in the ways of the world and with no ingrowing inhibitions, is smitten by Elizabeth's shyness and modesty, and the result is an immediate marriage. From the first moment trouble starts. Neither can adjust one's self to the other. Elizabeth is distressed by all sorts of things, Stephen's unshaven face in the morning, his clothing cheek by jowl with hers, his intimacies which disgust her, even the discussion of money matters which she does not think quite nice. In other words, she is 100 per cent. prude.

It is plainly the authors' [sic] intention to divert sympathy from Elizabeth, and in a measure she does so, although it is patent that Stephen, on his side, leaves much to be desired. He is callous and extremely self-centred, hardly making any allowances for his wife's distressful delicacy. His bohemian friends are constantly about, and this complicates matters. Elizabeth eventually runs away (as all wives in novels do), and while away on her own she has an opportunity to judge other men and get that education which her careful up-bringing had denied her. Then (again like all wives in novels) she bethinks herself that Stephen isn't so bad after all. The situations are amusing, and there is a lifelike quality in Miss Heyer's work, but it is impossible not to think that she is convinced that the typical wife should be a secondary party in the marriage contract.

The book is really well written, with a high degree of humor and a careful comprehension of consistent character development. Incident slips naturally into incident, and several of the personages besides the two principals stand out as results of genuine literary ability on the part of the author. Among them might be noted Stephen's mother, a delightfully vague and irresponsible person; old Mr. Hengist, always ready with his bald statements of truth; Cynthia, Stephen's cynical sister; even Nina, the thoroughly alert bohemian friend to Stephen, who aids him so much in his novel writing. Indeed, perhaps the weakest person in the book is Elizabeth, for it is rather difficult to believe that any intelligent young novelist in his right senses would marry her, and it is equally difficult to accept the suggestion that she could ever develop into a real personage. That she does so is more the deliberate plot adjustation of the author than any reasonable development on the part of Elizabeth. And even her development is an admission of failure as an individuality on her part. In other words, she makes up her mind to be the helpful secondary partner in the ménage, and not to call him from his work to tea, but just to chink the cup. One gets a picture of Elizabeth going placidly through life chinking the cup and yes-ing Stephen all the time. It is rather dreary to consider, for modern wives do not chink the cup.

**11.** *Wisconsin Library Bulletin*, **vol. 20, May 1924, p. 126:**

Heyer, Georgette. *Instead of the Thorn*. 1924. 345 p. Small $2.

Story of a young girl of today brought up by the conventional standards of Victoria's reign and of her difficulties in adjusting herself to life and marriage. Theme handled with restraint, but not needed in small libraries.

**12. "The World of Books,"** *The Springfield Republican*, **20 July 1924, p. 5:**

"A Shy Heroine. But *Instead of the Thorn* Is Highly Sophisticated."

The creation of a character so virginally shy as Elizabeth Arden could only be an author's protest against the vigorous modern female, the reader is inclined to believe after a perusal of Georgette Heyer's *Instead of the Thorn*. Surely no such fragile, rose-tinted creature could long survive in the morals of this sophisticated age with their exploitation of youthful sex clamorings. But one has sympathy with Elizabeth. Perhaps Aunt Anne is largely responsible for her outlook on life—Aunt Anne, who censors all her books, her clothes and her friends, and who sticks bravely to her decision that "it's foolish to tell young girls everything."

So Elizabeth is thrust into marriage romantically infatuated, yet unstirred by any emotion. Refusing to assume marital responsibilities, bewildered with the turn of affairs and angry at Aunt Anne for "letting her down" in such a shabby way, she decides to step out and show her husband that his love is nothing in her young life. Being a decent fellow he stands by, confident that she will return, yet fearful for her inexperience.

Elizabeth becomes involved with one of the several men that wander sketchily through the story, but finds out that his love is not unlike that human emotion she scorned in her husband and that a wedding ring brings much comfort, an accepted position in society and other earthly things so assuring to the feminine mind.

One's reactions to dainty Elizabeth are not unpleasant after so many months of the flapperish type of female, but, needless to say, the preposterous story only emphasizes sex in a different and even more prurient way.

## 1925

**13. Isabelle Wentworth Lawrence, "In the Days of Simon the Coldheart. A Chronicle by Georgette Heyer of Romantic Deeds During the Knightly Times of Henry the Fifth,"** *Boston Evening Transcript,* **23 May 1925, Book Section, p. 5:**

Hurrah for the days of old, so cold but bold! Simon lived when Henry was taking his soldiers across the sea to fight for France, unmindful that a mere lass of Domrémy [sic] would upset all his plans. He lived when wars were by arrows and swords, and eating was meat and bread, and drinking was good red wine. "He came walking from Bedford into Cambridge one May morning when the sun was still young and the dew scarce gone from the grass. His worldly possessions he carried on his back in an old knapsack; his short jerkin was stained and torn, and there were holes in his long hose!" What think you of this for a hero? Master threadbare and poor, say you? Not for long. He becomes knight and lord and grand marshal before we are done with him. He wins a great lady for his wife, and our hearts as well.

But at first it would seem that the title be justified. There is no denying that Simon appeared a gruff customer. Into my lord's presence he strode, even that of Fulk, the terror of Montlice, and demanded service. And "Away with you, sirrah," roared Fulk, as of course we knew he would do. Yet presently he was smiling at the impudence of the youngster, with his sturdy, "I hope to be a man, my lord, even as you. That is my ambition, sir, and so I come to seek employment with you."

"For that you beard the lion in his den, eh? I will eat you for my dinner, cockerel."

"So they said at the gate, my lord, but you will find me of more use alive than eaten." It worked. It always works, this happy vein of insolence and audacity.  All the young men in all the stories get their first jobs by just pushing into the office of the president of the company and making this sort of remark.  All the lovely authors, each in her own way, reassure us that this is the case.  The only time we did not know it to work was when we tried it once ourself, in real life.  We can confidently assure anyone who has any doubts on the matter that the method of procedure is like moonlight, warm on paper only.

However, here was Simon, admitted to my lord, and accepted by my lord according to all the tenets of the best stories.  Our only real quarrel is that Miss Heyer never shows us Fulk behaving like a genuine president of a company.  He never lives up to his ferocious name.  Probably, having established it, he did not need to, on the principle the country squires, with what one might call spats-lineage, can go round with perfect propriety in old golf stockings which do not match their plus fours.  Simon—we have left him o'er long hungrily cooling his heels—then set out to show the rest of the garrison how to do things better.  They accepted this tutelage with the same docility with which the stories show us officials accepting the overtures of the personality-plus expert.  They sat up and took notice.  Even my lord's son, Alan, the poet and ne'er-do-well, fell violently in love with his supplanter.  None of these things seem natural, yet one must accept them for the swing of the tale.  Simon was Simon, who always got his way, who had never been bested till he met the Lady Margaret of Belrémy.

Historical novels are of two kinds.  They show how things were different in days gone by, or they show how they were the same.  Sir Walter's were of the first variety, Sabatini's of the second.  A few rare people accomplish the improbable, by showing us both.  This is why we claim a certain greatness for Miss Heyer's books, despite the many conclusions with which it is possible to quibble.  With *Simon the Coldheart* we roam the ways of England and France in the days of Henry the Fifth, and see strange men with alien clothes and customs, but with *Simon the Coldheart* we love and fight and lose and win, exactly as it is done today.  Simon spent some time going up and down the land hunting him a manor of which to be the lord.  In just such fashion the coming man of today marks out the possessions and acquisitions which are to be his.  Then Simon thinks of a way of getting what he wants for nothing, and merely takes opportunity by the forelock when she knocks at the door.  Never tell us that all his trouble over securing the spy was for his king and country.  We rather resent the author's trying to do so.  We know our Simon by this time, and we see his little plan.  The king would be grateful and the king would then be approachable.  If you say to a man, "Here, I have saved your life and your kingdom," what can he reply except "What's your figure?"

Simon's was very modest, merely a confiscated property much in need of attention.  What a glorious time he did have getting the business into shape.  He kept the secretary and weeded out the steward, picked out the men who seemed solid, and insubordinated the rest, even showing up the ones who were interested in starting trouble.  His estate of a firm basis, he looked for more worlds to conquer, and in those days the one business of an estate was to take its men and go to war.  This Simon did, and went about successfully conquering everywhere, until he came to Belrémy.

So far our story has run like an old wives' tale, with a constantly returning refrain, until he came to Belrémy.  In truth it is well you should have your curiosity thus prepared, for in Belrémy Simon fell in love.  Not that he knew it!  Odds fish!  Our Simon never suspected a thing.  Cavalierly enough he set to work to undermine the lady's fortifications, and took her town.  The castle alone he could not take, for they had prisoner his beloved friend and companion-at-arms, Alan of Montlice, who merely tramped the wars because he did.  So Simon entered the stronghold alone, and, finding treachery, stuck his sword into Margaret, much as the heavy villain of today might hold the mortgage on the old homestead over her head.  Margaret, of course, would rather have died than yielded, but her friends counselled prudence.  Even so, she refused submission and was forced to a great adventure.

All this while we have neglected to mention that Simon had another companion who, loving Margaret's companion, Jeanne, comes into the story largely here.  Geoffrey was Simon's own half-brother.  They met for the first time on Simon's earliest field, in a hard fought fight, when

Simon helped him to a horse, at the cost of his own. Together they finished the day, and then the older man turned to the younger, "I had thought from thy bearing that a hundred campaigns had seen thee."
"Nay, but mine is fighting blood."
"Malvallet eyed him curiously. 'Is it? From what stock dost thou spring, I wonder? Methinks I have seen thy like before.'
"Simon gave his short laugh. 'Look in thy mirror, Geoffrey of Malvallet.'
"Malvallet nodded, not surprised. 'It struck me that that was so, a while back when thou didst come to my rescue. For which I thank thee, brother.' "

Thus these two become friends, though old Fulk of Montlice, who hated all the breed of Malvallet, was long in joining the friendship. His son, however, shared Simon's liking for his half-brother, and the three fared across the world together, King Henry being far too wise to separate them either in peace or in war. Another band of three musketeers were they, whose friendship would make a tale in itself, if the book lacked the chronicle of Simon, or the love adventure of Margaret of Belrémy, which it does not.

The period of the French wars has been little used on the English side, and Miss Heyer has a fresh field for endeavor. She knows her history thoroughly and seldom takes liberties with it. She makes the knightly days live again, but, better, she makes Simon and Margaret live, who never lived before.

**14. "Gentlemen Adventurers,"** *The Open Shelf,* **July 1925, p. 83.**

Heyer, Georgette. *Simon the cold heart* [sic].

How Simon Malvallet, a lad of fourteen, by "toil skill and valour," rose from page to knight; how as Lord of Malvallet he besieged the fair city of Belrémy and won great honor, and how Lady Margaret the Amazon melted his cold heart. A tale of chivalry and adventure in 15th century England and Normandy which older boys as well as lovers of romance will enjoy.

**15.** *Wisconsin Library Bulletin*, **21 (July 1925), p. 201:**

Heyer, Georgette. *Simon the cold heart* [sic]. 1925. 374 p. Small $2.

Historical romance of rather an old fashioned type with scenes laid in 15th century England. The love interest is introduced late, when the hero, who has scorned women, meets his match.

**16. "New Novels,"** *The Times Literary Supplement*, **19 November 1925, p. 770:**

*Simon the Coldheart.*

The historical novel has an appeal to two classes of readers: those who like a stirring tale of adventure, heightened by an infusion of "atmosphere," and those who are interested by a reconstruction of past times. Occasionally, but not very often, both are catered for by the same book. Of Miss Georgette Heyer's *Simon the Coldheart* (Heinemann, 7s.6d.net) one can only say that it is above the average of the former class of romance, and that it does make an attempt, not completely successful, to enter the latter. The hero rather resembles one of those over-successful warriors portrayed by Henty, save that he is more gloomy and stern and less disinterested than most of them. He fights his way dourly upward from the moment when, a boy of fourteen, he forces his way into the service of the Earl of Montlice as a page, till he is finally appointed "Lieutenant and Warden of the Sands and Marches of Normandy" by Henry V. A little too dominating, perhaps, is Simon and the better, we should have thought, for being taught that the greatest sometimes must suffer defeat; but otherwise we have no fault to find with him. The heroine is rather less realistic, a shrew of the shrews, who leads her men to battle, who attempts to stab her conqueror Simon in the back, who escapes from him in boy's clothes, and has to be rescued from the unspeakable Raoul the Terrible. Those who enjoy fighting at desperate odds, knowing that the best man will win, and in no doubt as to who is the best man, will be happy in Simon's company, though they may feel that the shrew and her tamer are an unconscionably long time in coming to terms. It takes us over 300 pages to reach the moment when

> the Lady Margaret stood by the sundial in her
> pleasaunce, gazing wistfully down at it. It was May
> now, and all about her flowers bloomed. . . .The sun
> shone warmly down upon the garden, and the birds
> sung [sic], but the Lady Margaret was sad.

Then we know that all will be well, and that the sundial has not many minutes more of sadness to record.

**1928**

**17. "The World of Books,"** *The Springfield Republican*, **13 May 1928, p. 7F:**

*"Helen."* Young Woman of Poise Amid People in a Whirl.

Helen was a 20th century girl in England and the story of her experiences is told by Georgette Heyer in *Helen* (Longmans,Green & Co., New York; $2). Helen's absorbing love for her father is presented as a father complex. Her mother dying at her birth, and Helen being the only child, she grows up under her father's tutelage on their country estate. She develops along lines that relieve her from many feminine foibles. She is accustomed to thinking matters out straight from the shoulder, is alarmingly pretty and not easily side-tracked.

Helen Marchant, like her father, is not talkative. As she tells one young man, she is not a "petter." Participation in outdoor sports is the sure way to her favor. Through the stress of growing up into a very popular and likable young lady, Helen never loses her father complex.

Then along comes the war, taking most of her friends away and plunging herself into war work in London. While she runs around with a rather hilarious set in London for a time after the war, she assures her father she is not "of it," merely carrying on for the adventure. Marchant is content to let her sow her wild oats, for he trusts her good sense and honesty, and stands by to lend a hand should there be need. The author shows this girl realizing the attraction of sex and refusing it as unsatisfactory. Companionship and friendship mean more to her than do the blandishments that pass for romance. However, there is an affair with an artist which is on the point of involving her deeply when she brings it to an end. All this time there has been one impatient young man waiting for her to realize that he is in the running. He is a neighbor with whom she has grown up and about whom she cherished no romantic feelings, but who always interested her more than anyone else and who knew how not to talk.

After Marchant's sudden death, Helen realizes the value of this disinterested friend. Running through the book is the admiration of Helen's chaperon governess for Marchant, which he never suspects, but of which Helen is aware. This situation brings about a queer friendship between the young woman and the older. One of the best bits of character sketching in the book is that of Mrs. Beazley, Helen's Aunt Mildred, tiresome, conventional and constant. Apart from this, the story is rather artificial.

**18. "New Books and Reprints. Fiction,"** *The Times Literary Supplement*, **17 May 1928, p. 380:**

*Helen*. By Georgette Heyer. 328 pp. Longmans. 7s.6d.n.

This story is described somewhat misleadingly on the paper cover as the study of a girl who had a "father-complex" which for a considerable time prevented her marrying. The natural affection and companionship that existed between Helen, a motherless only child, and her father did not for a moment keep away young men; nor was Helen's interest in them in the least perfunctory. She did not marry the first one that asked her, nor yet the second, but what proof is that that she differed in any way from the daughter of a widow?  Indeed, her relationship with her father is treated with such coolness and care—if anything under-emotionalized —that the reader can have no psychological qualms.  In due time Helen is bound to marry an exceptionally agreeable young man; all her training indicates such an end.  This being his inner conviction, the reader can take his time over this leisurely tale, which takes an even course through pleasant English scenes and shows us the growth and development of a thoroughly "nice" girl, candid, athletic, and affectionate.  Contrasted with Helen, who is perhaps just a trifle too worthy for deep interest, there is Miss Pilbury, a fantastically slangy and abrupt governess, whose abilities as a teacher and intellectual qualities we are obliged to take on trust, and a diverse lot of young men and maidens whose activities are sufficiently amusing to hold the attention.  Marchant himself, Helen's father, is very well drawn, with a quiet sincerity.  The War comes, and by the time it is over and Helen's hunters are back in the stables, the field of her admirers has been notably thinned.  Marchant remains, and so does Miss Pilbury—now a companion—and so does Richard Carmichael.  Then Miss Heyer remembers the "father-complex" theme, and ruthlessly sacrifices a normal and unselfish parent.  Marchant is given a day and a half of pneumonia; enters Richard the consoler.  The argument that while her father lived he would have satisfied Helen completely and prevented her marriage fails to carry conviction; otherwise this is a story which contains some good work.

**19. "Shorter Notices,"** *The New Statesman*, **19 May 1928, 204:**

*Helen*. By Georgette Heyer. Longmans. 7s.6d.

As a story of youth from the years immediately before the War to those immediately after, and as a record of the transformation in manners that took place during that period, this novel has its merits.  We see the shifting world through the eyes of Helen Machant [sic], who has been brought up by her father from infancy and has something of the character of a nice boy. The social values seem at times to be a little confused, but the author has an agreeable sense of character, her young men being exceptionally life-like.

**20. "Latest Works of Fiction,"** *The New York Times Book Review*, **27 May 1928, pp. 17 & 22:**

"Father and Daughter." *Helen.* By Georgette Heyer. New York: Longmans, Green & Co. $2.

The theme of this novel might be pounced upon eagerly by a psychologist of the Freudian school; yet the author shows little sign of being influenced by the doctrines of Freud. The theme is that of a father and daughter who become bound together with so close an attachment that the girl comes to regard her parent as all-in-all and appears incapable of adopting a normal attitude toward her various suitors. From childhood she has been her father's companion; and her devotion to him, arising in part from the fact that each had only the other to care for, is accentuated and fortified by their similarity of character and of inherent interests. Neither she nor her father seems to perceive the possible harm of their relationship; but the result is that, although she grows up to charming and vivacious womanhood, she still esteems her father almost to the exclusion of other men. She does enjoy masculine companionship, it is true, and on one occasion does find herself on the point of yielding to passion; but, on the whole, she regards her male friends as good pals rather than as possible lovers, and they find it impossible to batter down the barriers she has erected. Only after the death of her father, when she finds herself suddenly desolate, does she yield to the call of her more normal impulses and cry welcome to the advances of the man who has been waiting for her for years.

There are excellent possibilities, obviously, in this theme of a paternal complex; and some, but not all, of those possibilities have been utilized by Miss Heyer. She makes an arresting beginning and has depicted the childhood of her heroine interestingly and well; but, having reached midchannel, she does not progress with equal effectiveness, but conducts the reader with about the average degree of success through the mazes of her protagonist's social life. Here one will find stretches of the trivial and the tedious, though no more than in three novels out of every four; but one reads on in the hope that the author will yet redeem herself. This hope, however, is disappointed by a cheap and easy device: instead of traveling to the end of the path she was following and showing the logical effect of the paternal attachment upon the girl's life, the author summons in the pneumonia germ to assist her at a crucial moment; and, having thus removed the father with bacterial aid, she is able to proceed without the embarrassment of the situation which gives the book its sole reason for being. And thus she is able to reach an end not unlike that of the average romantic novel.

**21. *Wisconsin Library Bulletin*, 24 (July 1928), 224:**

Heyer, Georgette. *Helen*. 1928. 328 p. Longmans, $2.
   A well-told English story of a girl growing up from childhood under her father's care. The happy bond between the two, their friendly relationships with other nice people, and the final satisfactory termination of a love affair make it a pleasant story.

**22. *Boston Evening Transcript*, 7 July 1928, Book Section, p. 8:**

**Helen.** By Georgette Heyer. $2.00 New York: Longmans, Green, and Company.
   The unusual theme of parent fixation is chosen as the motive for this typical English story. According to eminent psychologists this is all wrong. A father complex, such as Helen possessed, is a thing to be shunned, for it indicates a decided lack in youthful training. Under pain of disagreeing with said eminent gentlemen, we are forced to admit, in this case at least, the author's handling has made Helen's love for her father a rarely beautiful thing. It is the moral yardstick by which she

measures the love of divers men, and finds each love lacking.

Deprived of her mother at birth, Helen's upbringing devolves entirely upon her father. Mr. Marchant is of the country squire type, clean living, clean thinking and with a tolerant viewpoint. Helen inherits his deep reserve and inability to be demonstrative; as a result of this she is adjudged austere. In reality, her emotions are deep-seated and sincere. During the war Helen becomes a nurse and finds time, amid her other multitudinous duties, to dash off a book. This rather upsets the popular fallacy that even a trashy book requires time and concentration. Helen's book was born of an impulse and matured in spare intervals.

There is much chit-chat relative to the decadence of the younger generation, a plentiful sprinkling of current English slang and many minor characters which tend to slow up the action at times. It is fairly agreeable reading but it is not the type of book which must be finished at one sitting. One reads it or leaves it alone with no strain on the will power.

## 23. R.A.T., "Fiction," *The Spectator*, 1 September 1928, p. 273:

*The Masqueraders*. By Georgette Heyer (Heinemann. 7s.6d.)

In *The Masqueraders* we find a certain confusion of sex; but a gay and superficial confusion arranged as a disguise. A sister takes her brother's sword, and the brother uses her fan. The time is the eighteenth century, just after the '45; and the masqueraders are the children of an adventurous father who has been implicated in the rising. They are charming young people; and the elegant life of the period sets them off very prettily, though sometimes embarrassingly. The figures point appearance in monstrous fine clothes like those in Aubrey Beardsley's illustrations to *The Rape of the Lock*. What with elopements, rescues, duels, and cards, the story goes excitingly; and finally the magnificent but dubious father proves himself a Viscount. It is a picturesque and engaging story.

**24. "New Books and Reprints. Fiction,"** *The Times Literary Supplement*, **20 September 1928, p. 669:**

*The Masqueraders*. By Georgette Heyer. 349 pp. Heinemann. 7s.6d.n.
The scene of this amusing story is London in 1746. Its amusing quality is due to "the old gentleman," as his son and daughter always call him. Tremaine, by birth an aristocrat, was by nature a clever, shifty, restless, boastful vagabond, a Cyrano de Bergerac grown elderly. Having made a runaway match with a farmer's daughter, wandered far, kept gaming-houses, and served in various armies, including the Pretender's in 1745, he found it convenient to hide his history while claiming his viscountcy, inherited at the death of his brother. So we find his madcap son Robin disguised as Kate and his staid daughter Prudence disguised as Peter carrying out the circuitous plans of their bewildering father, and slipping into embarrassing love-affairs of their own. There is much club life, dancing, duelling, and one rascal killed; for in novels miraculous swordsmanship always belongs to the virtuous party. The author works ingeniously up to her curtain, with the two young "masqueraders" restored to orthodox clothes and happily wedded, and the Old Gentleman planning to become at least an earl.

**25. "Shorter Notices,"** *The New Statesman*, **29 September 1928, pp. 768 & 770:**

*The Masqueraders*. By Georgette Heyer. Heinemann. 7s.6d.
The effeminacy of male attire in the fashionable London of the eighteenth century undoubtedly facilitated impersonation and interchange of identity between the sexes, but could scarcely have made it as preposterously easy as Miss Heyer assumes. The hero of her novel (who, as a matter of fact, is the heroine) carries the intrigue along merrily, sweeping blackmail, elopements, highway robberies, duels, murders, gossip at White's, Jacobite intrigues and violence to the officers of the law gaily before her. She and her brother, who makes a charming

woman, are the children of a fantastic father who is obliged because of many things, particularly his connection with "the Prince," to remain out of England. The girl becomes a member of White's, gambles and drinks, as much as she dares, with the best, and is saved from almost certain death in a duel by one Sir Anthony Fanshawe who, alone of all men in London, has seen through her disguise. He pieces the family history together, and even recognises the father in the cool, eccentric claimant to the title of Lord Barham. The claimant has no difficulty in proving his claim; indeed, he and his children have no difficulty in doing anything they want to do. Even the wily Sir Anthony has no desire to use his information for any other end than that of marrying the heroine. Miss Heyer has a lucid though artificial style sprinkled with irritating inversions; and she brings off the whole masquerade plausibly enough, but rather too glibly.

## 1929

**26. Gilbert Thomas, "Fiction," *The Spectator* 142, 11 May 1929, p. 755:**

*Pastel.* (Longman. 7s.6d.)

Miss Heyer proves once again that the oldest theme can yield new charm in the hands of a competent artist. *Pastel* is a simple tale of two sisters, the younger of whom outshines the older in fascination and threatens to monopolize the prizes. In the end, of course, Miss Heyer shows us that all that glitters is not happiness. Within her prescribed limits, she introduces us to real people and real scenes, all characteristically English; and, though she attempts no heights or depths, her plain is pleasantly fertile with humour and sympathy.

**27. *Boston Evening Transcript*, 15 May 1929, part 3, p. 2:**

*Pastel.* $2.00. New York: Longmans, Green and Company.

In *Pastel* may be found a thoughtful and realistic portrayal of the dreams and longings of a romantic girl who all her life has had to take second place. We sympathize with and love Frances because, whether we admit it or not, many of us have had similar longings and have had the same discouragements. The restful conclusion is a comfort, because it epitomizes a desire in the hearts of many, to be able to face life, undaunted and serene.

**28. "New Novels,"** *The Times Literary Supplement*, **13 June 1929, p. 472:**

*Pastel*, by Georgette Heyer (Longmans, 7s.6d.net), is a very readable, pleasant novel, which keeps to the surface of things and introduces us to some friendly and agreeable people. Its subject is the rivalry between two sisters. Frances, the heroine, is outdone in every way by her brilliant younger sister Evelyn. Evelyn is like a black-and-white drawing, while Frances is a pastel; but the sisters are all the same very fond of each other. A crisis comes for Frances with Evelyn's marriage to a handsome young man with whom Frances had been in love herself and who, until he met Evelyn, had seemed to like Frances. The marriage leaves her not really heartbroken but extremely disconsolate, and in this mood she agrees to marry Norman, the dull but excellent young man who has been in love with her for years. Up to this point the ups and downs of Frances's career have been very well described, and our interest in her has never been allowed to waver; but after Frances's marriage we begin to notice that Miss Heyer has a moral in mind and is writing with a purpose. Frances married Norman with many doubts and fears; and after her marriage she finds that the old rivalry with Evelyn still remains, for Evelyn's husband is much richer than Norman, and Evelyn's dinner-parties are much more successful than Frances's. But, on the other hand, Oliver is moody and bad-tempered, while Norman has all the solid virtues. So Frances settles down and decides not to envy Evelyn any more. The book remains readable to the end, but as soon as we begin to suspect the author's disinterestedness our belief in the story wavers.

**29. Alan Porter, "Fiction. Good and Middling Good,"** *The Spectator,* **14 September 1929, p. 344:**

*Beauvallet.* By Georgette Heyer. (Heinemann. 7s.6d.)
The two historical novels on our list provide a queer contrast. Miss Heyer's story is a pure fantasy, an Elizabethan adventure story with the most romantic ingredients. The detail is not free from anachronism. Did Elizabethan gallants go on the *Grand Tour,* as Miss Heyer asserts? The story is none the worse for these doubts; its rapidity carries us along as though enchanted. *Queen Dick* [by Alfred Tresidder Sheppard], on the other hand, is a *slow* story; and its erudition is great.

**30. "New Books and Reprints. Fiction,"** *The Times Literary Supplement,* **10 October 1929, p. 796:**

*Beauvallet.* By Georgette Heyer. 330 pp. Heinemann. 7s.6d.n.
The hero of any story of English piracy (for such it really was, no matter how Protestant and patriotic it might be in the eyes of contemporary England) on the Spanish Main in the spacious days of Good Queen Bess, can hardly fail to run the risk of comparison with Amyas Leigh. Miss Heyer is to be congratulated on having produced in Beauvallet one whom the great exemplar would not have disdained. Indeed, he seems to have been a shipmate of Amyas Leigh's in the *Pelican,* and only Miss Heyer's silence on this important detail prevents the reader from comparing the worth of the silver ship which Amyas Leigh and Salvation Yeo sailed into Bideford with that of the treasure brought by Beauvallet and his Joshua Dimmock into Plymouth after the sprightly knight had, in conformity with his promise, landed his future bride by night in Spain. Having done so, he naturally had to go back to Spain to find her, and Miss Heyer turns him into a gentleman of France, an identity thrust upon him complete with confidential dispatches by a fortunate but sanguinary hazard. In this guise Beauvallet is graciously received in audience by the gloomy King, whose beard he had been so busily engaged in singeing *in propria persona* at Vigo and in the Spanish

Indies, and is able to set on foot his plans for an elopement. All goes well until Beauvallet is recognized by an astonished Don who finds masquerading as a French envoy from the Duke of Guise the man who was known all over the Spanish Main as a devil-inspired English pirate protected from all good Catholics by enchantment. Thereafter the story becomes cinematographic with escapes, kidnapping, galloping, sword play and a breathless elopement. Miss Heyer has produced quite a pleasing story of great days.

**31. "Romance and Adventure,"** *The Springfield Sunday Union and Republican,* **20 October 1929, p.** 7e:

*The Masqueraders* is a gay swashbuckling romance of the Stuart rebellion days, when people counted all well lost for bonnie Prince Charlie, if need be. The tale, by Georgette Heyer (Longmans, Green, & Co., New York; $2), centers about the two young Merriots, a brother and sister, who to save their precious necks find it advisable to masquerade as one another. Their father, "the old gentleman," was a chronic masquerader, so his children were letter perfect in the art of disguise. Prudence Merriot was of Junoesque stature, while Robin, her brother, was a bit small for a man, hence the masquerade was possible, providing there was good teamwork, despite the fact that these were the days of high heels and hoop skirts and decidedly dandified dress for men.

Seldom is there a dull moment from cover to cover, for this author succeeds in crowding one event close upon the heels of another, and when there is a seeming quiet period it is to develop a new phase of the masquerade. There are occasions for thrills and for laughter in this tantalizing romance. Prudence sidesteps too much conviviality with Sir Anthony lest he surprise her secreta, [sic] and all the time she is falling in love with him.

1930

A CRITICAL RETROSPECTIVE


**32.** *New York Herald Tribune Books*, **30 March 1930, p. 16:**

"Marry, Coz!" ***Beauvallet.*** New York: Longmans, Green and Co. $2.50
     One might as well stop being annoyed at historical romances wherein
the supposed Elizabethans talk very bad Elizabethan and act like very
good Elizabethans—that is, like men who never were on land or galleon.
It's really just a gag, just good clean fun between author and reader. It's
really just fiction wherein the course of action doesn't grow from the
necessity of character in history, but the need of a plot all dressed up in
costume. If the characters act like human beings, as in *Andivius Hedullo,*
then every one rises and calls them "modern." If they strut about like
minions of the moon then the moderns never seem to know them for
misbegotten knaves in Kendal Green.
     The romance about Beauvallet, Drake's companion, is a very good
case in point. It's really very gay and exciting, and fun to read.
Beauvallet, a very devil with a heart of tenderness, captures the *Santa
Maria* and finds (as a stray passenger) the lovely Dominica, with a heart
of Spanish gold. She hates him for an Englishman, and right away loves
him for a man. Any fool can see that; but instead of heigh-ho for
England and married love, he gives her back grandiloquently to the
grandees and later (disguised as a French envoy) he comes to Spain,
duels, prisons, dragoons and all sorts of adventures just to prove to the
lady that he can win her in her own impregnable country and virtue, and
she loves him for it.
     Of course, the Elizabethans and others did all sorts of fantastical
enterprises. It's not what they do in historical romance, but the way they
do them and the way they talk about them. Beauvallet is just a moving-
picture hero and a "soundy" filled with windy phrases. Dominica is the
spitfire who suddenly becomes the tender wife—as if they ever did! She
coquets and he swashbuckles; and the author keeps telling you what it's
all about—as if you didn't know. It's not all about the Elizabethans or
anybody else. It's all about "romance"—once a proud maid, now a very
over-dressed wench. Even in his most extravagant stories Dumas never
does that sort of thing, not even in the novels he didn't write.

·

**33. "Brave Knights and Beautiful Ladies. Georgette Heyer Writes a Novel of Swashbuckling Adventures in England and on the Spanish Main,"** *Boston Evening Transcript,* **18 April 1930, Book Section, p. 1:**

*Beauvallet.* $2.50 New York: Longmans, Green and Co.

For several years Georgette Heyer has been proving herself a master of romantic fancy-dress fiction. What she does is always right, always highly flavored of her period, so that in some odd fashion the whole era is actually alive before you, and that with few descriptions. It is so easy that you are assured of long study in preparation, while there is no faintest trace of effort. In her last book, *The Masqueraders,* the very essence of eighteenth century dandyism walked abroad; in this we have swashbuckling days on the Spanish Main, and the merry England of Good Queen Bess. The style itself changes to fit the mood, though never for a moment does she lose the pervading sense of thrill. One cannot set down a book of hers if one loves the bright panache of days gone by, partly because the story is always too exciting to stop, and even more that the folk of the tale are too delightful to be lost sight of for a moment. Possibly—yes, of a certainty—it is that the spirit of one's own youthful dreams is here alive again, and one may dwell, for some three hundred and fifty large and well-written pages in one's own castles in Spain.

In the present story we are hurled at the beginning into a bloody, ravaging tornado of a sea fight, in which a mighty galleon is badly beaten by a small English vessel, which she unwisely attacks. The little *Venture* is the personal craft of that terror of the seas, Beauvallet, who had been pirate and privateer with Drake, and now runs the waters of the world for himself, preying upon the navies of Spain. His servant, Joshua, who followed him in all his adventures, lacked a family crest, but he had been told he should die in his bed, so he only worried about his master. Not that his faith in Beauvallet was dimmed, even by that frightful expedition into the heart of Spain, the jaws of the Inquisition, to steal a Spanish lady.

The lady, the lovely Dominica, was aboard the plundered Spanish vessel, with her father, an old Spanish governor of the West Indies, returning home very ill. Beauvallet, though five and thirty or more, had never before fallen to the wiles of woman, but within twenty-four hours he announced his intention to make an Englishwoman of the lovely signora. If he came to Spain to seek her, he demanded, would she come away with him? And Dona Dominica, bowing proud head, promised to follow him across the northern waters.

Of Beauvallet's doings at home, in that pleasant English countryside where his brother was a lord, of his visit to court to see the queen, and of his subsequent merry but grim masquerade as envoy from the House of Guise to the King of Spain, we may read with bated breath. And it is good to know, once more, that knights are brave and ladies beautiful.

**34. V. S. Pritchett, "Fiction. Great Demands," *The Spectator*, 26 April 1930, p. 713:**

*Barren Corn.* By Georgette Heyer. (Longmans. 7s.6d.)

If Mr. [Donald] Stewart demands too much [in *Sanatorium*] Miss Heyer offers too little. Can she really expect us to be interested in a heroine who can be driven to suicide because she has married above her and does not know which fork to use? That is virtually what happens, and if one needs lessons in deportment, etiquette and table manners, the lady's husband, "a Salinger," will instruct one in the smart way to behave badly. The heroine, for all the simple faithfulness of her love, is a dull creature and one regrets that Miss Heyer has wasted a pretty talent upon her.

**35. "New Books & Reprints. Fiction," *The Times Literary Supplement*, 22 May 1930, p. 436:**

*Barren Corn.* By Georgette Heyer. 282 pp. Longmans. 7s.6d.n

This novel recounts how Laura Bruton, a middle-class assistant in a Riviera hat shop, who resembled a Luini Madonna, had "generous curves," and at 30 was all simplicity, met Hugh Salinger, "one of the leisured class," a member of which "she had never imagined she would talk to. . .on equal terms"; how his intentions were strictly dishonourable;

how she withstood him and "the hunger to possess her grew more fierce"; how he proposed, the doubtful acceptance, and its result. Though her phraseology and her manners jarred on him, he very seldom troubled to correct her—" 'You never told me he was a lord.' 'Darling, not a lord; he's a baron' "—and they continued to jar. However, there were three months' "fleeting happiness" in Italy before their return to England, and Hugh's meeting with her family, who lived in Brixton and were dull, genteel, and anxious to please; though they are portrayed on the conventional suburban background of aspidistras and Nottingham lace curtains, their worried, petty, amiable figures are the most living in the book. Hugh was horrified by them and took Laura to stay with his incredible wax-work relations. At this point occurs the episode which prevents the book being a complete *rechauffé*. His cousin, Hylda, trying to make friends with Laura, says that she does not believe in class distinctions, outrages Laura's gentility, and deeply incenses her by the suggestion that she and Hylda alike are in no way superior to barmaids. After six weeks Laura and Hugh moved to London, and he grew gradually more and more bored with her. She did not get on with his friends, "the daring set" or "the hunting set" or "the Art set." He went about without her and was continually irritated by her presence. Finally she perceived she was a drag on him and contrived to commit suicide by an organized motor "accident."

## 36. "Romance and Adventure," *The Open Shelf*, May 1930, p. 80:

Heyer, Georgette. *Beauvallet.*
    A swashbuckling tale of England and Spain in the days when Drake and his followers roamed the high seas. Sir Nicholas Beauvallet vows that within a year he will wed Dona Dominica, a spirited beauty taken on a treasure galleon and chivalrously restored to her native shores by her captor. How he manages to enter Spain, his adventures there, and the way in which he fulfills his vow makes a story which older boys and girls will enjoy.

**37. Isabelle Wentworth Lawrence, "In a Fertile Field of Barren Corn. The Story of an Ill-Assorted Marriage With a Beautiful and Simple Young Woman,"** *Boston Evening Transcript*, **27 September 1930, Book Section, p. 3:**

*Barren Corn*. By Georgette Heyer. New York: Longmans, Green & Co.

On an average of every other day, with an extra thrown in for Sunday, one reads somewhere that all the plots in the world are as old as the Pyramids. Cheops wrote them on his walls, Caesar pondered them, while resting from his commentaries, Charlemagne would have read them while crossing the Alps, Lucretia Borgia took ideas from them for doing her best poisoning, Mussolini read all the best sellers before coup dictating Italy. There is, so they say, nothing new beneath the sun.

This being the case—and who would dare gainsay it?—it is idle to point out that Georgette Heyer, in her extremely vital story of modern English prejudice, has used a familiar theme. In it the hero is usually called King Cophetua and the heroine brought in under the modest appellation of the "beggar-maid." She named hers Hugh and Laura. But both deal with the rich young man who marries beneath him. There have been as many of these tales as of Burne-Jones's maidens climbing a winding stair. A goodly few of them have been as much alike as the aforesaid lovely but monotonous ladies. But Miss Heyer's is different. She turns the plot upside down until we are as dizzy with surprise as Humpty-Dumpty.

It was a far cry from Brixton to the south of France, where Laura served in a hat shop. But she had been in France before, during the war, and her French had made possible the transfer from London. The golden Riviera was enchanted country to her, but after she had had influenza, Madame, who knew a handsome woman when she had one, sent her off for a holiday at Villefranche. The season was over, anyway. She could be spared to regain her health.

Hugh came to Villefranche because he might as well be there as anywhere. His uncle paid all his bills without a murmur, and advised him to see the world, but to be careful about women. He was to take them, if he liked, but not to take them seriously. So Hugh went avoyaging with painting materials at his side, for he rather fancied himself as an artist. No one had ever told him anything to the contrary, for no one had ever shown him the seamy side of life at all. His uncle, Lord Salinger, spoiled him, because he was a black sheep himself, if you would believe what he said of himself, and he recognized the same strain in Hugh. My lord's only son, Roland, was a good young man, very much interested in hunting and tenantry, and in all the things which would make a good landlord of him when Lord Salinger died. But he was dull, and the tenth baron preferred something a trifle more dashing. He catered to human frailty, savoring it tenderly as congenial to his own. He encouraged Hugh's mother, Emmeline, in her extravagances. He paid for Hugh's little flapper sister, Joyce. He also supported his own sister, and her son and daughter, but they were plain and dull, too, and they bored him terribly. Indeed, his greatest amusement seemed to lie in spoiling Hugh, and Laura paid the piper.

For this story differs in that it is Laura who turns out to be a princess, and Hugh a blackguard. Possibly that is too strong a word. He does go on being kind to Laura until he feels that he cannot stand her any more. Perhaps that is all any of us would have done. But he breaks all codes of honor and dishonor by being that most detestable of human beings, a snob.

This, as we have said, [is] a study in English prejudice, or rather in what is to the English as natural as it is to the Hindu, the caste system. The classes and the masses, and the low and middle classes, of which Gilbert and Sullivan sang, do not appear to have been disturbed by war or Socialism, or by the general strike or the dole. It seemed inevitable to Hugh that his family should be horrified by his marrying a beautiful woman who had worked in a hat shop. They were, and it is quite evident that Miss Heyer understands their horror. Far better had he taken a painted and vulgar hussy from the chorus. She, at least, would be something they could manage. But Laura was that ghastly attribute, genteel. Laura was refined. When she poured coffee she crooked her little finger. When she talked she used more auxiliaries than the best usage requires. She was, alas, thirty, and quite too old to learn the easy familiarities of upper class intercourse. When she tried she grew stilted and lost all her charm. But it was worse than that. To her the ways of her husband's order were vulgar ways, lax ways, even immoral ways. She herself had been far better brought up in what constitutes godliness. In modeling herself to suit him she cast off much that she considered ladylike. But it was no use. She was born a lovely woman and no slapstick modes of life could contain her. In the end she took the only way for Hugh's relief, with a smile on her perfect lips, above the terror in her heart.

For she loved him for marrying her. At first he had not dreamed of doing such a thing. A woman from a shop! A creature with a family in Brixton! Delightful to flirt with, fascinating to kiss, regal to embrace, yes—but marriage was quite beyond the horizon. Then, when Laura fled away from him, Hugh found how much he wanted her. When he came to Nice and proposed, surprised at himself, fighting himself, darkly satiric, yet fiercely triumphant, she threw herself into the dust at his feet. And there she stayed. Whatever he asked, she did. Whenever he broke her heart, she held the pieces together lest their rattle disturb him. For him she broke with her family, though she knew the act beneath her dignity and his. For him—but what she finally did for him is for you to find out.

The story is beautifully written, with that smooth precision of Miss Heyer's which seems to be effortless. There is never a word too many. There is never a word too few. Underneath the somewhat cynical style with which she portrays England's Ruling Order, runs the same compelling force which makes her historical romances so unusual, and fascinating. Perhaps that force is a sense of romance in mundane times. Certainly it saves *Barren Corn* from being at all like any ordinary English story of an unhappy marriage. But what gives it distinction is that, hand in hand with the romance goes an astonishing outlook on society. The entire novel might be a treatise on socialism, were it not so aristocratic. The masses, to be sure, are disregarded, but the lower middle classes are painted, for all the horror of their gentility, as twice as good as you are, Gunga Din. Laura is worth six of Emmeline and all her like. Nevertheless, she obviously gives Miss Heyer "the horrors." She herself, who admires her immensely, could not have lived with her long.

91

Yet she makes us love and admire her. Quillinan, Hugh's friend, put it all in a brief flash. Hugh asked him what he thought of Laura. He told him, "I think she is far too good for you." Hugh was puzzled. Quillinan tried to explain. "You can have no notion of the beliefs that govern her class. None of them are yours. The niceties of social conduct as she understands them will constantly set your teeth on edge. . . . How will you convince her that the careful manners of her class, which she has been brought up to study, which she thinks true politeness, are wrong? She will be shocked by the more casual manners of our class."

Quillinan was right. Laura was more of a lady, to use the good old words, than Hugh a gentleman; she could not learn that it was the thing to run up debts, to live on other people's bounty instead of working for a living, to be careless of family ties and obligations and to swear easily.

Judged as a study in social condition, this has one fallacy. It does not allow that there is an old aristocracy, of which folk like the Salingers know nothing, which has ideals that are those of Laura. So, at least, it would appear on the surface. But when we realize that all our home truths are given from the lips of Quillinan, who is himself of the old nobility, and that Hugh is to break the heart of Stella, the fair neighbor next door, a quiet and lovely lady of Quillinan's ilk, we see that Miss Heyer has been laughing at us all the while. At the very end, in the midst of the inevitable melodrama of the climax, we suddenly know what she has been about. She has been showing us that while there is a firm and hidebound caste system, neverthless there is in reality no such thing as class. Laura and Stella and Quillinan are fine. The Tenth Baron has his moments of fineness. The rest are utterly negligible, however amusing and pleasant in their lives. That, of course, is true socialism.

But sometimes we wonder if what we like best is not just the story, much as we may admire the hidden meaning. It is very charming, in spite of Hugh's being a snob. He is rather nice, occasionally. Those honeymoon hours in the old Italian villa, those exquisite moments in the moonlight garden, appeal to the senses. And one more thing contributes unmistakably to our pleasure. We do like our heroine beautiful and our hero as handsome as a Greek god.

## 1933

**38. "New Books and Reports. Fiction,"** *The Times Literary Supplement*, **4 May 1933, p. 314:**

*Why Shoot a Butler?* By Georgette Heyer. 312 pp. Longmans. 7s.6d.n.
    There were plenty of reasons for shooting this one, though it would be unfair to disclose them. Other people in the book also deserve shooting and receive their deserts. There are a new and ingenious amateur detective, a suspected heroine, more foolish than most heroines and more attractive than the heroines of most detective stories, a motor race on land and sea, and a motive which, granted the obtuseness of most of the characters, becomes almost plausible. The story is readable and, in parts, amusing.

## 1935

**39. "New Novels,"** *The Times Literary Supplement*, **18 April 1935, p. 256:**

    Although Miss Georgette Heyer's publishers describe her latest book as "a thriller," it is more considerable and certainly more satisfying than the type of novel that commonly goes by this name. For *Death in the Stocks* is not only a very neat and mystifying detective story, it is also an excellent example of what can be achieved when the commonplace material of detective fiction is worked up by an experienced novelist. Miss Heyer's characters act and speak with an ease and conviction that is as refreshing as it is rare in the ordinary mystery story.
    The fact remains, however—and this is where Miss Heyer shows her gift for creating character—that it is very difficult, sometimes, indeed, impossible, to tell when the suspected parties are speaking the truth. Kenneth Vereker, suspected, and with good reason, like his sister Antonia and her *fiancé* Rudolf Mesurier, of the murder of his stepbrother, Arnold, is one of those "impossible" and hopelessly unworldly artists; his interest in the crime is a purely intellectual one;

fascinated by the problem, he refuses to pay any attention to the warnings of his cousin and solicitor, Giles Carrington, and those of the patient and worldly Inspector Hannasyde. His sister is almost equally unrealistic and casual in her attempt to explain away her presence at the scene of the crime. The consequences of their strange conduct are exceedingly baffling. Indeed, it is almost impossible to believe in the innocence of one of them until the very end of the book. This in itself is a rare enough achievement, seeing that in most detective stories the obvious suspects can generally be acquitted by an intelligent reader long before the author gives the correct verdict. The spectacle of Miss Heyer's lively young people merrily engaged in accusing each other and trying each other's nooses on is further enhanced by the well-timed entrances and exits of a variety of subsidiary characters, butlers, cook-generals, black sheep, bull-terriers, policemen and lovers, with their appropriate "business."

**40. Ralph Partridge, "Death Everywhere,"** *The New Statesman and Nation*, **4 May 1935, p. 646:**

*Death in the Stocks*. By Georgette Heyer. Longmans, Green. 7s.6d.

Mr. Hemingway, in his panegyric on bull-fighting, has impressed on us that no matador is worth a rap unless he goes in to kill *over the horn*. There are two awkward horns ever confronting the novelist who goes in to kill his man for our delectation, the dilemma of obviousness and dullness; and although both claim more victims than any bull-ring, it is distressing how many writers make thir choice of a slow death on the dull horn. Miss Heyer, however, fresh from her triumphs in the field of historical romance and thrillers, has taken a bold leap and gone straight in over the other horn. Whether *Death in the Stocks* has suffered any damage in the process it is for readers to decide; but whatever their individual judgments may be, I do not think one will disapprove of her having taken the risk. From the second page, where Arnold Vereker is found knifed in the village stocks of Ashleigh Green by the village constable, to the last (where all *my* dreams came true) there is not a tedious moment in the book.  The secret lies in Miss Heyer's remarkable gift for portraiture in the round; she makes the wayward Vereker family about whom suspicion hovers not only alive but positively frisky.  When one thinks of all those detective dummies going through the motions of sucking-up beer and tapping out pipes for twelve chapters, one overflows with gratitude to any writer whose characters would make sense whether suspected of murder or not.  But Miss Heyer must keep her talent under some restraint, or her excess of virtue will prove her undoing.  Once people in detective stories are made human, their behaviour has a certain consistency which protects them from their authors, who are no longer at liberty to force them into unnatural crimes.  Thus the range of suspicion is narrowed, and the author's task of avoiding the obvious solution even more difficult.  It is no longer a question of complicating a crime, but of subtilising a criminal; and *Death in the Stocks* for all its entertainment does not quite bring off that triumph of mystification.

If Miss Heyer may be said to offer us a neat little sum in subtraction, the rest of the books on this list provide plenty of unwarrantable additions and wild multiplication to the *n*th power. . . .

**41.   Will Cuppy, "Mystery and Adventure," *New York Herald Tribune Books*, 8 September 1935, p. 16:**

*Merely Murder.* 303 pp. Garden City: The Crime Club. $2.

Mustn't miss this, if you care for that brittle sort of thing in fiction, written in the vastly competent style so usual in British bafflers and so unusual elsewhere.  The brittlest people in it are Antonia Vereker (engaged to Rudolph Mesurier) and Kenneth Vereker (engaged to Violet Williams), step-sister and step-brother of Arnold Vereker, ye corpse, found stabbed to death in the stocks on Ashleigh Green.  They worry Superintendent Hannasyde almost nutty with their blithely sophisticated remarks about the case which, by the way, is solved by an assistant sleuth.  Antonia might have killed Arnold, who'd written her a nasty letter calling Rudolph a skunk and a thief, and Kenneth's pipe was found where it shouldn't have been, other clews being a pistol, marks on the blotter and a whisky and soda.  There's a second murder and a fine lot of snappy talk among the young lovers; once Kenneth and Violet have a slight tiff because he says her new green hat looks like a hen in a fit. The solution is so surprising that even Superintendent Hannasyde has to exclaim, "Good—God!" Miss Dorothy Sayers calls the book "an abiding delight," and she ought to know. Put it on your list.

**42. "The Criminal Record. The Saturday Review's Guide to Detective Fiction,"** *The Saturday Review* **12, 21 Sept. 1935, p. 18:**

*Merely Murder.* Georgette Heyer (Crime Club: $2.)
-*Crime, Place, Sleuth:* Arnold Vereker (nobody loved him) found quaintly slain. Debonaire detectives and callous kin wisecrack their way to killer.
-*Summing Up:* Much uncommonly good dialogue, an almost too gentlemanly sleuth, and a guessable but unconvincing end.
-*Verdict:* Diverting

## 1936

**43. "The Criminal Record. The Saturday Review's Guide to Detective Fiction,"** *The Saturday Review* **13, 22 Feb. 1936, p. 26:**

*Why Shoot a Butler?* Georgette Heyer (Crime Club: $2.)
-*Crime, Place, Sleuth:* Two menials murdered in English manor. Rude Mr. Amberley flouts police but drives criminal to *felo de se.*
-*Summing Up:* One of those missing will and wrongful heir yarns which in this case comes off rather well.
-*Verdict:* Engaging

**44. Isaac Anderson, "New Mystery Stories,"** *The New York Times Book Review*, **23 February 1936, p. 20:**

***Why Shoot a Butler?*** 332 pp. New York: Doubleday, Doran & Co. $2.
There might be many reasons for shooting a butler, but Frank Amberly [sic] cannot imagine any one of them as applying to the young woman whom he finds standing beside the car containing the body of a dead man. That is why, when he reports his discovery to the police, he fails to mention the girl whom he afterward comes to know as Shirley Brown. Amberly, who is a London barrister, is on his way to visit his uncle and aunt and, using a short cut recommended by his cousin, has taken the wrong turning that results in his finding the corpse in the car.

This is the second novel in which Georgette Heyer has employed a barrister-detective, but Frank Amberly is as different from Giles Carrington of *Merely Murder* as the two stories are different in motive and method. Carrington's cooperation with Scotland Yard was friendly and open. He concealed nothing from Superintendent Hannasyde and, in return, received that official's full confidence. Amberly, working with the more stupid local police, bullies them unmercifully and is not at all reticent in expression his frank opinion of their lack of ability. He tells them only so much as he thinks it is good for them to know and goes his own way with the investigation.

The stories are similar in presenting, in addition to puzzling problems in detection, groups of characters with distinctly marked individualities. None of the characters in *Why Shoot a Butler?* is quite so eccentric as are the Verekers in *Merely Murder*, but they are equally well worth knowing. Georgette Heyer's second novel is a worthy successor to her first one.

**45. "The New Novels: Detective Stories and Thrillers,"** *The Times Literary Supplement*, **6 June 1936, p. 479:**

***Behold, Here's Poison.*** Hodder and Stoughton. 7s.6d.
Widow Zoe Matthews, with her soulful ways and her resolve never to speak ill of or to anyone, and her sister-in-law, Harriet, with her endless small economies, one of which leads to her death, are interesting people to read about, even apart from the murder mystery. So is a third sister, the massive and implacable Mrs. Gertrude Lupton.

Gregory Matthews died of nicotine poisoning. No one regretted him, except because it brought Detective Hannasyde on the scene. Suspicion fell on Zoe, on her son Guy, on her daughter Stella, on Harriet, on Dr. Fielding, and on Gregory's other nephew Randall, who proved to be heir to Gregory's ill-got money. Randall's remark to "darling Aunt Gertrude" that if he was her husband he would keep several mistresses, is only a little ruder than most of his remarks. The author has two surprises for the reader: one is the murderer, the other is the marriage of Stella to Randall. The latter may be because their author dislikes them both.

**46. Ralph Partridge, "Detective Dozen," *The New Statesman and Nation*, 20 June 1936, Literary Supplement, pp. 973-4:**

*Behold Here's Poison*. Hodder and Stoughton. 7s.6d

Detection is supplied by Marks and Spencer this month. You will probably find several things you want on the counter, but once you have read them not one is likely to be remembered a year hence. But why grumble? The customer is always right; and that is why we are in the Woolworth period of detection. The reviewer, on the other hand, is almost invariably wrong, unless he manages to turn himself into an ugly customer. If he dares say a good word for some harmless, unpretentious detective story, he is bound to find that his intellectual friends, after refusing to be parted from the book during a couple of hours either for love or whisky, finally toss it contemptuously on the carpet with grunts of disgust, and then stride imposingly to the more respectable shelves for a breath of the classics. Therefore, with the usual diffidence, I put forward my own recommendations on the list: *Anthony Gilbert* for a *tour de force* in ambivalence, my favourite Mrs. Heyer for a sparkling novel crystallised round a thread of crime, *Post After Post Mortem* for the touch of excitement in the country house setting, *Murder in Triplicate* for one of those challenging American conundrums that derive from Ellery Queen, and *The Sutton Place Murders* for an orgy of wisecracks. . . .

Mrs. Heyer had me guessing in *Behold Here's Poison*. She has such a zest for characterisation that she is hard put to it to deodorise a murderer, so I felt confident of getting the poisoner's wind as soon as he or she crossed my path. How was I to know it was the garden path up which Mrs. Heyer was gently leading me? I recognised it, however, in the end by the delicious fragrance which Mrs. Heyer, in her incorrigible conscientiousness, felt bound to provide. Where, then, had my poisoner got to? How had I been misled? I regret to say that Mrs. Heyer was obliged through mistrust of her own terrible veracity to keep the culprit under cover by suppressing material evidence and compounding a felony. I do not blame her but I cannot praise. *Behold Here's Poison* is not for crabbed intellectuals, but anyone who can appreciate a delightful book will take it and like it.

**47. E. R. Punshon, "The Omniscient Detective," *The Manchester Guardian*, 23 June 1936, p. 7:**

*Behold, Here's Poison*. Hodder and Stoughton. 320 pp. 7s.6d.

That in a detective novel the detective should be superb in skill, in knowledge, in observation is as excusable a convention—though one of the great detectives of fiction, Dickens's Inspector Bucket, is not so depicted—as that in a love tale the heroine should be lovely as the dawn or that in an adventure story the hero should be a judicious compound of Hercules and Adonis. But this omniscience of the detective should always be germane to the tale, its display springing naturally from the story's complications. It should not, as in some American books, be flung at random at the reader, after the manner of the amateur who tunes in to every broadcast station available merely to display the efficiency of his set. . . .

Superintendent Hannasyde, in Miss Georgette Heyer's *Behold, Here's Poison*, claims our admiration by no display of superhuman acumen. He is simply a very likeable, lifelike policeman going about his job in a common-sense manner, even if he is rather inclined to overlook little things like safe deposits. Detective brilliance, indeed, is displayed not by him but by another character whom the reader will suspect of anything but that. Miss Heyer's description of family life would win the approval of Mr. G. B. Shaw, so thoroughly does she agree with his thesis that it consists chiefly of a competition in rudeness. But it is often amusing to read of people being rude to each other, and the story from that agreeable start works up to a grim and exciting climax. In fact, the whole thing is so good that one wonders why it is not even better till one realises that all of it—characters (the bully, the cat, the ditherer, the fool, the fop, and so on) and plot alike—comes too much from stock. There is about it a faint aroma of reminiscence, though the more or less familiar ingredients are so well and carefully mixed, the writing is so bright, and the solution so unexpected that the book achieves success and remains one no reader can fail to enjoy.

**48. "The Criminal Record. The Saturday Review's Guide to Detective Fiction,"** *The Saturday Review* **14, 5 September 1936, p. 18:**

*Behold, Here's Poison!* Georgette Heyer (Crime Club: $2.)
-*Crime, Place, Sleuth:* Elderly and obnoxious brother and sister mysteriously envenomed, leaving all heirs suspect and a pretty dish for Insp. Hannasyde.
-*Summing Up:* Randall Mathews, "amiable snake," dominates entire dazzling yarn, which is marvelous mélange of malice, murder, mystery, and mirth.
-*Verdict:* Priceless!

**49. "The New Novels: Detective Stories and Thrillers,"** *The Times Literary Supplement*, **31 October 1936, p. 885:**

*The Talisman Ring.* By Georgette Heyer. Heinemann. 7s.6d.
    This is partly a murder mystery, but much more a story in the manner of Jane Austen, of domestic comedy and love affairs notably devoid of heartbreaks. The date is about 1794, the people are Sussex landowners

and a few of their dependents. One of the two heroines, a romantic young half-French girl, lives in constant hope of adventure such as she has read of in Mrs. Radcliffe's novels. Unlike the similar heroine of *Northanger Abbey* she does find a few such adventures, for Miss Heyer does not avoid scenes of violence as carefully as Jane Austen. But the reader must expect more smiles than thrills.

The Talisman Ring of the title was an heirloom. Rash young Ludovic lost it at play to Plunket. Wicked cousin Basil murdered Plunket, took the ring and made Ludovic seem the murderer. Eustacie and her friends spent all the book proving the innocence of Ludovic (who had turned smuggler) and the guilt of Basil, obvious very early to the reader. "In an adventure," says Eustacie, "it is not proper to have everything quite easy;" and they do not; but the difficulties are never tragic.

**1937**

**50. Will Cuppy, "Mystery and Adventure,"** *New York Herald Tribune Books*, **21 February 1937, p. 16:**

*The Unfinished Clue.* 295 pp. Garden City: The Crime Club. $2.

Here's an elegant buy in smart, streamlined bafflement by the author of *Merely Murder*, *Why Shoot a Butler?*, and *Behold, Here's Poison!* Clever gabble, malicious characterization, fool-proof plot and high excitement are among the treats. Ye corpse is General Sir Arthur Billington-Smith, one of those "When I was at Peshawar" blighters, stabbed with a Chinese dagger in the midst of a week-end party, as he richly deserved. Something was bound to happen, if only because Geoffrey, Sir Arthur's son, had just brought home a Mexican fiancee, Lola de Silva, of the cabarets. "I love very often," says she, "and always passionately." "Brazen, painted hussy!" exclaims Sir Arthur. Lola was upset because there was no absinthe in the house; and there was no shower in her bathroom—which we, personally, regard as grounds for murder.

Miss Heyer provides a lot of assorted and entertaining personae, including the noble Stephen Guest, a strong and fairly silent man in love with Fay, Sir Arthur's young wife. ("With the exception of an incident in his youth, there had been no other woman in his life; he knew, beyond need of averring it, that there would never be another.") What will they do about it? In a sapient forward, J. W. P. observes of Miss Heyer's works: "To combine successfully mirth and murder is a feat that requires extreme technical adroitness in writing, and very seldom does a writer appear who has the ability to accomplish the task. . . . I can make a shrewd guess that her work succeeds as it does because she is canny enough to rely on character than on situation for the humorous aspects of her stories." Anyway, Miss Heyer is an author to read—this means you.

**51. "Rogue's Gallery,"** *Boston Evening Transcript*, **6 March 1937, p. 4:**

Perhaps a husband can forget a wife who deserted him, and a son can fail to recognize his mother. If so, then this new murder-mystery, *The Unfinished Clue*, by Georgette Heyer (Doubleday, Doran and Co., Inc., $2), of an unpleasant British Army officer, who is stabbed to death, is possible. Even if it is so, or not, the story has its points and runs along smoothly to an unexpected if debatable end. General Sir Arthur Billington-Smith is the boorish victim. Probably few English weekends ever had such an ungracious host. Indeed, it was small surprise to find him murdered in his study on the Monday morning. The difficulty young Inspector Harding of Scotland Yard faced was not that of finding suspects but of finding which one of everyone in the party was the murderer. Everyone: wife, sister-in-law, son, nephew, the son's fiancée and others, including a willing-to-be-mistress and her reluctant husband, and the wife's own determined suitor had both motive and opportunity.

And, Inspector Harding found further complications in a personal interest in one of the suspects, an interest, it is soon made evident, which was returned with interest. All the clues found—a torn check made out to the willing-to-be-mistress, the confession of the thief who stole money out of the General's safe, and so forth, all seemed to point to the murderer—but they all worked out to be useless. The only clue that the

102

Inspector could not solve was the unfinished word "There" scrawled upon a piece of paper by the dying hand of the General. When, finally, the Inspector's love-making was brought to a satisfactory conclusion, he managed to find time to take up anew the unfinished clue and so—not without surprise—he found the killer. Miss Heyer has the delightful talent of blending humor with mystery.

**52. "The Criminal Record,"** *The Saturday Review* **15, 13 March 1937, p. 18:**

*The Unfinished Clue.* Georgette Heyer. (Crime Club: $2.)

*-Crime, Place, Sleuth:* Domineering and generally disliked British knight slain at stock-model houseparty where almost all are suspect. Enter Scotland Yard.

*-Summing Up:* Barring the delightful Lola de Silva, self-confessed incomparable dancer, this is neither as cleverly plotted nor amusing as earlier Heyers.

*-Verdict:* Average.

**53. "The New Novels: Detective Stories and Thrillers,"** *The Times Literary Supplement***, 12 June 1937, p. 446:**

*They Found Him Dead.* Hodder and Stoughton. 7s.6d.

The author introduces us to enough live and interesting people to make the book attractive even without its ingenious detective plot. But the people need a genealogical table and the plot needs a plan of house and garden. Kane and Mansell were netting manufacturers in a small port in a south-eastern county. When Silas Kane fell off a cliff just after a party in honour of his sixtieth birthday it might be accident. But when his heir, Clement Kane, was shot in his study soon after, it was time for Hannasyde of Scotland Yard, whom we have met before, to take a hand.

Emily Kane, the rough-tongued matriarch, mother of Silas, was morally capable of murder, but perhaps not physically. Rosemary,

Clement's widow, was a beauty with Russian ancestry, analysed herself accordingly and pronounced herself a "courtesan manquée" and exasperated all other women. She rather wished to believe her lover the killer. Jim Kane, the next heir, was a good-tempered young man addicted to speed boats, but his mother Norma had enough energy to shoot pythons in the Congo, rush home to stand for Parliament and read *The Times* "from cover to cover every day," so she might have shot for her son's benefit. The unknown Australian cousin, or her still less known husband, might be there in disguise, to eliminate nearer heirs. Jim's schoolboy brother, Timothy, whose ardour in amateur detection provides several good scenes, proved to be some use after all.

### 54. *The Manchester Guardian*, 25 June 1937, p. 6:

The reader, too, will probably be quicker than was Superintendent Hannasyde in solving the problems met by Miss Georgette Heyer in *They Found Him Dead*. Culprit and motive are indeed soon obvious in this tale of how in sequence two senior partners of a business firm are murdered and how on the life of the third in the succession other murderous attempts are made. All that, however, goes for little compared with the excellence of the narrative, the grace and humour of the style, the growing tension of the story. Miss Heyer hardly shows that chessboard ingenuity some writers can display, nor is her work remarkable for originality of plot or characterisation, but within its limits it is of a high order and certain to afford pleasure and entertainment.

### 55. Isabelle Wentworth Lawrence, "In the Days of Ruffles and Ready Swords," *Boston Evening Transcript*, 10 July 1937, "Book Reviews," p. 4:

*The Talisman Ring*. New York: Doubleday, Doran. $2.
Like the hero of *Berkeley Square*, we yearn for the days of lace

ruffles, perukes, and ready swords, especially when we have been reading Georgette Heyer. That lady has her period at her fingertips, and the gift of laughter sparkles through it. The tale of the talisman ring, the finding of which would mean the freeing of Ludovic from a charge of murder, is the gayest bit of fooling we have happened upon in a long time.

To begin with, old Sylvester, Lord Lavenham, lay a-dying. On his death-bed he arranged a marriage between his grand nephew Sir Tristram Shield and his granddaughter, the charming Mademoiselle Eustacie, whose mother had been, according to Papa Sylvester, a fool: "Eloped with a frippery Frenchman; that shows you. What was his damned name?"

But Eustacie was lovely. Also, being French, she was easily reconciled to the idea of marrying a strange gentleman whom she had never seen. Only, she did like blond men. "It is a pity that you are so dark, because I do not like dark men in general. However, one must accustom oneself." Shield thanked her. Nevertheless, her cousin had one failing far worse than the color of his hair. He had no sense of romance. When she explained to him that she had been snatched from the jaws of the French Revolution, he showed no particular sympathy.

Nor did he sympathize when she told of her vision of going to the guillotine all alone in a tumbril dressed in white. "For me, I think one should wear white to the guillotine, if one is quite young, and not carry anything except perhaps a handkerchief. Do you not agree?" Sir Tristram said he would be sorry for anyone in a tumbril, of whatever sex, or however dressed. Eustacie pouted, "You would be more sorry for a young girl—all alone, and perhaps bound," she said positively. Sir Tristram merely remarked that she wouldn't have been all alone in a tumbril. "A Frenchman," said Eustacie, "would understand at once."

When grandpapa died, quite unintentionally, before he actually got them married, Eustacie was visited by a bold thought. She would run away to London, and be a governess. She would not even fear the Headless Horseman, who might come up behind her, and leap to the pommel of her saddle. At least, she would not after she had consulted her soon-to-be ex-fiancé, and been assured there was no such person. Sir

Tristram might not be romantic, but he was eminently respectable, and thoroughly dependable. So he proved when the matter of cousin Ludovic came up.

Ludovic had had a quarrel with a gentleman who was later found dead. Ludovic, accused of the murder, had to be smuggled out of the country. But he returned as a smuggler himself, and led the Bow Street Runners a merry chase. Of course, after Eustacie had ridden through the night with him, bullets flying in all directions, she loved him madly, and decided to save him. In this, she was ably assisted by the delightful Miss Sarah Thane, one of Miss Heyer's nicest characters, whom they chanced upon, when hiding at the inn. She knew just how you felt when your horse was maddened by fright and you were obliged to ride *ventre à terre*, and all that sort of thing.

All her life she had longed for adventure, and she had traveled about with her brother in search of it. Then Eustacie came into her life, and of course Ludovic followed—and then Sir Tristram Shield. On the cover jacket you will see the last two hunting a secret panel together. She understood just why Eustacie could not marry Sir Tristram in spite of being a well-brought up French miss. "He is thirty-one years old, and he does not frequent gambling-hells or cockpits, and when I asked him if he would ride *ventre à terre* to my deathbed, he said certainly not."

"This is more shocking than all the rest," declared Miss Thane. "He must be quite heartless." But she found she was mistaken.

We congratulate Miss Heyer on her competent vivacity, her delicious sense of humor, and her ability to string the sort of tale which always leaves us breathless with delight.

**56. Will Cuppy, "Mystery and Adventure,"** *New York Herald Tribune Books*, **8 August 1937, p. 13:**

*They Found Him Dead*. 275 pp. Garden City: Crime Club. $2.

Unless we err, *They Found Him Dead* is the big winner among current bafflers, with several miles to spare. It stands alone, you might say, in both composition and character, and there are no flies on the plot, either, if you're particular about the more childish side of your reading. Miss Heyer herewith returns to the manner of *Why Shoot a Butler?*—wasn't that her first success?—only more so, with bitter, realistic and amusing conversation all over the place, two killings and superior sleuthing by dear old Superintendent Hannasyde. Who murdered Silas Kane, rich netting manufacturer, discovered dead at the foot of the cliff (you don't really think he jumped off, do you?) and Clement Kane, his suspected heir (shot in the boudoir [sic]).

Miss Heyer also qualifies as part reviewer of her own book, by virtue of a candid letter written to her publishers before dashing off the volume. In this document she describes Paul Mansell, one of the suspects, as "a nasty piece of work," Betty Premble as "a damned fool and put in for light relief," Betty's husband as "more light relief" and Betty's two children (Jennifer and Peter) respectively as "repulsive little girl" and "repulsive little boy." Then there's Rosemary Kane, a sort of Ibsen lady with a comic slant, and a dozen other headliners, such as a sensible heroine, a hero of "handsome face and noble form," sinister extras and the diabolical skulking murderer, all done to a turn and with no truckling to the goofier fans. The whole affair is so admirable that it may be recommended even to mystery-haters, just to prove there are good ones now and then. In the words of her sample pre-review, also sent to her publishers, "This book will not disappoint Miss Heyer's many admirers."

**57. "The Criminal Record,"** *The Saturday Review* **16, 14 August 1937, p. 20:**

*They Found Him Dead*. Georgette Heyer. (Crime Club: $2.)
*-Crime, Place, Sleuth:* Mild-mannered Insp. Hannasyde, profiting by helpful hints of inept amateur sleuth, solves curious killings of British Uncle and nephew.
*-Summing Up:* Gala performance by all-star troupe of hierophants—mixing mystery, murder, young love, octogenarian crabbedness, boyish banditry, and much else.
*-Verdict:* Delightful

**58.** "Book Reviews. The Rogue's Gallery," *Boston Evening Transcript*, 25 September 1937, p. 4:

It is not an altogether simple matter to collect an ill-assorted group of characters, put them through their paces and then turn out an unusual and clever mystery. Yet this is just what Georgette Heyer has done in her highly amusing and exciting thriller, *They Found Him Dead* (The Crime Club, Inc., $2). In the first place, lest the reader has trouble in remembering who's who in the story, the jacket of the book contains the "Dramatis Personae" or list of those involved in the tale. Silas Kane, bachelor, was host at his sixtieth birthday party and his near relatives and business associates were his guests. That night, after his guests had departed, Kane went out for his usual before-going-to-bed stroll and in the morning his body was discovered at the foot of the cliffs near his home. An accident, evidently. Yet a few days later Clement Kane, heir to his uncle's fortune, was slain by a pistol shot as he sat at his desk in Cliff House. Murder, evidently.

The police were called into these cases, and Superintendent Hannasyde, assisted by Sergeant Hemingway found they were up against a mighty tough proposition and all their clues ran to dust but as luck would have it they chanced upon a lead which did the trick and Hannasyde vindicated himself. Characters to watch are fifteen year old Timothy Harte, Trevor Dermott in love with the beautiful Rosemary, Clement Kane's wife; Joe Mansell, a member of Silas Kane's firm. There are others too who may fool you unless you are cleverer than Hannasyde. This is a top notch thriller, free from messy details, humorous, speedy and completely logical in its outcome.

**59.** "The New Novels," *The Times Literary Supplement*, 13 November 1937, p. 869:

"A Story of Waterloo." *An Infamous Army*. Heinemann. 8s.6d.
Even at a time when a very fair number of good historical novels are

being published, Miss Heyer's latest one stands out. It is a story of the Hundred Days seen through the eyes of a group of aristocrats, civilians and soldiers, who are assembled in Brussels when the tale opens or arrive soon afterwards. Most of the characters are real persons, but those in the immediate foreground are creatures of the imagination. A very vivid imagination it is. Here is a romance of which the historical details are presented not merely with astonishing care and accuracy—bibliography and maps all complete—but with a comprehension of the essential features of the Waterloo campaign even more unusual, and which yet holds from first to last our keen interest in the fate of the principal personages.

The hero, Colonel Charles Audley, is a member of Wellington's personal staff. The heroine, Lady Barbara Childe, embodies all the extravagances of her epoch. She is a crazier, more obstinate and imperious Lady Caroline Lamb—who herself has a place in the background. To the horror of his relations and friends, Audley, immediately on his arrival from Vienna with Wellington, fell in love with this beautiful young widow, and was accepted by her. Audley, who is brilliantly drawn, was patient, gentle and humorous. He laughed her out of her escapades, or laughed at them if he could not. At length, however, in a passion at the very gentle remonstrance which he made about one of the worst, she broke off the engagement.

Meanwhile the legions were assembling and everyone was keyed up to the highest pitch of excitement. This period of preparations gives the author opportunity to form a striking picture-gallery, among the portraits in which may be mentioned those of Wellington, the Prince of Orange, Hill, Uxbridge, Seymour, the Belgian Constant de Rebecque and the German Müffling. The meaning of the opening moves of the campaign is better grasped than in some historical accounts, and there is even a sound criticism of Wellington's strategy. Quatre Bras is fought "off," but related with great effect to those anxiously waiting at Brussels, their legs still tired after the Duchess of Richmond's ball. For Waterloo we take our places on the field as spectators, and if a battle has ever, in fiction, been more vividly and accurately described from the point of view of a staff officer hurrying from one part of the line to another, one cannot recall an instance. The ordinary reader will find these trim episodes good, but he will not realize just how good they are. He may, however, realize more clearly than before how "near run" a thing it was. Charles Audley, desperately wounded towards the end of the battle and with his left arm amputated, was borne back to Brussels. Lady Bab, whose favourite brother was among the fallen, gave him the reception he deserved, and the Duke came into his sick-room to bless the mended match.

## 1938

**60. M. Persis Johnson, "Where There Was the Sound of Revelry by Night," *Boston Evening Transcript*, 30 April 1938, sect. 3, p. 1:**

*An Infamous Army.* By Georgette Heyer. New York: Doubleday, Doran, $2.50.

Brussels in the spring of 1815 was a gay city. The English gentry, chafed by their long confinement within the limits of their tight little isles during Napoleon's military operations on the Continent, had hastened to flock abroad upon the "little Colonel's" banishment to Elba. And the festivities attendant to the long-exiled King's reinstatement as King of The Netherlands plus the presence of the Army of Occupation in the Lowlands had made Brussels the logical goal for friends and relatives, pleasure-seeking ladies, and the mothers of marriageable daughters.

Even Napoleon's escape and the rumored threat of renewed invasions found the lords and ladies loath to leave Brussels to the Bruxelloise. Thus the hundred days that preceded the Battle of Waterloo found that city drawing strength from the presence of the seemingly imperturbable Duke of Wellington, while it turned somewhat hysterically to balls, teas and picnics to cover the nervous tension under which it lived.

This colorful period has provided inspiration for many an author, particularly English authors, not the least of whom was Thackeray. One of the latest writers to feel the drama of those days is Georgette Heyer. And the result of her interest is *An Infamous Army*—a historical novel that, upon its publication in England received acclaim not only for the agreeable mingling of history and fiction within its covers, but for the truly remarkable description it contains of the battle that "changed the fate of a continent"—the Battle of Waterloo.

Carrying on a private warfare during the tense One Hundred Days were the beautiful and daring widow, Lady Barbara Childs [sic], and a likable member of the Duke of Wellington's personal staff, one Colonel Charles Audley. Around these two imaginary figures Miss Heyer has woven a lively tale. For though it was a case of love at first sight for these two, their romance was far from tame. In fact, anything the impetuous Lady Babs had a part in was sure to be tempestuous, for her beauty and abounding energy in a day of feminine lassitude had already made her the toast of the town, while her complete disregard of Mrs. Grundy was fast making her the talk of the town.

Walking side by side with Lady Babs and Colonel Charles all through the pages of *An Infamous Army* are the outstanding personages of the Allied army, from the "crusty" Iron Duke and the Prussian Marshal Blücher, forever "stinking" of garlic, down to the youthful Prince of Orange. And under Miss Heyer's skillful pen these figures, both the true and the fancied, become distinct personalities; though cloaked in romance, they still have a deal of sturdy realism about them.

Climaxing the story is the previously mentioned description of the action at Waterloo. Here indeed Miss Heyer has breathed reality into the pages of history. Masterful handling of what would ordinarily be a mass of unwieldy detail has transformed it into a cohesive picture. The reader can see the scene of conflict, the red and gold squares of English soldiers forming and reforming on the plain as Napoleon's cavalry charges time and time again, the heroism of the Scottish brigades under murderous fire, the Iron Duke's bony nose appearing first here, then there, and the sound of his voice rallying the sagging lines. It is a gory scene, with officers and men dying by the thousands—a scene not soon to be forgotten.

In May, Wellington had called his force "an infamous army, very weak and ill-equipped." What could Napoleon have called it the morning after Waterloo?

**61. L. H. Titterton, "A Dramatic Tale of Waterloo. Georgette Heyer's *An Infamous Army* Is a Historical Novel of Unusual Interest,"** *The New York Times Book Review*, 8 May 1938, p. 6

*An Infamous Army*. By Georgette Heyer. 415 pp. New York: Doubleday, Doran. $2.50

In an author's note that precedes this historical novel, Georgette Heyer states that "the specter of Thackeray must loom over any one wishing to tackle the battle of Waterloo. . . . It is many years since I have read *Vanity Fair*; and although I have encroached on Thackeray's preserves, at least I have stolen nothing from him." Miss Heyer need not have made even this oblique apology for her distinguished novel; apart from the fact that *Vanity Fair* was concerned only to a minor degree with the social life of Brussels on the eve of the battle of Waterloo, and even less with the battle itself, there is no similarity whatsoever between the two books.

Miss Heyer has focused her readers' attention upon a strong and interesting story, around which she has built the complex happenings in Brussels up to and during the battle of Waterloo. And because she has chosen for her protagonist an officer on the staff of the Duke of Wellington—Colonel Audley—the battle itself is woven into the fabric of the story. Colonel Audley is the brother of Lord Worth, who, in common with a great many other members of society, had taken his wife to Brussels for a change of scene after their enforced absence from the Continent during the perilous days that preceded the departure of Napoleon for Elba. The Duke was off in Vienna, so his officers, with their ladies, were able to join the civilian visitors in making the most of what had already turned out to be a scintillatingly gay social season, in which balls and receptions followed each other with bewildering rapidity.

Among those staying in Brussels was Lady Barbara Childe, a singularly beautiful young widow whose elderly husband had died after a marriage of convenience that had lasted a very few years. A granddaughter of the Duke of Avon, Lady Barbara's behavior was everything that tradition frowned upon. She flirted indiscriminately with

112

single or married men, wore dresses so striking that the dowagers and her more conventional contemporaries, with one accord, agreed that she could have nothing on underneath them but the scantiest of garments, and, to everyone's amazement, threw over a Belgian nobleman of great wealth, who was quite certain he would end by making her his wife, in favor of Colonel Audley. Had Miss Heyer hammered on this triangle she would have produced the same familiar old melody which has only too often bored the hopeful reader, in spite of the unusual characteristics of the three individuals involved. But she has skillfully avoided doing so by the introduction of an amazing gallery of characters completely interesting in themselves.

Accordingly, the first half of her novel is an enchanting picture of mad gayety—colorful parties set against the background of the ominous return of Napoleon and his obvious intention of giving battle to the Allies. Many novelists have described great battles of the past, but Miss Heyer's description of Waterloo very definitely ranks her with the best of them. It is hard for a generation accustomed to think of warfare in terms of the trenches of Flanders to visualize two armies drawn up in full view of each other on opposing ridges with a valley in between, so that each could watch the other arranging its forces, bringing up its guns, and speculate with some degree of certainty upon the probable place of first attack. It is hard to think of soldiers going into action wearing steel breastplates, plumed helmets, white breeches, or scarlet coats, and even harder to visualize the British infantry forming hollow squares and remaining in this formation while the French cavalry charged them, swerved aside owing to the pointblank musket fire and the bayonets, and then rode around and around them, trying to break through into their centers. The very thought of the Duke of Wellington himself actually going to the aid of one of these squares and rallying it when it looked like breaking seems incredible in an age when general officers operate from far behind the lines. Yet when an artillery officer came up to the Duke and told him that he could clearly perceive Bonaparte and all his staff, and had no doubt of being able to direct his guns on them, he was met with a frosty stare and statement: "No, no, I won't have it! It is not the business of General Officers to be firing upon each other!"

113

The title of the book comes from Wellington's statement to Lord Stewart, in which he said, "I have got an infamous army; very weak and ill-equipped, and a very inexperienced staff," which is perhaps borne out by the fact that when brigade commanders were sending their staff officers in desperation to ask for orders, the Duke, knowing that nothing could be done but remain in position, replied, "There are no orders." The remark of a Highlander, when a Belgian brigade ran away without firing a shot, to the effect that the British didn't need foreigners to fight their battles, illuminates the problem faced by the Duke in commanding a motley army of troops from half a dozen nations fighting on Belgian soil.

Behind the comings and goings of the other major characters in the book there towers throughout the imposing figure of the Duke of Wellington. It is a mark of Miss Heyer's perfect craftsmanship that this character is so perfectly portrayed that the general order she has used as a climax to the book, bristling with discipline even in the hour of victory, seems inevitable and completely true.

### 62. *The Times Literary Supplement*, 28 May 1938, p. 372:

*A Blunt Instrument.* By Georgette Heyer. Hodder and Stoughton. 7s.6d.

Two "rules" often held up by critics before writers of detective stories are that every murder after the first is a weakness, and that the murderer must not turn out to be insane. Miss Heyer breaks both rules—and with every justification. Her second murder is not a despairing author's easiest way out, but a brilliant clue to the first; the murderer's insanity is not a sop to tender consciences but is—if the reader will only see it—implicit from the word Go.

A summary of the salient disclosable points of the plot of *A Blunt Instrument* would differ hardly at all from a similar summary of a thousand other detective stories. Suffice it to say that Miss Heyer's humorous Scripture-quoting constable is a grand addition to the cops' gallery of fiction (we could have wished for more of him); that the plot is watertight and as enthralling as the earlier Detective (now

Superintendent) Hannasyde stories; and that no blunt instrument has ever, in our recollection, more artfully escaped notice.


### 63. Nicholas Blake, "Romances of Detection," *The Spectator*, 17 June 1938, p. 1118:

*A Blunt Instrument.* (Hodder and Stoughton. 7s.6d.)

. . . Georgette Heyer, in *A Blunt Instrument*, gives a brilliant display of the most delicately pointed wit: she can be guaranteed to keep you in fits of laughter, but her detection is perfunctory, to say the least; and, among a small cast of charming and really live characters, P.C. Glass stands out oddly unnatural with his religious mania, his volleys of texts, his insubordination to his superiors. If we can't have discipline in the police force, where can we have it? Still, you should read this book . . . .


### 64. Ralph Partridge, "Detection," *The New Statesman and Nation*, 25 June 1938, Literary Supplement, p. 1077:

*A Blunt Instrument.* By Georgette Heyer. Hodder and Stoughton. 7s.6d.

Miss Heyer's publishers choose to list her detective novels as thrillers; a gross malclassification, since her art depends entirely on psychology, never on violence. In *A Blunt Instrument* she has set herself a most delicate task of mystification, one which requires a firm, light touch, such as Agatha Christie achieves once every five years. It would be unfair to Miss Heyer's chances of success to say more about her plot, but even if she fails, as she did with me, she is not disgraced. The pleasure of reading her spirited dialogue and meeting her enterprising characters is not affected by an early guess at the solution.


### 65. E. R. Punshon, "Literature and Mystery," *The Manchester Guardian*, 1 July 1938, p. 7:

*A Blunt Instrument*. Hodder and Stoughton. Pp. 288. 7s.6d.

Miss Georgette Heyer has won a popularity that entitles her to the position she assigns one of her characters in *A Blunt Instrument*, of being among the most successful crime novelists of the day. It is a well-deserved success, for she has always a good story to tell and she writes with vivacity and real humour, so that it is an invidious task to explain why the critic cannot fully endorse the popular verdict. But there does seem to be a certain lack of originality and of realism—the husband-and-wife scenes in *A Blunt Instrument*, especially in Chapter 12, are all too familiar, and such characters as the apparently frivolous nephew and the Scripture-quoting policemen, amusing as they are, have the flavour not of life but of fantasy. For all that, the reader will find both enjoyment and excitement in this story of the murder of a loose-living suburbanite, the subsequent investigation, and the surprise conclusion to a problem so fairly stated that the reader could deduce the truth for himself by a careful consideration of the times given.

**66. *The Times Literary Supplement*, 1 October 1938, p. 625:**

*Royal Escape*. By Georgette Heyer. Heinemann 8s.6d.

The escape of Charles II after the Battle of Worcester is an episode which affords great opportunities to the historical novelist. Miss Heyer takes full advantage of them. As is her wont, she bases her romance upon a considerable bulk of material; indeed, her tendency is to give her readers too much rather than too little history, and at times her theme and her personages become overloaded with detail. Yet *Royal Escape* will not be found lacking either interest or excitement.

The story opens with the last stage of Worcester fight. Then begin Charles's extraordinary wanderings, his hiding in woods and in priest-holes. We see him foiled in his attempt to cross into Wales, and on his famous ride to Bristol dressed as a servant with Jane Lane on a pillion behind him. That venture failed, too, and no ship was to be had. Charmouth and Southampton gave no better results. Meanwhile he had been recognized more than once and his foes were hot on his trail. It was almost—pious Royalists thought it quite—a miracle that he was at last got abroad. The portrait of the young king without a throne may be in some degree idealized, but his good temper and cool courage are not exaggerated. Nor are the heroic devotion and self-sacrifice of those who helped him, from wealthy squires down to humble yokels like the Penderels.

**67. "The Criminal Record,"** *The Saturday Review* **18, 8 October 1938, p. 18:**
*A Blunt Instrument.* Georgette Heyer. (Crime Club: $2.)
-*Crime, Place, Sleuth:* Philandering Britisher brutally bopped. Amiable Insp. Hannasyde and mixed-pickle assistants run ragged by antics of suspect.
-*Summing Up:* Double fracture of mystery story ethics only goes to show that if you're good you can get away with—murder.
-*Verdict:* Brilliant

**68. Will Cuppy, "Mystery and Adventure,"** *New York Herald Tribune Books*, **9 October 1938, p. 15:**

*A Blunt Instrument.* By Georgette Heyer. 310 pp. New York: The Crime Club. $2.
Miss Heyer seems to have returned, more or less, to the vein of her first big success, *Why Shoot a Butler?* In that work, you may recall, she captured every reviewer and most of the public with a couple of amoral characters, a special attitude toward crime and a species of extremely dry fun, not to mention other necessary ingredients. Here we have something of the same voltage, even more suitable, perhaps, to a wide audience, and hereby recommended. Our main suspect in the murder of Mr. Ernest Fletcher (all the ladies called him Dear Ernie), done in with a blunt instrument at Greystones, is Neville Fletcher, nephew of the deceased, an eccentric young man who may strike you at first as of unsound mind—he

got a half-blue at Oxford—and the one who should have been slaughtered. He has traveled in the Balkans, but he's probably joking about that Montenegrin with a knife at Skoplje. He has no alibi—says he was reading a book.

Anyway, Dear Ernie was seated at his kneehole desk when it happened, and within a few hours Superintendent Hannasyde has clews pointing to Mrs. Helen North, a foolish lady; Mr. North, her possibly jealous husband; Abraham Budd, who had called upon the deceased; Charlie Carpenter, an ex-convict, and a man of average height in a Homburg hat, seen leaving by the garden gate. We were inclined to quarrel at first with what looked like too much type casting and a slight staginess in some of the characters, but Miss Heyer won our vote as she went on with more and more genuine plot interest. Moreover, when the plot is all in, you can believe it—which is an almost unknown phenomenon in the mystery field. Perhaps our author resembles Sally Drew in the story—she's described as one of the six most important mystery writers. Miss Heyer is all of that.

**69. Marian Wiggin, "Book Review. Rogues' Gallery,"** *Boston Evening Transcript,* **15 October 1938, pt. 3, p. 2:**

When we find, on page five, that one of the major characters of a book is a "willowy young man in an ill-fitting dinner-jacket suit, who paused on the threshold, blinking long-lashed eyelids," we know with what we have to cope. Georgette Heyer doesn't help matters in *A Blunt Instrument* (Doubleday, Doran & Co., Inc.) by adding a female detective-story writer and a bobby (this is another English killing) who speaks almost wholly in Biblical quotations. Even the solution, meant doubtless to be a surprise, was only annoying.

**70. "Mysteries,"** *The New Yorker,* **15 October 1938, p. 72:**

*A Blunt Instrument*, by Georgette Heyer. A not very mysterious tale of murder in a London suburb. Miss Heyer has strained a point in an attempt to make her characters amusing. Pleasant enough reading, though.

## 1939

**71. Charles David Abbott, "King Charles on the Run," *The Saturday Review* 19, 4 February 1939, p. 7:**

*Royal Escape*. By Georgette Heyer. New York: Doubleday, Doran. 1939. $2.50

Worcester lost, his Scots army sullen and inimical, Charles Stuart the younger faced the same fate that had overwhelmed his father. It was the block that awaited him, and neither Cromwell nor other potent Roundheads would have shown any softening towards mercy. But this Charles was a more wary prince than his father. Wit and waggery were too much a part of his nature to permit the meek surrender. He could enjoy cheating his enemies with almost the same relish that he could bring to gaining his kingdom. Escape was so difficult as to seem hopeless, but it was in Charles to attempt the impossible. From sanctuary to sanctuary he fled, living only from one hour to another in some priest-hole or Cavalier hideout. Everywhere he was recognized and the pursuit followed relentlessly. A retreat to Wales was checked, Bristol was reached after endless hardships and mishaps but failed to provide a ship, Southampton was equally useless. Finally, from what is now Brighton, a barque carried him off to France and safety. Well-wishers to the Royalist cause called it a miracle; after 1660 even the church could refer to it as "the Royal Miracle." Miraculous or not, the escape was a feat of daring such as no English monarch, with the possible exception of the fabled Alfred, has ever accomplished, and it provides the historical novelist with a story that whips up its own suspense with artless speed.

Miss Heyer is adept at giving full-bodied reality to such a story. Casual readers who know her only in another role and who remember her only by such detective tales as *They Found Him Dead* will be prepared for the ease with which she develops her narrative, but they will be amazed at the learning which she displays so dexterously and so generously. She has taken her sources as seriously as would a professor of history, and has weighed all the evidence of those multitudinous tracts that, with the Restoration, celebrated Charles's miracle. Out of their confusion and their waywardness of detail she has built a plain, direct story which moves rapidly from one breathless episode to the next, each seemingly tragic and hopeless, until at last the *Surprise* with the king on board disappears into the gray of the Channel. It is Charles's triumph; he can laugh, as he doubtless did, at the unexpected joke the expense of which the solemn Cromwell could pay.

**72. Jane Spence Southron, in "'Royal Escape' and Other Recent Works of Fiction," *The New York Times Book Review*, 5 February 1939, p. 7:**

*Royal Escape.* 386 pp. New York: Doubleday, Doran. $2.50.

Perhaps democracy and humor go together. At all events, England's most naturally democratic King—a born democrat, whom circumstances confirmed in a personal idiosyncrasy—had not only the most irrepressible sense of humor of any personage of whom history tells but—and this is affirmed after mature consideration—of any Englishman past or present. It was a sense of humor that bore him up through years of miserable exile, pulled him out of difficulty after difficulty and did not desert him even when he was dying. It is this King, the young man of 21 whom Leslie failed at Worcester and who afterward went through six weeks of hairbreadth adventures that pale Hollywood's wildest stagings, of whom Miss Heyer writes in this exciting, authentic and extraordinarily fine historical novel.

It is Charles to the life; not the Charles who came back amid tumultuous rejoicings as King Charles II in 1660, nine years later, but the Charles of Cromwell's proclamation, the "tall man above two yards high," black-haired and, at first look, ugly but with a smile (or was it a grin?) that worked on folk like magic. There was a price on his head: a thousand pounds, a veritable fortune in those days; and the astounding thing was that though scores, perhaps hundreds, might have earned it none did. It was more than royalist loyalty that got him through. It was, not a doubt of it, personal devotion to a dare-devil youth who looked every inch a King but thought himself no better that the next man.

Charles's own story of his escape, Colonel George Gounter's account of the last act of it, in which he was the prime mover, and a number of other contemporary narratives, including a generous assortment of the young King's reputed sayings, were available as sources. There is such a wealth of material that it would seem to have been, largely, a matter of sifting, composing, unifying and, finally, dramatizing. In this dramatization, Miss Heyer's creative power has ample scope. Her people are fully rounded; completely alive. She has caught to perfection the trick of involving you in her plot, and the knowledge that it is a true plot only adds to your entanglement.

Even the two girls were to hand; lovely Jane Lane and fascinating Juliana Coningsby who, in turn, rode pillion behind the King, and, one must believe found it hard to treat him as the servant he was supposed to be. Here, but not unduly, Miss Heyer has indulged her imagination. Both girls—if we know anything of girls—must have thrilled to the adventure; and a weaker writer, relying on a superficial diagnosis of Charles's nature, might have made meretricious romance of it. Miss Heyer has shown greater insight. The Charles of *Royal Escape* is, above everything, a man with an unshakable purpose; to regain the kingdom his father had lost, and some day to repay those who now were taking their lives in their hands for him. It is brain, driving force, wise daring, and the ability to evaluate character that distinguish him no less than personal charm and a geniune liking for people.

What is specially notable in the novel is the clear, straight course steered through an amazing multiplicity of detail. From Worcester to Brighthelmstone—the little fishing village destined later to be Brighton—where the "escape" ended, was an intricate and long journey that meant doubling back, lying-up in wet woods, hiding in priests' holes

121

or in the famous "Royal Oak," riding, boldface, through rebel towns and rebel troops. The number of people in the secret grows daily. The King is passed on from one member of a family to another, from one friend to another. Poor, fat Lord Wilmot (veritable Falstaff of fun were he less tragic in his significance to the outcome) is forever pulling in some one fresh to help, not all of them useful. But though no spot and no person vital to the itinerary is omitted, there is no sense of over-crowding. It took talent of no mean order to differentiate among so many, so that the rustic Penderel brothers, the courtly Wyndham, sardonic Colonel Robert Phelips, staunch as any of them, Tom Gounter and his stout-hearted brother George besides, quite literally, scores more stand-out in vivid individuality, each contributing to the mounting excitement, furthering the plot and helping, implicitly, to explain an unprecedented historical situation.

*Royal Escape* does more than merely evoke a vanished scene. It puts you instantaneously and squarely in the past.

### 73. *The New Yorker*, 11 February 1939, p. 74:

*Royal Escape*, by Georgette Heyer.
The fortunes of Charles II of England from his defeat at the battle of Worcester on September 3, 1651, to his embarkation for France some six weeks later. Miss Heyer, who also wrote *An Infamous Army*, has a way with historical romance. She makes the King a fascinating figure, courageous, courteous, and charming, if a little short on gray matter. A first-class costume piece.

### 74. "Detective Stories. New Characters in Crime Fiction," *The Times Literary Supplement*, 24 June 1939, p. 375:

*No Wind of Blame*. By Georgette Heyer. Hodder and Stoughton. 7s.6d.
The best of this week's mystery stories are perhaps more noticeable

122

for the amusing personalities they embody than for a closely worked-out use of the mechanics of detection.  They stand out, however, from the mass of merely competent fiction by individuality and humour of different types, and by a swift movement that gives little time for critical analysis and never allows boredom.

In Miss Georgette Heyer's *No Wind of Blame*, the problem is that of the shooting of a most disagreeable and weak specimen of a man, husband to a rich, attractive and flamboyant ex-actress and stepfather to a very temperamental girl.  These two and their admirers form the main body of the suspects, though there are other possible murderers dotted about the neighbourhood in sufficient numbers and vagueness to be a great trouble to the police.  The eventual discovery of the method and identity of the criminal, though it is most ingeniously contrived, is the least of one's worries among the luxuriance of delightful characters that the book contains.  The widowed Ermyntrude, fantastic in her attitudes of grief; the wretched and unhappy Inspector whom her behaviour causes to feel like a leper; her irrepressible daughter Vicky, always playing a part and changing her role two or three times a day; the Georgian Prince who is a suitor for Ermyntrude's hand and fortune; even the unfortunate girl Janet who cannot stop talking—all these combine into one of the most amusing stories of its kind that has appeared for some time, and one that continues to hold the reader's attention.

**75. E. R. Punshon, "Courage and Fun in Crime Tales," *The Manchester Guardian*, 11 July 1939, p. 7:**

*No Wind of Blame*. Hodder and Stoughton. Pp. 320. 7s.6d.

Some of the purists of the detective novel have complained that Miss Georgette Heyer's detection is not according to the best examples, and indeed it is probably true that she owes much of her popularity to her lively writing and sense of fun.  In any case the purist's criticism is not one that applies to her new book, *No Wind of Blame*, in which the puzzle is both ingenious and fair. The story, which tells of the murder of the unsatisfactory husband of a wealthy wife, once a musical-comedy actress, opens slowly with scenes and dialogues surprisingly—since they are written by Miss Heyer—dull and lifeless.  But all that changes with the appearance on the scene of Vicky, a young lady who puts on a new personality with each new frock and who is indeed an ever-continuing joy.  The scene in which Vicky rescues her rich and now widowed mother from the attentions of a suspected fortune-hunter is one of the richest comedy.

**76. Ralph Partridge, "Frivolous Detection,"** *The New Statesman and Nation*, **15 July 1939, p. 96:**

*No Wind of Blame*. By Georgette Heyer. Hodder and Stoughton.  7s.6d.

We may deplore the dearth of serious detection nowadays, but it must be faced.  Either the authors cannot be bothered to invent the necessary brain-teasers, or the public can't be bothered to read them.  Whatever the reason—personally I suspect a contemporary drift from intellectual to emotional satisfactions—most of the modern detective stuff depends for its appeal on the trimmings and not on the crime.  The emphasis of criticism must be shifted, and we must judge the current output on its ornamental qualities, not on its structural stability.

In general it will be admitted that technical progress has been most marked in the handling of the love interest.  No longer are all the heroines a sickly blend of school-girl complexions and Victorian upbringing.  Miss Sayers sent her heroine to Oxford, and others have followed her lead.  The girls can now drink, flirt and become uncommonly good at games.  In return, the young men are allowed to take a few more liberties with them and drop the Galahad pose.  It is no longer obligatory to skip the romantic part of a detective story as being pure padding; sometimes it is the most entertaining feature of a book, *vide* Miss Sayers.

But the most remarkable, albeit questionable, innovation is the use of a murder plot as a vehicle for roaring fun.  The old masters of detection occasionally permitted a mildly humorous intonation to lighten their solemnity, but the modern school go all out for their laughs. Half the American detectives and a growing percentage of English advance to their objectives behind a creeping barage of wisecracks. The Dr. Watsons of today are chosen, not for their courage in the service of the Queen on the heights of Dargai, but because of their successful resemblance to music-hall knockabout artistes.

These reflections on the present state of detection are prompted by contemplation of the list under review. All are readable, some are very amusing, but not one of them is a sound detective problem, judged by the standards of fifteen years ago. . . .

Miss Heyer writes novels with crime in them; sometimes very good, sometimes not so good. *No Wind of Blame* is not so good because Miss Heyer introduces a tricky murder into her gay skit on the climbing attitudes of retired actresses in county society. The trickiness of the murder is the weakness: it is not subtle enough to hoodwink the average reader, but it occupies the authoress for a terrible time, trying to palm off her scientific explanation. But once you resolve to skip the details of detection, the rest of the book will be found very amusing. . . .

### 77. "Mystery and Crime," *The New Yorker*, 11 Nov. 1939, p. 92:

*No Wind of Blame*, by Georgette Heyer.

Lighthearted story of murder on an English country estate owned by a lady who isn't quite county. Very funny indeed, with the three women involved inspiring love in one form or another. For those who like diversion as well as deduction.

### 78. "The Criminal Record," *The Saturday Review*, 22 November 1939, p. 21:

*No Wind of Blame*. Georgette Heyer. (Crime Club: $2.)
-*Crime, Place, Sleuth:* Wastrel husband of rich and flighty Englishwoman pinked in neighbors' garden. Insp. Hemingway, despite

lunatic interruptions, solves it.

-*Summing Up:* Method of murder ingenious—if not quite believable. Priceless characters and spate of cock-eyed conversation make chapters hum.

-*Verdict:* Highly enjoyable.

## 1940

**79. "Historical. Love and Battle,"** *The Times Literary Supplement*, **13 April 1940, p. 185:**

*The Spanish Bride.* By Georgette Heyer. Heinemann. 8s.6d

Miss Heyer already has more than one historical novel to her credit, and in this romance of the Peninsular War she may be congratulated upon a success. The romance of the two fiery young lovers who, arrived at years of discretion, were later to stand godfather and godmother to two South African towns, Ladysmith and Harrismith, has the advantage of being a true one, and the further advantage of having been inimitably related by Sir Harry Smith in his own spirited autobiography. Miss Heyer has made good use of this, and of many other diaries and memoirs of the Peninsular War. Opening with the storming of Badajoz, where Harry Smith first met, and then and there married, his fourteen-year-old bride, Doña Juana Maria de los Dolores de León, she takes us with them through all the hardships of the campaign which culminated in the battles at Salamanca and Vitoria, then on into the Pyrenees, and, after much hard fighting and shocking weather, down into France, where the intrepid Juana takes her famous ride through disturbed country to return a looted Sèvres bowl. We see the passage of the Adour, the battle of Toulouse and the proclamation of the restored Bourbons. Then, after some years of absence on service in America, the gallant brigade-major rejoins his wife, and the story ends dramatically with their reunion on the bloody battlefield after Waterloo.

Miss Heyer manages a vast mass of material with considerable skill. Her military types are well characterized and differentiated, her battles lucidly described, as through the eyes of those engaged in them, and we are conscious all the time of the character of the country, which she manages to make us see very clearly. It was bold of her to risk comparisons with famous writers' accounts of Waterloo; but, by keeping quietly to the business in hand and following the point of view which she has adopted, she achieves an effective *dénouement*, while adding yet another to the ghastly pictures of war which no faithful account of the Peninsular campaigns can hope to avoid.


**80. G. M., in "The New Books. Fiction,"** *The Saturday Review* **23, 9 November 1940, pp. 19-20:**

*The Spanish Bride*. Doubleday, Doran. 1940. 397 pp. $2.50
   A good many people who keep up with Georgette Heyer's prolific vein of amusing light fiction concluded on finishing *An Infamous Army* that she was never happier than in writing of the Napoleonic Wars. She can make a battlefield piled with brightly uniformed corpses positively sprightly, and some of her thick-witted, hard-drinking officers of the line are as natural as anything since Charles Lever. This time, with the aid of considerable research in regimental memoirs, she has traced Wellington's army in the Peninsula from the bloody storming of Badajoz to the final invasion of France, following the fortunes of a British officer who married a fourteen year old Spanish girl after the sack and took her with him through the rough campaigns that followed. The hero and heroine, who have historical originals, are credible and amusing, but the best things in the book are the incidental pictures of British army life in Spain in that hearty, far away day: camp followers on the march behind the army, a regiment fording a swollen torrent, the commanding general's ball in a shell wrecked barn, a brisk skirmish with French hussars. The skirmishes are better than the battles, and Waterloo, again, at the end of the book, though seen this time by non-combatants, is neither Thackeray nor Victor Hugo, but again just good Charles Lever. Miss Heyer is best at surfaces; her people are not seriously enough studied to be anything but cleverly dressed puppets in an emotional crisis, but the costumes are

very good indeed, and the puppets lively and life-like. Perhaps the best way to forget about a real war is to read about a past one presented as a rough, good-humored lark.

## 1941

**81. Frank S. Ambrose, "Costume Piece," *Boston Evening Transcript*, 26 April 1941, section 5, p. 2:**

*Beau Wyndham.* New York: Doubleday, Doran. $2.

In the days when Beau Brummel [sic] set the pace for all Englishmen he had a friend, so the story goes. Sir Richard Wyndham, known as Beau Wyndham, creator of the Wyndham Fall, the most fascinating manner of tying a cravat. Bored and indifferent, Sir Richard, about to make a marriage of convenience, went to his club one night and got very drunk. On the way home adventures began which changed his life and attitude completely. A young girl dressed as a boy swung out of a window and landed in his arms. He forthwith offered his aid in her escapade and within a few days their coach was overturned in a ditch, they became acquainted with a very active thief, were the possessors of stolen jewelry, assisted at an elopement, discovered a murder, and fell in love themselves.

It is a gay tale of romantic costume comedy told in a sprightly and vivacious style for the amusement and entertainment of the readers. There is plenty of action, a lot of interesting people very well portrayed, and an engaging plot that holds your attention all the time. And of course the ending is all that it should be. If it never happened, that is just too bad; it should have.

**82. "Detective Stories. Toffs and Hatters," *The Times Literary Supplement*, 25 October 1941, p. 533:**

*Envious Casca.* By Georgette Heyer. Hodder and Stoughton. 8s.3d.

To give a house-party murder the appearance of originality needs skill. In this *Envious Casca* succeeds even though snow, holly and mistletoe recall other efforts of the same kind. To make a sealed-room mystery fresh enough to excite curiosity is also difficult, and here again the book succeeds because the characters are lively and distinct. But this type of story has a third handicap. Once the reader suspects that the action is to be confined within the same four walls, his imagination becomes restive. He may be interested in the beginning and the end, but the middle will find him impatient unless he is a most painstaking student of methods of investigation. Otherwise the temptation to skip pages may become too strong.

**83. "Battle of Wits,"** *The Times Literary Supplement***, 8 November 1941, p. 553:**

*Faro's Daughter.* By Georgette Heyer. Heinemann. 8s.

Miss Heyer is a most versatile writer whose works come under three very distinct headings. She is the author, first, of excellent detective stories which are justly popular for their amusing sketches of character; secondly, of seriously conceived historical novels; and thirdly, of cheerful romances against a period setting, which make no pretensions towards "importance" in any way. This present story falls into the third class, and is set in the late eighteenth century, a period of whose manners and customs Miss Heyer has made a particular study.

Deborah Grantham finds herself in the unfortunate position of running a faro-table in her aunt's polite and select gambling establishment; unfortunate, because, however polite and select the house may be, it is still undoubtedly a gaming-house, and a girl who helps to run it cannot be considered an eligible bride. The family of a certain wealthy young man becomes alarmed when it appears that she is trying to entangle him into marriage and the young man's trustee takes every possible measure to choke her off, succeeding only in rousing in her a storm of indignation at the idea that she should be thought open to bribes. There follows a most entertaining battle of wits, ending in a way which may be unexpected as far as the plot is concerned, but which will be no surprise to confirmed romance-readers. The story is redeemed from the ruck of such productions by the author's light-hearted wit and her peculiar skill in the delineation of silly women.

**84. Harold Brighouse, "Books of the Day. New Novels,"** *The* *Manchester Guardian*, **14 November 1941, p. 3:**

*Faro's Daughter*. By Georgette Heyer. Heinemann Pp. 274. 8s.

The mettlesome maid Deborah, though no better than a decoy in the gaming-house run by her aunt Lady Bellingham, was pleased to take umbrage when Mr. Ravenscar offered twenty thousand pounds for her relinquishment of all pretensions to the hand of the very young Lord Mablethorpe. The ending of *Faro's Daughter*, a Regency comedy, is early in sight, and the only question is how that ending is to be arrived at. Arrival is expertly made, with some good phrasing in dialogue but with invention hardly fresh enough. The sound construction calls for a compliment.

**85. Kate O'Brien, "Fiction,"** *The Spectator*, **14 November 1941, pp. 474-5:**

*Faro's Daughter*. By Georgette Heyer. (Heinemann. 8s.)

The other books are without value this week. *Faro's Daughter* may appeal to unsophisticated readers, for it is a lively enough effort in "period" stuff. High play, high life, high spirits, and all rather better done than in *The Man in Grey* [by Lady Eleanor Smith]. . . .

**86. John Fairfield, "Violent Deaths,"** *The Spectator*, **5 December 1941, pp. 539-40:**

*Envious Casca*. By Georgette Heyer. (Hodder. 8s.3d.)

. . . . The mansion of Envious Casca takes full marks, being not only

Tudor in period, but also a Manor, and one of the show-places of the neighbourhood. It is, curiously enough, haunted by the ghost of the Empress Elizabeth of Austria, who hangs about giving away the mechanics of the crime throughout the course of the action. The murderer is an agreeably loathsome character, but custom has very considerably staled the variety of his method: the reader is warned that this is a locked-room problem. . . .

**87. "Briefly Noted. Mystery and Crime,"** *The New Yorker*, **6 December 1941, p. 138:**

*Envious Casca*, by Georgette Heyer.

Nathaniel Herriard turns over his home near London to his jovial brother for a Christmas houseparty. The Herriards and their friends, a nasty lot, do their best to incriminate one another when Nathaniel is knifed in the back on Christmas Eve. Sharp, clear, and witty in the British manner. Recommended for readers who like to smile wryly.

**88. Will Cuppy, "Mystery and Adventure,"** *New York Herald Tribune Books*, **7 December 1941, p. 36:**

*Envious Casca*. 311 pp. New York. The Crime Club. $2.

After too long an absence from the criminous scene, Georgette Heyer returns with a killer-diller that picks up the season in grand shape. *Envious Casca* is a major Heyer tome, one of the best of the 1941 output and a must item for every fan in good standing. It's even timely, for the murder at Lexham Manor occurred on Christmas Eve while some of the Herriards were trimming the tree and some of them were sitting around sneering at the holly and mistletoe and making nasty remarks about Santa Claus. "I hate holly!" growls one of the characters on the first page, and we're not saying whether or not he got a dagger in the torso later on, as he so richly deserved. It looks for a time as though the Tudor mansion may be haunted, but maybe it's only the tension, what with guests all

131

hating one another and a certain person plotting slaughter in the midst of the Yuletide doings.

Seems to us that Miss Heyer has rather widened her appeal this time, without detriment to her tendency toward frivoling among the recently deceased. She provides half a dozen or more vintage characters full of the proper Heyer malice, patrician rudeness and nonchalant conversation, taking her fun where she finds it, but she never neglects her puzzle interest for more than a minute. All of which should be velvet for the brainier fans and also for those who sort of forget exactly who Casca was and what he was envious about. As for the personae, there's Uncle Nathaniel Herriard, with the family money; Stephen, a saturnine nephew with a line of pre-war sophistication; Paula, a niece with artistic aspirations; Edgar Mottisford, a business partner with something on his mind, and Willoughby Roydon, author of *Wormwood*, a drama in three acts deriving in part or entirely from Strindberg. At one point Willoughby reads his play aloud in the drawing room, and you wonder why people get bumped off. Sensible and effective detecting by Inspector Hemingway, love in sufficient quantities and all that quiet Heyer fun. Don't go elsewhere for Christmas murder.

**89. "The Criminal Record,"** *The Saturday Review* **24, 13 December 1941, p. 20:**

*Envious Casca.* Georgette Heyer. (Crime Club. $2.)
-*Crime, Place, and Sleuth:* English Christmas party of ravening relatives results in death and a job for detective Hemingway.
-*Summing Up:* Too-ready-to-talk suspects give detective tough but interesting job for sleuth. Good writing, considerable erudition, and workable plot.
-*Verdict:* Good stuff.

**90. "The World of Books. Mysteries,"** *The Springfield Sunday Union and Republican* **(Springfield, Mass.), 21 December 1941, p. 7e:**

*Envious Casca.*

The technic of Georgette Heyer is always intriguing but has never been so disarming as in *Envious Casca* a thriller blending both homicide and humor, as Scotland Yard tries to learn why and how the scrappy Herriard clan produced a murder when they were supposed to be having a Christmas reunion at the family estate. A few outsiders complicate things. There's not one of the clan that does not merit watching, for it is proverbial that the Herriards dislike one another and three of them go to great lengths to say so. Aunt Maud's tiresome hunt for a mislaid book seems at first to be just comic relief. But no indeed . . . .

## 1942

**91. Mort. Post, "Crimes of a Month,"** *New Republic* **106 (26 January 1942), pp. 125-126:**

Some of the bigger shots are back this month: Rex Stout, Georgette Heyer, John Rhode, Ngaio Marsh, John Dickson Carr. . . .

Georgette Heyer, most entertaining of the sophisticated mystery-mongers, is back from her amblings in costume romance with *Envious Casca* (Crime Club) as tart and juicy as a new apple. One of those house-party affairs, but peopled with a fine aggregation of pungent characters in a perpetual squabble. Brisk and amusing, with no nonsense.

**92. Lisle Bell, "New Popular Novels,"** *New York Herald Tribune Books*, **17 May 1942, p. 14:**

*Faro's Daughter.* 274 pp. New York: Doubleday, Doran. $2.

Georgette Heyer continues to delve with profit into the habits and manners of the Regency period when the marks of a gentleman were the quality of his tailoring, his horsemanship, his taste in women and his ability to live exceedingly well without soiling his fingers in trade or toil, and when a young girl's destiny was fulfilled when she acquired one of them as a husband. Her narratives reflect cushioned complacency of the upper classes, with their well stocked cellars and stuffy drawing rooms, their open fireplaces and their closed minds. It was a time when men still wore ruffles but it was no longer fashionable to carry a sword, when those of the old school still powdered their hair, but young blades had their locks cut in what was called the Bedford crop.

*Faro's Daughter* has the stock situations and entanglements —rivalries, flirtations, whispers of scandal, impetuous youth and shocked elders. Dashing young Lord Marblethorpe [sic] has stirred up a family hornets' nest by falling in love with Deborah Grantham, who operates a fashionable gaming place in London. An affair would have been winked at, but he wanted to marry the girl. His uncle tried to buy the young lady off and discovered that—whether or not she was a good match for the nephew—she was more than a match for him.

### 93. "Other New Novels. Near-Ruritania," *The Times Literary Supplement*, 31 October 1942, p. 537:

**Penhallow**. By Georgette Heyer. Heinemann. 9s.6d.

When Miss Heyer turns from the historical romances with which her reputation as a writer has been so far associated and gives us the story of a Cornish family in the year 1935, she still shows herself under the influence of her earlier work. With a few relatively unimportant alterations the drama of the Penhallows could have been played with equal, perhaps even greater, convincingness against the setting of life a hundred years ago, and although most of the characters speak in the modern idiom, such modern effects as motor-cars seem a little like an anachronism. The head of the clan, Adam Penhallow, a hard-drinking, hard-swearing, frankly unmoral man of sixty, takes a delight in keeping his family about him, six sons and a daughter by his first marriage and one son by his second. They are a very mixed lot temperamentally, but all the members of the first family are definitely Penhallows, with horses as their chief preoccupation. In the few months covered by the action various factors combine to bring matters to a crisis that is intensified by the surreptitious murder of old Penhallow by his oppressed, faint-hearted second wife, a crime for which we see that punishment awaits her, but not at the hands of the law. This brief summary does little justice to the development and movement of a plot that is sufficiently ingenious without being improbable; but the true value of the story depends primarily on the characterization and interplay of the many persons involved, all of them admirably portrayed and differentiated and, except for old Penhallow, only just perceptibly romanticized. None of them strongly invites our sympathy. They are all powerfully self-centred, with no interest in matters outside their own personal affairs. But we come to know them very well, and for some of them come to feel if not admiration, at least a certain liking—more especially for Adam's eldest son, who had to suffer so bitterly for his father's immorality. Within the limits she has imposed upon herself, Miss Heyer has built up an impressive drama of family life, though it is not representative of our own times.

## 1943

**94. "Fiction,"** *The Open Shelf* **(Cleveland Public Library), August 1943, p. 16:**

Heyer, Georgette. *Penhallow*.
Charmed with the idea of being mistress of a manor in Cornwall, nineteen-year-old Faith marries Adam Penhallow, a widower with seven children. "A fascinating study of a family that has held on to its feudal traditions and taken on none of the softness of the twentieth century."

**95. Margaret Wallace, "A Cold Cornish Spider," in "Latest Fiction,"** *The New York Times Book Review*, **15 August 1943, p. 12:**

*Penhallow*. 309 pp. New York: Doubleday, Doran. $2.50
To compare another novel to *Rebecca* at this date may seem a good deal like crying wolf. The parallel has been drawn a tedious number of undeserving times already. *Penhallow* really has a quality of sheer

narrative excitement which suggests it almost automatically. If it is less atmospheric than *Rebecca* and depends less upon an illusion dexterously sustained, it is also a sounder book, founded upon a deeper and more mature irony. It does not dissolve afterward as illusions are likely to do. In order to raise her story to its final pitch of interest, Miss Heyer takes her time about setting the scene. The reader may be forgiven for thinking at first that he has come upon another long family chronicle, quite picturesque and Cornish, in which a couple of weakly modern generations are dominated by a blustering and tyrannical old patriarch. Anyone who is discouraged by this impression or by Miss Heyer's rather ponderous and genteel prose will be missing the best psychological murder story of this and several seasons past.

The fact is that what may seem faults at first prove to be essential parts of Miss Heyer's plan. Bedridden Adam Penhallow sits in his manor of Trevellin like a gross and crafty old spider making life systematically miserable for his descendants. It is necessary for us to know them thoroughly in order to understand why any of their number had good reason for wishing him dead—a circumstance which makes a troublesome mystery for the police, though not for the reader.

Before we see the murder committed we are brought to the point of sympathizing with the murderer. Afterward, while the police pursue their investigation, we watch its fascinating consequences so far as the Penhallows themselves are concerned.

**96. "Briefly Noted. Fiction,"** *The New Yorker,* **28 August 1943, p. 66:**

*Penhallow,* by Georgette Heyer.

The psychological difficulties of the Penhallows, an old Cornish family whose members are mad, each in a different way. There is a violent, despotic father, who has been a gay dog in his day, a brood of grown sons (some legitimate, some not), a spineless second wife, a horsey aunt, plenty of privileged old family retainers, and so on. In the course of events, a murder is committed and the guilt is pinned on the wrong man. The story ends with only the reader knowing who really put the veronal in the whiskey decanter. Smooth enough entertainment if you don't expect too much of it.

**97. L. S. M., "Georgette Heyer's _Penhallow_," in _Springfield Union_, 29 August 1943, p. 7e:**

Like Hamlet's players, the novelist Georgette Heyer is adept at ". . . historical, pastoral, tragical historical, tragical comical historical pastoral . . ." and in _Penhallow_ she tries her skill at an elegant combination of _Wuthering Heights_ and _Rogue Herries_, plus a dash of plain mystery.

Old Adam Penhallow, the pivotal figure in the novel, is practically the last of England's feudal lords, giving no indication that he has heard of social revolution and ruling his large rebellious family as if the Magna Carta had never been signed, nor his England about to plunge itself into a second World War. All his family rebelled but all lived in the manor house under his tyranny, enduring his insults, his gross jokes, accepting his illegitimate offspring as servants in the house—and all waiting for Adam Penhallow to die.

An ideal setting has been provided for a murder, and Miss Heyer makes her Penhallow family a perfect group of potential murderers. Eldest Penhallow at Trevellin was Raymond, who ran the great, impoverished estate and fought constantly with his father, old Penhallow goading his son to violence and the young man avidly planning on his father's death, his own inheritance through entail and the opportunity to turn the other sycophant members of the family off the premises.

It is about Raymond and his great pride of race that the tragedy of _Penhallow_ has been centered and Miss Heyer has created the most intricate and melodramatic of situations. There are five other legitimate brothers, all greedily awaiting their father's death, yet fearing and hating the fact that it is Raymond who will inherit, and the half-brother Clay, ineffectual son of Adam's second wife Faith.

Adam's murder is inevitable, but the crux of the story is the macabre way in which the murderer's well-laid plans go awry and gothic horror is piled upon horror. There are no character shadings, no nuances among the unpleasant but nonetheless interesting characters who people the novel. All the Penhallows, all the servants, are pictured in high Victorian colors—there is even a sub-rosa romance between one of the younger Penhallows and a serving maid—and Miss Heyer has manipulated the mechanics of her highly melodramatic plot with considerable skill. Nevertheless *Penhallow* is an earnestly overwritten novel that just misses, by constant repetition of scene and motive, being grimly engrossing.

**98. "The 'Family Mansion' Formula,"** *The Chicago Sun Book Week*, **5 September 1943, p. 3**

*Penhallow*. By Georgette Heyer. Doubleday, Doran. 309 pp. $2.50

There is a curiously successful formula for writing best selling fiction which I have never seen adequately analyzed. In all of these books the action takes place in a big house (*Jalna*, *So Red the Rose*) and the family lives an anachronistic, feudal life.

Despite the presence of dogs, horses and lean fighting men, these books are not written for the infinitesimal proportion of the male population which reads romantic fiction. They are written for women who do not live in big houses, do not have an army of servants, and are not treated with chivalry (and brutally) by feudal males.

One might suppose that the women who read these books identify themselves with the heroine. This is sometimes called the "identification" theory, principal appeal of the Cinderella story in all its ramifications and mutations. But it is quite as likely that the women readers are identifying themselves less with the heroine than with the property. This would satisfy Veblen's theory that possessions become an intimate aura so identified with personality that we fight to the death for mere belongings.

*Penhallow* fits all the specifications. An old tyrant—Adam—rules the fantastic menage from his monstrous bed equipped with doors and drawers full of papers, money and gimcracks. His ineffectual second wife, Faith, his dark "eldest" son Raymond, illegitimate Jimmy, Eugene the self-imposed invalid son, Aubrey the dilletante, Charmain the masculine daughter—in fact, every member of the household has an excellent reason for murdering the old man.

Any pleasant evening in this English country house is filled with lethal argument; money, horses, love affairs and inheritance keep the tribe in a constant uproar.

When Jimmy finds Raymond trying to strangle Adam, the plot thickens. But the actual murder is not committed until the proper dramatic moment further along in the book.

Georgette Heyer, who has previously written several very good detective stories, merely uses murder to hold up her third act. She has written a dour novel of serious intent, better plotted than executed, but continuously entertaining. It should appeal to the thousands of readers who own vicarious estates all over England, Canada and the United States.

**99. Bess Jones, "Literary Pen," *The Saturday Review*, 18 September 1943, p. 24:**

*Penhallow*. New York: Doubleday, Doran. 1943. 309 pp. $2.50

This novel could have been a readable mystery story, or it could have been developed into what it pretends to be—a family story in which the expected conflict of the generations is complicated by the character of the dreadful old patriarch who rules the destinies of the household and by the size of the family itself, the products of two marriages and several unhallowed alliances. As it stands, it is simply so many pages of narrative that contains no suspense, family quarrels that are always the same and get nowhere, and dialogue that regards itself as very racy and bold because it is filled with hells, damns, bitches, bastards, and other terms of the sort.

The novel is laid in the sprawling country house of old Penhallow, a twentieth century survival of feudalistic living who has little love for his children but who perversely keeps them around him by never letting them have enough money to live independently of him.  His pleasures consist chiefly, however, in overeating and overdrinking, and in abusing his timid wife, twenty years his junior and a poor thing at best.  There are moments when the author manages to produce a scene or two that rise above the monotony of the violent language and of the repetitious unpleasantness of the family gathering, but for the most part the novel has little entertainment.

## 1945

**100. "Fiction," *Kirkus Reviews*, 1 December 1945, p. 534:**

Heyer, Georgette. *Friday's Child*. Putnam. $2.50.
A lightsome, brightsome comedy of Regency days, this makes merry with the marriage of Sherry (his hand refused by the Incomparable Isabella), and orphaned, seventeen year old Hero, country raised, naïve, unsophisticated, but virtuous. Sherry, and his fellow bucks, treat her like a younger sister, and she, adopting their language, attitudes and outspokenness, makes a romp of London society.  Her innate good taste and respectable upbringing, together with the loyalty of Sherry's friends, keep her from real trouble.  Sherry, continuing his debonair, wild ways, has trouble when Hero will not curb her pleasant, free ways, so she manages her misadventures, brings Sherry to heel and settles the fate of the Incomparable with true femininity.  Maybe thins out—but the period properties are colorful, and the protagonists likable.

## 1946

**101. "Briefly Noted. Fiction," *The New Yorker*, 16 February 1946, p. 96:**

***Friday's Child***, by Georgette Heyer. (Putnam)

If you have followed the graceless, lumbering pace of current historical novels, this nimble, light-hearted chronicle of high London society in the time of the Regency will seem almost too good to be true. The story (what there is of it) concerns a wealthy nobleman, his three fashionable boon companions, and an artless young wife who isn't onto the ways of the great world. It is the sort of cheerful company in which you might find Bertie Wooster or some of Mrs. Thirkell's decorous county people on an unexpected bender.

**102. Arthur Meeker, Jr., "Gay Regency Novel, British Style. Authentic Flavor Is Skillfully Conveyed,"** *The Chicago Sun Book Week***, 17 February 1946, p. 12:**

***Friday's Child***. By Georgette Heyer. Putnam. 311 pp. $2.75

They order these things better in England. *Friday's Child* is an excellent example of the pastime novel, transatlantic model; there's no doubt that it is an abler job of its kind, at once more tasteful and more workman-like, than anything we're showing over here this season.

No one—least of all, I am sure, the author—could take very seriously this pleasant story of Regency days. It concerns the runaway match of the dashing Lord Sheringham—known to his intimates as "Sherry"—who marries a portionless orphan, Miss Hero Wantage, out of pique because the beautiful Bella Milborne thinks she'd prefer a duke; takes his bride to London, where they share a house (but not a bedroom suite); educates her in the ways of the fashionable world; and, then gradually, without meaning to, falls in love with her.

The fable is pure romantic fluff, and the female characters are rather stereotyped, particularly Hero, the "Friday's Child" of the title, who seems too "loving and giving" to be quite credible. But Georgette Heyer knows the period thoroughly. Strangely enough, too, for a woman novelist, she has a very skillful touch with men. Sherry and his boon companions, Lord Wrotham, Gil Ringwood and the Hon. Ferdy Fakenham, are straight out of Wodehouse—if you can imagine

141

Wodehouse's young men transplanted to the Mayfair of 130 years ago. They are nonetheless amusing for that, and are admirably presented on their own farce-comedy plane.

The body of the prose is cast in a somewhat archly elaborate mold: all fawns are "startled," all shots "Parthian"; and we have numerous other noun-and-adjective combinations, such as "choleric eye," "afflicted parent," "burning desire," "inarticulate bliss" and the like, that have long since lost their freshness for the modern reader, but are well in place here, with their air of deliberate jocosity.

My only real complaint is that the book is a bit too long; however, Miss Heyer manipulates her strings with such deft good humor that somehow I kept on reading without becoming too impatient; and the closing chapters, where the scene shifts to Bath and comic complications pile up amazingly, are among the best. On the whole, here's cheerful and civilized entertainment for just a few too many idle hours.

**103. Rosemary Carr Benét, "London During the Regency," *The Saturday Review*, 23 February 1946, p. 39:**

*Friday's Child.* New York: G. P. Putnam's Sons. 1946. 311 pp. $2.75.

It is a relief to find a gay, light-hearted historical novel for a change, that is amusing to read, instead of the usual solemn, heavy-handed approach. Miss Heyer has thought of a new angle for her book about post-Waterloo London for we see it through the eyes of a Regency Dulcy. Like the poor, Dulcys are always with us and can be found in any age, in any period. This variant of the scatter-brained heroine is Hero Wantage, appropriately nicknamed Kitten, an attractive seventeen-year-old romp who is always getting herself into scrapes. This allows Miss Heyer to give a fresh, lively, sometimes mocking picture of the fashionable life of the time.

Hero, or Kitten, is poor, well connected, and doomed to life as a governess (for which she is ill prepared) or to marry a curate. When dashing Viscount Sheringham, called Sherry, saves her from this gloomy fate she is deeply grateful. Sherry's motives in the affair are mixed. He had been refused by the reigning belle of the moment, Isabella Milborne. Partly out of pique, partly out of avarice since he can get his inheritance when he marries, and only slightly out of chivalry, he elopes with the penniless but loving Hero. He regards the marriage as one of convenience but he soon finds that it is anything but that. When he takes his wife to London he has more than he bargained for on his hands. Kitten is pretty, naive, dotes on her husband, loves parties, loves life, and gets into one scrape after another always from the best and kindest motives. Her husband ends by telling her she is the most troublesome brat alive and trying to banish her to the country. Hero departs, taking, characteristically, an ormolu clock and a canary with her. Sheringham's struggles with the role of protector which fate thrusts upon him furnish a good deal of comedy. The ending, needless to say, is happy. If there are any movie directors in our audience, this would make a good picture since it has both action and humor, and the costumes are notably becoming.

The idea is engaging and is well carried out. The description of London a year or two after Waterloo is excellent. Miss Heyer manages to spoof the fashionable life of the time by presenting its foibles seriously. She does a wonderful picture of the current "Blood, or Tulip of Fashion, or Nonpareil," the sporting Club Member, touchy about his honor and supposedly dashing and reckless, but actually both stuffy and timid and conventional. All the details of dress and fashion are here but they are not dragged in unnecessarily. She tells us, for instance, exactly what a gentleman had to eat for dinner—"buttered crab, a dish of mutton fry with parsnips, a pheasant pie with several side dishes including some potted pie and a cold boiled knuckle of veal and a pig's face, washed down with some excellent chambertin"; but the only reason she mentions it is because the gentleman said he had a cold and that therefore he couldn't eat a thing.

Though light, this is good history and an amusing tale. The author has read Jane Austen to advantage, but so she should. She manages to keep the light tone and still paint a clear picture of the fashions and foibles of the time which is something of an achievement. The period itself is rewarding and there is just the right mocking slant here thanks to the artless Kitten.

**104. "Fiction,"** *The Open Shelf* **(Cleveland Public Library), March 1946, p. 8:**

Heyer, Georgette. *Friday's Child.*
Regency London is the setting for this rollicking, historical love story of Hero Wantage and Viscount Sheringham. A wholly delightful novel.

1947

**105. "Fiction,"** *Kirkus Reviews,* **1 January 1947, p. 11:**

Heyer, Georgette. *The Reluctant Widow.* Putnam. $2.75.
An assured touch for whimsical turns and a lively, amusing handling of historical romance for the story of Elinor, who arrives at the wrong house for a job. She is unavoidably married to a shocking fellow on his deathbed, and is led into involuntary participation in the ambition of the dead man's uncle, Lord Carlyon, to penetrate the treasonable activities of Bonaparte agents. All of a pucker, Elinor finds her enforced widowhood dominated by Carlyon, whose monstrous conceit and doubtful behaviour keep her enraged. She also finds that strange visitors to her new estate are murdered, that she is herself in danger, that Carlyon's brothers and sisters combine to placate her. She is at last persuaded that the day is saved for England and that Carlyon's conceits are chivalrous and her widowhood will end in a real wedding. Mistakes done to a turn, in Georgette Heyer's skilled manner.

**106. Mildred Peterson McKay (Librarian, New Hampshire State Library, Concord), in "New Books Appraised. Fiction,"** *Library Journal* **72, 15 February 1947, p. 319:**

144

Heyer, Georgette. *The Reluctant Widow*. Putnam. $2.75

Characters—a lord, an impoverished gentlewoman, a drunken cousin, an Oxford student sent down for his pranks and typical early 19th century persons. Place—English countryside, one well kept estate and another dusty and in disrepair but with a secret staircase. Plot—a missing paper from Wellington's files that Napoleon's agents desire. What more could a reader of a period piece require? A good romantic novel. Recommended.

**107. Ricker Van Metre, Jr., "Cinderella in English Castle. Preposterous Tale Is Pleasant Reading,"** *Chicago Sun Book Week*, **2 March 1947, p. 11:**

*The Reluctant Widow*. By Georgette Heyer. Putnam. 279 pp. $2.75.

This pleasant, preposterous period piece on Regency England may pass some otherwise tedious hours for the habitues of lending libraries with nothing better to do. It is not, strictly, a historical novel, though the Prince Regent, Bonaparte and Beau Brummel [sic] are occasionally mentioned. It is a novel of pure escape, based on the perennially "successful" Cinderella Theme.

Via a chain of rapid and highly unbelievable events, Elinor Rochdale, an impoverished girl of good but unlucky family, finds herself in the course of one hectic night, married, widowed and installed as mistress of an extensive estate . . . instead of as governess to a stuffy county family as she had intended.

Prime mover in this extraordinary turn of fortune is Lord Carlyon, handsome, strong-willed and sagacious. He desperately wanted a wife for his wastrel cousin Eustace, because, for reasons of his own, he did not want to inherit his cousin's estate. Elinor appears quite by chance; Carlyon seizes his opportunity and forcefully brings about her marriage to Eustace on his deathbed.

From this point, the plot boils merrily on to the obvious conclusion, complicated by night intruders seeking a lost document involving Wellington's plans to defeat the French, Bonaparte's agents, and a few other distractions for good measure.

All this strains the reader's credulity time and again. But if you want to read to avoid a chilling trip to the neighborhood movie—maybe this is your meat.

**108. "Regency Rakes,"** *The New York Times Book Review*, **16 March 1947, p. 39:**

*The Reluctant Widow.* 279 pp. New York: G. P. Putnam's Sons. $2.75.

Another Heyer novel with a Regency background, this lighter-than-usual romantic period piece is (as usual) laced with ribands of mystery and intrigue. You must enter the spirit of the tale whole-heartedly to feel the proper pangs for Elinor Rochdale, the virtuous little governess. By stepping into the wrong post-chaise and arriving at Lord Carlyon's house instead of the house of her new employer, Elinor finds herself reluctantly talked into marrying Eustace Cheviot, the dying cousin of Lord Carlyon. That Carlyon especially wants a widow for his expiring cousin so that he, Carlyon, *won't* inherit the Cheviot estate adds to the confusion: Elinor, of course, keeps her wits about her and wins Lord Carlyon's love to boot.

**1948**

**109. "Fiction,"** *Kirkus Reviews*, **1 January 1948, p. 6:**

Heyer, Georgette. *The Foundling.* Putnam. $3.

What happens when a many-titled Duke decides to play hookey from his suffocating dignity is the basis of this slight tale of Regency days. Gilly, to protect a young cousin, sets out to square accounts with a blackmailer, ends up with a kidnapping, a brainless, beautiful girl, and discovers that he is more than capable of taking care of himself in tight corners, and that his family's choice of a bride is absolutely perfect, even to helping him out of his scrapes. Done to a turn, in full period decor, this will appeal to those who like the lighter of this writer's work.

**110. Katherine Tappert Willis (Sp. Asst., Ferguson Lib., Stamford, Connecticut), in "New Books Appraised. Fiction,"** *Library Journal* **73, 1 February 1948, p. 197:**

Heyer, Georgette. *The Foundling.* Putnam. $3.

From Hertfordshire to London and Bath the quixotic Duke of Sales [sic], his family and friends and the beautiful Belinda, the foundling, move about in a world of early 19th century adventure that makes a very good tale. The technique of this story is much the same as that of the earlier novels of GH, if not the same period. Slow going at first, the novel moves along to a gay close and one is delighted that virtue is rewarded. For the general reader and general purchase.

**111. Richard Match, "Metamorphosis of the Duke of Sale,"** *The New York Times Book Review,* **21 March 1948, p. 20:**

*The Foundling.* 380 pp. New York: G. P. Putnam's Sons. $3.

"There's nothing like a glass of blood and thunder to put a cove in high gig," remarks one of Georgette Heyer's amiable Regency rascals in tribute to vinous spirits. The fellow was right, of course, but he neglected to add that, alcohol lacking, a Georgette Heyer novel will serve as a pretty good substitute for the cup that cheers. Miss Heyer writes cheerful and highly unorthodox historical novels, set in Regency England, in which people never lose their lives, their virtue, or even their tempers. The author of *The Foundling* is as much at home in Almack's Assembly Rooms and the Grand Pump Room at Bath as you would be in the Automat. But she likes her people and their century too much to take them seriously.

The Most Noble Adolphus Gillespie Vernon Ware, seventh Duke of Sale and Marquis of Ormesby, Earl of Sale, Baron Ware of Thame, Baron Ware of Stoven and Baron Ware of Rufford, was a timid young man known to his friends as Gilly. Orphaned at birth, bullied by his well-meaning guardian, hemmed in by the affectionate ministrations of a small army of family retainers, His Grace of Sale had reached the age of

24 without ever making a decision for himself. In all his life the titular master of Sale House, duke, marquis, earl, thrice baron, had never so much as selected a cravat for his own wardrobe.

Privately His Grace sometimes wondered what it would be like to have been born some quite unimportant person. "Not of too lowly a degree, of course," but just the same, not the seventh Duke of Sale. Could he get along without his valet, butler, steward, chaplain, footmen, grooms, gamekeepers, bailiffs, chief confectioner? One morning, in a moment of unaccustomed resolution, His Grace made up his mind. "I shall try to discover," he decided, "whether I am a man, or only a duke."

So saying, he was off to Hertfordshire, alone and incognito, to forestall a breach-of-promise suit threatening the House of Sale, to rescue a beautiful female foundling named Belinda, to deal with a plausible rogue named Swithin Liversedge and generally to acquit himself in a manner which would have made the first six Dukes of Sale proud of him. Georgette Heyer is writing about England after Waterloo; but don't expect anyone in her book to wrestle with postwar problems any more than you would expect Billy Rose to wrestle with Primo Carnera. Miss Heyer's talent is elegant farce, and she knows her craft well. It is, without apologies, a lighter-than-air craft.

**112. L. S. M., in "Recent Fiction," *The Springfield Sunday Republican*, 4 April 1948, p. 10B:**

*The Foundling.*
Wordy, but raffish and chattily entertaining, *The Foundling* by Georgette Heyer (Putmans [sic]; $3) narrates the adventures of a regency Duke who undertakes to rescue his cousin from the dewy-eyed innocent Belinda, the "foundling" of the title, who is ready to run away with any man who will give her a purple silk dress, but is encumbered by a guardian not averse to a spot of blackmail. It's all a great romp and the reader is far more entertained than he suspects at first glance when he starts to read this tongue-in-cheek, simonpure parody of regency rakes and a wronged, or nearly wronged, maiden.

**113.** "Period Pieces," *The Times Literary Supplement*, **24 April 1948, p. 229:**

Georgette Heyer: *The Foundling*. Heinemann. 10s.6d.

Both these books [the other is C. M. Franzero's *The Memoirs of Pontius Pilate*] may be described as historical novels, since they are fiction, and their scene is set in the past. But they are very sharply contrasted specimens of the art; and oddly enough a far greater success attends the frivolous production of Miss Heyer than Mr. Franzero's handling of an altogether more serious and important subject.

It cannot be denied that in *The Foundling*, as in her other novels of the same type, Miss Heyer writes to a romantic formula, and that her fantastic characters move in a perfectly artificial world, conveniently labelled "Regency." Nor do they bear any message or moral, but are all the more entertaining on that account, as they move on their gay, smooth and absurd career. Miss Heyer has given careful study to certain aspects of her favourite period, and she is sustained by a sense of style which is too often completely lacking in the authors of similar pleasant romances. There are frequent echoes of Jane Austen, for instance, in such a sentence as: "*She* will always be silly, but he appears to have considerable constancy, and we must hope that *he* will always be fond." The story of *The Foundling* is based on the familiar poor-little-rich-boy theme, the boy being a young duke who, too closely hemmed in by elderly well-wishers, breaks out into independence and succeeds in plunging into adventures and saddling himself with a beautiful young woman of quite transcendent silliness. And it is in the description of silliness that Miss Heyer excels.

**114.** *Wisconsin Library Bulletin* **44, May 1948, p. 105:**

Heyer, Georgette. *The Foundling*. 1948. 380 p. Putnam, $3.

Another of Georgette Heyer's amusing romances of the days of stagecoaches and footpads, noble heroes and lovely ladies in Regency England, with plenty of adventure. The charm of her tales lies as much in the tongue-in-cheek way she tells them as in the characters and the action.

**115. Margaret C. Scoggin, "Outlook Tower,"** *The Horn Book Magazine* **24, July 1948, pp. 291-92:**

Georgette Heyer. *The Foundling*. Putnam. $3.00

Twenty-four-year-old Duke of Sale, tired of coddling by relatives, servants, and lawyers, welcomes a chance to rush off unknown into adventure. The results are amazing. He outwits blackmailer and thieves, rescues runaway schoolboy Tom from various escapades, returns beautiful but foolish Belinda (the foundling) safely to her young man, wins the love of the girl he is to marry, and proves to everyone's satisfaction that he can take care of himself at all times. Light as fluff and sheer entertainment with delightful overtones of Jeffery Farnol and Charles Dickens.

### 1949

**116. "Fiction,"** *Kirkus Reviews*, **1 April 1949, p. 184:**

Heyer, Georgette. *Arabella*. Putnam. $3.00.

Another entertaining tale of Regency times, this deals with a beau's stratagem in deft manner. A country bred parson's daughter, Arabella is sent to her godmother in London, by her more worldly mother, in hopes of a good marriage, and en route accidentally meets the catch of the fashionable world, Beaumaris. But Arabella's highhanded treatment of the Nonpareil decides him it would be a hum to make her the most sought after female in London—and he proceeds to do so. Arabella saddles him with a chimney sweep she has protected, a cur she saves, and her younger brother's troubles after his disastrous stay in town, asks him to marry her so she can help the boy. Beaumaris provides a happy ending when he reveals he has visited her family and knows all her secrets. Well costumed period piece.

**117. Jean L. Ross (Head, Reference Dept., New Rochelle, NY, Public Library), in "New Books Appraised," *Library Journal* 74, 1 May 1949, p. 735:**

Heyer, Georgette. *Arabella*. Putnam. $3.

A rollicking Regency romance which will be a joy to Heyer addicts. Arabella, beautiful daughter of a country vicar, and the eldest of eight, is introduced to London society by her godmother, with the object of securing a wealthy husband. In a fit of pique she intimates that she is an heiress. Results are most entertaining. Not as interesting as some of its predecessors, notably *The Reluctant Widow* which it resembles, it is nevertheless a most welcome addition to the light fiction shelf. Recommended for public libraries.

**118. "Briefly Noted. Fiction," *The New Yorker*, 28 May 1949, p. 96:**

*Arabella*, by Georgette Heyer. (Putnam)

Miss Heyer seems to have hit upon a method of writing period novels that is much more successful than most, although limited in its possibilities of application. With pleasant directness, she adopts the most graceful literary mode of the period she has chosen to write about. The era she has selected in this case is that of Jane Austen, and her genteel Regency settings and people are good enough to fool any but the most puristic Janeite. The plot deals with a poor country vicar's daughter who snags a renowned London dandy, an event that is annotated with sufficient Georgian embellishment and wit to provide an exemplary piece of escapist literature.

**119. John Hay, *The Commonweal*, 17 June 1949, p. 250:**

*Arabella*. Georgette Heyer. Putnam. $2.

This is the story of the fair and proud Arabella, daughter of a country vicar, who leaves her home for a season at her grandmother's fashionable house in London.  In between going to a dazzling series of parties and balls, and listening to "anecdotes of ton" (not to be translated as stories of the town), she is much occupied with a Mr. Beaumaris, London's top swell, without whose exquisite attentions, as a matter of fact, her social success would be impossible.

Here is how the "nonpareil," as he is known to the London world, inspires Arabella upon their first meeting: "A very good form, too, she noted with approval.  No need of buckram wadding, such as that Knaresborough tailor had inserted into Bertram's new coat, to fill out those shoulders!  And how envious Bertram would have been of Mr. Beaumaris's fine legs, sheathed in tight pantaloons, with gleaming Hessian boots pulled over them.  Mr. Beaumaris's shirt points were not as high as Bertram's, but his necktie commanded the respect of one who had more than once watched her brother's struggles with a far less complicated arrangement.  Arabella was not perfectly sure that she admired his style of hairdressing—he affected a Stanhope crop—but she did think him a remarkably handsome man, as he stood there, laughter dying on his lips and out of his gray eyes."

Of course their human qualities bring these two proud people together in the end.  The struggle was never very great in any case, which may provide one of the explanations if the book does not sell as well in America as in England.  I cannot see *Arabella* advertised as an unbridled romance, or a novel of passionate nights, or as the story of a vicar's daughter who has all England at her feet.  The thing is contrived as light entertainment (let's have no comparisons with Jane Austen, an artist, and faithful to her own world), and hasn't quite enough gusto to put it on the best seller list.  But, as a neighbor of mine observed this morning, "You pays your money and you takes your choice."

### 120.  *The Open Shelf* (Cleveland Public Library), July 1949, p. 16:

Heyer, Georgette.  *Arabella*.

Arabella was just as unconventional as she was lovely—and Robert

Beaumaris, the Nonpareil, found life in Regency England quite unpredictable after he met her.

### 121. Catherine Meredith Brown, in "Fiction," *The Saturday Review*, 2 July 1949, p. 38:

*Arabella*, by Georgette Heyer. Putnam's. $3.

"R" is for Regency. Miss Heyer takes it away from there. The trappings are complete. Costumes emerge entire and detailed, manners of the period ooze on every page, and best of all there's a plethora of proper period phrases. All those jaunty words that wing us back in time are here to enjoy. The going is good, the living is easy, and there's luck to be found in London. Love, too, we can be sure of that.

The plot is all it should be. An eldest daughter of a modest county vicar comes to town for the season. Gambling her all on a wardrobe, backed by her titled godmother, her aim is to marry well. That she manifestly succceeds by catching the "nonpareil" of society may come as no surprise, but it gives pleasure. The tale weaves in and out of assemblies, at homes, drives, gaming tables, snubs, gossip, and talk, managing to amuse without either wit or real style. Agreeable and soothing stuff.

### 122. J. F. S., in "Recent Fiction," *The Springfield Sunday Republican* (Springfield, Mass.), 17 July 1949, p. 7B

*Arabella*.

A prolific reader browsing about a library picked up one of Georgette Heyer's books immediately became an ardent fan. Her newest, *Arabella* (Putnam's; $3), is definitely a fit companion for *Friday's Child, The Reluctant Widow, The Foundling* and *Faro's Daughter*. It relates the story of Arabella, oldest and most beautiful of the daughters of a poor Yorkshire clergyman, who goes to London to seek her matrimonial fortunes. The borrowed coach breaks down near the shooting box of rich and handsome Mr. Beaumaris, whose nod can make or break the social status of any young lady.

Arabella makes capital of the meeting and Beaumaris, who starts by making a game of presenting her to society, is soon so ensnared by her unpredictable actions, her malapropisms and her charmingly captivating self, that he is finally a very willing victim of the artful miss. Diverting, brimming over with entertaining characters, here is Georgette Heyer at her sprightly best.

### 123. Robert Kee, "Fiction," *The Spectator*, 22 July 1949, p. 122:

*Arabella*. By Georgette Heyer. Heinemann. 10s.6d.

Georgette Heyer, of course, we know too. She is a sort of Raymond Chandler at the other end of the scale. Her Regency story of the beautiful country rector's daughter who goes to London and takes the town and Mr. Beaumaris by storm is also the mixture as before—phaetons, flounces, faro and a happy ending in nice proportion. There seems little point in reviewing such a book. Those who have read Miss Heyer's other books will find *Arabella* delightful. Those who haven't won't dream of reading this one, for if it was the sort of thing they liked they would have discovered Miss Heyer long ago.

### 124. "Fiction. Historical Portraits," *The Times Literary Supplement*, 22 July 1949, p. 469:

Georgette Heyer: *Arabella*. Heinemann. 10s.6d.

Like her other works, Miss Heyer's *Arabella* is not so much a historical novel as a "period" novel, whose characters have no concern whatever with social trends or great events, but who merely skip lightly on the surface of the Regency scene. This they do, however, with a good deal of grace and absurdity, and, although this tale of a debutante from the country who is involved in great difficulties by giving herself out to be an heiress is not equal to Miss Heyer's best, it is adequately entertaining and gay.

## 1950

**125. "Fiction,"** *Kirkus Reviews,* **15 August 1950, p. 482:**

Heyer, Georgette. *The Grand Sophy.* Putnam. $3.

Another of the author's amusing fripperies, this is concerned with Sophy, whose continental upbringing under a father whose diplomatic career gave her more licence than any other English miss and whose peculiar talents are put to a wide use when she visits her aunt, Lady Ombersley. For Charles is running the household with far too strict a hand, and is engaged to far too straight-laced Miss Wraxton; his sister is in love with an impossible poet and cool to the man of her family's choice; Hubert is entangled with moneylenders; and Sophy—with unswerving determination—decides to put everything right. This entails her driving Charles' cherished horses, buying her own stables, giving an enormous ball, putting a moneylender in his place, and stage-managing the break-up of Charles' engagement, the proper course of his sister's—and a successfully caught husband for herself. Amidst the fustian of the period Sophy's naturalness contrasts with the simpers and high flights, and sad puckers and sad tangles are routed in a lighthearted manner. Effervescent.

**126.** *The Open Shelf* **(Cleveland Public Library), October 1950, p. 2:**

Heyer, Georgette. *The Grand Sophy.*

Lively, impulsive, wealthy Sophy's unconventional up-bringing on the Continent had not prepared her for the restrictions of society in Regency London or in the family of her aunt, Lady Ombersley.

**127. "Fiction,"** *The New Yorker,* **7 October 1950, p. 133:**

*The Grand Sophy*, by Georgette Heyer. (Putnam).

A readable, if somewhat overstuffed, novel of eighteenth-century London. The people in the plot are all of the upper class, and most of them have titles and money, and sense enough to make way readily for Miss Heyer's Sophy, who is almost six feet tall and possessed of the rowdy and rebellious charm that twentieth-century readers like to see in a historical heroine.

## 128. Kelsey Guilfoil, "Entertaining 18th Century English Life," *Chicago Sunday Tribune*, 22 October 1950, pt. 4, p. 4:

*The Grand Sophy*, by Georgette Heyer. Putnam, $3.

Once again Georgette Heyer has demonstrated her amazing ability to make English life in the late 18th century as real as today's news, flavoring it well with the spirit of that earlier day, and making of the whole a piece of delectable entertainment. If this is not the highest art, it is certainly a relief for the reader, jaded with novels that try to deal significantly with sordid elements of life in our times, whether their approach be sound or sensational.

Miss Heyer can always be depended on to produce as a principal character a young woman who combines a great deal of charm with strength of personality, and the grand Sophy of this novel is such another. To be honest about it, Miss Heyer is in some danger of becoming a formula writer, and there are aspects of Sophy's character and actions, as well as situations, in this book to remind the reader that Miss Heyer has used much the same material before.

But what of that? I'm sure that many people will come to a first reading of Miss Heyer's work with this story, and those who have read her other novels won't mind another serving of the same palatable fare. And the author makes of Sophy so vivid and forthright a person that she has individuality enough and to spare.

Sophia Stanton-Lacy, the grand Sophy, only child of Sir Horace

156

Stanton-Lacy, comes to live with her aunt, Lady Ombersley, while her widowed father journeys to Brazil. Sir Horace has reared this young lady himself, including in her training such accomplishments as riding and shooting like a man, and in general has taught her to conduct herself with a degree of propriety but not the feminine dependence and decorum expected of young ladies of her time.

In her aunt's family Sophy finds a household torn by financial difficulties, a wastrel husband, an elder son who has assumed control of the family purse, and a young son and daughter with problems of their own.

In this bedeviled family group Sophy is like a fresh breeze blowing out the smoke and cobwebs. She just takes hold and starts managing everything for everybody. They like it, too; altho her cousin Charles, holding the purse of the family, feels that she is encroaching on his domain. But Sophy's highhandedness and goodness of heart prevail, and the family's destinies are all comfortably rerouted by the end of this gorgeous tale.

There is more to this than superb entertainment, for Miss Heyer's art is a facile and limber one. It is no small feat to make Regency London come to life, and to make its characters speak and act as did the people of that time and place, without too much quaintness or strangeness of manner. But what am I saying? It's a highly enjoyable story; that's enough.

**129. S. M. Neal, "*The Grand Sophy*, Law Unto Herself," *The Springfield Sunday Republican* (Springfield, Mass.), 22 October 1950, p. 4D:**

Enthusiastic readers of *Friday's Child* and *Arabella*, both by Georgette Heyer, will find *The Grand Sophy*, her current novel, rewarding. Historical research makes this author pre-eminent as a period writer and the atmosphere she reproduces is the last word in its field.

"The Grand Sophy" is financier, horsewoman and social leader on the continent and in her home surroundings in London. She is a willful, albeit sensible and expert girl, upsetting the fundamentals of a stuffy household, where the will of one son is law for everybody, except Sophy. This son has the family's money but Sophy proceeds to defy him and scandalize London and the family. It is a book full of fun and romance.

That the grand Sophy is a law unto herself is true, but everyone benefits by the many social reversals due to her clever manipulations. Old Heyer fans will enjoy this book and new ones wonder how they missed Miss Heyer before.

**130. *Wisconsin Library Bulletin* 46, November 1950, p. 18:**

Heyer, Georgette, *The Grand Sophy*. 1950. 307 p. Putnam, $3.

Kirkus calls it "another of the author's amusing fripperies". Laid chiefly in London during the Regency period just at the close of the Napoleonic wars, this is certainly up to the standard, with a heroine as charming as she is saucy.

**131. Elswyth Thane, in "Fiction," *Saturday Review*, 16 December 1950, pp. 15, 37:**

*The Grand Sophy*, by Georgette Heyer. Putnam's. $3.

Sophy is a delectable heroine. She was brought up like a boy by her widowed father, in the midst of Wellington's Peninsular Army, where she was taught to ride, drive a spirited team, and shoot a pistol. She was at Brussels during Waterloo. And she arrives like a gay landslide into the conventional London household of her Aunt Lizzie, where everything is at sixes and sevens and everyone is in love with or engaged to the wrong person. Sophy begins at once to put everything to rights. She is not one to mind a good rousing scene and takes particular joy in baiting her domineering Cousin Charles, who, of course, is destined to be humanized by the treatment. She "borrows" his precious horses and drives them through London traffic and in the Park as well as he can. She purchases her own perch-phaeton and pair and threatens to drive four-in-hand, which no female should contemplate at all. In the end she nearly precipitates pistol duels and fisticuffs between sober men who hitherto had been the best of friends. And there are quite heavenly passages between her and the humorless, interfering heiress who means to marry Charles. The plot, as such, is not the important part of Miss Heyer's books. What recommends them most in this dreary world is the sheer fun of them.

The Regency period is peculiarly Miss Heyer's own, and *The Grand Sophy* is one of her very best. No one is more adept at combining the amusing idiom of the time with an undated wit to make dialogue that crackles with life. No one creates characters so entirely without anachronisms yet so convincingly flesh and blood. There is nothing of the egad-forsooth style in her books, but the very essence of the swaggering, coaching, gaming set is on every page. If there is any justice in the writing world, which is sometimes questionable, Miss Heyer's public will continue to increase substantially.

## 1952

**132. "Fiction,"** *Kirkus Reviews* **20, 1 February 1952, p. 86:**

Heyer, Georgette. *The Quiet Gentleman*. Putnam. $3.50.

There's less bounce in this newest Heyer and more of a touch of Thirkellian social scenes but the story of Gervase Frant, Lord St. Erth, and his assumption of his role of master of Stanyon, has its moments of gay character conflict. For Gervase is a complete hand at taking in people by his mild compliance and his step-mother, the Dowager, finds her powerful monologues thwarted, Martin, her indulged halfling son, is put in his place and the two ladies in his life, Drusilla and Marianne, cannot be sure of his affections. Attempts on Gervase' [sic] life, Martin's jealousy and dislike, Drusilla's rational unfemininity add to the damned hum, and, no bamming, Gervase turns tables prettily. With his life saved and the would be murderer packed off, it is the gently assertive Drusilla for whom the wedding bells will ring. Genteel melodrama, completely in period, for those with an acquired taste.

**133. Henry Cavendish, "Authentic Atmosphere in Delightful English Tale,"** *Chicago Sunday Tribune,* **9 March 1952, pt. 4, p. 5:**

*The Quiet Gentleman,* by Georgette Heyer.  Putnam, $3.50

William Lyon Phelps once reported that after reading some 200 pages of one of Thomas Hardy's novels he arrived at a place where "it appeared that the heroine and the two heroes were in a most unpleasant predicament; I myself saw no way out, but I had read so many novels where unpromising situations were neatly changed that I read on in a fool's paradise, thinking the author would exert his magic in the right way."

Devoted followers of Georgette Heyer's delightfully fabricated prose will proceed all the way through 289 of the 315 pages in *The Quiet Gentleman* before arriving at an impasse similar to that encountered by Prof. Phelps in *A Pair of Blue Eyes.*

The exasperated response produced by the contemporary English author's otherwise absorbingly interesting portrayal of English country life in the early 19th century arises from the fact that she builds up an air tight pattern of circumstantial evidence pointing to one of the characters as villain.  In the final pages, she upsets all this, and on nothing more substantial than a train of presumptive conclusions.

*The Quiet Gentleman,* it should be noted, is a comedy of characters developed around a mystery plot.  The seventh earl of St. Erth, veteran of the campaigns against Napoleon, returns to claim his patrimony of Stanyon castle.  His underlying ruggedness is illusively covered over with a patina of London dandyism resulting from his handsome appearance, his stylish clothes, his chivalrous manners.  Around him is grouped a lifelike cast of characters, each sharply delineated.

Somewhere in the galaxy is the murderous individual who—so the reader is led to believe—has attempted on no fewer than four occasions to bring about the violent death of the heir to the family fortunes.  The identity of this individual is projected in some 10 of the last 25 pages, but the disclosure appears rather as a plant than as any unfolding of supporting evidence hitherto suppressed or unnoticed by the reader. As a result, *The Quiet Gentleman* comes through the greater part of the book as fascinating reading.

**134. Harvey Curtis Webster, in "Fiction," *Saturday Review* 35, 22 March 1952, pp. 19, 44:**

*The Quiet Gentleman.* By Georgette Heyer. Putnam's $3.50

When Gervase St. Erth returns from the Napoleonic wars to assume his earldom, his ferocious looking half-brother exclaims, "The fellow's nothing but a curst dandy!" Nearly everyone in the huge Gothic castle, complete with drafty halls and secret passages, has reason to resent his return alive. The half-brother hoped to inherit, his formidably unpleasant mother wants him to, while even the pleasant-seeming cousin, Theo, knows he would inherit if the other three were dead. But the quiet, soft-spoken dandy quickly reveals himself as a combination of the best of Beau Brummell and Hercule Poirot. Surviving countless attempts on his life and winning all but one heart by his skill at everything from dueling to conversation, he eventually uncovers his would-be murderer and marries the girl one does not expect him to.

Historical novel addicts, particularly those who read *Arabella* and *The Grand Sophy*, and those who love a mystery may find Miss Heyer's blending of the two forms as good as a sedative. There are plenty of not-to-be-taken-too-seriously shivers, period descriptions of clothing, hunting, castles, and love of the most unimpugnable kind (sex stops with hand kissing and men only look at hands and faces). Some of its readers may doubt, however, that it quite gives the "fine combination of the best of both Dickens and Jane Austen" one reviewer found in *Arabella*. I find myself unable to do more than praise it with faint damns.

**135. Margaret C. Scoggin, "Outlook Tower," *Horn Book* 28, June 1952, p. 187:**

Georgette Heyer. *The Quiet Gentleman*. Putnam $3.50

Mystery and romance tricked out in early 19th century costume and language as a young English nobleman returns to claim his ancestral castle and finds himself the object of several murder attempts. Suspicion falls upon his younger half-brother, but there are other odd characters among his relatives who keep the reader guessing. A mannered piece with enough humor and light romance to please older girls.

**136. Mary Dodge Read, "Young People. Adult Books for Readers from Fourteen to Eighteen Years of Age,"** *Library Journal*, **July 1952, pp. 1215-16:**

Heyer, Georgette. *The Quiet Gentleman*. Putnam. 315 pp. Cloth. $3.50

An earl returns to his home to find himself the object of several murder attempts. Naturally he tries to solve the mystery. The action takes place in the early nineteenth century and is told in a slow and leisurely manner. Older teenagers will like this.

**1953**

**137. "Fiction,"** *Kirkus Reviews*, **15 February 1953, p. 132:**

Heyer, Georgette. *Cotillion*. Putnam. $3.50

Another in the Regency panels repeats the theme of country mouse (Catherine Charing) who comes to London, cuts a swathe in the Polite World and lands in the arms of the man of her choice. Kitty is heir to a fortune IF she marries one of Mr. Penicuik's great-nephews: she turns down the offers as they are made and offers herself to fashion-plate Freddy for a month in London on the basis of an engagement which will be repudiated at the end of that time. She involves herself in the affairs of Dolphinton who is attempting to escape his Mama with one who is not of the *bon ton*: she champions the romance of Olivia and a gambler who is posing as a gentleman: she wakes up to the fact that her old love, Jack, is a cad and worthy only of being trampled on:—and in all this pulls unwilling Freddy in her wake. Freddy is the one who ties up the loose ends of her plotting, sets her straight on clothes and manners, and wins her heart for safe keeping. A diverting hum for those with a feeling (or a failing) for Heyer's costume pieces.

**138. *The Times Literary Supplement*, 20 February 1953, p. 117:**

Georgette Heyer: *Cotillion*. Heinemann. 12s.6d.

In Miss Heyer's new Regency novel she once more dresses the kind of story dear to all daydreamers with some able character studies and an admirable knowledge of her period. The heroine is not an intellectual girl, but she is never slow at repartee, and her manoeuvres in face of her guardian's decision that she shall marry one of his nephews or lose her heritage are entertaining enough. Readers will find in *Cotillion* an evening or two of pleasurable escape as they drive in imagination with Westruther, that splendid "Corinthian," in his curricle to Richmond, or accompany Kitty in the scandalous excitement of attending a public ball, or watch Madame Fanchon, "one of London's most renowned modistes," as she brings out her display of exotic gowns, "figured, embroidered, flounced and braided."

**139. Henry Cavendish, "All Skip and Dance—a Sort of Literary Bubble Bath. Georgette Heyer's Novel—With 18th Century Slang," *Chicago Sunday Tribune*, 12 April 1953, pt. 4, p. 4:**

*Cotillion* by Georgette Heyer. Putnam. 320 pp. $3.50.

A cotillion, as defined by Milord Webster in the *New International Dictionary*, is "an elaborate and complicated dance, executed under the leadership of one couple, consisting of dances of several kinds, and marked by the giving of favors and frequent changing of partners." All of which provides a very apt description of Georgette Heyer's latest excursion into the lighter side of early 19th century English manners.

The book is, if not exactly an elaborate and complicated dance as indicated by the title, at least a tale in which the characters skip and dance rather than plod about. The plot development, moreover, is executed under the leadership of one couple (Freddy Standen, heir to Lord Legerwood, and the intriguing Kitty Charing, brunette ward of miserly old Uncle Matthew Penicuik). Likewise, *Cotillion* consists, if not of dance routines of several kinds, then of vividly contrasting narrative patterns. And it is certainly marked by the giving of favors and the frequent changing of partners—dashed if it ain't!

Possibly the most entertaining thing about the book is the subtle way it steams along under a full head of the colloquial slang of the period, the generally understandable distortions of the king's English cloaking a rapidly developing network of plot complication. Characters put themselves in puckers, they get in queer stirrups, and they go on mops. They make cakes of each other, shell out the blunt, and become nicely bubbled without resort to alcohol.

Beneath this pattern of frothiness, Kitty, half French and volatile, rejects the half witted, stiff necked, and rascally suitors that Old Moneybags dangles before her at his country estate of Arnside. With a flashing show of ingenuity, she engineers her removal to London, and quickly loses the pastel shades of her country upbringing, meets the tip nosed matchmakers of tony society, and goes refreshingly in for a bit of matchmaking on her own.

The book, in sum total, stacks up as something of a literary bubble bath, wherein readers so inclined may take a delightful and frothy dip among the gayer aspects of the author's favorite and well worked Regency period. The intellectual content is pitched at about the same level as a remark that Freddy makes about one of the balmier members of the cast: "Of course he ain't a lunatic! Got no brains, that's all." But don't be deceived about frolicsome Freddy; he's the lad who turns all the tables.

**140. "Steeped in Regency Style,"** *New York Herald Tribune Books*, **24 May 1953, p. 10:**

*Cotillion*. 316 pp. New York: G. P. Putnam's Sons. $3.50

In her long list of amusing Regency novels, Georgette Heyer has become steeped in that period.

In her latest novel, however, Miss Heyer has perhaps leaned a little too heavily on stylization. This story of Kitty Charing and her guardian's curious will is an almost too artificial one. Matthew Penicuik, Kitty's guardian, was a mean, but exceedingly well-to-do man and had a whole horde of nephews who hoped for his legacy. But Penicuik had undertaken to bring up a half-French orphan—Kitty—and he determined that his fortune would go to her and whichever one of his nephews would marry her. Naturally this placed the whole family in a dilemma. There was the clergyman nephew who was unctuous in offering his protection; the half-witted Earl whose Mama drove him into offering for Kitty's hand; the London rip whom Kitty really adored, and who preferred to make no move at all; as well as foppish, foolish Freddy who because of an involved set of circumstances had to pretend to be Kitty's fiance, although he of all the nephews had no need of Uncle Matthew's money.

It all adds up to a somewhat absurd situation, and Kitty does not have the character to carry it—as some of Miss Heyer's other heroines might have done. The result is a novel which has many of the charms of its predecessors, but is far too confined to a contrived pattern.

## 141. E. H. D., in "Recent Fiction," *The Springfield Sunday Republican* (Springfield, Mass.), 7 June 1953, p. 8C:

In *Cotillion* (Putnam's; $3.50) regency England is again the background for a delightful novel by Georgette Heyer. Kitty Charing, the gay and spirited ward of old Matthew Penicuik, is the heroine, she being the half French, half English daughter of his friend.

The life of London in the regency period and the customs of the "ton" (high society) make a gay picture, and the narrow escapes Kitty has as result of her kindhearted efforts to help the strange friends she makes provide a wealth of interest and humor.

**142. Margaret C. Scoggin, "Outlook Tower," *Horn Book* 29, August 1953, p. 289:**

Georgette Heyer. *Cotillion*. Putnam. $3.50

   Georgette Heyer's books start a bit slowly for some readers because the characters are always garbed in the costumes of Regency England and their language, like their clothing, is somewhat mannered. However, once past that hurdle, girls may settle down here to a delightful bit of humor and confusion. Penniless Kitty Charing will inherit her guardian's fortune only if one of his nephews marries her. She is secretly in love with the one dashing nephew who makes her no offer, counting on his ability to marry her whenever he chooses. In her eagerness to get away for a season in London, Kitty persuades good-natured nephew Freddy to pretend an engagement with her. He does, and Kitty is at once plunged into all the intrigues, petty scandals and match-making of the society crowd. Gives her heart away, too, in the end and, surprisingly enough, not to the cocky Jack. Of course, there are some allusions to the seamy side of Regency life but always delicately handled.

## 1954

**143. "Fiction," *Kirkus Reviews*, 15 July 1954, p. 450:**

Heyer, Georgette. *The Toll-Gate*. Putnam. $3.50.

   Another Regency rollick when Captain John Staple tries to account for some kind of bobbery that has caused eleven year old Ben's father to disappear. His impersonation of a toll-gate keeper leads him to Nell Stornaway, whose bedridden grandfather is unable to prevent his heir, Henry, from foisting unpleasant Coate on their home, Kellands. The peculiar questions of one Stogumber, who turns out to be a Bow Street Runner, indicate devilish havey cavey [sic] afoot and Staple is right-handed by highwayman Chirk in his investigations which lead to the hold-up and robbery of a government coach carrying newly minted, new coinage. Marriage to Nell on her grandfather's deathbed and a promise to protect the Stornaway name provoke Staple to fast action but he clears Chirk, protects Henry, pays off Coate and writes an end to Stogumber's assignment. The cant of the day makes this a flash tongued romance-adventure tale—which has humor and intelligence.

**144. "Briefly Noted. Fiction,"** *The New Yorker*, **4 September 1954, p. 76:**

*The Toll-Gate*, by Georgette Heyer. (Putnam).

A rather mechanical but cheerful extravaganza about an aristocratic young veteran of Waterloo who disguises himself as a gate-keeper in order to protect a squire's granddaughter from an assortment of rogues. Miss Heyer is a witty writer and an expert at this kind of story, and the reader can just skip over the chunks of period slang she has forced into the dialogue and not miss a thing.

**145. Lucy Black Johnson, "Spritely Fun,"** *New York Herald Tribune Books*, **12 September 1954, p. 6:**

*The Toll-Gate*. 310 pp. New York: G. P. Putnam's Sons. $3.50

Georgette Heyer has a knack for writing escape reading. She gives us an attractive hero and heroine, usually in pleasant revolt against some of the stricter etiquette of English Regency society. She surrounds them with a flashy set of villains, rogues and ruffians as well as outspoken, faithful retainers, steadfast friends and lively urchins. And she builds a tale on which amusing details about the manners, morals, styles and language of the period rest lightly.

Her best efforts have been set in or near London and peopled for the most part with the fashionable world. *The Toll-Gate* is located in the wilds of Derbyshire, where Captain John Staple, recently returned from the Napoleonic Wars and now bored with polite society, discovers mysterious doings at the toll house and a damsel in distress at the Hall. He stays to set everything to rights and marry the lady. His adventures involve a delightful Bow Street runner, the highway robbery of pound pieces fresh from the Mint, a high-class shill for a villain, some eerie underground caves, and murder most foul. All very spritely and good fun, but the only genuine Corinthian in the book, the Honorable Wilfred Babbacombe, has a very small role indeed and the presence of an honest highwayman named Chirk doesn't make up for the lack of fribbles and rattles who would populate a town drawing room. Heyer readers will, of course, enjoy this one, but they will look forward to a return to the London scene.

### 146. Henry Cavendish, "19th Century Uppercrust Fun," *Chicago Sunday Tribune*, 19 September 1954, pt. 4, p. 4:

*The Toll-Gate*, by Georgette Heyer. Putnam, 310 pp. $3.50

Once again Georgette Heyer has directed her comic genius along the fictional highway of early 19th century England, but this time with a new twist. In *The Toll-Gate*, a fun speckled piece with a more prosaic title than the action warrants, Mrs. Heyer abandons the courtly glitter of aristocratic London salons. Instead, she cleaves with refreshing persistence to the commoner levels of life flowing along one of the rural turnpikes of the Regency period.

The introductory pages, while a bit confusing at first, set up the signposts for this new turn. The sixth earl of Saltash, deeming his betrothal to the somewhat colorless Lady Charlotte Calne "a matter of considerable family importance," assembles a choice collection of uppercrust stumblebums at Easterby.

The earl, "seated at the head of a table loaded with plate, and bearing as a centerpiece an enormous epergne, presented by some foreign potentate to the fifth earl," looks around with a smugness that fires the tinder of the book's dry wit.

One evening of the anticipated week-end gathering is too much for the earl's 29 year old cousin, Capt. John Staple, a curly haired giant and veteran of the Peninsular fighting that led to Napoleon's defeat at

Waterloo. Staple, seeking entertainment somewhat more suitable to his manly nature, ducks out the next day and heads for the Leicestershire hunting seat of his erstwhile army crony, Wilfred Babbacombe. He becomes lost in the mist and reins in at a toll gate along the turnpike to find the keeper gone.

Eventual solution of this initial mystery builds up into a narrative that portrays the human side of plebian life flowing along the turnpike, takes Staple and tall, chestnut haired Nell Stornaway over the hurdles of romance and adventure, develops a parallel romance between a gentlemanly highwayman and a plumply proportioned lady's maid, and leads on to robbery and triple murder.

The climax is pitched in a grimly tense discovery scene in an abandoned cave when the villain and his pasty faced accomplice get what's been coming to them all along.

Despite the grimness in the latter phases of the plotting, the handling is characterized thruout by a frothy vein of comedy.

**147. *The Open Shelf*, December 1954, p. 37:**

*The Toll-Gate* by Georgette Heyer. Putnam. $3.

A former captain of the Dragoons in the Napoleonic wars tangles with hold-up men, bags of new currency, and the granddaughter of the local squire.

**148. Margaret C. Scoggin, "Outlook Tower," *Horn Book* 30, December 1954, p. 464:**

Georgette Heyer *The Toll-Gate*. Putnam. $3.50.

Here is a costume piece set in an era of gallant highwaymen, young gentlemen with a nose for adventure, and sprightly heroines. This one follows Captain John Staples [sic] in his search for a missing toll-gate keeper. He avenges a murder—narrowly escaping with his own life—finds a lost treasure, and rescues a lady in distress. It is set in early

19th-century England with the conversation a bit mannered at times, but it should appeal to older girls with a taste for old-fashioned romance. (For me it has echoes of Farnol and Walsh.)


**149. Grace P. Slocum (Superintendent, Work with Young Adults, Brooklyn Public Library), "Young People," *Library Journal*, 15 December 1954, p. 2503:**

Heyer, Georgete [sic]. *The Toll-Gate*. 310 pp. Putnam. $3.50

Another witty novel of Regency England in which a young aristocrat disguises himself as the local gatekeeper to cover the mysterious disappearance of the man formerly in that position. He immediately becomes involved with highwaymen, stolen gold, and a beautiful young lady. Written in the vernacular of the day, this novel presents an entertaining and authentic picture of a romantic society.


1955


**150. "Fiction," *Kirkus Reviews* 23, 1 July 1955, p. 446:**

Heyer, Georgette *Bath Tangle*. Putnam. $3.00

. . . in a flutter of flounces and petticoats, when two Regency heiresses, stepmother Fanny, Lady Spengrove, younger than Serena, her stepdaughter, leave London and the dullness of their mourning to take up residence in Bath. Serena meets an old love, attractive and protective Hector and her secret engagement to him is countered by her arrogant, ex-suitor, now the trustee of her fortune, who becomes the fiance of a young debutante. Spits and spats ensue when Serena takes timid Emily in hand and berates Rotherham for his treatment of the girl; a pretty state of affairs blows up when Emily "elopes" with Rotherham's ward—for Serena goes in pursuit. Hector discovers he really loves Fanny, and Rotherham is strong in his persuasion that Serena loves none but he . . . More leisurely incident here than in other Heyer titles, with the social

170

comedy along Thirkell lines, this will give her audience a somewhat slower-paced story that relies more on character than drama and action.

**151. A. F. W., "Fun at the Spa," in "Fiction," *Saturday Review* 38, 3 September 1955, p. 32:**

In the newest of her Regency harlequinades, ***Bath Tangle*** (Putnam, $3.50), the indefatigable Georgette Heyer rings a variation on the familiar triangle. Instead of three lovelorn characters she uses three mixed-up couples who can't get themselves sorted out till the last suspenseful pages. Heroine of the romantic tangle is short-tempered, hoydenish Lady Serena. The temper has not been improved by her father's will: Serena can come into her inheritance, due her on marriage, only with the approval of the imperious Marquis of Rotherham. Papa, it seems, died displeased that his daughter had broken off her betrothal to the Marquis.

Chaperoned by her stepmother, an ethereal charmer two years her junior, Serena visits Bath. Partly because mourning becomes them, the becreped young ladies are drawn into the whirl of spa society. An old beau of Serena's turns up and wins her promise of marriage, whereupon the Marquis announces his engagement to a chit. The chit's callow suitor, Rotherham's ward, takes drastic action. Everyone gallops off in pursuit of everybody else, the fragile stepmother gets her man, Serena and Rotherham resume their Kate-Petruchio courtship. In short, Miss Heyer's Pump Room chronicle sails along on a gale of high Regency spirits. Gale and regale is this storyteller's formula, and she has thirty-five puckishly entertaining novels to prove it works.

**152. Henry Cavendish, "A Frothy Bit of Life and Love," *Chicago Sunday Tribune*, 4 September 1955, pt. 4, p. 3:**

*Bath Tangle*, by Georgette Heyer. Putnam, 327 pp. $3.50
Georgette Heyer, mistress of the sheerest kind of romantic fluff, has

established herself firmly as Britain's foremost contemporary exponent of what may be referred to metaphorically as lightly threaded literary needle point.

In a brilliant series of frolicsome novels—I can remember *The Foundling, Cotillion,* and *The Toll-Gate*—she has portrayed with admirable humor the frothier side of early 19th century English manners during the period of George III's reign.

*Bath Tangle* introduces readers to a strange feminine combination as a result of the demise of the earl of Spenborough in his mid-50s. His 25 year old daughter, Lady Serena Carlow, is a titian haired heroine whose temper belies her name. In striking contrast, the widowed Fanny, stepmother to Serena altho several years her junior, is a docile individual with a "general air of youth and fragility."

The action opens as the two tire of Spenborough's estate and move to the more sociable environs of nearby Bath. There the tangles of the title quickly develop into a maze of lover's mixups along tempestuously romantic pathways.

Resolution of the intertwining amours is left mostly to the author's ingenuity in the plotting, and all ends well with the beating of the final heart throbs. The book adds up to a sparkling story light as cheese souffle and as mischievous as a kid snapping bubble gum.

**153. Ethel Dexter, "An English Story in Romantic Vein. Novel by Georgette Heyer, *Bath Tangle*," in "Book Reviews," *The Springfield Sunday Republican* (Springfield, Mass.), 9 October 1955, p. 10C:**

Known for her tales of the Regency period and as a prolific writer of good novels, Georgette Heyer in *Bath Tangle* (Putnams; $3.50) has produced a very English and very readable story in a charming setting. Here are portrayed two distinctly opposite characters in the persons of the widow, Fanny, and Serena, the daughter of her recently deceased husband, the Earl of Spenborough, as they sit pensively in the library of their home, the country seat Milverley Park.

Six years the junior of her daughter-by-marriage, Fanny is shy, retiring and charming in her heavy widow's weeds.  On the other hand, Serena, a titian haired beauty of 26 summers, is like a spirited horse, held in check by the reins of convention.  Much as she adored her father, she resents with everything within her the final provision of the will just read which states that all of her great fortune will be held in trust by her cousin (and a rejected suitor) the Marquis of Rotherham, to be given to her at her marriage and then only if her chosen one shall meet with his approval.

Since Serena has but recently in a stormy interview broken her engagement to the fiery but attractive young lord there seems little chance of receiving his approval of anyone whom she may choose.  The proviso in the will is one of the marquis's chosing [sic], for he feels, as does Serena, that the will is a clever way arranged by her father for mending the broken engagement, of which he had much approved.

Resourceful and determined, Serena arranges for her young stepmother to chaperone her in a house hired for the period of mourning in the city of Bath, where even in mourning it is proper to retire to drink the healthgiving water.  *Bath Tangle* tells what happens when a former admirer, Maj. Hector Kirkby, appears, pays court, and to the disgust of Lord Rotherham is accepted by Serena.

**154. Margaret C. Scoggin, "Outlook Tower," *Horn Book* 31, December 1955, p. 469:**

Georgette Heyer *Bath Tangle*. Putnam. $3.50

A merry tongue-in-cheek period piece which scrambles and unscrambles two sets of young lovers.  Brusque imperious Ivo, Marquis of Rotherham, treats Serena with disdain but is secretly drawn to her; fiery-tempered impetuous Serena resents Ivo's calm superiority and is furious that her fortune depends upon his consent to her marriage but she misses him when he courts another girl; handsome correct Hector worships Serena from afar but finds her deucedly difficult when he is with her and turns to gentle pretty Fanny for consolation; Fanny strives long to keep from losing her heart to Hector.  19th-century Bath is the setting; gay blades, aristocrats, fortune hunters, social climbers throng the scene. Light and entertaining for the more sophisticated girls who enjoy mannered romance.

## 1956

### 155. "Fiction," *Kirkus Reviews*, 1 July 1956, p. 451:

Heyer, Georgette *Sprig Muslin*. Putnam. $3.75.

A Regency romp through the English countryside is sparked by the over-imagination of Amanda "Smith" who starts the mischief by running away from her grandfather who will not let her marry Neil. Her stories and escapes involve Sir Gareth Ludlow, who realizes she must be protected, Lady Hester for whom he has offered and been refused, and young Hildebrand Ross whose attempts to forward Amanda's efforts to find Neil end in the accidental shooting of Sir Gareth. Amanda's request that Hester come to nurse the patient frees Hester from family duties and the four's enjoyment of an idyllic hideaway is shattered as families catch up with them and Amanda is restored to Neil while Gareth proves he wants Hester for love and not companionship. Pleasant pleasantries here.

### 156. Katherine Tappert Willis (Readers Advisor, The Greenwich Lib., Greenwich, Conn.), in "New Books Appraised," *Library Journal* 81, August 1956, pp. 1790-91:

Heyer, Georgette. *Sprig Muslin*. 276 pp. Putnam. $3.75.

The setting of GH's new story is in the same delightful Regency London and the nearby country known so well through English fiction. Sir Gareth Ludlow's family and the Earl of Brancaster have all of the problems of romance and marriage that usually filled the lives of youth in the early 1800's, but the problems are solved in GH's inimitable manner. A pleasant novel—not dull in spite of the familiar scene. For general purchase, and may well be added to young people's collections.

**157. S. P. Mansten, "Fiction. Also Noted," *Saturday Review* 39, 25 August 1956, p. 27:**

*Sprig Muslin*, by Georgette Heyer (Putnam, $3.75), serves up a nineteenth-century romance enlivened by a comic chase that sees Sir Gareth Ludlow on the track of the unpredictable Amanda. This impish young lady teases a score of admirers and elopes with a "greybeard" uncle before Sir Gareth finally corners Amanda's affections. This is Miss Heyer's twenty-sixth novel and should satisfy readers with a taste for a gay, amusing, and unpretentious reading-lark.

**158. Henry Cavendish, "Rollicking Novel of Regency Period," *Chicago Sunday Tribune*, 2 September 1956, pt. 4, p. 4:**

*Sprig Muslin*, by Georgette Heyer. Putnam. 276 pp. $3.75.

Georgette Heyer is the English author of some of the most pleasantly amusing contributions to the comedy of manners on record. In *Sprig Muslin* she returns to the early 19th century Regency period, long familiar to her readers, and performs with lightly touched nimbleness an astonishing feat of costume camouflage.

The central feminine character, a saucy minx who takes the name of Amanda Smith for stage purposes, is introduced on the approaching eve of her 17th birthday. She has large, dark eyes, a misty gaze, a lovely willful mouth, and an obstinate chin. "A picture of pretty mulishness," she is attired in a becoming gown of sprig muslin as she engages in a stormy scene with the lug-headed landlord of a wayside inn.

Obviously a lass of quality, Amanda has a yen to get married, is being thwarted by her crusty old grandpapa, and is engaged in an ingenious campaign of fabrications to obtain her own way. Her dusky ringlets dance under the brim of her chip-straw hat, and tears sparkle at times "on the ends of her long eyelashes." The author teases readers thruout with a captivating characterization of the bewitching miss. But not until the closing pages is Amanda's real identity undraped.

Acting opposite the fetching young figure is the more subdued but resourceful Sir Gareth Ludlow, a man-about-London—"never too high in the instep"—who is still benumbed romantically by the death, in a carriage accident some years earlier, of his beloved Clarissa. Now in his mid-thirties, Sir Gareth calls at the Mount St. home of his sister, Mrs. Wetherby, to announce his intention of seeking the hand of a lady of breeding, good manners, and amiable disposition, but little fortune and no prospects. His objective, he explains laconically, is to perpetuate the Ludlow family line.

"Not Lady Hester," the nephews and nieces chorus. Their adored uncle, redoubtable possessor of a princely fortune, is firm, however, and sets forth for rural Cambridgeshire to press his suit. On the way, he encounters Amanda at the height of her stormy scene with the posting house landlord; and from this stems a generally hilarious series of adventures which go to make up the narrative complication.

As the curtain falls, Sir Gareth, rebuffed at first by his rather dowdy spinster love, wins Lady Hester in what steams up into an amorous match. And Amanda, revealed as the granddaughter of the august and eminent Gen. Summercourt, gets her youthful veteran of England's Peninsular campaign against Napoleon. It all adds up to as zany, frothy and rollicking a tale as Mrs. Heyer has ever penned.

**159. Ethel Dexter, "English Romance in *Sprig Muslin*," *The Springfield Sunday Republican* (Springfield, Mass.), 4 November 1956, p. 32A:**

*Spring Muslin* [sic] (Putnam's; $3.75), a light but entertaining novel, is Georgette Heyer's contribution this season. Laid in England early in the 19th century, this romantic story concerns a charming but too imaginative young lady of high society calling herself "Amanda Smith." To satisfy her love for adventure and to fulfill her avowed intention of marrying her soldier finance [sic] she runs away from her grandfather's sumptuous home. Her adventures become more than even she could have anticipated.

She gets lost and literally throws herself into the arms of the dignified Sir Gareth Ludlow for protection. Chivalry demands that he accept this responsibility, but it greatly disrupts his own plans for the courtship of the dignified Lady Hester Thale.

In this gay and delightful story this attractive but irrepressible young woman leads everyone a merry chase over the English countryside from castles to hostels. Everything ends happily, however.

## 1957

**160. Daniel George, "New Novels," *The Spectator*, 11 January 1957, p. 59:**

*April Lady*. By Georgette Heyer. Heinemann 13s.6d.

The new Georgette Heyer is what might have been predicted, an historical romance—her twenty-fifth apparently. Conscientiously period—

> They saw badger-hunting in the reeking squalor of Charles's, where a man must be a very fly-cove to avoid having his pockets picked; they rubbed shoulders with bing-boys and their mollishers in the sluiceries; became half-sprung on blue ruin in these gin shops; and, wandering eastward, deep-cut at the Field of Blood.

—it is an entertainment for a reader who can still take to such people as Lord Cardross (with mistress) married for his money (to save her father and brother from disgrace) by the eighteen-year-old Lady Helen (Nell to us). The thing is that Giles (Lord Cardross) really does love Nell and vice versa, and after a more or less regulation amount of mis-understanding they achieve a proper *modus vivendi*—at least, the butler surprises them "locked in a crushing embrace." Discreetly retiring, he fumbles with the door-handle when he returns, this time to find that "My lord, before the mirror above the fireplace, was pensively absorbed in some delicate adjustment to the folds of his cravat; my lady, a trifle dishevelled, but otherwise a model of fashionable decorum, was seated in a large armchair." Being a "period" novel, it has no bedroom scene; but it is undoubtedly the stuff to give them as likes it.


**161. "Past Tenses,"** *The Times Literary Supplement,* **18 January 1957, p. 33:**

Georgette Heyer: *April Lady.* Heinemann. 13s. 6d.

*April Lady* is a tale of true love in the high society of Regency days, a genre in which Miss Heyer is accomplished. The story is exciting and gracefully told, with a liberal seasoning of the slang of the period. Such a careful writer should not introduce a Foreign Office clerk who expects to be sent abroad on a diplomatic mission; but in other respects the picture of the times is attractive and accurate.


**162. Katherine Tappert Willis (Trustee, The Morristown Library, Morristown, N. J.), in** *Library Journal,* **July 1957, p. 1778:**

Heyer, Georgette. *April Lady.* 256 pp. Putnam. $3.75.

What difference if some of the detail of GH's last of many Regency novels is not accurate! This is, as usual, graceful and exciting with all problems solved so satisfactorily that the novel is the best kind of "escape" story—fine for adult and for adolescent. The world knows, by this time, that any one seeking problems of the day and dissertations on economy and social and cynical-sentimental affairs in the most serious way is not to be led to GH. A useful, and to-be-purchased writer for all public libraries.


**163.** *Kirkus Reviews,* **1 July 1957, p. 451:**

Heyer, Georgette. *April Lady*. Putnam. $3.75.

Lady Helen lands in a pretty to-do over her debts, over her brother Dysart's borrowings and her husband's strictures about no further financial failings. For Earl Cardross is hesitant to show he loves his Nell and his Nell has been instructed by her worldly mother to keep her feelings hidden, and there is always the taint of her family's profligate and expensive heritage—so when Nell is pressed by a dressmaker, when Dysart attempts a highwayman holdup to help her, and when Nell attempts to borrow from moneylenders—there's quite a stir and quite a bit of dodging so that Cardross be kept ignorant. Cardross' ward, the Lady Letitia, who is also his half sister, adds to the confusion by her passion for the respectable but unworthy civil servant Allendale and, in trying to protect her from the gossiping "ton", Nell's small dissemblings come to naught until Cardross breaks down and love shines through. A taming of the Regency rakes here but still "high in the instep."

**164. Henry Cavendish, "It's Daffy, Dandy, and Downright Delicious," *Chicago Sunday Tribune*, 1 September 1957, pt. 4, p. 5:**

*April Lady*, by Georgette Heyer. Putnam, 254 pp. $3.75

Georgette Heyer, whose *Sprig Muslin* was one of the most delightful bits of flimflammery this side of P. G. Wodehouse in his early days, has done it again. This English author, who has been specializing in the Regency period as setting for the last half dozen or so of her costume novels, goes back once more in *April Lady* to the days of a century and a half ago in England, when dandies were really Dandies and Vivacious Ladies were always Pertly Impertinent.

The 30 year old earl of Cardross opens the action by severely rebuking his bride of a year (the 18 year old Lady Helen, better known as Nell) for financial extravagance. Toted up against her are her carefree dealings with dressmakers, milliners, and her improvident rakehell of a brother, Viscount Dysart.

Nell thinks his lordship wed her in a marriage of convenience, because Mama has warned her not to be disturbed if she discovers her handsome husband has Another Interest outside the marital bonds. The earl, in turn, gives way with gradual inevitability to the conviction that his lovely but designing bride has married him for his money.

With these growing factors of complication setting the stage for entirely innocent misunderstandings, the plotting wends along its merry way. Nell endeavors to extricate herself from the predicament of mountainous bills without his lordship finding out about them.

A dark haired soubrette—Cardross' vivid, 17 year old half sister, Lady Letty—pursues willy-nilly her own amorous attachment to a suitor with no means and less prospects. There's a comic opera holdup, and a necklace of emeralds and diamonds disappears mysteriously and is as mysteriously recovered. At the moment of crucial darkness the lights come on and it all ends happily. The earl and his golden haired bride, you see, have been wildly in love with each other all along.

In a melange of daffiness of this sort the plotting doesn't really matter. It's the sheer fun of reading on a high entertainment level that's the thing. For such an experience *April Lady* is tops. It's sure-fire guaranteed to afford even the sourest of pusses a refreshing evening of kittenish enjoyment.

**165. S. P. Mansten, "Duly Noted,"** *Saturday Review* **40, 14 September 1957, p. 50:**

*April Lady*, by Georgette Heyer (Putnam, $3.75), is a comedy of errors involving elderly Lord Cardross and his young wife who mistakes [sic] each other's marriage motives. The high and low life of England's Regency period are given a gay whirl by Miss Heyer, a specialist at this sort of thing. Her twenty-seventh novel is utterly feminine and best read with a side-dish of bonbons.

**1958**

**166. *Kirkus Reviews*, 1 February 1958, p. 90:**

Heyer, Georgette. *Sylvester*. Putnam. $3.95.

Another Regency romp pursues the obstacle course of true love in the marital stakes of Sylvester, Duke of Salford, and authoress-incognito, Miss Phoebe Marlow. Phoebe has been a little dab of a country girl but her book, with the Duke as a villain, is about to be published when he comes with the possibility of offering for her. She flees with her childhood friend Tom Orde and they both are rescued by Sylvester who is shocked and delighted with her impropriety and candor. Once in London with her grandmother she learns more about her villain-hero, is forced to take his scoldings when her book creates a scandalous stir and, with Tom, is kidnaped by Sylvester's widowed sister and her new husband. In France, caring for Sylvester's nephew, it is Tom who whips the two embattled lovers into line. Nothing to put you in a gudgeon [sic] but a pleasant entertainment for Heyer's following.

**167. Margaret M. Mulcahy (Formerly Washington, D.C., Public Library), in *Library Journal*, 15 March 1958, pp. 844-45:**

Heyer, Georgette. *Sylvester or the Wicked Uncle*. 309 pp. Putnam. $3.95

Period romance of Regency England. Sylvester, Duke of Salford, cold-bloodedly seeking a suitable wife, is directed to Phoebe, daughter of his mother's dearest friend. She is a young female of unfashionable aspect who dislikes him and leaves home rather than accept his suit. Phoebe has also written a gothic novel in which he recognizably appears as villain. Considerably shaken, Sylvester falls in love with Phoebe; she also has a change of heart, but the publication of her novel sets in motion various complications. All ends happily. Frothy, readable, and full of delightful Regency dialogue. For general library purchase.

**168. Margaret C. Scoggin, "Outlook Tower," *Horn Book* 34, June 1958, pp. 221-2:**

Georgette Heyer. *Sylvester*. Putnam. $3.95

Another involved but entertaining period piece of Regency England dealing with the "pride and prejudice" of hero and heroine. This time a plain but witty girl is sought in marriage by a wealthy, somewhat arrogant Duke. Unfortunately he has snubbed her once and she has never forgotten or forgiven him. She has written a novel, too, and has put him into it thinly disguised. When the Duke comes to make an offer for her hand, Phoebe runs away from home. There follows a series of amusing events. She and the friends who are helping her are snow-bound and it is the Duke who rescues her. Later she tries to rescue his nephew from a scatter-brained mother and again finds herself in the Duke's company. All ends well, with pride and prejudice dissolving. Not for every girl but certainly for those who enjoy mannered gaiety and romance in costume.

**1959**

**169. *Kirkus Reviews*, 15 January 1959, p. 61:**

Heyer, Georgette *Venetia*. Putnam. $3.95

Miss Heyer is moving over into Thirkell's domain and her Regency comedies are taking on a more concentrated pattern. Here, it is Venetia Lanyon, whose devotion to her invalid brother, Aubrey, along with the selfishness of her older brother, Conway, and her father's lack of interest, about whom ideas of marriage revolve. There are two suitable choices but when she meets the dreadful ogre, an expert in the art of dalliance, and shadowed with a lurid reputation—Lord Damerel—she proves that a green girl living a restricted life in the country can make a romantic, intelligent decision about a husband. There are obstacles—Damerel's horrid past, the secret about Venetia's own background, the installation of Conway's bride and her impossible mother, and the general family perturbation that hound Venetia before she can achieve the life she wants. Gay—mannered and attractive.

**170. Henry Cavendish, "Wonderful Nonsense,"** *Chicago Sunday Tribune*, **22 February 1959, pt. 4, p. 4:**

*Venetia*, by Georgette Heyer. Putnam. 308 pp. $3.95

In an imposing parade of wonderful nonsense, England's Georgette Heyer has proved herself over the years to be a past master of the art of ruggle-buggle which may be defined rather broadly as P. G. Wodehouse transplanted back into the 19th century English Regency period (circa 1815), with touches of Ed Wynn, Eddie Cantor, and *Hell-za-poppin'* tossed in for good measure.

In ruggle-buggle, gentlemen of quality "offer" for the ladies of their selection and proud parents make the decisions for their darling daughters. The trouble with this is that when lass of undeniable beauty blends a flash of independent spirit with the gleam in her eye, there easily may be complications.

*Venetia*, Miss Heyer's latest in a long line of Regency comedies, combines in some degree or other all of these literary elements. Against a verdant Yorkshire background Venetia Lanyon, shining with the glory of guinea-gold hair, the enchanting arch of a pretty mouth, brilliant eyes, and the sparkle of irrepressible fun, is perilously close to being on the shelf as she reaches the age of five and 20 years without having made a suitable match.

She has suitors, tho: a stiffnecked stodge-podge of 30, and an insufferable adolescent six years her junior.

Into this un-Edenlike scene enters "the wicked baron," Lord Damerel, wastrel owner at 38 of the neighboring estate, and an admitted rake of well worn points. He is such a one as shocked the countryside in his puppyhood days by running off with a married lady. The latter, it develops in partial mitigation of his lordship's offense, was "a little, plump, black-eyed slut . . . whose marriage ring and noble degree hid the soul of a courtesan."

Obviously almost anything can happen in a situation such as this, and in Miss Heyer's latest offering it does. Let it suffice to say that virtue triumphs, the beast turns out to be beauty incarnate, and the reader has a fine time posting thru pages of well loaded triviality.

**171. Alberta M. Lockwood (Librarian, Ft. Branch, Indiana, Public Library), in *Library Journal*, 1 March 1959, pp. 777-8:**

Heyer, Georgette. *Venetia*. 308 pp. Putnam. $3.95

In her usual setting—19th-century England—prolific Miss Heyer has done it again in this vivacious story of Regency society. Venetia Lanyon, a fatherless (motherless too she thinks, but that is part of the intrigue), 25-year-old beauty, manages the family estates during the continued absence of her older brother Conway, and cares for her precocious crippled younger brother. An amazing woman even for today she refuses to accept either of her addled suitors just to be a married woman. Then her true love appears on the scene—Lord Damerel, a rake with a past; their path to each other is beset with every obstacle. But by plotting deviously, and fearlessly risking her reputation, Venetia wins him and he wins her. An appealing story, apart from our reality. For those who want a costume story or a tale of love.

## 1960

**172. *Kirkus Review* 28 (1 March 1960), p. 197:**

Heyer, Georgette. *The Unknown Ajax*. Putnam. $3.95

Here, within a long series of Regency romances and romps, the whole action is kept on the Kentish coast and activities of the "free traders" complicate the situation facing the inhabitants of Darracott Place. The old lord is acknowledging his rightful heir, Hugo, but is determined to lick him into shape so that he may support the character of a gentleman.

Hugo, with his bulk, his smothering Yorkshire accent and locutions, and his instructions to marry his cousin, Anthea, whose temper and tongue put him in his place, is the catalyst who keeps his two beau monde cousins, Vincent and Claud, on guard for his gaucheries, his younger cousin Richmond almost ready for hero worship, and his other relatives in a state of utter incomprehension. When it is revealed that Hugo is neither an impostor nor a usurper, that his speech and education can pass muster, and that his fortune is considerable—he still has not won recognition. His handling of young Richmond's rebellion against the old lord's restrictions—by a play that hoaxes the Riding officer of the Customs Land Guard ready to prove a smuggling charge—proves to the Family that his caprices have wisdom behind them and Anthea happily capitulates to her destiny. This fancy moves lightly and with a flourish.

**173. Henry Cavendish, "Comedy in Regency Era Novel,"** *Chicago Sunday Tribune***, 22 May 1960, pt. 4, p. 7:**

*The Unknown Ajax*, by Georgette Heyer. Putnam, 314 pp. $3.95

In the wonderful world of Homer, Ajax was a warrior of tremendous physical proportions. He was such a one, I suppose, as would clobber enemies with a fence post instead of dallying around with a rubber truncheon.

It seems entirely appropriate, therefore, that Georgette Heyer should refer to the hero of her latest excursion into the froth and frippery of Regency England as "The Unknown Ajax."

Maj. Hugh Darracott, heir to his venerable nibs, Lord Darracott, is certainly an individual of appropriate physical proportions.

Yet as he faces the quizzing-glasses of the other gentlemen of the family, there is "something rather bovine" in the blankness of his blue eyes that masks whatever thoughts may be revolving behind them.

The stage for high comedy based on misunderstanding is quickly set following introduction of the characters. The narrative reveals that Hugh's father, a military man, married—while stationed in Yorkshire years earlier—a weaver's daughter. He was killed, conveniently, in action in Holland.

Thereafter, the son—with two others ahead of him in the family line—had been reared quietly in his native environs, with the stigma of being a "weaver's brat" attaching to him.

A boating mishap removes—with seeming misfortune for the family line—the two heirs ahead of Hugh, and Lord Darracott has the problem of upgrading his unwanted grandson to qualify him socially for the succession.

The solution is to bring the major to the family estate and, after preliminary polishing, marry him to his cousin, Lord Darracott's impishly lovely granddaughter, Anthea.

The accomplishment of this objective—threaded with clownish complications as the major tries to play out his assigned role as weaver's brat—makes a story that displays the author's usual frolicsome mood.

As with Mrs. Heyer's other Regency period comedies, this one is guaranteed not to strain the intelligence. Yet it will provide the reader with wonderful entertainment from first page to last.

**174. *Library Journal*, July 1960, p. 2686:**

Heyer, Georgette. *The Unknown Ajax*. 314 pp. Putnam. $3.95

Another of Miss Heyer's delightful novels of Regency England, this adds an adventure in smuggling to its gay love story. Recommended where good light fiction with historical background is needed.

**175. Margaret C. Scoggin, "Outlook Tower," *Horn Book* 36 (October 1960), p. 420:**

Georgette Heyer *The Unknown Ajax*. Putnam. $3.95

Another "Regency" tale dealing with young bloods and fine families. This time the death of the old Lord's eldest son brings an unknown grandson to aristocratic Darracott Place in Kent. Hugh is a giant of a man whom all his cousins consider a crude, uneducated chap. Little by little, as he exerts friendly but unmistakable authority, his supercilious cousin Vincent and his elegant cousin Claud and his daredevil young cousin Richmond sense he is not exactly what they thought him. Even his cousin Anthea, infuriated when her grandfather had first suggested that she marry Hugh, begins to think this may be a good idea. Hugh's true self emerges when he saves Richmond from a smuggler's fate through quick wits and a neat strategem. I thought this slow in starting and too "talky" at first, but I liked it better as the plot unwound. Older girls who like other Heyer books or period settings or light reading will enjoy this.

**176. Eric Keown, "New Fiction," *Punch* 239, 6270 (23 November 1960), p. 756:**

Georgette Heyer, *Pistols for Two*. Heinemann, 15/-

After a gruelling course of modern fiction it is a startling experience to pass into the rosy world of Georgette Heyer, where love-lorn maidens of the highest degree find themselves moving smartly towards Gretna Green in the sporting curricle of a Nonpareil with dazzling Hessians and thirty thousand a year. This is the first collection of Miss Heyer's short stories, and each is guaranteed, after coins have been flicked to expectant ostlers and the viscount with a rueful smile quivering at the corner of his supercilious mouth has caught up with the lovely governess in the post-chaise, to end with romance neatly tied up in pink ribbon. Except one, "Night at the Inn," which shows how much better Miss Heyer could be if she could forget the exotic blooms of Georgian courtship.

## 1961

**177. *Kirkus Reviews* 29 (1 December 1961), p. 1056:**

Heyer, Georgette, *A Civil Contract*. Putnam. $4.50

Differing from previous Regency romances in its theme of a marriage of convenience, this follows Capt. Adam Deveril, Lord Lynton, in his decision to sell his title and wed the daughter of wealthy Cit Chawleigh. His heart lost to the beauteous Julia Oversley, and she lost to him through his dead father's debts and the responsibility to maintain Fontley Priory and provide for his two sisters and mother, Adam is accepted by Jenny who, with more sense than sensibility, proceeds to make him most comfortable. Her father however with his massive generosity is an obstacle, while Julia's lingering charms are a threat, and it is to Jenny's calm determination and Adam's ability to feel sympathy for his vulgar father-in-law that the civil contract turns into a lasting, respected bond. There's more substance to this spirited picture of London and Lincolnshire life, of the *ton* and its mannered ways, of the give-and-take that "golden shackles" demand. Likable.

## 1962

### 178. H. B. H., *Springfield Union*, 14 January 1962, p. 4d:

*A Civil Contract*, Georgette Heyer.

In *A Civil Contract* (Putnam; $4.50) Georgette Heyer writes another entertaining romantic novel about England in the early part of the 19th century, similar in tone and style to her several other popular books about the Regency period.

This story starts when Adam Deveril, an officer with the Duke of Wellington's army in the Peninsula, is obliged to sell his commission and return home to take over management of the family's large but heavily mortgaged estate after the death of his father in a hunting accident. As the new Viscount Lynton of Fontley Priory, the young war veteran is faced with a serious problem of salvaging the family fortunes. This leads to negotiations with a wealthy London businessman with a daughter for whom he seeks a marriage into the nobility.

In Miss Heyer's capable hands, this situation is expanded into a skilfully-plotted, amusingly told tale, richly highlighted with old English background material which again displays this writer's talent for social comedy with an aristocratic setting.

**179. Henry Cavendish, "A Formula for Fiction That Endures Repetition,"** *Chicago Sunday Tribune,* **21 January 1962, pt. 4, p. 3:**

*A Civil Contract* by Georgette Heyer. Putnam. 394 pp. $4.50

Georgette Heyer again displays her mastery of Regency period manners in *A Civil Contract.* She uses the same formula as in such frothy social comedies as *Spring Muslin* [sic], *Cotillion, Bath Tangle,* and *April Lady*—without the slightest sign of the formula's being shopworn thru repetition.

In this latest example of her metier, the hero is youthful Adam Deveril, sixth Viscount Lynton, of Fontley Priory in Lincolnshire. He returns from service with the duke of Wellington in the Spanish peninsular campaign to find that his noble father, killed in a hunting fall from his horse, had wasted the family fortunes in the feckless circle of the prince regent. What to do to restore the debt burdened estate?

Miss Heyer provides an ingenious answer by addition of an entirely new character to her already rich assembly of regency comedians. Robust old Jonathan Chawleigh is a hard riding operator in the London financial district. While gifted with a heart of gold, he is endowed with such business acumen as to have piled up material riches beyond the wildest dreams of the wealthiest nobility.

Unmindful of social ambitions on his own part, Chawleigh will have nothing but the best for his plain but comely and tractable daughter, Jenny. He bluntly proposes a marriage to Deveril whereby Jenny will gain a vaunted title and the doting old financier will underwrite the wasted Lynton family fortunes. Unoffended by the offer, his youthful lordship accepts in a down-to-earth spirit of sensibility.

The rest of the story is devoted to the heart warming episodes wherein Adam gradually detaches his heart from a blighted earlier affection, and he and Jenny solve all their problems in a spirit both of gentleness and civilized gentility. The resourceful young peer even puts one over on benevolent old Moneybags in a financial coup that ties up all loose ends as the curtain falls. In a word, *A Civil Contract* is a five-star job of sheerly delightful romance writing.

**180. Phoebe Adams, "Potpourri," *The Atlantic Monthly* 209, 3 (March 1962), p. 150:**

Readers who recall that Georgette Heyer once wrote exceptionally amusing and puzzling murder mysteries may be tempted, by opening hints of hanky-panky in the hunting field, to essay her latest novel, *A Civil Contract* (Putnam, $4.50). They will be disappointed. It is woman's-magazine pastry with an elaborate Regency setting. Togetherness in the curricle, you might say.

**181. "The Children's Section," *Library Journal* 87 (15 March 1962), pp. 1334-35:**

Heyer, Georgette. *A Civil Contract*. 393 pp. Putnam. $4.50
    The mixture as in her previous books, but that doesn't matter to Heyer fans. Adam Deveril, Viscount Lynton, late of the Duke of Wellington's forces, on the edge of financial ruin, contracts a marriage of convenience with the daughter of a city man. Told with Miss Heyer's usual charm and knowledge of the period.

1963

**182. Brigid Brophy, "A Sight of Intriguers," *New Statesman*, 25 October 1963, pp. 578-9:**

*False Colours*, by Georgette Heyer. Bodley Head. 18s.
    There is a new Regency Georgette Heyer—a piece of childish let's-pretend, but blessedly unpretentious, about an inheritance and handsome twin brothers. Nimble to the point of wit in copying period detail, it calls the twins as alike "as fourpence to a groat."

**183.  Henry Cavendish, "Frothy Comedy of Regency England,"** *The Chicago Sunday Tribune*, **31 March 1963, p. 9:**

*The Nonesuch*, by Georgette Heyer. Dutton. 300 pp. $3.95

Georgette Heyer, past mistress of the frothy comedy of manners played out against the backdrop of early 19th century England, is at her frothy best in this latest of her costume romances.

For hero, she presents "The Nonesuch," a designation defined by Webster's New International Dictionary (second edition) as something "unequaled, unrivaled, matchless."  Still a bachelor at 35, Sir Waldo Hawkridge is famed in London high society for his wealth (a town house, a toney estate in Leicestershire, and another estate that has been in the family "since the Lord knows when").  He has looks, social charm, and can ride, hunt, box, and drive a spanking team of fours to perfection, and is a smart cookie to boot!

As heroine, the lovely and resourceful Miss Ancilla Trent, now around 26, is the niece of a famous military general, but (in straitened family circumstances) is governess-companion of tempestuous Tiffany Wield, a juvenile enchantress at 17, who has glossy black hair, blue eyes, and the feminine form divine, but is something of a spoiled minx just the same.

There also are Sir Waldo's handsome younger cousin, Lord Lindeth, the latter's starry-eyed inamorata, Patience Chartley, daughter of a Yorkshire rector, and other characters ranging from muddle-headed to mildly intelligent.

The action moves strictly along the lines of comedy complication. Sir Waldo inherits another estate, Broom Hall, in rural Yorkshire.  He decides to convert it into an asylum for homeless orphans, his favorite charity.

Miss Trent, who quickly gets in his hair, mistakes an innocent reference to  Sir Waldo's "wretched brats" at a crucial point when he is seeking her hand in marriage.

All sorts of heart-rending misunderstandings arise.  The utterly ruthless but beauteous Tiffany adds to the trouble by trying to take Patience away from Lord Lindeth and Sir Waldo away from Miss Trent.

191

As a finale, she stages a runaway to London without proper chaperonage, only to be caught up within 20 miles.

As the tale winds wicky-wacky along to a happy conclusion in the best Heyer tradition, all the good characters win out, all the bad ones are put in their places, and the reader has an enchanting evening.


## 1964


**184. Elizabeth O'Rourke (New Brunswick, N. J.), in *Best Sellers* 23, 23 (1 March 1964), p. 414:**

Heyer, Georgette. *False Colours*. Dutton. 317 pp. $3.95

Georgette Heyer is a popular author with many historical novels and mysteries to her credit. All of her recent books have been set in the Regency Period in England, an era in which Miss Heyer feels comfortable and at home. Her novels are minutely detailed and reveal thorough and painstaking research, but how she is able to come up with a fresh plot and story-line in each novel is amazing.

In *False Colours*, we have a charming and delightful family—an irresponsible mother of identical twin sons. Kit, the younger of the twins, returns from the Continent to find his usually gay mother anxiously awaiting the return of Evelyn, the older twin, who has mysteriously disappeared. When Kit agrees to save his mother and Evelyn embarrassment by taking Evelyn's place at a party where Evelyn was to be presented to his fiancée's family, many complications arise and as the two, mother and son, get involved more deeply in the deception and involve more friends and relatives, the plot thickens.

The plot is almost predictable, so it will not be any injustice to the reader to disclose that Kit and the would-be fiancée of Evelyn fall in love; that Evelyn finally returns only to reveal that he too has fallen in love with another girl; and the problem which is the cause of all of this—Lady Denville's debts—is still unsolved. Of course, the dilemma is finally resolved in a highly romantic, though improbable, manner.

This novel cannot be dismissed as just another historical novel. It is excellent in its genre. Miss Heyer has the ability to transport the reader back to the early 19th Century and actually sense the elegant mode of living during that time. Her novels abound with great houses staffed by servants and lackeys, with a society moving about by season from city to the country, to Bath or Brigthton, to the races. The houses sparkle with the gentry of their guests. There is continuous dining and visiting. There are balls. There are beautiful and modish clothes and decor.

It is also interesting that Miss Heyer's style of writing is indigenous to the period of which she writes. *False Colours* is written in a leisurely detailed manner, reminiscent of Jane Austen. However, it is a comedy rather than a satire. The principal characters, the twins and their mother are likeable, attractive people, who have a warm, loyal attachment for one another. Their peccadillos and shortcomings are treated lightly and humorously and in good taste.

If the modern reader can adjust himself to the slow pace of this novel, he will find it soothing, enjoyable and worthwhile.

### 185. Henry Cavendish, "Regency Comedy in a Proven Formula," *Chicago Sunday Tribune*, 1 March 1964, p. 9:

*False Colours*, by Georgette Heyer. Dutton. 317 pp. $3.95

Georgette Heyer, prolific English author of droll fripperies in fiction, has a simple formula for the Regency costume romances she has been writing for more years than this reviewer can remember offhand.

She dreams up an amusing situation (such as a romantic mixup of identical twins with lovely lassies, as in the current production); then sets it against the background of uppercrust England somewhere between 1815 and 1820, and writes about it amusingly. In *False Colours*, she scores again.

The handsome and socially charming Fancot twins, Evelyn and Christopher (Kit), are, at 24, the pink of the London vogue. Evelyn has just succeeded to the title of earl of Denville upon the death of his father shortly after Waterloo, and Kit has inherited a more than modest competence from his godfather.

The trouble is that Mama, threatened with being side-lined as the dowager countess of Denville after the death of her husband, still is utterly exquisite tho in her forties and is as rattle-brained as they come.

Unfortunately, too, Mama has run up debts of around $100,000 without her husband's knowledge during his later years. The debts Evelyn—as the new head of the clan—is determined to take care of to preserve the family honor.

He proposes a marriage of convenience with Miss Cressida Stavely, not so much a beauty as well endowed with both papa's money and common sense. Evelyn, however, messes things up at the start by going on a harum-scarum mission to redeem a bauble Mama Denville had pledged at gambling.

His carriage overturns and he is laid up with injuries, just when he is due at a fancy dress party to meet the Stavely in-laws. At that point, Kit shows up in the middle of the night from a diplomatic mission to Vienna, and he substitutes for Evelyn.

The rest of the zany tale is concerned with Kit's rising romance with Cressy and Evelyn's defection to a Quaker-like beauty during his convalescence in the provinces. Mama succumbs to a filthy-rich elder suitor who had pursued her before she married Denville 25 years earlier. And the Stavely clan concurs in all the plot-resolving shenanigans the author can devise.

It is all utterly ridiculous—and delightful.


**186. Martin Levin, "A Reader's Report,"** *The New York Times Book Review*, **5 April 1964, p. 48:**

What Edgar Rice Burroughs was to the African Jungle, Georgette Heyer is to Regency England. Neither writer had actually *been* there, but so far as legions of devoted readers are concerned they might have been. And who is to say whether Tarzan's gorilla-dialect is any less authentic than Miss Heyer's Regency dialogue? ("We shall be at fiddlestick's end, for she is obviously starched-up, you know, and I collect, from something Stavely said to me, that she already doesn't like it above half.") In *False Colours* (Dutton, $3.95) Evelyn Fancot tries to extricate his Billie Burke-ish mother from near bankruptcy by marrying a young lady for money. But when Evelyn does not show up at a crucial audience with his intended, one Cressida Stavely, his place is taken by his twin Kit—and, by Jupiter, there is a proper mishmash. Evelyn, who is willing to sacrifice himself for a favorable balance of credit, is in love with another; brother Kit, who understudies him, is in love with Cressida; Sir Bomany [sic] Ripple, who has plenty of loot himself, is in love with mother Fancot; and plenty of period palaver is exchanged before everyone pairs off for the happy finale. Miss Heyer is in her element, which is somewhere between Jane Austen and Jeffrey Farnol.

### 187. "Viking Books, Recommended for Young Adults," *Library Journal* 89, 15 April 1964, p. 1881:

Heyer, Georgette. *False Colours*. 317 pp. Dutton. $3.95

When sober Kit takes the place of his high-living and mysteriously missing identical twin so that the latter's brand-new fiancee and her family will not learn of Denville's disappearance, the ensuing mix-ups and romance may be counted on to end happily with all couples properly paired. A comedy of manners in Miss Heyer's usual witty and polished vein.

### 188. M. C. Scoggin, "Outlook Tower. Something for the Girls," *The Horn Book* 40 (June 1964), p. 306:

Georgette Heyer. *False Colours*. Dutton, $3.95.

When Kit Fancot comes home on a visit from his diplomatic post abroad, he finds that his brother, the Earl of Denville, has vanished at a most crucial time. The Earl is about to become engaged to a wealthy girl whose fortune *could* bail their mother out of vast indebtedness, but the

Earl must appear at the engagement party; otherwise, no engagement. Kit, somewhat reluctantly, agrees to masquerade as his brother, as the two are identical twins. When the Earl delays his return, complications mount. So it goes—Regency England with its costumed artistocracy is re-created in a lighthearted, wholly improbable tale, which ends with all themes neatly tied into a pretty bowknot. Heyer has fans among the girls, and I thought this one of her best stories.

**189. Elizabeth O'Rourke (New Brunswick, N. J.), in *Best Sellers* 24, 10 (15 August 1964), p. 189:**

Heyer, Georgette. *Pistols for Two*. Dutton 249 pp. $3.95

Once again, Georgette Heyer takes us back to the graceful, elegant Regency period. This time, she has left the milieu of the novel and has given us eleven sparkling short stories. These stories are wrought with the precision of an O'Hara. They take the reader into the early 19th Century of the Brontës and Jane Austen. Miss Heyer, of course, does not write from the insulated viewpoints of those two women (nor with their genius), but in a much broader concept and with tongue-in-cheek. She pokes fun at dashing dandies, cavaliers, innocent heroines, fainting mothers, spinster sisters, domineering fathers, and elderly men who are all of *45*. Each story has a Regency theme, a romantic center, a (not always unexpected) twist ending, an undercurrent of seriousness and an understanding of human nature.

The characters are many. There are the loyal, dedicated sisters and daughters, such as Miss Tresilian in "A Clandestine Affair," and Miss Trent, in "Snowdrift," who are not left to a life of frustration by the author, but manage to capture eligible, handsome bachelors before the stories end. Then, there are the older, plain sisters, such as Augusta in "The Duel," and Miss Clara in "A Clandestine Affair," who have recourse to illness and hysteria and are left to unloved and unloving ends by the author (which, we suspect, they justly deserve). There is the unselfish widow, Mrs. Wingham, in "A Husband for Fanny," who, in encouraging Lord Harleston's suit for her beautiful young daughter's hand cannot understand why she herself (unconscious of her suppressed jealousy), is depressed when all seems to be working out well. There are the young lovers in "A Clandestine Affair," the boy likable and easy-going, the girl strong-willed, dominant (a well-matched pair). There are the hard-drinking young rakes, Lord Saltwood in "The Duel," spoiled and wayward with underlying steel in his character, and the weakling, Sir Ralph Morland, in "Hazard," who offers his pretty half-sister as a stake in a drunken poker game.

The stories run the gamut from cloak-and-dagger in "Night at the Inn," to whimsical-comedy in "Full Moon," but each of them has an upbeat ending.

Regency English expressions are delightful, but puzzling, and part of the fun of reading Georgette Heyer is guessing the meaning of the obsolete words and expressions. Clothes, which are an indication of class, are described in detail—the plain, drab pelisse of the governess in "Night at the Inn," the cloak of velvet on the girl of quality in "The Duel," the neckcloth on the young counting house clerk in "Night at the Inn"—which was tied "with more regard for propriety than fashion"—; the driving coat of many capes and the faun pantaloons of the young Nonpareil in "Full Moon," are a few examples of Miss Heyer's descriptive prose. The characters' names have a Dickensian flavor—Waggleswick, the Bow-Street Runner in "Night at the Inn," and Criddon, the butler, in "The Duel," to cite two. Then, there are the various modes of transportation of the period—carriages, curricles, tilburys, phaetons, post-chaise-and-fours. Marriage matches (that were planned in infancy) result in defiant elopements to Gretna Green.

This is primarily a book for the young or for women. It is a very feminine book in appearance with its pale pink jacket and chartreuse drawing of a garland of ribbons, crossed duelling-pistols, riding crop, lorgnette and mask. Recommended especially to the tired business-woman or school teacher, harrassed housewife and/or mother. Instead of the evening cigarette, cocktail, or tranquilizer, try one of Georgette Heyer's short stories.

**190. Robert Maurer, "The flag says bang,"** *New York Herald Tribune*, **"Book Week," 16 August 1964, p. 12:**

*Pistols for Two and Other Stories*. By Georgette Heyer. Dutton. 249 pp. $3.95

Georgette Heyer, whose thrillers and Regency period romances sell well here and in England, appears now with her first collection of stories. To use a popular commercial term, these 11 pieces are "genuine facsimiles." With no attempt at a contemporary or any other meaningful viewpoint, Miss Heyer plunges boldly into a milieu of masked balls and duels of honor, recreating in miniature those gooey marble-backed novels which when read by Jane Austen's flightiest heroines inevitably caused their catastrophic elopements to Gretna Green with ineligible suitors.

Quite conveniently, the tales have interchangeable characters, dialogue, themes, plots, texture. One summary can do for all. In "Bath Miss," Sir Charles Wainfleet (he of the shapely leg and dazzling Hessian boots) is obliged by protocol to escort home Miss Nan Massingham (she of the incorrigible frankness and well-turned ankle), a parlour boarder at Miss Titterstone's seminary in Bath. In some consternation Sir Charles sets off, sniffing his snuff with more vigor than is his wont and disturbing plans with his fiance [sic], Lady Almeria Spalding (she of the impoverished Earl of Alford's family). When Nan is injured, forcing the couple to spend an unchaperoned but uneventful night at an inn, who turns up but Lady Almeria, leaping to unwarranted conclusions (as is *her* wont), breaking the engagement, and opening the way for Sir Charles' proposal to Nan as the two move off in his curricle, presumably leg to ankle.

The moral of this digest is obvious, or was meant to be: best turn back to the real thing, beginning with *Sense and Sensibility*.

**191. Henry Cavendish, in "Books Today. Other Books Briefly,"** *Chicago Sunday Tribune*, **23 August 1964, p. 9:**

***Pistols for Two, and Other Stories***, by Georgette Heyer. Dutton. 249 pp. $3.95

In a series of costume novels based on the Regency period of early 19th century England, Georgette Heyer has produced some of the zaniest light froth ever to come from a typewriter, fountain pen, or stubby pencil. In this collection of 11 short stories, she demonstrates she is quite as adept at the shorter form of fiction.

Mistress of mirth in the realm of period manners, the English author presents two delightful excursions into the misty balminess of romance and nonsense to open and close her book. In "Pistols for Two," which provides the collective title, two young sprigs of half-baked parsley air their differences over a nice dish of lettuce against an early dawn landscape. But a smartly attired London smoothie, stealing into this provincial setting, mixes all the metaphors and takes the cake—with most of the icing as well! In "Full Moon" at the close, a bit of moon madness combined with the scent of roses serves to cap romance in a garden at midnight as a handsome young lord fills a slightly fractured engagement.

In between there's a variety of moods and manners having in common only the scrambling and unscrambling of romantic complications.

Mrs. Heyer proved by past performances that she is in sure possession of her Regency period details and background. To this she adds a clear narrative line, and a writing style as smooth as a jet flying at 30,000 feet. It all adds up to a pleasant romp through hours of wonderful reading.


**192.** *Library Journal* **89, 15 October 1964, p. 4227:**

Heyer, Georgette. ***Pistols for Two***. 249 pp. Dutton. $3.95

Georgette Heyer has written another delightful book about Regency times. Even better news is that it is a collection of short stories, all in the inimitable Heyer vein. Newcomers reading this delightful assortment of tales will join the Heyer crowd.

## 1965

**193. Elizabeth O'Rourke (New Brunswick, N. J.), in *Best Sellers* 25, 1 (1 April 1965), pp. 7-8:**

Heyer, Georgette. *The Spanish Bride* and *An Infamous Army*. Dutton. 390 pp. & 421 pp. $4.95 ea.

Miss Heyer's two novels, originally published 25 years ago and now being published again in the U.S.A., are historical romances in the true tradition. According to the "Author's Notes," a tremendous amount of research was done and reading accomplished in order to accumulate background material. Obviously, the greatest source of material for Harry and Juana Smith's love story was Harry Smith's own *Autobiography*. Obviously again, the greatest sources of technical detail were Wellington's Dispatches and Supplementary Dispatches. The author states that "wherever possible, I have allowed the Duke to speak for himself, borrowing freely from the twelve volumes of the Dispatches."

Miss Heyer's characters, whether drawn from reality or her imagination, are for the most part lively, energetic, young people, who love life, adventure, and duty, and they spur the stories along.

### The Spanish Bride

When the British under Wellington were besieging Badajos on the Spanish peninsula, Brigade-Major Harry Smith unexpectedly and impulsively acquired a bride, a 14-year-old girl who had sought the protection of the British. Loved and respected by his men, hardworking, loyal, energetic, apparently so valuable to the commanders he served that he was allowed the eccentricity of an entourage of a string of greyhounds, a stud of horses, a batman, a groom, and, after the acquisition of his young wife, a maid,—Harry Smith is the hero of this novel. The heroine, of course, is Juana, the Spanish bride. A tiny, convent-bred child-woman when she married Harry, she developed into a thoroughbred, who learned to ride, keeping up with the hard-marching Army through parching heat, freezing snow, and chilling rain. Fording rivers, climbing treacherous mountain paths, staying in the rear only when fighting takes place and at Harry's command, always priding herself on being a good soldier and obeying orders immediately, the pet of all the men in the Light Division, mending, cooking, sleeping in castles, when they can be commandeered, or rolled up in the blanket on the ground, Juana endured all with the wonderful resilience of the young.

With this delightfully romantic plot, Miss Heyer also tells the story of the Allied British, Spanish and Portuguese Peninsular campaign against the French from Badajos on the Portuguese border, over the Pyrenees, to Toulouse in France, where word of Napoleon's abdication and exile to Elba ended Wellington's march.

An interesting facet of this novel is the evolution of character sketches of the various officers under whom Brigade-Major Smith served. Among them: Vandeleur, Skerrett, Colborne, Barnard, and, of course, the Commander, the Duke of Wellington, of whom a member of his staff said:

> . . . You could not look at his calm profile without acquiring a feeling of boundless confidence, and he had a knack of appearing without warning amongst hardly-pressed troops which always turned the tide in favour of the Allied army. Nothing ever ruffled his calm in battle. You would not have known him for the same man who, in his office, displayed such alarming irritability whenever anything went awry. He could rally demoralized troops by merely putting himself in their midst; and if, in the stress of circumstances, their fire grew ragged, he could steady it just by saying in his loud, cheerful way: "That's right, my lads; take your time! No hurrying now!" as though they were at target-practice.

### An Infamous Army

Brussels, preceding the famous Battle of Waterloo, was gay and brimful of activity. Many English families were visiting the Capital of

201

Belgium in that Spring of 1815 and one of England's renowned regiments was headquartered there. There were also Dutch, German, and, of course, Belgian troops quartered in the surrounding area. The Duke of Wellington and his staff were attending a Congress in Vienna, when news of Napoleon's escape from Elba and landing in the south of France filtered into the Belgian capital. Thus, Miss Heyer had a perfect setting for her novel and, gradually and suspensefully, moves the plot toward the day of the famous battle. The romantic escapist reader will revel in the balls, the luncheons, the picnics in and about Brussels, all the while tension and anxiety are mounting with rumors of Napoleon's approach to Paris and the massing of the French troops.

The author's account of the Battle of Waterloo doesn't let the reader down. Graphically described are the combined allied forces lined up in full battle regalia and colors, regiment after regiment. There are dragoons, cavalry, artillery, infantry, horse guards, light bobs, and riflemen. There is the excitement of the men and horses. There are the generals, all ready at their command posts. There is Wellington, in his conservative attire and with his innate ability to rally and inspire his men, riding from position to position wherever the forces needed encouragement. There is the impact of the overwhelming majority of the French forces.

With the exception of Wellington himself, fictional characters predominate in this novel: Colonel Audley on Wellington's staff, and Lord Worth's brother, shocks his family and the rest of Brussels by becoming engaged to the naughty Lady Barbara Childe. Babs, an incorrigible flirt, reaches the zenith of impertinence in a flirtation with Lady Worth's brother, Sir Peregrine, whose wife, the mother of two children and expecting a third, is not in a happy frame of mind to begin with. Naturally, the engagement is broken.

There is the usual Heyer twist in plot here, however, with the goody-goody protegé of Lady Worth, Miss Devinish, doing something horrible—contracting a secret marriage with Lord George Alastair!—and the beautiful selfish Lady Babs, rising to the occasion in a novel manner when the wounded soldiers drift back to Brussels during the Battle, by assisting Lady Worth to bind their wounds, give them cheer, ease their death, and prove to all that she *is* worthy of the Colonel!

One suspects from the epic nature of these two novels and their romantic plot that the author may have had the movies in mind when they were written 25 odd years ago. Despite the lapse of time, however, they have stood up well as novels. Always entertaining and a good storyteller, Miss Heyer has delineated here a detailed slice of British history, as well as the British national character. Timely, too, in view of the recent resurgence of interest in British history due to the death and funeral of Sir Winston Churchill, these two novels are recommended to all.

**194. "Fiction,"** *Kirkus Reviews* **33, 1 September 1965, p. 938:**

Heyer, Georgette *Frederica*. Dutton, $4.95.

The plot of Miss Heyer's latest *jeu d'esprit* is so light that it floats off the page. In this lavender-sprinkled world of Regency froth, foppery, tone and entrenched virginity, live girls whose delicate existences are "quarrels about rosebuds and pink gauze", and young men with unimpeachable intentions. The clockwork story reveals the social-climbing ambitions of Miss Frederica Merriwell. Frederica has brought her adorably irresistible sister Charis into London and hopes that their cousin, the Marquis of Alverstoke, will arange that Charis have a proper coming out, or social debut. Meanwhile, the Marquis is being harassed by a sister and a cousin for aid in *their* daughter's [sic] coming out parties. Frederica, 24, is the head of a small family, which includes besides Charis, three very bright brothers. For the interminable revelation of personal relationships, Frederica is an apt device, as the determined girl runs on like a fiddlestick. Artifice is all and the climax is an aborted elopement cross-indexed with Frederica's capitulation to the Marquis . . . . For the carriage trade, an audience which is readily identifiable as Miss Heyer's very own.

**195. Elizabeth Bower,"Romantic Reading," *Punch* 249, No. 6530 (3 November 1965), p. 666:**

*Frederica*. Georgette Heyer. Bodley Head. 21/-

Regency *ton*: cynical and of course highly eligible peer involves himself with poor but intelligent heroine, who hopes to marry off extremely beautiful sister. The plan fails but she marries instead, after allowing young brother to go on near tragic balloon ascent. Stylish, witty and bang up to the mark for all Heyer fans.

**196. Elizabeth O'Rourke (New Brunswick, N.J.), *Best Sellers* 25, 17 (1 December 1965), p. 351:**

*Frederica*. Dutton. 384 pp. $4.95

Indubitably, her most engaging heroine, and also one of her most entertaining novels, *Frederica* is Georgette Heyer's latest book. In it, Miss Heyer has managed to bridge the gap between the beautifully elegant Regency period, at which she excels, and the upcoming industrial age.

About the plot—Frederica, an older sister, has been left with the responsibility of raising three younger brothers and a debutante sister. She is most anxious that Charis, an unspoiled beauty, shall have her chance at a brilliant match, so she takes her and her teenage brothers to London where she applies to her distant cousin, a confirmed, cynical bachelor, the Marquis, for an introduction to society. By a twist of fate, it is Frederica who is on the brink of a brilliant marriage at the end of the story, and Charis who is involved in a romance with a handsome, though not affluent suitor.

Just as interesting are the lively, energetic young brothers—Jeremy [sic] destined for the cloth and a scholar, and Felix, the 12-year-old potential inventor and explorer. It is Felix who introduces the Marquis, steeped in the tradition of early 19th Century England and reluctant to accept change, to the intricacies of a foundry.

And it is here that Miss Heyer has departed from her previous Regency novels, for, obviously, without actually mentioning dates, the author means to convey the advent of the industrial-revolution. Interwoven into the plot through the ebullient enthusiasm of Felix are locomotives, steamboats, and a hair-raising balloon ascension. Of course, there are the usual balls, dinners, and parties with which Miss Heyer's Regency novels abound. Miss Heyer has spanned the Regency period of spoiled dandies and matchmaking females and the mechanical-transportation era most successfully, all the while producing a bright, colorful novel.

**197. Katherine Tappert Willis (Trustee, The Morristown Lib., Morristown, N.J.),** *Library Journal* **90 (15 December 1965), p. 5416:**

Heyer, Georgette. *Frederica*. 384 pp. Dutton. $4.95

Regency London and the country are never dull in a novel by the famous Georgette. "The Season" with its balls and operas and the race meetings is the setting for the gay Frederica and her impecunious Marriville [sic] family—brothers and sister Charis who is to be the belle of the season. There are ups and downs, of course, but as in every Heyer novel all comes right and the Marrivilles are fairly well settled in life as the story ends. Every fiction collection will add one or more copies of *Frederica*. It is a gay, amusing, and useful novel without one touch of today's agonies which recommends it to more readers than at first seems possible—or likely.

**1966**

**198. Elizabeth O'Rourke (New Brunswick, N.J.),** *Best Sellers* **25, 23 (1 March 1966), p. 440:**

Heyer, Georgette. *The Corinthian*. Dutton. 244 pp. $3.95

*The Corinthian* is a 1966 reissue of a novel originally published in the

United States in 1941 under the title *Beau Wyndham*.

This is a light, frothy novel lacking the virtuosity in plotting and the colorful detail of some of Miss Heyer's other books. Yet, as is the case with all of Miss Heyer's novels, this book is recommended for its sheer entertainment value.

The plot involves a runaway heiress, Penelope Creed, and The Corinthian, a young man of fashion, who unwittingly, while he is quite drunk, catches her as she descends, via knotted sheets, from the window of her aunt's London home.

Discovering they are both in the same predicament—Wyndham's mother and sister having badgered him into proposing to an unwanted fiancee and Pen's aunt pushing her into an unfortunate marriage with a cousin—they flee London, disguised as a young student and his tutor. As the plot develops, they take the stagecoach to the scene of Pen's childhood, where she thinks her childhood playmate will be awaiting her. The stagecoach overturns and seeking lodging in an inn, the two runaways become involved with a Bow Street Runner and a group of thieves. Ultimately, they reach Pen's old home to find her sweetheart involved in another romance; there is a murder, apprehension of the thieves and of course the inevitable romantic ending.

Miss Heyer's fans will enjoy this novel, but may be a little disappointed that it does not come up to her usual standards.


**199. Jessie Kitching, "Forecasts (Fiction)," *Publishers Weekly* 189 (20 June 1966), p. 77:**

*These Old Shades*. *Devil's Cub*. Georgette Heyer. Dutton, $4.95, each.

Fans of Georgette Heyer have a five-fold treat in store for them this fall. Dutton is bringing out in the U.S.A. five of her bright, entertaining novels. *These Old Shades*, a period romance set around 1750, and *Devil's Cub*, a sequel about some of the same people 25 years later, both will be published August 31. On October 14, *The Conqueror*, a novel about William of Normandy, will appear. The last two to be published here this year will be *The Convenient Marriage*, a late 18th century story, and *Regency Buck*, set in 1811. These will appear December 2, priced at $4.95 each.

## 200. Leonore Fleischer, "Forecast of Paperbacks," *Publishers Weekly* 190 (26 September 1966), p. 137:

*Frederica*. Georgette Heyer. Avon Books, $.75.

Miss Heyer's Regency romances are delightful; like sherbet on a hot day, they melt on contact with the mind and leave a refreshing aftertaste. This, her latest, was a #1 best seller in London last year. With wit and style, she stages a battle of the sexes between London's leading beauty and London's most notorious rake, as Frederica schemes to marry off her sister well, and affluently.

## 201. Genevieve M. Casey (State Librarian, Michigan State Library, Lansing, Mich.), *Best Sellers* 26, 16 (15 November 1966), pp. 309-10:

Heyer, Georgette. *The Conqueror*. Dutton. 377 p. $4.95

Nine hundred years have passed now since the Battle of Hastings, which seated William of Normandy on the throne of England. No more graceful [?] of this anniversary could be imagined, than Georgette Heyer's fictional biography, *The Conqueror*.

William emerges as a strong, complex, imaginative man. When his mother, the daughter of a burgher, presented her little illegitimate son with love and pride to his father, Count Robert of Normandy, she predicted to everyone's astonishment that her child would be a king. From the moment when the infant grasped his father's sword with a strength unusual in so young a babe, William showed himself a leader among men.

Georgette Heyer reveals William through the admiring eyes of the knight Raoul de Harcourt, son of a Norman nobleman, who became William's man and friend, giving him perfect loyalty all his life. It was

Raoul who watched over William's sleep when barons in his own retinue would have murdered him in the night to prevent his mastery of all of Normandy. It was Raoul who perceived William's sanity and gentleness. Raoul who realized that because William was a strong man, more able than his brutal contemporaries to take the long view, he could treat his enemies with impersonal mercy.

It was to Raoul that William confided his revolutionary idea of using archers in battle. For the first time warfare became a matter of guided missiles, as it were, instead of hand-to-hand combat. Whether this advance in military tactics, which had its modern fruition in Hiroshima and now in the inter-continental ballistic missile, has in fact served the course of human civilization, could be questioned; but there is no doubt that it led William the Norman directly to victory over King Henry of France and to his coronation, one cold Christmas day in Westminster Abbey, as King of England.

Love, as well as war, was brutal in the Eleventh Century. The time of the troubadors strumming out songs of love beneath a lady's window had not yet arrived. When Matilda, Duchess of Flanders, haughtily refused William's proposal of marriage, with reference to his bastard birth, William wooed her with a show of Norman armies and a whipping in the presence of her ladies-in-waiting. Nevertheless, Matilda came to William willingly, loved him truly, and bore him many children.

William the Conqueror was an interesting man, far ahead of his times in subtlety, in military strategy, in political acumen and Georgette Heyer catches his complexity.

Her novel is primarily valuable, however, not so much as a portrait of a man, as it is a portrait of a period in the history of Western Europe. *The Conqueror* grew out of an incredible amount of historical research into the way of life, the way of speech, the way of thought, and feeling, and praying in the Eleventh Century. Without sacrificing the flow of her plot, Miss Heyer conveys an understanding of this period, more authentic as well as more colorful than many historical tomes. It is obvious in reading this novel that Georgette Heyer, who has previously published over 30 of the historical romances, is indeed a mistress of her craft.

**202. "Paperbacks. General Fiction,"** *Best Sellers* **26, 18 (15 December 1966), p. 354:**

*Frederika* [sic] by Georgette Heyer is a charming and expert historical novel (Avon. $0.75).

**203. Rollene W. Saal, "Pick of the Paperbacks, Fiction,"** *Saturday Review,* **17 December 1966, p. 36:**

*Frederica.* By Georgette Heyer. Avon. $.75
    The latest recipe from the queen of the Regency, a delight for her multitude of admirers, contains the staple ingredients—romance, adventure, maidenly modesty, and gallantry, all askew.

**204. Leonore Fleischer, "Forecast of Paperbacks. Fiction,"** *Publishers Weekly* **190 (26 December 1966), p. 101:**

*The Reluctant Widow.* Georgette Heyer. Ace Star Books, $.50
    Another delightful comedy-romance from this mistress of escape reading. As usual, the setting is Regency England, where young Elinor makes a very strange marriage that leaves her a widow on the same night that she becomes a bride; she finds herself mistress of a huge estate and in love with her late husband's cousin, who has mysterious plans . . . involving her.

### 1967

**205. Barbara A. Bannon, "Forecasts. Fiction,"** *Publishers Weekly* **191 (23 January 1967), p. 256:**

*Black Sheep.* Georgette Heyer. Dutton, $4.95
    Miss Heyer has never been in better form than in this very funny Regency romance set in Bath, wherein a seemingly sedate maiden lady who is all of "eight and twenty" undertakes to save her young niece from a "ramshackle youth" who is a fortune hunter. In doing so she, herself,

falls victim, very prettily, to the young man's "black sheep" uncle. The conversation is delightful, full of all sorts of quizzical period slang, and the hero and heroine (older style) make a most spirited Beatrice and Benedict.


**206.** *Kirkus Reviews* **35 (1 February 1967), p. 155:**

Heyer, Georgette. *Black Sheep*. Dutton, $4.95
   This is one of Georgette Heyer's dimpled diversions, indeed, sunny as a buttercup, somewhat more simply plotted than some of her earlier low intrigues in the high society of Bath during the Regency. For the most part it concerns Miss Abby, "a mere twenty-eight years in her dish," and the surrogate guardian of her niece Fanny whose mother committed some unidentified indiscretion. Fanny now falls in love with Stacy Calverleigh, a fortune hunter, who proposes—heavens, horrors, an elopement to Gretna Green, while Abby falls in love with his uncle who is none other than the man Fanny's mother had run away with . . . . *Black Sheep*, more lace than wool, and triumphant trivia.


**207.** *The Booklist* **63, 14 (15 March 1967), p. 765:**

Heyer, Georgette. *The Convenient Marriage.* 1966. 279 pp. Dutton, $4.95.
   Similar in style to the author's *Frederica* . . . , *Regency Buck*, . . . and her many other Regency novels which combine humor, suspense, and romance. Here, Horatia Winwood rescues her older sister from an undesired marriage to Lord Rule by proposing to Rule herself. After the marriage Horatia's friendship is subtly sought by Lord Lethbridge, Rule's enemy. Light entertainment for women, especially Heyer devotees.
—*Regency Buck*. 1966. 332 pp. Dutton, $4.95
   Light and frothy, in the vein of the author's other Regency novels,

this follows the fortunes of Miss Judith Taverner and her brother, Sir Peregrine, recently orphaned and appointed wards of the elegant Lord Worth, a stranger to the young Taverners. A mystery develops as Lord Worth turns away Miss Taverner's suitors and it becomes apparent someone is trying to kill Peregrine. A good introduction to Heyer's period stories. . . .

**208. Barbara A. Bannon, "Forecasts. Fiction,"** *Publishers Weekly* **191 (5 June 1967), p. 169:**

*The Talisman Ring* and *Faro's Daughter*. Georgette Heyer. Dutton. $4.95 each.

To this reviewer, reading Georgette Heyer is the next best thing to reading Jane Austen. Dutton is going to make her steadily increasing band of fans madly happy by bringing back into print in early August two earlier Heyer Regency romances formerly published in this country by Doubleday (the first in 1937, the second in 1942), both long out of print.

In *The Talisman Ring*, a long-lost family heirloom, a young heir falsely accused of murder, a band of smugglers, two utterly delightful Heyer heroines, a taciturn but highly resourceful older gentleman—all play their parts in a tale funny enough to have you laughing aloud. We particularly enjoyed the conversation of pert Eustacie, a refugee from the guillotine, who speaks a most delightful *franglaise* at times, and English Miss Thane, who has been longing all her life for a Romantic Adventure.

*Faro's Daughter* introduces a heroine who is even more dashing than most Heyer girls. She is nothing less than a faro dealer in a notorious London gambling establishment run by her aunt. Needless to say, this leads to all sorts of complications, not the least being that her virtue is continually being called into question. Deb is equal to all challenges, however, and trumps the hand of her most persistent antagonist in a fine romantic faradiddle. *Dutton now has 157,000 copies of all its Heyer books in print.*

**209.   Barbara A. Bannon, "Forecasts. Fiction,"** *Publishers Weekly* **191 (19 June 1967), p. 87:**

*Devil's Cub. These Old Shades. The Corinthian.*   Georgette Heyer. Bantam Books, $.75 each title.

With these three, Bantam joins Ace in publishing Miss Heyer's work. As far as we know, there will be no overlap of titles; you can buy it in Ace or Bantam but not both.   These novels are the popular Regency romances; they sell quite well, as do the Ace titles.  But we *must* put in a word about the covers, since many paperback buyers *do* judge a book by them. These are insipid, chocolate-boxy, pretty-pretty, silk-and-satin-and-pink jobs, *à la* Emilie Loring, stressing the romantic, ladylike aspects of the novels.  Miss Heyer deserves better than this.  Her books sparkle with wit and style, and many intelligent readers who aren't familiar with her work will be turned off by these covers.  On the other hand, the ladies who devour pink-and-blue romances will get rather more than they paid for.   Don't hesitate to recommend these to the most discriminating reader of fiction, cover or no cover.

*Arabella.*  Georgette Heyer.  Ace Star Books, $.60.

Another of Miss Heyer's famous and justly popular Regency romances, in which a young girl meets and conquers the suitor of her choice.  In this one the heroine is a charming young thing from the country; the man she's set her bonnet for is a sophisticated London bachelor and a confirmed one.  Will she get him?  You can bet your pantalettes she will! Georgette Heyer tells the story with wit and style.

**210.   Elizabeth O'Rourke (New Brunswick, N.J.),** *Best Sellers* **27, 9 (1 August 1967), p. 171:**

Heyer, Georgette. *Black Sheep*. Dutton. 255 p. $4.95

*Black Sheep* is another of Georgette Heyer's delightful frothy Regency romances, replete with a high-spirited heroine, a rakish hero, an intriguing plot and wonderful characterizations.

This new novel is set in Bath, where Abby Wendover lives with her older sister Selina and her niece Fanny. At 28, Abigail, witty, attractive, and still sought after, has no inclination to marry but expects to devote herself to hypochondriac Selina, while finding a suitable match for her heiress niece, Fanny. Returning from a visit to London, Abby finds Fanny infatuated with a very attractive but undesirable young man, Stacy Caverleigh [sic], and after appraising the situation, she is for once in accord with brother James's opinion that young Stacy is a fortune-hunter. Although absent on the family estates in Bedfordshire, James Wendover's presence is felt and opinion is weighed before any decision is made by the Wendover sisters.

Quite unexpectedly, Caverleigh's uncle, Miles, the "black sheep" of the Caverleigh family has come to Bath with no knowledge of his nephew's involvement with the Wendovers, or presence in Bath, for that matter.

From then on, the delightful plot and counter-plots develop, with Miles courting Abby to the consternation of Selina, James, and their conservative Bath friends.

Illness, circumventing Fanny's elopement with Stacy, allows time for the intervention of another supposed heiress, who attracts Stacy's attention, thus disillusioning Fanny.

Finally, all of the problems are happily resolved, and after a surprise climax, there is the inevitable happy ending.

Miss Heyer's thorough knowledge of the Regency period provides this novel with an authentic background. However, in this book, she does not allow herself to overindulge in descriptive passages, nor the language of the era, which in some of her former novels had a tendency to intrude on the story line.

A thoroughly enjoyable book, *Black Sheep* is recommended for summer reading.

**211. Barbara A. Bannon, "Fiction Forecasts,"** *Publishers Weekly* **192 (11 September 1967), p. 67:**

*Royal Escape* and *The Masqueraders*. Georgette Heyer. Dutton, $4.95 each

Most of the Georgette Heyer novels Dutton has been bringing back into print have been sparkling Regency comedies. These two move backwards in time to the romantic days of the ill-fated Stuarts. *Royal Escape* is a very well-written historical novel dealing with Charles II's escape after the Battle of Worcester. Those gallant, doomed Cavaliers and ladies who gave their all for the Stuart cause are re-created with great charm, and the King, himself, emerges as an appealing and tragic human being.

*The Masqueraders*, which dates from 1928, is pure romance all the way, the kind of light, frothy, never-never-land fiction that no one is writing nowadays. It all has to do with a brother and sister, adventurers both, the children of the rogue adventurer of them all, who are fleeing a secret Jacobite past. To escape, they exchange roles, and if in the context of 1967 this sounds sniggeringly suggestive, all we can say is that in Miss Heyer's deft hands it is quite delightful. No end of quixotic adventures ensue, with the boy proving himself very much a man, and the girl succumbing to love in a most feminine fashion.

**212.  Lucille G. Crane (Scottsdale, Arizona), *Best Sellers* 27, 12 (15 September 1967), pp. 229-30:**

Heyer, Georgette. *Faro's Daughter* and *The Talisman Ring*. Dutton, 278 and 297 pp., resp., $4.95 each

In a world that is concerned with the intense and serious problems of world peace, a war that is not a war, racial injustice and civil disobedience, an escape into the world of Georgette Heyer's Regency period has some merit in itself. As she describes it, everyone knows his place in the social structure and therefore can enjoy society of man in its fullest. The results are amusing and wholly enjoyable. The requirements for enjoyment, however, are an interest in things English and romantic.

*Faro's Daughter* hinges on the desire of Max Ravenscar to save his cousin, still a minor, from marrying a lady who is considered unsuitable because she lives with and helps an aunt who runs a gambling house. The fact that Deborah Grantham, who is a highly honorable young lady, has never had any intention of marrying Lord Maplethorpe precipitates the conflict. She takes offense when Max tries to bribe her. Each then tries to best the other and misunderstandings result on both sides. Ravenscar, who is excessively wealthy and seldom opposed by anyone, finds his match in the lively Miss Grantham, who is highly intelligent and almost as willful as her foe. They eventually recognize their true feelings and fall in love. Lord Maplethorpe, in the meantime, with some assistance from Deborah, meets and marries a fragile lovely thing that brings out his sense of responsibility and has the approval of his mother and cousin. The battle of wits is delightful.

*The Talisman Ring* is a mystery of sorts in which the heir to Lavenham Court cannot claim his due because he has been accused of murder. The real murderer has stolen the ring and it must be found in his possession to clear Ludovic. The spirited young buck has his own ideas of proving his innocence, all of them without consideration for his safety; but his cousin Sir Tristram comes to his assistance in a more practical and staid manner. Their efforts are often helped and hindered by their cousin Eustacie who is a refugee from the French Revolution and wants adventure in any shape or form. Sarah Thane innocently enters the scene and becomes embroiled in the hi-jinks that follow. The solution is satisfactory to all concerned, including the reader. The true culprit is arrested and the proper couples fall in love. The comic character of Sarah's brother is quite hilarious. The setting is the country and almost entirely in a village inn. It all is too full of fun and comedy to be concerned with a capital crime, but the nature of the people makes it quite plausible.

The people in these two novels, as well as others in Miss Heyer's long list of books, are stock characters and are much the same from book to book. The conclusions are usually predictable, but that does not lessen interest in the action. It is the prancing good nature of the tales that pleases. You come away chuckling at the foppishness of the beaux, the liveliness and beauty of the heroines, the strength of the heroes.

Everyone recognizes the need for suitable marriage and the novels are concerned with this problem, with class lines kept very distinct. The homes are described well and are usually in Grosvenor Square (London) or a mansion in the country. The clothing is minutely detailed for both men and women, but the description of men's attire has caught Miss Heyer's imagination and she loves to explain the folds of the cravat and the cut of the coat. The slang, which should puzzle the American reader, does not. In itself it brings alive an era, all gaily packaged for our entertainment.

These two novels are reprints of works previously published. When I read them in their English edition the print was poor and the binding and paper inferior. This new edition has much improved the print, binding and paper. Obviously, the publishers have recognized the consistent popularity of Miss Heyer's work (as I have also observed over the years) and produced a welcome reissue for the old and new Georgette Heyer fans. A firm and grateful thank you.

**213.** *Best Sellers* **27, 17 (1 December 1967), pp. 345-46:**

Heyer, Georgette. *The Masqueraders* and *Royal Escape*. Dutton. 288 and 430 pp. resp. $4.95 each

The reissue of these early (1928 and 1939 respectively) Heyer novels is testimony to the popularity of this facile writer, an enduring popularity.

*The Masqueraders* takes an incredible plot and deftly makes it plausible and amusing—a young man, not yet 20, after involvement in the 1749 Jacobite uprising in England, has to take to flight dressed as a girl while his sister, who accompanies him, pretends to be a boy; they rescue an heiress, for whom the disguised brother forms a great affection, while the sister-masking-as-a-boy falls for the heiress's supposed fiance.

*Royal Escape* however centers around the historical incidents of Charles II's flight after the defeat of his armies at Worcester in 1651 and around the loyal men and women who helped him, risking their lives to do so. Charles makes a dashing hero, even in flight, even hiding for a day in a leafy tree.

## 1968

**214. Lucille G. Crane (Scottsdale, Arizona),** *Best Sellers* **27, 23 (1 March 1968), p. 451:**

Heyer, Georgette. *Beauvallet* and *The Black Moth*. Dutton. 244 and 326 pp. $4.95 each

The reissue of Georgette Heyer's early historical novels is a welcome event. The two under consideration here are of 1920 vintage and show the author at the beginning of her career as the writer of the ever popular Regency novels. Her later books show a refinement of technique which is lacking in these earlier efforts; but her romantic formula is much the same in all.

*Beauvallet* precedes the author's favorite historical period by several dynasties. Beauvallet is the contemporary of Drake and Raleigh and the scene shifts from the privateer *Venture* to the Court of Elizabeth I and Spain of the Inquisition. The beautiful Senora Dominica is the cause of the hero's adventures. He captures and sinks the ship in which she and her father are returning to Spain and he gallantly offers to sail them home himself. That he falls in love with the heroine at first sight is inevitable and he promises to come to Spain for her within a year. Beauvallet's daring disguise and cleverness bring him success in spite of imprisonment and flashing blades.

The author's creation of environment based on her solid knowledge of the social history of the past gives us, among other things, the impression of the richness of the silk materials, the grandeur of aristocratic living and the London of this period.

There is much that is enjoyable here, in spite of the stock characterization. The British Protestant point of view is reflected in the description of the Spanish Inquisition, but since the religious and political parts of the novel are only minor, not much can be made of the matter. This is entirely a story of adventure and romance.

*The Black Moth* brings us to the Regency period of knee breeches. The Black Moth, Lord Andover, is the villain of the novel; but he is a gentleman of high birth living within a code that he and those he opposes accept and understand, so that he seems about as dangerous as a moth. The story is advanced by action, rather than by psychological interpretation. Lord John has taken the blame for his brother Richard's cheating at cards and, according to the code, goes into self-imposed exile on the Continent. When he returns to England and becomes a highwayman for the fun and adventure he thwarts the kidnapping of the fair Diana by Lord Andover and John is wounded. Nursed back to health by Diana, he feels he cannot marry her because of his disgrace. Another kidnapping by Andover lets John come to the rescue with sword flashing. It is all very melodramatic and one wonders at oneself enjoying this kind of thing.

Georgette Heyer has a following that will be delighted with these two additions to the American bookshelves. What she writes currently shows growth and skill in handling a story which is more compact and more filled with witty conversation. The earlier books have stilted conversation and do not produce the chuckles one has learned to expect. Miss Heyer's efforts are always enjoyable, however, in spite of the defects in technique we are all so fond of criticising. My recommendation is: Read and Enjoy!

**215.** *Kirkus Reviews* **36 (15 April 1968), p. 486:**

Heyer, Georgette. *Powder and Patch*. Dutton $4.95
    One of the new appearances of one of the favorite old ones, for her retinue.

**216. Barbara A. Bannon, "Forecasts. Fiction,"** *Publishers Weekly* **193 (13 May 1968), p. 54:**

*Powder and Patch*. Georgette Heyer. Dutton $4.95
    An early (1923) Georgette Heyer novel, originally published as *The*

*Transformation of Philip Jettan*, this amiable trifle is a pretty little pink and white bonbon, merely a foretaste of the elegant Heyer wit to come. Nevertheless, its tale of a country bumpkin transformed into a sophisticated 18th century gallant so that he may win the lady of his choice, does have a period charm that will please all Miss Heyer's devoted fans.

**217.  *Best Sellers* 28, 6 (15 June 1968), p. 128:**

Heyer, Georgette. *Powder and Patch*. Dutton. 233 pp. $4.95

Under the original title of *The Transformation of Philip Jettan*, this novel was first published in England in 1923. It is, therefore, one of the earliest of Georgette Heyer's pleasantly amusing historical novels which critics have recognized as in the tradition of Jane Austen. It is an unabashed romance about a country girl coming into London to enter its social life and a young dandy who, to woo and win her, adopts extremes of the current fashions of the Regency period, only to find that his tactic repels the object of his affections. She, Cleone, becomes so confused that she gets herself engaged to two other men, neither of whom she likes enough to marry. Of course, it is Philip Jettan who finally straightens things out and all ends happily as anyone could have predicted. Not perhaps as finished or as subtle as her later novels, this is still skillfully done and makes pleasant and chucklesome reading. This is its first publication in the United States.

**218.  Barbara A. Bannon, "Forecast. Fiction," *Publishers Weekly* 194, 9 September 1968, p. 55:**

*Cousin Kate*. Georgette Heyer. Dutton, $4.95

Departing, only momentarily, we hope, from the elegant quadrilles and polished flirtations of her amusing Regency romances, Miss Heyer serves up a very different sort of tale in the same period setting, nothing less than a full-fledged Gothic. And a very expert job she does of it, too,

219

complete with remote and forbidding country house, screams in the night, dark hints of something best left unmentioned in a family heritage, and one of those plucky Heyer heroines, Cousin Kate, a poor relation brought into the aristocratic Broome household with a very nasty fate indeed planned for her. No Heyer girl was ever downed so easily, however, and gamine Kate, aided by a dashing cavalier and the earthy family of her old nurse, wins out. The Gothic gloom and doom is nicely leavened with wit, romance and wonderful period slang. This is Miss Heyer's first new novel since *Black Sheep*. Dutton now has 21 of her titles in print.

**219.  *Kirkus Review* 36, 15 September 1968, p. 1073:**

Heyer, Georgette. *Cousin Kate*. Dutton $4.95

Even though T. E. White said he couldn't read Georgette Heyer without a nose clip, there's a wide audience that inhales happily, not only smelling salts and arnica, but whiffs of green goose and calves' feet, not to mention aromatic romance. Actually this is a simpler story than any Georgette Heyer has done, not all those Regency Wodehousehold mixups, and it concerns Kate Malvern, unmoneyed but a "precious lambkin" all the same and her stay at Stapleton with her ambitious Aunt Matilda and ailing Uncle Timothy. Aunt Matilda's generosity and graciousness are not altogether unmotivated—she would like Kate to marry her son Torquil, a definitely erratic boy who proves to be totally unhinged (a murderer). Instead there's Philip, a cousin, whom Kate finds at first "odious" but then decisive and attractive. You know it well—muslins starched along with backbones and the Heyeroglyphics are just as easy to read as they are to decipher.

**220.  Sumika Yamashita (Oakland Public Library, Calif.), *Library Journal* 93, 15 November 1968, p. 4427:**

Heyer, Georgette. *Cousin Kate*. 318 pp. Dutton. $4.95

A writer whose forte is Regency period manners, mores and romance includes those elements in this novel but gives emphasis to a grim plot about succession and madness. Kate, an orphaned and penniless young lady, is befriended by a hitherto unknown aunt and installed in luxury at Staplewood. She begins to suspect that her aunt's kindnesses cloak a cruel plan and finds that she is the intended bride of her beautiful but mad young cousin. With the aid of Philip, her new fiance, she is able to escape this fate, but not before a sad and gruesome climax. Y[oung] A[dult] girls who delight in witty Regency pieces will be interested in this slightly different piece from Miss Heyer.

## 1969

**221. *Kirkus Reviews* 37, 9 (1 May 1969), p. 534:**

Heyer, Georgette. *Duplicate Death*. Dutton. $4.95

This while modern (originally 1951) is still one of Miss Heyer's relatively older-fashioned auctions and Whissht you're off in that elegant world where a mesalliance is almost a dirtier word than murder. . . the former when baronet-to-be Timothy is about to marry a social unknown Beulah Birtley. . . the latter when the lady for whom she works and a guest are strangled at and following a duplicate Bridge party. . . . Even double dummy it's hard to reconstruct but it will be surely enjoyed by the large audience who find her "Such a pet."

**222. "Clue Works," *Best Sellers* 29, 6 (15 June 1969), p. 117:**

. . . In an intricately devised plot, written as usual in her definitely elegant style, Miss Heyer triumphs once again in her earlier metier. The duplicate-bridge party given by a dubious social-climbing hostess is the scene for double murder. Inspector Hemingway is at his rueful best in sorting out the grab-bag of ill assorted characters, all of whom have very good reasons for not being entirely cooperative. In attempting to beat the Inspector at his own game, the reader has no easy task, particularly as the second victim seemed the logical choice in accounting for the first murder. *Duplicate Death* (Dutton. 271 pp., $4.95) is an intriguing story.


**223. "Fiction. Schemes & Schemata: Mysteries & Science Fiction," *Kirkus Reviews* 37, 12 (15 June 1969), p. 654:**

Heyer, Georgette. *Detection Unlimited*. Dutton. $4.95
In Miss Heyer's detective novels, as well as her romances, conversation and speculation lend themselves to purposeful gossip, this time in a small, inveterately British community where one Sampson Warrenby—"bit of an outsider" and "dreadfully underbred" is murdered. Then there's his niece, "no oil painting," along with other residents—among them a young couple and baby with an undisclosed past and a writer with a gimpy leg and a nasty tongue whose brother committed suicide. Or did he? Artful deceit for the Heyerarchy.


**224. Barbara A. Bannon, "Fiction Forecast. Mystery and Suspense," *Publishers Weekly* 195 (30 June 1969), p. 62:**

*Detection Unlimited*. Georgette Heyer. Dutton, $4.95
The first American publication of a Georgette Heyer mystery originally published in Britain in 1953, this is agreeable escapism, light summer fare for those who enjoy reading about the English country gentry, tennis and lawn parties, genteel murder. There is something of the flavour of Angela Thirkell's romantic comedies to Miss Heyer's tale of an ingrown village society where everyone tries to play detective and not even sudden death can disturb the local caste system. A period piece in a way, but a pleasantly engaging one.

**225. Allen J. Hubin, "Criminals At Large,"** *The New York Times Book Review,* **24 August 1969, p. 22:**

Owing to a lingering fondness for duplicate bridge, I was prepared to like Georgette Heyer's *Duplicate Death*, a 1951 novel now disinterred by Dutton ($4.95) for first publication in this country. And I was not disappointed, for Miss Heyer presents an admirable puzzle concerning an unlovable specimen about whose neck someone looped a length of piano wire while he absented himself from the table. The proceedings are adorned with acid observations on the antics of the upper British crust around a deck of cards, and the diverting verbal sparring between Inspectors Hemingway and Grant. But take note: Miss Heyer's amusing style is not designed for skimming, and she seems capable of challenging Victor Hugo in the long-sentence stakes.

**226. "Clue Works,"** *Best Sellers* **29, 11 (1 September 1969), p. 203:**

. . .Georgette Heyer's *Detection Unlimited* (Dutton. 288 pp., $4.95) dates itself by reference to ration requirements in England early in the 1950s, but is published here for the first time. Set in the small village of Thornden, it involves the murder of a most odious sort of social climber and gives Chief Inspector Stanley Hemingway one of his "nice" problems. Hemingway is worth meeting. He has humor and wit and a way with him that should charm readers, even if the murder and its consequences (the entire village starts theorizing about "who-dun-it") may be a bit tedious . . . .

**227.** *Library Journal* **94, 1 November 1969, p. 4029:**

Georgette Heyer's *Detection Unlimited* (Dutton. $4.95) shows a more orderly England [than Gordon M. Williams' *The Siege of Trencher's Farm*] with Inspector Hemingway at work in the village of Thornden after the body of solicitor Sampson Warrenby is found in his

223

garden. No one in the village liked Warrenby, and everyone has his own solution for the crime. Leisurely and entertaining.

**228. "Fiction,"** *Kirkus Reviews* **37, 24 (15 December 1969), p. 1343:**

Heyer, Georgette *The Unfinished Clue*. Dutton $4.95
    The unfinished clue in this British-country-house do, by chatty Miss Heyer, is an incomplete word scribbled by the dying hand of thoroughly nasty General Sir Arthur Billington-Smith, cordially hated by family and house guests (including a dance hall siren of voluptuous charms and hilarious vulgarity). Inspector Harding—gentry himself—rattles the teacups. Good fun—tiffs amongst the toffs.

## 1970

**229. Barbara A. Bannon, "PW Forecasts,"** *Publishers Weekly* **197 (12 January 1970), p. 60:**

*The Unfinished Clue*. Georgette Heyer. Dutton, $4.95
    Dutton, which is reissuing old Georgette Heyer mysteries, after her Regency and other romances, has come up with a 1934 example of the English country house party thriller that is such a marvelous period piece by 1970 standards it almost reads like pure camp. Stuffy old Sir Arthur, a mean martinet who is ruining the lives of his family, is done in by a Chinese dagger. A dashing Scotland Yard detective unravels the whole thing and finds romance in the process. Miss Heyer does a lovely satire of a 1930's Mexican dancer of the Lupe Velez-Yvonne de Carlo school.

**230. Sergeant Cuff, "Fiction. Criminal Record,"** *Saturday Review*, **31 January 1970, p. 38:**

***Detection Unlimited***. By Georgette Heyer. Dutton. $4.95
   Reading from left to right: the squire, the vicar, the family solicitor, the chief, and the body on the garden seat with a bullet through its brain. Now who could ask for a finer curtain-raiser than that?

**231.** *Kirkus Reviews* **38, 5 (1 March 1970), p. 282:**

Heyer, Georgette. ***Death in the Stocks***. Dutton $4.95
   Amateur sleuth Giles Carrington acquits himself as a pro in springing Cousin Tony [sic] and his charmingly scatterbrained sister Antonia from a murder charge anent the dispatching of their half-brother Arnold Vereker, found slumped in a village green stocks. Along the way another half-brother shows up and is similarly silenced. Much intra-familial bickering but Miss Meyer [sic] does rather better in country houses than in mod flats. After the stocks discovery—a rapid decline.

**232. Haskel Frankel, in "Criminal Record. Fiction,"** *The Saturday Review* **53, 25 April 1970, p. 61:**

*The Unfinished Clue*. By Georgette Heyer. Dutton. $4.95
   You know the setup: the English country weekend with an assortment of guests, including one sufficiently detestable for the others to want to murder. Well, it takes Georgette Heyer, who has written enough historical romances and thrillers to stock a library, seventy-seven pages to get someone to knock off Sir Arthur. The novel is, of course, professionally handled and the solution satisfactory, but one suspects the book will appeal more to the ladies than to the men.

**233. "Clue Works,"** *Best Sellers* **30, 3 (1 May 1970), p. 58:**

   Georgette Heyer, so long known in the U.S. as a specialist in Regency period fiction, is also a more than competent mystery writer. The publication of a new edition of her 1935 *Death in the Stocks* has a dimension that is often lacking in detective fiction, that is humor and, in this instance, a rather wild humor derived from the characters of the Vereker brother and sister, the two most suspect of the murder of their wealthy half-brother, who was found stabbed to death and sitting in the stocks near the green of Ashleigh Green not far from Hannaborough. Inspector Hannasyde of Scotland Yard and Giles Carrington, a barrister acting for the Verekers, solve the case, but still fail to explain how Arnold Vereker got put in the stocks.

**234. "Fiction. Fate Accompli: Mysteries," *Kirkus Reviews* 38, 11 (1 June 1970), p. 626:**

Heyer, Georgette. *A Blunt Instrument*. Dutton $4.95
Among the silly but engaging toffs and those of lowlier station (including a policeman who bleakly quotes Scripture) it's not too difficult to put the finger on the wielder of the blunt instrument—who did in womanizer Ernest Fletcher and finished off his blackmailer. For fanciers of willowy young men and lady novelists who wear monocles. Vintage 1938.

**235. Barbara A. Bannon, "Forecasts. Fiction," *Publishers Weekly* 198 (27 July 1970), pp. 66-7:**

*Charity Girl*. Georgette Heyer. Dutton, $5.95
This is the most delightful new Georgette Heyer Regency romance in several years. It is witty, full of dashing period slang, and it trifles with the affairs of several maids and men with such style and gentle irony that readers of good "ton," as Miss Heyer herself might put it, will find reading it a very "comfortable cose" indeed. It all begins when a chivalrous and rich young gallant takes pity on a pathetic poor relation in a neighboring family. Before long he is so entangled in his efforts to

help her that every step he takes leads to some hilarious new confusion. There is an engaging cast of supporting characters, including an old miser and the girl's rapscallion father. The romantic conclusions are not what you may expect, but that adds to the fun.

**236. "Fiction," *Kirkus Reviews* 38, 15 (1 August 1970), p. 822.:**

Heyer, Georgette. *Charity Girl*. Dutton $5.95.

Miss Heyer, in spite of her opulent output, is hardly at Point Non-Plus. This time Gretna Green is mentioned but once—when Lady Silverdale of the self-cosseting vapors fears the worst, since pathetic little Cherry, whom she had been talked into taking under her protection, and her son, disappear simultaneously. But Henna [sic] Silverdale, sensible and charming, knows better. Also Viscount Desmond [sic] who gallantly conveyed the orphaned Cherry from a Cinderella existence with a nasty aunt. It's mostly Des's bumble-broth in attending to Cherry's dreadful relatives, including Father, who turns up a barndoor savage, not to mention a fleamint, hog-grubber and lobcock. Escape-prone matrons may unpack their quizzing-glasses.

**237. "Fiction. Macabracadabra: Mysteries, Science Fiction," *Kirkus Reviews* 38, 17 (1 September 1970), p. 989:**

Heyer, Georgette. *No Wind of Blame*. Dutton $4.95

A re-issuing from Miss Heyer's Country House Party period in which limp Wally Carter, who married wealth in the still impressive form of Ermyntrude, a good hearted widow and ex-chorus girl, is done in on a rustic bridge. Inspector Hemingway politely riffles through sane and shady sorts and finally grapples with the matter of a murder weapon and a murderer with no tenable connection. Dear dead Morning Room days—unrushed, unruffling.

**238.** *Best Sellers* **30, 13 (1 October 1970), p. 267:**

*The Spanish Bride* is one of Georgette Heyer's more elaborate historical novels.


**239. Ruth A. Grossman (Milwaukee, Wisconsin), *Best Sellers* 30, 14 (15 October 1970), p. 273:**

Heyer, Georgette. *Charity Girl*. Dutton. 254 p. $5.95

For the coterie of Georgette Heyer fans, another divertissement, *Charity Girl*, has appeared on the literary scene. Essentially it is a comedy of manners, and if there is any redeeming social significance in the plot, it is that we consider the plight of the poor relation, forced to live on the largesse of any relative who will grant her shelter. And that is bestowed, more often than not, out of selfish ulterior motives, rather than generosity of spirit. The charity girl is an unpaid servant, forced to "fetch and carry" for the entire family, governess for the young, nurse for the ill, subject to the whims of her patron. She has no status above or below the stairs in the highly structured society of the Regency Period of England.

Such is the plight of aptly named Charity Steane, abandoned daughter of an unconscionable rake, Wilfred Steane, who in turn was disinherited by his irascible, miserly father, Lord Nettlecombe. Her maternal aunt, Lady Bugle, an ambitious, grasping woman with five daughters for whom she must make suitable marriages on the modest income of a small inheritance, takes her in and treats her unmercifully. When the situation becomes untenable for Charity, she runs away, with plans to throw herself on the mercy of her grandfather.

Viscount Desford, a man of impeccable antecedents, handsome, intelligent, independently wealthy, a "pink of the ton," a catch of the first water, happens upon Charity on the road to London. Taking pity, he magnanimously offers her refuge at the estate of his old and dear friend, Henrietta Silverdale, whom he cherishes as a sister, and whose hegemony is as flawless as his own.

228

After depositing Cherry, as she is known, he sets off to track down Lord Nettlecombe, who has left London to take the waters. Tearing around England in his curricle with his perfectly matched horses, he manages to overtake Cherry's grandfather at Harrowgate, only to discover that the Lord has married his common housekeeper, and that were Cherry to live under his roof, she would only be exchanging one form of bondage for another.

Meanwhile Wilfred Steane has returned from the Continent, chances upon Simon Carrington, Desford's amiable younger brother, and demands to know Desford's whereabouts, so that he can force him into marriage with Cherry to redeem his little girl's reputation which he claims has been hopelessly compromised. To forestall this, Simon fibs that Desford is indeed engaged to Henrietta, that he acted only with the purest motives.

At the final confrontation, it is revealed that Cherry, with her tarnished bloodlines, has found a suitable mate in a likeable commoner, of good nature and sturdy yeoman stock; and that both Desford and Henrietta find that Simon's little lie has much merit, and so all ends happily.

Because of the heavy reliance on coincidence and chance, it is impossible to take the excessively romantic plot of *Charity Girl* seriously, but one must be impressed with Miss Heyer's scholarship, for it is evident from the detail throughout the novel that she has made a comprehensive study of the manners of the Regency Period.

Those who read Heyer faithfully will find *Charity Girl* agreeable; those who read it as escape will find it high camp.

**240. "Serious Fiction. Paperbacks,"** *Best Sellers* **30, 16 (15 November 1970), p. 363:**

Among the reprints of interesting historical novels, there is Georgette Heyer's *Royal Escape*, concerning Charles II (Bantam. $0.95)

Typical rather than distinguished is the British-country-house mystery by Georgette Heyer, *Envious Casca* (Bantam. $0.75)

## 1971

**241. "Paperbacks. Adventure,"** *Best Sellers* **30, 21 (1 February 1971), p. 484:**

*Detection Unlimited* by Georgette Heyer is a mild story of death in an English village, with everybody working on a solution. (Bantam. $0.75).

**242. Rollene W. Saal, "Pick of the Paperbacks. Fiction,"** *Saturday Review*, **27 March 1971, p. 42:**

In *Frederica* (Avon, 75¢) the title character, one of Georgette Heyer's more adorable heroines, takes her younger sister to London for the social season, where she considers herself too long of tooth to be more than an escort (she's twenty-four, but then, this was Regency England). However, the aging chaperone has some fun, as will the reader. Though *Frederica* is a reissue, we wanted to be certain no loyal Heyer fan missed it.

**243. Rollene W. Saal, "Pick of the Paperbacks,"** *Saturday Review* **54, 27 November 1971, p. 48:**

*Five Mysteries of Georgette Heyer* (Bantam, 5 Vols. Boxed, $4.75).
Many of Georgette Heyer's millions of fans in both the U.S. and England know her for her Regency novels. How many know her detective stories? How many should? The solution can be found in this fivesome, which offers *Envious Casca*, *No Wind of Blame*, *The Unfinished Clue*, *Death in the Stocks*, and *They Found Him Dead.*

## 1972

**244. *Kirkus Reviews*, 40 (1 August 1972), p. 887:**

Heyer, Georgette. *The Toll-Gate*. Putnam $6.95

A brace of culls hop the twig before adventuring Captain Staple, formerly of the Dragoons, who hates *suitable* marriages, finds one to suit, in this re-issue of Ms. Heyer's 1954 romance. Heyer fans are insatiable.

**245. "Fiction," *Kirkus Reviews* 40 (1 September 1972), p. 1044:**

Heyer, Georgette. *Lady of Quality*. Dutton $6.95

No here and thereian but slap up to the mark is Georgette Heyer who has been playing variations on the Regency romance for lo these many years. Miss Wychwood, still unmarried though not yet "an ape leader," is almost thirty. Possessed of a considerable independence, she has left her brother's estate to set up housekeeping in Bath, chaperoned by the garrulous Miss Farlow who is "more like a skinned rabbit than a woman and a regular gabble grinder into the bargain." The rest in standard Heyer, as the beauteous Miss Wychwood takes a runaway seventeen-year-old heiress under her wing and then falls inevitably in love with that young lady's guardian. The usual elegant trifle.

**246. Barbara A. Bannon, "PW Forecasts. Fiction," *Publishers Weekly* 202 (4 September 1972), p. 40:**

*Lady of Quality*. Georgette Heyer. Dutton, $6.95

In this delectable new Georgette Heyer novel of early 19th century Bath, a "sweet hornet" of "a certain age" (29) meets up with the "rudest man in London." Despite the intrusions of a priggish "gabble-grinder" of an old maid companion and a "young sprig" and "green girl" who have their own "amusing rattles" to pursue, the lady of quality and her bit-of-a-rake swain are the ones on whom our eyes are fixed. They don't play us false. Miss Heyer is in top form in this, her umpteenth period novel of early 19th century England, romantic, amusing and full of tart-tongued comment on the mores of the time. Any number of emancipated young women of the 19th century will still encounter more than a twinge of sympathy with Miss Wychwood, whose brother and sister-in-law *will* insist on telling her what is best for her to do with her spinsterhood. Perhaps the reason Georgette Heyer's novels sell so superlatively well is not simply their elegant escapism, but the fact that they always touch upon a very human situation. *Special Literary Guild selection.*

**247. Sr. M. Marguerite (RSM),** *Best Sellers* **32, 17 (1 December 1972), p. 400:**

Heyer, Georgette. *Lady of Quality*. Dutton. 255 p. $6.95.

Nineteen seventy-two: in the midst of the "Middle East Situation" and election crises and threat of total war, Georgette Heyer can continue to write her delightful novels of manners, morals, and styles in a never-never land of dignity, class distinction, rigidly observed customs in "society."

This, according to the fore page, is her thirty-sixth "historical novel"—not much history, just a graphic description of royalty and near-royalty, persons with vast estates and plenty of servants who are willing to climb four flights of steps to administer a soothing wet cloth for a headache or a restoring cup of tea; people with no more harrowing concerns than whether to wear a certain dress to the Assize Ball, or whether one's protegée would be a social success, or whether one's near relative would behave in such a manner as to earn the disapproval of "society," and therefore would not be able to contract a suitable marriage.

Miss Heyer adheres (one supposes) to the kind of slang and colloquial expressions used in the time of George III and IV; she describes the prevailing styles of clothing, makes it of paramount importance that her heroes and heroines (but especially the heroines—it was a man's world) should make the correct contacts, act in an acceptable manner.

It was all taken for granted that servants should climb those four flights of steps to bring one a cup of tea, that grooms should accompany

232

young ladies on their morning rides, that "nannies" should have enough control over their young charges to keep them out of sight, out of mind unless especially called for, and should be on twenty-four-hour duty, especially in the case of illness.

People talked in such stilted phrases as: "I am much obliged to you (ironically). You have relieved my mind of a great weight. Perhaps you will add to your goodness by explaining what you imagine I have done to put you out of temper?"

It is a good story—undoubtedly authentic with regard to manners, morals, customs, and styles of the Regency Period. Miss Heyer can spin a romance out of ordinary circumstances, detailed items of daily occurrences. It is all fascinating because it is made to seem ordinary, yet it is far away from society, prices, customs, every detail of life as we here and now in America know it.

The Lady of Quality is a Miss Annis Whychwood [sic]: wealthy, independent—and twenty-nine! She is finally mastered by her love for the pseudo-villain who of course reforms in order to win her after she has won his admiration by "sparring" with him in what he calls a hornet-like manner of conversation.

In the midst of so much that is sordid, unsafe, confusing, it is good to have occasional escape reading of a far-away and far-from reality way of life.

## 1973

**248.** *Kirkus Reviews* **41, 15 February 1973, p. 215:**

Heyer, Georgette. *April Lady*. Putnam $6.95

Another flurry "slap up to the echo" in this 1957 Regency romance in which relentlessly talkative ladies stoop to miniscule follies.    The audience is constant and insatiable.

**249. Irene N. Pompea (Colorado Springs, Colo.), *Best Sellers* 33, 2 (15 April 1973), p. 39:**

Heyer, Georgette. *April Lady*. Putnam. 254 pp. $6.95

This novel, first published in 1957 and now reissued, proves that Georgette Heyer has long been skillful in the writing of romantic intrigue.

Thinking that his charming young bride, Lady Helen, has married him for his money, Lord Cardoss tries not to show his real feelings; Lady Helen, in the meanwhile, having been warned by her mother that this is a marriage of convenience, keeps her ardor concealed—especially after she gives her brother money to pay his gambling debts and then finds that the rest of her generous allowance will not pay for her extravagant clothing. The tradespeople come to her husband to be paid and he is convinced that Helen really did marry him for his money.

Letty, the young, flighty sister of Lord Cardoss, who lives with him and his bride, is passionately in love with diplomat Jeremy Allandale who is leaving for an assignment in South America. Letty wants to marry and accompany him. Her brother thinks that she is too young. Love and a cunning, obstinate female intrigue work on Cardoss to change his mind.

Dysart, Lady Helen's brother, becomes part of the intrigue as he tries to help her to get money for a gown so that she will not have to account to her husband for the expense. He tries to steal her jewels, is recognized, and then pretends it was all a prank. When a valuable necklace is missing, Lady Helen thinks Dysart stole it, Lord Cardoss thinks that his wife has sold it. Then comes a solution and a happy ending—one can imagine the characters taking bows at the final curtain.

**250. Irene N. Pompea (Colorado Springs, Colo.),** *Best Sellers* **33, 4 (15 May 1973), 91:**

Heyer, Georgette. *Why Shoot a Butler?* Dutton. 262 pp. $5.95

Oh, what a tangled web an author must weave when she sets out to write a mystery! Clues planted here and there, but not too obvious. The bumbling police! Georgette Heyer indeed presents a challenge to the reader as she weaves a classic tale of crime and detection in *Why Shoot a Butler?* At seventy, she is still active in the writing field, having just had a new Regency novel published. *Why Shoot a Butler?* is the eleventh and last of Miss Heyer's mysteries that Dutton is reissuing.

In this reverse twist of the butler getting done in, instead of doing it, the body is discovered on the third page, and then it's away we go. There are hidden clues with the characters looking for them, and then there is the secret clue in the book, a masquerade party with an uninvited guest, attempted murder in the dark of night, and a secret meeting in the country. All the props of a mystery are there, used very cleverly. And of course one must stir in a bit of romance with the mystery. If genteel mysteries are your cup of tea, you have here a steaming teapot just waiting to be poured!

**251.** *Kirkus Reviews* **41, 1 July 1973, p. 716:**

Heyer, Georgette. *Venetia*. Putnam $6.95
Venetia, the lively 'un and Lord Damerel with the rake's reputation, are badly foxed by fate's bludgeonings which include the return of an important relative. Lord Damerel proposes four times and Heyer collectors will easily accept this the second time around.

**252. "Paperbacks. Fiction,"** *Best Sellers* **33, 17 (1 December 1973), p. 407:**

*Lady of Quality* is not only an adequate title but it describes the sort of lady who is usually the subject of a Georgette Heyer romance—this one is late-eighteenth century in England with an independent woman of twenty-nine and a villain who, naturally, turns out to be a hero (Bantam. $1.25).

**1974**

**253. "Paperbacks. Fiction,"** *Best Sellers* **33, 21 (1 February 1974), p. 495:**

Fashionable in the Georgette Heyer style is her *Frederica*, though the Regency period is ending and the Industrial Revolution is beginning; there are parties and balls and a couple of romances (Bantam. $1.25).

**254. Sr. Marguerite (RSM, Baltimore, MD),** *Best Sellers* **34, 2 (15 April 1974), p. 45-6:**

Heyer, Georgette. *The Unknown Ajax*. Putnam. 314 pp. $6.95

One does not have to eat a whole pie to find out what the pie tastes like; and one does not have to read a whole book (I did, though) to make a review and criticism.

Miss Heyer has a good thing going: she sets her stories in the time of the Regency; her characters are all members of fine old families with their faithful retainers, their elegant estates, same sorts of characters, all credible and amusing. I take it for granted that her descriptions of fashions, scenes, and conversations are authentic. Such words and expressions as "La!," "I collect," "a miserable squeeze crab," "game as a pebble," "put to the blush,"—and "slumguzzled"—must actually have been used in the communications of the time. The plots, too, are predictable: always a stranger, a non-conformist, or an erratic appears in the midst of a conservative group, time, and/or community and wins acceptance through some act of generosity, courage, or unexpected condition.

This is not to denigrate Miss Heyer's style, policy, or talent; we need more novels like hers. We need more wholesome details of ideal or idealistic living, more reticence, less blatant emphasis on dirt whether moral or physical. We need to be transported to a world where crime is not considered cute and criminals, drug addicts, and clever politicians are not the heroes.

The book jacket notes that Miss Heyer has lived in such seemingly inaccessible parts of the world as Tanganyika and the Macedonian-Bulgarian border. Perhaps her experiences in these countries enable her all the more by way of contrast to depict the characters, times, and customs she so graphically presents.

We need more novels like this.

## 1975

### 255. R. M. Franklin, "A Family Romance," in *The Times Literary Supplement*, 21 November 1975, p. 1379:

Georgette Heyer: *My Lord John*. 383 pp. Bodley Head. £3

Evidently some historical novelists, like many historians, have a hankering to work on periods remote from their central research interests. In her last historical romance, published posthumously, Georgette Heyer abandoned her familiar Regency background for the fourteenth and fifteenth centuries. *My Lord John* is based on the life of John, Duke of Bedford, the third son of Henry IV, and follows his career from his birth in 1389 to 1413. In a preface Miss Heyer's husband, G. R. Rougier, explains that it is only the first part of what was to be a trilogy covering the whole span of John's life, but which remained uncompleted on Miss Heyer's death.

In 1413 the most interesting parts of John of Bedford's career, as companion-in-arms of his brilliant elder brother Henry V, and above all as ruler of those great tracts of French territory which passed into English control as a result of Henry's victories, still lay in the future. In consequence the novel has an air of anticlimax about it, and more than once themes are indicated which vanish inexplicably. There are compensations, however. Because John of Bedford was so far from the centre of the historical stage for most of the period covered here, Miss Heyer was at liberty to build up a very full background to his life without straying from the realms of the historically possible into those of the manifestly untrue.

In doing so she was able to use a formidable knowledge of the period, acquired by a long process of reading and research to which her husband pays tribute. The course of events is from time to time altered to meet the requirements of the plot but beyond this it is very rare to find her in error on a matter of fact. Her approach was particularly appropriate for a period when the passions and decisions of a comparatively small group of individuals had a crucial role in determining events. Miss Heyer sets John of Bedford's life firmly within the circle of his immediate family, with all their close loyalties and jealousies. One may quarrel with some of the detail in her account of how those emotions operated, but the basic outlines of what she has to say are sound and it is salutary for the professional historian, as well as the general reader, to be reminded that the great of this world have not only mothers but also brothers and sisters. This portrait of a family is the core of the book, and by far the most enjoyable and worthwhile aspect of it.

On matters of more general interpretation, however, Miss Heyer's judgment was often seriously awry. Few historians would agree, for example, with her opinion that the wardship system of the late Middle Ages was seldom badly abused. Both Parliament and the common people play far too small a part in her vision of the age. There are descriptions of executions in the novel, traitors' heads are impaled, children are taken hostage, yet she failed to convey—this is perhaps the novel's most important failure—a real sense of the claustrophobic web of distrust, vengefulness, and fear which was closing round the court at the end of the fourteenth century, and was to form the context of its life for most of the fifteenth century.

Miss Heyer was an outstanding storyteller, here as in her Regency novels. Whether one enjoys her deliberate use of archaic words and phrases must obviously be a matter of taste. There can be no mistaking the fact that this style came naturally to her, or that she had absorbed a wide vocabulary of early English. But if one thinks of the austere elegance of fourteenth-century prose at its best—that of Margery Kemp, for instance—Miss Heyer's pastiche begins to jar.

238

**256.** "Fiction," *Kirkus Reviews*, 15 September 1975, p. 1014:

Heyer, Georgette. *My Lord John*. Dutton $8.95

Georgette Heyer, who died in 1974, was absolute monarch of her small but fertile field of the Regency romance, that lovely fluff produced for those who harbor an 18th-century fantasy of eloping to Gretna Green. This, her last novel, is a more serious work, set in the Middle Ages at the height of Lancastrian power, beginning with the infancy of the children of Henry of Bolingbroke and left unfinished by the author before the death of Bolingbroke as Henry IV. Miss Heyer chose to view the maze of political, military and court events through the career of John, Henry IV's third son, but in general the slant is influenced by Shakespeare. Henry IV is haunted throughout his reign by the death of Richard II, whose crown he usurped, and the death, though never solved here, is forecast by the King's words: "I would he *were* dead, but not by my hand!" However, we do meet a vigorous John of Gaunt and Harry (later Henry V) displays a forthright devotion to Richard: "He piles wrong on wrong. . . . But I love him, still or loud!" John is the ever-faithful servant to the realm and brother Harry, methodically going about his duties as pacifier and governor of the Scottish Borderland, acting as all-around confidant and moderator. This is a generally unaccented account of the events of the period—the fall of contentious nobles, uprisings quelled in Wales and Scotland, dealings with France and Rome, the spread of the Lollards, etc. A reasonable reading of the times, but one wishes for less stately converse, more consolidation of material into the dramatic confrontations which were Heyer's forte. Even the inclusion of such marvelous Middle English words as "orgulous" ("over-proud," the glossary tells us) doesn't serve to move matters along, but predictably this is more respectable in scope and scholarly responsibility than most, and will not diminish the luster of Miss Heyer's perdurable happy gestes.

**257. Barbara A. Bannon, "PW Forecasts. Fiction,"** *Publishers Weekly* **208 (15 September 1975), p. 46:**

*My Lord John*. Georgette Heyer. Dutton, $8.95

This posthumously published final novel from Georgette Heyer is very different from anything else she ever wrote, excellent entertainment even though it remains unfinished, but much more serious, more intensely dramatic than her delightful Regency romances. Miss Heyer was long fascinated by the medieval period of English history in which she steeped herself with a scholar's thoroughness. Out of it she has woven here a colorful pageant dealing with the House of Lancaster, from the last days of Richard II to the time just before Henry V's accession to the throne. The central figure is Henry's loyal and honorable third brother, John Duke of Bedford, and in telling his story from childhood to young manhood and that of Richard, of Bolingbroke, who tumbled Richard from his throne, and of John's brothers, a rich panoply of every aspect of medieval life emerges, from the intrigues and lusts of the court to the gamy stews of London, the lot of the commoners of the day, the life of the soldier, the monk, the barons. What is often hard to come by in this kind of historical fiction—a sense of family relationships—Miss Heyer achieves immediately and her young "lordlings" [sic] step out of history to become for us very real human beings. *First printing, 30,000; ad appropriation $20,000.*

### 258. Philippa Toomey, in "Fiction," *The Times*, 2 October 1975, p. 9:

*My Lord John*. By Georgette Heyer. Bodley Head, £3

This is the last novel that we shall have from Georgette Heyer. In an introduction, her husband, G. R. Rougier, tells us that in spite of the success of her Regency historical novels, she herself preferred the Middle Ages, and was particularly fond of the House of Lancaster, planning a trilogy on the life of John, Duke of Bedford, younger brother of Henry V. A meticulous researcher, she would have liked to spend five years on these books. Interrupted twice—each time by another Regency story—she wrote only the first book, *My Lord John* and did not live to complete it.

A complex cast of characters merits the four pages devoted to a list giving their titles and relationships, followed by a family tree and a glossary. Not one of the airy but delicious trifles she used to put together for our enjoyment, therefore, but a more serious book altogether. It begins with the "lordings" Harry, Thomas, John and two year old Humfrey in the garden at Kenilworth, welcoming their grandfather, Bel sire, as they called him, John of Gaunt, as we know him—on a visit to their father Henry, Earl of Derby, later Duke of Hereford, later still, Henry IV. Seen through the eyes of the children, the relationships, shifting loyalties, friendships, treacheries and dangers, Cousin Richard's strange behaviour as king, are absorbed almost painlessly. Harry, the eldest, the future Henry V, is taken into King Richard's court. The children are separated when their mother dies young, as so many did. Bel sire himself had three wives and three families.

John is the central figure, at 14 made Warden of the Eastern Marches and Captain of Berwick. We see him grow up quickly in the arts of diplomacy and war in the north, which was more loyal to the Percys than to the King, though Hotspur was dead. Scots, Welsh, French battles were fought and won—but the human side is there, too. The character of Harry, much loved, but never understood, even by his closest friends, is subtly drawn, and Henry IV's second wife, the beautiful and extremely tiresome Joanna of Brittany is shown with the light touch we remember so well.

It takes a little time to adjust to the archaic forms of speech used—but it is with a real sense of disappointment that the end, in mid-sentence, is reached. *My Lord John* sends us rushing back to the history books to find out what happened next. I hope Miss Heyer would have liked that.

**259. Eleanore Singer (University of Western Ontario Library, London, Canada),** *Library Journal* **100, 15 November 1975, p. 2172:**

Heyer, Georgette. *My Lord John*. Dutton. 383 pp. $8.95

Despite the fame for her Regency novels, Heyer was actually more interested in the Middle Ages and was at work on a fictional trilogy about the House of Lancaster when she died. *My Lord John* is the first (and the only finished) part of that work. It deals with John, Duke of Bedford, brother of Henry V of England; the period covered is 1393 to 1413. In the preface, Heyer's husband describes her as a perfectionist whose research was "enormous and meticulous." Indeed, she uses so many words of the period that one has to constantly flip to the glossary at the end of the book to make sense of a phrase or passage. This is well-documented historical writing, but as a novel it doesn't have enough dramatic or narrative flow to keep it from being often boring, and it falls far short of that superb blending of history and compelling story-telling that characterizes successful examples of the genre, like the medieval novels of Zoe Oldenbourg.

## 260. Geneva Stephenson, "Last Heyer Novel, A Period Panorama," *Columbus Dispatch*, 23 November 1975, p. K-8:

*My Lord John*. By Georgette Heyer. Dutton. $8.95

Now published posthumously, this last work of the author's more than 50 novels, is fascinatingly different from all her previous work. Many of her great successes dealt in light, romantic vein with the Regency period in England. This book also has an English background, one that has fascinated authors all the way from Shakespeare to Gordon Daviot (Josephine Tey).

The chief characters are the Lancaster family: Richard II, Henry IV who usurped Richard's throne, and Henry's four sons—Harry who became Henry V, Thomas, Humpfry, and the Lord John of the title, all of whom held various dukedoms and other titles.

Scores of characters appear: Harry Hotspur, Owen Glendower, Mortimers, Arundels, their many lovely or not so lovely wives and progeny; there is an amusing, touching portrait of Geoffry Chaucer, one of Froissart, and other notables of the period including some pitiful, humble martyrs of religious bigotry.

Plots, counter-plots, real friendship and base treachery, the scope of

Lancastrian ambitions from France where England still held territory, to Ireland, Wales, and Scotland—included also are some accounts of far reaching travels and forays into the remote eastern lands beyond Europe.

With incredibly extensive scholarship, Miss Heyer tells the drama of an entire era, seen through the eyes of the four young sons of Henry IV, to their maturity—even at 15 given responsible government posts and titles—extending through the last of Richard II's reign to the death of Henry IV.

One would call this a narrative rather than a novel, were it not for the in-depth characterization, the movement, the color, the motivation.

Miss Heyer steeped herself in the lore of the period for years, concluding this final, vigorous manuscript at the age of 71. In private life she had long been the wife of G. R. Rougier, a Commander of the British Empire.

A family tree and also a listing of the principal great houses involved is furnished, also a brief glossary of the occasional, usually trenchant, rare or obsolete expressions.


**261. "PLA," *The Atlantic Monthly* 236, 6 (December 1975), p. 118:**

*My Lord John*, by Georgette Heyer. Dutton, $8.95
Ungrateful to mention it, when the late Georgette Heyer gave so much pleasure with her Regency comedies, but this endless novel about a brother of Henry V is a terrible bore. To represent a gaggle of Plantagenets as amiable youths doing their virtuous best in difficult times was (see glossary) a sleeveless notion.


**262. Jane Aiken Hodge, "Historical Novels," in "Book Reviews," *History Today* 25, 12 (December 1975), pp. 857-8:**

*My Lord John*. By Georgette Heyer. 384 pp. Bodley Head, £3
The historical novel's worst danger, and worst defect, is probably dullness. In a modern *Dunciad* there would be a special section for

authors who drown in their own research, and pull the reader in after them. It is the soft, disastrous under-side of the enormously hard work that goes into books like Edith Pargeter's *The Dragon at Noonday* and Georgette Heyer's posthumous *My Lord John*. Each of these books takes a considerable slice of history for its subject; each suffers from the difficulties involved in simply covering the ground. . . .

Georgette Heyer, too, thought much about style in the historical novel. Her Regency books are triumphs of a language that never was on sea or land; her attempt at doing the same thing for her story of Henry the Fifth's brother John is less successful. Maybe all the words she uses can be found in contemporary sources; knowing her work, I think it most likely. But they are scattered with too lavish a hand. "Bonchief or mischief . . ." "boldrumptious . . ." "witterly . . ." "orgulous . . ." Her hero princes are "lordings" throughout the first section of the book; their grandfather, John of Gaunt, "bel sire." It grates, at last. But her worst trouble is with time. The unfinished book begins in 1393, when John was four, and takes him up to 1413, when, proved a brilliant and beloved administrator, he is holding the Scottish border for his ailing father, Henry the Fourth. Despite some happy moments of unmistakable Heyer humour, all too rare in the historical novel, I am afraid this novel will not hold a young reader for long.

**1976**

**263. Pauline J. Earl (Clarks Green, PA), in "Fiction,"** ***Best Sellers*** **35, 10 (January 1976), p. 302:**

Heyer, Georgette. *My Lord John*. Dutton, 384 pp. $8.95
    This is Georgette Heyer's last novel. It was envisioned as part one of an historical trilogy with John, Duke of Bedford (1386-1435), third son of Henry IV and brother of Henry V, as the central character. The novel is unfinished, even breaking off mid-sentence; however, a short historical postscript brings the story to a logical conclusion.
    The book is historically overwhelming, scrupulously researched, and

meticulously detailed. Miss Heyer brings the spirit of the Middle Ages to life in every chapter, and genuine historical personages become very familiar personalities. The plot can be found in any good English history text, and all the political, papal, and personal intrigues are artfully woven into the saga of *My Lord John*.

However, all this attention to detail may prove detrimental to the success of the volume, for if a person does not have a basic understanding of the English genealogy of the era he will find himself adrift in a sea of names and relationships. The text incorporates vocabulary common to the early fifteenth century, but contemporary readers may find words such as "bratchet," "caltraps," "drammocks," "gainbite," "murrey," "ventosity," etc. comprehensible only after a trip through the five-page glossary.

The author published more than fifty books of which a large portion are historical romances set in Regency England. *My Lord John* proves this successful writer to be a scholar as well as a story teller. Her death prevented the book from reaching any literary climax, but it is an educational experience, and to a devotee of English historical fiction, the reading effort is a rewarding one. Miss Heyer will be missed.

## 264. Edmund Fuller, "Hercule Poirot's Last Case," *The Wall Street Journal* 187 (14 January 1976), p. 12:

*My Lord John*. By Georgette Heyer. 384 pp. $8.95

The late Georgette Heyer, a prolific writer, may well be called the historical romancer for the scholar and intellectual, among which groups she enjoyed an enthusiastic following rare to writers of that genre. She appealed, of course, also to all lovers of historical romance, and it is characteristic that her fans often include two or three generations within a family. The milieu of the great volume of her work is the Regency, an era replete with color and scandal, rich in personality, significant in politics and culture, of all aspects of which Miss Heyer had a profound knowledge to underpin her talents as tale-spinner.

Her last book, posthumously published, is *My Lord John*. Surely her devoted readers will want it, but many of them may be startled by its departure from the Regency scene and the inevitable differences in manner, style, and vocabulary.  Its central figure is John, Duke of Bedford, third son of King Henry IV, most trusted of the brothers of Shakespeare's Prince Hal, later King Henry V.

Miss Heyer's husband, G. R. Rougier, tells us that this period of "armour" was her heart's true love.  The present work was conceived as a trilogy on the House of Lancaster, of which this is but the first third which, alas, stops in mid-sentence.  He says, "The penal burden of British taxation, coupled with the clamor of her readers for a new book, made her break off to write another Regency story."  That happened more than once. "So a great historical novel was never finished."  She uses a rich, archaic vocabulary (there's a glossary) which enhances her evocation of the age.  The book will give particular pleasure to devotees of Shakespeare's chronicle plays, though there are many contrasts due to her greater authenticity.

These three books [the other two are Agatha Christie's *Curtain* and Janet Hitchman's biography of Dorothy L. Sayers] are the work, or are about the work, of three unusual, gifted British ladies whose followings are large and loyal.

**265.  Margaret W. Reid, "Georgette Heyer's last novel,"** *Wichita Falls Times*, **15 February 1976, Sunday Magazine, p. 4:**

**My Lord John**. Dutton, $8.95
*My Lord John* is Georgette Heyer's last book.  The popular Englishwoman who wrote more than fifty historical novels, most of them set in Regency England, died in July, 1974.  This posthumous novel, only recently released, was not quite finished, and her editors have added an historical note to tell readers how John and his famous family fared in their last years. She had been working on the story for many years, according to a note from her publisher, and "became as familiar with its period as she was with Regency Bath and London."

246

John was the third son of England's King Henry IV (1399-1413), the first Plantagenet king of the Lancastrian branch. Readers meet the family while the children ("four nobly born imps") were still young, attended by nurses and a "damsel," and follow their fortunes through about two decades. John, second son, dominates the novel, of course, was bright, intensely loyal to his father, and while still very young fought against invading Scots and disloyal Englishmen. John's older brother, whom he called Harry, became king in 1413, after their father's mysterious death, and John became Duke of Bedford.

The real charm of the story lies in the vivid portrayal of life in the Middle Ages, the dominance of the church, and the character of John whose responsibilities seem heavy for his years. Childhood was short, apparently, in those long-ago times. And Miss Heyer's use of words and expressions is fascinating, a constant reminder of the period and how language changes.

Georgette Heyer wrote her first book when she was only 17; it was published in 1921. Her last Regency romance, *Lady of Quality*, was published in 1972. Her books, famed for their entertainment value, have been immensely popular in England, and after Dutton became her American publisher have gained enthusiastic new readers year after year in this country book after book . . . for the regency novels are "concerned with love and marriage among the British aristocracy . . . [and] swarm with lively heroines, and in her stories no one is vicious, no one suffers, no one is depressing or boring."

Some readers admit to feeling a special kinship with Georgette Heyer. An American who discovered her books was so pleased with them that she worked with dealers for two years, urging them to stock everything Heyer had written. Most of the novels are now available in paperback. A member of my own family has collected Heyer for years and on a trip to London found some of the earlier volumes she did not have.

Miss Heyer's husband, G. R. Rougier, formerly Queen's Counsel, judge, and presently a Commander of the British Empire, has written the preface to this last novel and says, in part: "Her research was enormous and meticulous. She was a perfectionist. She studied every aspect of the period—history, wars, social conditions, manners and customs, costumes, armour, heraldry, falconry and the chase . . . . She learnt to read medieval English almost as easily as modern and amassed a large vocabulary."

Farewell, Miss Heyer. May your books long remain in print, both in this country and abroad.

## 1979

### 266. "Fiction," *Kirkus Reviews*, 1 October 1979, p. 1157:

Heyer, Georgette. *Simon the Coldheart*. Dutton $10.95

A re-issue of a 1925 medieval romance (never before published in the U.S.)—in which Heyer runs with a welter of solemn "sooths" and "mayhaps" rather than her later, classier Regency jargon. He of the frigid ticker is neglected bastard Simon Beauvallet—tough, ruthlessly fair, proud, mighty in battle—who comes at age 14 to the Earl of Montlice (known as "Fulk the Lion") for employment. And under the Lion's hard regimen and increasingly affectionate discipline, Simon grows to manhood. At an early age he will nip in the bud a plot to overthrow Henry IV, distinguish himself in the field, set to rights the slovenly caretakers of a lordless estate which he has been given by the king; and finally he will march against the French enemy at the castle town of Belrémy where dwells the Lady Margaret—proud, brave, and full of fight. Hitherto not interested in women, Simon sets out to conquer Belrémy and Margaret; she attempts to escape from him; but then he rescues her from a cruel tyrant and before long there's a rapid thaw in frozen bosoms. Heyer herself did not wish to see this book reprinted, but though certainly far from her peak, there's that ever-popular appeal of clanking armor and trembling wimples. And, however elementary the tale, it's told without slack: perfectly acceptable goods for the castle-and-moat consumer.

**267. Barbara Kemp (University of Michigan Library, Ann Arbor), in "Book Reviews,"** *Library Journal* **104 (1 Nov. 1979), pp. 2370-71:**

Heyer, Georgette. *Simon the Coldheart*. Dutton. 286 pp. $10.95
Heyer fans are in for a treat! This novel, originally published in 1925, has never been published in the United States. One of her early works, it still displays her talent for characterization and her ability to make the past come alive. The story is set in Heyer's favorite period, the Middle Ages, rather than the more familiar Regency period. Simon rises from page to lord and advisor to King Henry by dint of hard work and real ability. His singleminded quest for advancement leaves no room in his life for women—until he meets the Lady Margaret. A spirited, independent woman and leader of Simon's French foe, Margaret is hardly an easy conquest, but Simon thrives on such adversity. If the plot seems familiar, it is, but Heyer makes us care about Simon and Margaret.

## 1986

**268. T. J. Binyon, "Criminal proceedings,"** *The Times Literary Supplement*, **25 April 1986, p. 454:**

Georgette Heyer. *Footsteps in the Dark*. 289 pp. Grafton. £8.95
*Footsteps in the Dark* was Georgette Heyer's first detective story, originally published in 1932. The plot is indescribably ridiculous. Four bright young things—2m, 2f—inherit an ancient, rambling manor house in the country, complete with ruined gothic chapel, secret passages, ghosts, master criminals, drug-crazed French artists, bumbling local policemen and mysterious clean-cut hero. She was to do far better than this. Nevertheless, both characters and narration are still bright and effervescent enough to keep one going through the worst the story has to offer.

## 1987

**269. Charles Shibuk, "The Paperback Revolution,"** *Armchair Detective* **20, Winter 1987, p. 99:**

This popular author's first essay into crime fiction, *Footsteps in the Dark* (1932) (Berkley), has just received its first American publication. It's a light-hearted tale, set in an old English priory mansion with a reputation for being haunted, and features a cowled intruder called "the monk" who might be a ghost—or something else. This is not a major rediscovery, but it is a pleasant minor work.

## 1989

**270. Sheldon Kaye (Portland Public Library, Maine), in "Audio Reviews,"** *Library Journal* **114, 15 September 1989, p. 150:**

*A Blunt Instrument* 6 cassettes. unabridged. 8 hrs. Chivers Sound & Vision, dist. by G. K. Hall Audio, 1989. $44.95

One first wonders if Georgette Heyer's 1938 English mystery novel, with its reliance on the artificial plot device of split-second timing as well as its late 1930s sensibilities and dialog, will work for contemporary readers. This question is soon replaced by worry that none of the many suspects who had access to Ernest Fletcher during the half hour before he is found bludgeoned could have "done it." By taking the period and his eccentric, fully realized characters seriously, injecting just the right hint of melodrama into his fluent delivery, narrator Hugh Dickson brings out a great deal of fun in this classic whodunit.

## 1992

**271. Nancy R. Ives (State University of New York at Geneseo Library),** *Library Journal* **117, 1 June 1992, p. 204:**

***Duplicate Death***. 8 cassettes. unabridged. 12 hrs. Chivers Sound & Vision, dist. by G. K. Hall Audio, 1992. $69.95

A guest is murdered at a fashionable society bridge party, thus initiating a series of events certain to entertain listeners as they try to guess the murderer's identity. This British murder mystery, complete with all the conventional characters of the genre—social-climbing mother, debutante daughter, ambitious secretary, and shady bachelor—makes an ideal audiobook. Author Heyer leads listeners through the course of the chief inspector's investigation, keeping them guessing until the end. The straightforward plot, while not innovative, is nevertheless effective for this medium; more intricacy might be confusing. Clifford Norgate, with his fine British accent, reads particularly well, varying his tone and articulation for each character. The tape quality allows Norgate's voice to be heard with clarity, precision, and no background noise. This mystery is particularly suited to the audio format and is recommended for general collections.

### 1993

**272. Preston Hoffman, "Book Sounds. Spoken-Word Audio Reviews,"** *Wilson Library Bulletin* **68, December 1993, pp. 9, 101:**

Heyer, Georgette. ***Behold, Here's Poison***. Chivers North America, Inc. 6 cassettes. 8 hrs. 15 min. $49.95

Mystery novels seem especially suited to the audio format. Numerous polls have shown they are one of the most, if not the most, popular genres in library collections. There is something about a mystery that makes it particularly appealing to listeners. Or is it that lovers of mysteries are also audiophiles? Perhaps the important exercise of remembering the characters, their personalities, and the clues they leave prepares listeners for the similar demands of the audio format. This ability to remember details is a useful skill when reading, but it is absolutely essential when listening. Also, many mysteries follow a classic form that makes them easy to digest and perhaps functions as a mnemonic aid, much as the epic form assisted bards in remembering oral poetry.

The mystery novel as we know it has been brought to perfection by the British, and appropriately their audio books are among the best. I admit to a weakness for Robert Barnard's mysteries, which are comedies of manners—with a corpse both to capture your interest and to provide a plot. . . .

Georgette Heyer's *Behold, Here's Poison* is a mystery from the classic period that has been reinvigorated by Hugh Dickson's definitive reading. He has many voices at his command, which results in characters that are not only differentiated, but also defined and made almost tangible. The problem, and it is a major one, is that there are so many characters (twenty-two are introduced in the first chapter alone) that it is very difficult to keep them straight. I needed to listen to the first cassette twice to make sense of it, though it was still enjoyable the second time. The solution to this problem seems simple. As was common with texts of novels at the time of *Behold, Here's Poison*'s original publication (1936), a character list should be provided. This could appear in print on the back cover or, even better, utilize the touch-and-talk technology popular in children's audio books. One would touch the name "Randall" on a cover panel, and the appropriate voice would say something like, "I, Randall Matthews, am the nephew of the victim and tend to be supercilious and even smarmy, without actually being hateful." The listener could then identify the person by name, vocal quality, or even personality.

## 1994

**273. Nann Blaine Hilyard (Auburn Public Library, ME), in "AudioReviews,"** *Library Journal* **119, January 1994, pp. 184-85:**

*Envious Casca*. 10 cassettes. unabridged. 13 hrs. Chivers Audio Bks. 1993. $79.95

The extended family of wealthy, irascible Stephen Herriard [sic] gathers at his rambling house in Hertfordshire for an unforgettable Christmas celebration. The host is found murdered in his locked bedroom. Who did it, and why? Georgette Heyer's classic country house mystery translates well to audio. Clifford Norgate reads this period piece with the good-humored, dramatic flair it deserves; characters' voices match their descriptions with pinpoint accuracy. This will be a popular addition to audio-book collections.

# III. *Obituaries and responses*

**Hugh Hebert, "Postscript," *The Guardian* (London), 6 July 1974, p. 11:**

England lost one of her great queens of popular historical fiction when Georgette Heyer died late on Thursday night. She was 71 and for half a century she clocked up an average of a book a year—two a year in the mid-thirties. They swashed most famously through tales of Regency times and buckled through the Battle of Waterloo, and 11 of them were detective stories written to plots concocted by her barrister husband, Ronald Rougier.

Recently her books have been selling 100,000 copies in this country in hardback alone—many more in paperback. They boomed in America and Germany, and even penetrated Czechoslovakia. Her headier fans compared her with Jane Austen, and even her detractors would find it difficult to dismiss the books with the novelettish end of the romantic fiction market; because she always did her homework.

Her heroines might tend to have quantities of soft brown hair and an irrepressible sense of humour, her heroes to be immaculate and a trifle world weary: page one might tend to introduce a member of the nobility and the last page to clinch a marriage, with varieties of elopements, convenient accidents to carriages, duels and chases in between. But she had the reputation of being a meticulous searcher.

She would note the words and the phrases as she researched, but without noting their origin. So when an Israeli barrister wrote to her last month: "The language is particularly enchanting. Where did you find the delicious word 'thatchgallows,' for which I looked in vain in the OED" the answer sent on her behalf was that the OED might not have it, but you could bet your bottom dollar it had existed.

She was utterly professional, said her agent, Mrs Deborah Owen, yesterday. "When she turned in her finished manuscript, she had checked every word and punctuation mark. It was a rare moment when somebody had to move a comma. She was a complete perfectionist."

She was also a very private person. She never gave interviews, and one semi-apocryphal story says that once when her publisher tried to manoeuvre her into a slap-up publicity lunch at the Savoy, she threatened to wear such scandalous clothes that she would never be allowed through those doors again:

"I have no hobbies," Miss Heyer once said, "and play no ball games. I belong to no societies, and I make no personal appearances." What she loved doing in her spare time was watching sport on TV—preferably golf and cricket. Yet she is remembered as a charming and extremely witty person, whose interests ranged well outside the Regency-romantic-writer label with which she was usually stuck. She was planning a trilogy set in medieval times, her favourite period. But it became clear that she would never write it.

She was born in Wimbledon, and she started her first book—*The Black Moth*—when she was 17 as a serial story to cheer a convalescent brother. It was published two years later, and it still sells.

The last novel came out in 1972—*Lady of Quality*—and it sold as well as ever. And the chances are that many of them will go on selling and being borrowed by the army of admirers who wrote her reams of letters and for whom she made history a soothing, glittering entertainment.

**Unattributed, "Miss Georgette Heyer,"** *The Times* **(London), 6 July 1974, p. 14:**

Georgette Heyer, who died yesterday at the age of 71, was born in London in August, 1902. Her first historical novel, *The Black Moth: A Romance of the Eighteenth Century* when she was 17, was written as an entertainment for an elder brother who was recovering from a serious illness. It was published in 1921 (and is still in print). It proved to be the start of a long career as a popular and prolific novelist. There were more than 50 books, many of which have been translated and sold all over the world.

Educated privately, Georgette Heyer married George R. Rougier in 1925. He was then a mining engineer, and the next six years were spent in London, Tanganyika, and Macedonia. Later they returned to England, and she persuaded her husband to give up mining and read for the Bar. He was called to the Bar in 1939, took Silk in 1959, and was chairman of Cambridge and Isle of Ely Quarter Sessions at his retirement in 1971. Their only son, Richard, was born in 1932.

For 25 years the Rougiers lived in Albany. "I have no hobbies, play no games. I belong to no societies, and make no personal appearances," Georgette Heyer would say. She refused all personal publicity, regarding her fame with a certain amount of sardonic amusement, saying that her readers would find all they needed to know about her through reading her books. She was never interviewed, though *The Times* did persuade her to be photographed in 1970.

She was witty, amusing, charming, generous, delighting in the grand manner, a "lady of quality" to quote the title of her last book. The almost annual novel which appeared regularly from 1921 until 1972 came in several forms: the historical—(as in *An Infamous Army*, a story of the year of Waterloo) the detective story—there were 11 of these, and she relied on her husband for plots and details of police procedure—and the always popular "Regency" romances.

Popular her novels were, but there was also a firm core of scholarship and expert knowledge of the Regency period, its fashions, politics, military and social history, modes of speech, even agricultural policy, on which to hang the slender stories of love or hate at first sight, elopements, abductions, duels, gambling debts and happy endings. She kept notebooks of the turns of phrase and slang current for the particular year she was writing about, and a glimpse of her methods may be obtained from the Author's Note to *The Spanish Bride*, the story of the courtship of Harry and Juana Smith during the Peninsular War. There is not a complete list of authorities, but a number of sources—Harry Smith's own Autobiography, Napier and Sir Charles Oman on the War, and "I have not, to my knowledge, left any of the

Diarists of the Light Division unread." These include Kincaid, George Simmons, Edward Costello, Rifleman Harris and Quartermaster Surtees, and reference is also made to regimental histories, journals and lives of the commanders, and the dispatches of Wellington himself.

Her plots were seldom original, and indeed there was more than a little duplication in the rakes and Regency bucks, the eloping 17-year-olds, the ladies of Bath, highwaymen and Bow Street Runners. The excellent, easy style developed early—*Devil's Cub*, one of her best, was published in 1932. There were historical novels of other periods—notably the Elizabethan *Beauvallet* and the Stuart *Royal Escape*, but somehow the result was not quite so happy.

"Another Georgette Heyer" was greeted by her readers with joy and phenomenal sales. She gave her name to a recognizable genre of fiction, but no rival managed to achieve the touch which charmed both men and women from all levels of society. It was rumoured, at one time, that a group of Oxford dons met regularly to discuss her novels, and though it may be an apocryphal story it is not totally unlikely. Her family and many friends, together with her devoted readers, will be saddened to know that there can never be another Georgette Heyer to delight us.

**"Georgette Heyer,"** *The Times* **(London), 12 July 1974, p. 20:**

Max Reinhardt writes:
Your perceptive and affectionate obituary of Georgette Heyer will be appreciated by her many friends and admirers. If I offer any further contribution it is only to amplify some of your remarks.

The story of Oxford dons meeting to discuss her novels which you call apocryphal, I believe may well have been true, because her male dialogue was always extremely good and backed by extremely subtle wit. In fact, although she had many extremely good friends of both sexes, she particularly liked male conversation, and that was reflected in her novels. I remember one year in a West Indian island we were told that a famous Canadian mining tycoon was due to arrive in his private jet plane from Montreal. He was soon lying next to her on the beach, and as he unpacked his bag there were half a dozen Georgette

Heyer novels. Later in the day when I met him and he realized that I had the privilege of knowing her well, he asked me if I would be kind enough to tell her that she had given an enormous amount of pleasure to him and all his tough mining colleagues over very many years. That was the kind of fan letter that she most enjoyed receiving.

As for her professionalism, it was impeccable. She always told me when she was starting a novel, but she always warned me that she didn't know how long it would be and she always wanted a deadline because she realized how important it was to get it out in time for Christmas. I remember a crisis that we had to face because the novel that she was writing at the time and expected to be short developed into a long one. (In fact, it was one of her best.) She asked me what was the latest date that we had to have the book to publish it for Christmas. She had a great following overseas, so the determining factor was always the date of shipment to Australia, the most distant of the important overseas markets.

I told her that there was a ship leaving for Australia on August 14 and that if she delivered the typescript on July 7 in the morning, we would be able to print it, bind it and deliver the copies to the ship on time. (One must realize that her first printings were of 65,000 or 70,000 copies.) I know how tremendously hard she worked to get the book finished. It arrived in an impeccable state on the morning of July 7, went straight to the printers, and was ready to be shipped on August 14.

**Duff Hart-Davis, "20th century Jane Austen,"** *The Sunday Telegraph* **(London), 7 July 1974, p. 8:**

"I have no hobbies and play no ball-games. I belong to no societies and make no Personal Appearances."

Thus, with the little ironic flourish of the extra capital letters, Georgette Heyer once summed up her own character in a letter to her agent; and to the day of her death last week, at the age of 71, this outstandingly successful historical novelist carefully kept her private self hidden from the public eye.

Scarcely a single reader set eyes on the author whose books sold

100,000 hardback copies in this country alone, who was immensely popular in America and Germany, and whose annual income must have been well into six figures.

She was a tall, slim woman of striking appearance and great determination. Her husband, George Ronald Rougier, was first a mining engineer and then a lawyer, and during their first years together his career repeatedly took him to outlandish places. In Macedonia and Tanganyika she lived for six years in utterly primitive conditions.

Later she lived for 25 years in Albany, where she shared her house with a ghost whose manifestations were conventional but friendly.

Her first book was published in 1921, when she was 19, and among her early works were 11 detective stories, for which her husband supplied the plots. But it was in the field of historical romances that she left almost all competitors standing, and for these her secrets were, first, her cool wit, and second, her immensely detailed research. She travelled enormously, keeping elaborate indexes of the information which she gleaned.

She never wrote in summer (which, even in England, she considered too hot for real concentration), but started each book in the late autumn and worked right through the winter, staying up far into the night and visibly draining herself with the intensity of her effort.

The absence of long or serious reviews never worried her. What mattered was the fact that her stories sold in ever-increasing numbers—and it must be a unique achievement that 48 of her books—that is, all but five early ones, which she herself suppressed—are still in print.

She was slow to make friends. But once she had made a friend, her loyalty was indestructible, and her marriage brought joy and inspiration to both partners. Thus reinforced, she had no need to seek the limelight and sometimes at home she would bring her irony to bear on authors who deliberately courted publicity. Small wonder that she was sometimes known as the 20th-century Jane Austen.

**"Georgette Heyer: 20th century Jane Austen,"** *The Sunday Telegraph* **(London), 14 July 1974, p. 11:**

I, and I expect at least a thousand Jane Austen fans, would like Duff Hart-Davis to give one reason for saying that the late Georgette Heyer was a "20th Century Jane Austen."—(Miss) M. Miller, Edinburgh.

Duff Hart-Davis writes: For at least 20 years reviewers have compared the writing of Georgette Heyer with that of Jane Austen, and many leading critics, among them Marghanita Laski, have commented on the ways in which Miss Heyer was influenced by her Regency predecessor.

The delightful stories of Georgette Heyer have given me many hours of pleasurable reading—characters, indeed phrases, remain in mind long after the book is finished. Truly a "Lady of Quality."—Winefride Chapple, Stoke, Devon.

**Unattributed, "Obituary Notes," *Publishers Weekly* 206 (29 July 1974), p. 16:**

GEORGETTE HEYER, author of over 50 novels, all of which are in print in the United Kingdom, the U.S. and Germany (with the exception of a few titles which had not been reprinted at her own request), died July 4 in London. She was 71.

She was 17 when she started writing her first book, *The Black Moth*, to amuse a convalescing brother; it was published by Constable in 1921 and is still selling. In the United States her publishers were Putnam and Dutton; her most recent novel was *Lady of Quality*, published in 1972 by Dutton. Although she was known primarily for her historical novels set in Regency London, she also wrote 11 detective stories, relying on her husband, a barrister, for the plots.

Of a retiring nature, she once declared, "I have no hobbies and play no ball-games. I belong to no societies, and make no personal appearances."

# *IV. Reference works*

How to deal responsibly with the treatment of Georgette Heyer in reference works? I looked first in the index of my multi-volume paperback *Pelican History of English Literature* (3$^{rd}$ edition, 1978)—nothing there. I looked in the 15$^{th}$ edition of the *Encyclopaedia Britannica*, which was, after all, published in 1974, the year of Georgette Heyer's death. Surely, considering her popularity at the time—no, nothing there. So who *was* there? Dorothy Sayers, Agatha Christie, and Margery Allingham all had respectable entries, and they were all mystery writers contemporary with her. On the other hand, another contemporary, romance writer Barbara Cartland, who was even more prolific than Georgette Heyer and not at all averse to personal publicity as Heyer had been, was not mentioned. Clearly, a visit to the local university library reference section was in order.

As so many of the citations in this book attest, Georgette Heyer has been best known for her many Regency romances, not for her less numerous mysteries or historical novels. Indeed, very early on, her name became linked with Barbara Cartland's for the former genre, and both were discounted as writers of nothing but the most frivolous merit. Surely, I thought, time and intelligent readers have corrected this injustice; if so, something as general as the 1999 *World Book Encyclopedia* (which caught my eye as I entered the library) should testify to that fact. Sure enough, the entry there describes her briefly as "an English novelist who gained fame for her mystery stories and her historical fiction. . . a respected authority on the Regency. . . ." Heartened, I turned to the shelves more specifically devoted to writers in English, and before long found fourteen reference works which included

Georgette Heyer.

Of the five on twentieth-century crime fiction, four were from the 1970s and early 1980s, as if readers and writers had become aware of a gap to be filled; one specifically opined that although Heyer was more widely known for her romances, her mysteries were actually better crafted. The fifth, published in 1994, focused on women mystery writers, and it was surrounded—in time, if not precisely on the shelves—by other reference works also devoted to women writers and, of all things, writers of romances and historical novels: surely an outgrowth of the increasing feminist consciousness, and evidence of growing recognition of women's writing and tastes. In the meantime, two additional, more general reference works from the 1980s showed that Heyer had certainly been recognized in the literary sphere, if not exactly accepted into the canon.

The first mention of Georgette Heyer I found in a reference work, then, was in *A Catalogue of Crime*, by Jacques Barzun and Wendell Hertig Taylor, published in 1971. It had lasting influence, partly, I presume, because of the growing interest in crime fiction as a genre, but also because Jacques Barzun was already a widely recognized scholar and authority in the humanities. Barzun and Taylor's introduction of Georgette Heyer reads as follows:

> The republishing of her detective *corpus* in the mid-fifties—that is, some twenty years after their first appearance—attests to the sterling merits of this inadequately prized writer. She ranks with Sayers, Allingham, and Marsh, possessing the sure touch of the first and avoiding the occasional bathos of the other two.

High praise indeed. There follow brief plot summaries of each of Heyer's twelve mysteries, wherein *A Blunt Instrument* and *Death in the Stocks* are ranked as her best and *Duplicate Death* and *Detection*

262

*Unlimited* as her worst. Her characters, her wit, and her "born detective mind" are mentioned repeatedly, and the recurrence of the two detectives from Scotland Yard, Hannasyde and Hemingway, is duly noted. Interestingly, there is also an entry for *Pistols for Two*, which says, "Too bad. . . some dueling but no detection," as if the book's title had been misleading. (See Chapter V for more from Barzun and Taylor.)

Eight years elapsed until, in 1979, Allen Hubin's *Bibliography of Crime Fiction 1749-1945* listed all twelve of Heyer's mysteries, giving publication dates and, again, noting the presence or absence of Hannasyde and Hemingway. His bibliography is strictly that, however, and he included neither biographical data nor commentary for any writers listed.

Three years later, H. R. F. Keating's *Whodunit?* was more personal, but less complete. Keating described Heyer in a short paragraph as "above all [a] Regency romance writer" whose detective stories nevertheless "were in the Golden Age tradition and popular." He goes on, "Country houses figure largely and the puzzle is all, but the style is light and agreeable and many of the characters deftly comic." Only *Death in the Stocks* is mentioned specifically, and on Keating's rating scale receives nine stars for "readability" and two for "tension," though that would seem to contradict his emphasis on the puzzle. Plot and characterization receive seven and six stars, respectively.

The other two entries I found on Georgette Heyer in crime fiction reference works were written by continuing scholars in the field, Kathleen G. Klein in *Twentieth Century Crime and Mystery Writers* (2nd edition, 1985) and Elaine Bander in *Great Women Mystery Writers* (1994). Klein was the editor of the latter work, and Bander had already published elsewhere on Heyer (see Chapter V). Both benefited from intervening publications on her, the most ambitious being Jane Aiken Hodge's biography in 1984.

Klein and Bander took different approaches to Heyer, however. Klein included very little biographical information and focused primarily on her craft as a novelist:

> The dozen detective novels of Georgette Heyer
> illustrate perfectly the development of the mystery
> genre in the Golden Age of the 1920s and 1930s....
> [They] rely on stock plots and characters so deftly
> handled and so cleverly written as to seem unique.

She particularly notes the eccentric, comic characters, delighting especially in Vicky Fanshawe in *No Wind of Blame,* and singles out *Penhallow* as unusual and "rare in . . . allowing only the reader to know the whole truth: the convention of 'justice done' is forcefully challenged."

Bander, too, acknowledged Heyer's place as "a significant contributor to the Golden Age of English detective fiction, wedding comic romance (and occasionally melodrama) to classic detection," and praised particularly "the ironic wit and antisentimental love interest" which distinguished her mysteries as well as her Regency romances, "a genre Heyer virtually invented and perfected." But throughout her discussion she draws in biographical details and conjecture about Heyer herself, most notably,

> . . . her point-of-view characters tend to share her
> distaste for social hypocrisy. Nevertheless, Heyer is
> not above snobbery, and her writing reflects the
> prejudices of her time and class. Her servants are an
> inferior species. Similarly, her ethnic characters are
> caricatures: an egotistical Mexican cabaret dancer, a
> specious White Russian prince, a Gaelic-spouting
> Scottish policeman. Police detectives are usually
> clever tradesmen outwitted by barrister-heroes.

Also in contrast to Klein, Bander dismisses *Penhallow* as "stock melodrama with little detection, and repetitive to boot."

In 1980, the multi-volume bibliography *Contemporary Authors* contained an entry on Georgette Heyer which included not only a full bibliography of her novels, but also a list of fifty-five reviews and three obituaries—something completely new. Following the work's general format, the entry's author, Martha G. Winkel, provided only a very short biographical paragraph on Heyer and an essay based on and liberally quoting from the cited reviews, both positive and negative.

Then in 1986, the eminent *Dictionary of National Biography 1971-1980* included an entry on Georgette Heyer by her publisher and friend Max Reinhardt, based on "private information; personal knowledge." What could be more definitive, though perhaps from a not altogether impartial perspective? Regarding her craft, Reinhardt described Heyer as "one of those rare novelists who are able to create a totally convincing world of their own." He goes on, "Perhaps the most memorable characteristic of the Regency novels . . . is their sparkling wit and pace, and it is this verve and the sound common sense and knowledge of human nature that lie beneath it that distinguish her books from those of her many imitators." Regarding Georgette Heyer herself, Reinhardt summarized her life and publishing history, but then went on to describe his experience of her thus:

> She confined herself to a small, select circle of friends whom she trusted, and this may have made her appear to the outside world a little aloof and detached. She had a great sense of fun, and was thrilled when after the Queen had asked her to one of her informal lunches, she was told that Her Majesty had bought a number of her latest books to give away for Christmas, and had commented that she seemed to be a formidable person. "Me, formidable?" said Georgette Heyer, completely astounded.

The later reference works seem to follow the aforementioned "feminist thread," all the more evident in the fact that so many reference

265

works now focused specifically on women writers and reading material traditionally considered as belonging to women, i. e. romances and historical fiction. In 1988's *An Encyclopedia of British Women Writers*, Paula Connolly went into greater depth than had previously been seen, using *The Nonesuch* as an example of Heyer's work and to show how she "develops the potential of the genre by mirroring characters and relationships—the Nonesuch and Ancilla Trent with the young Lord Julian and Patience Chartley, the coquette [Tiffany Wield] with the gentle beauty, fashion with foppery." Connolly summed up Heyer's strengths as "wit, clear characterization, and closely defined social scene."

In *Twentieth Century Romance and Historical Writers* (2nd edition, 1990), Joan McGrath was more interested in the phenomenon of Heyer's plots:

> If plot were all, the popularity of Heyer's work would be totally inexplicable, but her countless fans could explain that plot has very little to do with it. It is the bubbling good humour, the endlessly complicated social situations, the inspired silliness of the lovely creatures who perform these fantastic courtship rituals, that brings them back time and again for another of her stories.

In a particularly personal tone, McGrath concludes, "Heyer's work is intended to amuse rather than to enlighten, and if there ever was a writer who could brighten a grey day, it is she."

1993's *The Oxford Guide to British Women Writers*, by Joanne Shattuck, offered nothing new, though Shattuck seems to have carefully avoided the term "romance" in favor of "historical novel."

The specifically feminist perspective seems to appear first in Laura Marcus's entry in the 1989 *British Women Writers: A Critical Reference Guide*, which asserts that "in. . . *Regency Buck* (1935), the heroine is 'tamed' by her guardian and love and marriage come with female submission to the stern but dashing hero." I could wish that people would not persist in generalizing about Georgette Heyer on the basis of *Regency Buck*, but I suspect those who do of having chosen a "typical" Heyer on the basis of its title, and never reading further. In her selected bibliography, Marcus also appears to have been unaware that *The Corinthian* and *Beau Wyndham* are the same book, and she attributes to Heyer something called "*Freedom* (1965)," which error demonstrates effectively, I think, the depth of her acquaintance with the author.

In like manner, the unattributed Georgette Heyer entry in the 1990 *Feminist Companion to Literature in English* appears to have been written by someone who had read more *about* the author than *by* her. The most interesting (to me) excerpt reads as follows:

> She gleaned authentic detail from first-hand sources. . ., presented it with verve and style, delighted in duels, gambling, disguise, rescue, and the peerage, set her lovers to overcome initial dislike or misunderstanding, and indulged in cautious explorations of gender (some boyish heroines, some effeminate heroes).

No mention is made of the dialogue, nor the interaction of characters.

1994 brought a third edition of *Twentieth Century Romance and Historical Writers*, this one with a new entry on Georgette Heyer by S. A. Rowland, who was certainly an enthusiast, whether or not one entirely agrees with her. She divides Heyer's work into three categories: "the early swashbuckling romances (*Beauvallet*); [the] Regency comedy of manners, sometimes combined with a mystery story (*The Reluctant Widow*); and the late comedies of humour and feeling (*Frederica*)." She discussed how Heyer treated romantic conventions with irony, for example in *The Talisman Ring*, and exploded even her own romantic clichés, as in *A Civil Contract*. Rowland's social and/or feminist conscience led her to describe Heyer's created world as an artificial one in which

> . . .[s]ociety is run happily by males born to privilege and duty while females are confined to the domestic and romantic spheres. . . .However bold the heroines, their independence always proves a chimera when they find true love.

I think there is room for discussion here, and also regarding Rowland's summing-up below, but surely few readers would disagree with the very last words:

> Essentially a writer of adult fairy tales in a credible historical setting, Heyer created a unique world of delightful artifice. . . . [S]he was a true artist of comedy where laughter and love (not sex) always prevailed. She is sorely missed.

# V. *Other articles and books*

As I have stated before, my intention with this book is less to draw conclusions than to provide the raw material from which the reader may draw his or her own. There are some three dozen pieces represented here, most of which deal with Georgette Heyer's romances, but a surprising number of which are concerned specifically with her mysteries. Others are even more specialized, such as the two rather esoteric article excerpts analysing minutiae in her use of language. While most are appreciative or even grateful, some, if not altogether critical, certainly leave a negative flavor behind. Others are neutrally observant in a scholarly way.

There are particularly notable names, including novelists A. S. Byatt and Jane Aiken Hodge; scholars Germaine Greer, Jacques Barzun, Lillian Robinson, and Elaine Bander; and Georgette Heyer's own son, Queen's Counsel Sir Richard Rougier—not to mention less well-known names and comparative obscurities taking up a cause.

Among the recurring motifs are Georgette Heyer's relationship to Jane Austen, the presence of sex in her novels—or the lack thereof—her attitudes toward social class, and the relative emancipation of her heroines. *Regency Buck* crops up with what I feel is unfortunate frequency as the one novel out of all fifty-six to generalize upon. Most of the material here appeared originally in the 1980s; in the 1970s, it seems, Heyer was just gaining recognition beyond the romance-reading public, and as the 1990s progressed, she was increasingly accepted and even taken for granted.

I would like to express my particular gratitude to Eileen Kendall, Susan Faust, Sheri Cobb South, and especially to Jay Dixon for bringing to my attention important items I had not found on my own; and to Helen Hughes, Barbara Bywaters, and Marlo Newton for concentrating their material into a form I can include here. As so many of the writers represented here have said, there can be no more Georgette Heyers, but I hope this book can help extend our pleasure in her. Read, react, enjoy!

**A. S. Byatt, "Georgette Heyer Is a Better Novelist Than You Think" (in *Nova*, August 1969, pp. 14-22; reprinted as "An Honourable Escape: Georgette Heyer," in *Passions of the the Mind. Selected Writings* [New York: Turtle Bay Books, 1992], pp. 233-40):**

The only responsible position I ever held at my respectable boarding-school was a place on the Library Committee. I was relieved of it after one term. I assumed that this was because of general incompetence, but discovered later that it was because I had vetoed the purchase of Georgette Heyer's books, which the staff had taken as conclusive proof of intellectual arrogance, narrow-mindedness, the moralism of the Cambridge English school creeping up on me already. The truth was exactly opposite. The sharpness of my veto was a desperate attempt to conform to what I took to be *their* moralism. I had read every word of Georgette Heyer. I was a secret, illegal member of two circulating libraries to get more of her books. I had purloined exercise books to write two Regency romances and half a novel about the amours of Charles II. These were shockingly bad, and their badness led me to realise how difficult good escape literature is to write. Georgette Heyer still seems to me a superlatively good writer of honourable escape. This article is an attempt to exorcise my own past cowardice and hypocrisy by trying to say why.

Escape literature can exist to satisfy people's fantasies—sexual and social—at the expense of probability and "truth." But there is another kind, which exists less to satisfy hidden desires than to provide simple release from strain—the story with simple streamlined rules of conduct and a guaranteed happy ending. Both kinds like to create other worlds—imaginary lands of legend and fairy-tale, the past, the future, outer space, Tahiti, the aristocracy, the desert of the sheikhs and the American frontier.

270

There are various uses of costume drama. Much of it depends on the universal childhood desire to be someone else, somewhere else, usually someone more powerful and important. An incredible number of people claim to be reincarnations of Cleopatra, and even more read novels about her. Purely sexual costume drama probably derives from a time when there was more licence to describe sexual activity in other periods than in our own—which produced a spate of watered-down versions of Fanny Hill and Moll Flanders. A bastard version of these is the pruriently suggestive novel for nice girls, which has it both ways—describes the life of some great whore, courtesan, society lady, with suggestive details but has a moral scheme which ensures that the sex is narrowly avoided (except perhaps once), the tart has a heart of gold and *really* loves her dull, neglected husband all the time. There is straight cloak and dagger, as in Baroness Orczy; there is real curiosity about shifting cultures and beliefs, as in the best of Scott. There is "serious" work "explaining" some glamorous figure of the past in terms of modern psychiatry and sociology. The film *The Lion in Winter*, with its simplified Freudian explanations of Richard I's homosexuality and the power structure of mediaeval Europe, is one of these. It is bastard Albee—the "family romance," infantile needs controlling the language and behaviour of big business, the "deals" dictated by terror of incest and sibling rivalry. It diminishes both big business and the Plantagenets in the process.

Which brings me back to the "serious" literary-critical dismissal of escape literature. The Penguin literary history's *Modern Age* imperceptively lumps Georgette Heyer together with several other historical best-sellers as a "formula" writer who simply dresses up "modern bodies and feelings" in period disguise. It claims that the values and drift of her dialogue are essentially modern, despite the Regency phraseology. This, although true of the ponderously significant *The Lion in Winter*, does not seem to me to apply to Miss Heyer's lighter fantasies. They satisfy, too, much simpler emotions: the perennial need for a happy ending and, increasingly, a curiosity about historical facts of daily life and thought.

It is necessary to distinguish between her books. The earliest seem to be written out of a simple desire to create more of Baroness Orczy's

271

world of bright colour and danger—rather as my unsuccessful Regency pieces were written out of frustration because I could get no more Heyer. She began by adapting Baroness Orczy's solid, large English hero, whose lazy good looks and "inanity" hid a keen intelligence and a grip of iron. (Other descendants of this aristocratic hero are Lord Peter Wimsey and Albert Campion in their version of the streamlined escape world.) The heroes of *The Black Moth* (gentleman turned highwayman) and *The Masqueraders* are of this kind. In *The Masqueraders* the lazy, large gentleman casually unmasks the girl, who is disguised, for no very good reason, as a man.

In Miss Heyer's early novels great use is made of the fantasy-fulfilling cliché of sex-changing disguise; later she gets too subtle to need it. Romantic heroines in real life were clearly possessed by the same need to get into the comparative freedom of the man's world: both Mary Queen of Scots and Lady Caroline Lamb were fond of disguising themselves as beautiful page boys.

Another costume-novel cliché which appears in Miss Heyer's early work is the villain with the fascinating sneer, cold thin mouth, complete *sang-froid* and complete ruthlessness—except to his lady. The rather mechanically wicked villain of *The Black Moth* was resuscitated with a new name as Justin Alastair, Lord Avon, or Satanas, in *These Old Shades* and *Devil's Cub*. I imagine that the charm of Justin Alastair and his reckless son, Dominic, accounts for the names of small sons of many of my contemporaries.

In these two books Miss Heyer comes her nearest to playing with her readers' sexual fantasies. She is so successful because she avoids coming very near. In the first, the young heroine-disguised-as-a-boy, with conventionally flaming hair and huge violet eyes, is rescued, unmasked and finally married to a coldly "wicked" father-figure. This provides the faint *frisson* of danger which appeals to female masochism, and the appeal of achieving the impossible which (psychoanalysts would say) satisfies the Oedipal desires. In *Devil's Cub* Miss Heyer uses one of the stocks-in-trade of the romantic novel: the characters are in close proximity and without a chaperon almost from the beginning. This provides a sense of danger and drama and heightened expectation—the declarations of love, and the bedding, are of course delayed by points of honour and twists of the plot until the end.

Both these novels are successful escape literature—particularly the second—for two reasons. There is the minimum of sexual titillation—only, indeed, the proximity and the romantic appearance of the hero—and there is an increasing clever balance between geniune romance and a saving comic mockery of romance within romance.

*The Convenient Marriage* (1934) and *Friday's Child* (1944) both play with a variant of the delayed bedding trick: this one has been used by romantic novelists from Ethel M. Dell and Marie Corelli onwards. Hero and heroine are married for purely practical reasons at the beginning of the novel, but declarations of love are postponed to the end. No clue is given as to whether these marriages were consummated, although the reader must clearly be wondering and imagining. In *The Convenient Marriage* I *think* we are meant to assume that the hero—a gentleman and a Marquis—is waiting with superhuman patience until his schoolgirl wife really trusts him: this trust is delayed by the dastardly plotting of his ex-mistress and one of her beaux.

In *Friday's Child*, a much more successful novel, Georgette Heyer blandly and blatantly ignores the sexual issue until she makes a light joke about it on the very last page. In this novel the hero's ex-mistress is only mentioned when his wife asks at the Opera if *that* is his opera-dancer. Her sexual jealousy is sketched in very lightly indeed—but his rage at her public *faux pas* is crushing. Miss Heyer is beginning to employ the technique of her most successful work—the shifting of attention from the sexual imagination to the details of conventional behaviour and daily life. She employs increasingly less of the props of high passion—highwaymen, Jacobites, duels and disguise. She is playing romantic games with the novel of manners.

Miss Heyer is most successful with the artificial conventions of fashionable Regency society—a world of elegance, good taste, meaningful trifles and the high significance of *manners*. It has been said that in no other period were the ruling classes so secure in wealth, privilege and power. Some were politically active, many were without

273

responsibilities except their estates, which they often left to others to manage. They developed eccentricities and mannerisms to use up their time and wealth. Lord Petersham collected snuff boxes, Lord Alvanley won a bet that he could produce the most expensive dish at a meal (a pie made from three hundred small back pieces of thirteen different birds and costing £108 5s). The Green Man of Brighton dyed his clothes, furniture, carriages, livery and hair bright green. "Romeo" Coates took the Theatre Royal in Bath to play Romeo himself and drove an all-white curricle shaped like a shell. Max Beerbohm described an ordinary day in the life of a rich man:

> To spend the early morning with his valet, to saunter round to Whites for ale and tittle-tattle and the making of wagers, to attend "a drunken *déjeuner*" in honour of "la belle Rosalie," to drive far out into the country in his pretty curricle followed by two well-dressed and well-mounted grooms . . . and stop at every tavern on the road . . . to reach St James's in time for a random toilet and so off to dinner . . . dinner done, to scamper off to Ranelagh to dance and sup.

Into this leisured world Beau Brummell introduced the ideal of artfully achieved simplicity. He had clean, starched neckcloths, perfectly cut plain clothes, perfectly shining boots, and, unusually, he *washed*. "No perfume, but clean linen, plenty of it, and country washing." A biographer explains his success as "the perfect art which conceals art, that satisfying spontaneity which can be achieved only by taking intense thought."

The description would, curiously, fit the novels of Brummell's contemporary Jane Austen, who also held up the perfect manners of the perfect gentleman as an aesthetic and moral ideal.

In Jane Austen's world, as in Brummell's, keeping off boredom is a major emotional force—Emma's silliness, Anne Elliot's solitary pensiveness, Darcy's distant pride are functions of boredom. Nobody *need* work; neither men nor women were exhausted by hours of office labour like Dickens's heroes, let alone those career men and women with whose devotion of the major part of their lives to the strife of job and ambition the modern novel, serious or romantic, is singularly incompetent to deal. And in such a world marriage, the rituals of courtship and the subsequent family life were much more real, much more essentially important than they are now.

Georgette Heyer's awareness of this atmosphere—both of the minute details of the social pursuits of the leisured classes and of the emotional structure behind the fiction it produced—is her greatest asset. Her most attractive heroes are lazy, bored men—dandies, Corinthians, entirely in control of their clothes and amusements, enjoying them—but in need of something more. Her heroines are lively, resourceful girls, usually not rich, with natural moral taste combined with a certain unworldly innocence that arouses the masculine protectiveness of the heroes.

In these novels, besides the leisurely, decorous good-temper of the plots, it is the details of life which are satisfying. It has been said that Miss Heyer's slang—boxing cant, thieves' slang, the fashionable adjectives of the *ton*—is right to the year in which her book is set. Her clothes are certainly right—anyone leafing through the contemporary periodicals *La Belle Assemblée*, *The Lady's Magazine*, the *Beau Monde* after reading her novels will discover, as I did, a world of details of tissues, trimmings and cosmetic hints, already familiar turns of phrase, twists of the language I had always known through her novels. She can do shops and entertainments—fashionable milliners, the Pantheon Bazaar, Astley's theatre. The mechanical genius's interests in *Frederica* are fully documented. He wants to see a pneumatic lift in Soho and Trevithick's steam-locomotive—*not* the Puffing Devil, which burnt itself out on the road, but the one that was exhibited on its own track near Fitzroy Square.

W. H. Auden said that Jane Austen was good at describing "the amatory effects of brass." Miss Heyer is good at money and the lack of it, too. In *Black Sheep* there is an excellent portrait of a gentleman Nabob from India, who has made his fortune and is prepared to throw over certain conventions. In *Frederica* and *Arabella* there is a wealth of

275

fascinating detail about how to contrive ball dresses on a tiny budget. And she is aware of, and knowledgeable about, the ways in which men of birth used up their energy when not devoted to leisure or politics, the army and agriculture. She knows all about sheep-breeding, the "new" crops of turnips, swedes and mangel-wurzels, about Coke of Norfolk, Tull's Drill, manures and rotation of crops. Her two most realistic novels deal with the army and with finance. These are the early *An Infamous Army* and the fairly recent *A Civil Contract*.

*An Infamous Army* is a skilful reconstruction of the battle of Waterloo—included in the bibliography of Lady Longford's new biography of Wellington. It is meticulously researched and documented: the Iron Duke, Miss Heyer tells us, says nothing in the novel that he did not, in fact, say at some point of his life.

*A Civil Contract* comes nearest of Miss Heyer's novels to abandoning the streamlined escape world for real emotion and real causation. It deliberately reverses the romantic bed-trick of *The Convenient Marriage*. Adam inherits his father's title, estates and very heavy debts. He marries Jenny, the daughter of a rich Cit, despite his love for the beautiful Juliana, to save his estates. Jenny's father wants the title for Jenny; Jenny, who loves Adam, can only aspire rather bleakly to "make him comfortable" and give him an heir—both of which she does. She never becomes beautiful; although slightly improved by contact with Adam's family she remains essentially tasteless about clothes and flashy horses, although the crimp in her hair, the number of her jewels and her plumes are reduced. Adam copes with her generous, blundering, vulgar father with his own innate moral taste: he suffers because he is taking everything and really giving nothing—and since he does not come to love Jenny, only to settle with her, this problem has no easy solution. Sex enters this book more than any other, but on the same practical, flat, anti-romantic note. The couple are seen, apprehensive and nervously polite, heading towards a purposeful but unromantic honeymoon. There is no kiss, no sudden tension as in the novel of delayed romantic recognition—but Jenny's pregnancy, a sickly one, is documented in detail with appropriate medical regimens and errors, and Adam's protectiveness comes out. In this novel the denouement is provided not by love but by economics. Adam, a military man, is warned by his father-in-law to sell government stock in the panic before Waterloo; instead, gambling on his own professional skill and knowledge of Wellington, he *buys*, and repairs his fortune. I know of no other romantic novel in which the high tension is supplied by the Stock Exchange. And throughout the book attention is concentrated on daily life, family life, financial repairs, domesticity and agriculture.

Romantic love of Jane Austen's kind, if not of Caroline Lamb's, is an ideal image of a society which often had to make do with marriages of this kind. Miss Heyer knows about the relationship between the ideal and the actual; Jenny knows what she has got, and does not deny the reality of what she has not got.

Marghanita Laski has said that Georgette Heyer is a genius and defies description. I am painfully conscious that my description of her world leaves out the sparkle and comfort of the flesh and blood for the sake of largely irrelevant literary-critical bones. Why *is* she so good? Partly because she has good taste—her stories are deliberately innocent, not because she does not know about the seamier side of Regency life, but because she chooses to hint mockingly at it or ignore it.

Partly because she is neither prurient nor working out fantasies—her own or the reader's—and by deflecting attention from the passions to the daily life of her romantic characters, she manages to create an escape world of super-sanity in her fantasy. I think the clue to her success is somewhere here—in the *precise* balance she achieves between romance and reality, fantastic plot and real detail. Her good taste, her knowledge and the literary and social conventions of the time she is writing about all contribute to a romanticised anti-romanticism: an impossibly desirable world of prettiness, silliness and ultimate good sense where men and women really *talk* to each other, know what is going on between them and plan to spend the rest of their lives together developing the relationship. In her romantic novels, as in Jane Austen's, it is love the people are looking for, and love they give each other, guaranteed by the cushions, bonnets, and dances at Almack's and by the absence of sex-in-the-head. It is a myth and an idealisation, but it is one we were brought up to believe whether or not we really had Jane Austen in our

277

schoolroom. And because of Georgette Heyer's innocence and lack of prurience we can still retreat into this Paradise of ideal solutions, knowing it for what it is, comforted by its temporary actuality, nostalgically refreshed for coping with the quite different tangle of preconceptions, conventions and social emphases we have to live with. Which is what good escape literature is about.

**Germaine Greer, *The Female Eunuch* (New York: McGraw-Hill Book Company, 1970, pp. 167-85, 342-3):**

. . . Exploiting the sexual success of the Byronic hero in an unusually conscious way, Georgette Heyer created the archetype of the plastic age, Lord Worth, the Regency Buck. He is a fine example of a stereotype which most heroes of romantic fiction resemble more or less, whether they are dashing young men with an undergraduate sense of humor who congratulate the vivacious heroine on her pluck (the most egalitarian in conception) in the adventure stories of the thirties, or King Cophetua and the beggar maid.

> He was the epitome of a man of fashion. His beaver hat was set over black locks carefully brushed into a semblance of disorder; his cravat of starched muslin supported his chin in a series of beautiful folds, his driving coat of drab cloth bore no less than fifteen capes, and a double row of silver buttons. Miss Taverner had to own him a very handsome creature, but found no difficulty in detesting the whole cast of his countenance. He had a look of self-consequence; his eyes, ironically surveying her from under world-weary lids, were the hardest she had ever seen, and betrayed no emotion but boredom. His nose was too straight for her taste. His mouth was very well-formed, firm but thin-lipped. She thought he sneered.

> Worse than all was his languor.  He was
> uninterested, both in having dexterously averted an
> accident, and in the gig's plight.  His driving had
> been magnificent; there must be unexpected strength
> in those elegantly gloved hands holding the reins in
> such seeming carelessness, but in the name of God
> why must he put on such an air of dandified
> affectation?[1]

Nothing such a creature would do could ever be *corny*.  With such
*world-weary lids*!  With the features and aristocratic contempt which
opened the doors of polite society to Childe Harold, and the titillating
threat of *unexpected strength*!  Principally, we might notice, he exists
through his immaculate dressing—Beau Brummell is one of his friends—
but when he confronts this spectacle—

> She had rather have had black hair; she thought
> the fairness of her gold curls insipid.  Happily, her
> brows and lashes were dark, and her eyes which were
> startlingly blue (in the manner of a wax doll, she once
> scornfully told her brother) had a directness and fire
> which gave a great deal of character to her face.  At
> first glance one might write her down a mere Dresden
> china miss, but a second glance would inevitably
> discover the intelligence in her eyes, and the decided
> air of resolution in the curve of her mouth.[2]

Of course her intelligence and resolution remain happily confined to
her eyes and the curve of her mouth, but they provide the excuse for her
naughty behavior toward Lord Worth, who turns out to be that most
titillating of all titillating relations, her young guardian, by an ingeniously
contrived mistake.  He, confronting her in this charming dress—"a plain

---

[1] Georgette Heyer, *Regency Buck*, (London, 1968), p. 15.
[2] *Ibid.*, p. 5.

round gown of French cambric, frilled around the neck with scolloped lace; and a close mantle of twilled sarsenet. A poke bonnet of basket willow with a striped velvet ribbon. . ."[3]—and most compromisingly placed shaking a pebble out of her sandal, and so having to hide her stockinged foot in her skirts, sweeps her up into his arms and hurls her into his curricle (for at this point neither of them knows their relationship) where he "took the sandal from her resistless grasp, and calmly held it ready to fit on her foot." Then to provoke her charming indignation still further he kisses her. At such a rate of conquest the novel would be merely twenty pages long, if it were not that as her guardian Worth is too much of a man of principle to pay his addresses to her. She becomes, with his help, given sternly and diffidently, the belle of the season, wooed by all but loving none (but him). She has eighty thousand pounds a year, which is the motive for one sort of suitor; lustful desire for her is the motive of the rest, the most remarkable being the Prince of Wales, whose advances are so repugnant that she faints dead away, to be brought around and carried home by her masterful father-lover, who alone loves her without greed or self-interest (being fabulously wealthy, steadfast and strong). He protects her all the time, even though most of the time she is unaware of it, until her majority when, after a moment of looking down into her face, he sweeps her into his arms. Georgette Heyer has a streak of discretion, or perhaps prudery, which prevents her from exploiting the sexual climaxes in the writing: Barbara Cartland, on the other hand, overwrites the imagery of embracements and thereby reveals much more of the essential romantic preoccupations. In *The Wings of Love* she [Cartland] divides the love interest in two with Lord Ravenscar the forty-year-old lecher who covets tiny Amanda's lovely body. . . .

Miss Cartland's taste for titillation as far exceeds Heyer's as Heyer's researches into historical color exceed her own. . . .

Both these books I bought for three and sixpence in a supermarket, but it could not claim to have been a random choice, because I remembered those names, Heyer and Cartland, from my fantasy-ridden

---

[3] *Ibid.*

teens. . . .

This is the hero that women have chosen for themselves. The traits invented for him have been invented by women cherishing the chains of their bondage. . . .

Although romance is essentially vicarious the potency of the fantasy distorts actual behavior. The strength of the belief that a man should be stronger and older than his woman can hardly be exaggerated. . . . Ballroom dancing is an extraordinary capitulation on the part of society to the myth of female submissiveness; the women travel backwards, swept along in a chaste embrace, their faces close to the men's but not actually touching. Such dancing, which is only as old as Heyer's *Regency Buck*, may be seen as the expression of middle-class manners, for the aristocratic modes of dancing were formal while the lower orders allowed an independent part to the woman, involving greater or lesser exertion. There is no folk dance or native dance that I have ever heard of in which the man takes over the automotion of the woman. . . .

The most significant operation of the romance myth, however, is in the courting situation. Boys, unless they are consciously exploiting female susceptibility, have little idea what the kiss means in the romantic canon. For them it is a beginning, a preliminary to intimacy; for the girls it is the crown of love to be staged at climactic points. . . .The impulse to yield militates against the impulse to impose the right form on the circumstances, and most often a girl breathing out her soul on the lips of her callow lover seduces herself with an inflated notion of what is really happening. She offers at one time both more and less than he is asking. The baffling scenes that ensue when boys violate sentimental protocol testify to the fantasy operations of romance. It is such a simple role that more cynical young men fake it deliberately: the veriest tyro soon learns the best line is the suppressed-but-almost-uncontrollable-desire line, which a little heavy breathing and significant glancing can put over. How about the Cartland line, "If I kiss you I won't be answerable for the consequences"? Such dialogue could be dynamite. For all their prudish insistence on blushing and the excision of any suggestion of less intense and less decorous human contact, Cartland and Heyer are preparing the way for seducers—not lovers, seducers. But while they make the handsome man's job easier they put even more obstacles in the way of the homely male. Although the romantic male is not so invariable a stereotype as the characterless, passive female, he has certain indispensable qualities. He is never gauche, although he might be insolent or even insulting; he is never nervous or uncertain or humble, and he is always good-looking. In the tribal teenage situation there are some boys with whom one does not go out; they are not acceptable, being homely, or corny, or eager. Actual debauchery is less of a disqualification than any of these.

Settings, clothes, objects, all testify the ritualization of sex which is the essential character of romance. Just as the Holy Communion is not a real meal that satisfies hunger, the Almighty Kiss stands for a communion which cannot actually be enjoyed. . . .

Women's magazines treat the same story over and over again, changing the setting, inventing more and more curious combinations of circumstances to vary the essential plot; but falling in love, the kiss, the declaration and the imminent wedding are the staples of the plot. Other stories treat ancillary themes, of adulterers, of delusion and disappointment, or nostalgia, but the domestic romantic myth remains the centerpiece of feminine culture.

If female liberation is to happen, if the reservoir of real female love is to be tapped, this sterile self-deception must be counteracted. The only literary form which could outsell romantic trash on the female market is hard-core pornography. The titillating mush of Cartland and her ilk is supplying an imaginative need but their hypocrisy limits the gratification to that which can be gained from innuendo: by-pass the innuendo and you short-circuit the whole process. I and my little friends swapped *True Confessions* back and forth because we were randy and curious. If you leave the *Housewives' Handbook*[4] lying about, your daughter may never read Cartland or Heyer with any credulity.

---

[4] Rey Anthony, *The Housewives' Handbook on Selective Promiscuity* (Tucson, 1960, and New York, 1962).

**Marghanita Laski, "The Appeal of Georgette Heyer" (in "Books," *The Times* [London], 1 October 1970, p. 16):**

*Charity Girl.* By Georgette Heyer (Bodley Head, 30s).

Ever since the serious novel deprived itself of the pleasure of the shapely story satisfactorily resolved, serious but compulsive novel readers who need the shapely story as a drug have had to turn, for this part of their need, to the popular novel. Often it is easy to see why such books appeal to both non-intellectual and to intellectual: the gratifications to be gained from many thrillers, detective stories, science fictions and, of course, from Hornblower, are easy to discern.

The Regency novels of Georgette Heyer constitute another and more difficult case. Their appeal to simple females of all ages is readily comprehensible. But why, alone among popular novels hardly read except by women, have these become something of a cult for many well-educated middle-aged women who read serious novels too?

For men, a brief description may be helpful. Among other books, including detective stories, Georgette Heyer has for some 40 years been producing novels set in a kind of Zinkeisen-Regency England of which the latest, *Charity Girl*, is published today. They are entirely concerned with love and marriage among an upper class that ranges from wealthy dukes to wealthy squirearchy. The heroes, usually demoniac but occasionally gentle, are invariably dandies. The heroines may be spirited and sophisticated, spirited and naive, or, increasingly of recent years, common-sensible. By miscomprehension and misadventure, hero and heroine fail to achieve mutual understanding until the end.

Since nothing but the Regency element distinguishes these books from the best of the many thousands that used to fill the "B" shelves in Boots' Booklovers Library, it must be this element that gives the stories their special appeal, and this element is very odd indeed, for Miss Heyer's Regency England is not much like anything one infers about that time and place from more reliable writings, whether fiction or fact.

That Miss Heyer has done a lot of work in the period is obvious. Any of her characters may talk more "Regency English" in a paragraph than is spoken in Jane Austen's entire corpus. Real people often appear, such as Beau Brummel [sic] and Lord Alvaney and, of course, Lady Jersey, since whether or not the heroine will be admitted to Almack's is often a grave crux—she always is. Any individual Heyer novel can be an extremely enjoyable pastime, but the more Heyer novels one reads the more one recognizes the same limited props, slightly rearranged on the stage. Smart chairs are covered in straw-coloured satin, smart gloves of York tan are negligently pulled on, buttered lobsters are toyed with at elegant meals. Hardly a hero but has a multi-caped coat tailored by Weston, is envied by young cubs for his mastery of the neckcloth. Hardly a dashing heroine but takes the ribbons of a phaeton. Hardly a novel but introduces a Tiger or Game Chicken to exemplify the language of the Fancy in which Miss Heyer is especially deft.

But those aspects of life on which Miss Heyer is so dependent for her creation of atmosphere are just those which Jane Austen (and other novelists for years to come) referred to only when she wanted to show that a character was vulgar or ridiculous. Food, clothes, furnishings, transport—it is because those matters engrossed a Lydia Bennet, a John Thorpe, a Mrs. Elton, that we know them to be morally and socially worthless. Though Jane Austen's letters show how greatly clothes and furnishings, at least, interested her personally, it would obviously be entirely improper for them to interest her in relation to commendable characters. It is possible, even probable, that Fitzwilliam Darcy wore a many-caped coat built by Weston; it is unthinkable that we should know that he did.

It is not, then, in respect of decorum that Jane Austen has influenced Georgette Heyer but the influence is there, at least in the early books, in some balance and turn of sentences: "We talked of all manner of things until I was comfortable again, and I do not think there was never anyone more good-natured."—There is certainly an echo of Harriet Smith here. But "her characters was no *use*! They was only just like people you run across every day," as Kipling's soldier said of Jane Austen; they are several social steps below Miss Heyer's chosen ambience, and infinitely less glamorous. A model nearer in feeling and event would be Fanny Burney's much earlier Evelina.

But not there, or in Jane Austen or Maria Edgworth [sic] or even Harriet Wilson does one find Miss Heyer's extraordinary dandified heroes. There *were* dandies, but they were jokes, not heroes. Is it the shade of Sir Percy Blakeney that knocks at Miss Heyer's door? If so, his shadow is the only one that falls on this pseudo-Regency in which there is almost no dirt, no poverty, no religion, no politics (a short step to silence in books for women). I have still got no nearer to discovering why Miss Heyer's books appeal to so many educated women, but I know what lack of shadow it is that makes them of only limited appeal for me. It is because they have no sex in them

Now I realize that the popular romantic novel must be without overt sex, especially if it is to sell in that holy of holies of the trade, Irish convents. But not to say anything nasty is not necessarily the same thing as not to imply that sexual drives exist. In a good popular novel, be it overtly as clean as a whistle, we should never doubt that to put in the dirty bits would be merely to expand it and not to alter it or, as it would be in Miss Heyer's case, to shatter it. We have never doubted the sexual passion that linked Sir Percy and Lady Blakeney throughout their alienation. Stanley Weyman's depressed heroes suffer from real lust, his heroines are in danger of real rape. Even for Charlotte Yonge the sexual relations of her characters were at least implicit (and for what can be achieved within reticence, try her historical novel *Love and Life*). A counterbowderizing [sic] expansion could be undertaken on any lastingly worthwhile popular novelist.

But if ever Miss Heyer's heroines lifted their worked muslin skirts, if ever her heroic dandies unbuttoned their daytime pantaloons, underneath would be only sewn-up rag dolls. Her *mariages blancs* could run till doomsday without either partner displaying nervous strain; her heroes can, as in this latest, roam the country with unprotected young girls who need never fear loss of more than a good name. Certainly the odd hero may have had his opera dancer before he enters the heroine's (and our) ken, but not inside these covers. So long as the puppets are out of their box, a universal blandness covers all.

Were we to take Georgette Heyer simply as a novelist for women whose only novel-reading was popular romance, she would deserve the highest praise. As the genre goes, her books are better than most, and more complicated: it often takes a couple of chapters to guess who will finally marry whom. The Regency element is pleasantly novel and the props, if limited are genuinely period pieces. But the appeal to educated women who read other kinds of novels remains totally mysterious unless—is it?—could it be?—these dandified rakes, these dashing misses, the wealth, the daintiness, the carefree merriment, the classiness, perhaps even the sexlessness, are their dream world too?

**Erik Routley, *The Puritan Pleasures of the Detective Story* (London: Victor Gollancz Ltd., 1972, pp. 181-82):**

. . . Another author who combined historical fiction with a side-line in detection was Georgette Heyer. Her long series of historical novels has aroused contradictory opinions: it probably depends on what you think history is. If you feel that history is best related by reference to the more articulate and influential sections of society in whatever age is being put under review, then the Heyer novels give a faithful enough record and an adequate impression of their subjects: it is when one seeks a view of history that includes other people besides Regency bucks who were alive in 1815 that impatience begins to rear its head. She is probably better than her enemies suggest, and less admirable than her immense popularity implies. Anyhow, what is interesting from our point of view is what she made of the detective story.

She certainly tells a good story in the small handful she wrote in this form: but she stands with Agatha Christie as an assistant priestess of the cliché. Agatha Christie gets away with it (we have said) because she is such a fiendishly clever and formidably just plot-maker. Georgette Heyer's stories are as countrified and as county as the Poirot situations of 1920, but the detective interest that kept Mrs. Christie running never really gets off the ground in Heyer. For the rest—think of any detective-story cliché, any stock character, and you'll find it in her stories: the not-too-well educated policeman, the country vicar with the neurotic wife, the fast-talking competent sister of a heroine goaded near insanity by her husband's brutality, the exotic and outrageous Spanish dancer (called, of course, da Silva—Spaniards in thrillers are always that, or Garcia). It's all perilously near what used (until the *Nova* revolution) to be called "women's magazine" style—West End, rustic high life, able young asses who teach the police their job, loads of money, and butlers, butlers, butlers (yes, even a Shot Butler). In one book the characters in order of appearance bear the names Amberley, Brown, Collins, Dawson, Fountain, Gubbins, Harper, Jenkins, Ludlow, Matthews. Some better historian will surely tell me that that's been done before; all I can say is that this is where I first noticed it. And yet Georgette Heyer has a quite remarkable gift for reproducing the brittle and ironic conversation of the upper middle class Englishwoman of that age (immediately before 1940). I am bound to say that Vicky Fanshawe in *No Wind of Blame* (1939) is very nearly the funniest fictional female I have ever met—and it needs exquisite judgement to create a convincingly comical young woman in any kind of novel.

**Unattributed, "Vacuum-packed passions" (in *Times Literary Supplement*, 30 August 1974, "Fiction," p. 923 [a review of Rona Randall, *Dragonmede*]):**

The late Georgette Heyer was a writer of the highest craft, much underrated by most critics of fiction. To entertain, as she did, with novels of manners of impeccable period accuracy, and which often described individuals of unfashionably strong character or with strong "faults" of character coming to terms with a rigidly hierarchical society, is no casual feat. Her stories were encased, furthermore, in a believable, if pragmatic, moral code. She could even at times risk a realistic story of compromise (as in *A Civil Contract*) rather than the narcissistic finales of perfect happiness demanded in the usual romantic novel. In these respects she had much in common with Daphne du Maurier, another entertainer.

Between them, they have spawned yet another sub-genre of the modern romantic novel, the Gothic romance. Rona Randall's

*Dragonmede*, a selection this past spring of the American Literary Guild, is an example. It is peculiarly undistinguished, marked only by a certain imitative crispness. The plot has everything, including insanity, fratricide, and significant, deliberate, plotted coincidences, as well as judicious doses of the "purple heart throbs":

> With one swift movement I was off the couch, restoring order to my disarranged skirts, smoothing my hair, turning my back upon him as I drew my torn bodice over my breasts and hid from him the tears which disillusion brought.

It is an ingredient of such novels that the characters, unlike those of Miss Heyer, exist in a vacuum, the subject of the novel being only their own domestic needs and emotions. For one reason or another heroines are often outcasts. Women of good birth forced to earn their living are frequent, governesses obligatory. In *Dragonmede*, this claustrophobic isolation is induced by the social ostracism in which the sub-heroine, Luella Rochdale, mistress of a gambling house and thus outside polite society, exists. The novel concerns her successful efforts to marry off her daughter Eustachia (who narrates), and the events which spring from the consequences of Eustachia's grand marriage.

Sympathy is engaged by the simple disparity between the readers' knowledge and grasp of the web of coincidence on which the plot depends and the knowledge and understanding of Eustachia herself. If we are interested at all, it is to cheer Eustachia feebly on. The motivation of the characters is elementary, basically that of survival without the loss of public esteem. The plot moves from Eustachia's growing comprehension of the cruelty and callousness of her husband, Julian, her understanding of the family she has married into where nothing is as it first seemed to her as a bride, and her further realization of her mother's reasons for engineering the marriage in the first place.

Throughout all this melodrama, the period detail—we are told the novel is set in the mid-1800s—is not at all well done: the novel is really set in no-time. The psychological insights and observations occasionally muttered by the narrator are totally out of keeping with her supposed station, time and education, although they do add a certain spice to the almost unimaginable blancmange that is the texture of the book.

The real interest of this slight work is in the indisputable fact that it will have so many readers. And this in spite of the fact that unlike the best romantic thrillers or romantic novels *Dragonmede* neither delights us with facts or technical descriptions of specialized groups in society, nor interests us in the development and conflict of characters. Its only virtue is that it is smoothly and grammatically written, seldom a feature of the present-day romantic novel. The lowest common denominators of the genre will interest future social and cultural historians; the authors' assumptions about what women really want to read, at least, are accurate enough. It is Janet and John with sex thrown in, and if the results read as though they were written by committee or computer, it is this which ensures their commercial success. It is only authors of exceptional talent, like Miss Heyer, who can be literate, amusing, witty, as well as romantic—and successful.


**A. S. Byatt, "The Ferocious Reticence of Georgette Heyer" (*Sunday Times Magazine* [London], 5 October 1975, pp. 28-38):**

*Georgette Heyer's last novel,* My Lord John, *was posthumously published three days ago. Although she is as widely read as any contemporary writer, she had a horror of personal publicity and almost nothing is known about her private life. With the co-operation of Miss Heyer's husband, Ronald Rougier, the novelist A. S. Byatt provides the first biographical portrait of this formidable figure, and a critical appreciation of her work. It is illustrated by photographs from the Rougier family albums. Above: Georgette Heyer as a young woman. Above right: Ronald Rougier, photographed after his wife's death in their London flat by David King.*

When Georgette Heyer died last year, aged 71, she had written over 50 books. She was one of the great bestsellers, but refused to give interviews and was very rarely photographed. Anything anyone needed to know about her, Miss Heyer said, could be found in her books. But part of the charm of the books is that they have the anonymity of good comedy. They tell you as much and as little about their creator as Jeeves or Mr Pickwick. Such reticence, in such an author, seemed admirable and proper. It was also somewhat ferocious. In 1955 she wrote to a prospective interviewer:

> As for being photographed At Work, or In my Old World Garden, that is the type of publicity which I find nauseating and quite unnecessary. My private life concerns no-one but myself and my family; and if, on the printed page, I am Miss Heyer, everywhere else I am Mrs Rougier, who makes no public appearances and dislikes few things so much as being confronted by Fans. There seems to be a pathetic belief today in the power of personal publicity over sales. I don't share it, and before you assure me how mistaken I am I beg you will consider the case of the late Ethel M. Dell, about whom the public knew nothing, and whose colossal sales we should all of us be glad to have had. . .
>
> Console yourself with the thought that my answers to the sort of questions Fans ask seem to daunt them a bit! Not unnaturally, they expect me to be a Romantic, and I'm nothing of the sort.

Ronald Rougier, Georgette Heyer's husband, has now decided that it is proper that there should be some kind of record of his wife's life and way of work, and very kindly allowed me to see her books and notebooks, as well as talking to me himself and arranging for me to speak to her close friend, Carola Oman, and her publisher for 20 years, A. S. Frere, of Heinemann. I saw also her present publisher, Max Reinhardt of The Bodley Head, and Joyce Weiner, who, as her agent, protected her for many years from fans, journalists, intruders. All these people were very courteous and helpful; almost all were alarmed, in somewhat similar ways, at the breaking of a way of conduct Miss Heyer had decided upon. I said once to Mr. Rougier: "I don't feel even now that I *know* your wife at all. But then, she wouldn't have liked that." "Well," he said, politely, "shall we say, not too intimately." What follows is a not too intimate account of what I have learned about Georgette Heyer.

She was born, in Wimbledon, on August 16, 1902, the year of Edward VII's coronation. She was the daughter of George Heyer, M.A., MBE, and Miss Sylvia Watkins. On George Heyer's side she was of Russian extraction—her paternal grandfather had, according to Mr Rougier "emerged from Kharkhov," married a Miss Roum, of an old English Norfolk family, and settled on Blackheath. Sylvia Watkins's family had for generations owned the tugs on the Thames, and had indeed been responsible for the transport and installation of Cleopatra's needle on the Embankment. Mrs. Heyer studied at the Royal College of Music and was a talented cellist, one of the three outstanding pupils of her year. There were two younger brothers, one four and one nine years younger than Georgette, both with one English and one Russian name, George Boris, and Frank Dmitri. George Heyer, the father, read Classics at Cambridge and was brought up to be a gentleman: later, when the family suffered financial reverses he became a schoolmaster, and came to teach at King's College, Wimbledon. Georgette Heyer seems to have been deeply attached to him, and he to her. When she started telling the story of *The Black Moth* to her elder brother, when she was 17 and the brother was recovering from a serious illness, it was her father who encouraged her to prepare it for publication.

George Heyer fought in the First World War (Georgette was in Paris in 1914 and claimed to have heard Big Bertha) and died, suddenly, in June 1925, after playing tennis with Ronald Rougier, one month after his daughter's engagement, and two before her marriage. In 1958 Georgette Heyer, writing to Mrs Frere about the relationships between parents and children, wrote roundly that it was nonsense to imagine that a daughter pined for sympathy from her Mama. "Frere may tell me that I don't know because I haven't *got* a daughter (and a lucky break for that daughter that is!) but he forgets that I have *been* a daughter. Boys tell their Mothers, and Girls tell their Fathers." With her mother her relations were less enthusiastic and cordial. "A love-hate relationship," Mr Rougier called it, and said that for obscure reasons Mrs. Heyer had been very hostile to her daughter's writing in its early days, although very proud of her later. Mrs Heyer was a widow for 49 years, living in various Kensington hotels, and devotedly cared for by her daughter, who also made over to her the American rights to her novels during her lifetime.

*Photos: Georgette Heyer with her mother and brother; her father, a few hours before his death; Ronald Rougier, shortly after his marriage to Georgette Heyer, in Tanganyika; Georgette Heyer, Ronald Rougier, their son Richard, his wife, the latter's family; a late snapshot of Georgette Heyer taken by her husband while on a Scottish holiday; Georgette Heyer's favorite photograph of herself; on a rare public appearance, with the writer Kay Dick at a literary party; Mr. and Mrs. Rougier in Venice—an unusual holiday—she much preferred the North; Mr. and Mrs. Rougier playing a game of bridge with their son Richard and a friend.*

Ronald Rougier, like his wife, was of Russian descent. He was born in Odessa, and his family, who were in business, later moved to Northumberland. The Rougiers met at the Bushey Hall Hotel where both families had gone for Christmas. Ronald Rougier was at that stage a mining engineer and it is clear that he was fascinated by George Heyer as well as by his daughter. He described him as a born teacher, whatever he was brought up to be, a man given to explaining history, recommending books, quoting the *Iliad*, offering information, lines for further thought on things "in which my own family weren't really interested." Mr. Rougier became Georgette Heyer's official dancing partner. After five years' acquaintance they became engaged and then married. Two months later he went abroad, prospecting on the Caucasus, where his Russian was useful. He was back in the summer of 1926 and in the autumn went out to Tanganyika. In spring 1927 Georgette Heyer went out to join him. She was then 24, and had already published *The Black*

*Moth, Powder and Patch* and *These Old Shades*, as well as *Simon the Coldhearted* [sic] and *The Great Roxhithe* [sic], which she later suppressed.

Photographs of her at this time show a tall, slender, elegant woman with a shingled head of dark hair, and an expression at once shy and composed. Carola Oman, a lifelong friend, says she first met her when Georgette Heyer was 17, "in a cloud of hair," and the two of them used to meet in Wimbledon and read their work in progress to each other. I borrowed from Mr. Rougier a novel published by Georgette Heyer in 1929, and set in a suburb called Meldon which was clearly Wimbledon transposed. Bad works by good writers are always very instructive. *Pastel* is concerned with two sisters, one, Evelyn, fashionable, witty, daring, "modern," attractive, given to scarlet and brilliant yellow, the other, Frances, sweet, girlish, shy, pretty, "pastel" indeed, naturally inclined to domesticity and motherhood but without Evelyn's "flair" for a place-setting, a ball dress, driving a sportscar. Evelyn gets the beautiful Viking blond young barrister Frances wanted: Frances "makes do" with Norman who has always been there and never wavered in his devotion. She reflects that reality is better than romance, or at least reliability is, and gives birth to a daughter, reflecting later that Evelyn would no doubt have "a male child," but that she is satisfied. She feels her creator is punishing her, and also punishing Evelyn, the one for living without style and vitality, the other for concentrating on modern trivia, terrible plays about psychic projections, claustrophobic "arty" parties. Neither Meldon domesticity nor Chelsea chic clearly attracted the author of this remorselessly, vehemently lifeless work very much. The novel is informed by a sense of something missing for all its heroine's protests about being satisfied with life as it is. Many of Miss Heyer's heroines complain of lack of adventure, protest against its arrival, and meet it with aplomb.

Tanganyika was certainly not Wimbledon. The Rougiers were there for two years, living in a hut made of elephant grass, in a compound in the bush, prowled round by lions, leopards, and rhinos. There was one other white man in the compound, a "rough, Cornish miner"; the natives had never seen a white woman; the nearest white people, the District

Officer and Game Warden, were 150 miles away. Mr. Rougier went on safari, prospecting for tin. Mrs. Rougier sat in the grass hut, with her books, and wrote *The Masqueraders*. Once she went on safari too, travelling 18 miles one day and 22 the next, over very rough ground, on one water-bottle a day. She did not complain once, of heat or difficulty, but did not go again. *The Masqueraders* turned out to have only one anachronism, despite the circumstances of its writing—White's Club had been made to open a year before it did.

After Africa, in 1929, the Rougiers went to Macedonia, again mining. As usual Mr Rougier preceded his wife; *The Masqueraders* came out while he was in Macedonia and she in England: his telegram on receiving his copy reached her as "Congratitations. Find Mahineroders excellent" [sic].

What scanty press material there already was about Georgette Heyer agreed that it was she who had decided that they settle in England. I asked Mr. Rougier why: he replied that she had said that it was impossible to start a family unless they did. Carola Oman said that Georgette Heyer, although she could put up complete barriers around certain topics which were then never discussed, could be both forceful and outspoken about others, and instanced the decision to have a baby.

Mr Rougier had always wanted to be a barrister; it had simply not been the kind of profession his family had been able to imagine for him. He now began to read for the Bar—supported by his wife, and her earnings—and was called in 1939.

Their only son, Richard, now also a very successful Q.C., was born in 1932. His mother was clearly passionately devoted to him (though there were nannies, and governesses). He went to Marlborough, like his father, and to Cambridge with an Exhibition in Classics. He is a skilled bridge player, also like his father, and played in the Olympic Bridge Trials.

As well as playing cards, the Rougiers were given to playing guessing games with Shakespearean quotations in the evenings. Mr. Rougier says that his wife knew most of Shakespeare by heart—although her son accused her of not understanding tragedy, when she expressed dislike of *Anna Karenina* and scorn for the idiocy of the characters in *Othello*.

For 10 years the family lived in Sussex, and then moved to the

294

Albany, where A. S. Frere was also living. For the last 15 years of her life Georgette Heyer was in ill-health and the 70 stone steps to their set of chambers in the Albany became too much. She dispatched her husband to hunt for flats—finally, finding one she did not "spit at the idea of," they eventually settled at Parkside, Knightsbridge.

What was she like, and how did she live? One is hesitant about asking such questions about anyone who so resolutely refused to answer them, and indeed, made it seem an instance of very bad *ton* to ask them. Certain words recurred. She was clearly formidable, she was clearly witty, she was clearly a woman of intense loyalties to her chosen circle of friends and relatives. She was, her former agent, Miss Weiner said, Mr. Rougier himself said, a "recluse." This clearly meant more than that she rejected any kind of publicity. Even in private life, she was a very private person. She "did not like meeting new people." She was, A. S. Frere said, one of those people who are much better hosts than guests, happy on her own ground, in company she knew and had selected, among people who shared her own kind of joke or style of conversation. She was not a snob but, as Joyce Weiner says, her motto might have been "*odi profanum vulgus*" and she clearly did not suffer fools gladly. Towards those whom she did admit to her friendship she was clearly absolutely loyal and extremely generous.

Men tell you that she did not like women. A. S. Frere said that it was a good thing she had a son, not a daughter, as she used to terrify women. Particularly younger women, like her son's girl-friends. Max Reinhardt says she preferred male conversation. Women credit her with "masculine" characteristics—a "masculine mind" Miss Weiner said, "a *man's* good manners," Mrs. Frere (the literary critic, Pat Wallace) said. "I wouldn't have called them a man's good manners," said her husband, "but *you* may say so of course." "She liked," A. S. Frere said, ". . . what was that phrase she used in her novels? To depress people's pretensions." "To give a 'masterly set-down,'" I said.

It was clear that many people found her alarming. Her letters to Frere about pushing journalists (characterised as S. Bs for Silly Bitches) run on in a spate of gleeful and half real, half mock—irritable contempt. But the ultimate example of Georgette Heyer's capacity to alarm people is worthy of one of her own works.  Max Reinhardt described how she was invited to lunch at Buckingham Palace.  She telephoned him to ask, should she go, would he have lunch afterwards to talk about it?  She went, elegant in a very large sloping hat—everyone agrees that she had excellent taste in formidable hats.  She came back, charmed by Her Majesty, who had read and enjoyed her books.  And was told that the Queen, doing her Christmas shopping a week later in Harrods, had ordered a dozen copies of her latest book and had told the saleswoman: "She came to lunch with me last week and I found her *very* formidable." "Do you think I could terrify *anyone*?" Georgette Heyer asked Max Reinhardt, in, as he put it, "her loud clear voice, terrifying every waiter."

*Photo: Georgette Heyer, beneath her own portrait, with her husband and her son.*

In her private life, besides her work, she seems to have liked things that required skill, or style, or precision, from jigsaws, to cards, to complicated kitchen gadgets—she collected, Mr Rougier says, a variety of tin-openers, bains-marie, fish-kettles, and rejoiced in a waste-disposal unit; she was interested in her husband's and son's golf and was a passionate watcher of television sport—particularly cricket and show-jumping.  She liked to choose clothes and was known to castigate people for wearing topaz with pearls, or patterned fabrics, even by Emilio Pucci.  She liked to choose meals, always appropriately with vegetables in season, and carefully thought-out wines.  She liked window-shopping and taking her grandsons—two boys from her daughter-in-law's earlier marriage, and her own grandson—to Harrod's.  She had—as far as I can see—the true letter-writer's gift of making the loss of a borrowed handkerchief, the re-covering of a screen in gold brocade, into comic and absorbing adventures.  If she was a formidable presence, and had a scholarly mind, the writer of the domestic letter is recognisably the same as the one who describes the refurbishing of Arabella's limited wardrobe, or the Reluctant Widow's struggles with decayed furniture and lofts of junk.

Her literary tastes, too, show catholic admiration of precise competence. She liked Alistair Maclean and Richmal Crompton, G. B. Stern and E. F. Benson, Noel Coward, Raymond Chandler and Ivy Compton-Burnett. All, at least, superb craftsmen, and several creators of idiosyncratic languages.

The interest in skill, precision, competence, centred on her own work. Her success was phenomenal, though not immediate—it began, Ronald Rougier says, with the sales of *These Old Shades* in Australia, from where she received a letter saying that she was "a bonzer woman" and that the writer, a librarian, "noticed that all the girls who read the filthiest books like yours." Her sales were enormous, although, as Frere says, she never had a review in a serious paper, and vetoed most publicity. Max Reinhardt says they sell between 65 and 80 thousand copies of her books in hard covers: Frere said he had to decide whether to print 80, or 100, or 120 thousand, and that her runaway best seller was printed in the year of the General Strike with no newspapers, no trains, and no post. Paperbacks sell over half a million at least and The Bodley Head have received their biggest paperback offer ever for the coming *My Lord John*.

She was, apparently, most punctilious to deal with, always presented perfect MSS on the deadline, and never needed any correction. I wonder, reading part of her correspondence with Frere, looking at her card-indexes, her library, her notebooks, whether the very magnitude of her popular success made her doubt the value of her work. She was certainly ferociously derisive of, and angry about, other popular novelists who without her learning cashed in on her success, plagiarised or adapted her plots and period language. But she referred to her own work with a persistent, broadly funny self-mockery which, I feel, hid a sense that it had more real value than was acknowledged. Her contempt for most of the fans, came, I think, from the same knowledge that she was not, as she said she wasn't, a Romantic. Joyce Weiner said that she always answered fan-letters that required historical information. Max Reinhardt qualified this. She answered them "if the question was intelligent enough and rightly put."

Typical of her self-deprecating sharpness is this remark about *Venetia*, addressed to Mrs. Frere: "I dislike the book as much as I disliked *Sophy*, or even more, shouldn't be surprised if the fans do too.

Except that my hero is a Rake, which always gets my silly sex. Of course I don't let him do anything worse than kissing the heroine on sight, and getting mildly tight: all his rakishness lies in the Past, and I've given him a very good reason for going to the Dogs, because however written out I may be I do still know my onions!" Or, of *April Lady*: "Oh, yes, I can explain *April Lady's* success! Almost the Top of the Popular-Appeal Stakes (amongst females) is the Rift in the Married Lute—provided it All Comes Right in the End, and was never serious in the first place." And "Would you believe it? My Mama loved *April Lady*! There, I feel, speaks My Public—also feeble-minded!"

An editor at Heinemann who once mistakenly, in Frere's absence, asked Georgette Heyer to write her own blurb received by return of post a caustic, witty and mocking description of the book as the usual folly. But Max Reinhardt, attempting to offer helpful editorial suggestions about the language of the first of the novels he published, was told roundly that no-one in the country knew more about Regency language than Miss Heyer, and that there was no point in pretending anyone did. No more editorial suggestions were made.

Towards the end of her successful career Georgette Heyer was bedevilled by income tax problems. What she saw as her major work—the trilogy on the life of John, Duke of Bedford, Henry V's younger brother—was constantly being laid aside so that another Regency romance could be produced to satisfy the tax man. Some of these unwilling romances show signs of fatigue—*April Lady*, whose plot is a rehash of the earlier *Convenient Marriage*, is a case in point, and both she and Mr Rougier felt that this was so. She wrote to A. S. Frere in 1955:

> I never felt less like writing a gay romance, and am churning out heavy pastry in a slow laborious fashion, and am quite likely to go into strong hysterics if anyone speaks a harsh word to me. Or any other kind of word that I don't happen to want to listen to. I suppose the book [probably *Bath Tangle*, again a tired book] will get itself written in the end. . .

> But when I sit and try to think about it, I find, after
> half an hour, that I have mentally written the whole
> of Henry V's death-bed scene. Blast everything!
> When I once again laid John of Lancaster in
> lavender, I felt as I did when I saw Richard off to his
> Prep school for the first time.

It was part of Georgette Heyer's sense of style not to appear to take
her romances seriously—or herself. She disliked most writers and the
public pretensions of writers—Frere said that she was "good company"
because she had not the self-absorption, or sense of the paramount
importance of her work that almost all of them had. She referred to
writers as Inkies—her first letter to Max Reinhardt begins, "So Frere
thinks it is a pleasure to deal with me, does he? He must have forgotten
how broad a view I've always taken of his duties towards me. My own
opinion is that all Inkies are hell, and ought to be incarcerated." Or, to
Frere, making a lunch date, she suggests that she could engineer
publicity, for him, by appearing with a monstrous wolf-hound, "or shall I
just come as Little Ma—really the *simplest* of creatures, happiest when
pottering about my kitchen (my books just seem to *come* to me, you
know) but just *too* touched and happy for words to think of the pleasure
I've given to the Feeble-minded?"

But, of course, her books did not just come to her. They were worked
for, and worked at. She was one of those rare writers who create an
idiosyncratic world, recognisably their own, a world with its own laws
and language. What I learned from looking at her papers and talking to
Mr. Rougier about her working methods was that her life-style, too, was
in its way a creation of a world of her own, with its own laws and
barriers to the outside world.

She was, of course, very fortunate in having a husband who was truly
and deeply interested in what she was doing. With all her detective
stories, except the first, he provided the plots, from his legal and other
knowledge. I asked him, did he or she invent the characters for those
joint works, and he assured me that the people were her work—he called
them A, B, C, D, and she would give them flesh and feelings, and then

change his plots, or request alternatives because A or B "could *never* have behaved like that." But he shared, too, her interest in history, and in the collection of facts. He still has the map they used of the Old English roads when they followed, together, all the movements of Charles II after the battle of Worcester, visiting every inn and priest's hole. And many of the books in Georgette Heyer's collection were happy *trouvailles* of his own—including the monumental *Master of Game* by Edward, Second Duke of York, which plays a part in the language and plot of *My Lord John.*

I had imagined that Georgette Heyer researched in libraries, maybe studying in the British Museum. Miss Weiner assured me that she would not have tolerated such a *public* activity. She had her own idiosyncratics and impressive library of about 1000 historical books among which she sat to write. The OED, the DNB, Lemprière, dictionaries of slang, dialect, Anglo-Saxon, Fowler, Roget, Debrett, Burke, an 1808 dictionary to the House of Lords, proverbs, place-names, foreign phrases. She had standard historical works in both the mediaeval and 18th-century periods, as well as more recondite histories of snuff-boxes, of sign-posts, and coaching. There are several shelves on costume from Planché's two-volume *Cyclopedia of Costume* (1876) to Alison Adburgham on *Shops and Shopping*, from Grand-Cartaret, *Les Elégances de la Toilette* to *The History of Underclothes*. She wrote at a Norwegian oak desk which looks rather like a drinks cabinet, and opens to display two wings of bookshelves, between which she sat, with dictionaries and reference books to hand, and drawers and shelves of paper, glue, pins around her. Another enclosed world.

Her notebooks are the work, not of a professional scholar, although they are precise, orderly and passionate about accuracy, but of someone interested in two main things—the bringing to life of the matter-of-fact which is the stuff of fiction, and vivid language. The Regency notebooks are indexed collections of words and figures, under headings like Boots and Shoes, Beauty, Colours, Dress, Hats, Household, Prices, Shops. Slang items, or catching similes for fatness, or dishonesty, or folly cover pages of notes. There are careful records of the cost of keeping a carriage—in the country £213 p.a., in London, over £500 p.a. Or of

300

lights, candles, spermacetti, common oil, lamp oil, cotton for lamps.

The work—the life-work—for the mediaeval novel is more detailed and more extensive.  There are large card indexes, containing a biographical card for each of a huge list of characters, embellished with their coats of arms, carefully drawn by Georgette Heyer.  There are cards for every year from 1390 to 1495, the year of the death of John of Bedford and the beginning of the fall of the House of Lancaster.  On these cards, month by month, she listed the events she read about.  There are small notebooks of phrases, as in the Regency period, under headings such as: Forms of Address, Archery, Chivalry, Church, Dress, Drink, Endearments, Exclamations and Expletives, Food and Cookery, Fools, Furs, Furniture, Games, Hawking, Horses, Materials, Measures, Medicine and Sickness, Music, Naval, Proverbs and Sayings.  It is not scholarly, in the sense that method and proportion are subordinated to imaginative vitality, but it is dense, detailed and even the lists have a combination of verbal dash and concrete reality, which is one of the merits of her books.

Looking through these papers, remembering *Pastel*, I had a sense that this real other world was what had been missing, and that the very act of research was for Georgette Heyer, the act of recreating a past to inhabit.  It was the froth or smoothness of the wish-fulfilment of her plots that she mocked about her work:  never the recreation of history, certainly never the prose.  She despised, sometimes, their appeal to foolish females, but history she took seriously.

The opposition between masculine and feminine elements in her work is largely misleading.  Her letters are feminine, her preference for male company seems to have been very feminine, her depiction of the relations between men and women, feminine.  Precision and forcefulness are not exclusively male characteristics, nor, even, is a capacity to delineate a battlefield or describe generalship.  Men who don't like her romances do like her military books—*An Infamous Army* is a tour-de-force in its dovetailing of a romantic plot into a detailed depiction of Waterloo, vividly brought to life.  But men did like her romances, for their wit, their poise, their historical accuracy.

What *she* did not like, Mr. Rougier said, was female gushing about her plots (she was nauseated to overhear someone describe *A Sprig of Muslin* [sic] in Truslove and Hanson as "such a sweet, pretty book"). Men who wrote to her asked precise questions, which she answered. She is on record as saying the women in the Middle Ages, with dowers and the management of castles or conduct of sieges, had considerable independence and power. The bad days set in with Queen Victoria's romantic over-dependence on Prince Albert. Law Lords, Mr. Rougier remembers, prized Miss Heyer's work. Lord Justice Somervell bequeathed his Georgette Heyer collection to the library of the Inner Temple Bench. I cannot imagine this happening to most writers for the titillation of the Female Heart. Miss Heyer had a toughness and independence like her more resourceful heroines.

In what sense, then, was it true that she could be found in her books? I think there are various things that the books and their author, so determinedly reticent, had in common, one of which, as I have just suggested, was a liking for the closed, yet lively fictional world of the past. Georgette Heyer liked form and style, both in chivalry and mediaeval courtesy, in the manners and social nuances of the 18th century, in a modern world she felt to be disintegrating into formlessness.

She admired the Queen Mother, and what she stood for: she was sharp about Princess Margaret's attempt to create a modernised, dashing or informal royal image. She knew how a good letter should be written and commented tartly to Frere when his subordinates wrote her a bad one, either over-gushing or over-bold. She disliked, Max Reinhardt says, the modern world, especially "the anxiety with which we want to reach equality." Her tax grumbles included: "I'm getting so *tired* of writing books for the benefit of the Treasury and I can't tell you how utterly I resent the squandering of *my* money on such fatuous things as Education and Making Life Easy and Luxurious for So-Called Workers." Any interest in style, especially style in the past, is a way of fending off the threats or demands of a world which style distances, controls, or makes easy to judge. In that sense, Miss Heyer, and her work, for better or worse, are conniving in escape, and escape literature.

It occurred to me, writing this article, that "escape" literature is too broad a category to be useful. Escape from what? The humdrum, the

302

tedious, into a bright world of perfect hats and wise, considerate lovers, of money and wit and gaiety? Yes, although the brightness and gaiety have their roots in realities of common sense, plausible conduct, quite unexplored by the real bosom-flutterers of the profession. But there are worse things, from which we all must escape—illness, mourning, horrors. And Georgette Heyer seems to be, as well as a courageous woman, a provider of courage in others. Among her papers are two moving tributes. The first by Lady Ellenborough (Rachel Law) was sent to Ronald Rougier after his wife's death. In this Lady Ellenborough points out that Georgette Heyer remains readable even when one is in hospital beds awaiting drastic surgery. Shakespeare slips away, she says; pornography, at the other end, is no good because "sex is cut down to size when the swish of the scythe sends a draught down the corridors." But Georgette Heyer's comedy, archetypal, external, has a kind of earthy vigour which is sustaining.

This is something I have found to be true myself—she remains tolerable, interesting, gripping when things are so bad that most high literature seems irrelevant and bad entertainment drives one insane. The fan letter she herself kept, and by which she was deeply moved, was a letter from a woman political prisoner in Rumania who had been incarcerated for 12 years with no access to books or visitors, and had kept herself and her fellow-prisoners sane by reciting *Friday's Child* as a kind of endless serial. Good escape literature has subtle relations to what it is measured against; it knows, secretly, what that is. It is interesting that Georgette Heyer, for all her Russian ancestry, was "(I say it defiantly) wholly Allergic to Russian literature, drama, and art . . . I loathe and despise their silly Fatalism. In fact, I am glad to think that I inherited less of my grandfather's Russian temperament than any other of his descendants." She adhered to the English virtues, good taste, unobtrusive courage, the saving joke.


**Jacques Barzun and Wendell Hertig Taylor,** *A Book of Prefaces to Fifty Classics of Crime Fiction 1900-1950* **(New York/London: Garland Publishing, Inc., 1976, pp. 63-4):**

Georgette Heyer
*A Blunt Instrument*

The work of Georgette Heyer shows that the commonplace idea of what is or is not consistent in human character has no basis in reality. Biographers keep telling us that their subject was "a bundle of contradictions": all this ever means is that the biographer's notion of life is preshrunk by faulty logic. There can be no contradictions—that is, mutually exclusive forces—in a going concern such as a human being. The "contradiction" of this nonexistent kind in Georgette Heyer is that her agile mind alternately produced flimsy historical romances, chiefly about the Regency period, and modern tales of detection of the most solid kind.

Though her fame in the latter genre is not as widespread as that of Sayers, Christie, Marsh, and Allingham, she unquestionably belongs to that remarkable company. Her output of just a dozen choice works puts her precisely next to Sayers. In both, undiluted quality marks each tale, whereas the other three much more prolific women, who at their best equal the distinguished pair, fall below them again and again. But the artist, unlike the artisan, is to be judged only by his superior work. The rest, which is negligible, should be respectfully neglected.

Miss Heyer's position being such, her admirers experience the same difficulty in choosing her topmost performance as they do when faced with a like demand about Sayers'. Fortunately, "undiluted quality" is not synonymous with complete success, and for one reason or another, two or three of Georgette's murders (like Dorothy's) can be put on the second shelf. Even so, when all has been scanned and weighed, two of Heyer's—*Death in the Stocks* and *A Blunt Instrument*—stand there like twin peaks of equal height and radiance.

After much debate internal, the critic resigns himself to giving the edge to *A Blunt Instrument*, for reasons in part technical, in part tangential. In this story, Miss Heyer sets herself the challenge of the least likely and least suspected villain and meets it with a dazzling response. It resembles in audacity and success—though not in plan—another famous piece of sleight of hand, which in the interest of suspense may not be even hinted at here.

The tangential merit is this: from her "Regency days" our author developed a penchant for sardonic beaux who play the fool or worse and turn out efficient angels in disguise. She does them, it must be said, with enormous verve; their insufferable ways entertain even as they infuriate. In *A Blunt Instrument* there is one such character; in *Death in the Stocks*, there are two, the double dose justified by their being boy-and-girl twins [sic]. It seemed wiser to elevate above the other the story with the lesser charge of an irritant that is an acquired taste.

Besides, the present tale contains the person and the aphorisms of P. C. Glass, who is as good as Wilkie Collins's Betteredge in *The Moonstone* and who deserves as wide a renown. All these fine points, of course, would be nothing without the well-knit plot, the clues flawlessly handled, and the suspense undiminished by an ironic treatment of character, which taken together make this favored work *the* classic among a splendid dozen.

Georgette Heyer (Mrs. G. R. Rougier, 1902-1974) was educated "at numerous high-class seminaries" but never went to college, though she attended college lectures in history. Her first novel, written at seventeen, was published when she was nineteen. She married at twenty-three and lived with her husband in East Africa for three years. Her preferred author was Jane Austen, and her first popular success in detective fiction was *Death in the Stocks*, published in the United States as *Merely Murder* in 1935.

**Nancy Wingate, "Georgette Heyer: A Reappraisal" (unpublished paper presented at the annual meeting of the Popular Culture Association, April 1976):**

The enterprise of rescuing an author of lapsed reputation is one of peculiar peril, for there is more than a good chance that the obscurity is deserved. But the case of Georgette Heyer is unusual in that what is unappreciated today is only her detective fiction. The main body of her writing, her "Regency romances," far from disappearing, has been popular for 45 years, with no sign of diminishing now. These, with titles like *Sylvester, or the Wicked Uncle* and *Regency Buck* are silly tales which more than live up to the archness and artificiality promised by such titles, and have not encouraged discriminating readers to try her detective fiction. But they mislead. Her detective work, consisting of twelve novels written between 1932 and 1953, is different in kind and quality and is well worth bringing back to mystery fans' attention.

Georgette Heyer was born on August 16, 1902, in London in an upper-middle-class family. She was educated at various schools but never attended college. Like Margery Allingham and Ngaio Marsh, she was encouraged to write from childhood and wrote her first novel at 17. In 1921, at the age of nineteen, she published her first novel, *The Black Moth*, a swashbuckling historical romance. In 1925, she married G. R. Rougier and went with him to East Africa, remaining until 1928, when she spent a year in Yugoslavia. Few facts are available and, except for the birth of a son in 1932, her life was apparently varied only by the publication of an occasional detective story in between some 45 Regency romances, until her death in 1974.

These detective fiction books cannot be said to have disappeared wholly from view, as Bantam Books currently have editions of eleven of the twelve in print,[5] but they are not considered important by today's critical arbiters, despite the opinion of so influential a critic as Jacques Barzun, who, in his monumental *Catalog of Crime*, speaks of the "sterling merits of this inadequately prized writer...[who] ranks with Sayers, Allingham and Marsh, possessing the sure touch of the first and

---

[5] It should be noted that while there were 12 mysteries, we will discuss only eleven; apparently the first one, *Footsteps in the Dark*, was a rather awkward first attempt which has not been re-issued since its 1932 printing. All references in this text will refer to the paperback Bantam Book editions, except for *Death in the Stocks* (Heinemann, Ltd., 1952) and *Duplicate Death* (E. P. Dutton Co., 1969).

avoiding the occasional bathos of the other two."[6]

I will identify for you what I consider those "sterling merits" to be, but we should logically begin with a glance at contemporary judgments of the books when they were published. Apparently, judging from the remarks of Will Cuppy, and other British and American reviewers, her reputation was quite good, and the books were valued as much for their wit and comedy as for their well-woven plots. Although the reviewer for the *Manchester Guardian* pointed out in reference to her fourth book, *Behold Here's Poison*: "The whole thing is so good that one wonders why it's not better until one realizes that all of it—the characters . . .and plot alike—comes too much from stock . . . ," he concludes that ". . .these more or less familiar ingredients are so well and carefully mixed, the writing is so bright and the solution so unexpected that the book achieves success. . ."[7] On the whole, that's a pretty fair estimate and describes the elements that most forcibly strike the modern reader.

She is not original about murder methods, motives, or, usually, characters. In the eleven books, there are seven shooting murders, two of which feature virtually identical hair-trigger devices to set the guns off and thereby create alibis. Her most original murder method, which earned her much praise, was in her fourth book, *Behold Here's Poison*. The murderer plants a tube of toothpaste, poisoned with nicotine (one of the first uses of nicotine as the poison). In a grisly coda, a second death follows, because the dead man's sister, in clearing up his things, decides not to be wasteful—and uses up the toothpaste. Her only other really clever murder method is in the eighth book, *Envious Casca*. It is original in its use in a detective story, but was actually based on a historical incident, in which the Empress of Austria was stabbed by an Anarchist on a dock and did not realize it. She continued onto the boat and only after ten minutes or so felt faint and was discovered to have been stabbed. In the book, the murderer stabs his brother, who continues into his room, locks his door, and promptly expires, leaving the poor police

---

[6] Jacques Barzun and Wendell Hertig-Taylor, *A Catalog of Crime*, Harper & Row, 1971, p. 234.
[7] *The Manchester Guardian*, June 23, 1936.

with a false locked-room murder.

It is in the area of motive that she is most repetitive. In seven out of the eleven books, the murder is committed for the sake of an inheritance. But oddly enough, her welter of other possible motives is always so good that it is only upon a careful compiling that the reader realizes this lack of originality, and in fact, she is so knowledgeable about inheritance laws that it is always quite interesting. For instance, in her next to last book, *Duplicate Death*, a young Lord murders to keep it from being revealed that he was in fact born out of wedlock and subsequently legitimized. According to British law, in such a case, the child is considered legitimate, but can inherit neither title nor estate.

In fact, the only motif she overuses enough to arouse the reader's suspicion is that of the long-lost "next-in-line" heir, who appears in the story in an assumed role. This happens in five of the books, so that after the first two or three, any mention of an Australian branch of the family immediately triggers a knowing "ah-ha!" In fact, a couple of times this "out of the past" motif is a little strained; e.g., in *The Unfinished Clue*, the murderer turns out to be the vicar's wife, who is in reality the long-unheard-of first wife of the murdered man, who has been living in the village for two years, completely unrecognized by either her ex-husband or her son. Heyer stresses how much she had changed and faded in the intervening 16 years, but still. . . . And in another example, in *Why Shoot a Butler?*, the long-lost grandson and granddaughter are the hero and heroine, who get into all kinds of [obvious] scrapes trying to get the missing halves of the will that proves their rights to the estate.

The settings of the books are also completely typical of the "golden age" detective stories, always being either London, a village, or a house-party.

In all but three of the books, the detective work [and the deduction] is done by Inspector Hannasyde, and Sergeant, later Inspector, Hemingway. Hannasyde is rather colourless, but Hemingway is a delight, with his hobby-horses of psychology and the theatre, and his droll but not unkind habit of baiting his underlings.

Having examined the "family likeness" to other "classic" or "golden age" mysteries in these plot motifs, another homogeneity strikes us: the inevitable upper-class British assumptions about class. Snobbery, in short.

*Death in the Stocks*, published in 1932, exhibits the class prejudice which runs through all her books; indeed, through all the books of all the British "golden age" writers. This prejudice is usually directed toward servants and foreigners, but can encompass the police and anyone who is not quite "quite." *DITS* is true to form, cf. the passage of Sergeant Hemingway interviewing a housemaid who has just found a body: "...she had come to 'do' the flat at seven o'clock that morning and had found the poor gentleman dead in his chair. She did not suppose that she would ever recover from the shock." (p.203) Dry as it is, that sentence illustrates the unexamined contempt for the servant class illustrated so unrelentingly in British fiction,[8] that I can think of only one housemaid in all the books who is described as "intelligent, attractive and interested."[9]

But an even more scathing dismissal demonstrated in the book is that of the heroine's erstwhile fiancé, whom she describes as ". . . showing his teeth too much when he smiles, and wearing the sort of smart clothes that one's own men don't wear." (p. 183) A friend of hers is quoted as saying "He wanted to know why he had such wavy hair and said he didn't like it..." (p. 186) and even the supposedly impartial Sergeant Hemingway is quoted by Hannasyde, "Hemingway fancies Mesurier more than I do. He will have it the man's a dago." (p. 129)

In 1939, in *No Wind of Blame*, there is a cold-blooded look at how "society" worked that is a little shocking to a reader bred in today's

---

[8] See *Murder on the Menu*, Scribner's, 1972, in which Jeanine Larmoth details the ordained roles of hysterical housemaid, bad-tempered cook, uppity housekeeper, and snobbish butler.

[9] Ngaio Marsh, *A Man Lay Dead*, Little, Brown & Co., 1932, p. 69. This excepts also such characters as Lucy Eylesbarrow, the Oxford graduate in *What Mrs. McGillicuddy Saw* who goes into domestic service to make money, and the upper-class girl who becomes a maid in *The Mysterious Affair at Styles* and winds up marrying the hero. These two heroines are not really "maids."

nominally classless society. The central character is Ermyntrude Carter, a character so vivid that she is one of the reasons Jacques Barzun gives such high marks to the book.[10] Ermy is an ex-actress who had married money long ago, and is generally regarded as hopelessly common, but truly generous and good-hearted. In an opening scene, Lady Dering, a neighbor and meant to be a pretty likable character, breaks it to her resentful husband that they are going to dine at the Carters', saying that it's because a Russian prince is to be one of the other guests, and she doesn't want to "miss anything as rich as that." Sir William, to his credit, replies: "Dash it, you can't accept people's hospitality just to make fun of them!" She replies that she is just going to be "gloriously entertained." When he expostulates further, demanding to know the real reason, as surely it isn't for the prospect of seeing a Russian prince, she explains:

> "Dear William, I like you so much when you're stupid. The amazing Ermyntrude is going to build the hospital for us...Not with her own fair hands, dearest. She's going to give us a really big cheque, though. I don't call a few dinner-parties much of a price to pay."
>
> "I call it disgusting!" said Sir William strongly.
>
> "You may call it what you please, my dear, but you know as well as I do that that's how these things are done. Ermyntrude's a kind soul, but she's no fool, and she has a daughter to launch. I don't in the least mind being useful to her if she'll make our hospital possible." (pp. 14-15)

It's very satisfying to note that the daughter she mentions winds up engaged to Lady Dering's son.

The "closed ranks" attitude is more vicious in that book against an unfortunate girl who's gotten "in the family way" by Ermyntrude's reprobate second husband. Even the heroine, Mary, painted as kind-

---

[10] *Catalog of Crime*, p. 236.

hearted and common-sensical, dismisses her from consideration. Only the quiet doctor has any kindness to spare for her: "I think it's very hard luck on Ermyntrude, but I also think Gladys Baker has been grossly imposed upon." Replies Mary: "Yes, if she'd been a sheltered plant, but as far as I can make out, she's nothing of the sort, but perfectly able to take care of herself." "You're not in a position to judge of that," he replied. Nobody else has any concern to spare for Gladys, and in the general clearing up at the end, she is quite forgotten. (p.66)

In her last two books, which were written in 1951 and 1953, Heyer's underlying and not unnatural bitterness at the changes which had by then taken place in Great Britain shows through. In *Duplicate Death*, we hear for the first time the much-vaunted snobbery of the servant class. The butler is unfailingly condescending to his social-climbing employer. "He was always very polite, for this was something which he owed to himself, but he deeply despised her." (p. 33) Indirectly, this is ascribed at least in part to the economising made necessary by the post-war period. "The economies which [she] practised behind the scenes, and, too often, at her servants' expense, never failed to mortify him, for Such Ways, he said, were not what he had been accustomed to." (p. 33) In the same context, the housekeeper gives her views on What The World Is Coming To.

> "All this talk about the Workers!...Anyone 'ud think the only people to do a job of work was in factories, or dockyards, or plate-laying! No one bothers about people like you and me, and my brother, who's doing a jobbing-gardener's work, because no one can't afford to keep a head-gardener like him, that was always used to have four under him! It makes me tired, Mr. Thrimby."

The Butler's half-hearted "Ah, well, it's Progress, Mrs. Foston. . .," she quite rightly snubs with:

> "Yes, and I suppose it's progress that makes any little chit that hasn't had any more training than that

311

> canary of mine waltz in here asking as much money
> as a decent housemaid that's worked her way up from
> between-maid!... Something for nothing!  That's
> what people want nowadays... I've no patience with
> it!" (p. 172)

It's a revelation—were it not for *Upstairs, Downstairs*, we Americans would probably never have known that one had to, or could, work one's way up from tweeny or scullery-maid.[11]

In the last book, *Detection Unlimited*, Heyer has Hemingway, now an Inspector, observing the run-down condition of the local Squire's home, echo Mrs. Foston's sentiments:

> "Progress," said Chief Inspector Hemingway.
> But he said it to himself, well knowing that his
> companion, inevitably reared in the hazy and
> impracticable beliefs of democracy-run-riot, would
> derive a deep, if uninformed, gratification from the
> reflection that yet another landowner had been
> obliged, through excessive taxation, to throw out of
> work the greater part of his staff.
>
> As though to lend colour to these sadly
> retrogressive thoughts, Constable Melkinthorpe
> said... "They say the squire used to have half a dozen
> gardeners, and I don't know how many grooms and
> gamekeepers and such.  Of course, things are
> different now."
>
> "They are...and the people as notice it most are
> those gardeners and grooms and gamekeepers.  So
> you put that into your pipe, my lad, and smoke it!"
> (pp. 129-130)

---

[11] Her snobbery does not extend to her heroines' names:  several of them—Beulah Birtley, Dinah Fawcett, Mary Cliffe, Mathilda Clare and Shirley Brown—sound like typical servants' names to me.

Yes, as Anthony Boucher said, the British detective story makes it abundantly clear ". . . that the British caste system was inviolate and a Good Thing. . . ."[12]

A motif that is her own, and not simply a characteristic of the "genus golden age," and one that she uses to considerable effect in several of the books is that of rudeness as a character-revealing device within the social class she's writing about. Generally, either one character is unabashedly cutting to everybody in sight or else one character is so unrelentingly obnoxious that everybody in sight is rude to him or her (and there is one transitional book, *Behold Here's Poison*, with both an egregiously rude and an egregiously obnoxious character). The rudeness gives her an opportunity for wit, which is consistently entertaining, and even, in a couple of the books, carefully worked into the plot.

In the first several books, the rudeness derives variously from the child-like frankness of the Verekers in *Death in the Stocks*; from the conceit of Frank Amberley, who honestly considers himself far cleverer than the police or anyone else and is charming in spite of it in *Why Shoot A Butler?*; and from the equal conceit of Randall, in *Behold Here's Poison*. Randall, however, is simply poisonous to everyone and renders it quite unconvincing that his cousin, whom he has picked on ever since they were children, should fall happily into his arms when he proposes, out of the blue. He has spent several chapters caustically finding fault with her hats, her dress, her manners and her attempts at rational thinking. Her question, "But why would you want to marry me?" is exactly what's bothering the reader, and goes unanswered. This is a failing that shows up consistently in the "Regency romances" but almost never in the mysteries. In fact, in the far better *Envious Casca*, a similar love-hate relationship is very well-rendered, and a parallel love scene goes off quite nicely.

With *They Found Him Dead*, she reverses course and introduces the

---

[12] Anthony Boucher, "The Ethics of the Mystery Novel," in *The Art of the Mystery Story*, edited by Howard Haycraft, Simon & Schuster, 1946, p. 386.

opposite device: a character so obnoxious that he or she asks for it. In this book, that character is a sister-in-law, whose egotism and fatuity is so well drawn that the reader waits impatiently for her next come-uppance, which comes variously from the impertinent teenager, the vinegary eighty-year-old *grande dame* of the household, or the generally calm and self-contained elder brother, but most delightfully from the young "companion," Patricia Allison. Sample dialogue:

> "The trouble is that I've got terribly extravagant tastes—I admit it freely, and I wish to God I hadn't but the fact remains that I have. That's my Russian blood again. It's an absolute curse."
> "Yes, it does seem to be a bit of a pest," agreed Miss Allison. "All the same, you've got any amount of English blood as well. Why not concentrate on that?" (p. 11)

One regrets that Heyer has Miss Allison draw it so mild, but she is constantly aware of her equivocal position as "hired help" in the house and is therefore held back from expressing herself as freely as doubtless would one of the young "gentry."

In general, the rude character is the cleverest one, and therefore the hero or heroine. But Heyer, banking on the unthinking acceptance of this convention, fools the reader in *Detection Unlimited*, in which the poison-tongued Gavin turns out to be the murderer, and in *Envious Casca*, in which the bumbling Uncle Joseph, who drives everyone crazy with his tactless attempts to "smooth things over" turns out to be a calculating murderer who knew all along that this kind of behaviour was guaranteed to get under everyone's skin in a way that ordinary rudeness wouldn't. In fact, the only thing that doesn't happen in relation to the rudeness motif that one might expect is that none of her maddeningly stupid or maddeningly egotistical characters is ever killed (excepting the accidental death of the maddening sister in *Behold Here's Poison*).

A problem with the first two books, which she more or less successfully solved in the later ones, is that of what constitutes the proper

314

number of suspects. In *Death in the Stocks*, the cast of characters is so limited that one fixes on the murderer by default. There are the lovers Antonia and Giles, obviously out; the temporarily estranged lovers Kenneth and Leslie, just as obviously out; the nanny, not shown to be round the bend, so out; Roger, who gets killed and so is out, and Rudolph, the erstwhile fiancé, whose "not one of our kind" dismissal is so pointed that presumably even in this flowering of English insularity Heyer would have blushed to make him the guilty party. And that leaves—*voila!*—Violet, who's never been particularly likable anyway, and whom we could all see with half an eye was not at all suitable for *her* erstwhile fiancé Kenneth anyway.

Of course, in some of the later books, she errs a bit too much in the opposite direction, with often an unlikely number of suspects, all with perfectly good motives and bad alibis. For instance, in *They Found Him Dead*, her nine suspects include a teenage boy and a half-crippled octogenarian. It's a relief to the reader that in *Detection Unlimited* she provides her two love-interests with the only solid alibis in the book and drops all pretense of letting them be suspected.

But all this light-hearted wit and cleverness is a quantum leap away from her most original book: the long psychological mystery, *Penhallow*, published in 1942. The book is unusual in many ways: a genuine servant girl is the heroine; there is a fairly constant nibbling at the question of the propriety or silliness of social conventions which were then just beginning to disappear, and there is the unusual circumstance of the murder's not taking place until page 183—practically heretical in a day when many mysteries opened with the discovery of the body. But the most striking thing about the book is that the murderer gets away with it, which, while it is not unknown in mystery fiction, is unusual enough to deserve very close examination.

In *Murder on the Orient Express*, Poirot lets the murderers "get away with it" because he feels justice has been satisfied, albeit vigilante-style. Miss Pym permits it in *Miss Pym Disposes* (published four years after *Penhallow*) for reasons which are as vague as Miss Pym's thought-processes. And in *Penhallow*, Heyer permits it—but with a difference. Not only does the murderer get away with it, with never a breath of

315

suspicion against her, but the book ends with no one in possession of all the facts. In short, with the truth unrevealed. This doesn't just go against the rules of the game, it violates the nature of the game, so that we have to try to adduce why she has done it.

The rules of the game might be described as necessitating: a crime to be solved, logical deductions, honest clues, and a final solution. Heyer departs from the convention by 1) letting us read the murderer's mind before, during and after the crime and by 2) leaving the facts of the case unrevealed to the rest of the characters, including the police.

W. H. Auden has given us an oblique sidelight on this question of what constitutes a detective story in his brilliant essay, "The Guilty Vicarage." "The interest in the study of a murderer is the observation, by the innocent many, of the sufferings of the guilty one. The interest in the detective story is the dialectic of innocence and guilt."[13] Both of these interests are satisfied in *Penhallow*, with the added *cachet* that the guilty one whose sufferings are "observed" by the other characters is not in fact guilty, while the reader observes the agony of the guilty party. Also, the effects of the crime on the people round it are given precedence in an unusual way. Generally, in country-house murders, there are a few perfunctory signs of grief, and some suspicious glances darted from the corners of eyes, but the writer's (and the reader's) attention is quite rightly focused on the ensuing investigation rather than on what it would really be like to wonder incessantly if one of your family is a murderer. Writers generally get over this unnatural heartlessness by having the characters exhibit an inordinate amount of light-hearted flippancy—and I'm not condemning this. This is all part of the never-never-land pleasure of detective stories, and the reader quite rightly wants to get on with the investigation, and spare the tears, please.

All of this has to do with what Auden calls the "magical function" of the detective story. He says that "the magical satisfaction [detective stories] provide [which makes them escape literature not works of art] is

---

[13] W. H. Auden, "The Guilty Vicarage," *The Art of the Essay*, ed. Leslie Fiedler, Thomas Y. Crowell Co., 1958, p. 444.

the illusion of being dissociated from the murderer."[14] He contends that the reason the reader is satisfied with the typical detective story, in which one identifies, if at all, with the detective, is because "The identification of phantasy is always an attempt to avoid one's own suffering; the identification of art is a compelled sharing in the suffering of another."[15] As an example of the kind of "art" he's referring to, he mentions *Crime and Punishment*. Now *Penhallow* is obviously no *Crime and Punishment*, but it is a successful attempt at an unusual and difficult rendering: a satisfying novel of psychological realism, clothed in the dress of the typical English country-house golden age detective story, and certainly to be judged on its own merits rather than condemned out of hand because it doesn't "fit the canon."[16]

In brief, what takes place in the story is that quarrelsome, tyrannical old Adam Penhallow is poisoned by his weak, downtrodden wife; she is never suspected, because he had had a terrible quarrel with his eldest son the day before his death and everyone thinks the son did it. The son ends up killing himself because of his father's harrowing revelation during that last quarrel that he is really a bastard with no rightful claim on the estate he's been raised to believe is his, which knowledge sends him into despair. With the suicide, the police, who have had no direct evidence against anyone, conclude that he must have committed the murder and shot himself out of remorse.

What is important is how Heyer uses this plot structure to get at two

---

[14] *Ibid.*, p. 452.

[15] *Ibid.*, p. 453.

[16] The only other novel so similar to *Penhallow* in psychological realism and concern with the perception of guilt that it comes readily to mind is Francis Iles' brilliant *Before the Fact*, the story of a wife who spends years facing the fact that her beloved husband is a murderer, then months realizing that he plans to kill her, and in the end helps him to accomplish it. It later became the movie *Suspicion* by Alfred Hitchcock, starring Cary Grant, but the movie is marred by the decision to change the ending to a conventionally happy one: it was felt (probably rightly) that Cary Grant's fans would not be able to bear with his playing a murderer.

questions: that of the perception of truth and that, less often given attention, of murder as "problem-solver in human relations."

About the first: ironically, when the rest of the family consider the wife's hysteria over Penhallow's death and all the ensuing strain, they put it down to hypocrisy.

> "I haven't the smallest doubt that she is quite sincere in her present grief, just as I am sure that she was equally sincere when she thought herself unhappy with Father. Her nature is shallow; she is easily swayed, and extremely impressionable. She is the sort of woman who, having complained of her wrongs for God knows how many years, will now spend the rest of her life telling herself that she was always a perfect wife to Father." (p. 256)

The police are equally misled about her part in the murder: "[The Inspector] did not exclude her from his list of possibles, but he did not consider it likely that, having borne patiently with Penhallow for twenty years, she should suddenly have taken it into her head to murder him." (p. 262) Were it not that that is precisely what did happen, these conclusions about her character and motives would be perfectly accurate. On the opposite side of the coin, the family's inability to believe that Raymond, their brother, did in fact poison his father is more accurate than they know. In short, Heyer is saying, how little we may actually see—and perhaps by implication—how fortuitous the times when the pieces do come together so that the detective can say in the end "The truth is known, the guilty are punished, the innocent are set free, and order is restored." How plausible it always is, and how equally plausible her rendering of the opposite, tragic denouement.

The other question I mentioned is that of murder as problem-solver, by which I mean that there is very often a tacit assumption in mysteries that the murderee has been rightfully removed—that life will just be better all round without him. Heyer does such a good job of painting the misery and confusion and hostility that Penhallow rouses in virtually

318

everyone who knows him that the reader even goes along with this assumption, and in a way, rather hopes along with the wife that the murder will never be discovered, a common element in the pleasure of mysteries. It seems to the reader as well as to the wife that

> ". . . if he were to die, as the doctor had hinted that he would, every trouble would vanish, and they would be free, all of them: free to disperse, to follow their own inclinations; free from the fear of Penhallow's wrath; free from their degrading dependence upon him for their livelihood. . .if only he would fulfill his doctor's expectations, and drink himself to death!" (p. 170)

From these reflections, it is but a step to wishing one of the sons "...would do something desperate, desperate enough to enrage Penhallow into bursting a blood-vessel. No one could think it a crime to put an end to a life so baleful..." (pp. 172-173) When she suddenly thinks of "putting a painless end to herself" and then gets the idea of poisoning Penhallow with her sleeping-drops, she goes over all the "good" reasons for doing it—and the reader concurs, as is usual with "bad-guy" victims, although the run-down usually comes at the end of the book.

> "With fatal clarity, the very means by which she could hasten Penhallow's end (for it was no more than that, she told herself) showed themselves to her, so that it almost seemed as though she were meant to take this course... He would not suffer... It appeared to her that if he felt no pain she could not be thought to have committed so great a crime. She was sure that she had many times heard him inveigh against the life he was forced to lead, saying that the sooner he died the better pleased he would be, and if her brain could not quite accept this declaration at its face-value, at least it was ready to receive it as a half-

excuse for what she meant to do." (p. 180)

For awhile, the reader is convinced still that the murder, though it was of course a drastic step, was the right thing to do, and will help straighten out the lives of all the characters. But the results of the murder gradually seem more terrible to the murderess than the original, seemingly unbearable, situation with Penhallow. She is horrified that everyone believes Raymond, the son, to be a murderer—but despite her guilt, cannot bring herself to tell the truth, especially after his suicide, when it would do no good anyway.

> She had thought that in hastening Penhallow's end she would be bringing peace to his whole family. Instead of this. . .the consequences of her action were as appalling as they had been unforeseen. . .When she saw that Raymond was being harried by the Inspector. . .when she realized that Clara and Bart had loved Penhallow, and bitterly mourned him. . . when she saw the growing suspicion of one another in the faces of her stepsons, she regretted her mad deed as she had never thought it possible that she could. If she could have called Penhallow back to life, she would have done it. . . . (p. 265)

The after-taste of the book reminds one of the statement of Sir Ronald Howe, Deputy Commissioner at Scotland Yard, in 1955, when he was asked to write "A Personal Reaction" for the detective fiction section of *The Times Literary Supplement*. He said: "I wish that the creators were not so preoccupied with murder. . . .All murders are sad, sordid affairs, and to one in the detective trade a good thumping fraud is far more interesting and full of excitement."[17]

---

[17] Sir Ronald Howe, Deputy Commissioner of Scotland Yard, "A Personal Reaction," *The Times Literary Supplement*, Detective Fiction section, February 25, 1955.

We certainly don't want every book to be a *Penhallow*—in fact, we don't want any others to. As Dr. George Dove said when he had just finished reading *Penhallow*, ". . . thank goodness this one never became a convention. There must be hundreds of stories in which the murderer commits suicide, but to have an innocent person do so and thus seem to 'solve' the mystery would not be very good for business."[18]

Perhaps that is the "magical function" of *Penhallow*: we are associated with the murderer more than in virtually all other mysteries, and we come out chilled with that identification, and the reminder that the "never-never-land" of detective fiction is precisely that. But we don't need more than one book to do that for us, do we?

**Lillian S. Robinson, "On Reading Trash" (in her *Sex, Class, and Culture* [Bloomington/London: Indiana University Press, 1978], pp. 202, 207-222):**

. . . What is unusual about my own literary education is that I encountered the male literary tradition against a background filled with trashy popular fiction by, for, and about women. The result is a rather different perspective than I am supposed to have on the two parallel traditions of English literature. Most of this essay will be focused on a contrast between the works of Jane Austen and those of Georgette Heyer. The pairing is honestly come by, in my own history, but I believe it has larger implications as well; the concentration on women as they appear in both high and popular fiction makes possible some useful distinctions between the two and forces a reconsideration of such categories as literature, entertainment, and propaganda. Once the absurd incongruity of any connections between the two writers is duly acknowledged and assigned its proper weight, it has much to tell us about female literary experience. . . .

If the drugstore Gothic can trace its origin back through modern

---

[18] Personal letter of Dr. George N. Dove, East Tennessee State University, September 2, 1975.

revivals of the Brontës to the romantic fiction that flourished in eighteenth-century circulating libraries, its counterpart among historical romances claims a similarly elevated lineage. Around 1966 Georgette Heyer's novels were issued in paperback for what I believe was their first mass distribution in the American market. The cover of each novel proclaimed it—and Heyer's Regency fiction generally—to be in the tradition of Jane Austen. Subsequent novelists who treat the Regency period have been described by their publishers as following in the romantic tradition of Georgette Heyer. Like the Gothics, then, these novels are products whose peddlers stress their resemblance to others of the kind, by the same author or by other established specialists in the genre, rather than emphasize the innovative uniqueness of each product. The appeal is to familiarity and success, assured by reference to places, customs, and ideas well known from earlier productions of the same type. Georgette Heyer is the acknowledged Queen of the Regency romance (later paperback editions make some such peculiar claim), and it is a clear selling point to say that the book you are touting is just like "a" Georgette Heyer, has the same Regency background, and affords (therefore) the same "delight." But for Heyer herself there can be only one predecessor sufficiently glamorous and sufficiently connected in the public mind with the Regency period and that is Jane Austen herself, whose heroines, her own contemporaries, did, unquestionably, live out their personal dramas during the years that the future George IV reigned in the place of his mad father.

As a selling point the comparison can only prove disappointing, for Heyer's novels concentrate on precisely those minutiae of dress and décor that Austen takes for granted. Not even in *Northanger Abbey*, where Mrs. Allen is satirized as a woman obsessed with her own gowns and trimmings and, for a secondary interest, those of her young charge, Catherine Morland, does Jane Austen bow to the necessity of describing a single garment in any of her novels. A bit of dialogue about fashions may serve to delineate character—as when Mrs. Elton simultaneously fishes for praise of her gown, deprecates the necessity of being so ornately dressed, and plans aloud to add some more trimming to another dress—but they are of scant interest in themselves. Heyer (and, with even less skill, her sister Regency buffs) tells us about colors, cut, fabric, and trimming, about half-boots, pelisses, and cloaks, not only because the acquisition and display of clothing are more central to the existence of Heyer's heroines than they are to Austen's, but in order to invest the novels with that meretricious quality Henry James would have called "the tone of time."

Similarly, in Jane Austen's novels, the varieties of carriages are used as a social marker (Mr. Collins drives a gig, the Bennets keep a closed carriage but have to use farm horses to pull it when they want to pay a call, and so on). Elsewhere, conversation about horses and vehicles reflects the personality and temperament of various characters (John Thorpe mistreats his horse and gig and boasts about his trading in these matters; Mrs. Elton can never forbear to mention that her rich brother-in-law, Mr. Suckling, keeps two carriages, including a barouche-landaulet). In Georgette Heyer's novels, however, the niceties of phaeton and perch-phaeton, of driving to an inch, and of membership (in appropriate and fully described costume) in the Four Horse Club are built directly into the texture of events as they make up the narrative.

Perhaps because she was writing for contemporaries who knew what the world of the Regency period looked like, but more likely because these facts inform her historical sense in a deeper and more thoroughgoing fashion, Austen is able to make a more complex use than her imitators of the aesthetic culture of her own time. The mourning Captain Benwick in *Persuasion* has been reading so much Scott and Byron that Ann Elliott recommends a therapeutic dose of prose; Byronism has affected *Sanditon*'s Sir Edward Denham less innocently, as he plots a cut-rate abduction; Fanny Price knows Cowper; and, of course, the young ladies in *Northanger Abbey* read all the "horrid" novels they can get their hands on.

But drawing, music, literature, even amateur theatricals tend to be an organic part of life to the people Jane Austen writes about. Everyone in Bath goes to the theater and the concerts. Catherine Morland's recital of her week's schedule (the Upper Rooms Monday, the theater Tuesday, the concert Wednesday) to an amused Mr. Tilney is no less true because it can be so mechanically evoked. And the musical evenings attract social climbers like Sir Walter Elliott and his eldest daughter quite as naturally as they do someone like Anne, an able musician herself who can translate Italian songs at sight. Highbury, remote though it may be, shelters not only Jane Fairfax, who is an accomplished pianist, Emma Woodhouse, who would play better if she applied herself, and Mrs. Elton, who is determined to signal her entry into the married state by abandoning her music, but amateur critics like Harriet Smith, who knows she is supposed to throw around terms like "taste" and "execution" although she is unsure just how to recognize these qualities when she is exposed to them. Appreciation of cultural productions, opinions and attitudes about them, thus becomes another attribute of character.

The only remotely comparable cultural attribute in the works of Georgette Heyer is a taste for the fiction of Jane Austen herself. Thus, in *Regency Buck* Judith Taverner is delighted by an ironic passage in the copy of *Sense and Sensibility* she comes upon at a circulating library. Jenny, in *A Civil Contract*, prefers the same Jane Austen novel to the Byronic effusions her friend Julia adores; *Sense and Sensibility*, she believes, is down to earth, deals with real people—precisely the qualities that make Julia feel it is flat and prosaic. After her marriage Jenny tries to read her husband's agricultural manuals, sweetening the task by alternating it with chapters from the newly published *Mansfield Park*. Those of Heyer's heroines who read Jane Austen share some small part of that author's ironic social vision, but once we understand that a taste for those novels signifies humor and good sense—personal traits that Heyer always values—there are no further subtleties to be revealed by her heroines' choice of reading matter.

However superficial this use of taste to illuminate character, it remains the only reference to contemporary culture that serves any purpose beyond historical decoration. When Lady Serena, in *Bath Tangle*, reads Lady Caroline Lamb's *Glenarvon* and delights in identifying the models for that roman à clef, the incident serves simply to "place" her and her mismatched fiancé, in their respective social and moral spheres. Reading Byron becomes the mode in several novels, but it really is a fashion like those concerning dress and has rather less influence over what actually happens than the vogue for a certain shade

324

of blue or the choice of a gentleman's tailor. Literature, which is pressed into service rather frequently as the source of historical color, and the theater and fine arts, which are referred to somewhat less often, furnish detail rather than depth, and a kind of detail, moreover, that tends to support the general picture of women's lives that emerges from these novels.

The niceties of social behavior, like the references to artistic production, serve quite different purposes in the historical romance than they do in the novel of manners. Jane Austen could assume that her readers knew the rules of polite social intercourse. When an impromptu dance is held at *Mansfield Park*, Maria Bertram knows it would be incorrect to dance only with her foolish betrothed, Mr. Rushworth, and uses that knowledge to claim her share of Henry Crawford's attentions. Mrs. Norris and Mrs. Rushworth chat about the proprieties of the matter, but the real tension subsists in the rivalry of the two Miss Bertrams, in Maria's impatience with Rushworth and her hopes of Crawford, and in Fanny Price's feelings as she watches the action. Who dances with whom—at Mansfield, Netherfield, Highbury, or Bath—is always of greater significance than the way a Regency gentleman craves the honor of a dance or the fact that partners are invariably paired off for two dances at a time.

Not only are such regulations and breaches thereof more central to the action in Georgette Heyer's novels, but there are more of them. The reader of Heyer and of her Regency sisters rapidly learns that the coveted vouchers to Almacks could be obtained only from one of the aristocratic patronesses (and she learns those ladies' identities, habits, and crotchets); and also that, once accepted, gentlemen must wear knee breeches, not pantaloons, there; that alcoholic beverages are not served; and that a young lady may not waltz until her doing so has been approved by one of the patronesses. All this comes under the heading of what I would characterize as pseudoinformation not because it is untrue (repetition, at least, would suggest that what these books have taught me about Almacks is accurate) but because, ultimately, it reveals nothing about the society that fostered an institution like Almacks as its elite marriage market. Yet the pages of Georgette Heyer's works are full of passages in which character is defined through young men's boredom at a club where the card room stakes are so low and the refreshments so mild, and entire plots turn on their being refused admission for being improperly dressed or arriving after 11:00 p.m.[19]

One result of this passion for the specific fact without concern for its significance occurs in the matter of sexual morality, precisely the area of life that the social proprieties are intended to regulate and define. Georgette Heyer's high life is a great deal higher than Jane Austen's, embracing those segments of aristocracy and fashion that in fact represented an extravagant and dissolute threat to the sort of country families with whom Jane Austen is most at home. Gentlemen in Heyer's universe are expected to have experience with loose women at various levels of society, but however daring her ladies may be, they never actually breach the double standard. Indeed, in their innocence, they have the rare gift—albeit commonplace in women's fiction—of being able to captivate and hold on to the most experienced and worldly males. Her gentlemen are considered morally acceptable because they are candid and generous with their mistresses. The heroines who eventually enchant them are daring in their wit and, sometimes, in their knowledge of the existence of sexual misbehavior. But they kiss passionately only at the end of the book when love has terminated in betrothal, and they are revolted by sexual advances made on the mistaken assumption that they are of the class that is assumed to be universally available to gentlemen.

Jane Austen's people do not giggle over "crim. con." stories; their

---

[19] Unlike the true historical novelist (even one writing for women), the Regency *romancière* does little research. (Some of the hastier books seem, indeed, to have been based on reading exclusively in other novels about the period.) Even Heyer, the best of the lot, relies on a fixed repertoire of historical facts and characters on which she rings (eventually predictable) changes. Thus, when Beau Brummell appears—as he does extensively in *Regency Buck*, for instance—all conversation that is not directed to one of the fictional characters comes directly from the four or five best-known anecdotes about the man, precisely the ones retailed in Virginia Woolf's brief essay on him.

world is superficially a great deal more straitlaced. In her fiction, however, the facts of life—the real ones, free of rakes who can be instantly reformed by refreshing virgins and of the knowing virgins themselves—are never far below the surface. Seduction, elopement, illegitimacy, divorce, living in sin are not alluded to in every chapter of a Jane Austen novel. Nonetheless, *Northanger Abbey*, which began, after all, as a youthful burlesque, is the only one of her books that does not include a major incident or character touched by one of these breaches of the sexual code. Sexual misconduct, moreover, is not limited to the unknown "bits of muslin" or the discarded aristocratic mistresses who populate Georgette Heyer's pages, but involves people—although never heroines, of course—whom the reader has come to know as characters. One does not like Maria Bertram, Lydia Bennet, or Mrs. Clay, but all are fully developed persons, not symbols, and their motives and emotions are no less complex than those of any of the other women Jane Austen depicts. Not even Mrs. Clay, who is announced as "designing" before she makes her first appearance in *Persuasion*, is reduced to the purely sexual component of her misdeeds. The social distance between a sexually virtuous woman and one who has "fallen" is much more palpable in the novels of Jane Austen than any twentieth-century novelist writing about Austen's period can adequately imagine. The gulf, however, the difference between one kind of person and another, is a great deal easier to bridge when we are reading the real thing than in any modern imitation.

In Georgette Heyer's fiction, the public events of the day—economic, political, or military—are very much to the fore, although Heyer necessarily betrays a far more shallow sense of their significance than does Jane Austen, who barely mentions them. Thus, for example, Viscount Linton, the hero of Heyer's *A Civil Contract*, an aristocratic ex-officer with heavily mortgaged ancestral acres, turns to scientific farming. Against the advice of his bourgeois father-in-law, he adds to his shares in government bonds at the moment when it looks as if Wellington may have lost at Waterloo. He thus lays the foundation for a renewed family fortune based on the old values (loyalty to his country, his party, and his former commander), shoring up the new (the land is still mortgaged and its owner is introducing modern agricultural methods, with their attendant destruction of a way of life and a livelihood for the rural population). Some historical "color" is provided by references to Tull's drill, Coke of Norfolk and his experiments in farming, the effect on the stock market of defeatist military rumors, and the Corn Law riots. Similarly, the plot of *The Toll Gate* [sic] revolves around the theft of some cases of newly minted (and not yet circulated) gold sovereigns; the characters in several novels (*The Unknown Ajax, The Talisman Ring,* and *The Reluctant Widow* come immediately to mind) have dealings with French brandy smugglers; and the Bow Street Runners, the new national police, figure in these four novels, as well as in several others. But in all this there is no hint of how deeply the events reflected by the specific details influenced and altered the entire fabric of the society in which they occurred.

In Jane Austen's novels, the details are always basic to our understanding of characters or plot, for she is aware that new social forces do encroach on the way of life—prosperous, decorous, and cultivated—that is the common heritage of Mansfield, Pemberly [sic], Hartfield, Kellynch, Norland, and Northanger. These places and the style of living they simultaneously shelter and reflect are menaced by political-economic developments external to the English country house and its usual surroundings. Sir Thomas Bertram, for instance, must see to his Caribbean property (who works his plantations, what do they produce, and just what *was* he saying about the slave trade that interested Fanny Price far more than it did his own daughters?). John Dashwood's first action at Norland, after dispensing with his stepmother and half-sisters, is to apply capitalist values and methods to his inheritance, enclosing Norland Common and adding to his holdings by engrossment. At Kellynch, it is Sir Walter Elliott's own extravagance, which might be interpreted as an inability to make the rents from an inherited estate cover all the temptations of modern life, that necessitates the family's removal to Bath and their rental of the house to a retired admiral made prosperous by England's naval wars. Questions of taste and manners, which are, at the deepest level, questions of class, are always dependent, in Jane Austen's works, on the material situation created when the gentry are placed in relation—and very often in confrontation—with the conditions of insurgent capitalism.

Jane Austen, like Heyer, focuses on getting her heroines married for love to suitors whose fortune and character are both adequate. The historical context in which the eventual marriages are achieved, however, has a far more profound significance for her than it ever could for Heyer. Heyer's characters may marry for money, as in the case of Adam Linton; or marry for love and find great wealth as well, as with the majority of her heroines; or marry, as happens in *April Lady*, *The Convenient Marriage*, and *Friday's Child*, for immediate material motives and find love through the marriage; or be frankly pursued for their own fortunes, as in *Regency Buck* or *The Quiet Gentleman*; but any understanding of why some groups are poor or rich—even when they are newly so—has no place in her kind of fiction. By contrast, Austen's novels are rooted in an understanding of the fact that cataclysmic social changes were affecting not only relative wealth and poverty, but also class definitions and class relations, sources and amounts of income, and the cultural life informed by these forces. Austen could hardly share the modern reader's knowledge about the eventual direction and meaning of these changes, but she has and communicates a far more vivid sense than we can attain to of the daily reality that the new conditions demanded.

After Sir Walter Elliott's financial difficulties necessitate his renting the family estate to a retired admiral, we are privileged to overhear the baronet's fatuous strictures on a profession that enables men who merely have uncommon abilities—rather than gentle birth—to rise above "their betters." Sir Walter's porings over the Baronetage are far less rewarding in human qualities than the roster of naval officers that Jane Austen brings to our attention. But although the author does not join her character in deploring the fact that England should have fallen into the hands of men of intelligence, courage, good will, and enterprise, she is nonetheless aware of the larger social and economic changes behind this shift. Her doubts about the new culture are embodied in the Miss Musgroves, the refined descendants of honest country squires. She sees the generations of the Musgrove family, in fact, as representatives of the old England and the new, reflecting that the ancestors whose portraits hang in the parlor must be surprised to witness the goings-on of the young generation. The chief difference is that the two Miss Musgroves have been away to school and learned accomplishments. Those accomplishments sit lightly on them, to be sure, but the result is, in fact, that they can live "to be fashionable, happy, and merry." They have leisure, whereas the older generations of Musgrove ladies, gentlewomen though they were, were also mistresses of their rural households, with real work to do.

The fine articulations of class society are important to both authors, although this concern reflects quite different views of what a social order is and what purposes it serves. Georgette Heyer's preferred milieu is what her characters would call "the first circles" of English society (and, in the novels with eighteenth-century settings, of French society as well). All of her heroes belong to this class; most of them are earls, although there is at least one baron, one viscount, and one marquis among them, as well as several dukes, some baronets, and a few younger sons of the nobility. The heroines are not quite so uniformly placed: if they are from equally aristocratic backgrounds—or even the country gentry—their families are poor; if heiresses, they are not usually from the very highest levels of society. In almost no case is the Cinderella theme entirely absent, and it is frequently the central device of Georgette Heyer's plots.

The emphasis on "the first circles" implies, of course, the existence of other circles. Heyer concerns herself principally with those just beneath the tier occupied by her main characters. Thus, in addition to Almacks, there is the Pantheon Ballroom, an inferior and unexclusive establishment more often referred to—as a kind of negative social touchstone—than visited. When a heroine takes part in a masked ball there, as at least two do, she is stared at and accosted by rude, vulgar "cits," the same fate, indeed, that attends a well-born lady in Heyer's works whenever she is in a situation where she may meet men of the middle classes.

Men of the bourgeoisie and below are usually unmistakable in their crudity even when they are not drunkenly pawing the heroine. When Heyer portrays characters who lack polite manners and an elite education she can never resist making them stupid as well. Thus, Jenny's father in

*A Civil Contract*, who we are supposed to believe is a brilliant and shrewd financier, one of the new self-made capitalists, is by turns short-tempered, irascible, babyish, foolish, and awkwardly falling all over himself with whatever emotion is dominant at the moment. Middle-class women are either unshakably practical, of-the-earth earthy, or deficient in judgment, their poor grammar being only the outward sign of an inward vacuity that not infrequently fades off into viciousness.

These careful distinctions among the first, the second, and the third ranks and among the overlapping layers in the first are really where the action is. The poor are people, of course, but no sense is conveyed of what their poverty means or how it interlocks with the lives of the very rich as this fiction depicts them. A few characters, to be sure—Arabella in the novel named for her, Sir Waldo Hawkridge, the Nonesuch for whom another novel is titled—engage in philanthropic ventures, but a hero or heroine need not spare a thought for the sufferings of the masses in order to be considered wholly admirable. There are chimney sweeps and children working in mines and factories, but such matters are alluded to only if an aristocrat, in the course of advancing the real plot, rescues one or two of them from that fate. There are also country folk, innkeepers, and, of course, servants by the score, because they are required for the support of a lavish style of life, and there are a few lumpen characters who live in alleys and swill gin, but they have neither identity nor brains. Low status (whether the possessor is a Bow Street Runner or Leaky Peg, a kindhearted backstreet girl), is invariably accompanied by low intelligence.

Georgette Heyer introduces us to characters who speak of fashions and fashionables as being "of the first stare" or "highly select" and she can bring in figures who are indeed at the very peak of the social order. In *Regency Buck*, Judith Taverner receives the marriage proposals of the Duke of Clarence; Heyer's fictional creation thus has the opportunity to become the morganatic Queen of England. As long as she does not tamper with history to the extent of bringing about such a marriage, the twentieth-century novelist can place an actual historical figure in the picture, put all manner of foolish speeches into his mouth, and have him rejected by Miss Taverner. Jane Austen could hardly take the same

331

liberties with a royal duke who was her contemporary—not simply because decorum forbade them, but because her sense of both fictional and social order would have made it inconceivable *and unnecessary* to do so.

Yet the same issues that are so important to Georgette Heyer—the size of dowries and the income of estates, the pretensions of the newly rich, and the impact of conflicting class styles on the marriage market—are also important to Jane Austen. The difference resides not only in the less elevated social and economic level that Jane Austen's characters occupy, but also in the reasons why social distinctions are so much to the fore. Fundamentally, Jane Austen shows us snobs and social climbers, but she is not one herself. Indeed, no character whom the reader is expected to admire has aspirations to associate with anyone above her own station, and it is a sign of vulgarity to be overly concerned with adding to or demonstrating one's own social importance. Not even the interests of an advantageous marriage can move Jane Austen's heroines to seek company above their own rank and, again, ardent pursuit of an eligible *parti* is one of the chief touchstones of poor breeding and defective character in any young woman.

Heyer's heroines are at once more pragmatic and less realistic. They take part in the London "Season" in full knowledge that it is their *job* as well as their role to find a husband through the process of social mating that is one function of the brilliant assemblies they attend. Her novels are about love, successful, lasting love, but Heyer and her heroines are well aware that, for Regency society in general, love is only incidental to the functions of the institutions of courtship and marriage. With the energy they devote to the social round, however, and the passionate detail with which Heyer describes the events and the costumes that so absorb them, a completely artificial world of balls and parties comes into being. Heyer's novels introduce the modern reader to a Who's Who of Regency high life where fashion is elevated to the position of a major social force. Her heroines want love; some of them even read books and want also the more esoteric pleasures of rational intercourse and virtuous conduct. But in the novels there is no other measure of success for an individual, a party, or a custom, than to be accepted by those who are identified as leading, making, or following the mode.

The problem is that Heyer realizes how important this sort of success is for the kind of heroine she chooses and almost mass-produces. Yet on some essential level she does not know what to do with that understanding, because she does not know what a society is. Thus, she shows a society articulated by class and one in which class feeling, especially snobbery and ambition, runs high, without conveying any sense that class is something other and more than style. Jane Austen's world is less fashionable, though by no means less class-conscious, than that of the Regency romance; there is no possibility, however, of her readers' confusing class itself with its most superficial expressions, because the novels make it clear that everything they are about—ethics, manners, attitudes, sentiments, distinctions—has its basis in class. Understood in this way, class in Jane Austen's novels becomes, as it is in actual human history, the defining and motivating force of society itself.

I can imagine no greater waste of energy than an elaborate demonstration that Jane Austen is a better writer than Georgette Heyer. In drawing so extensive a comparison between the two, my intention has not been to belabor the obvious points about what makes a great writer great, but rather to approach the question of women's light reading from a perspective that avoids the pat formulas about "escape" and "vicarious experience." That there is some overlap between the present-day audience for both kinds of work is reflected not only in the early advertising of Heyer's books but also in the marketing of Jane Austen's works. Two unfinished Austen novels, *Sanditon* and *The Watsons*, have been completed by twentieth-century authors and are now available in mass-market paperbacks, with cover illustrations and (grossly exaggerated) plot descriptions that seek to render them indistinguishable from their presumed pop-fiction successors. And they are displayed side by side with romances by Heyer and her imitators. I wonder what happens to a reader who picks up one of these books—both, admittedly, containing a rather denatured product—instead of one of its shelf-mates? (Say, the novel called something like *Bath Cotillion* by one of the Heyer epigones that I bought at the Indianapolis Airport and, having finished, left on the plane and that made so slight an imprint on my consciousness that less than two weeks later, I almost bought it again at Hengerers department store in Buffalo.) Does the reader who relished *Bath Cotillion* find that the issues and problems Jane Austen raises stand in the way of her story? Does the more elegant style interfere as well? Or do the superfluous elements of superior character, incident, and analysis simply go unnoticed? If this last is the case, as it must be for one segment of Jane Austen's modern readers, then it becomes somewhat more challenging to examine both the Regency romance itself and the sources of its appeal.[20]

If it is possible to read Jane Austen for the same reasons one reads Georgette Heyer, then coming to understand what makes it possible suggests some conclusions about what women read and why. In both its high and its popular avatars, this sort of novel centers on the private concerns of women, domestic, marital, and personal. For Heyer, these concerns must be bolstered by a mass of sartorial and decorative detail that Austen readily dispenses with in order to underscore the true ethical context in which the action unfolds. Both novelists, however, are saying that the personal *matters*, and those twentieth-century novelists who choose an historical period when great public events were in the making seem to be saying it with particular force. Historical incidents become the backdrop for that message, and exalted social position serves to enhance the argument itself.

At the same time, the import of historical fiction for women is to reinforce the notion that the public world, however much its vicissitudes may influence women's lives, is always at one remove from women. And, conversely, women remain at one remove from it. Larger political considerations may affect what happens to a woman, but her participation in history, as chambermaid, queen, or the Cinderella who is transformed from one to the other, consists in being a female, dressed—always—in appropriate period costume. It is not so much that this kind of fiction

---

[20] The problem is becoming acute, moreover. I recently saw a vending machine called a Convenience Center in the lobby of a Holiday Inn. It dispensed such items as body lotion, hair spray, tampons, deodorant, and copies of *Pride and Prejudice*!

"tells" or "teaches" women something about their nature, role, and sphere. Rather, it repeats what direct experience and dominant ideology have already succeeded in communicating. In this sense, it would appear that female readers do not seek out trashy novels in order to escape or to experience life vicariously, but rather to receive confirmation, and, eventually, affirmation, that love really is what motivates and justifies a woman's life. At best, it is much too slight a compensation for the weight of stiff velvet and the chill insubstantiality of sprig-muslin into which our historical imaginations have been laced.

**Nancy Wingate, "Getting Away With Murder" (in *Journal of Popular Culture* 12, 4 [Spring 1979], pp. 590-1):**

In this book [Anthony Berkeley's *Trial and Error* (1937)] . . . we are satisfied with the "murder as problem-solver" ethic, since life improves for everyone after the murder, and quite believably too. Georgette Heyer's *Penhallow* (1942) takes the same concept and provides a far more realistic resolution. A long-suffering wife has killed her husband, a selfish, trouble-making old tyrant, to free her children from his constant meddling in their lives. The reader is at first lulled into sharing her conviction that the murder will solve all the family's problems, but both the murderess and the reader are unpleasantly surprised: the children are grieved over the loss of their father and suspect each other of murder. The mother is even more horrified when her innocent stepson commits a timely but unrelated suicide and is marked as the murderer. She had expected the death to be put down to accident and is heartsick that he is considered guilty, even though he's dead and can only suffer in his family's recollection. Heyer counters the notion of the efficacy of "murder as problem-solver" with the traditional argument that the end cannot justify the means because we can never predict the consequences of our actions and so never know if our desired end will be reached.

Heyer offers a new reason for the difficulty of finding out the truth: the sheer weight of the prejudices human beings bring to the investigation of crime, as they bring them to anything else. Because of their preconceived notion of her character, neither the police nor her family ever consider the wife seriously as the murderer. The inspector "did not consider it likely that, having borne patiently with Penhallow for twenty years, she should suddenly have taken it into her head to murder him."[21] By the same token, the family's acceptance of the notion that their brother comitted [sic] suicide because he had murdered their father is equally unjustified; their faith in him is well placed, but there is no way they will ever find out. The mother is too terrified to confess, especially once the police have fastened on the stepson's suicide as clear evidence of his guilt. The police conclude that it's "a very unsatisfactory case" (p. 298) as does the reader, and in this instance I think it's purely because of the truth's not coming out. We're upset that the family considers their innocent brother a murderer, but, since he's dead, we are not as upset as in a case in which someone's future life might be ruined. It's simply that the notion of the detective in the case being baffled and misled is unpalatable. This book would produce a completely different effect if an infallible detective, for instance Poirot, were to figure out that the wife had done it, get her confession and then get the police to put it down as accident or suicide. She is a sympathetic character, the murder is one we can identify with, and our pity for her is greater than our desire for her punishment. But we want someone to *know* what really happened.

This desire to have the detective know what really happened is satisfied in E.C. Bentley's *Trent's Last Case* (1936) . . . .

**Erik Jorgensen, "Some Notes on Negated Comparatives (+ 'than')" (in *English Studies* 61 [1980], pp. 543, 550):**

1.   Apart from a few references made in passing, the following observations leave out of account cases where *no(t) more (less) than* is followed by a numeral or another indication of quantity  (or an entity viewed as quantity—in the widest sense of the term). Such cases will in

---

[21] Georgette Heyer, *Penhallow* (1942; rpt. New York:  Bantam Books, 1972), p. 262.

general hardly offer any particular interest beyond what is usually stated in current handbooks.

Cases of the following type may, however, require some brief mention in this connection:

> Philip had done no more than say that he wished to enter his new abode on Thursday. (Georgette Heyer, *Powder and Patch*, William Heinemann Ltd., 1951, p.131).

> . . .had done no more damage than burning a cigarette streak in the bureau top, . . . (Patricia Highsmith, *The Cry of the Owl*, Pan Books, 1965, p. 15).

*No* is here a pronominal adjective, and in the first example, *more* is a substantive, in the second, an attributive adjective. In both cases, the *more*-element may be said in itself to fill the place of the first term of the comparison; the second is virtually, if not formally, a quantitative entity. . . .

5. Negated comparatives of the type dealt with above, i.e. cases where *more* is functionally an adverb, whereas *less* may be an adverb, an adjective, or a substantive, and cases where we have a synthetic comparative, also negated, present the following characteristics:

If the comparative in itself is felt as having a "positive" value (as e.g. "more mature" as opposed to "less mature," "better" as opposed to "worse"), a clear distinction between *no* and *not* as negatives is as a rule strictly observed. There is normally in current usage a striking difference in content between the two constructions. "*No* + comparative" has usually, with very few exceptions, an absolute negative effect, denying the reality of the two terms of the comparison or, in the case of the first category mentioned in section (1), stating the total absence in the two persons or things compared of the quality, etc., in question. "*Not* + comparative," reversely, has always a positive, affirmative effect as far as the two terms of the comparison are concerned, with, in addition, the

337

possible or probable implication that the second term may even exceed the first.[22]


**Hanna Charney, *The Detective Novel of Manners. Hedonism, Morality, and the Life of Reason* (London/Toronto: Associated University Presses, 1981, pp. xxiv-xxv, 79-82):**

Introduction

. . . In detective fiction, as I understand it, action, necessary though it is, is still refracted by the mind.

This reflexive quality opens the detective novel in a number of different directions, all of which lead far from the short story. In the present study, we follow authors who have shaped and developed the forms of the genre, with all its special modern possibilities, since the 1920s—Margery Allingham, Josephine Bell, Robert Bernard, Nicholas Blake, Agatha Christie, V. C. Clinton-Baddeley, Amanda Cross, E. X. Ferrars, Erle Stanley Gardner, Michael Gilbert, Georgette Heyer, Michael Innes, P. D. James, Harry Kenelman, Emma Lathen, Elizabeth Lemarchand, Frances and Richard Lockridge, Ross Macdonald, J. J. Marric, Ngaio Marsh, Patricia Moyes, Maurice Procter, Ruth Rendell, Dorothy L. Sayers, Simenon, Maj Sjöwall and Per Wahlöö, Rex Stout, Phoebe Atwood Taylor, Josephine Tey, Patricia Wentworth, Sara Woods—to name, as the saying goes, only a few. Their pseudonyms are kept intact, since we are dealing with the products of their imagination as

---

[22] Of course it does not follow that both constructions are logically practicable in all contexts. For instance, in the example from Phyllis Bottome quoted in section (1), *no more* with its absolute negative effect, would be at variance with the preceding positive statement. Reversely, in a case like the following *not more*, with its positive implication, would be impossible: ". . . Selina knows no more than the man in the moon where her cousin may be!" (Georgette Heyer, *April Lady*, Pan Books, 1970, p. 199).

presented in their works. The range is wide, although it comprises only certain areas on the historical map of crime fiction. Boundaries shift as we enter the psychological, moral, and philosophical province of the detective novel of manners. . . .

### Social Worlds: The Microcosm and the Larger Reality

As in all novels of manners, there is a constant interplay in detective fiction between the customs and mores of a certain milieu and psychological and ethical realities. The murder is the breach that violently breaks open this microcosm and forcefully brings in the outside world. Even in the hospital, where death is a regular occurrence, murder brings a frightened hush and destroys the balance. What commonly happens in an English village, where the police seem part of the family, is that Scotland Yard must be called in. Scotland Yard is the medieval war alarm, the signal that the comfortable values of the town will be violated by rude inquiry, tactless probing, and intolerable suspicion. The fine distinctions of a society in which every member has his consecrated place will no longer be observed. The respected old butler will be interrogated with the youngest scullery maid and the masters themselves will be under more or less polite suspicion. The style in the conversations will change abruptly. The accepted small talk of tea parties—roses, fairs, the latest indisposition of Mrs. X's Pekingese—will yield to straight questions in an unfamiliar dialect or a neutral language that reeks of London talk.

In a small American town, the inspector may be a New York Jew, whereas among bankers under suspicion, he may be a stocky Irishman with a large family. In the world of advertising, he may be a down-to-earth skeptic with little patience for the frills of greed. The question of communication runs through the minds on both sides. Will the gruff policeman understand the delicate duties of the secretary of an important executive? Will he grasp how much a nurse can or cannot reveal about a doctor? Does he know how complicated is the matter of inheritance for a pair of stepbrothers? The policemen also may have trouble finding their way. Is adultery still a motive for murder among the fashionable rich?

Do members of the jet set suffer from jealousy? How can a painting be worth millions of dollars? Why do people become so agitated about some old pages of manuscript left in an office drawer? Would a lawyer protect a criminal client? Are actors always playing a part, even in their private lives? Do scholars and writers care more about a real death than about what happens in their books? Would a bishop shield the wealthy trustee of one of his churches?

The gravity of the situation demands that communication be established. . . .

By whatever means, the elements of the situation must become understandable and open to the investigation of the law of the land. This process of making understandable, of making us see, is symbolically that of the novel itself. The reader is also the outsider penetrating into an originally closed society with its own languages, manners, and morals. And although the action opens this closed society up and shows it to be a microcosm of society at large, it is still presented for itself as the scene of the action in its own particular colors and nuances. Sometimes we are jolted into awareness from the very beginning as in *The Unfinished Clue* by Georgette Heyer:

> It was apparent to Miss Fawcett within one minute of her arrival at the Grange that her host was not in the best of tempers. He met her in the hall, not, she believed, of design, and favored her with a nod. "It's you, is it?" he said ungraciously. "Somewhat unexpected, this visit, I must say. Hope you had a good journey." (p.1)

Miss Fawcett is accustomed to her brother-in-law's rude ill humor, but the readers watching the curtain rise on this aristocratic country house setting have to readjust their expectations. The readers cannot smoothly glide into a scene of welcoming "Dahlings," drinks offered, or a polite butler's deft hand removing the luggage.

Forms are strictly observed in the host Sir Arthur's house. "But in spite of the fact that Sir Arthur's principles forbade him to quarrel on the

Sabbath, Sunday had not been a happy day." (*The Unfinished Clue*, p. 40) Quarrels are contained, but they seem near explosion. Innuendos abound at parties about the general's much younger wife and his desire to disown his son from a former marriage. The seething of passions and conflicts reaches a high point on page 62: "Really, it's more like a home for mental cases than a house-party," Dinah thinks. The English upper classes are often presented in this way. There is a crescendo of satire, constantly puncturing the outward forms observed by tight-lipped ladies, choleric army officers, and frivolous wives. Then, in turn, the satire is punctured as the investigation starts, and all the characters have to reveal themselves slowly through the traumatic events surrounding the murder. . . .

### Earl F. Bargainnier, "The Dozen Mysteries of Georgette Heyer" (in *Clues* 3, 2 (Fall/Wtr 1982), pp. 30-39):

Although she is much more widely known for her forty-five Regency romances, Georgette Heyer was also the author of twelve mysteries, ten in the late classical detective mode and two not.[23] Elaine Bander has

---

[23] The editions of Heyer's novels used for this study are listed below, preceded by the original date of publication. All quotations will be cited in the text using, where necessary for clarity, the abbreviation given after the entry.

> 1932 *Footsteps in the Dark* (NY: Buccaneer, 1976) (*Dark*)
> 1933 *Death in the Stocks* (NY: Bantam, 1971) (*Stocks*)
> 1935 *Why Shoot a Butler?* (NY: Dutton, 1973) (*Butler*)
> 1936 *Behold, Here's Poison* (NY: Bantam, 1973) (*Poison*)
> 1937 *They Found Him Dead* (NY: Bantam, 1970) (*Dead*)
> 1938 *The Unfinished Clue* (NY: Bantam, 1971) (*Clue*)
> 1938 *A Blunt Instrument* (NY: Bantam, 1966)
> 1941 *Envious Casca* (NY: Bantam, 1970) (*Casca*)
> 1942 *Penhallow* (NY: Bantam, 1972)
> 1951 *Duplicate Death* (NY: Bantam, 1970) (*Death*)

provided a convenient term for Heyer's mysteries: "the 'What Fun!' school of detection, in which, instead of issuing appropriate sounds of outrage and anxiety, the suspects cracked jokes over corpses and honed their wit upon blunt instruments, burlesquing but not injuring the once-solemn conventions;" the reference to "blunt instruments" would indicate Bander's thinking of Heyer, if she did not add, "The 'What Fun!' school thrived in the hands of Georgette Heyer."[24] It is doubtful that Heyer was consciously burlesquing the conventions of interwar detective fiction—and the term does not apply to one novel, *Penhallow*—but "What Fun!" does indicate one, and the most important, of the three fictional components which give Heyer's work a distinctive quality, and that is comedy, specifically comedy of manners (which in her work is accompanied by an unpleasant snobbery) as well as some characters from farce. The other two components are melodrama and romance. Heyer's combining these three elements, in varying degrees, with the formulas of classic detective fiction creates the nexus of her mysteries.

They have received little critical attention, aside from the championship of Jacques Barzun and Wendell Hertig Taylor.[25] Perhaps

---

1953 *Detection Unlimited* (NY: Bantam, 1971) (*Detection*)
[24] "The English Detective Novel Between the Wars: 1919-1939," *The Armchair Detective* 11 (July 1978), 271 & 272.
[25] The most extensive study thus far of Heyer's detective fiction is an unpublished essay by Nancy Wingate, "Georgette Heyer: A Reappraisal," presented at the meeting of the Popular Culture Association, April 1976. I am indebted to Ms. Wingate for providing me a copy, and much of my study reflects views similar to hers. The major exception is our differing judgment of *Penhallow*, which she considers Heyer's masterpiece; I do not. I agree more with Barzun and Taylor, who describe that novel as "A long study about a family of terrorizing and oversexed males, embroiled with one or two victimized females, halfwits, illegitimate boot boys, and others." *A Catalogue of Crime* (New York: Harper & Row, 1971), p. 236. One should also see Kathleen Gregory Klein's entry on Heyer in *Twentieth Century Crime*

the reason is their being generally so predictable and, at the same time, containing so much comedy, which has an uneasy relationship with crime at any time, and so much "blasted romance," which critics of detective fiction have been condemning since the 1920s. (I bought *The Unfinished Clue* at a second-hand book store; on the inside of the front cover was a comment by a former purchaser: "Another one I couldn't read.") They certainly offer nothing particularly new to detective fiction as a genre—unless it is that combination of romance, melodrama and comedy. Otherwise most are conventional (pardon the pun) in structure, setting, characters, style and mysteries to be solved.

Heyer specializes in upper class family murders and is often repetitive. Her victims are domestic tyrants—one is called "a pocket-Hitler," blackmailers or weaklings. Her murderers are often of the least likely type, but can be spotted by that very fact. Since she is so fond of the device of the hidden heir, the murderer is rarely of the immediate family, the major exception being *Envious Casca*, which contains her cleverest portrait of a murderer, one who is variously Pickwickian, "The Ideal Polonious!" (3), and a "Sort of Peter Pan" (118). Her settings adhere to the closed circle convention, albeit with a larger than usual number of suspects, and are invariably upper class, whether in London or at the ubiquitous country house. Among many repeated structural devices are the birthday party of the elderly victim (*They Found Him Dead* and *Penhallow*), the rigged gun or false shot to provide an alibi (*They Found Him Dead, No Wind of Blame* and *Detection Unlimited*), the evidence concealed in a safe deposit box (*Behold, Here's Poison* and *Detection Unlimited*), and, straight from Victorian melodrama, the opening introduction of major characters through a servant or companion (*Behold, Here's Poison, They Found Him Dead* and *Penhallow*). Heyer's repetitiveness also extends to style; just one example is the continual use of one form of transition which appears again and again in all the novels: a character is thinking or talking about something and the scene shifts to another thinking or talking about the same thing or a

---

*and Mystery Writers*, ed. John M. Reilly (New York: St. Martin's Press, 1980).

character wonders what another is doing and the answer is given by shifting to that person:

> "But they haven't anything like enough on you yet, Stephen!"
> Oddly enough, Inspector Hemingway had reached much the same conclusion . . . (*Casca*, 199).

> "I should like to know what those detectives were doing up the lane, and what they're up to now."
> They were, in fact, being driven back to Bellingham . . . (*Detection*, 220).

Heyer does follow the rule of fair play; a good instance is the statement when the false shot is used in *They Found Him Dead*: "a sudden report, as from a gun" (67). On the other hand, to solve the murder in *Envious Casca* the reader needs to know the circumstances of the assassination of the Empress Elizabeth of Austria.

These few examples of the conventionality of Heyer's work indicate their typical Golden Age nature. Though some might disagree, Erik Routley's evaluation seems both fair and honest:

> [S]he stands with Agatha Christie as an assistant priestess of the cliché. . .but the detective interest that kept Mrs. Christie running never really gets off the ground in Heyer. . .think of any detective-story cliché, any stock character, and you'll find it in her stories: the not-too-well educated policeman, the over-sophisticated policeman, the country vicar with the neurotic wife, the fast-talking competent sister of a heroine goaded near insanity by her husband's brutality, the exotic and outrageous Spanish dancer . . .It's all perilously near what used. . .to be called "women's magazine" style—West End, rustic high life, able young asses who teach the police their jobs,

> loads of money, and butlers, butlers, butlers (yes,
> even a Shot Butler).[26]

As detective novels *per se*, they are hardly more than perfunctory; it is in the blending of melodrama, romance and comedy with the conventions of detective fiction that Heyer achieves at times a quality that deserves to be called Heyeresque. Implicit in Routley's statement is the relationship between Heyer's mysteries and her romances, which (from the three I forced myself to read) are also melodramatic. These two elements will be considered before examining the novels' comedy, but before them the least attractive element of Heyer's work must be noted.

That element is the overt snobbery which is present and which takes three forms. Least offensive are the statements about the decline of aristocracy and its values, the loss of the proper work ethic among the lower orders, and the evils of progress. Such statements are especially prevalent in the two post-World War II novels. In *Detection Unlimited* Inspector Hemingway considers the decline of an estate, but keeps his opinion to himself, "well-knowing that his companion, inevitably reared in the hazy and impracticable beliefs of democracy-run-riot, would derive a deep, if uninformed, gratification from the reflection that yet another landowner had been obliged, through excessive taxation, to throw out of work the greater part of his staff" (129). The bitterness is obvious. Another form of snobbery is the attitude toward characters who are "not quite quite." Ermyntrude Carter of *They Found Him Dead* [sic] is the most developed example, but there are others, including Rudolph Mesurier of *Death in the Stocks* and Willoughby Roydon of *Envious Casca*. It is never made clear exactly why these characters are the butts

---

[26] *The Puritan Pleasures of the Detective Story* (London: Victor Gollancz, 1972), p. 182. Routley gives credit to Heyer for her "quite remarkable gift for reproducing the brittle and ironic conversation of the upper middle class Englishwoman of that age (immediately before 1940)," and he finds Vicky Fanshaw of *No Wind of Blame* "very nearly the funniest fictional female I have ever met" (182). I find her silly and deserving of a good spanking.

of other characters' mockery or contempt, except that they do not conform to the image of lady or gentleman in a rigidly stratified society. If such characters seem unfairly treated by the upper class "in group," even more so are the lower classes, whose presentation is the third, and most deplorable, form of snobbery.

In the first novel is the following statement, significantly made by the detective: "Pocket combs studded with paste, puff-boxes, and all that sort of meretricious junk that's designed to catch the eyes of city typists, and domestic servants" (279). There is no deviation from this sneering point of view. The last novel has Hemingway glimpsed by two stenographers and an office boy, who are thrilled and terrified. One of the stenographers says that if he questioned her, "she wouldn't be able to speak a word, on account of her being very high-strung," while the office boy, after boasting that no detective can scare him, has "a horrid fear that from so high-ranking an official not one of his youthful peccadilloes could remain hidden" (110). Between these two novels, the working class, and particularly servants, are consistently figures of either contemptuous humor or sheer scorn. They are vacuous, cowardly, affected or untrustworthy. They are unreliable witnesses, for their inevitable reaction to murder is a mingling of terror, often hysterical in the case of women, and a kind of secretly sadistic or masochistic enjoyment:

> The girl, after the manner of her kind, was torn between excitement and a conventional impulse to burst into tears (*Casca*, 64).

> The footman. . .looked somewhat scared, as though all these dramatic proceedings were to him a fearful pleasure (*Clue*, 74).

> It was shocking, awful, and yet thrilling. . . .She didn't want to have anything to do with it; she wouldn't be out of it for worlds (*Poison*, 6).

346

One cannot but wonder what was Heyer's attitude toward her own servants—and what theirs toward her. The impression given by the novels is of a world in which only those who have money, manners, position and lineage matter; all others are to be used when needed, laughed at and about, and then discarded without thought or feeling.

## Melodrama

Since *melodrama* has come to have such a broad meaning—some might say that all detective fiction is melodrama—the specific concept indicated by the term here requires explanation. It is used to refer strictly to features of plot and character which are direct descendants of Victorian drama and fiction, particularly devices, techniques, and elements of sensationalism and sentimentality; it is not used in the wider sense, which would include stereotyped characters (though they are certainly present), their histrionic behavior and the shortest route, ignoring cause and effect, to a satisfactory conclusion, that conclusion being virtue triumphant. Obvious examples of melodramatic technique are that in seven of the twelve novels inheritance is the motive and that a hidden or long-lost heir appears in five. These two staples of nineteenth-century drama and fiction—in which money is so important—are employed by Heyer in the same way that they were by the earlier melodramatists: to provide conflict and mystification. The late *Duplicate Death* offers another illustration. In that novel neatly paralleled are two women with a past, that favorite character of the 1890s. The heroine has been in jail and frantically wishes to conceal the fact. Of course, it develops that she was "cooked," i.e., framed, and is totally innocent. Conversely, the first murderer, also the second victim, is a society woman who appears to be a sister of Braddon's Lady Audley and Shaw's Mrs. Warren, especially of the latter since there are delicate hints that she may have been in Mrs. Warren's profession, as well as in the drug traffic. Other such melodramatic features can be found in nearly all the novels, but the four most explicitly melodramatic are the first two, *Footsteps in the Dark* and *Why Shoot a Butler?*, *The Unfinished Clue* and *Penhallow*.

GEORGETTE HEYER:

Among the melodramatic elements of *Footsteps in the Dark* is the pseudo-Gothic setting, The Priory, which contains secret panels, underground cells, tunnels entered through a hinged tomb, and a skeleton inside a priest's hole. Such unlikely items in the 1930s are eventually explained as "supernatural" cover for crime, organized by a master criminal, called The Monk, who is suave even when arrested. He is opposed by two couples: frightened Celia, sensible Charles, adventurous Peter and romantic Margaret. The two men have the characteristics of adult "Hardy boys," while Margaret falls in love with a mysterious stranger, appropriately named Strange, who is actually Inspector Draycott of the C.I.D. He is assisted by a comic ex-criminal, who with a cowardly butler, a scatty aunt, and a clumsy constable provides farcical interludes, as similar characters did in Victorian melodrama. This obvious apprenticeship mystery of Heyer is occasionally amusing, but reads much like a book for juveniles. Better, and more typical of her fiction, is *Why Shoot a Butler?* It has the romance and comedy of later novels, but it also contains much melodramatic coincidence, including the opening scene, a plot hinging on a will which has been torn in two—still another Victorian favorite—and the single most sensational episode of any of them: Frank Amberley's mad automobile dash to the coast, with a comic and cowardly Constable Gubbins, for a nick-of-time rescue of the heroine from the villain's attempt to drown her in a sinking boat. (It is never satisfactorily explained why Amberley uses the twisting back roads to reach the coast, since he has already reconnoitered the boat and its docking site. The only reasons are to heighten the melodramatic suspense and to make the drive more thrillingly dangerous.)

The plot premise of *The Unfinished Clue* is a simple variation on Mrs. Henry Wood's *East Lynne* (1861). That teary story of Lady Isabel's leaving her family to run away with another man only to return to watch over her child as Madame Vine, not being recognized by her former husband or friends, is paralleled in Heyer's novel by a runaway wife's returning and murdering her former husband to prevent his disinheriting their son. Again, she is unrecognized by any of her former acquaintances; aside from the murder, Heyer's major change is to make the errant woman not a governess on her return, but the Vicar's wife!

348

The last line of *Penhallow* states, "A very unsatisfactory case" (298). It is unsatisfactory, not that the murderer is never discovered by the other characters, but that either Heyer could not decide what kind of novel she wished to write or she let the melodrama take control. The Brontesque *Penhallow* family belong to the middle of the nineteenth century. When after some forty pages there is mention of cars and telephones, the reader becomes disoriented, but until then there has been no indication that he is in the twentieth century. This is especially true because such a tremendous amount of detail is devoted to physical objects in the novel. One is introduced to a Gothic manor in Cornwall where horses are raised; the house itself consists of oaken stairs, small windows set deep in stone walls, an uncomfortable lay-out, and massive mahogany furniture. Included are numerous lists of clutter of the untidy household, very little of which is "modern." The entire aura is of the last century. (The cover of the 1972 Bantam edition contributes to the confusion: it presents a blonde young woman in a long dress and shawl standing on the terrace of a Tudor mansion; again, nothing indicates a time later than 1860.) Populating this setting are a group of totally disagreeable, unpleasant, scheming people; the only likeable character is Inspector Logan, and he is a failure. The tyrant father, the neurasthenic stepmother, and the brood of brutal, grasping, domineering, lesbian, homosexual, hypochondriacal, jealous and weak children, as well as the father's bastard who serves as bootblack, must rank among the least empathic families in detective fiction; it is impossible to care what happens to any of them. They are also very melodramatic in their actions and reactions to one another. The menage at Wuthering Heights is serene compared to that at Penhallow. Altogether this novel is Heyer's most melodramatic, least comic, and far from her best.

## Romance

Heyer's favorite author was Jane Austen, and her Regency romances, whatever one may think of them, are evidence of her admiration. When she turned to the mystery, she did not abandon the romantic formulas she had developed from Austen. In fact in nine of the novels she

GEORGETTE HEYER:

incorporated what might be called the "pride and prejudice" formula, generally adding features of a Beatrice and Benedick relationship: apparent overt dislike or indifference, with waspish or scornful repartee, gradually transformed into affection. Both the young men and young women are distinct types, which are repeated over and over, and though they may be suspects, they are never guilty.

As in the romances, the heroines play a lesser role than the heroes. It is enough that they are beautiful, desired and usually persecuted in some way, but they are also independent, often witty, and, most evident in the mysteries, sensible. Additionally, in three novels they have less social status than their male counterparts: Pat Allison of *They Found Him Dead* and Beulah Birtley of *Duplicate Death* are companion-secretaries, each of whom marries one of the Harte brothers of a titled family; Shirley Brown, the poor, dispossessed heroine of *Why Shoot a Butler?*, is rescued and presumably wed by Frank Amberley of a country family, who also retrieves her fortune. Others are more equal, as Dinah Fawcett of *The Unfinished Clue*, who marries the Roderick Alleynish Inspector Harding; Mary Cliffe and Dr. Maurice Chester of *No Wind of Blame*; and Sally Drew, "one of the six most important crime novelists," and Neville Fletcher of *A Blunt Instrument* (23). In three, the lovers are cousins: Antonia Vereker and Giles Carrington in *Death in the Stocks*, Stella and Randall Matthews in *Behold, Here's Poison*, and Mathilda Clare and Stephen Herriard in *Envious Casca*. As stated, these young women are sensible, yet they may be deliberately surly or offensive to the man, as Shirley Brown or Stella Matthews, or strangely oblivious of his interest in her, as Mary Cliffe or Antonia Vereker. But whether they raise bull terriers, as two of them do, cater to the whims of an older female employer, or just like to spar with the disagreeable, they demand to be won in the game of love for themselves, as they are. In the slang of the 1930s, they are "spunky," but they are also typical heroines of the comedy of manners.

That the young men are from the romances is made clear by Timothy Harte in *Duplicate Death*—he returns as an ex-commando hero of 27 after having been the teenage "Terrible Timothy" of *They Found Him Dead*: "He began to think rather badly of a state of civilization that made

350

it impossible for him to pick a quarrel with Seaton-Carew upon frivolous grounds, and then inform him that his friends would wait upon him in the morning" (51). Like Giles Carrington and his older brother James Harte, Timothy is a pleasant chap and, in spite of his statement, is not one of Heyer's transported Regency rakes as heroes, such as Frank Amberley, Randall Matthews, Neville Fletcher and Stephen Herriard. But all are the decent and ultra-chivalrous hero, even when that chivalry is hidden under what has been called a "snake" façade.

Randall Matthews is "one of Georgette's favorite 'snake' types, who turn out decent once the motive for the foulness is made clear."[27] Indeed he is described as "poisonous-tongued" and "an amiable snake." Similarly, Amberley is called "the rudest man in London" (*Butler*, 331), and Herriard is characterized by "his careless rudeness, his roughness, the indifferent sardonic gleam in his deep-set grey eyes" (*Casca*, 26). Fletcher is the ne'er-do-well nephew, who likes to travel in the Balkans and is always flippant. (The only "snake" character who is a murderer is not given a heroine to woo; nor is, for special reasons, the non-guilty but exasperatingly facetious Kenneth Vereker of *Death in the Stocks*, but in *Behold, Here's Poison* it is learned that he has wed "the plain but deserving" girl who has always loved him.) What is immediately striking about these men is that they are neither particularly "manly" or "unmanly"; rather they are men who go their own way, do as they please—until they meet the right woman, and care nothing for social convention. In creating them, Heyer added a new male figure to detective fiction.

These couples enliven Heyer's novels, for though they are stereotypes, they are original ones for pre-world War II mystery stories. They are certainly less insipid than many of the lovers of more widely read mystery novelists, and the major reason is they are characters of comedy of manners, whether dramatic or fictional, however transformed for Heyer's purposes.

---

[27] Barzun and Taylor, p. 235. Wingate states, "In general, the rude character is the cleverest one, and therefore the hero or heroine" (8).

## Comedy

The comedy or "What Fun!" element is generated not by the action but by the personalities and dialogue of the characters. The attitude of many of the characters is that a murder case is something to be enjoyed. Mrs. Haswell and Miss Potterdale of *Detection Unlimited* express what is almost a general view; they agree that "although it was disagreeable to persons of their generation to have a murder committed in their midst, it was very nice for the children to have something to occupy them" (95). The young people in that novel and most of the others do seem to enjoy the excitement, the chance to play amateur sleuth, and the opportunity to trade quips about everyone involved. Heyer's suspects and witnesses and her major detective, Inspector Stanley Hemingway, provide the bulk of the comedy. That she was thoroughly conscious of their essentially comic roles is shown by her playing with names. In *Why Shoot a Butler?* the characters in order of appearance are named Amberley, Brown, Collins, Dawson, Fountain, Gubbins, Harper, Jenkins, Ludlow and Matthews.[28] For some reason she liked her own final initial for her policemen. Inspector Hannasyde appears in four novels, Hemingway in eight, Harding in *The Unfinished Clue* and in *Detection Unlimited* Hemingway is assisted by Inspector Horace Harbottle and Constable Hobkirk and is directed by Superintendent Hinckley. In that last novel she carries such naming to excess in the dogs of Mrs. Drybeck, whose kennel designation is "Ultima" and whose dogs are named Umberto, Ulysses, Una, Uppish, Umbrella, Ursula, Urban, Urania, Uriah, Ulrica, Unready, Uplift and Ullapool. Hemingway calls Mrs. Drybeck "Ultima Unlikely," and the repetition of the "U's" is apparently the only purpose of the title *Detection Unlimited*.

The personalities of the suspects and witnesses, especially family members, naturally vary considerably, but a very large portion of such characters are in the same way comic: whether a ludicrous vamp, as Lola de Silva in *The Unfinished Clue*, an empty-headed debutante as Cynthia Haddington of *Duplicate Death*, the "God-controlled"—today it would

---

[28] Routley, p. 182.

be "born again"—Connie Bawtrey of *No Wind of Blame*, or the monocle-wearing Miss Potterdale of *Detection Unlimited*, who owns two goats with the Shakespearean names of Rosalind and Celia. Among the men are the boastful-cowardly Constable Gubbins of *Why Shoot a Butler?*, such indignant and ineffectual "haw-haw" types as Sir Humphrey Matthews of the same novel and Sir Charles Carrington of *Death in the Stocks*, the absurdly phoney Prince Varasashvili of *No Wind of Blame*, and the moth-hunting Mr. Titmarsh of *Footsteps in the Dark*. Such families as the Verekers of *Death in the Stocks*, the Matthews of *Behold, Here's Poison*, and the Kanes of *They Found Him Dead* offer a plethora of comic types. Most can be described by one word, which adequately sums up the basis of their presentation: irresponsible Kenneth Vereker, impervious Roger Vereker, feckless Guy Matthews, domineering Gertrude Matthews, self-dramatizing Zoë Matthews, self-analyzing Rosemary Kane and globe-trotting Lady Norma Harte, a Kane by marriage and mother of "Terrible Timothy." These and other characters by their overtly comic personalities give Heyer's mysteries much of their mannered, non-threatening ambience.

Since there are so many eccentrics, it is not surprising that they say exactly what they think—no matter how outrageous. They do not hesitate to discuss who among them may have committed the crime and how, even with the person being discussed present. Nor do victims escape their inappropriate—but comic—remarks. Miserly Harriett Matthews' comment on her brother's death is "Now he's dead, and there are two beautiful lamb cutlets gone to waste" (11). Though *Death in the Stocks* contains more comic dialogue than any of the others, as a result of Verekers' skewed ways of thinking and their determination not to take the case seriously, it is found in all of the novels—even *Penhallow*—and justifies the term for them of "What Fun!" mysteries.[29]

Stanley Hemingway, who is progressively Sergeant, Inspector and Chief Inspector, is not only Heyer's major detective, but also her major

---

[29] It would be a waste of space to quote passages of comic dialogue out of context as illustrations; for any effect, they must be part of the total work and accumulative.

comic character. He is not a great detective, in spite of his statement, "I'm never wrong" (*Casca*, 115). He solves only four of the eight cases in which he is involved: his early superior Hannasyde, who is much like Christie's Superintendent Battle or Crofts' Inspector French, solves two and Giles Carrington and Randall Matthews each solve one. Rather he is a genial master of ceremonies for the fun.

Hemingway is cheerful, brisk, bright-eyed, birdlike, infinitely talkative, and "incorrigibly flippant." He disarms hostility with "a certain engaging breeziness of manner," even though it is "the despair of his superiors" (*Wind*, 140). This breeziness is a part of what he calls his flair, about which he holds no doubts. One of his two principal interests is the theatre, and he likes to treat cases in stage terms; the case in *Behold, Here's Poison* reminds him of that in *Death in the Stocks*, and he says that "when I got the hang of the decor here, and a squint at some of the *dramatis personae* that's what flashed across my mind" (69). He likes cases with a "classy décor" and believes the more tangled a case becomes the easier it is to solve. His second interest is psychology, the terms of which he enjoys sprinkling into his conversation, but Hannasyde says that his knowledge of psychology extends only to "a strange realm of bastard words and lurid theories" (*Blunt*, 85). His droll humor is seen in his treatment of and quarrels with his various assistants, usually a mixture of patronizing and facetiousness. Particularly good examples of this aspect of his personality are his encounters with the Bible-quoting Constable Malachi Glass in *A Blunt Instrument* and the Scots Inspector Sandy Grant in *Duplicate Death*. Another instance of his drollery is his coining of alliterative epithets for persons in an investigation: "Henna'ed Hannah," "Pretty Paul," "Granite-faced Gertrude," "Dismal Desmond," "Mr. Silent Steele," and many others. These few elements of Hemingway's personality demonstrate his significance in creating the "What Fun!" tone of the novels in which he appears. Whatever his deficiencies as a detective, he is a success as a likable, comic policeman.

Barzun and Taylor rank Heyer with Sayers, Allingham and Marsh, but it is difficult to understand such high praise. She is major only in her effective use at times of the comic and the romantic as elements of detective fiction, for many others have used melodrama. When she blends the three well with the conventions of Golden Age detective fiction, she does create a few works that are distinctive. (To choose, I would say her best are *Behold, Here's Poison, A Blunt Instrument, Envious Casca* and *Duplicate Death*.) The problem is that her works are often such an uneven mixture that one can never know what to expect. Perhaps this uneven mixture contributes to the inability of Bantam Books to decide upon suitable covers. Setting aside the already mentioned Gothic cover of *Penhallow*, in the early 1970s most of the covers emphasized the romantic more than the mysterious with long-haired young women prominent. A new series of covers began in 1979, eliminating all human figures and displaying weapons and blood. What is most notable about the first two in this new series, *Envious Casca* and *Detection Unlimited*, is their nineteenth century quality, one featuring a kerosene lamp and the other an antique desk, neither object playing a major role in its respective novel. Apparently the artists have been unable to determine a way of indicating the "What Fun!" nature of the mysteries, their distinguishing characteristic. The uneasy relationship of comedy and murder would probably make such covers offensive to many. Nevertheless the fact remains that Heyer's achievement in mystery fiction is most evident in her ability to combine comedy and her special type of romance with the conventions of the genre as practiced between the two World Wars.


**Rachel M. Brownstein, *Becoming a Heroine. Reading About Women in Novels* (New York: Viking Press, 1982, pp. 29-31):**

I expect that my thoughts about women and fiction will be interrupted by a visit to Doctor T., but it turns out I am wrong. Showing interest in the patient as a person, he asks me what I am up to. Writing a book, I tell him, about English novels. "Georgette Heyer?" he supposes with a very cute wink. When I ask him if he reads her, he says of course not, but Sarah (nodding toward the door to the outer office), Sarah does. He assumes that as a writer I also am in a position to look down at Sarah. Then to save his nurse's face he adds that he doesn't think she does so much, anymore.

I have not meant to write about Georgette Heyer, but with characteristic sauciness she seems to be intruding herself. I read Georgette Heyer when I was in college; I traded volumes with a friend who was a lawyer, a woman in her late twenties. We were obliged to stoop thus, we reasoned, because Jane Austen had gone and died after only six books, and the pleasures of rereading were limited. Georgette Heyer is not like Barbara Cartland or Victoria Holt or Rosemary Rogers. Her prose has pretensions to wit, her characters are respectful of artifice and irony, and she makes a show of scorn for sentimentality. Reading Georgette Heyer, my doctor's nurse does not, I bet, merely escape a hard world owned and operated by the likes of her condescending employer. Her fantasy is not simply of being young again, and beautiful and loved this time round, although that, of course, must figure in it. Georgette Heyer appeals to the reader who enjoys being reminded how well she knows the elegant manners of an era when women who used English well had power.

Part of the pleasure of reading Georgette Heyer (and other romance writers, too) is the pleasure of predictability: the exotic details of eighteenth-century card games and cosmetics with which the novels are salted are the only elements of the unknown they contain. The reader's foreknowledge, her recognition of this as a variation on a theme, is depended on: of course the beautiful, intelligent, spunky, hard-pressed young woman disdained by the corrupt matron will in the end marry the arrogant, wealthy man distinguished by a pair of good legs and a sneer whose vigorous, contemptuous curl hints at his capacity for passion and even true love. In the fantasy life such novels feed, dreams of adventure and being swept away are mixed with dreams, just as powerful, of knowing, controlling, and containing: the reader enjoys what feels like a novelist's sense of satisfaction when she matches up new characters to the various obligatory parts she anticipates, when the action turns out as it has to. The Georgette Heyer setting, the world of Regency high society as it has been portrayed in comedies of manners, is meant to be bracing, not lulling: wit is the heroine's most prized characteristic, and sometimes also the hero's and the villainess's. The reader is flattered to imagine that like those crisp-souled eighteenth-century types she, too, scorns the spinelessly sentimental, the simply romantic. The first sentence of *Faro's Daughter* dismisses the sort of novels a Georgette Heyer reader is proud to condescend to:

> Upon her butler's announcing the arrival of Mr. Ravenscar, Lady Mablethorpe, who had been dozing over a novel from the Circulating Library, sat up with a jerk, and raised a hand to her dishevelled cap. "What's that you say? Mr. Ravenscar? Desire him to come upstairs at once."

Lady Mablethorpe is glad to be saved from fiction by real life—by sparring in her drawing room with an ominously named man; the reader is cheered by the promise that this fiction will be more exciting than a novel from the Circulating Library. Georgette Heyer is no Jane Austen. But the reader of Jane Austen will recognize in her romances not only eighteenth-century types and manners, and the marriage plot rewritten, and the familiar Cinderella figure, but also the reminder of superiority to other, falser, softer, more commonplace fictions, the kind, a heroine is aware, that most women read.

**Harmony Raine, *The Georgette Heyer Compendium* (Cutchogue, NY: Buccaneer Books, Inc., 1983, n.p.):**

When Georgette Heyer died July 4th, 1974, at the age of 71, she had written more than fifty books. She was one of the world's best sellers, but refused to give interviews and was very rarely photographed. Anything anyone needed to know about her, Miss Heyer said, could be found in her books.

Of Russian extraction, she was born in Wimbledon on August 16th, 1902. In 1925, at age twenty-three, Miss Heyer married George Ronald Rougier and accompanied him to Tanganyika, and in 1929 to Macedonia. After finally settling in England, their son, Richard George, was born in

1932.  Over her lifetime, their flats were in Sussex, Albany and, finally, Parkside, Knightsbridge.

Miss Heyer wrote fifty-seven books, most of them historical novels, with many set in Regency England.  She also collaborated with her husband in writing eleven detective novels.  She was only seventeen years old when she began her first novel, *The Black Moth*, as a serial story to amuse her brother who was recovering from a serious illness. Her father encouraged her to work on it with a view to publication, and it appeared in 1921.  Her success was phenomenal, though not immediate—it began, her husband has said, with the sale of *These Old Shades* in Australia.

Toward the end of her successful career, Georgette Heyer was bedevilled by income tax problems.  What she saw as her major work, the trilogy on the life of John, Duke of Bedford, Henry V's younger brother, was constantly being laid aside so that another Regency romance could be produced to cover taxes.

It was part of Georgette Heyer's sense of style not to appear to take her romances, or herself, seriously.  Although her favorite author was Jane Austen, along with William Shakespeare (most of which she knew by heart), and others, she referred to most writers, and herself, as "Inkies."  But her books did not just come to her.  They were worked for, and worked at laboriously.  She had an impressive library of about one thousand historical books among which she sat to write.  They included dictionaries of slang, dialect, Anglo-Saxon, Roget, an 1800s dictionary to the House of Lords, proverbs, place names, foreign phrases, several shelves on costuming, and more.  The most well-known period of which she wrote, Regency England, was indexed in notebooks under such headings as *Boots and Shoes, Beauty, Colours, Dresses and Hats, Household, Prices*.  But the cataloging of the House of Lancaster which was her life's work, and is partially found in *My Lord John*, was the most detailed and extensive.

Although she is known for her "Regency Romances"—so called because the stories take place during the Regency of George IV, 1811 to 1820—her other books cover diverse eras.  The reign of Charles II is found in *The Royal Escape* [sic] and *The Great Roxhythe*; medieval

England in *My Lord John* and *Simon the Coldheart*. And, of course, we have her detective novels set against the 1920s.

We all have our favorites, and are sorry when we come to the last page, for her characters seem to live beyond it. And, in the end, isn't that the definition of a good writer?

**James P. Devlin, "The Mysteries of Georgette Heyer. A Janeite's Life of Crime" (in *The Armchair Detective* 17, 3 [Summer 1984], 300-315):**

EDITOR'S NOTE: *Solutions to several of the mystery novels of Georgette Heyer are contained in the following article.*

> "I could not sit down to write [seriously] under any other motive than to save my life; and if it were indispensable for me to keep it up and never relax into laughing at myself or at other people, I am sure I should be hung before I had finished the first chapter."

The words are those of Jane Austen, who never wrote a mystery novel, but the sentiments are also those of Georgette Heyer, who wrote a dozen, although she first made her name as a writer emulating Austen's work.

Georgette Heyer was an active writer from 1921 until the time of her death in 1974. Her work as a detective novelist spans only twenty of those years—1932 to 1953—but places her, by period and quality, as part of the "Golden Age." Most of the rest of her career was dedicated to those bubbling fictions which led to her proclamation (by one of her publishers, no doubt) as "England's Mistress of Romance."

Although Miss Heyer's plotting is generally far more intricate than Austen's, the two ladies share a delicious use of dialogue and humor, ranging from the deliberately absurd to jokes so subtle that you wonder if they were actually intended, as in this example from *The Conqueror*:

> Watching from the narrow windows of the house

> where she lodged ashore, Matilda's straining eyes
> saw the banners slowly rising to the mastheads. . .
> She stood motionless until the *Mora* had become a
> speck on the horizon. . .thinking how she might stitch
> the scene with threads to make a tapestry worthy of
> her skill.  She would do it, she decided, she and her
> ladies, while they were left lonely and anxious in
> quiet Rouen. . . .It would take a long time, she
> thought, but the end would justify the labour.

Were we meant to chuckle at this picture of the Rouen Sewing Circle, or is this a serious account of the origin of the Bayeux Tapestry?

If the majority of Miss Heyer's nearly sixty titles are the historical romances once inaccurately described as trifles "where no one loses their virtue, their lives, or even their tempers," we will not make the mistake of treating them too lightly.  Most of them are set in England during the Regency (the last nine years of the reign of King George III, ending in 1820); the author's knowledge of the history, customs, and language of this period is considerable, and provides a firm foundation of detail for the romantic and comedic escapades of her lords and ladies.  This thoroughness is also an asset to Miss Heyer as a mystery writer.

Although most of the Heyer crime stories take place in the present, suspense and violence are very much a part of her romantic world.  Much of the action of *The Unknown Ajax* (1960) centers around the conflict between smugglers and revenue agents; the Black Moth, in the novel of the same name, is an infamous highwayman.  Among other novels having a particularly criminous flavor are *The Masqueraders* (1928), *Regency Buck* (1935), *Faro's Daughter* (1942), and *The Foundling* (1948).

Some biographical data: Georgette Heyer was born in Wimbledon, Surrey, England, in 1902, one of three children.  She married the late George R. Rougier in 1925; they had one son.  The couple lived in East Africa (Tanganyika) for three years after their marriage, and then in Macedonia and Yugoslavia.  Later, and finally, they made their home in London, at the Albany in Picadilly.  Miss Heyer's early seminary education was supplemented by her own reading and research, which her husband described as "enormous and meticulous."

Her first novel, *The Black Moth*, a Romance of the 18th Century, was written in 1919 to amuse a convalescing brother; offered for publication two years later, it was accepted immediately. Following in 1923—and leading off a fifty-year career—were *The Transformation of Philip Jettan* (*Powder and Patch* in later printings) and *The Great Roxhythe*. Although a few of the earliest romances have contemporary settings, by 1930 she had securely established her reputation as a writer of historical pieces.

Although Miss Heyer "shunned public attention," her work became popular and well known in England; it was through her mystery novels, however, that her writing came to the American notice. Then, when she returned to the mystery form in 1951—after an absence of nearly ten years—two publishers began to reissue her books here, interspersed with new stories.

"Her publisher described her, despite her shy nature, as a very bright and amusing person to meet," said the New York Times, in its obituary notice, "with conversation which sparkled with verve and wit. She worked quickly, they said, and made few corrections."

Readers of the Heyer "thrillers" may be disappointed that there weren't more of them, but Miss Heyer did not consider herself a mystery writer. In fact, according to her son (in a letter to this writer), "she regarded the writing of mystery stories rather as one would regard tackling a crossword puzzle—an intellectual diversion before the harder tasks of life have to be faced." It must have been a relief for her occasionally not to have to concentrate on the Regency period and its details, but to write from a modern frame of mind.

Miss Heyer's first try at a thriller—never reprinted, alas, and missing from the Library of Congress since its 1982 inventory—seems to have been *Footsteps in the Dark* (1932), subtitled "a novel of mystery." *The Catalogue of Crime* calls the book "a less than successful effort to combine banter with spookery, and to ring the changes on the old dodge of covering up criminal activities in a ruined abbey by ghostly happenings that should scare away the new tenants." The author is commended for a "born detective mind," however, "thinking of clues even after they don't matter." *Footsteps in the Dark* was most likely a trial balloon for a different type of story from what Miss Heyer had been writing by that time for ten years. But Miss Heyer once said that readers would find all they needed to know about her in her books. . .

*Why Shoot a Butler?* (1933), although still somewhat experimental on Miss Heyer's part, shows her moving toward the later puzzle stories. The central character is Frank Amberly [sic], who is a barrister, not a professional detective. This is the only one of Miss Heyer's regular mysteries in which the bulk of the detective work is done by an amateur; in the stories that followed, the detecting is always done—at least officially—by policemen.

The title of the book is itself one of Miss Heyer's jokes; the author removes the butler from suspicion in the first chapters—by making him the victim. But as soon as another butler arrives on the scene, the police are ready to pin the crime on him:

> "I don't mind telling you I got my eye on that butler. That's your man, Mr. Amberley, you mark my words!"
>
> "I think, Sergeant," said Amberley, swinging round a sharp bend, "that you are nearer the truth than you know."

The pun may not be so easily caught by the American reader, but the new butler is Amberley's manservant, brought up undercover from London.

The story begins with Amberley's discovery of the corpse of the butler of the title in an automobile by the side of the road to his uncle's country house. Near the car is a sullen girl with a gun; Amberley believes her when she tells him she didn't do it, and does not mention her presence to the police when he reports the crime.

To the official theory of murder, Frank explains that the motive for the murder was theft of a different kind: "When you have discovered the answer to that riddle, you will in all probability have discovered your murderer" (p. 69). He also predicts that the murder itself "is likely to prove the least interesting feature of the whole case" (p. 82).

The stolen item (although the reader doesn't learn this until the end) is half of a will which cuts Basil Fountain out of his expected inheritance in favor of his cousins, Mark and Shirley "Brown." Two of the family servants, Dawson and Collins, have torn the document in half; Collins is blackmailing Fountain with his half, while Dawson is threatening to sell his portion to the Browns.

Dawson (the butler) is killed by Collins but manages to tell Shirley (the sullen girl) where his half is hidden. The plot becomes so thick at this point that to attempt to describe it would be counter-productive: it mostly involves the progress of the will from one place to another in an intricate series of misunderstandings. Fountain, trapped between blackmail and exposure, kills first Collins and then Mark Brown.

Although Amberley knows by now who is responsible, he still needs proof for the police. He sets a trap to catch Fountain in an attempt to kill Shirley, but both the attempt and the trap fail. While he is in London investigating the will (this is the first of Miss Heyer's law-laden motives), Shirley is kidnapped. A suspenseful chase ensues, with Amberley and the unfortunate Sergeant "hurtling along at over fifty miles an hour" (p. 217). Shirley is saved, of course, and Frank proposes to her. Fountain, finally confronted by the police, kills himself.

*Why Shoot a Butler?*, like the early Agatha Christies, shows the strong influence of Sir Arthur Conan Doyle. Amberley works a lone hand, although enjoying official cooperation. Like Holmes, he knows—almost from the beginning—who the guilty party is and conceals several pertinent facts from the police (and the reader) for reasons of his own.

At a costume ball celebrating the engagement of Fountain's step-sister, Amberley guesses who Shirley really is when he sees the resemblance in a portrait of Fountain's great-grandmother. Shortly after this, Shirley comes up to the picture gallery to find Dawson's half of the will; by switching the point of view from Frank to Shirley, Miss Heyer not only glosses over Amberley's recognition but also conceals from the reader the fact that he has already found and taken what she is looking for.

One might consider this dodge justified by the fact that Amberley is

363

going to keep his find a secret until the very end of the story, and of course it is necessary to the plot, but it is a little exasperating to the reader who is accustomed to the "fair play" detective novel. This kind of trick—and it turns up again, only legitimately—is made easier for Miss Heyer by her stylistic trait of never using a first-person Watson.

Another, deliberate, Sherlockianism occurs when Fountain gets away from Amberley's trap at Shirley's cottage:

> Amberley said over his shoulder: "I would like to draw your attention to one small but significant point. The man who broke into this place tonight did not know of the existence of Bill."
>
> The sergeant cast an eloquent glance at Corkran. "And who," he inquired, "might Bill be, sir?"
>
> "Bill," said Mr. Amberley, "is Miss Brown's bull-terrier. Think it over."

Miss Heyer also takes an amusing poke at "a novel in a lurid jacket":

> Sir Humphrey put on his pince-nez and took the book. *"The Stalking Death,"* he read. "My dear, surely this doesn't entertain you?"
>
> "Not very much," she admitted. "The nice man turned out to be a villain after all. I think that's so unfair, when one had become quite fond of him."

There are, in addition, several nods cast in Jane Austen's direction by her loyal admirer. Like Mr. Darcy in *Pride and Prejudice*, Frank Amberley is referred to as the rudest man in London. There is even a direct quote from *Emma* by Sir Humphrey, who, "like Mr. Woodhouse, was of the opinion that the sooner every party breaks up the better."

*Why Shoot a Butler?* is, by the standards of the later Heyers, unusually action-packed. She went on to make the later mysteries uniquely her own in style, depending less on physical excitement and more on dialogue, humor, and suspense.

*Publishers Weekly* in 1970 described her next mystery, *The Unfinished Clue* (1934), as "such a marvelous period piece . . . it almost reads like pure camp." Certainly, Miss Heyer could have been amused by this description, since comedy plays a relatively small part in this book, which is a very standard country house party puzzler. Sir Arthur Billington-Smith is found stabbed (not shot, as according to *The Catalogue of Crime*) in his study, and, with the exception of his sister-in-law Dinah Fawcett (who also has an alibi), there seems not to be a person on the premises who didn't have a reason to wish him dead.

The first part of the story, typically, sets up the host and his assemblage. Sir Arthur is the perfect victim for murder, the kind of man who marches around shouting, "In this house my word is law," and offending and bullying everyone in sight, family or friend. The long-suffering Fay is his second wife; Geoffrey, who is under constant threat of being cut off without a cent, is his son by his first wife, who walked out on him.

His nephew Francis has come to hit up the old man for money; when he doesn't get it, he robs the safe in the study. The general is quite willing to give large checks to Camilla Halliday, however, despite the violent objections of her husband Basil. Completing the party are Stephen Guest, who is in love with Fay, and Lola deSilva, an exotic entertainer who is engaged to Geoffrey. Also around and about are the vicar and his wife, Hilary and Emmeline Chudleigh, and Julia Twining, an "old friend."

Having rendered the general thoroughly dislikable to the reader, Miss Heyer disposes of him with his own Chinese letter opener. The investigations of the local police turn up little more than Sir Arthur's dying message—the inscription "THERE. . ." scrawled on a piece of paper, so the Yard is called in. Inspector John Harding seems at first the type who will solve the case through persistence rather than brilliance:

> Miss Fawcett, realizing that her frank stare was being
> returned with a rather amused twinkle, had the grace
> to blush. She stepped forward, and held out her hand.
> "How do you do?" she said politely.

365

"How do you do, Miss Fawcett?" said Harding, shaking hands with her.

"How on earth did you know I was Miss Fawcett?" asked Dinah, visibly impressed.

"The butler told me he would fetch Miss Fawcett," explained Harding gravely.

"Oh!" said Dinah, disappointed. "I thought you were being frightfully clever."

"No, I'm afraid I wasn't," said Harding apologetically.

The second phase of the plot now begins—the game of questions and answers played between the suspects and the police. The inspector is normally cordial, but he has another side when the occasion calls for him to show it:

"There are two ways of giving evidence to the police," continued Harding in his even voice. "One is to answer the questions that are put to you, and the other is to have the truth pulled out of you. I recommend the first of these. You will find it less unpleasant."

While there is some amusing conversational by-play in *The Unfinished Clue*, the questions and answers are mostly serious. Throughout the book, the major comic relief is supplied by the colorful Lola deSilva, whose speech is completely frank and whose behavior outrages the more old-fashioned members of the party. "I love very often, you understand," she tells them, "and always passionately." She cannot understand why there are no showers in the house, or why the cocks crow all morning in the country. She is perfectly willing to be arrested for Sir Arthur's murder, but only after she has consulted with her publicity agent.

Nearly half the book is taken up with Inspector Harding's interviews of the people involved in the case, all of which lead nowhere, although he does score neatly from time to time:

Harding moved several of the papers on the table, and chose one from amongst them. With his eyes on it he said: "You hadn't at any time during the weekend allowed Sir Arthur to kiss you?"

Camilla, her gaze also riveted to the paper, hesitated. The Sergeant, aware that amongst the various statements before Harding there was none in the least relevant to the question, nodded his head slowly in appreciation of this stratagem . . .

"I don't know who's been spying on me," Camilla said, "but I think it's the absolute limit!"

Harding did not pursue the question any further. He laid the paper down again and sat back in his chair.

"The trouble is they're all lying," Harding tells Sergeant Nethersole, without making any attempt to tell him, or the reader, who is lying the most. Suspicion is balanced pretty evenly until Mrs. Chudleigh, in an attempt to provide an alibi for Geoffrey, inadvertently tells a *truth* that breaks the case.

The last portion of the book contains just about the only real action in the entire story. While Harding investigates this alibi, a last-minute red herring by Miss Heyer is supposed to distract us from the fact that Mrs. Chudleigh, by protecting Geoffrey, has effectively confessed to the crime herself. It is at this point that the story—as a mystery—falls apart.

The reader is faced with another Conan Doyle situation when he learns that Harding has guessed, from the paper on the general's desk, that Mrs. Chudleigh is really *Theresa*, the general's first wife (perhaps he had read *A Study in Scarlet*, where the dying inscription turns out *not* to be part of a woman's name). He never explains what put this thought into his mind ("something Geoffrey said . . .") nor does he present—even at the end of the story—any more solid a motive for her than he could for any of the other characters, who had just as much opportunity.

Not to worry about the absence of clues: Mrs. Chudleigh, confronted with her guilt, kills herself (which has always seemed a tacit admission by the novelist that his detective's case doesn't really have a leg to stand on). She has thoughtfully written out a confession for the Inspector, however, which he turns over to his Superintendent. The book ends with Harding's proposal to Dinah Fawcett, with whom he has meanwhile fallen in love.

It is with *Death in the Stocks* (1935) that Miss Heyer comes firmly into her own as a mystery writer. In the best known of her early thrillers, she brings the "comedy" to the fore, while skillfully weaving it through the "action" of the plot. The *New York Times* later remarked, "Rarely have we seen humor and mystery so perfectly blended . . . Some of the humorous episodes which seem least relevant actually contain the clues which lead . . . to the correct solution of a very difficult problem."

She also introduces, on this occasion, the main characters for the rest of her detective novels: Superintendent Hannasyde and Sergeant (eventually promoted to Chief Inspector) Hemingway. *Death in the Stocks*, finally, is the book which, under the title *Merely Murder*, established the Heyer reputation in the United States: *Why Shoot a Butler?* was not published here until the following year.

Like *Why Shoot a Butler?*, *Death in the Stocks* starts right off with the discovery of the body of the victim. The word-picture drawn in the first few pages is positively cinematic, as the moonlight glides across the village green, finally revealing the macabre figure of Arnold Vereker, dead in the stocks, in full evening dress.

There are only a few principal characters in the story, which makes the least-likely-person dénouement all the more surprising, even more since murderer and motive have been in fairly plain view the entire time. Antonia and Kenneth Vereker are the half-sister and -brother of Arnold; Rudolph Mesurier and Violet Williams are their respective fiancées [sic]. Giles Carrington is their cousin and solicitor; Roger Vereker is Arnold's brother, at first believed long dead, and later genuinely so.

Hannasyde's efforts to clear up the murder are hampered by the steadfast refusal of Kenneth and Antonia to take seriously either the murder or the possibility of their own arrests. Their constant arguing and fantasizing about the case enable Miss Heyer to throw literally dozens of red herrings about. When the others express shock, Tony replies, "Arnold was our relative, and if we don't mind discussing the murder, why should you?"

The motive for the crimes is the ownership of the Shan Hills Mine Company, left to Arnold by his father but understood to be left to Roger, and then Ken, in the event of his death. Kenneth's fiancée, Violet, has killed Arnold so that she and Ken will be able to live in the style in which she is interested. The unexpected return of Roger throws a monkey wrench into her plans, so he has to go, too, in a faked suicide.

At the end, an astounded Hannasyde tells Giles, "But—she never came into the case at all!" Here, however, Miss Heyer has been more than fair with the reader, throwing into apparently casual conversation clues which are, in fact, unavailable to the police (Hannasyde is, in the end, given the solution by Giles). We see, more than the official investigators, what Hemingway calls "psychology—which the Superintendent here doesn't hold with" but which shows why a person might commit murder: "If you'd been born with a taste for nice things, and never a penny to spend which you hadn't worked and slaved for, you'd feel the same . . . I want all the nice things that make life worth living . . ."

Even while Miss Heyer is using the squabbling of the Verekers to befuddle the police, she is tossing out clues for the benefit of the alert reader: "My fiancée says it's such a rotten story, you're bound to believe it. She reads about seven detective thrillers a week, so she's pretty well up in crime." Violet herself even makes the remark, after Roger's death, "It seems to me that anyone of normal intelligence can get away with murder."

Here again, a few words on "point of view" as utilized by Miss Heyer will not be out of place. The style of the story (as noted before) is very cinematic. Nothing that takes place "on screen" is concealed from the reader. Of course, there is a certain amount of direction of our attention, just as there would be in a film. The treatment does not focus on the police, even though they are ostensibly in charge of the investigation; nor does it really focus on any one of the other main characters (the focus in *Why Shoot a Butler?*, by contrast, is almost always on Frank Amberley).

The advantage of this method is that it makes the novel more of a "fair play" puzzle simply by its style. If, in the first-person story, we can see only what the "Watson" sees, here we see everything, apparently indiscriminately. If Violet Williams seems never to come to the center of the frame, it is because we find the antics of Kenneth and Antonia Vereker more interesting.

Those readers of a classic bent will recognize the quotations from *Hamlet* with which the participants bedevil each other in Chapter XIV and will also recall a similar exchange in Dorothy L. Sayers's *Busman's Honeymoon*, not published until 1938.

It should be noted that the solution in this case is based on a solid piece of evidence, fairly presented (although certainly easy enough to miss) and conclusive of guilt. Giles's presentation to Hannasyde is logical and clearly done. Every piece of the puzzle fits neatly into place, and Miss Heyer has produced the first of her masterpieces.

A theatrical version of *Death in the Stocks*, adapted by A. E. Thomas, and produced in New York with the title *Merely Murder* on December 3, 1937, was less of a masterpiece. Thomas makes the play a comedy, not a mystery, adding characters not in the book and setting the entire show in the Vereker flat, thus losing the pace of the original story altogether. (Those curious about this can find a typescript of the play in the Billy Rose Collection at the Library of Performing Arts at Lincoln Center.)

One of the most interesting reviews of the show was written by Richard Lockridge, then a drama critic for the *New York Sun* (later, of course, the famous mystery writer):

> Georgette Heyer's *Merely Murder*, carefully strained of all solid particles by A. E. Thomas, was presented as a play last evening . . . Admirers of Miss Heyer's neat tight little mystery may want to know how Mr. Thomas has accomplished this . . . [By] leaving out all the action and emphasizing the patter, thus cleverly turning the tables on Miss Heyer, who wrote it the other way around . . . They may also want to know why, but there, I am afraid, I cannot help them.

*Merely Murder* closed after only three Broadway performances, thus fulfilling the prophecy of another critic, who described the show as "one of the casualties of the . . . season."

The next year—1936—brought two crime stories from Miss Heyer. *The Talisman Ring*, although clearly cast in the mold of the romantic stories (its original title page calls it "an exciting and witty romance of the period of formal manners and informal morals"), offers a classic thriller situation: how to unmask a suspected murderer and retrieve a missing family heirloom.

Eustacie de Vauban, fleeing a *mariage de convenance* with her older cousin Tristram Shields [sic], encounters a band of smugglers (they prefer to be called "free traders") in their woods. Their leader also turns out to be a cousin of hers: Ludovic Lavenham, who was thought to be in exile in France, suspected of the murder of Sir Matthew Plunkett, who had won the Ring of the title from him in a game of cards. The ring itself disappeared after the murder.

Eustacie and Tristram determine to clear Ludovic's name by pinning the crime on the real killer—their cousin Basil (yes, another cousin), known without affection as "the Beau"—by finding the ring, which they believe he stole after despatching Plunkett. In this they are assisted by one Sarah Thane, her brother, and the usual assortment of Heyer characters, as the danger to Ludovic, who has been wounded in a battle between the free traders and the excisemen, grows greater and greater.

While not a mystery in the "detective" sense of that word, this is surely one of Miss Heyer's liveliest stories, in which the comedy and suspense are mixed in just the right proportions, and the plot always takes precedence over the romantic elements. An anxious break-in at Basil's house and an attempt to murder Ludovic at the inn where he is hiding are balanced by the hilarious masquerades of first Ludovic and then Sarah Thane as Eustacie's (non-existent) maidservant, to confuse a rather slow-witted pair of Bow Street Runners.

The Talisman Ring is finally discovered in a rather clever hiding place, Basil is tricked into admitting his guilt, the romantic couplings line up as they should, and all ends happily.

In *Behold, Here's Poison* (the title is from the first act of *Pericles*), her other mystery for 1936, Miss Heyer introduces a new element into her stories. The question in the other mysteries has always been simply "who done it?" but now she adds "how did they do it?" to the puzzle.

The victim is one Gregory Matthews, who, we are told, "had many sterling qualities. It wasn't his fault that he was brought up to be selfish through and through." Making up his household at the time of his death are his sister Harriet, "the elderly lady with the economy mania," and his sister-in-law Zoë, who "had contrived to make herself, if not the mistress of the house, at least the cherished guest whose comfort must be everyone's first consideration" and her children Guy and Stella.

Although Stella's fiancé, Dr. Deryk Fielding, thinks at first that Matthews's death is due simply to syncope, Gregory's other sister, Mrs. Lupton, "a massively-built woman of about forty-five, reinforced wherever possible with whalebone," demands a post mortem. The result: nicotine poisoning—"one of the earliest uses of nicotine as a despatcher," according to the *Catalogue of Crime.*

Hannasyde's investigations, made with the aid of Giles Carrington, who turns out to have also been solicitor for Matthews, unearth a business associate—Mr. Hyde—no one in the family has ever seen or heard of, and whom no one can locate. Nor is Hyde the only skeleton in the family closets: the meek Henry Lupton is keeping a mistress on the side, and Dr. Fielding is concealing the fact that his father died in an Inebriates' Home.

> The Sergeant opened his eyes at that. "What things they do get up to in the suburbs!" he remarked admiringly. "Now, some people might call that blackmail, Super."
>
> Hanasyde nodded. "I do myself."
>
> "Blackmail's one of the most powerful motives for murder I know, Super."
>
> "Admittedly . . . "

Although Hannasyde and Hemingway do not find out until much later, Matthews—under the rather obvious name of Hyde—has indeed been carrying on a lucrative trade as a blackmailer. When his nephew and heir, Randall, described variously as "an amiable snake, smooth and fanged . . . utterly poisonous," finds this out, he does some investigating of his own and soon concludes that the murderer is their neighbor, Mr. Rumbold, who "seemed to have been created especially to be a Friend of the Family. . .[If] he found the recital of other peoples' troubles wearisome . . . he was far too well-mannered to show it." This position he has carefully built up over a period of four years, while waiting for an opportunity to eliminate his blackmailer.

Randall, who hated Gregory anyway, is prepared to let well enough alone; sooner or later, the police will have to give it up. So he keeps his information from the authorities (and, of course, from the reader) while the others go through the repeated questionings and the ordeal of the inquest:

> Mrs. Matthews came up to suggest that they should all of them devote the rest of this unhappy day to meditation, but . . . since Guy . . . flatly refused to meditate with his mother, and Stella could not be found, abandoned the idea of a contemplative day, and ordered the chauffeur to motor her to town for the purpose of buying mourning clothes.

A second death, however, upsets the apple cart. When Harriet Matthews dies, Dr. Fielding immediately calls the police. Hannasyde is now able to discover that the poison had been injected into a tube of Matthews's toothpaste, which Harriet took for her own use rather than see wasted—a grim confirmation of Hemingway's "psychology!"

Randall now confronts Rumbold and extracts a written confession from him. The murderer's subsequent suicide effectively closes the case, as Randall explains to an irate Hannasyde.

Hannasyde certainly has every reason to be annoyed, and so has the reader, as Miss Heyer has reverted to some of her worst Sherlockianisms in this story. Here is the crucial clue in the case:

> The drawer held an untidy collection of oddments. Hannasyde turned over a packet of labels, disclosing a pair of horn-rimmed sunglasses underneath, a scattering of paper-clips, and a tube of seccotine. For the rest, there was a quantity of stamp-paper, some sealing wax, a pen-knife, a bottle of red ink, and a roll of adhesive tape . . . Randall was looking at the heterogenous collection, a slight frown between his eyes.

Even though Hannasyde sees Randall make the connection, he is unable to guess what it is: "I wish very much that I knew what Mr. Randall Matthews found to interest him amongst this collection . . . [W]hether it was in something he saw, or in something he expected to see, and didn't, I don't know."

Randall, who knows that his uncle hated sunglasses and never wore them, links Matthews—by this simple means of disguise—with the mysterious Hyde. By getting to Hyde's papers before the police, he uncovers (and then conceals) the blackmail records. The reader can only feel cheated at this, and at Randall's conniving at Rumbold's "escape" from justice.

On the other hand, the idea of putting the poison in the tube of toothpaste is, at the same time, both hilarious and horrifying. Like the hiding place of the Talisman Ring, it is simple enough to be practical and not to tax belief, but unexpected enough to be dramatically effective. Miss Heyer's best effects are usually the most simple at bottom, although they may be carefully and cleverly tangled in details. The novel which followed *Behold, Here's Poison*, however, comes close to sinking under the weight of its own complications and plot contrivances.

*They Found Him Dead* (1937), according to the original American edition, "contains, in the words of the author herself, a real surprise: 'Dear old Superintendent Hannasyde . . . [who] might be allowed to solve the mystery, just for a great treat. He has never solved one yet, and I'm afraid they'll leave him out of the C.I.D. if I don't let him do some good once in his life'. . ." In spite of this wry preface, *They Found Him*

*Dead* contains an unusually small amount of the Heyer wit; indeed, after the last few stories, it is almost disappointingly straightforward in the telling.

It is almost as if, having proved that she could spoof the pants off the detective story, she was now going to show that she could do it straight, too. *They Found Him Dead*, if it does let us down in some respects, is an illustration of the red herring raised to the level of a fine art. Oscar Roberts, the murderer, has not even appeared as a character when Silas Kane apparently suffers a heart attack and falls to his death at his family's seaside property; but this is fair enough, since no one even considers the possibility of murder at this point. Nor is this terribly odd, since Silas is the first person murdered in a Heyer novel who has not made the world a significantly better place by leaving it.

The centerpiece of the plot, however, is the murder of Silas's nephew, Clement Kane, who succeeds to his shares in the partnership of Kane and Mansell. Although Clement is obviously shot, with people all around his study, no one sees the perpetrator making his escape:

> Miss Allison . . . picked up the detailed list for Clement and was about to take it into the study when . . . Oscar Roberts stepped over the threshold. Roberts smiled at Miss Allison and was about to follow the butler when a sudden report, as from a gun, startled them all into immobility.
> Then Pritchard . . . ran to the study door . . . Clement Kane lay crumpled across his desk, one arm hanging limply at his side . . .

The gimmick here is a sort of reverse alibi: not so much to prove the murderer elsewhere at the time of death, but to shift the apparent time of the crime itself. The "report" that the people hear is produced, not by the actual shot, but by a blasting cap attached to a three-minute fuse concealed near the study window. This trick came from Miss Heyer's husband, who was her uncredited collaborator (although it was no secret) on the mysteries. Their son says: "My father. . . worked out how the

375

murder was committed. At one stage in his life he had been a mining engineer . . ."

Hannasyde catches on to this trick after he makes a simple but logical deduction about the location of the missing gun, which is then found with a silencer still attached. This opens the formerly narrow field of suspects to include almost all of the characters again, but then Roberts makes a stupid psychological mistake, which Hemingway picks up: "He . . . went to some trouble to demonstrate how unlikely it was that two such dissimilar murders should have been committed by the same man. Until that moment, he had insinuated that Paul Mansell was responsible for both deaths."

Perhaps a little more of the Heyer fun would have covered some of the rampant implausibilities in this tale of a man who has traveled halfway around the world, and murdered two people, so that his estranged wife could come into the Kane fortune. There is no denying that motive is usually the weakest link in Miss Heyer's mysteries when it is founded in some legal complication.

Another big problem is the ruse by which Roberts insinuates himself into the circle of the Kanes and Mansells, as the representative of an Australian firm interested in handling the nets the company makes. The coincidence of Roberts working for the firm which wants to do business with Kane's outfit is almost on a par with the passenger list of the infamous Calais Coach. On the other hand, we dare not assume this story to be a complete fake, since it could be so easily disproved, but, astonishingly, no one in the novel—not even Hannasyde—ever questions Roberts's *bona fides*!

Probably the worst obstacle to credibility in this story is the extraordinary amount of luck that attends Roberts in his murderous plans: after only one visit to the Kanes, he knows that Silas invariably takes a solitary constitutional before retiring; the night he chooses for the murder is further blessed with a dense fog. In the second murder, no one happens upon the body before he has set up his fuse gimmick; no one sees him skulking about the house—even though the place is crawling with people; the fuse operates as set (not an infallible assumption!); and all the timings of all the other people's actions fall right in with the length of the fuse. Finally, in two separate attempts to kill young Jim Kane, who unexpectedly turns out to be ahead of Roberts's wife in the line of succession (the property is entailed, like in *Pride and Prejudice*), he is able to sabotage first a large boat and then Jim's roadster without being observed.

Very little of this is apparent on a first reading, since the reader is caught up in the suspense of the story; it is only on reflection that we see how action has been substituted for probability. Most of the other details of the crimes are neatly worked out, however, and the red herring—the business deal between Kane and Mansell and Roberts's firm, which seems to be the motive through the story—actually points at the real killer without implicating him.

In place of the usual comedy, Miss Heyer has given us some very well drawn characters, even if a few do verge on caricature. Young Timothy is every bratty young relative you ever knew, peppering his conversation with expressions from American gangster films; the embittered old lady, Emily Kane, is also good. Even the people who are a little far-out have their moments of truth. Rosemary, Clement's wife, dramatizes herself beyond belief, and Lady Harte, "the African explorer," is just too good to be true. Yet, when they come together, they produce the following exchange, quite different from the usual Heyer repartee:

> "I don't suppose you even feel the atmosphere in this awful house," said Rosemary, shuddering . . . "I expect you have to be rather sensitive to feel it."
>
> Lady Harte raised her eyes from the cards. "I do not in the least mind being thought insensitive, Rosemary; but as I fancy you meant that remark as a slur . . . I can only say that it was extremely rude . . ."
>
> "Of course, I know I'm very selfish," replied Rosemary with the utmost calm . . .
>
> "You are not only selfish," said Lady Harte; "you are indolent, shallow, parasitic, and remarkably stupid . . ."
>
> "When you have seen your husband shot before

your very eyes," said Rosemary, a trifle inaccurately, "perhaps you will have some comprehension of what it means to suffer . . ."

"My husband, as I think you are aware, died of his wounds twenty years ago. I saw him die. If you think you can tell me anything about suffering, I shall be interested to hear it."

Although all her mystery thrillers are set in the present, Miss Heyer's use of invective remains almost historically elegant; it is not until *Envious Casca* that she allows one of her characters to refer to another as a bitch.

For someone whose avowed specialty was the past, Miss Heyer shows on more than one occasion that she was never far out of touch with the present: "Mr. Harte said he hadn't had such a cracking nightmare since the occasion when Jim took him to see *The Ringer*." This must have been the English Players' production, since Miss Heyer was out of the country when the Edgar Wallace play was originally produced in 1926. The novels are filled with references to plays, and her son told this writer that she read a great deal: "She was a great admirer of Raymond Chandler, and, to a slightly lesser extent, Agatha Christie, Erle Stanley Gardner, and Patrick Quentin."

It might be well to state, right off, that *A Blunt Instrument* (1938) is this writer's choice for Miss Heyer's real masterpiece. There are no unacceptable contrivances here, no gimmicks, just a brilliant bit of misdirection sustained through to the end—when the case is even solved by the detective in charge. The reader who has never read this novel is advised to skip the following paragraphs, so that he can enjoy the book when he does so.

The story begins with P. C. Malachi Glass standing over the body of the late Ernest Fletcher only moments after the murder; the local police, however, quickly call in the Yard, and, before too many pages have passed, our old friends Hannasyde (for the last time) and Hemingway are on the scene.

The murder seems, at first glance, to be fairly simple: Fletcher was beaten over the head repeatedly with the proverbial blunt instrument.

378

Yet, although no fewer than four people were known to be in or near the deceased's study at the critical time, no firm evidence can be found as to the killer's identity—nor can any trace of the weapon itself be located!

P. C. Glass, who speaks in a Biblical language of quotations, aphorisms, and other pieties, is assigned to help the Yard men in their investigation, but, the deeper the three dig, the more difficult the case becomes. Hemingway complains at one point that "the only conclusion I've come to is that the whole thing's impossible from start to finish. Once you start putting all the evidence down on paper you can't help but see that the late Ernest wasn't murdered at all. Couldn't have been."

Their assistant, who has a scriptural reference for every occasion, is also a constant source of irritation to the other two policemen:

> Hannasyde said: "Why do you encourage him, Skipper. . . I believe you enjoy him. . ."
> The Sergeant grinned. "Well, I've got to admit it adds a bit of interest to the case, waiting for him to run dry. . . He hasn't, though. I certainly have to hand it to him: he hasn't repeated himself once so far."

A second murder only adds to the confusion, until Hannasyde suddenly sees the "common factor" in both cases. The final confrontation between the man from the Yard and the killer is wonderfully managed; Glass's statement that "I alone know the murderer" and the questions which follow heighten the suspense until Glass himself is finally revealed as the villain. Again, the death weapon—a policeman's truncheon—is horrible in its simplicity, and so much a part of him as to be, in effect, invisible.

The *Saturday Review* originally disparaged the solution as "a double fracture of mystery-story ethics," but a second reading will show that this is merely due to the reader's assumption—taken into account, and carefully fostered by Miss Heyer—that a policeman must be above suspicion. Of course, there is no legitimate reason for this to be so; besides, the author makes a pretty clear distinction between her detectives, Hannasyde and Hemingway, and the other police in the story.

To put the reader even further off the trail, Miss Heyer uses Glass throughout for comic effect, as a foil for Hemingway and Neville Fletcher, the dead man's nephew. Her humor does not mock the Bible itself, nor geniune religious belief, but rather that certain type of pious fanatic who can practice intolerance—and even murder—in the name of religion. The point, of course, is that we are cleverly led not to take Glass too seriously.

Yet, in view of *Roger Ackroyd*, it is the reader's place to suspect *everyone*, and all the clues are perfectly fair. It is the mystery novelist's job to deceive the reader by any legitimate means available—and Miss Heyer succeeds here, admirably.

After *A Blunt Instrument*, *No Wind of Blame* might seem to be rather a let-down. The novel's chief interest, for the detective story fan, will be in the mechanical contrivance by which the murder is committed. No matter how well drawn the characters are, however, 107 pages of them is quite a bit to bear before Wallis Carter is finally sent to meet his Maker.

When Carter is shot dead on the footpath near the Dower House of his wife's country property—with no one anywhere near him—the stage is set for another Heyer entertainment . . . and "stage" is the word. If *Death in the Stocks* was conceived in cinematic terms, *No Wind of Blame* and its successor *Envious Casca* are theatrical, from their Shakespearean titles on.

Everyone in *No Wind of Blame* is playing a part, either literally or figuratively. Carter's widow, Ermyntrude, is a former actress who has never lost her love for the Grand Scene; her daughter Vicky ("I'm hardly ever 'Victoria'") acts out her life as a succession of different characters.

Early on in the investigation, an attempt by Inspector Cook to question Ermyntrude ends in total chaos as the two ladies give full rein to their thespian inclinations. Mrs. Carter is particularly amusing, as she alternately swears that she will say nothing and delivers tirades on every subject going.

There are also a great many references to plays and acting. "I remember I saw a play once," says Wally, "about speaking nothing but the truth . . ." (probably W. S. Gilbert's *Palace of Truth*). He also opines: "Don't ever marry an actress, unless you're the kind of man who likes having a wife who carries on like Lady Macbeth and the second Mrs. Tanqueray and Mata Hari, all rolled into one! Before breakfast, too!"

Inspector Hemingway, who is the Yard officer on the case—not appearing until page 186!—also relies heavily on theatrical terminology: "Now let's go over the dramatis personae . . . I'm bound to say I don't fancy him for the chief part . . . Decor and scenery are my specialties."

Hemingway, now out from under the shadow of the more sober Hannasyde, begins to develop a character of his own: the "brisk and bright-eyed Inspector," accompanied by Sergeant Wake, "disarmed hostility by a certain engaging breeziness of manner, which had long been the despair of his superiors." Nor does he forget to refer to his "psychology."

The investigation, which turns up nothing of any value until almost the very end of the book, centers mostly on securing the best possible motive for the crime. Wally is described as having "no moral sense whatever, and [was] as weak as water." Almost everyone (as usual) has one reason or another for wanting him dead: Prince Alexis Varasashvili, the Carters' house guest, who is wooing Mrs. Carter almost openly; Robert Steel, who is also enamored of the former Mrs. Fanshawe; Mary Cliffe, Carter's ward, and the supposed heir to his alleged fortune; Percy Baker, whose sister is thought pregnant by Carter—and these are only the more likely ones.

The point here seems not to be the detective work, but the entertainment. If Miss Heyer were conscious of the structural deficiencies of her criminal plot, she made up for it in the dialogue, the characters, and the continuous wit of the telling. Two examples are particularly reminiscent of Jane Austen's gently satiric style of humor:

> Wally was pardonably affronted, and animadverted bitterly upon the license permitted to the young in these unregenerate days. Upon which austere pronouncement he strayed away grandly, but a little uncertainly, in the direction of his bedroom.

> As Alan had expressed his intention of starving
> before he ate another meal at the Dower House, Janet
> did not think he would appear again until suppertime.

The motive, when it is finally revealed (in a phone call from Hannasyde, who has stayed in London), turns out to be one that has not even been hinted at in the story: an obscure bit of legalizing which provides that Harold White, one of Wally's neighbors, will inherit a large fortune if Carter dies before his senile aunt. This confuses the reader as much as it does the police, since Miss Heyer has been at great pains all along to show us that White could not have pulled the trigger on the gun that killed Carter.

At this point, Miss Heyer plays a clever game on one of the most famous Sherlockianisms, the one about the dog in the night-time from *Silver Blaze* (which she had also used in *Why Shoot a Butler?*). Here, Vicky Fanshawe's dog has given no alarm when the two of them arrive at the death scene, which at first is taken to mean that the killer is someone the dog is well acquainted with (as in Doyle). Hemingway turns it neatly around: suppose it means that no one was there at all?

Hemingway and Wake now piece together a few odds and ends and produce the *deus ex machina*—an infernal machine responsible for the shooting, operated by remote control, electro-magnetically. This idea was definitely supplied by Miss Heyer's husband, the former mining engineer; their son says that "this accounts for the considerable expertise in the method of killing in *No Wind of Blame*. They actually got the experts at the Home Office to try it out, and it worked."

There is nothing in *Envious Casca* (1941) that Miss Heyer hasn't used before, yet the wonderfully grotesque situation of a murder at Christmas—which ought to shock us profoundly—is instead turned into a piece of great fun.

The theatrical types from *No Wind of Blame* are back again, as is the legal motive; again we have the house-party murder, and the belated appearance of Hemingway on the scene; as in *Why Shoot a Butler?* a book figures prominently in the complications, and the killer, like the one in *A Blunt Instrument*, is a person we have been led not to take seriously.

382

Nathaniel Herriard, the owner of Lexham Manor, has been prevailed upon by his brother Joseph to throw the house open for a "real English Christmas [which] meant, in his experience, a series of quarrels between inimical persons bound to one another only by the accident of relationship, and thrown together by a worn-out convention which decreed that at Christmas families should forgather."

Yet Joseph, who "was like a clumsy, well-meaning Saint Bernard puppy, dropped amongst a lot of people who were not fond of dogs," has his way, and Nathaniel invites his business partner, a distant cousin, and his nephew and niece to Lexham to spend the holidays. Stephen and Paula bring their respective fiancées, of course, a bubble-headed socialite and a penniless dramatist, putting the fat well in the fire. Mathilda Clare, the cousin, later describes the results to the police:

> "Miss Herriard treated the assembled company to a dramatic scene—she's an actress, good in emotional roles. I wasn't present, but I'm told she and Mr. Herriard had a really splendid quarrel, and enjoyed themselves hugely."
>
> "Seems a funny way to enjoy yourself, Miss."
>
> "It would seem funny to you or me, Inspector, but not, believe me, to a Herriard."

The festivities reach their apex two days before Christmas, when the young playwright reads his exceedingly modern and realistic piece, entitled *Wormwood*, to the guests at the Manor. The unpleasantness which follows is capped by Nathaniel's murder—in an apparently locked room—only a few hours later.

The early investigation is in the hands of a local inspector, deputizing for his chief, who is "in bed with influenza. It wasn't as though the case was likely to do him much good . . . The Chief Constable would be bound to call in Scotland Yard, he thought, and some smart London man would get all the credit . . ." After about fifty pages of entertaining stalling, this is exactly what happens; not that our old friend Hemingway accomplishes very much at first either.

Joseph's wife, Maud, immediately singles out the Inspector as the logical person to find her copy of *The Life of Empress Elizabeth of Austria*, which is unaccountably missing. "And it . . . belongs to the lending library, and if it is lost, I shall be obliged to pay for it. Besides, I hadn't finished it." No one is very inclined to hunt for the book, from which Maud has been reading passages aloud for several days.

What suspense there is in the story comes from the fact that almost everyone suspects Stephen of the murder, and his attitude is certainly very bad. On the other hand, although he feels that he has at least four good suspects, Hemingway admits that he is unable to actually prove anything about the crime:

> The Inspector, with the simple intention of unnerving the household, was spending the morning pervading the house with a notebook, a foot-rule, and an abstracted frown. His mysterious investigations were in themselves entirely valueless, but succeeded in making everyone. . . profoundly uneasy.

Like its immediate predecessor, *Envious Casca* is short on clues and real detection but long on clever and amusing talk—not any substitute, but enjoyable after all on its own terms:

> "I'm blessed if I know how we're ever going to make any headway."
>
> "That's right," said Hemingway cheerfully. "And all the time I wouldn't be surprised if the clue to the whole mystery has been under our nose from the outset. Probably something so simple that a child could have spotted it . . ."
>
> "If it's as simple as all that it's a wonder you haven't spotted it," said the Sergeant sceptically.
>
> "It's very likely too simple for me," Hemingway explained. "I was hoping you'd hit on it."

Hemingway talks about "psychology" and "flair" but doesn't use them until the very end, when Nat's will is discovered to be invalid, thanks to a brilliantly managed bit of stage business which tips him off that, in fact, "Uncle Joe" is too good to be true.

With his motive finally in hand (the best of all Miss Heyer's legal trickeries), Hemingway happens upon the single genuine clue in the entire story, which gives him the means in a case "which reminds me of the Hampton Court Maze more than anything else."

The only question left at this point is: how was the locked-room business arranged? Well, it wasn't at all. If you'd been paying attention, you would have realized that Maud's book had to be missing for a reason. Hemingway comes to this conclusion and looks up the Empress in an encyclopedia. There he finds that Nat's murder has been based on an historical incident in which the victim was stabbed without realizing what the pain was from. Nat obligingly locked himself into his room, and died according to plan.

Rather thin, when all is said and done, but amusing in the accomplished hands of Miss Heyer, who has her detective complain about "all those thrillers that get written nowadays by people who ought to know better than to go putting ideas in criminals' heads . . ."

After these two lesser efforts, Miss Heyer changed tactics. *Penhallow* (1942) is unique among her thrillers in that it is not a detective story at all. Our friends Hannasyde and Hemingway are absent, and the police on the case accept a totally incorrect solution of the crime. Since the reader watches the crime being committed, it is not even a mystery.

Instead, *Penhallow* is a simple story of suspense, of a large country family held in thrall by old Adam Penhallow, and an account of how his power over them extends even beyond his death. Although bed-ridden for much of the book (and dead for its last third), he fills the story, as he dominates the characters, especially his second wife, Faith:

> No spirit ruled at Trevellin other than Penhallow's,
> and the tyranny he exercised was so complete that it
> left no member of the household untouched. . . The
> wounds his rough tongue had dealt during the years

of his rampant strength and health had seldom been
intentional; now that his health had broken down, and
his strength had failed, nothing seemed to please him
more than to. . . upset the peace of mind of any of his
household. . . as if he were bent on revenging his
physical helplessness on his family.

At one point, the only mystery in the story seems to be: *who* is going to kill Adam Penhallow? Margery Allingham wrote, in *Black Plumes*: "A gread deal has been written about the forthrightness of the moderns shocking the Victorians, but there is no shock like the one which the forthrightness of the Victorians can give a modern." Adam's last—and ugliest—act of ill-will in the book is to reveal to Raymond, his oldest son, the true story of his birth. The almost casual cruelty is the culmination of a series of incidents in which none of the principal characters emerges unhit.

Faith goes from expecting Adam's death to wishing for it:

If he were to die, as the doctor hinted that he would,
every trouble would vanish, and they would be free,
all of them: free to disperse, to follow their own
inclinations; free from the fear of Penhallow's wrath;
free from their degrading dependence upon him for
their livelihood . . . She saw clearly that Penhallow's
death would be a universal panacea . . . No one could
think it a crime to put an end to a life so baleful;
indeed, if Penhallow's brain were going, it would
almost be a kindness.

The thought soon becomes father to the deed, and the old man gets his when Faith poisons him by dumping a bottle of her sleeping draught into his liquor decanter. She little dreams that the horror will only begin with the death of Penhallow. Her dream of all the family members going their merry ways is gradually destroyed as she comes to realize that Trevellin is the only thing that makes them a family at all.

Raymond Penhallow suffers as much as Faith. Adam's revelation is the end of Ray's world, since he has expected to inherit the estate. As the police investigation seems to be drawing nearer and nearer to the truth, he fears that he will not be able to keep the matter a secret, and kills himself. This is taken by the others as an admission of his guilt in Adam's death.

Far from freeing herself from Penhallow, Faith has tied herself to him until her dying day, with the additional burden of Ray's unnecessary death to bear . . . a considerable punishment for one who might otherwise be said to "get away with murder." The awful irony, saved by Miss Heyer for the last page, is that the police never do discover Raymond's secret.

The light touch is not absent from *Penhallow*, but it is never allowed to distract from the tension and suspense of the story. The juxtaposition of the stylish talk of the city dwellers and the blunt frankness of their country cousins jolts the reader more than once. There are also multiple examples of the elegant phrasing and quick wit we have come to expect from Miss Heyer:

> In their several ways, they were all of them imperceptive, and insensitive enough to make it impossible for them to understand why anyone should be hurt by their cheerful brutality.

> Red to the ears, Clay played first with the idea of murdering all his half-brothers, and then with that of committing suicide; while Penhallow made the Vicar sheer off from his side in a hurry by once more stating his doubts of Clay's parentage.

> "I am afraid my errand to your father was sadly unexciting. Tut, tut! you silly child, have you been picturing a mystery? The influence of the modern crime novel."
> "I never read them."

The character of Adam Penhallow is one of Miss Heyer's most fascinating creations. He behaves like "an eighteenth-century squire," in a house which has been rendered an anachronism by design—there is no electricity, no telephone service, no central heating, and the hot water system isn't much good either. Since horseflesh is one of his passions, it's almost out of character for him to own an automobile. This suspension of time is all part of the atmosphere Miss Heyer creates for the tale—floating Trevellin somewhere between World War One (which is mentioned) and World War Two—which was going on at the time but is never even referred to, much as Jane Austen ignores the wars of her own time.

Miss Heyer was certainly aware of the conflict, however. A 1942 plug for the Crime Club describes Heyer and Allingham as "on voluntary leave of absence from heavy writing schedules . . . doing war work in England." 1943, in fact, was the first year since 1927 which did not see a new Heyer novel. She continued to produce romances during the war years, but not at the pace she had maintained previously. Heyer was not to write another mystery until 1951.

Once back in the game, she presented the world with three suspense stories in a row, two with Hemingway and one a romantic novel. The first two, unfortunately, are below the standards set by previous works.

One wishes that Miss Heyer's return to the detective novel could be more in the nature of a triumph, but when she notes at the beginning that the book was written "in response to the representation of certain members of the Bench and Bar," the reader may know, with a sinking feeling, that he is in for another obscure legal motive.

*Duplicate Death* brings back Chief Inspector Hemingway (he'd *have* to have gotten a promotion in ten years), who has now been granted the first name of Stanley, and the Kanes, who find themselves involved with the murder of Dan Seaton-Carew, an unpleasant customer who traffics in drugs and homosexuality.

The "gentleman" meets his end during a bridge party (the first pun in the title) given at the house of Mrs. Haddington, a real social climber, and her daughter Cynthia, the descriptions of whom show that Miss Heyer has lost none of her comic touch:

> [Mrs. Haddington's] beautifully waved hair showed no grey streaks, being of a uniform copper, and if it occasionally seemed to be rather darker toward the roots this was a blemish which could be, and was, very easily rectified.

> Those who disliked [Cynthia] said that she was totally devoid of intellect, but this was unjust. Whenever she had a few minutes to spare between her various engagements she would turn over the pages of society journals, even reading the captions under the pictures; and she never entered her room without turning on the radio.

Hemingway has barely gotten the suspects in the first death settled in his mind when Mrs. Haddington herself is murdered, in precisely the same fashion as Seaton-Carew—strangulation (the second pun)—and there doesn't seem to be anyone who could have committed both the murders.

It's a nice situation, and Miss Heyer milks it for all it's worth. For sheer storytelling, *Duplicate Death* ranks with any of the other novels, and the characters are all good. Only the solution fails.

Just when we're ready for Miss Heyer and Hemingway to pull a really neat trick out of their sleeves, it is admitted that there isn't anyone who could have been responsible for both the crimes: Mrs. Haddington herself killed Seaton-Carew, who had been giving her daughter cocaine; her death is completely unrelated to his, except in the copying of method.

The less said about the second murder, the better; huddled and almost perfunctory, it isn't nearly as interesting as the first. The personal element is replaced by the legal, and the substitution is no improvement. The wrap-up is much like *Why Shoot a Butler?* which is a real disappointment after so much good work in this book.

This occasionally terrifying but ultimately unsatisfactory tale was followed the next year by *The Quiet Gentleman*, hailed by the *Saturday Review* as "for those who love a mystery." In fact, however, neither the romantic nor the criminal outcome of this story will escape the reader for long.

Gervase Frant, also known by his title Lord St. Erth, has come home to claim his estates after some years of soldiering, during which his father has died. His half-brother Martin has had free rein of the property in the meantime and resents St. Erth's return. The strength of this resentment comes under much discussion as a series of attempts is made on the Earl's life, but, since all the signs so obviously point to Martin, even the least alert reader will quickly transfer his suspicion to the only other possible miscreant. Although the story takes one or two clever turns, Miss Heyer's tricks are for some reason inadequate to this lengthy novel.

Perhaps her mind was already otherwise occupied. It was at about this time that she began work on "the *magnum opus* of my latter years," a medieval trilogy, the first volume of which was eventually to be published as *My Lord John*. These three novels were to cover the great years of England's House of Lancaster, 1393 to 1435. Miss Heyer's plan to devote five years of work to this trilogy did not take into account "the penal burden of British taxation, coupled with the clamor of her readers for a new book," according to her husband. So the Middle Ages—actually her favorite historical period—were laid aside for another Regency novel. Her return to the trilogy was again interrupted, as, apparently, were the mystery stories; *Detection Unlimited* was to be the last Heyer crime book.

The only thing keeping *Detection Unlimited* (1953) from the list of Miss Heyer's classics is her apparent uncertainty whether she was writing a mystery or a comedy. Her dedication is a joke ("To all such persons as may imagine that they recognize themselves in it, with the author's assurance that they are mistaken"), and the original British dust jacket shows five people—and a number of disembodied hands—all pointing away from themselves.

Certainly, the author does a pretty good job of having it both ways. She doesn't do much more than set up the *dramatis personae* (as Hemingway is fond of calling them) before the murder of Sampson Warrenby occurs. Soon the Chief Inspector, assisted by Inspector Harbottle, is on the scene, and the "detection" begins. Everybody in the village has his own idea of who committed the crime; most of their time and conversation is occupied in trying to focus Hemingway's attention on someone else—for spite, for amusement, out of fear for themselves.

This goes on for quite some time, with little sign of progress, even though the case seems dreadfully simple: "a plain case of shooting . . . no locked rooms, or mysterious weapons, or any other trimmings." Although he has to listen to a lot of apparently pointless conversation, Hemingway says he likes the case—"Why shouldn't I, when I've got half a dozen people doing my job for me?"

Once again, Miss Heyer has based the telling of the story on the method of the murderer, who has set up the crime to look as if it took place at a different time than it actually did—not so much to alibi himself as to drag as many people into the affair as possible. Thus the story itself reflects that confusion, until the police catch an important clue.

The architect of this bizarre situation is Gavin Plenmeller, a detective-story writer who is also what Barzun and Taylor call "one of Georgette's favorite 'snake' types, who [usually] turn out to be decent once the motive for the foulness is made clear." Gavin goes about making just the type of remark this character has always made in her stories: "I never heard her say an unkind word about anyone. There is no affinity between us . . . The people of Thornden are too respectable for me, I won't say dull, leaving that to be inferred . . . You know very well that I find not the smallest difficulty in saying to people's faces precisely what I say behind their backs." It's no wonder that another character is given to ask Hemingway "whether these fellows who are so damned clever at murdering people on paper ever put their methods into practice. . ."

Although, in any other Heyer novel, this type of behavior would immediately disqualify Plenmeller as a suspect, he is in fact guilty of two murders, and Hemingway settles down to pin them on him. At this point, much of the comedy subsides, and the murder turns out to have been part of an elaborate scheme which Hemingway is able to peel away bit by bit. "The mistake we've been making . . . is to have paid a sight too much attention to what you might call the important features of the case, and not enough to the highly irrelevant trimmings . . . I ought to have spotted at the outset that it was much *too* simple."

Elaborate though the whole thing is, it all hinges in the end on a single item that Hemingway is unable to find, and the tone of the story changes again, into a battle of nerves:  he has the evidence that will prove the old murder but needs the gun used to kill Warrenby. Finally, Hemingway pulls one of the oldest tricks in the book, based on his famous "flair;" Plenmeller falls for it, and the case is over.

Hemingway's last assignment blends humor and detection as well as many of the earlier mysteries, with—oddly?—a bit of nostalgia:  he refers more than once to those past cases—*No Wind of Blame*, *Envious Casca*, *They Found Him Dead*, and *Duplicate Death*. There are good, fair clues to what's going on slipped in among the chatter, and the wonderful irony of the over-clever novelist tripping up at the end.

It may be noted that the taxation problems alluded to were already being felt, since Miss Heyer, in Hemingway's person, takes the opportunity to make a complaint about them:

> The road had led them past a small horse-farm . . . and what had once been an extensive vegetable garden, with an orchard beyond it; and had reached the front-drive by way of the stableyard, where weeds sprouted between the cobblestones, and rows of doors, which should have stood with their upper halves open, were shut, the paint on them blistered and cracked.  Where half a dozen men had once found congenial employment one middle-aged groom was all that was to be seen.  "Progress," said Chief Inspector Hemingway.  But he said it to himself, well-knowing that his companion, inevitably reared in the hazy and impracticable beliefs of democracy-run-riot, would derive a deep, if uninformed, gratification from the reflection that yet another landowner had been obliged, through excessive taxation, to throw out of work the greater part of his staff.

In view of Miss Heyer's statement that readers would find all they needed to know about her in her books, it is rather tempting to read between the lines of that passage . . .

Although her "life of crime" ended with *Detection Unlimited*, Miss Heyer continued to work for another twenty years, turning out the light novels in which she specialized and even a book of short stories. We must not picture her, either, just dashing off any old thing to keep ahead of the tax man—*The Unknown Ajax* (1960) and *False Colours* (1963) are as neatly plotted and amusing as anything in her entire output.

The collection *Pistols for Two* (1960) is an excellent introduction, for the mystery fan, to the "other" Georgette Heyer; most of the tales are simply romantic escapades, but "Night at the Inn" is not only a neat little thriller but a virtual lexicon of the slang and cant of the period.

Miss Heyer had still another surprise in store for her readers—*Cousin Kate*, published in 1968—a rather grim-shaded Gothic story, complete with mad relations and an old dark house. Her last complete novel was *Lady of Quality* (1972); *My Lord John*, still unfinished at the time of her death two years later, was published in 1975 with notes by her husband.

Although she might have been disappointed not to have done more serious historical work, she took to the end a craftsman's pleasure in her writing and refused to allow certain of her earliest books to be reprinted, which might had given her time to complete the trilogy.

In any event, the work she left behind, in both the comic/romantic and detective fields, is substantial in quality. Miss Heyer has earned a special place in many readers' affections by combining them into what one writer (Elaine Barder [sic], *TAD*, July 1978) has called the "What Fun!" school of detection, "in which, instead of issuing appropriate sounds of outrage and anxiety, the suspects cracked jokes over corpses and honed their wit upon blunt instruments, burlesquing but not injuring the once solemn conventions." Surely, after Miss Heyer, there would be no excuse for the detective story to take itself too seriously again.

But this, after all, is in keeping with the spirit of Jane Austen, whose own defense of her work—from Northanger Abbey—might be a fitting conclusion to this survey:

Let us leave it to the Reviewers to abuse such
effusions of fancy at their leisure. . . [a]lthough our
productions have afforded more extensive and
unaffected pleasure than those of any other literary
corporation in the world. . . there seems almost a
general wish of decrying the capacity and
undervaluing the labour of the novelist, and of
slighting the performances which have only genuine
wit, and taste, to recommend them. . . I will not adopt
that ungenerous and impolitic custom.

**Jane Aiken Hodge, *The Private World of Georgette Heyer* (London: The Bodley Head, 1984, pp. 5-12, 207-8):**

Georgette Heyer was an intensely private person. A best-seller all her
life without the aid of publicity, she made no appearances, never gave an
interview, and only answered fan letters herself if they made an
interesting historical point. Having scored an instant success with *The
Black Moth* at the age of nineteen under her own name, Georgette Heyer,
she experimented with a pseudonym, Stella Martin, for her third book,
published by Mills & Boon, then achieved a permanent alias when she
married Ronald Rougier at twenty-three. From then on, Georgette Heyer
wrote the best-sellers, while Mrs. Ronald Rougier led the deeply private
life. She never talked about her background and early years, giving only
the barest facts of her life in eighteen lines of *Who's Who*. After her
death, A. S. Byatt, the critic and novelist, wrote an invaluable long
memorial piece for the *Sunday Times*, based on interviews with her
husband, her friend Carola Oman and her two good publisher friends, A.
S. Frere of Heinemann and Max Reinhardt of The Bodley Head. This is
the only source for much of the information about her early life, about
which she herself never talked. I have been able to supplement it by
talking to her surviving family and friends (her husband and Carola
Oman are now both dead) and by reference to her letters and to the four
early novels she later suppressed.

394

Her own invariable answer, when asked about her private life, was to refer the questioner back to her books. You will find me, she said, in my work. So should one now, almost ten years after her death, try and look behind the curtain of privacy in which she shrouded herself? My first instinct, when I started work on this book, was to concentrate entirely on the work, merely giving the barest facts of her life as a foreword. Then I began to talk to the people who knew her, and to read her letters. Everyone who knew her had loved or respected her, and they all seemed glad that a book should be written about her. But her own letters settled the question. She may have been a private person socially, almost a recluse, but on paper she was a compulsive communicator. And she wrote, her son says, just as she talked. Her letters to her publishers are full of sidelights on her own life and pungent comments on the world at large. They confirm, in short, her friends' unanimous description of her as shy on the surface, but a formidable, positive person underneath, with strong views and a great sense of style.

It hardly sounds the description of a purveyor of romantic froth. But in fact, for those with eyes to see, the strong character is there in her books, even in the lightest and most frivolous of them, and an awareness of the kind of person she was adds a new dimension to one's enjoyment of them, or, perhaps, helps to explain just why one does enjoy them. She may have been a compulsive writer, but she was also an immensely skilled and meticulous craftswoman. She did her best to conceal her high standards and stern moral code behind the mask of romantic comedy, and succeeded, so far as her great fan public was concerned. But she had a smaller audience among dons and journalists, among her husband's legal associates, among intelligent women everywhere, and even among feminists, who enjoyed the romantic syllabub all the more because they were aware of the hard core of realism underneath.

Naturally, it was the ravening fan public that made its voice most clearly heard during her lifetime, and its adulation served both to drive her further into herself and to put off readers who might have enjoyed her as they do Jane Austen or even Ivy Compton-Burnett, a favourite of hers. There is a terrible snobbery in the average intellectual reaction to her work. It is not everyone who has given her name to a type of novel, and it is unfortunate that that name should tend to provoke an uninformed, unjustified sneer. My aim in this book is to try and redress the balance by giving a feeling of her and of her work, as far as possible through her own words in the extensive correspondence which her publishers have kindly made available to me and her letters to friends. Some of her friends, though happy to talk about Georgette Heyer, have felt that she would not have wished her letters shown or quoted, and this is a feelng that must be respected. Her letters to her publishers, on the other hand, are part of the professional world she enjoyed, and unless otherwise indicated all the quotations in this book are from them.

Unfortunately, hardly any letters survive from before the 1940s, when she herself was in her forties and had been a best-seller for years. By this time she was taking a sadly deprecatory line about her own work. Speaking of *Friday's Child* in 1943 she says: "Spread the glad tidings that it will not disappoint Miss Heyer's many admirers. Judging from the letters I've received from obviously feeble-minded persons who do so wish I would write another *These Old Shades*, it ought to sell like hot cakes. I think myself I ought to be shot for writing such nonsense, but it's unquestionably good escapist literature, and I think I should rather like it if I were sitting in an air-raid shelter, or recovering from flu. Its period detail is good; my husband says it's witty—and without going to these lengths I will say that it is very good fun."

The statement sums up the problem she had with her readers. The dons and lawyers mostly kept quiet. The more vociferous of the fans tended to like the wrong books for the wrong reasons. They kept asking for swashbuckling romance when she was writing neat romantic comedy in the vein of Congreve and Sheridan. The reviewers, too, failed to appreciate the style and craftsmanship of her work as it developed into what would be known as "the Georgette Heyer." It is no wonder that she turned against publicity of any kind.

As well as the letters, Georgette Heyer left the unfinished typescript of about half of what she had planned as a serious mediaeval book, since published as *My Lord John*; a remarkable research library of some thousand volumes (now unfortunately dispersed); and a small but highly signficant collection of papers, to which her son has kindly given me access.  There was no attic full of carefully hoarded manuscripts and first drafts.  A flat-dweller since 1939, she found the proliferating copies of her published books problem enough without indulging in the sentiment of keeping old papers, however fascinating they might have proved to posterity.  She saved a few reviews, and one fan letter.  It was from a woman who had kept herself and her cell-mates sane through twelve years in a Romanian political prison by telling the story of *Friday's Child* over and over again.

There was an impressive collection of her own research material.  About three-quarters of this was the detailed and meticulous work for what was to become *My Lord John*.  The rest, even more immediately fascinating, consists of the files devoted to research for her eighteenth-century and Regency novels.  There is also a group of short stories that have never been published except in magazine form; two articles published in *Punch* and one from the *Sphere*, and five articles that have never been published at all.  The stories are typical Heyers, and it is surprising that they have not been published as a companion volume to *Pistols for Two*, but Georgette Heyer never thought much of her short stories, dismissing them as mere pot-boilers.  The articles—critical, personal and political—are an interesting experiment that apparently did not come off.  We should probably be grateful.  If *Punch* had gone on publishing her in 1954 we might have gained an essayist and lost some of her best work.

She might have turned "respectable."  After its heyday in the nineteenth century, the historical novel had fallen into disrepute in the early years of the twentieth, and this was particularly true when Georgette Heyer started to write.  She herself was obviously influenced by popularizers like Baroness Orczy and Jeffery Farnol, but they had helped to give the genre a vulgar name.  Her planned book about John, Duke of Bedford, was to be respectable:  a very early example of the more serious kind of historical novel that would be developed by people like Zoë Oldenbourg and Mary Renault.

Her books may not have received critical acclaim, but they sold.  When she died, at seventy-one, in 1974, she had fifty-one titles in print in hard covers or paperback and had been translated into at least ten languages and pirated in others. She was that rare thing, a steady best-seller. Hyped single titles come and go. Even in the current climate of sex and violence, her books are still solidly on the shelves. In fact, she now has more titles in print that she did when she died, since *My Lord John* has been published and *Simon the Coldheart*, an early historical novel, reprinted. Her name is a household word, used in *The Times* crossword puzzle in the Thirties and in the *New York Times* one in 1982. She is a literary phenomenon that demands investigation.

I have indulged myself, for the purposes of this book, in reading her entire output in chronological order and it has proved a rewarding experience as well as a delightful one. There are, to begin with, four early novels which she later suppressed. *Instead of the Thorn*, *Helen*, *Pastel* and *Barren Corn* were all written in her late teens and early twenties and are about the experiences of young women growing up in the complex social scene of the years after the First World War. Inevitably they and the detective stories she wrote mainly in her thirties throw a certain amount of light on the early years of her own life about which she would never talk. Her surviving brother, Frank Heyer, has confirmed that there is a considerable autobiographical element in the novels, particularly in *Helen*.

What she did not choose to write about is almost as interesting as what she did. Like Jane Austen, she knew her own limitations to a nicety. She spent the early years of her married life under primitive conditions in the wilds, first in Tanganyika, then in Macedonia. She was the only white woman for miles in Tanganyika, and nearly died in a dentist's chair in Kratovo. But she recognized this for experience she could not use. No heroine of hers would ever sit in a grass hut writing a novel.

She would write only of what she knew, or could find out about. The meticulous research shows how hard she worked for the background of her eighteenth-century and Regency novels, as well as for the more serious historical ones. Aside from a few excursions to France, where she had been as a child, her early books are set largely in London and the Sussex country she knew so well. She then widened her field gradually as she came to know other parts of England. Her son went from

Marlborough to Cambridge and his mother's novels follow him. And a whole new burst of country opened up for her when she and her husband started going to Scotland for his golf and toured the north of England researching the landscape and its castles for her long-projected mediaeval book. *The Quiet Gentleman, The Toll Gate* and *Venetia* all have North-Country backgrounds. Interestingly enough, though she and her husband spent many summers at Gullane in Scotland, and she loved the Scots, she never set a book in Scotland. Perhaps she looked on this time as pure holiday, or perhaps she sensibly blenched at Scottish dialect. Regency speech was enough for her. She used an Irishman, just once, in *Faro's Daughter*, but never again.

Most interesting of all is the change and development in her work over the fifty-odd years of her writing life. "Another Georgette Heyer," the critics used to say, with that fatal note of patronage, when each new title appeared. No wonder if it infuriated her. There is a clear line of development in her work, from the early stories of romantic adventure through the light-hearted comedy of her middle years to a warmer and graver type of book towards the end of her life. The emphasis shifts a little, too, from the dominating hero to the interesting heroine, and hero and heroine alike grow a little older with a younger couple often introduced to keep the balance. I hope to trace the thread of this development through her writing, published and unpublished, with the known facts of her life sketched in, simply, as background to her work. I think this is what that very private lady would have wished. . . .

A measure of her popularity in the United States had been the proliferation of fake Heyers there, which, fortunately, did not reach its peak until after her death. For a while there was a real risk that they would destroy what they fed on, but it now seems unlikely. To turn from one of their cardboard copies to the elegant, ironic originals is to turn from candle to sunlight. In a few more years, the imitations will have sunk without trace, but Georgette Heyer's well-ordered world will still be there for those with the luck to find it. After her death, Rachel Law, Lady Ellenborough, sent an unsolicited tribute to her publishers. Georgette Heyer, she said, was the only reading for a hospital bed. "Sex is cut down to size when the swish of the scythe sends a draught down the corridors. . . .Comic characters are more enduring and archetypal than tragic ones. Tears may fall from heaven but laughter is the earth's underground, inexhaustible spring." People like Lady Ellenborough, and the Romanian political prisoner, and many others, men and women, dons and lawyers and high-powered business men, will go on finding refreshment in Georgette Heyer's elegant romantic comedy and comfort in its strong moral framework. Highbrows who couple her books with the illiterate output of mass-market romancers merely betray that they have never read them. The romantic story is there, right enough, to keep children from play and old women from the chimney corner, but it is told with a style and humour that put her work in a class of its own. And the rules and customs of her private world can stand the test of time. She was not the only author of her day to create a private world as an escape from moral chaos. P. G. Wodehouse, C. S. Forester and Angela Thirkell did it too; Dick Francis still does, creating a small world at a time, as do the writers of science fiction. But Romantic novelists write mainly for women, or are held to do so, and their form of escapism has never in this century achieved the status of the detective story, the sea tale, or science fiction.

If anyone could make the romantic novel respectable, it should have been Georgette Heyer, unacknowledged moralist and stylist extraordinary. It did not happen in her lifetime, and she minded silently, added her own denigration to that of the critics, indulged her mediaeval dream, and lived her intensely private life. In many ways, she was a very lucky woman. She made for herself the life she wanted; she combined career with marriage brilliantly; and she did not live to see the publication of *My Lord John*, and the end of her mediaeval dream. She wrote mainly for women, but lived all her life among men, whom she preferred. She gave an immense amount of pleasure to all kinds of people, and must have known she did. It would be a suitable irony, and no surprise, if a reappraisal in the next few years were to give her work the critical acclaim it never achieved in her lifetime. The need for escape is not likely to grow less.

A sampling of reviews of Hodge's *The Private World of Georgette Heyer*:

Kathy O'Shaughnessy, "Rogue Males," in *The Spectator* 253, 8 September 1984, p. 28:

Georgette Heyer's novels are usually found in the obscure, badly-lit section of the bookcase, revealingly well-thumbed but ruthlessly demoted to second-class status, the not-quite-literature category. Whether or not Heyer's novels are "literature," they have been and continue to be so popular that they enlist recognition of a kind. The populist argument is a weak one (Harold Robbins, for example, has genuine delusions about his Shakespearian merit, because of the number of people who read his books), but Heyer's novels have created a *genre* in their own right. Their distinctive quality is apparent in the dialogue:

> "Amanda Smith, I regret to be obliged to inform you
> that you are a shockingly untruthful girl," said Sir
> Gareth calmly.

This is the voice of the hero who never, to use the colloquial phrase, loses his cool. His more rakish alternative has deep sneer lines on his face and swears oaths when he returns from a long journey, his top-boots splashed with mud. So successful was this voice and these heroes that her books bred a host of plagiarists, whose feeble imitations irritated her enormously.

Jane Aiken Hodge traces her life from its beginning in 1902 to her death in 1974, by which time she had 51 novels in print, translated into at least ten languages. For 50 years she produced best-sellers, priding herself on meticulous historical accuracy, gradually accumulating her own reference library. In fact, she hated the 20th century and called it "filthy." Regency England provided the perfect distant setting for her fiction. Without poverty, politics, sex, violence (the working classes intrude occasionally to touch their forelocks, and to demonstrate the author's knowledge of Regency slang), her books are more safely escapist than fairy-tales, since these include subversive creatures of the darker imagination, such as witches, wizards, and goblins.

Georgette Heyer's legendary success is due partly to the careful limitations of her fictional world, and her astonishingly predictable female readership. She had an astute understanding of their demands, and responded with a brilliant, rigid formula. For example, she has two kinds of hero. The first is "suave, well-dressed, rich and a famous whip"; the second is brusque and savage, with a foul temper. The heroine, on the other hand, is a fresh-faced chit just out of the schoolroom. She is physically delectable, and sometimes guilty of extravagance and wilfulness—faults which enhance her attractiveness. She is sexually chaste, while he has a degenerate past, and she finally redeems his jaded life. The plot is the sequence of obstacles that stands in the way of their union. The social standing of both hero and heroine is equivalent and impeccable.

It is a mistake to envisage Georgette Heyer as a sentimental woman. She was not inclined to examine critically her saturnine hero and his fictive success (in real life, she herself declared, he would be a nightmare), but she was a realist both about his effectiveness and the process of identification in her readers:

> He is the rugged and dominant male, who yet can be handled by quite an ordinary female: as it might be, *oneself*! He is rude and overbearing, and often a bounder; but these blemishes, however repulsive they may be in real life, can be made, in the hands of a skilled novelist, extremely attractive to many women.

She never questioned the significance of her stereotyped characters, or her wish fulfilment plots. Later she cast an amusingly knowing eye at Charlotte Bronte's [sic] creation of the original prototype, Rochester:

> She had the genius to state that he was not a handsome man, thus lifting him out of the ordinary run of heroes. What, in fact, did this ugly hero look

> like? Had he a squint or a harelip? Charlotte knew
> her job better than that! "He had a dark face, with
> stern features and a heavy brow". . . like Jane, we
> succumb to this splendid creature.

In real life, Georgette Heyer did nothing of the kind. She married
Ronald Rougier, a barrister, after a sedate, protracted courtship. She
dressed not in Barbara Cartland pink but in "a correct coat and skirt by
day and a dark grey dress at night. . . impressive, rather than elegant."
Her fans expected her to be romantic: "I am nothing of the sort," she
declared brusquely. She had a low opinion of her fellow authors, calling
them "inkies," and was prone to forthright statements such as "My own
opinion is that all Inkies are hell, and ought to be incarcerated." She
seemed to lead a rather dour existence, her husband Ronald remaining
colourless, at least in this book, to the last. She hated publicity of any
kind, and was always Mrs. Rougier in private, spending quiet holidays at
a golfing hotel in Scotland, doing tapestry or the *Times* crossword. She
never gained critical esteem, and even denigrated her own work: "I think
myself I ought to be shot for writing such nonsense."

In this biography, Jane Aiken Hodge has undertaken to redress
matters. Thus she comes armed with assumptions about her reader (as a
creature who views Miss Heyer with contempt), and a defensive attitude.
Quoting a passage from *Sylvester* she concludes defiantly: "How many
readers would recognise this passage as Georgette Heyer's if they
encountered it in a literary quiz?" (Now surely this is a double-edged
sword: the passage, she thinks, is better than Heyer, thereby implying
detrimental things about Heyer.)

Miss Hodge is herself an author of romance novels. This shows a
little in her prose, which has a tendency to lyricism, as when she twice
refers to Heyer's comic touches: "Laughter, like sunlight, broke out
again." She gives a pleasant account of Mrs. Rougier's life, but spends a
great deal of time telling us about the various plots of various novels.
This is not, by any stretch of the imagination, a work of literary criticism,
yet as a biography there seems too much about Heyer's plots, a quantity
of detail that interferes with the story of her life. Miss Hodge idealises

Georgette Heyer, linking her with Jane Austen, which is preposterous, all in all, rather killing her with kindness (she talks about Heyer's "passionate accuracy"). To me, the mystery remains a mystery. Mrs. Rougier sounds so robust, austere and rational that you wonder what or who it was that wrote these romances so adeptly and at such high speed. She had the gift of invention, but she never could take it beyond two-dimensional character and formulaic plots. The nature of those limitations is also interesting.

**Unattributed, in *Publishers Weekly* 226 (14 September 1984), p. 133:**

The British writer whose name is synonymous with a "recognizable genre of fiction," the historical romance, was a very private person. Wildly popular in England and the United States because of her finely researched novels, Georgette Heyer, sometimes called the 20th century Jane Austen, was a family woman whose married name was first revealed in her obituary in 1974. Her respectful biographer explores the many ambiguities of the prolific best-selling author who was shy, formidable, opinionated, devoted to only a few friends and her craft. Put off by fans who acclaimed her novels for what she considered the wrong reasons, Heyer also suffered the criticism of reviewers who dismissed the professional quality of her historical romances. Heyer, through excerpts from her many works, correspondence with publishers, and anecdotal recollections, is viewed here as an independent person, author of elegant, ironic novels (*Spring Muslin* [sic], *The Nonesuch* et al.) that create a small world where readers find comfort and refreshment.

**Gillian Avery, "The very pink of propriety," in *The Times Literary Supplement* (London), 21 September 1984, p. 1064:**

A taste for historical romance—which was based on a view of history that after the Regency period we entered the modern age—was symptomatic of the state of illusion that the middle-brow, unreflective

404

middle classes were living in in the 1930s. Hitler was in power, war was rushing towards us, but there we were immersed in stories about bygone and not particularly edifying aristocrats. All the popular fiction seemed to be set in an upper-class never-never-land—Dornford Yates, John Buchan, Wodehouse, A. E. W. Mason, P. C. Wren. The criminals were gentlemen—Raffles and the Saint—as were the detectives, when they weren't noblemen. Georgette Heyer, whose books equally suited my father and my schoolgirl contemporaries, never to my knowledge hinted that there was any poverty or unrest in the eighteenth and early nineteenth-century world that she depicted in nearly forty novels. Occasionally one of her exquisites wrinkles a delicate nostril and exclaims "faugh" as he steps into a particularly insalubrious inn, but there is no mention of the way of life of the masses who do not possess curricles and abigails and coats by Scott or Schultz [sic], let alone any reference to Tom Paine and his disciples. We are shown a world where the aristocracy are the only beings of interest, happily ministered to by the lower orders who exist solely for their support and convenience, and the bourgeoisie are pretentious buffoons where they are not downright nasty (though they are never allowed to be sublimely wicked; that is the privilege of the Duke of Avon or the Marquis of Vidal). Georgette Heyer was not unusual in this; it was the fashion of the time. Readers would not have identified with the boorish and sycophantic middle-class characters in Heyer's novels: they assumed that if they had lived in Regency times they would have been frequenting White's and Almack's, and from time to time buying duelling pistols at Manton's Shooting Gallery.

Schoolgirl light reading in the 1930s and during the war seemed largely historical: romance in costume was considered peculiarly adapted to their needs and was prominent in school libraries and there was a feeling that a historical setting was both educational and edifying. The works of Harrison Ainsworth (who for some curious reason was much reprinted where Wilkie Collins was not) were very much school library fodder, and the accounts of torturings in the Tower of London, plague pits and supernatural happenings mildly amused some. To those who discovered her, D. K. Broster made a very powerful appeal. Patricia

Beer was one of these who identified with the Jacobite cause because of *The Flight of the Heron.* "Looking back I feel sad. The feelings it roused in me were not about anything real yet I have experienced nothing stronger since," she wrote in *Mrs. Beer's House,* an account of her youth. Broster, whose output was only a quarter of Heyer's, never attained a tenth of her popularity. She wrote in a very different style. Whereas Heyer's books are light-hearted skirmishes with love or with adventure, as deftly constructed as any detective story (she wrote those very competently too), Broster's books betrayed deep feeling—passionate loyalty to a cause, the hero-worship of an older man by a younger. And they often ended tragically, whereas Heyer distanced herself from emotion or tragedy.

Perhaps part of the attraction of Georgette Heyer was that her novels are all optimistic; even the apparently most vicious men are capable of reform. In *These Old Shades* we meet the Duke of Avon, a languid and, we are told, licentious man of the world, a patron of the gaming table, up to the neck in unregretted amours. He himself says: " 'My reputation is damaged beyond repair. I come of vicious stock, and I have brought no honour to the name I bear. . . . To no woman have I been faithful; behind me lies scandal upon sordid scandal. I have wealth but I squandered one fortune in my youth and won my present fortune at play.' " But when the red-headed Léon whom he adopts as his page turns out to be a girl (and Léonie), he treats her with the greatest decorum and expects decorous behaviour from her. Eventually, her true, aristocratic parentage being irrefutably established, he marries her saying, " 'Since you will stoop to wed me, I pledge you my word that you shall not in the future have cause to regret it.' " No reader doubts that he will keep his word, and when we meet him again in *The Devil's Cub* [sic] it is clear that though his authority is as awful as ever and the thought of his displeasure unnerves or even terrifies all about him, he has been a blameless husband. It is now the turn of his son to be wild and reckless. He kills a footpad in the first chapter, desperately wounds an acquaintance who accuses him of cheating at cards in the fourth (" 'Damn you, Vidal, I believe you have killed him!' Rupert said angrily. 'I'm very nearly sure of it, dear uncle,' said the Marquis") and flees to France with a girl whom he supposes to

406

be a vulgar trollop on the make. Only when she turns out to be a "cit" but not a trollop (taking after her father's gentlemanly forebears rather than her mother) he is appalled: " 'I don't ruin persons of your quality.' " Thereafter he makes careful arrangements so that the proprieties shall not be offended, and when after many misunderstandings and hair's breadth escapes she agrees to be his wife (having to witness a duel fought over her with rapiers first) she appears confident that she is marrying a reformed character. Similarly at least two novels, *The Foundling* and *Sprig Muslin*, feature a duke and a baronet respectively who encounter deliciously silly young persons at large, and conscientiously insist on being their protectors (against the giddy creatures' wishes) enduring every sort of inconvenience and misunderstanding in order to turn them over to suitable authority.

For underneath all the dash and sparkle, the duelling and curricle-racing, the gaming, the disguises and elopements, Georgette Heyer was the very pink of propriety. She supported marriage (her own was very happy) and she was dismayed when her son proposed to marry the estranged wife of one of his colleagues. The stability she gave to the world she described and her belief in its institutions seem now to belong to some remote dreamland, but was a commonplace in books at least until the 1950s; our schoolgirl reading made us feel very safe in spite of the war around us.

But she never intended to write for schoolgirls and seems to have been dismayed at their enthusiasm. She would have liked to think that her readers were fastidious and cultivated men rather than women—barristers and dons and such—who could appreciate the accuracy of her historical detail, her wide reading, and she seems to have had the greatest contempt for most of her fans (the few who were introduced to her had to be warned not to mention her books)—the societies in America who dressed up and acted Heyer; the writers of gushing letters. The fact that Lord Justice Somervell bequeathed his collection of her novels to the library of the Inner Temple must have been very gratifying.

There can be few popular writers who maintained such a high standard of professionalism over all her output. Her plots are tours-de-force, gathering in pace as the work proceeds with an ever-present element of surprise, until in the final chapters we have all the cast assembled, ejaculating their explanations and exclamations like the finale of some Rossini opera. She took immense pains with her historical detail, never obtruding it, but weaving it into the background so that one dates the books from some casually mentioned fact, like the death of Princess Charlotte. If she names the brand of polish that a valet uses for his master's Hessian boots one can be sure she has got it right. She was more interested in such details than in political history. She had never, for instance, heard of Lord Rockingham, and having bestowed his title upon the hero of *Bath Tangle* had (loudly lamenting, for she was proud of the fittingness of her names) to substitute the name of Rotherham. She rarely used historical characters. *The Infamous Army* [sic] is one of the few exceptions, and though held in esteem by some of the perceptive (the description of the battle of Waterloo is accurate enough for it to have been used at Sandhurst for lectures on military history) the Duke of Wellington himself does not seem as solid as some of her fictitious characters. She did not herself consider she was writing romance, though it is not clear what else she thought her books were. Perhaps comedies of manners; certainly there is comedy and certainly they are mannered.

Despite the title of her book, Jane Aiken Hodge is able to show very little of Georgette Heyer's private world. All that is known of her childhood and youth is contained on two pages. She was born in 1902 in Wimbledon, the daughter of George Heyer who, it is surmised, was the formative influence of her early years, though even this has to be inferred from her novels. She never went to university, and when she was nineteen wrote her first book, *Black Moth* [sic], a dashing story of a gentleman highwayman who is really an earl in disguise and who, having taken the blame for his brother's dishonourable conduct has gone into hiding. It was originally made up to amuse her little brother Boris, and all her life she was to lavish tender care on her family. Indeed her worries about individual members of it and her fury about income tax matters occupied most of her thoughts when she was not writing, if we are to believe the correspondence quoted. She was successful from the very beginning of her career, and it was the income from her novels which supported her husband throughout his early days at the Bar. Their tastes were for that quiet simplicity that takes a great deal of money to support, and the British tax system being what it is, the more she wrote the more she had to write—which she did, savagely reviling the Inland Revenue and the various governments of her time for the ridiculous uses to which they put her money. But she would probably have written in any case; clearly she loved this world she had created, indeed one could say that this fictional dreamland was her private world though she took care that no serious feelings should obtrude.

Lacking anything much to say about Heyer's life, Mrs. Hodge has concentrated on the novels, and discusses each one, demonstrating their admirable craftmanship, their humour and strong dramatic line. Feeling perhaps that the subject is a rather lightweight one, the publishers have chosen to make a picture book out of it, throwing in lavish quantities of portraits of personalities of the Georgian period which sit rather oddly beside the occasional family snapshot, and prints of fashionable Regency life with somewhat faint-hearted captions such as "The Royal Academy Summer Exhibition . . . Like Jane Austen's, Heyer heroines were seldom particularly artistic or musical." But the book looks handsome, and one guesses it would have satisfied this most fastidious author.

**Patricia Altner, (National Defense University Library, Washington, D.C.) in *Library Journal* 109, 1 November 1984, pp. 2066-2067:**

Best known for her Regency novels, Heyer placed a high value on privacy and categorically turned down all requests for interviews. This personal reclusiveness has made it difficult for biographer Hodge; therefore, she has written less a biography than a survey of Heyer's works interspersed with glimpses of the author's life as gleaned from her letters and from interviews with family and friends. Although largely unacknowledged by critics, Heyer's novels were witty, well written, and meticulously researched. This shy yet formidable lady, who died in 1974, spawned many imitators, but none has matched her grace or style. Hodge's beautifully illustrated volume is a welcome tribute. Would-be romance writers will find this work of special interest.

**Patricia Ann Reilly, O.P. (Associate Professor of English, St. Thomas Aquinas College, Sparkill, New York) in *Best Sellers* 44, January 1985, pp. 378-79:**

Here is a charming biography of a very private British lady who has been called "the 20th-century Jane Austen."

Jane Aiken Hodge, daughter of Conrad Aiken, the American poet, is well suited to write of this novelist, as she herself has written fifteen historical novels, three suspense, and a biography of Jane Austen.

Georgette Heyer, a best-seller for fifty years, never made a public appearance or gave an interview. Only after her death in 1974 did her fans learn her marriage name from the published obituaries. Ronald Rougier, queen's consul, was her devoted husband and best proofreader for almost fifty years. In fact, he collaborated with her in providing plots for her detective stories. When she died at age 71, she had published 51 literary gems—historical romances, thrillers, and short stories—translated into at least ten languages. She was a literary phenomenon—a steady best-seller.

Born in the prosperous London suburb of Wimbledon in 1902, Georgette had published five novels by the time of her marriage in 1925. When asked about her private life, her inevitable reply was, "You can find me in my work." This, Jane Aiken Hodge did; but she also talked to those who knew her. Hodge found that anyone who knew her loved and respected her. Friends unanimously concurred that Georgette's shyness masked a strong positive person with definite views and a great sense of style.

Strong views on world matters were expressed by Heyer in letters to her publishers, which served as another source for this biography. Heyer kept only one fan letter among her few surviving manuscripts. The letter was from a Romanian woman who kept her cell mates "sane" by repeatedly telling the story of *Friday's Child* throughout their twelve years of political imprisonment.

Hodge deftly traces the development in Heyer's work over the half-century of her writing. From the early stories of romantic adventure she progresses through the lighthearted comedy of her middle years to a warm, graver type of book toward the end of her life. The author interlaces the thread of the development of her writings with the known facts of her life.

This study reveals the meticulous literary craft which conceals Heyer's high standards and the stern moral code behind the mask of romantic comedy. Her Regency novels of manners and morals were written in the vein of Congreve and Sheridan wherein laughter is the great corrective and healer.

The charming jacket print from Ackerman's "Repository of Arts, Literature,. . .1818-1828," courtesy of the British Museum, fittingly enfolds *The Private World of Georgette Heyer*.

**Katya Watter, "A Secret Career," in *The Times Educational Supplement*, 5 April 1985, p. 37:**

"Christ, why did I have to be born into this *filthy* age?" Jane Aiken Hodge quotes Georgette Heyer as saying. She would have preferred to live in the Middle Ages. As it was she set about creating her own world and contrived throughout her life to keep this world private. She gave no interviews and with consummate tact combined the secret career of a best-selling novelist with the more conventional one of a wife playing second fiddle to a well-known husband.

Jane Aiken Hodge, with a delicacy Georgette Heyer would appreciate, has produced an account of her life and writing that makes use almost exclusively of what can be called public facts, letters and other records. For example, her private correspondence with family and friends remains, for the most part, private, but her vigorous, decided letters to publishers are extensively quoted. Apart from revealing as much of *The Private World of Georgette Heyer* as the subject herself would have tolerated, J. A. Hodge has written a workmanlike, if brief, critique of her work, which, though it does much to "redress the balance"

411

of adverse opinion, still fails to do justice to Georgette Heyer's sensitive ear for dialogue and the accuracy of characterization revealed by its means. The trouble with attempting to give a true picture of Georgette Heyer as a writer is that whereas her plots were mostly "my usual froth," her style and characterization (with some exceptions) can be compared with Austen, Coward or Sheridan. She herself claimed that her style was a mixture of Johnson and Austen. Her serious admirers who could appreciate her distinction kept quiet, but her "ravening fan public" were vociferous and the result is a reputation much below her deserts.

**Kay Mussell, "Fantasy and Reconciliation. Contemporary Formulas of Women's Romance Fiction"** (*Contributions in Women's Studies*, no. 46. Westport, CT: Greenwood Press, 1984):

pp. xiii-iv, xvii:

The most interesting romance writers of the past thirty years are Mary Stewart, Georgette Heyer, and Anya Seton because these three writers rarely succumb to the most limiting formulaic conventions. Mary Stewart's originality derives from her delineation of complex settings and character types, her use of a wide range of literary models, and her graceful and stylish prose. Georgette Heyer, while working in a limited field—the Regency romance—has nevertheless made it her own; virtually every Regency writer covets the accolade "in the tradition of Georgette Heyer."[30] Her heroines are appealing and spunky; her men, vulnerable and tender. Her wit and humor, if not up to the standard of her inspiration, Jane Austen—and who could write so well?—is at least crisp, pointed, and original. Anya Seton specializes in thoroughly researched historical novels about women, and she has written many fewer books than most other romance authors because of her careful preparation for each book. She chooses a different historical period for each novel, and she makes it live.

---

[30] Barbara Cartland, *The Innocent Heiress* (New York: Pyramid, 1950, repr. 1970), front cover.

412

pp. 55-59, 61:

Innumerable writers have employed the conventions of historical romance in many periods of history, and a comprehensive analysis of all types would be both unending and redundant. For the past fifteen years, however, one particular historical romance subformula has been so popular and so pervasive that it represents the approach of all. The Regency romance, set in that most ambivalent period between the relative license of the Stuart and early Georgian eras and the repression and respectability of the Victorian age, was elaborated most fully in the work of Georgette Heyer. Heyer's romances are set between 1775 and 1825, although the Regency period actually lasted from 1810 to 1820. The majority, and the best, of her novels occur from about 1800 to 1816, prompting inevitable—and only partially unfair—comparisons with Jane Austen.[31] The popularity of Heyer and other Regency writers spawned American imitations; and today, almost a decade after Heyer's death, many writers still attempt to reproduce her fictional world and her success.

The Regency period is no more appropriate for romances than many other eras, but Heyer showed exceptional skill in suggesting its fictional possibilities. Regency romances transport readers to England, often London, to a society in which women contract suitable marriages through participation in a structured social ritual—the marriage market represented by the London season. A courtship ritual dominates the action of each book and provides a value system against which characters' behavior can be measured. Some heroines flout convention more than others, but all are in danger of ostracism for inappropriate behavior.

The vocabulary of Regency romances, seen outside the context of the novels, may seem arch and sometimes confusing; but for devotees, the language enhances the illusion of being admitted to a secret and special world. Characters care about social status, and encroaching persons may be fended off with "setdowns," clever verbal insults that depress

---

[31] For an extended comparison of Austen and Heyer, see Robinson, "On Reading Trash," 200-22. . . .

GEORGETTE HEYER:

pretensions. An "accredited Beauty" is the hit of the season; a woman who lacks beauty may be described as "elegant" or as "having countenance." A plain woman is an "antidote." Eligible men may be "Corinthians," who wear impeccable but restrained clothing tailored by Weston, drive their teams of horses "to the inch," and "peel to advantage" in Gentleman Jackson's boxing saloon. Their only flaw is that they become quickly bored with the silliness of women who "set their caps" for them. A proposal of marriage is called "making an offer." A less respectable proposition "gives a woman carte blanche." Ineligible men are vain and silly, often described as "Tulips of the Ton," who dress outrageously in an exaggerated manner and are convinced, against all the evidence, of their own grandeur.

Heroes and heroines stand out from other characters, who are silly at best and stupid at worst. Heyer was particularly adept at creating dialogue for "chuckleheads," or for a character described as "hen-witted," or "a beautiful peagoose," or "a slow-top." A character may be "prosy," or boring, given to speeches and the issuing of offensive, unnecessary advice. Protagonists rise above the foolishness of other characters because they see through the sham yet still behave impeccably by their own standards. If they transgress the rules of the courtship ritual, they do so for the best of reasons. Most Regency heroines also pass the domestic test.

Publishers and reviewers frequently identify Regency romances with the work of Jane Austen, a more appropriate analogy for Georgette Heyer than for other Regency writers such as Barbara Cartland, Clare Darcy, Caroline Courtney, or Jane Aiken Hodge. For most Regency authors, the comparion derives more from the chronological setting of the novels than from similarities between Austen's novels and modern Regency romances. Certainly not even Georgette Heyer at her best threatens Austen's reputation, but both Heyer and Austen use similar conventions and employ social satire to construct their plots. For Austen, of course, those materials were the stuff of everyday life. For Heyer, they remain historical conveniences.

Heyer and Austen both write about young women of marriageable age whose conventional attributes put them at a disadvantage in the

414

marriage market. Their mothers are either absent or unfit to ease their way, and they must depend on their own wits. They face a similar set of options: marriage, teaching, service, or spinsterhood. Some of Heyer's stock characters are reminiscent of Austen's creations, and her "prosy" bores are similar to Mr. Collins of *Pride and Prejudice*, although not so finely drawn. Her attractive young rakes resemble Frank Churchill of *Emma* or Mr. Wickham of *Pride and Prejudice*. She uses characters of virtue but little understanding like Mr. Bingley. Her older heroes have the maturity and competence of Mr. Knightley.

Austen sets no novels in the highest social circles of Regency England, for Almack's and the London season mean little to her characters. Her men do not have titles, although they are genteel, respectable, and occasionally rich. Although most of her heroines marry above their social status, Austen cares more for their achievement of a satisfying marriage with a guarantee of financial security than for social climbing. Her provincial settings—the countryside, small villages, Bath, and Lyme Regis—differ from the fashionable world of Regency romances, for when Heyer uses these same settings, she does so with numerous references to the glamorous world of London. Austen does not mention the Prince Regent in her work, while modern Regency writers refer to him as a symbol of the titillating corruption of the age.

Austen rarely describes clothing except when characters' preoccupation with dress demonstrates their debased or frivolous values. Balls and dances occur in her novels as the social setting for people in country villages rather than as the fashionable events of Heyer's marriage market. Austen employs much richer material and offers a more varied cast of characters and a sharper, more realistic vision of human foibles. Set against Austen's satire, Heyer's humor has a slapstick quality instead of Austen's finely honed irony. However, Austen and Heyer both delineate silly, fatuous, and restricted social conditions for their protagonists.

A book that spans the range of conventions used by Austen and Regency writers is Austen's unfinished novel *Sandition*, completed anonymously a few years ago by "Another Lady." Austen wrote most of the first eleven chapters before she died; and, although the fragment is not superior Austen, a reader can imagine how the elements of this book might have come together had she lived to finish it. However, when "Another Lady" picks up the tale, the book degenerates into stock Regency romance, perhaps a little better than many because of the constraints of extending Austen's unique plot line. But Austen would never have used the abduction scene that finishes this book. Her ineligible man would have transgressed the social code more subtly than the character imagined by the later writer. The sober and serious heroine becomes a caricature, and the manipulative and impetuous hero could never compare with Darcy or Wentworth. The satire, even when it builds on Austen's base, is thin and silly, and the characters lose their depth and moral ambiguity when the modern author picks up the tale. At the end of an Austen novel, characters get what they deserve but without the unambiguous absolutes of Regency romance.

The unknown collaborator remains anonymous, but she is clearly familiar with Regency romance conventions. Based on internal evidence, she is neither Heyer (no humor) nor Cartland (too clever); but she may be another writer such as Jane Aiken Hodge, who has written a popular biography of Jane Austen. As with Charlotte Brontë and the gothic romance, Austen inspired the modern Regency formula even though the modern writers are less subtle and less profound. However, as Lillian Robinson suggests, both Austen and Heyer

> are saying that the personal *matters* . . . the import of historical fiction for women is to reinforce the notion that the public world, however much its vicissitudes may influence women's lives, is always at one remove from women. And conversely, women remain at one remove from it. . . . It is not so much that this kind of fiction "tells" or "teaches" women something about their nature, role, and sphere. Rather, it repeats what direct experience and dominant ideology have already succeeded in communicating.[32]

[32] Robinson, "On Reading Trash," 221-22.

p. 79:

. . .In Regency romances, the code of the ton contrasts with the corruption of the Prince Regent's set, as if the stiffly correct social world were a reaction against the publicized lapses of the corrupt upper nobility. Although many heroes of Regency romances are respected by the Prince and his friends, especially for athletic prowess and fastidious taste, they do not participate in the most corrupt of the Regent's activities. Heyer's heroes are experienced men of the world, but they are also mature and sensitive. They never confuse lust with love or deal dishonestly with a woman.

pp. 98-100, 115:

In a few romances, usually those with historical settings, heroines may be homely or plain. Unattractive women pass an explicit domestic test to make plausible the heroes' attraction to them. In Georgette Heyer's *A Civil Contract*, the heroine is the daughter of a vulgar but well-meaning businessman, who offers the titled hero money to save his estate if he will marry Jenny and give her increased status as his wife. Heyer describes Jenny as almost hopelessly unattractive; however, since she has intelligence and common sense, she accepts her weaknesses and compensates by being an excellent wife and mother. She wants to make her husband comfortable, and she does not waste time trying to compete with more fortunate women. She also understands her husband's loss of pride when he accepts money from her father, so she sensitively makes it easier for him to take the needed aid without incurring intolerable emotional obligations. Eventually, her husband sees the benefits of having a wife like Jenny and gives up his infatuation with a more beautiful woman.

Although romance heroes may be initially attracted to or repelled by a woman's appearance, they recognize superficiality and appreciate women with feminine qualities beneath the veneer. Unworthy men are never so perceptive. Beautiful women can learn to protect themselves from wrong choices, while ordinary women become beautiful in the eyes of men who love them. Plain women find that the men they love do not need beauty in a wife. In a culture that values both youth and beauty, romances reassure women that they need not be beautiful to succeed. It does not matter, so women are told, that they may not have inherited perfect features or acquired glamour. Men who make appropriate husbands will recognize worth despite the exterior package.

These patterns work most overtly in historical romances with unusually independent heroines who do not follow society's prescriptions for proper female behavior. In Heyer's *Sylvester, or the Wicked Uncle*, for example, the heroine is slightly older than the average debutante. She has had one London season, but she "didn't take." When the hero's mother asks if Phoebe is beautiful, Sylvester replies:

> "No. Not a beauty, Mama. When she is animated, I believe you would consider her taking. . . . She blurts out whatever may come into her head; she tumbles from one outrageous escapade into another; she's happier grooming horses and hobnobbing with stable-hands than going to parties; she's impertinent; you daren't catch her eye for fear she should start to giggle; she hasn't any accomplishments; I never saw anyone with less dignity; she's abominable, and damnably hot at hand, frank to a fault, and—a *darling!*"[33]

To love such a woman, whom he describes in terms that seem more appropriate for a much-loved and indulged child, Sylvester must look beneath the surface. Phoebe has none of the conventional qualities that would lead a man like Sylvester to marry her. She has no interest in marriage, and she intends to set up housekeeping with her sympathetic governess and support them both by writing romantic novels. Despite her lack of social graces, however, Phoebe is more intelligent, more modest, and more honest than other women in the book. And she deserves to be a wife, for she demonstrates her femininity through

---

[33] Georgette Heyer, *Sylvester, or the Wicked Uncle* (New York: Ace, 1957), 272.

nurturing Sylvester's heir, the son of a silly, vain, and unfit mother.

p. 129, 144:
. . . Georgette Heyer rarely alludes to sex, even when other authors would do so. In *A Civil Contract*, her most explicit scene occurs when the husband in an arranged marriage speaks to his shy bride at the beginning of their honeymoon.

> "But first let me tell you that I'm not blind to the evils of *your* situation. We are barely acquainted, as you have said yourself; it must be very uncomfortable for you indeed!" He smiled at her, not lovingly, but very kindly. "*That* evil will soon be remedied. In the meantime, don't be afraid. I won't do anything you don't like."[34]

End of discussion; end of sex. . . .

pp. 136-7, 144:
Through their climactic scenes, the final few pages when the characters acknowledge their love, romances offer a vicarious fantasy or recapitulation of the exquisite moment of being chosen. In the reconciliation between lovers, the hero's authority is crucial, for a heroine may be oblivious to the signs of love. She may understand neither her own feelings nor those of the hero, and her acknowledgment may depend on his perception as he instructs her to recognize the truth. In Georgette Heyer's *Frederica*, the hero teaches the heroine the nature of love when he proposes to her. Frederica says she has not thought about marrying him. Alverstoke says, ruefully, that he knows that. She suggests that he thinks he compromised her when they spent time together without a chaperone; he denies it. She tells him that he does not want to marry her; he agrees, adding that since everyone apparently believes he will, he will be humiliated if she rejects him. She says that

---

[34] Georgette Heyer, *A Civil Contract* (New York: Ace, 1961), 94.

she has to take care of her two young brothers, and he says he wants to help. When she accuses him of marrying her out of compassion, he again demurs. Finally, she says that she cannot believe he loves her.

> "Oh, not in the least," he assured her cheerfully. "It is merely that I find I cannot live without you, my adorable Frederica!"
>
> "Is it like *that*? Being in love? You see, I never was in love, so I don't know. . . .It has always seemed to me that if one falls in love with any gentleman one becomes instantly blind to his faults. But I am *not* blind to your faults, and I do *not* think that everything you do or say is right! Only—Is it being—not very comfortable—and cross—and not quite *happy*, when you aren't there?"
>
> "That, my darling," said his lordship, taking her ruthlessly into his arms, "is *exactly* what it is!"
>
> "Oh—!" Frederica gasped, as she emerged from an embrace which threatened to suffocate her. "*Now* I know! I am in love!"[35]

Alverstoke seems less authoritarian than some other romance heroes because he does not know how Frederica feels, but he has enough authority to define love for her and to give her the information she requires to respond properly to his proposal. Male knowledge and authority in matters of love are constants in romance fiction; but, paradoxically, expertise in human relationships belongs to woman's sphere. Conventionally, in the act of being chosen—when the hero makes his declaration—a woman knows she has earned the right to take on the responsibilities inherent in her intuitive expertise. He bears the responsibility of making the choice before she can perform her womanly duties.

---

[35] Georgette Heyer, *Frederica* (New York: Avon, 1965) 348-50.

**Philippa Toomey in "Correspondence,"** *The Times Literary Supplement* **(2 November 1984, p. 1249c):**

Sir, - Without making any kind of claim that Georgette Heyer was a social historian rather than a romantic historical novelist, it does seem hard on her that Gillian Avery, in her review (September 21) of Jane Aiken Hodge's *The Private World of Georgette Heyer*, should say that she "never to my knowledge hinted that there was any poverty or unrest in the eighteenth and early nineteenth century world that she depicted in nearly forty novels."

To my knowledge, here and there were a number of amiable young ladies who took pity on climbing boys, homesick servant girls, juvenile delinquents, stray dogs, even someone known as "Leaky Peg." And injudicious reference to "Waldo's brats" caused great grief until it was revealed that they were inhabitants of the orphanages maintained by a nobleman, following the philanthropic example of his mother.

Men were killed or wounded in wars in Heyer novels, and noblemen did occasionally find themselves slumming and having to manage without a valet (with amusing and salutary consequences). For other social classes, there is a train of servants (mostly, it must be admitted, of the devoted category), old soldiers taken on as grooms, and a gallery of amusing low-life charcters, including con men, Bow Street Runners, near-villains in an old tradition of grotesques.

Jane Austen was far less forthcoming.

PHILIPPA TOOMEY

**E. R. Glass (Università degli Studi di Lecce) and A. Mineo (Istituto Universitario Orientale di Napoli), "Georgette Heyer and the Uses of Regency," (in** *La performance del testo: atti del VII Congresso Nazionale dell'Associazione Italiana di Anglistica [A.I.A.],* **Siena, 2-4 Novembre 1984 [Siena: Libreria Ticci succ. A. Giubbi & C., (1986)], pp. 283-292):**

> "*The Times* thought it was a huge joke, and drew
> a male elitist distinction between 'bodice rippers' and
> the works of 'serious authors,' but whether domestic,
> gothic, melodramatic or plain Cartland, forty percent
> of Britain's most borrowed novels happen to be
> historical romances, according to a Public Lending
> Right survey published in September."[36]

Among these popular and prolific writers, Georgette Heyer occupies an interesting position which we could compare to that of Dorothy Sayers in detective fiction, another interwar writer popular with a middle-class, educated public, whose novels have never fallen out of fashion with readers. Georgette Heyer is still published and read, with suburban libraries often lending from four to six copies a day and sales averaging 400 a month, and is recognised as the forerunner of a school of Regency romance. It appears significant, in view of the lack of previous attention, that her attractively illustrated biography[37] published ten years after her death, was greeted by full-page reviews in both *The Times*[38] and the *TLS*[39], plus a long radio programme.[40] Not only do we find a dearth of qualified research on romantic fiction as a whole, compared with more "legitimate" fields such as detective or science fiction, but within the genre, scant consideration has been paid to middlebrow historical romance.[41]

---

[36] See D. Hewson, "Romantic fiction is borrowers' choice," *The Times*, September 17 [sic; actually September 25], 1984.

[37] J. Aiken Hodge (1984).

[38] See A. Huth, "The compulsive storyteller wrapped up in an enigma," *The Times*, August 31, 1984.

[39] See G. Avery, "The very pink of propriety," *TLS*, September 21, 1984.

[40] An hour-long BBC Radio 4 programme in the series *Bookshelf* on October 7, 1984, was devoted to Georgette Heyer.

[41] The only critical study of Heyer found so far is "On Reading Trash" in L. S. Robinson, *Sex, Class, and Culture*, Bloomington, Indiana U. P., 1979.

Out of Georgette Heyer's forty historical novels published between 1921 and 1975, we decided to concentrate on the bulk of her production set during the first two decades of the nineteenth century, as well as the few which have the last half of the eighteenth century as a background, leaving out eight novels set in other periods, which are constructed round real historical events. The analysis refers to twenty-eight out of the thirty-two "Regency" or near-Regency novels.[42]

Considering the "uses of history" in romantic fiction generally, it is evident that historical setting equals exoticism for most writers, and it is usually evoked in undigested, improbable and anachronistic fragments, the novels thus presenting a marked hiatus between the simple modern language and characterisation and their historical pretension, as in Barbara Cartland's nineteenth century excursions into Ruritania. Georgette Heyer's use of a historical setting is much more complex, as with the intention of being taken seriously, she researched her work exhaustively. She rapidly collected texts on language, style and behaviour, and filled notebooks with detailed drawings of dress, and with slang expressions. This effort resulted in a coherent amalgam of description and dialogue, albeit limited to an upperclass pleasure-seeking milieu.

Her novels set in the latter half of the eighteenth century show an obvious debt to Baroness Orczy, creator of the adventurous Scarlet Pimpernel. According to her biographer, Georgette Heyer was actually most fascinated by medieval history, but was unable to reproduce a plausible medieval language and atmosphere.[43] In addition, other factors appear to have contributed to her shift to Regency. Firstly, as Panek points out with regard to detective fiction, most writers of popular genres in the 1930s gravitated towards restricted and elaborately described setting.

They were aware that the romance could never be

---

[42] . . . All the quotations are taken from the Pan Books paperback edition of Georgette Heyer's novels.

[43] Aiken Hodge (1984: 76-77).

> important literature, and while they wrote romance
> elements into their novels, they also nudged them
> toward a more acceptable literary tradition—the
> novel of manners. [44]

Secondly, when she started writing, while the Victorian era was considered too modern and too close, the beginning of the nineteenth century was far enough away to be "historical." It was, however, not too distant or bizarre, as Heyer herself tacitly admitted when she abandoned her much loved and re-worked medieval novel, which was published posthumously as *My Lord John* in 1975. During the interwar period, nostalgia for the pre-industrial "organic" society—one of the available readings of the past—when combined with a reaction against Victorian puritanism and earnestness, would have fostered the illusion of a more lightweight, elegant and aristocratic atmosphere. Today, World War II is perhaps still our most prominent collective watershed, with the result that our sense of the past has been pushed forwards, and the Victorian and Edwardian eras have been incorporated into historical novels at all levels from John Fowles to the much read Catherine Cookson. Another historical parameter is formed by our perception of where costume ends and fashion begins, which, in this shortcut to the past, is largely at the mercy of the visual media. Costume is in fact a central element of all historical romance, as not only does it enable the reader to visualize the hero, the heroine and the social setting in detail which never dates, but it also enhances a specific sense of period. Furthermore, this commonsense notion of history *sells* at the station, the supermarket or the local library, especially when translated into atmosphere-evoking adjectives by blurb writers who know that their contribution is decisive. "I never read anything before Victorian," said one woman, firmly expressing her

---

[44] Panek, L., *Watteau's Shepherds: the detective novel in Britain 1914-1940,* Bowling Green: Bowling Green University Popular Press, 1979 p. 27.

preference for Catherine Cookson.[45]

The third reason for Georgette Heyer's shift to regency was the soothing and inspiring influence of Jane Austen,[46] which she herself acknowledged.[47]

In tracing her progress from the picaresque tale such as *These Old Shades* (1926) or *Regency Buck* (1935) to the novel of manners like *Venetia* (1958) or *Black Sheep* (1966), or from action to psychology, we have analysed both Georgette Heyer's narrative strategies and use of language. Traditionally, the narrative scheme of any romantic novel can be expressed by the simple formula "meeting - obstacles - happy ending." In Heyer's early production, the nature of these obstacles is primarily physical, often represented by the misdeeds of villains, thieves or highwaymen, and by the presence of duels or fights, and violent death. Paralleling this type of action, we find a rapid narrative pace with radical changes of scene and long eventful journeys, usually giving the main characters an opportunity to meet as the result of an accident, as fugitives, or at an inn.

The second phase we have identified is characterized by a sharply decreasing number of adventurous elements overall, which also change qualitatively. For example, the violent elements disappear completely, while other narrative devices such as accidents, elopements and short journeys become less spectacular, and being largely relegated to the subplot, also less prominent. In this second phase, a more evolutive pace emerges, with a greater psychological exploration of each narrative episode which accompanies a more restricted, or drawing-room situation.

---

[45] This episode occurred while we were looking for readers to interview. Besides our textual analysis, a pilot study of fruition was carried out in Britain, both in local libraries, and with the information obtained from a dozen questionnaires. Any references we make to reader "use and gratification" stem from this small survey.

[46] All Jane Austen's work is pertinent to our study of the development of Georgette Heyer's narrative structures, but the closest prototypes are provided by *Pride and Prejudice*, *Emma*, and *Persuasion*.

[47] Aiken Hodge (1984: 50).

Furthermore, a modification in the simple formula above goes with these developments, and from *Arabella* (1949) onwards, a narrative scheme based on Jane Austen's *Pride and Prejudice* is adopted with increasing frequency. The new scheme can be synthesized as follows:

[See diagram on facing page]

In all romantic fiction, the reiteration of verbal duelling between the two main characters until the final resolution forms the backbone of the narrative. The denouement itself can be of two types, which Greimas defines as *confrontation polémique* and *confrontation transactionelle*.[48] The former implies that one of the antagonists gains a mastery over the other at the end, while the latter implies a negotiation instead. Previous studies of romantic fiction agree on the existence of a resolution which corresponds to the *confrontation polémique*: the heroine always yields to her master.

In this respect, however, Georgette Heyer is atypical, since in most novels she appears to share the Austen *confrontation transactionelle* epitomised by Elizabeth Bennet's musings in *Pride and Prejudice*. "It was a union that must have been to the advantage of both" signifies a negotiated resolution, despite the didactic undertone, also present in Heyer. Her exchanges often approximate more to the much-exploited theme of the 'Taming of the Shrew,' counterbalanced by that of the 'Reform of the Rake,' than to the varied, complex and dynamic relationship depicted in Jane Austen's novels. In fact, Georgette Heyer's heroines are doomed to a relative capitulation by the mandatory happy ending, as their unusual liveliness and enterprise stays within the limits of marriageable convention. For readers, a vision of independence may

---

[48] We are indebted to Pozzato (1982) for this reference, taken from A. Greimas and J. Courtés, *Sémiotique. Dictionnaire raisonné de la théorie du langage*, Paris, Hachette 1979. We found the same definition in Greimas' preface to Courtés (1976: 11).

| meeting | verbal duelling | hero's first declaration of love | moral/psych. obstacles | hero's good deeds | recognition of the hero | happy ending |
|---|---|---|---|---|---|---|
| | | heroine's refusal | | heroine's inner conflicts | capitulation of the heroine | |

Narrative scheme based on Jane Austen's *Pride and Prejudice*, visible in Georgette Heyer's works from *Arabella* (1949) onward. (Glass/Mineo) be "secretly and enjoyably subversive," as Tony Davies suggests[49], but could never be put into practice. Actually, our interviews suggested that the reader is offered a vicarious experience of self-assertion, which in reality, she feels would lead to rejection by her partner.

Moving from the plot to the characterization, we detected a change in the portrayal of the hero and heroine, from a combination conducive to violent clashes of temperament and behaviour to a more subtle psychological matching. Georgette Heyer's heroes and heroines fall into three main types, which we have classified as follows:

## HEROES

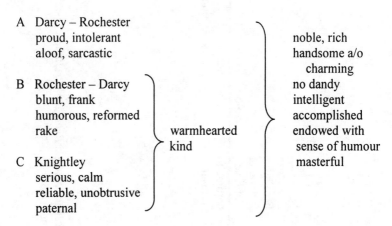

A  Darcy – Rochester
proud, intolerant
aloof, sarcastic

B  Rochester – Darcy
blunt, frank
humorous, reformed
rake

C  Knightley
serious, calm
reliable, unobtrusive
paternal

warmhearted
kind

noble, rich
handsome a/o
   charming
no dandy
intelligent
accomplished
endowed with
   sense of humour
masterful

---

[49] T. Davies, "Transports of Pleasure," in *Formations of Pleasure*, London: Routledge & Kegan Paul, 1983, p. 55.

HEROINES

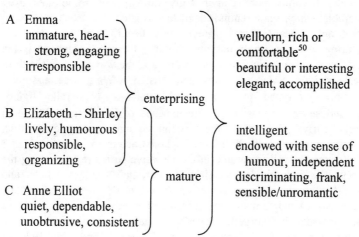

A  Emma
   immature, head-
     strong, engaging
   irresponsible

           enterprising

B  Elizabeth – Shirley
   lively, humourous
   responsible,
    organizing

           mature

C  Anne Elliot
   quiet, dependable,
   unobtrusive, consistent

wellborn, rich or
comfortable[50]
beautiful or interesting
elegant, accomplished

intelligent
endowed with sense of
  humour, independent
discriminating, frank,
sensible/unromantic

We know that Heyer aspired to literary dignity, despising fans who only read romance and swashbuckling adventure into her novels, while neglecting her accurate descriptions and humour. Hence, along with the more adventurous narrative mode of her earlier novels, she began to experiment with a vein of elegant comedy, which came to prevail. In the first phase, we discovered a prevalence of heroes and heroines of type A, and even where types B and C appear, they are less rounded than in later novels, and relatively subordinate to the sequence of events, whereas in the second phase, the neat interaction between psychological conflict and the situation arising from it, reverses this relationship. The A's have become extinct, and the B's and C's appear in matching couples, assuming more Austenian features. In fact, we can trace the prototypes of Georgette Heyer's heroes from the Scarlet Pimpernel and Mr Rochester, to Knightley by way of Darcy. Similarly, features of Shirley, Emma, Elizabeth Bennet, and Anne Elliot are discernable in her heroines.

---

[50] In the 28 novels analysed, there are only three poor heroines.

Just as the main characters undergo a clear development, the secondary characters become more convincingly drawn, and sometimes even memorable, which again reminds us of Jane Austen. Not only does Georgette Heyer rely heavily on Jane Austen's structuring, but she also relies on the same themes. Marriage is the central issue in romantic fiction generally, and the way it is dealt with in Heyer's writing owes much to Jane Austen. We notice a similar importance attributed to money and rank—no Cinderella figures here—and sense emphasized at the expense of sensibility. While in Heyer's early production, these connotations remain embryonic, conferring a touch of originality on stock characters and situations, later on they become well-integrated in the narrative structure, qualifying the characters as individuals, stressing the heroine's inner conflicts, and adding to the psychological tension between the male and female protagonists, of course within the limits of a comedy of manners.

An analysis of Georgette Heyer's language demonstrates both her craftsmanship in the construction of Regency, and the lack of conjunctural and cultural specificity inherent in her vicarious approach. The feeling of Regency is mainly conveyed through language; in fact, Heyer, who acknowledged Johnson's as well as Austen's influence on her style, created a coherent but completely artificial language.

In her reconstruction of a Regency language, the rhythm is the most successful feature. Georgette Heyer obtains an echo of Jane Austen by creating a measured pace with a sequence of subordinate clauses. With this pace and relative lack of metaphors and abstractions, the concrete neatness of most of Heyer's writing offers a plausible version of a neo-classic prose style. Straightforward and comparatively concise passages alternate with elaborate concatenations which have a graduating and accumulating function, often promoted by the use of passive constructions, negatives, relative clauses and strategically placed adverbs.

> The news that Mr Calverleigh had left Bath was brought to Sidney Place by Miss Butterbank on the following morning. She was a little disappointed to

> find that Miss Wendover was already aware of it, having received a brief note from him excusing himself from attending her rout-party; but as he had not divulged his reason for leaving Bath, his destination, or the means by which he proposed to travel, she was quickly able to repair two of these omissions. She was known, behind her back, as the Bath Intelligencer, but although she could tell Miss Wendover that Mr Calverleigh had set out on the London Mail Coach at five o'clock on the previous evening, she had not discovered the nature of his business, and could only advance a few conjectures (*Black Sheep* 1966: 157).

Dialogue constitutes a large proportion of each novel, enriched by wit and elegant comedy, which, however entertaining, eventually becomes idiosyncratic cliché.

> She was by now extremely angry, but for the second time she was obliged to choke back an involuntary giggle. She said unsteadily: "Talking to you is like—like talking to an eel!"
>
> "No, is it! I've never tried to talk to an eel. Isn't it a waste of time?"
>
> She choked. "Not such a waste of time as talking to you!"
>
> "You're surely not going to tell me that eels find you more entertaining than I do?" he said incredulously.
>
> That was rather too much for her: she did giggle, and was furious with herself for having done so.
>
> "That's better!" he said approvingly. (*Black Sheep* 1966: 44)

The sense of timing is accurate, but the incessant gurgling, chuckling

431

and giggling indulged in by female characters in response to the more sober twinkle in his eye or amused twitch at the corners of his mouth, which pepper their encounters, distract the reader from a basic shallowness. This is Heyer's own style, laced with twentieth century upper-class English, and patently not derived from Jane Austen. It has a double function within the narrative of stressing the underlying affinity between the main characters, which is one of Georgette Heyer's most important values, and emphasizing the very unsentimental treatment of the love theme.

The use of period lexicon and expressions help to convey the sense of Regency, embroidering a language which is entirely her own creation in this respect, too.

> "Take a damper!" Kit advised him. "I'm entirely at one with you in believing that Papa was grossly to blame; but dearly as I love Mama I can see how maddening she must have been to a man of his cut! You think he could have taught her to hold household: you may be right, but I doubt it. Now, don't fly up into the boughs again! None of that signifies today: it's past mending. What we have to do, Eve, is to find a way to tow her off Point Non-Plus now . . . ! (*False Colours* 1963: 212)

Even more bizarre epithets and expressions like "leg-shackled," "flummery," "pompous lobcock," "gone to pigs-and-whistles," "hagged," and so on, are easily understood in their context, while distancing the reader from everyday life very effectively.

Unlike traditional romantic fiction, historical or otherwise, irony plays an important role. Like Jane Austen, Heyer's irony is aimed at the social milieu: its social climbers, dandies, hypochondriacs, and the morbidly romantic. However, from the cultural viewpoint, Jane Austen was able to convey the subtlety of dialectical ambiguities in social values, whereas Georgette Heyer grafted her sense of humour on to her monolithic vision, thus producing a static and predictable set of values.

432

It is interesting to note how, in the end, her irony proves ineffectual in expressing an alternative ideological message, since the ironical treatment of "sensibility" in the subplot or in romantic minor characters, and the heroine's sensible and practical attitude only temporarily displace the emphasis on the romantic undercurrent. This contradiction which is easily discerned by careful readers well before the inevitable happy, if humorous ending, is evident, for instance, in *Black Sheep*, where the heroine, Abigail Wendover, ridicules the sentimentality of both her niece and her elder sister, while secretly waiting for the right man to turn up. Here she is considering the pros and cons of marrying one of her admirers.

> He would be a kind if unexciting husband; he enjoyed all the comforts and consequence of a large house and an easy fortune; and in marrying him she would remain within reach of Selina. On the other hand, no romance would attend such a marriage (*Black Sheep* 1966: 32).

Although Georgette Heyer's irony does not challenge her traditional values, it is irony, together with the neatness of her plots, which gives readers "a humane and civilised pleasure," in A. S. Byatt's words[51], and makes her writing rise above the average historical romance.

In spite of the atypicality when compared with most romantic fiction, Georgette Heyer's predictability of language, character, and situation gives her novels a static, one-dimensional and inward-looking quality. In fact, we have come to the conclusion that narrative elements were transposed from a text that Jane Austen never wrote, a compositive and sedimented mythical vision constructed by Janeite cult critics and readers who appreciated the novels mainly as comedies of manners, a longlasting phenomenon which Mudrick aptly described as "Gentle Janeism"[52]. The

---

[51] In the radio programme referred to in Note 5, [renumbered 40] above.

[52] Discussed in L. Trilling, "Emma and the legend of Jane Austen," in *Beyond Culture*, Harmondsworth: Penguin, 1977, p. 43.

problem is, that in the absence of lived culture as the basis of creative authenticity, an author who attempts to reconstruct the narrative modes of the past at whatever level, needs strategies which give his or her work an autonomy beyond simple imitation. Unlike John Fowles, for example, who in *The French Lieutenant's Woman* consciously invested his own operation of pasticheur with irony and ambiguity, Georgette Heyer never queried her method, and repeatedly used the same formula, however much she tried to refine it. Furthermore, the absence of social conflict and everyday routine in her static society provides a gratifying vehicle for escapist entertainment. Although escapism is a common denominator in all reading of romantic fiction, our interviews show that an educated reader finds aesthetic pleasure, entertainment, and even a sense of history in Heyer's detailed descriptions and dialogues. Readers do not feel ashamed of Georgette Heyer, as her elegance of style and structure tally with values which reach them surreptitiously, creating an escapist atmosphere at a different level from Barbara Cartland, for instance, who proves unreadable for the same readers.

In analogy with a Centre for Contemporary Cultural Studies analysis of Barbara Cartland[53], which relates her language and ideologies to elementary school English as it was taught from the '30s to the '50s and the domestic values it conveyed, we would suggest that Georgette Heyer's particular brand of "literary" English restates traditional British elitist ideologies of hierarchy, decorum and restraint in both personal and social relationships.

**Erik Jorgensen, "The Pattern 'in charge of' and Its Variants in Contemporary English" (in *English Studies* 67 [1986], p. 358 fn. 9):**

The definite article is never used when the pattern has the active function. . . . In the case of the alternative active pattern, *to have c. of*, a number of examples with the definite article have been registered, all of

---

[53] See S. Hall et al. (eds), *Culture, Media Language*, London: Hutchinson, 1980, pp. 256-268.

them, except one, from some of Georgette Heyer's "Regency novels," and occurring concurrently with cases without the article. For instance, in *Cousin Kate* (Pan, 1969), p. 44, we find: "She said that I was too young to have the charge of her grandchildren. . . ," but a moment later in the same conversation: "And as for me being too young to have charge of the children. . . "; at least three other examples with the definite article have been found in Georgette Heyer's "Regency novels." This is presumably to be understood as one of the many deliberate archaisms to be found in this branch of the writer's production. Elsewhere in contemporary English this usage seems to be extremely rare. Only one case has been registered in the present inquiry: "You had the charge of a young girl, a subnormal but very rich girl" (Agatha Christie, *Dead Man's Folly*, Pan, 1968, p. 185), whereas the usage seems to have been fairly common earlier on in the period of modern English: ". . .she was indeed not the mistress of this great house, but had only the charge of it" (Charles Lamb). . .


**Elaine Bander, "'What Fun!': Detection as Diversion" (in *Comic Crime*, ed. Earl F. Bargainnier. Bowling Green, OH: BGSU Popular Press, 1987, pp. 44-53):**

Detective fiction is always fun for readers. Why else do readers so cheerfully feed their addiction? And most detectives in literature, from Dupin and Holmes to Archer and Wolfe, whether amateur or professional, enjoy their vocation. Only in "What Fun!" detective fiction, however, do the *other* characters—official mourners, witnesses, suspects—respond to murder in their midst with gusto and delight. Whereas in traditional detective fiction most characters greet the discovery of a violent crime with expressions of horror and fear, either out of genuine conviction, respect for social conventions, or (in the case of the criminal) as protective colouring, the characters in a "What Fun!" novel rub their hands in gleeful anticipation of a puzzle.

These characters view crime and detection as a diversion at least on a par with tennis, cocktails, and fast cars. Their attitude, as well as their ironic, reflexive commentary on the detection process, increases our own delight in detection, so that readers, detectives, and suspects can all join together to exclaim, "What fun!"

Although elements of whatfunity can be found in many detective novels, the "What Fun!" school of detective fiction really belongs to a particular time and place: England between the wars. H. Douglas Thomson, the man who invented the label in his pioneering study of detective fiction, *Masters of Mystery* (1931), describes the rise of "What Fun!" detective fiction after the Great War:

> The "holiday spirit" permeated the underworld and the annals of crime. By this I mean not only that the detective story was written in a lighter vein as an August companion, but also that the characters of the detective story began to treat the murder just as light-heartedly as the reader, and their desire to solve the mystery did not arise from righteous indignation so much as from the crossword complex.[54]

"Detective-fever," of course, was first diagnosed by old Gabriel Betteridge in Wilkie Collins's *The Moonstone*, and the contagion has been around in one form or another ever since. Holmes and Watson were no strangers to the affliction, nor were their scores of imitators. Then just before the First World War, E. C. Bentley wrote *Trent's Last Case*, which came close to being a "What Fun!" novel. The hero, Philip Trent, could qualify as a "What Fun!" detective, for he's an irreverent amateur (a serious painter and occasional journalist). When his publisher asks him "to do some work" by investigating the death of Sigsbee Manderson, Trent replies, "Some play, you mean."[55] He takes the job for a lark, then loses his detachment when he falls in love with the lovely widow. But

---

[54] *Masters of Mystery: A Study of the Detective Story* (London: Collins, 1931), p. 72.
[55] *Trent's Last Case*, in *Three Famous Murder Novels* (New York: Modern Library, 1941), p. 247.

while Trent is jolly and unconventional, at least until he becomes emotionally involved in the case, the other characters take the business-at-hand in dead earnest. Certainly no one but Trent looks upon the murder investigation as "play."

The distinctive qualities of "What Fun!" detective fiction do not emerge until the post-war publication of A. A. Milne's *The Red House Mystery* (1922). Indeed, this novel gave the sub-genre its name when Thomson wrote:

> *The Red House Mystery* is a fine example of the "Lord, what fun!" type of detective story where detection is the amateur's recipe against rainy day ennui, and the murder is acclaimed as a happy stroke of Providence.[56]

In *The Red House Mystery* the murder of Mark Ablett is solved not by a policeman or professional detective, but by Antony Gillingham, a clean-cut, eccentric young gentleman who has chosen to work variously as a *valet de chambre*, a newspaper reporter, a waiter, and a shop-assistant. He becomes a detective through pure chance. One summer day he leaves a train at Woodham "because he liked the look of the station." Discovering that he is near The Red House, Stanton, where his young friend Bill Beverley is staying, he decides to walk over and call, thus arriving in time to help discover a murder. Since he is between jobs, Antony takes up the new profession of "private sleuthhound." (No one, it should be mentioned, has offered to pay him a fee.) As an outsider, he can "consider the matter with an unbiased mind." To begin his investigation, Antony questions Bill closely about the household.

---

[56] *Masters*, p. 164. Earl F. Bargainnier generously attributed the term to me in his article, "The Dozen Mysteries of Georgette Heyer," *Clues: A Journal of Detection*, 3:2 (Fall/Winter 1982), 30. In fact I took it from Howard Haycraft, *Murder for Pleasure* (New York: Appleton-Century, 1941), p. 151, who was in turn citing Thomson's study.

> Bill looked at him eagerly.
> "I say, are you being the complete detective?"
> "Well, I wanted a new profession," smiled the other.
> "What fun! I mean," he corrected himself apologetically, "one oughtn't to say that . . . ."[57]

Of course one oughtn't—but one does, over and over in "What Fun!" novels of the Golden Age.

The detective novels of Georgette Heyer are typically "What Fun!," beginning with her second, *Death in the Stocks* in 1935, and continuing beyond the interwar period with her final detective novel, *Detection Unlimited* (1953).[58] Many of her characters express the "What Fun!" sentiment outright. In *A Blunt Instrument*, for instance, languid Neville Fletcher remarks, "Aren't we having fun," as he trails a policeman around the grounds of his murdered uncle's house (15). In the same novel, when detective-novelist Sally Drew suggests blowing up the dead man's safe, Neville exclaims, "What lovely fun!" (30). In *They Found Him Dead* young Timothy Harte speculates on the possibility of a murder happening in his grand-uncle's house. "'Of course, I know there won't be one really, but all the same, it 'ud be jolly good fun if there was,' said Mr. Harte wistfully" (18). Timothy is wrong; two murders ensue, and Timothy, "his blue eyes sparkling with pleasurable anticipation," asks, "I

---

[57] *The Red House Mystery* (New York: Dutton, 1922), p. 58.
[58] The editions of Heyer's novels cited in this essay are listed below, preceded by the original date of publication. All quotations will be cited in the text using, where necessary, the abbreviation given after the entry:

> 1935 *Death in the Stocks* (Granada, 1963)
> 1936 *Behold, Here's Poison* (Granada, 1963)
> 1938 *A Blunt Instrument* (Bantam, 1973) (Blunt)
> 1938 *They Found Him Dead* (Bantam, 1970)
> 1939 *No Wind of Blame* (Granada, 1963)
> 1941 *Envious Casca* (Panther, 1961)
> 1953 *Detection Unlimited* (Granada, 1961) (Detection)

say, do you think there's a Hidden Killer in the house?" (165).

In *Envious Casca* even characters who feel conventional distress at
the violent death in their family are touched by detective-fever. Paula
Herriard says to sardonic Mathilda Clare, "Do you wonder which of us
did it?" Mathilda admits that she does, and Paula adds:

> "I know!  Ah, but it is interesting, isn't it?
> Confess!"
> "No, it's vile."
> "Oh—vile! . . . If you like!  But psychologically
> speaking, isn't there a fascination?" (110-111)

Nearly all of the villagers in *Detection Unlimited* share Terrible
Timmy's ghoulish interest in murder and detection. Thus Mrs. Haswell
and Miss Patterdale "were agreed that although it was disagreeable to
persons of their generation to have a murder committed in their midst, it
was very nice for the children to have something to occupy them . . ."
(89). When proper Major Midgeholme remarks, very properly, "Sad
business, this," cynical Gavin Plenmeller corrects him: "'What a
mendacious thing to say!' remarked Gavin. 'When we are all perfectly
delighted!' " (82).

Agatha Christie also practiced Golden Age whatfunity, less in her
Hercule Poirot books than in those novels detailing the adventures of
high-spirited, high-born young ladies. . . .

[Dorothy L. Sayers] was practically a charter member of the "What
Fun!" school. [Lord Peter] Wimsey, who makes his first appearance in
*Whose Body?* (1923), is a cross between quotation-spouting Trent and
Ass-About-Town Bertie Wooster, at least in the early novels. . . .

Only later, beginning with *Strong Poison* (1930), does Wimsey
express ambivalence about his role of detective, an ambivalence which
haunts him for several more novels while he courts Harriet Vane. In
*Strong Poison*, for example, Wimsey again has a "personal interest," as
Bunter had called it in *Clouds*, for he has fallen in love with the murder
suspect, Harriet Vane, and must save her from the gallows. For the first
time in his life, however, he recognizes that what has been "fun" for

himself has been a life-or-death matter for others concerned: "I'm beginning to dislike this job of getting people hanged. It's damnable for their friends . . ." (92).

Sayers deliberately transformed the character of Wimsey from a one-dimensional comic instrument ideally suited for "What Fun!" detection to a complex human being, whose flippant wit in the early novels is retroactively cast as a protective pose, a mask worn to disguise a vulnerable sensibility. In subsequent novels like *Have His Carcase, The Nine Tailors, Gaudy Night,* and *Busman's Honeymoon,* Peter Wimsey and Harriet Vane continue to discuss the ethics of detection; eventually both Peter and Harriet accept the legitimacy of his job—but by this time his "What Fun!" days are behind him, and Sayers's fiction has lost most if not all of its "What Fun!" characteristics.

Heyer's output, meanwhile, remained faithful to the "What Fun!" spirit; her last detective novel, *Detection Unlimited,* was as full of whatfunity as the early *Death in the Stocks*; her characters exhibited the "What Fun!" attitude that criminal investigation is an amusing pastime and that an ounce of cynical wit is worth a pound of trite moralizing. In short, just as the detective problem in the novels frustrates readers' plot expectations, so too the comedy in the novels works by reversing the conventional pieties readers expect in detective fiction.

Gavin Plenmeller and Neville Fletcher are typical of Heyer's unconventional young men, languid, even epicene, whose witty reversals of conventional attitudes sound as though they had wandered off the set of Oscar Wilde's *The Importance of Being Earnest.* Their lives are a series of poses, and they view murder as high theatre. This decadent aestheticism is generally innocent, meant merely to baffle and disconcert the other players, but it can also conceal guilt. The murderer, of course, is by definition playing a role: each of the other characters may appear guilty from time to time, but he or she alone is guilty, yet he or she must always act the role of the innocent; sometimes that role can mean acting the part of an innocent person who pretends to be guilty for the theatrical value, or the fun of it. Confusing? Of course. Since Golden Age detective fiction depends on bluffing readers, Heyer's readers cannot dismiss the whatfunity of her characters as a mere pose; it might also be a most deadly serious disguise.

In *Death in the Stocks*, for example, Antonia and Kenneth Vereker disdain to pretend grief for their murdered half-brother or to disguise their relief at his death. Indeed, they cheerfully assess the evidence against themselves, bristling with indignation at the suggestion that they might not be capable of murder. Their more conventional cousin Giles recognizes what he calls their "purely intellectual attitude," which baffles the police and annoys Kenneth's resolutely genteel fiancée, Violet—ironically so, since she is in fact the murderess. Thus the one character determined to observe the niceties of social hypocrisy is also the one who has committed murder.

Kenneth, a painter, views the murder aesthetically; "I won't have seedy strangers butting in on a family crime. It lowers the whole tone of the thing, which has, up to now, been highly artistic, and in some ways even precious" (85). His perspective is similar to De Quincey's in *Murder Considered as one of the Fine Arts*:

> Everything in this world has two handles. Murder,
> for instance, may be laid hold of by its moral handle
> (as it generally is in the pulpit and at the old Bailey),
> and that, I confess, is its weak side; or it may be
> treated *aesthetically*, as the Germans call it—that is,
> in relation to good taste. [59]

This "aesthetic" view is of course the view of detective fiction readers and writers; it is also the view of many characters in "What Fun!" books.

Typical of this aesthetic detachment in Heyer's novels are Neville Fletcher and Sally Drew. When Neville announces his uncle's murder, Sally says to him:

> "You'd better tell me all about it. It might be

---

[59] Thomas De Quincey, *On Murder Considered as One of the Fine Arts*, Vol. XIII, *The Collected Works of Thomas De Quincey*, Ed. David Masson, 14 vols. (Edinburgh: Adam and Charles Black, 1890), p. 13.

good copy."
"What a lovely thought!" said Neville. "Ernie has
not died in vain."
"I've always wanted to be in on a real murder,"
remarked Sally thoughtfully (*Blunt*, 21).

When told that Ernie was killed by the eponymous "blunt
instrument," Sally nods "with the air of a connoisseur." She tells
Neville, "I hope you get pinched for the murder," and he replies, "It
would be awfully interesting" (21). The two compare their real selves
unfavourably to the resourceful characters in Sally's books. They enjoy
the murder in the same spirit as they would enjoy reading—or writing—a
work of detective fiction. By the end of the novel, however, Neville has
completely lost interest in the investigation. He doesn't even wait to hear
the name of the murderer. Newly engaged to Sally, he tells the
astounded Inspector Hannasyde, "I can't be bothered with murder cases
now. I'm going to be married" (246). Clearly *his* handle on murder is
aesthetic, not moral. Even Sergeant Hemingway partly shares this
aesthetic view of crime. Hemingway wants an *artistic* case: "I don't like
the setup. Ordinary, that's what it is. . . . Give me something a bit
*recherché* and I'm right on to it" (34).

In *Detection Unlimited* Heyer really lets loose. The entire village of
Thornden succumbs to detective-fever after the murder of the unpopular
Sampson Warrenby: hence the title. Everyone has a different theory,
and amateur detection becomes everyone's favourite pastime, quickly
eclipsing tennis:

The murder of Sampson Warrenby naturally formed
the sole topic for conversation. . . . Abby said simply
that she had never hoped to realize an ambition to be,
as she phrased it, mixed up in a murder-case. Miss
Patterdale . . . very handsomely said that she was glad
it had happened while she was there to enjoy it. (46)

Here the narrator shares the "What Fun!" outlook of her characters, adding that the murder "naturally" was on everyone's lips and that Miss Patterdale's comment was a handsome one. This satiric inversion of conventional values (one would expect a well-bred maiden aunt to apologize if violent crime marred her niece's visit) is typical of "What Fun!" literature in general, and Heyer's books in particular.

In Heyer's novels, however, the "What Fun!" attitude is not always a genuine expression of cynicism, aestheticism, or satire. It can mask more serious emotions, even blood guilt. In *Detection Unlimited*, for example, Gavin Plenmeller appears to be yet one more of Heyer's clever, cynical, languid young men who scorn social and moral hypocrisy, whereas in fact he is a murderer who tries to divert genuine suspicion from himself by deliberately calling attention to the evidence against himself, such as his lack of an alibi. During one of the general discussions of the case which occupy the villagers throughout the novel, Plenmeller says: "*Surely* the police cannot overlook my claims to the post of chief suspect? I write detective novels, I have a lame leg, and I drove my half-brother to suicide. What more do the police want?" (49). As he anticipates, the others put his remarks down to plain bad taste. The idea that he could be telling the truth is never seriously entertained. He is just one of the villagers making his peculiar brand of fun out of the fortuitous murder, or so they think. So he wants them to think.

It is rare, however, to discover a murderer lurking beneath a "What Fun!" façade. More commonly, a character whose flippancy and cynicism is (at least in part) a pose is disguising more benign emotions, such as fear lest the police wrongly suspect himself, or concern for another character, or even atavistic horror of death. When Neville Fletcher first learns of his uncle's death, for example, he remarks casually to Sergeant Glass, "I don't like murders. So inartistic, don't you think?," thus adopting the aesthetic pose, but "it was plain that under his flippancy he was shaken" (*Blunt*, 5). Later he tells Sergeant Hemingway, "You mightn't think it, but I'm frightened of you. Don't be misled by my carefree manner: it's a mask assumed to hide my inward perturbation" (114). Kenneth Vereker, too, plays a game with police in *Death in the Stocks*. Like Plenmeller, he calls attention to the case against himself. His sister Antonia recognizes the method to Kenneth's madness: the police don't know how to take him and hesitate to arrest him partly because of his unsettling attitude.

Guy Matthews, weak and dependent, tries a "What Fun!" pose in *Behold, Here's Poison*, but he has trouble carrying it off. After his initial questioning by Detective-Superintendent Hannasyde, Guy remarks to the household, "Aunt was scared. . . , but personally I found it rather amusing" (47). His next remarks, however, belie his detachment. His cousin Randall's flippancy is more effective, because rooted in a more genuine cynicism. After startling Hemingway and Hannasyde by admitting that he, as heir, had a strong motive for wishing his uncle dead, Randall adds, "Now do let us understand each other! There's not the least need for you to ask me careful questions. I shall be delighted to answer anything you choose to ask me. In fact, I'm burning to assist you to track down the murderer" (63). Ultimately, it is Randall who successfully does the tracking, not in a spirit of "What Fun!" but in order to suppress the fact that his uncle had been a blackmailer. Randall's pose, moreover, unlike Guy's, remains consistent. When asked if he will attend the inquest, he yawns, "If nothing more amusing offers, I might" (90). Clearly, though, he is aware of the stakes. When congratulated upon inheriting his uncle's fortune, he replies "in a bored voice" that "It puts strange ideas into the heads of policemen, . . . and that, though amusing up to a point, is apt to become a nuisance" (120).

Stephen Herriard in *Envious Casca* also adopts a casual "What Fun!" pose, conscious of the effect he creates. When asked, "Who did it?", he replies, "'I've no idea!'. . . He took a cigarette from the box on the table and lit it. 'Interesting problem, isn't it?' he drawled." Stephen then looks around "in malicious amusement at the various countenances turned towards him" (57). His sister Paula's histrionics are instinctive, for she's an actress. Her brother, on the other hand, is conscious that, as his dead uncle's heir and the one to discover the body, he is the most likely suspect. His casual attitude masks anxiety lest police suspicion fall upon himself.

Indeed, with so many characters playing roles, consciously or unconsciously, it's not surprising that murder and detection are often viewed as mere backdrops for theatre. Sergeant Carsethorn, commenting to Chief-Inspector Hemingway on Gavin Plenmeller's perverse behaviour, says it perfectly: "Anyone would have thought the whole thing was a play, and we was having drinks between the acts, and talking it over" (*Detection*, 59).

In *No Wind of Blame* Vickie Fanshawe is continually role-playing and isn't above casting the police into subordinate roles in her little dramas. After goading Inspector Hemingway to declare her an official suspect, she casts herself "upon the maternal bosom" and plays out a scene for her mother's benefit, accusing her mother's suitor of implicating her. She has a good time acting, and incidentally prevents her mother from marrying a fortune-hunter. For Vickie, her stepfather's murder is a stroke of good fortune, ridding her mother of an unsatisfactory husband and providing herself with scope for her talents.

Perhaps the best explanation for the "What Fun!" pose is provided by Dame Agatha in *Why Didn't They Ask Evans?*. Bobby's conservative clergyman father says of the dying stranger whom Bobby discovers, "What a tragedy!" and he deplores Bobby's own flippant tone. Bobby cannot explain what he really feels, but thinks, "If his father couldn't see that, of course, you joked about a thing because you had felt badly about it—well, he couldn't see it!" (14).

As many commentators have pointed out, Golden Age detective fiction flourished partly because the trauma of the Great War left ordinary, educated readers hungry for a literature drained of profound emotions, a literature which would assuage doubts and reinforce social prejudices, at a time when modernism was stripping "straight" literature of all its familiar landmarks. Detective fiction filled this need. At the same time, the post-War generation could not think and feel as their fathers had done. "What Fun!" detective fiction allowed such readers the best of both worlds: the surface iconoclasm of its characters and the reassurance of a world in which all problems have rational solutions and all evil-doers eventually pay for their crimes. By allowing the reader's own "What Fun!" attitude into the detective story, "What Fun!" authors made explicit the comic world-view implicit in all detective fiction.

**Victoria Nichols and Susan Thompson, *Silk Stalkings. When Women Write of Murder. A Survey of Series Characters Created by Women Authors in Crime and Mystery Fiction* (Berkeley: Black Lizard Books, 1988, p. 38):**

HANNASYDE and HEMINGWAY
1935-1953  8 books  English
Georgette Heyer

The series featuring Superintendent Hannasyde and Sergeant Hemingway can best be described as drawing room crime. The suspects are invariably related to one another and the scene is the country home or London house of a wealthy individual or family. The related suspects are usually eccentric. The heir may disdain his anticipated wealth or be brusque to the point of rudeness toward his benefactor. Other members may be vague and flighty or their nerves so highly strung that when the crime—always murder—is discovered, they dissolve into tears and remain prostrate for most of the rest of the novel, except for meals. There is a liberal dose of romance, as a rule, between two people who haven't the slightest idea that they are attracted to one another. They spit and snap at each other but the threat of incarceration for one of the pair brings out the other's true feelings. The unknown beloved is defended and at the end true love is recognized for what it is and the happy couple are united.

The first four books feature the detecting duo of Hannasyde and his sergeant, Hemingway. The last four have Hemingway, now promoted to inspector himself, on his own. Hannasyde's appearance is limited to brief conversations over the phone with either his former sergeant or the chief constable of the locality which requires expert assistance. These detectives are personifications of the Yard and their personalities rarely intrude upon the case. They are pleasant and have great appreciation for a good lie. Hemingway tends to favor a psychological approach to suspect and victim alike. His flair leads him toward the belief that when a case seems most hopelessly confused, it is near its conclusion. Hannasyde is more prosaic and gives Hemingway's theories short shrift.

Both men are methodical though not to the point of tedium. Their lives outside the investigation seem nonexistent.

Locked rooms, missing weapons, and airtight alibis for all potential suspects provide the necessary bafflement. The solution requires some solid knowledge on the author's part of pathological motivations and infernal devices. These stories are neat puzzles, in the classical form, with the emphasis on character and well-devised plot. The victim is well out of the way and the perpetrator deserves all he gets in consequence of his crime. Love is requited and all ends happily.

**Teresa Chris, *Georgette Heyer's Regency England* (Illustrations by Arthur Barbosa. London: Sidgwick & Jackson, 1989, pp. 6-7):**

For more than fifty years, millions of readers worldwide have enjoyed the Regency romances of Georgette Heyer. Her audience continues to grow with each generation as her fans, old and new, reread the novels, appreciating the sheer elegance and wit of her prose style, and relating to the wonderfully vivid characters who stay alive to us long after the last page is turned.

Georgette Heyer created her own special Regency world based on an exact knowledge of the period. We, the readers, can escape completely into this world, as she vividly conjures up the mores of the time, the preoccupations of the people, the language in which they conversed, and the niceties of their social intercourse. It is a world which is fascinating to us, even today, because such severe order was imposed and everybody knew their place. The "ton" set the standard, from the select dances at Almacks to the propriety of racing down to Brighton in a curricle. The term "the ton," from the French word meaning everything that is fashionable, had come into usage in England in the latter half of the eighteenth century and by the Regency period it denoted the cream of society. Georgette Heyer's appealing characters are bound by the conventions of this world but more often delight us by rebelling against it.

Georgette Heyer died in 1974, so there is a finite number of her

Regency romances that we can enjoy; we are, in fact, lucky to have as many as we do. She was an extremely private, if prolific, person and didn't, outside her books, spend much time commenting on the world she had created. Of the over fifty novels which Georgette Heyer wrote, twenty-four are set in the Regency period. She was a stickler for accuracy and compiled copious notebooks full of details of Regency life, including drawings of items of dress and the different carriages used in the period. She meticulously researched her facts, and knew, for example, every turnpike on the Great North Road. The odd, but memorable, expressions her characters used were culled from her extensive reading and jotted down for future use.

The contemporary detail enhances the credibility of the novels and increases our pleasure in them, but it is the characters who give the novels the unique life which makes her readers lifelong fans. Georgette Heyer's heroines are often young and spirited, appealing in their inventiveness, and for falling into social scrapes from which they constantly need to be rescued. In the later novels, however, a new maturity is seen. The heroines are older and wiser, "no longer in their first bloom," often financially independent. They confront the hero on a more equal footing and the relationships which develop are surprisingly akin to those that men and women experience today. Georgette Heyer brings them all convincingly to life but unfortunately these characters live only between the covers of each book.

There is however one element in her books that is real and still exists for us today and that is the settings where her characters fell in love, strolled to the library, met the Prince Regent, sheltered from the rain, or fought their duels. London, Brighton, Bath and other locations all around England are rich in Regency heritage and hence rich in memories for fans who can recall each nuance of their heroines' romances or adventures. This book will explore the settings of that world so that the reader may once again enjoy parts of the novels in the places where they actually happened.

So often, whilst in the street, by raising the eyes above the modern frontages and switching our perception, we can plunge ourselves into Georgette Heyer's Regency England, and experience her world anew. In some places, like Bath, it is even possible to have afternoon tea and to listen to a quartet in the Pump Room while remembering how Abby who was "neither in her first bloom" nor "an accredited beauty" agreed to take a stroll about the room with Miles Calverleigh, the Black Sheep of the title, allowing herself to be beguiled by his iconoclastic remarks and droll wit.

Whilst many of the settings are still the same as they were over one hundred and fifty years ago, it is, in some cases, only a name that will connect us with a familiar scene. Where possible a number of gentle walking tours have been included in this book, pointing out the Regency landmarks mentioned in the novels, and recalling the most romantic, exciting or funny scenes that happened there.

*Georgette Heyer's Regency England* will give pleasure to anyone who has read Georgette Heyer's work and wanted more.


**Helen Taylor, *Scarlett's Women: "Gone With the Wind" and Its Female Fans* (New Brunswick, N. J.: Rutgers University Press, 1989, pp. 204-205):**

. . . As with romances, critics have long scorned those historical novels popular with women and little serious attention has been paid to writers who have been staples of women's reading, such as Georgette Heyer, Norah Lofts, and Jean Plaidy. In recent years, however, feminist critics have turned their attention to historical novels and films in order to understand their power over women. They have shown that the roles female characters play in such historical romances—such as mistresses, wives, mothers, or daughters of famous men, confined to the margins of major affairs of state, wars, or kingships—assure readers that "the personal *matters*," and "nothing is personal which is not also *social*."[60]

---

[60] Lillian S. Robinson, "On Reading Trash," in *Sex, Class, and Culture*, New York and London, Methuen, 1986, pp. 221; "Towards a Feminist Cultural Studies: Middle-Class Femininity and Fiction in Post Second

Intimate relationships, family structures, and women's influence (albeit at various removes from the centre of power) have significance for historical events and transformations.


**Marlo L. Newton, "Romancing the Tome: The Novels of Georgette Heyer" (abstract of M.A. thesis in History, University of Melbourne, Australia, 1991):**

Romance novels have been dismissed as homogenous formulaic texts, suitable only to while away an idle hour. "Romancing the Tome" contends that there are specific categories of romance, as evidenced by modern booksellers, who distinguish between both genre—e.g. Regency, Historical, Contemporary, Young Adult—and degree of eroticism. Further, the argument runs that certain individual authors are the original creators of a particular style, which is later so imitated that it becomes a genre in its own right. Readers of romance and their detractors both know what they mean by a "Barbara Cartland" romance, or a "Mills and Boon" scenario.

In the specific case under examination in this thesis, the discussion is of the author Georgette Heyer. Her published work spans from 1921 until 1975, and reprints of her works are still available. She is most famous for her Regency romances, which form approximately half of her creative output.

The thesis examines why Heyer began writing, and why a twentieth century author wrote mainly of the Regency period in England. It contends that Heyer grew progressively appalled by the societal changes of her own era, and used the historical novel to create a more ordered and mannered past. In the process, she defined what we understand to be "Regency" in manners, morals and atmosphere.

While Heyer's work is a byword for historical accuracy of detail—the coats, houses and carriages of the beau monde all meticulously

---

World War Britain," *Englisch-Amerikanische Studien* 1 (1987), pp. 58-72.

correct—her universe is an artificial creation, where the gentry controls society, vulgarity is punished and heroes and heroines find true love allied to class values. Heyer's Regency may bear little resemblance to the historical period of 1788-1820, which was a turbulent and controversial era, yet her enduring achievement was the creation of a literary sub-genre, the Regency Romance.

The thesis discusses the worth of romance fiction, its place in social history, and the developmental changes of the genre. It then moves on to Heyer's created world, discussing the parallels between post WWI England and the Regency, and explores the books for class consciousness. Finally, the thesis examines the heroes and heroines of Heyer's novels, with respect to gender roles, and the place of women.

The major conclusions drawn are that Heyer has an enduring appeal that is due to the quality of her writing. She created the Regency genre and used it to write what her biographer Jane Aiken Hodge called "honourable escape" fiction. "Romancing the Tome" attempts to explore the complexity of vision possible in an individual author, the presentation of an ideology of romance, and the place of a popular writer in a discourse on history.

**Kathleen Gilles Seidel, "Judge Me by the Joy I Bring," in *Dangerous Men and Adventurous Women. Romance Writers on the Appeal of the Romance* (ed. Jayne Anne Krentz. Philadelphia: University of Pennsylvania, 1992, pp. 175-176):**

. . . In real life, people respond to loveliness in complex ways. Some become conciliatory and fawning; others become defensive. This doesn't happen in a romance. . . .

The fantasy, I believe, is not to be beautiful, but to have an identity for yourself that is not caught up in your appearance. Romance heroines rarely know how beautiful they really are. This isn't because they are too stupid to look in a mirror or too low in self-esteem to understand what they see there, but because they are presenting the fantasy of being something other than body, of not having any of this cosmetic-

451

advertisement stuff matter.

My editors at Harlequin used to joke that they could always tell when a man had written a manuscript. Somewhere in the first fifty pages the heroine undressed in front of a mirror. . .and liked what she saw. That sounds like a good idea, having a body that you can admire when you are buck-naked in your own bathroom. But what clearly seems a better idea, a more appealing fantasy, is to walk by that mirror and *simply not care.*

One heroine in romance literature who knows exactly what she look like—and she is the homeliest of them all—is Jenny Chawleigh of Georgette Heyer's *A Civil Contract.* She's "already plump, and would probably become stout in later life" [New York: Ace Books, 1961, p. 57]. What makes her such an appealing heroine is that she utterly accepts her appearance. She chuckles at how dreadful she will look in her Court dress. She knows that she has many other abilities and—this is crucial—*values herself for them.* She and the physical accident of her short neck and mouse-colored hair don't have much to do with one another.

This fantasy is not limited to the romance genre. Sue Grafton, Sara Paretsky, and the other creators of the hard-boiled female detectives are also presenting heroines without much anxiety about their physical appearances. . . .

Kay Mussell and Tania Modleski, feminist scholars, blame repetitive reading on the ending of the book.[*] The fantasy of the happy ending, they assert, is precarious, even false, as it is based on "the failure of a patriarchy to imagine a wider vision of women's lives" and "the insistent denial of the reality of male hostility towards women." The ending, although it provides temporary relief, is thus inherently unsatisfying, "so unsatisfying that the story must be told over and over." "Readers must

---

[*] Rather than reproducing several footnotes, I simply refer the reader to Tania Modleski, *Loving With a Vengeance: Mass-Produced Fantasies for Women* (Hamden, CT: Archon Books, 1982, pp. 57, 111), and to Kay Mussell, *Fantasy and Reconciliation: Contemporary Formulas of Women's Romantic Fiction* (Westport, CT: Greenwood Press, 1984, pp. 164, 184.

constantly return to the same text (to texts which are virtually the same) in order to be reconvinced." The endings have so little to do with life that they are believable only fleetingly, and the desperate reader must seize another book to try to recapture that brief—and false—pleasure.

I don't dispute the authenticity of Mussell's and Modleski's reading experience; the pleasure they feel at the endings of the books may well be undercut by a profound political uneasiness. I don't feel that way. In a well-done book, the happy ending becomes for me a satisfying, convincing, imaginatively realized fantasy. And I don't think that the habit of repeated readings necessarily proves that hundreds of thousands of American women read like them, not me.

Their argument, by focusing only on the political message of the ending, ignores the fact that the pleasures of fantasies pervade the book. It is fun to read, early in Georgette Heyer's *The Devil's Cub* [sic; London: Pan Books 1969, pp. 62, 77-80], the Marquis of Vidal's cool resolve to race his curricle to Newmarket immediately after fighting a duel. It is even more fun to follow the restrained, ironic language in which his ducal father afterwards banishes him to the Continent. Romances are full of delicious moments, some funny, some heartwarming, some sensually evocative. That's why I reread *The Devil's Cub* every few years. I am not desperately seeking out the ending so that it will assure me that it is possible to be happy within our patriarchal culture's institutions. I am relishing the book's entire experience with the ongoing accumulation of fantasy's pleasures, small and large.

**Dan Crawford, "Crimes of the Heart" (*The Armchair Detective* 25, Summer 1992, pp. 360-66):**

The mystery novels of Georgette Heyer (1902-1974), once dismissed as formulaic and flippant, are now in print again and gaining some respect. Appreciation of her sense of humor and character portrayal are on the rise, and her detectives, Superintendent Hannasyde and Inspector Hemingway, bid fair to be admitted into a minor pantheon of favorite sleuths.

Most critics will mention, in passing, that Georgette Heyer was more famous for her historical novels, particularly those set in England's Regency period, the second decade of the nineteenth century. As a matter of fact, Georgette Heyer and Barbara Cartland, between them, carved out a new subgenre of the paperback romance: the Regency romance, which is now published by the boxcar-loads. Georgette Heyer is to the Regency what Agatha Christie is to the English cozy and Babe Ruth is to the home run: the standard against whom all newcomers are measured. There were those who practiced these things before and after the magic names; some were better and some worse, but Heyer, like Christie, is the icon in her field. (I don't know what this makes of Barbara Cartland. The John Creasey of Regencies? The Erle Stanley Gardner? Perhaps the Carolyn Keene.)

There seems to be something of a wall, though, between the mysteries and the Regencies. Even the excellent article "A Janeite's Life of Crime" by James P. Devlin (*TAD* 17:3), in covering Heyer's mysteries, slights the Regency novels, giving extended coverage to only one, *The Talisman Ring.* And, if mystery critics pass over the romances, romance aficionados tend to bypass the mysteries: the mysteries were mere playthings, plotted by her husband and tossed off by Heyer to fill the time between important books. (According to Jane Aiken Hodge's biography of Heyer, the author considered her medieval novels, particularly the massive one left unfinished at her death, to be her "important" work. There's always something.)

S. A. Van Dine and Raymond Chandler, among others, felt that there was no room for romance in the mystery. Even if that is true, the reverse is not. Every good romance novel needs at least two plots: Plot A, which is about the hero and heroine falling in love, and Plot B, which can be anything so long as it distracts the hero and heroine from Plot A. It can be a battle to save the family farm, a romance between secondary characters, a hostile takeover of someone else's business. Or it can be a mystery.

Georgette Heyer took a mystery plot into her historical romances several times and added suspense thereby. Of course, if you [sic] mind works that way, any romance can be considered a suspense story: will she or won't she, and with whom? A mystery, however, generally demands a crime, and, in the words of Van Dine, "hidden forces that are not revealed until the dénouement." The Regency mysteries have these, though they seldom include detectives. There will be the occasional character who investigates clues and tracks down information, but these efforts are occasional and rarely extend the length of the book.

The novel closest to a detective tale is probably *The Toll Gate* [sic] (1954), which is something of an inverted mystery: not a whodunit, but a what-was-done? John Staples, like the reader, knows at the outset that the two undesirables, Henry Stornaway and Nathaniel Coate, are up to something. And, since this is fiction and not mere history, the reader can be certain that it is no coincidence that Ned Brean, the keeper of the toll gate, is missing. But did two men come from London to Yorkshire simply to kill a gatekeeper? If so, why? If not, where is Brean? Matters are complicated by a mysterious stranger, one Stogumber, who is ambling about just a little too casually to be merely a tourist.

Some of Heyer's best work is on display here. There is a tall, self-reliant heroine, a friendly highwayman, a marriage by night in a dying man's bedroom, and an engaging scamp of a boy. (Heyer shows no evidence of any interest at all in small girls, but schoolboys frequently pop up in her stories.) And, which is rare in her largely nonviolent books, there is a chill corpse, a violent tussle in a dark and freezing cavern, and two more deaths.

*The Talisman Ring* (1936) is more of a romp. The only corpse in this story was buried years before the story begins. Sir Matthew Plunkett's mistake was winning a medieval talisman ring at cards. Three men might have killed to get the ring; the case against one of them was so strong that he fled the country. The two remaining men gather to attend the deathbed of Sylvester, Lord Lavenham. Sylvester is one of the most engaging of Georgette Heyer's domestic tyrants. She has had an amazing variety of them, male and female, detestable to marginally lovable.)[sic] Sylvester has decided to provide for his granddaughter Eustacie, a French refugee, by marrying her to the phlegmatic Sir Tristram Shield.

Eustacie is much younger and more romantic than Sir Tristram and, after incurring one too many pragmatic remarks from him, decides to run away. She runs into her cousin, Ludovic Lavenham, who has become a smuggler since he left England. Learning that Sylvester is dead, and that he is now Lord Lavenham, he resolves to discover who really did kill Sir Matthew Plunkett. He thinks that Sir Tristram, who collects medieval rings, is the man; the other suspect, his cousin Basil, always believed in his innocence, while Sir Tristram simply bustled him from the country.

But Ludovic is wounded by anti-smuggling forces and must flee to an inn, where he and Eustacie are befriended by the remarkably calm Sarah Thane. She is not at all disturbed by the presence of a wounded smuggler and agrees to help them investigate Sir Tristram. Tristram, however, arrives and prevents Ludovic's arrest. And at this point, the further progress of the story must be as clear to the reader as it is to Sarah Thane. Sir Tristram will marry Sarah and Ludovic will wed Eustacie. All that remains (and this takes nearly two-thirds of the book) is to find out what Basil did with the missing ring.

*The Talisman Ring* can hardly be considered strictly a Regency romance, as it is set just after the death of Louis XVI, more than a decade before the Regency. *The Masqueraders* (1928) reaches back still further, to the years just after the debacle at Colloden and the last gasp of hope for a return of the Stuart monarchy. Jacobites, the fleeing supporters of the wrong side, are hunted down and hanged for treason.

There is romance and adventure aplenty in *The Masqueraders*; many of Heyer's earliest works are straight swashbucklers of high quality. But at the core of this one is a mystery, a Mr. Colney. Mr. Colney is a Jacobite. But he is not being Mr. Colney at the moment; just now he claims to be Lord Tremaine of Barham, a long-lost brother of the late Viscount Tremaine. The reader knows that this is merely the latest in a series of Mr. Colney's identities. He has had many names, and played many games and, though he is magnificent, he is simply a con man. Can he convince the law, as well as a suspicious Rensley, who will be Lord Tremaine if this claimant is proved an imposter, that he is the missing heir, without revealing any of his other identities?

Well, he simply has to, of course, for he is the father of the hero and heroine, Peter Merriott (really his son Robin) and Kate Merriott (his daughter Prudence) [sic]. And he does, managing on the way his daughter's romance with Sir Anthony Fanshawe, his son's connection with flighty Letitia Grayson, and the murder (well, killing) of the man who holds the one piece of evidence that could ruin all his plans.

"I am a great man," he admits, at the end of the book. The reader can only agree. (You would not have liked the man who was killed; really, almost anyone murdered in a Heyer novel was asking for it.)

It was not her intention to write a series of Regency novels: as seen by the preceding two books, she dabbled in several eras. When she did start to specialize, it took a few tries before she made the decade her own. *Regency Buck* (1935) is one of her earliest attempts, and it shows it. There is a great deal of inconsequential namedropping, and, at the climax, she repeats the ending of *The Black Moth*, with the hero arriving through the window in the nick of time.

Judith Taverner, surely one of Heyer's dimmer heroines, has been left the ward of the Fifth Earl Worth. Her father, when writing his will, had really meant to appoint an old drinking buddy, the Fourth Earl Worth, but his memory was not very good, and he made the mistake. He then had the bad taste to die just after the Fourth Earl did, which meant that his daughter, as well as his son Peregrine, were left in the guardianship of a gratingly autocratic and unscrupulous man.

Judith has several battles of wills with this pompous rake, but her problems are only beginning. Her brother, though under-age, is nominally master of a large fortune. Several people might benefit by his death—her uncle, her cousin, and Lord Worth—and Perry begins to have some very close brushes with death. The reader is made privy to information which Judith does not have; we are allowed to watch as one of the three suspects confers with a would-be murderer, and, later, as he dopes and kidnaps Perry. Even then the reader is left a little in the dark, and, when all is explained in the end, one is inclined to cry, with Judith, "It's not fair!"

*The Reluctant Widow* (1946) assembles much the same cast and puts them through a similarly Gothic ordeal, but Heyer has honed her talents, and the result is a stirring tale of espionage and murder. Cheerful

Peregrine Taverner has become the sunny Nicky. The autocratic Lord Worth has become the autocratic Lord Carlyon. There is a smooth cousin, an absurd uncle, and a host of sinister forces behind the scenes. The heroine is made of considerably sterner stuff, however, and that makes all the difference.

Elinor Rochdale gets into trouble by climbing into the wrong carriage. She has been hired as a governess, but Lord Carlyon assumes that she has answered his advertisement for a young woman of quality to marry his dissolute cousin Eustace. If Eustace dies unwed, his estate will fall to Lord Carlyon, who does not at all want to inherit it. Elinor declines this position, and Lord Carlyon accepts her decision.

He does, that is, until his brother Nicky rushes in, in a panic. There has been a brawl, and Nicky has inadvertently put a carving knife deep into cousin Eustace. Learning that Eustace is still barely alive, Lord Carlyon bustles Elinor into his carriage, and, in a few short hours, Elinor finds herself wife, widow, and mistress of a ramshackle estate known as Highnoons.

If that were not enough, a mysterious visitor begins to appear at Highnoons, at one point shooting Nicky. What is the man after? The reader can guess. Authors do not drop remarks about stolen battle plans simply for a lark. The reader knows very well that Eustace had something to do with the missing documents and that they will be found at Highnoons.

But then the mysterious visitor is murdered. Which one of Eustace's relatives is not only a spy but a murderer as well? The obvious suspect is cousin Francis, a fop who exposes his villainy when he tries to beat Nicky's dog, Bouncer, and admits that he prefers cats to dogs. (There are also no cats in Heyer novels, except for a few kittens who are more props than anything else, but dogs both bound and abound through her pages.) Lord Carlyon's chief concern, however, is the scandal. How can he quiet the uproar that must follow should it come out that two of his relatives, at least, are spying for Napoleon? He does it, to the astonishment of his family, by turning the stolen papers over to cousin Francis. His explanation proves a nice grasp of detective work.

This book is entirely a Regency thriller, a Regency Gothic, perhaps.

So much goes on that there is almost no room for the romance, which is tacked on, a little unconvincingly, in the last three pages. (Personally, I feel that that is just the way Lord Carlyon *would* conduct a romance.) When this book was adapted for the movies (the only Heyer novel to be so treated), it had to be spiced up considerably, to the author's annoyance.

The above are the chief among the mysteries set in the Regency period. Others which may be included are *Cousin Kate* (1968), the relatively late Gothic, with its title character almost forced into marriage with a mysterious, and possibly dangerous, cousin, and *The Quiet Gentleman* (1952), in which someone schemes against Lord St. Frant [sic]. Other books have brief mystery subplots. In *The Corinthian* (1940), a continuing subplot includes a stolen necklace and a dead body, but it is really only one more complication besetting the hero and heroine. *The Grand Sophy* (1950) has a marvelous scene in which the heroine extorts at gunpoint a ring and an I.O.U. from a loan shark. One of Heyer's most perennially popular books, *These Old Shades* (1926), has its hero (if that is the word) plumbing the mystery of his page, Leon Bonnard. Justin Alastair is one of her greatest characters, and one of the few who appears in more than one Regency. (A virtually identical character, with another name, was the villain of *The Black Moth* [1921], and Alastair himself reappears in *Devil's Cub* [1932], in which his son kidnaps a woman.) Alastair, the Duke of Avon, has figured out Leon's secret by page 2 of *These Old Shades*, leaving the reader to puzzle it out alone. The secret is revealed a third of the way through the book, allowing the reader, and Alastair's allies, to sit back and watch as he closes his grip on the perpetrator of the crime. The climactic scene has been given the compliment of blatant imitation by several subsequent Regency novelists.

*The Unknown Ajax* (1960) is also concerned with a mystery to some degree. Is the heroine's younger brother, one of those madcap youths whom Heyer liked to include in her cast of characters, just playing practical jokes or is he in league with a band of smugglers? The main plot, however, is concerned with a massive practical joke played by the hero on the family.

459

Arguments could be made, perhaps, for including others among the novels. At any rate, the point has been made that Georgette Heyer did not wholly abandon the mystery when she plunged into historical fiction. There is certainly enough to reward anyone who ventures over to the Romance rack at the bookstore in search of mystery. Besides a good mystery, there are generous dollops of humor and historical accuracy that would do credit to a writer in any genre.

This accuracy will have its drawbacks for some readers. Those who insist on contemporary crime will be disappointed, of course. Further, Heyer is writing of a period when what have been called "anti-humanist values" were the accepted way of life. The line between male and female roles in society was a thick, impenetrable wall. Heyer turns this to her advantage; her heroines frequently express amusement (mixed with envy) at the bizarre world of men, which sometimes seems to them to be composed solely of horses, bad brandy, and women of the night. They generally conclude, with a sigh and a shake of the head, that there is simply no understanding such a strange sex.

Harder to swallow are the equally clear lines between classes of society. Heyer takes no particular trouble to hide her obvious satisfaction with a world in which people knew their place. She regrets the plight of the urban poor in the Regency period; several of her heroes and heroines take arms against the hunger and disease rampant in London's slums. Yet she keeps the boundaries clear; those who are not gently born are "nobody." Of course, this is an accurate portrayal of society at the time, but, although one knows that a Justin Alastair would have felt that way, one can forgive him almost every vice but his snobbery.

Anyone taking up the cudgels for a writer of romances must approach the question of formula writing. All paperback romances (there are still some people who insist "all paperback fiction") are written to formula, are they not? The hero must be a certain age and height, the heroine younger and shorter; there must be a rival, a duel, and so forth, right?

This article has not helped matters at all by pointing out that Georgette Heyer had several favorite character types: the domestic tyrant, the schoolboy, the rash young man. There were others: the well-informed and pompous bore, the stiff prude, the dimwitted dandy, and

460

the romantic girl. (In Heyer novels, "romantic" is almost always a synonym for "silly.") She herself said that she had only two heroes: the affable giant and the cool aristocrat. She claimed that she arrived at her stories by simply combining one of these with one of her two heroines: the meek, sheltered miss or the daring nonconformist.

But Heyer was too good a writer to fall into the trap of endless repetition. Her characters are recognizable types but are not interchangeable. Sylvester Lavenham, the tyrant who will not be crossed in *The Talisman Ring*, is not much like Lord Darracott, who handles that role in *The Unknown Ajax*. Eugenia Wraxton, the stiff prude of *The Grand Sophy*, is obviously different from her counterpart in *Venetia*, Edward Yardley. Heyer's plots, too, escape from formula; she even had the strength of humor to occasionally let the dimwitted dandy get the girl, while the cool aristocrat went away disappointed.

Had formula been foremost in her mind, Georgette Heyer would have written more Regency mysteries, or fewer. As it is, she wrote just enough to deserve notice and appreciation from those who enjoy her modern murders.

**Kathleen Bell, "Cross-Dressing in Wartime: Georgette Heyer's *The Corinthian* in its 1940 Context" (in *War Culture: Social Change and Changing Experience in World War Two Britain*, eds. Pat Kirkham and David Thomas. London: Lawrence & Wishart, 1995, pp. 151-159):**

[from the introduction: ". . . Kathleen Bell examines a single example of the most popular of 'female' genres and reading habits, the historical romance, written by leading author, Georgette Heyer, in which the heroine cross dresses."]

Georgette Heyer's *The Corinthian*, her second novel of 1940 and published in November of that year, negotiates and addresses a number of social and political debates current at the time, which it may have been difficult to consider overtly. At first glance, *The Corinthian* seems to merit the adjective 'escapist,' fulfilling a need to take refuge in fantasy from such anxieties as the black-out, the blitz, food shortages, rationing, and the fear of German invasion. This label would seem to be endorsed by the subject of the book; both principal characters and many minor characters directly enact escapes of various kinds and the words "escape" and "escapade" occur frequently in the text. Moreover the story, set in the early nineteenth century, seems at first consideration far removed from World War Two. Its two main characters, the Corinthian Richard "Beau" Wyndham and the 17-year-old heiress Pen Creed, are both under pressure to enter into marriages that will further their families' interests. Wyndham, hours away from proposing to the frigid Melissa Brandon, is wandering home, drunk, when he observes what he at first takes to be a young man escaping from the upstairs window of a house. The "youth" turns out to be a young woman, Pen Creed, who has donned masculine clothing in order to travel safely to meet her childhood sweetheart, Piers Luttrell, whom she has not seen for five years. They travel cross-country by stagecoach, heading for Piers' home, with Richard acting in turn as Pen's tutor, guardian, and uncle. The plot is complicated by a series of episodes concerning the upper-class but impoverished Brandon family, bringing Pen into contact with a thief, a Bow Street runner, a stolen necklace, and a murder. When Piers is finally discovered, it turns out that he has entered into a secret betrothal with the ultra-feminine and unadventurous Lydia Daubenay—a discovery that frees Pen who realises that she is now in love with Richard.

Certain staple elements of romantic fiction are present—the young woman slowly realising her love for the older, protective man and the need to assert freely-chosen love over compelled marriage—as well as detective story puzzles about the theft of the Brandon necklace and the murder of Beverley Brandon. These offered a degree of escape in that they were familiar plot elements pointing to reassuringly familiar conclusions. At the same time, however, comparisons with wartime circumstances are frequently implied, as, for example, when Pen, perpetually hungry, eats her apples core and all.[61] Indeed, the novel

---

[61] *The Corinthian* [1948], pp. 45 and 137.

offers the fantasy of a constant supply of large meals ranging from a hamper on a coach to a breakfast of "lavishly" buttered bread with "several slices of ham"—goods that were rationed in 1940.[62]

The era in which *The Corinthian* is set suggests further comparisons with 1940. Military service in Wellington's Peninsular Army is offered as a means to personal redemption, drawing on the further parallel of Napoleon's conquest of Europe and threatened invasion of Britain with contemporary fears of invasion—a parallel frequently invoked at the time.[63] Comparisons with the Napoleonic Wars also offered the happy conclusion of Allied victory at Waterloo. Heyer's first novel of 1940, *The Spanish Bride*, had been a fact-filled historical romance set in the same period. Based on Harry Smith's marriage to the 14-year-old Juana, it recounted hardship shared in campaigning, the separation of the married couple, and finally victory at Waterloo. The book was a best-seller[64] and therefore Heyer's regular readers could be expected to pick up the significance of *The Corinthian*'s occasional references to the Peninsular Wars.

More intriguingly related to the events of 1940 is the introduction of a cross-dressed heroine at a time when the suitability of women for war-work, as well as femininity itself, was a subject of public debate. Heyer had created two cross-dressed heroines more than a decade previously:

---

[62] For details of rationing, which began in early 1940, see Norman Longmate, *How We Lived Then*, Hutchinson, London, 1971, chapter 13, pp. 140-155.

[63] For instance in many press references and in Winston Churchill's enthusiasm for and conviction of the propaganda value of the film *Lady Hamilton* (1941).

[64] The "In the Bookshops" column in *The Observer*, 14 April 1940, lists *The Spanish Bride* as the book most in demand from libraries and as one of the seven top-selling novels of the week. Present-day readers may be startled by early passages in the book which depict British soldiers in disorderly activities ranging from looting to raping nuns but the conduct of the troops undergoes a marked improvement in the course of the novel.

Léonie in *These Old Shades* (1926), her first big success, and Prudence in *The Masqueraders* (1928), who was, less usually, accompanied by her cross-dressing brother, Robin. Tales involving cross-dressing were not unusual in the inter-war years[65] and its resonances varied from the erotic to the political. The heroines of *These Old Shades* and *The Masqueraders* used their masculine disguises to enter male territory; Léonie, serving as the Duke of Avon's page, accompanied him to brothels and gambling clubs and relished lessons in sword-fighting, while Prudence, disguised as an adult male, encountered men as equals in the world of male clubs, joining them in drinking, gaming and—less successfully—fighting. In these two novels the assumption of male clothing is concealed from other characters for a long time and even, to some extent, from the reader. Ambiguity about gender, and doubt about the hero's knowledge of the heroine's true identity, adds a layer of erotic interest to their encounters.

But Pen Creed is different from earlier transgressive heroines. Her assumed masculine identity brings her few of the advantages or erotic encounters afforded the others. She willingly places herself in a subordinate position in relation to the older Richard, adopting the role of pupil or ward. Apart from a few scenes of farcical confusion in which she enacts the role of Lydia's would-be seducer, Pen's assumption of masculine identity allows her no more freedom than the indulgence of a healthy appetite and the occasional walk at night, with Richard as protector always close at hand. Even the erotic possibilities of the scenario are limited by Richard's (and the reader's) immediate identification of Pen as a female. Instead of being put forward as a figure whose gender is uncertain, Pen is quickly established as the boyish girl, able to fit into the male world—but never quite as an equal. While Heyer novels were not noted for their emphasis on sexuality, even within Heyer's *oeuvre* the romance between Richard and Pen is signally lacking

---

[65] Examples of novels include: D. K. Broster, *Mr. Rowl* (1924), Virginia Woolf, *Orlando* (1928), while notable instances of cinematic cross-dressing can be found in *Queen Christina* (1933), *Morocco* (1930), *Sylvia Scarlet* (1936) and *First a Girl* (1935).

in erotic interest. When it is suggested that Richard and Pen (at this stage travelling as schoolboy and tutor) should share a room,[66]there is not any embarrassment in their laughter; they are simply amused at the impossibility of the situation and Richard rapidly puts forward an alternative suggestion.

This surprisingly unadventurous combination of elements may derive from popular uncertainty about what role women were to be given as their country waged war. While in the later war years younger, childless women were conscripted and others encouraged to seek paid employment, the beginning of World War Two saw an increase in female unemployment.[67] Employers reportedly preferred cutting back on production to engaging women workers, provoking an active lobbying compaign from the Federation of Business and Professional Women.[68] In January 1940, Winston Churchill appeared to endorse their aims in a widely-reported speech, although he also offered reassurance to any who feared the permanent loss of the pre-war status quo:

> Nearly a million women were employed in the last war in 1918 under the Ministry of Munitions. They did all kinds of things that no one had ever expected them to do before and they did them very well.
>
> But after the war was over they went back home and were no obstacle to the resumption of normal conditions of British life and labour.[69]

Churchill's speech stimulated national debate, but he did not become

---

[66] *The Corinthian* [1948], p. 59.

[67] For a detailed analysis of changing employment patterns in World War Two and their causes see Penny Summerfield, *Women Workers in the Second World War*, 1984, especially Chapter 3.

[68] This is chronicled in the editorial pages and correspondence columns of *Time and Tide* for 1940.

[69] Churchill's speech, given in Manchester on Saturday 27 January 1940, was fully reported in *The Observer*, 28 January 1940.

prime minister until May of that year and it was not until 1941 that women were subject to conscription. Instead the emphasis was on women selecting themselves as capable and volunteering for service—as civilian workers and as soldiers.

As the debate continued, questions raised included national need, the rights of women to equal treatment and, inevitably, the danger that female sexuality posed to men.[70] Pre-war prejudices against women working continued to surface. On 13 July *Time and Tide* reported an incident which it considered representative of the country's unwillingness to allow women to take on "unsuitable" jobs despite the anticipation of invasion:[71]

> Cornering women out of the war has become a regular fetish with officialdom. The latest evidence comes from a town in the Eastern Counties, where women who responded to the "dig for defence" appeal to civilians were told to go back home. Women, it seems, are not fit to dig or fill sandbags. They are not fit to co-operate with I.D.V.s In some districts they have even been deemed unfit to hold important A.R.P. posts. Meanwhile women are deluged with "pep" talks on the radio, designed on special homely lines which it is hoped no doubt will

---

[70] The concern that women's irregular sexual activities may weaken the resolve of their soldier husbands by causing "trouble at home" is expressed by an article sent to *Time and Tide* by "the Archbishop of York who vouches for the writer" and published on 31 Akugust 1940, p. 886.

[71] After the fall of France the Government was concerned to advise the population of how to react when the Germans landed. George Orwell's letter to *Time and Tide* (22 June 1940, p. 662) recommending arming the populace in response to the "almost certain" invasion of Britain stimulated debate about the possible arming of Britain, including calls that women be equipped with hand-grenades.

> penetrate to their sub-human understanding.
>
> What a mercy the bold Mrs. Cardwell did not have to ask officialdom before she arrested an armed parachutist. It certainly would have been forbidden . . . unseemly, unsuitable, and quite beyond her powers.[72]

*Time and Tide* goes on to praise the action of Churchill in cutting through the usual red tape to secure an OBE for the intrepid Mrs. Cardwell. Here, as elsewhere in *Time and Tide*, Churchill functioned as a hero despite its largely feminist and left-leaning agenda. Yet Churchill's call for female labour and female involvement in the war effort had been couched in conservative terms; similarly Heyer's representation of Pen Creed can be read as an attempt to allay male concerns while praising certain of her qualities as "unique."

> "I am afraid," confessed Pen, "that I am not very well-behaved. Aunt says that I had a lamentable upbringing, because my father treated me as though I had been a boy. I ought to have been, you understand."
>
> "I cannot agree with you," said Richard. "As a boy you would have been in no way remarkable; as a female, believe me, you are unique."
>
> She flushed to the roots of her hair. "I *think* that is a compliment."
>
> "It is," Sir Richard said, amused.[73]

In the context of 1940, Pen's assumption of a masculine character posed little danger to the established order. However, for the female reader of the time and/or the would-be wartime volunteer, Pen legitimises difference, exceptionality, and the desire to function in a male world. But

---

[72] "Time and Tide Diary," *Time and Tide*, 13 July 1940, p. 727.
[73] *The Corinthian* [1948], p. 58.

the limits to female aspiration are clearly defined. As a boyish woman, Pen is marked out as praiseworthy because she achieves the virtues of an average, unexceptional boy and, within a system of values which views men as superior to boys as well as women, there is never any danger of her competing with or equalling grown men. Nevertheless, her aspirations are endorsed precisely because they relate to masculine virtue. It is important to note that this is not a fixed scheme throughout Heyer's work. In novels as diverse as *Devil's Cub* (1932), *Sylvester* (1957), and *Frederica* (1965), men are seen as in need of the domesticating and civilizing force of femininity while *Faro's Daughter* (1940) and *The Grand Sophy* (1950) allow their powerful and active heroines a combination of conventional feminine attributes with an understanding of and adherence to aspects of the masculine ethos. It seems reasonable, therefore, to link the attitudes to masculine prowess and, by implication, feminine weakness in *The Corinthian* to the situation in contemporary England.

While boyishness is treated as praiseworthy in *The Corinthian*, it is set against two other, less approved models of femininity: the masterful woman whose qualities are thrown into relief by the weak men around her and the more conventionally feminine woman who uses her appearance of weakness to manipulate people. These types are common both to Heyer and the genre but are treated less sympathetically than usual. Louisa, Wyndham's sister, who falls into the first category, may possess a "leavening gleam of humour"[74] but has no rapport with her brother, being chiefly concerned to push him into an unwelcome marriage. Melissa Brandon, the bride chosen for Wyndham by his family, is described as "hard," "contemptuous," and an "iceberg."[75] Lady Luttrell alone, making a belated appearance in the final chapter, redeems the model of this type, but only by endorsing Wyndham's judgement and taking more interest in his love-match with Pen than she does in the elopement of her own son.

More conclusively dangerous is the exaggerated and manipulative

---

[74] *Ibid.*, p. 6.
[75] *Ibid.*, pp. 20, 22, and 13.

femininity of Lady Wyndham, using her apparent frailty as a "subtle way of getting her wishes attended to." The "delicate state of her nerves," indicated by handkerchief, vinaigrette, and hartshorn, has, we are warned, a "sinister message."[76]  As she fades from the plot, another feminine manipulator intervenes in the love story.  Lydia Daubenay's frilled garments[77] indicate her concentration on her own desires.  Having run away and fainted at the sight of violence, Lydia attempts to use tears to win the support of Pen, only to be condemned as an "unprincipled liar."[78] In the younger woman feminine weakness is significantly connected with a lack of that important wartime quality, public spirit.[79]

Yet this public spirit, which Lydia is condemned for lacking, proves an elusive concept in *The Corinthian*.  While this novel lacks the adherence to the strict standards of social etiquette proclaimed in most other Heyer novels—Pen is the only Heyer heroine to effect a successful escape from her bedroom window while Piers and Lydia set off to commit the *faux pas* of a Gretna Green marriage—social hierarchy and class interest still prevail.  At the end of the day public interest (represented by the magistrate and the Bow Street runner) is at odds with and subordinated to the needs of the upper classes to maintain their public image.[80]  Richard, acting as the text's ethical arbiter, is prepared to co-

---

[76] *Ibid.*, p. 6.

[77] For a midnight assignation, Lydia is described as wearing "a white muslin dress, high-waisted and frilled about the ankles, and with a great many pale-blue bows of ribbon with long fluttering ends" (p. 128). Needless to say one of her major concerns is that the grass might stain her dress.

[78] *The Corinthian* [1948], p. 132.

[79] Pen and Richard happily assume that she would be unwilling to perform the public duty of identifying Captain Trimble (164).

[80] In the detective novel of this period the reader would expect that while the magistrate and the Bow Street runner might not be able to ascertain the truth without the air of the amateur sleuth, the sleuth would share their value system.  In the detective sub-plot Richard functions as

operate with the magistrate over the murder of Beverley Brandon but, openly preferring class solidarity to public justice, he works to cover up Beverley's earlier crimes thus averting public disgrace for his family. Although public-spiritedness is seen as a masculine virtue to which women should aspire, the degree to which it is genuinely public is a matter for men to determine. Women must take their part in public-spiritedness at second hand; Richard defines what is best for the proper ordering of society while Pen and Lady Luttrell defer to his judgement.

This concentration on class may echo concerns about changing class relations in wartime. While government-backed propaganda did not deny class difference, a new emphasis was placed on classes working together.[81] In practical terms people from different classes were asked to work alongside each other; the officer class, for example, was enlarged to include those with relevant ability and experience. Objections were raised to the preservation of narrow peacetime hierarchies in the wartime situation.[82] But against this concern that ability be given priority over social standing was the fear that women who had achieved professional status in peacetime (a status barely open to women of working-class or lower middle-class origins) should lose that status as unqualified women were taken into the workforce.

---

aristocratic sleuth but clearly separates his value system from those held by the forces of law and order.

[81] In such films as Humphrey Jennings' *London Can Take It* (1940) the stress is on the shared experience of Londoners regardless of class. Other films dealt less happily with the need to address all social classes as Jeffrey Richards and Dorothy Sheridan's *Mass Observation at the Movies*, RKP, London, 1987, illustrates, especially in Section D "Ministry of Information Shorts," p. 424ff.

[82] For example, *Time and Tide* was concerned that "the recruiting of officers for the W.R.N.S. has taken place practically entirely from the wives and daughters of existing naval officers" and expressed particular concern that commissioned rank had been recommended for "a schoolgirl barely eighteen." "Families in Uniform," *Time and Tide*, 30 December 1939, p. 1647.

Set in the context of this debate, Pen Creed's position is that of the very young, enthusiastic, aristocratic amateur. Her class origins, which are the same as the hero's, hark back to an older world in which aristocratic position is the best guarantor of intelligence and the security of the aristocracy the only surety for a happy and well-ordered society.

For the first part of the novel Richard and Pen escape from society and its rules; as Richard observes, "it was good for a man to be removed occasionally from civilisation."[83] But the use of Richard to represent civilisation in the latter half reveals a deep fissure in the novel since he stands both for the values of civilisation and the need to escape from it; indeed, it is only his escape and his refusal to make the socially-approved marriage with Melissa Brandon that enables him to function as protector of the Brandon Family's reputation. There are two reasons for this. Firstly, the civilisation from which Richard is escaping is a world of female rule and dominating domesticity. This was, of course, the very "escape" being asked of men recruited and conscripted into the armed forces as well as an "escape" which some women were also demanding for themselves. Given the heterosexual conventions of the genre, female escape can best be achieved by a romance whose heroine has been brought up by her father and who dresses, thinks, and acts like a boy. But she is represented as an immature male; s/he defers to Richard as her/his superior and is dependent on his advice and commands. The relationship Pen and Richard achieve is asexual; Pen's chief attraction is her boyishness—which partly denies her sexuality. Although Pen is at one point accused by Richard of a "feminine trick"[84] (the word "trick" is significant) there is no traditional transformation of the "tomboy" into a beauty in petticoats. But she does get her man, romance and, the reader is given to assume, sex; the last reference to the couple is to a "golden-haired stripling . . . locked in the Corinthian's arms being ruthlessly

---

[83] *The Corinthian* [1948], p. 83.

[84] She does no more than pat her curls into order before the mirror (p. 162). The comment may seem a trifle unfair from a man who requires the minimum of an hour in which to dress himself.

kissed"[85] to the amazement of a stagecoachful of passengers. The text implies that feminine women are powerful and dangerous but women prepared to be lesser men can be trained to obey male commands and absorbed into male hierarchies without danger. They also get some rewards.

Secondly, the journey of escape undertaken by Richard and Pen, which introduces them to experiences not usually encountered by members of their class, can be related to a journey recommended to the British wartime population as a whole. They journey away from civilisation and their customary comforts in order that civilisation (or the pre-war status quo) may be restored. Discomforts are made light of while the benefits of the journey are lauded. Men escape from the powers of womanly women into an arena in which they can take control while women who give up the delights of femininity are promised its conventional rewards.

**" 'Georgette Heyer made me a good judge of character.' Cassandra Jardine meets Mr. Justice Rougier, whose mother's influence led him to speak out against the system," in *The Daily Telegraph*, 19 December 1996, p. 18.**

"A judge's life," says Mr. Justice Rougier, "is a desperate attempt to keep your head below the parapet." This week, he broke his own rule.

As he sentenced a 17-year-old murderer to be detained at Her Majesty's pleasure, he spoke out against the "grotesque" bureaucracy that had allowed the youth to elude justice for so long. Darren Lawrence, he said, had a record of violence, and yet no charges had ever been brought over previous incidents.

"I am informed that, if a young person is to be prosecuted for an act of violence, then no fewer than 46—yes, *46*—different forms have to be filled in to fulfil the paper lust of the bureaucratic element in our criminal justice system," he said.

---

[85] *Ibid.*, p. 207.

Only extreme outrage could have goaded Sir Richard to such an outburst because he has an abhorrence of self-publicity—a trait he shares with his late mother, the novelist Georgette Heyer. Just as she always told inquirers that "you will find me in my books," he prefers to do his job unobtrusively.

The biggest controversy in his 10-year career as a High Court judge, Queen's Bench Division, was unintentional. In April 1995, he had been the judge who sentenced Jonathan Jones to life imprisonment for the "pitiless execution" of his girlfriend's parents, Harry and Megan Tooze. But afterwards, he wrote privately to the Home Secretary and to the defence QC, John Rees, expressing "some surprise" at the jury's verdict.

He was angry when the letter was made public, yet his "bold and brave action," as it was later described by the former Bar chairman, Anthony Scrivener, contributed to Jones's release this year.

It was not the first time that Sir Richard had shown independence of mind. He once sentenced a rapist to a year in prison, which he admitted was a gamble, and, two years ago, ordered a man to pay £4,000 to a burglar he had shot.

Last year, he admitted during a court case to never having heard of a bouncy castle. But then, like his mother, who died in 1974, Sir Richard holds much of popular culture in distaste. Rock music, for example, he describes as "jungle noises designed to annihilate thought. I disagree with the idea that judges should be up to the moment. Fads come and go. Judges ought to have an element of continuity and tradition."

His own sense of historical continuity was fostered by his mother, who brought him up eating Regency dinners, and hearing the slang of the beaux and ostlers. His weekends were spent looking at period houses and inns; his playtime enriched by snippets of research recounted to him by his mother. "Did you know that, in 1818, it cost 16 pence a mile to hire a chaise and four?" he asks.

Sir Richard's flat in west London is full of Regency memorabilia, from period fashion and a copy of a Stubbs, to tomes of research material left to him by his mother, who all but lived in the era.

"She was never happy in post-war Britain. She would have preferred to live in the Regency; it was a romantic period and she was a romantic with a strong practical streak. Perhaps I'm a romantic, too, at heart. I am 64 but have the attitudes of an older generation: old values, old morals. Like her, I have strong views. I despise dirt and squalor and the rat race. The attitudes of the war years and those that followed were far healthier and considerably safer. I dislike the current lack of respect for people, the awful 'I, I, I,' the total lack of restraint."

Reformers, he feels, should be treated with caution. Too often, he believes, they are inspired by a desire for fame. "And nothing is more contemptible than a man on the make—that, by the way, could be my mother talking."

A portrait of his formidable parent dominates the sitting room, glaring out "as if someone has just trumped her ace." With her caustic wit and her tendency to talk non-stop to hide her shyness, Heyer terrified many of his friends, but not her son. He was "very, very fond" of his mother and, while reticent about himself, he loves to talk about her.

Even her faults, he says, were endearing. "She was a snob, but not a cold snob." Brought up in genteel poverty, as the daughter of a teacher, Heyer loved the correctness of the Regency period, with its strict manners and mores. "She wouldn't have taken kindly to a young man who said 'Pardon' or wore his signet ring on his fourth finger. 'My dear, he drinks his own bathwater,' she would say. I have no idea why, but the meaning was clear."

Heyer was already well known by the time her only child was born in 1932. *[The] Black Moth*, her first novel, was written to entertain her sickly younger brother and published when she was 19. By the time she married Ronald Rougier, her dancing partner, she had already written *These Old Shades*, one of her most enduringly popular novels. When Ronald threw up his job as a mining engineer to train as a barrister, she supported the family, constantly complaining about having to write "for the taxman."

"A fiercely devoted mother," she would work from 9pm to 5am—so as not to disrupt family life. "And she always looked fresh at breakfast."

In Richard's nursery, she would recount to him her latest plot while playing patience. Often, a single historical detail, such as the introduction of the guinea, would prove a spur to invention and, knowing she had a large audience among adolescents, she was always keen to hear her son's opinion of a story.

Biographers have suggested that Heyer suffered from a broken heart which led her to fantasise about witty young women winning the hearts of difficult men. But Sir Richard rejects that. If there is a secret that explains her retreat into history, he feels it probably lies with her beloved father, a keen scholar. "The cataclysm of her life was that her father died suddenly and unexpectedly when she was 22." He had had a heart attack after a game of tennis with Ronald. "She was devastated."

"My parents were close. Her heroes were modelled on Charlotte Brontë's Mr. Rochester, and my father was nothing like that. He was a good-looking man, very well read and intelligent, but perfectly reasonable to live with, which many of her heroes were not."

The atmosphere in their Albany flat was studious. "My mother was emotionally inhibited; she never spoke of her feelings. If my parents quarrelled, it was over issues like the Divine Right of Kings." Richard had a facility for translating into Greek and Latin, and a retentive memory that served him well. On one occasion, he avoided a beating at prep school by learning 580 lines of poetry.

Inspired by his mother's passion, he tried his own hand at writing. His childhood efforts included a book on British birds and a poem about Caractacus. "I have her discipline, but not her imagination," he says regretfully. So, when the time came for him to choose a career, he followed in his father's footsteps.

As a barrister, he specialised in medical insurance and pharmaceutical cases, before he "turned referee." "It suited my temperament. I like talking, and life at the Bar is intellectually exciting."

As a judge, he deals with criminal cases. "You have to guard against a warped view of life because you see more than most of its downside," he says. Occasionally, he has been criticised for lenience: "I'd like to think that prep school, which was barbaric, has made me more sympathetic to those who are without supporting family in a hostile environment."

Apart from divorce and a second marriage this summer—"a romantic story, but I won't say more"—Sir Richard's life has been quiet. He has one son, Nicholas, and two stepsons from his first marriage.

"My father regarded golf as the only human activity of any worth, but I'd rather fish. I share my mother's interest in odd pockets of history like the Albigensian crusades." His bridge playing was once good enough to earn him a place on the national team.

Heyer's 54 [sic] books line his shelves, but they have not lined his pockets. While she was alive, they topped the best-seller lists in hardback, outselling Graham Greene. But she was an extravagant woman, who didn't like to think twice before buying a Georgian coffee service.

When she died, it was the era of super-tax. Paying 98.5 per cent tax on her books' projected earnings "all but landed me in Carey Street," he says. He was forced to sell the rights to many of them, some of which he has recently bought back.

Despite their continuing popularity, only *The Reluctant Widow*, starring Douglas Fairbanks [sic], has been filmed in Hollywood. But recently, a script of *The Grand Sophy*, Sir Richard's favorite, has been approved, and *These Old Shades*, which he dismisses as "girl meets boy in fancy dress," is in the hands of a producer.

When he retires from the bench, Sir Richard's ambition is to write. Not, he says quickly, his memories of legal life. He intends to study the grandes horizontales of the belle epoque, a project that would undoubtedly have shocked his mother. Her characters, she used to say, "did not exist below the waist."

But, as he has shown this week, Sir Richard has an independent mind.


**Carmen Callil, from "Subversive Sybils: Women's Popular Fiction This Century," a talk for The British Library Centre for the Book (London: The British Library, 1996):**

Women's popular fiction is an imperfect genre, close to life itself and to our dreams, as faulty and erratic as we are ourselves. And so the writers I'm going to discuss—Georgette Heyer, Jackie Collins, Colleen McCullough, Judith Krantz, and Celia Brayfield—do not represent the literary canon of fiction written in English. What they represent is the entertainment canon: they're storytellers who want to entertain us, and most of them would fall over in a heap if their books were taught in schools (though I think some should be).

It goes without saying that being a popular novelist, rather than a literary one, doesn't mean the said novelists cannot write well. They can, and many do, though it's hard to find a literary critic who thinks so, as we shall see. These particular women writers are very much a part of a venerable female literary tradition. . . .

Women writers have used popular fiction to take by the scruff of the neck the rules and regulations of the society which governs them and to shake the life out of said rules and regulations while seeming not to do so. In that way, popular women's fiction has always been a way of encouraging women to behave badly. Behaving badly are two words often used to describe people who are not fitting in with the wishes and desires of others.

One does not have to be a raving feminist, in fact one does not need to be a feminist at all, to note that women are gradually moving themselves into the twenty-first century on terms which allow them, more than ever before, to control their own lives.

These changes have always been greeted with fear and scorn, nowhere more so than in the critical appraisal of popular women writers. The abuse heaped upon them by critics, then and now, can only be because they threaten the status quo. . . .

Georgette Heyer wrote romantic comedies of manners, stories set in the Regency period. She always wrote love stories, and the novels concentrated on marriage, money, property, and love. Every heroine had to get married; that was the sole aim in life. One should never marry for money, but it was essential to pursue it, as it was nice should the ownership of dukedoms, baronetcies, and the other paraphernalia which decorate the upper crust, go with it.

However, none of this was of any worth to her heroines, unless accompanied by love, true love. Marrying for money was out of the question. Georgette Heyer wrote forty-odd novels on wide variations of this single theme. What makes them special, of course, is her delicious and perfect recreation of Regency England, down to the smallest detail of dress, food, conveyance, and language, and then too, her writing style. In Georgette Heyer we certainly have a popular writer whose command of the English language was near perfect, and worthy of imitation. Heyer is an author I would certainly teach in schools.

Here is a tiny example from a favourite novel, *Regency Buck.* Our heroine, Miss Taverner, is at dinner.

> Everyone was acquainted; nothing, Mrs. Scattergood declared, could have been more charming. Lord Alvanley, except for his habit of putting out his bedroom candle by stuffing it under his pillow, must always be an acceptable guest; Lord Petersham, the most finished gentleman alive, was courteous and amiable; the Earl was a calm but attentive host; Mr. Brummell was in a conversable mood, and a pleasant evening was spent in one of the saloons, playing cards, drinking tea, and chatting over a noble fire.

Translate the same punctuation and use of words to a booze-up in the pub after a football match, and we would have a nation of literate children.

I first read Georgette Heyer when I was eleven, and gobbled up all her novels, which I read again and again before I was twenty, when I stopped, mostly I think because other matters took over. Nevertheless, I'm certain that while she influenced my writing style, she left me, too, with something else: a feeling that a real heroine should only marry on her own terms. Despite the fact that marriage was the great goal, somehow, insidiously, she made me think otherwise. How could this be? Where did I get this idea from? I had no idea until many years later, when I read the only biography of her—an authorised one—which has been allowed. Written by Jane Aiken Hodge it's called *The Private World of Georgette Heyer* (1984). It has to be said that there is very little private in it, but what we do learn about her, which is of interest, is as follows:

Georgette Heyer was a Daddy's girl: she adored her father; it's hard to discover what she felt about her mother (shades of Margaret Thatcher here). She disliked women and women's concerns, and mostly despised her readers, whom she thought to be either women, or beneath her: she was a snob. She married happily and had one son, but expressed many times her relief that she'd had a son, and not a daughter. In addition, she was of severely masculine appearance, and many of her novels describe a mannish heroine such as she: a woman who spends her life among men, and who wants to be—and often is—like them. In some of her early novels, her women dress like men too—a particularity she shares with Daphne du Maurier. She was an obsessive, meticulous researcher and writer, yet she called her novels "another bleeding romance."

I hope this is sufficient to give you an idea as to why I found the vast dose of Georgette Heyer I injected myself with, subversive. For me, she gave out mixed messages. There has been no one faintly like her since her death in 1974. Georgette Heyer is underrated, and deserves renewed attention. . . .

Georgette Heyer, Jackie Collins, and Judith Krantz do not tinker with the most important social institutions which arrange women's lives. . . .

Celia Brayfield recently published a study of popular fiction, *Bestseller Secrets of Successful Writing* (1996). She says that "popular culture circulates ideas for millions of people. Those ideas are our modern mythology . . . [they tell] society how to survive. . . . Society changes at dizzying speed . . . [and] a great many modern stories address the fears aroused by those changes . . . . [T]he classic romance story appeals to the sense of powerlessness which many women still feel."

It's a measure of how successful these subversive sybils have been that so much scorn and derision has been poured upon them: because, apart from entertaining their audience with fantasy or storytelling, or both, they have used their power and influence to change the way women view themselves and live their lives in the late twentieth century.

**Susanne Hagemann, "Gendering Places: Georgette Heyer's Cultural Topography," in** *Scotland to Slovenia, European Identities and Transcultural Communication.* **Proceedings** *of the Fourth International Scottish Studies Symposium* **(Frankfurt a. M.: Peter Lang, 1996, pp. 187-199):**

Georgette Heyer was born in Wimbledon in 1902 and died in 1974. She wrote twelve detective stories and made a few attempts at "serious" historical novels, but she is best known for her historical romances, often set in Regency England. The romances range from adventure tales such as *These Old Shades*—with an exchange of babies, a heroine masquerading as a boy, an abduction and pursuit through England and France, intrigues and counter intrigues, and a suicide engineered by the Mephistophelean hero—to novels of manners such as *Lady of Quality*, in which on the physical (as opposed to the psychological) level there are no events more dramatic than a bout of influenza. Heyer's romances are carefully researched as far as material culture (e. g. clothes or carriages), social behavior, and period language are concerned; her heroines as a rule have more personality than those of run-of-the-mill love stories, and she makes much use of humour and irony. On the other hand, she has been criticized on the grounds that her irony is temporary and superficial, her language is mere pastiche, her characters and situations are predictable, her neglect of social conflict and everyday routine makes for escapist entertainment,[86] and her period colour is "pseudoinformation [...] because, ultimately, it reveals nothing about [...] society."[87] Her work has been aptly characterized as "middlebrow."[88]

---

[86] Glass, E. R. and A. Mineo, "Georgette Heyer and the Uses of Regency," La Performance del Testo: Atti del VII Congresso Nazionale dell'Associazione Italiana di Anglistica (A. I. A.), Siena, 2-4 Novembre 1984, ed. Franco Marucci and Adriano Bruttini. Siena: Ticci, 1986, pp. 288-290.

[87] Robinson, Lillian S., "On Reading Trash," *Sex, Class, and Culture*, Bloomington: Indiana University Press, 1978, p. 212.

[88] Glass/Mineo, p. 283.

The protagonist of Heyer's romance *The Foundling* is described as slightly built, delicate, pale, quiet, and diffident[89] as having the gift of empathy, as gaining points by what an uncle calls "coaxing" and "caressing" ways (300, 343) and as suffering from "periodic headaches" (207). All this would be in no way remarkable—if the protagonist were not a man. In the following, I shall argue that his feminine traits are closely connected with the fact that his main place of residence is in the country, in other words, away from London. More generally, I shall look at correlations between place and gender, particularly in those of Heyer's works which are based on an opposition between "London" and "non-London."

I shall begin by examining the foundations of identity in Heyer. Much is made of the characters' gender and geographical-cum-cultural affiliations. Gender at first sight appears to be a relatively unstable category: in *The Masqueraders*, a brother and sister exchange roles, and in both *These Old Shades* and *The Corinthian*, the heroine disguises herself as a boy. However, such cases should be examined in the larger context of part-playing, since the motif is a quite frequent one in Heyer's romances: the eponymous hero of *Beauvallet*, an Englishman who penetrates into the Spain of Philip II using French papers, and the protagonist of *False Colours*, who steps into the shoes of his twin brother, are only two examples; many more might be adduced. What virtually all of these masks have in common is that they are assumed in order to achieve a clearly defined goal (more precisely, two goals: the one pursued by the character, in the case of *The Corinthian*, for instance, escape from a tyrannical aunt, and the one pursued by the narrator, namely the eventual union of hero and heroine) and can be discarded without leaving any substantial traces when they have served their purpose. Similarly, in the course of a novel, a heroine chafing at the restrictions imposed on her may well express a desire to be a man (cf. e.g. *Regency Buck*[90]) or behave in an "unfeminine" way (cf. e.g. *The*

---

[89] Pan edition, 1963, pp. 6, 20.
[90] Mandarin ed., 1991, p. 191.

*Grand Sophy[91]*); but the ending invariably shows her happily engaged, and usually subordinated, to the hero. Moreover, a narrowly gender-oriented reading of such cases would ignore the fact that Heyer's heroines also voice other unrealizable desires (concerning the colour of their hair, for example: cf. *Regency Buck* 1) and that her heroes are just as given to defying convention (cf. e.g. *Devil's Cub[92]* or *Black Sheep[93]*). Focusing on the gender issue alone, we might be tempted to interpret the heroines' occasional display of "masculine" paraphernalia and attributes as an indication of covert transsexual desires on their part and of homoerotic ones on the part of the heroes; but if we look at the patterns of behavior in their entirety, we can conclude that gender identity is securely founded on the characters' sex—sex being treated as pregiven.

Having shown that a binary and essentialist ideology characterizes the approach to gender prevalent in Heyer's romances, I shall now turn to the main subject of my paper—place—and attempt to demonstrate the set of gendered assumptions at work here. A considerable number of Heyer's works are based on an opposition between "London" and "non-London." "London" and masculinity are in many cases closely linked through the person of the hero, who tends to be a prominent member of high society. "Non-London," by contrast, often serves as the heroine's home. This set-up occurs, for example, in *Arabella*, where the heroine is sent from Yorkshire to London to find a suitable husband. She fulfils her task admirably by attracting the attention of the most sought-after bachelor in the capital. A movement in the opposite direction, from London to Yorkshire, can be found in *The Nonesuch*, but the topography of gender remains the same: it is the hero who comes from London, and the heroine who resides in Yorkshire.

"Non-London" is thus feminized through its frequent association with female protagonists. A second method of feminization, and one worth looking at in more detail because it is much less obvious, is the ascription of "feminine" traits to male characters brought up, living, or desiring to

---

[91] Heinemann ed., 1950, pp. 60, 92-3, 201-9.
[92] Heinemann ed., 1932, pp. 61-63.
[93] Bodley Head ed., 1966, pp. 44, 70-71.

live outside London. This method, which is used most frequently in those novels which directly contrast "London" and "non-London," can be shown up by applying the frameworks of classic images-of-women criticism to the male characters in question. (It seems advisable to focus on male characters because Heyer's women tend to be "feminine" irrespective of their geographical base.)

Women have often been described as emotional and irrational, sometimes to the point of madness. This complex of stereotypes recurs in connection with "non-London" men in Heyer. Significantly, if a heroine from the provinces has a brother, he is usually her junior, embodying youthful immaturity as opposed to the hero's worldly wisdom. Immaturity often takes the form of emotionality, coupled with an inability to think and behave rationally. When young Bertram Tallant in *Arabella* comes to London for the first time, he immediately runs up heavy debts by gambling; seeing no way out of his difficulty, he indulges in drink and wild talk until his future brother-in-law arrives to rescue him. In similar financial straits, Sir Peregrine Taverner, the Yorkshire-born younger brother in *Regency Buck*, reacts to his guardian's reprimands in a way represented as distinctly childish: "Peregrine swung over to the window, and stood staring blindly out, one hand fidgeting with the curtain-tassel. His whole pose suggested that he was labouring under a strong sensation of chagrin." (107) Time does not make Sir Peregrine less youthful: when he reappears in *An Infamous Army*, set a few years after *Regency Buck*, he is still as naïve and thoughtless as he was in the earlier novel. In *The Unknown Ajax*, set in rural Kent, Richmond Darracott, yet another younger brother of a heroine, being forbidden by his grandfather to join the army, reacts irrationally by turning to smuggling in search of adventure. *Frederica* takes the motif a step further by providing the heroine with three younger brothers, two of whom are still schoolboys, epitomes of immaturity. A different type of immaturity is exemplified by Lord Dolphinton in *Cotillion*, who is mentally retarded. His dominant emotion is fear of his overbearing mother. She forces him to live in London, but his great desire is to breed horses on his country estate. The estate, incidentally, lies in Ireland—a location which serves to marginalize Dolphinton even further.

Like young men from rural areas, Heyer's male Londoners can on occasion display emotionality and irrationality, but they do so more rarely, and there is a significant difference between the two groups insofar as the destructive potential of these qualities tends to be turned inwards in the case of the former and outwards in the case of the latter. Bertram, Peregrine, and Richmond are in danger of harming themselves in the first place; their London counterparts are much more prone to vent their feelings on their environment. For instance, the London-based hero of *Devil's Cub*, in a state of intoxication, nearly kills a man in a duel and later abducts the virtuous heroine in a fit of fury; similarly, a minor London character in *Friday's Child* is in the habit of challenging friends to duels whenever despair at (seemingly) unrequited love overcomes him. It may be fanciful to describe this difference in terms of stereotypes of female masochism and male aggression, but the parallel works surprisingly well.

As far as the motif of madness (a variant of irrationality) is concerned, there is only one character in Heyer's romances who has what politically correct usage terms difficult-to-meet needs: Torquil Broome in *Cousin Kate* attacks animals and humans, and ends up committing suicide after killing his mother. Not surprisingly, he has his home in the country. The fact that he behaves violently there could tempt a reader of Sandra Gilbert and Susan Gubar to apply the framework of their classic study *The Madwoman in the Attic* to his position. Gilbert and Gubar argue that the madwoman or monster-woman in literature "embodies intransigent female autonomy"[94] and "seeks the power of self-articulation" (79). They have been criticized, e.g. by Toril Moi[95] for their assumption that the madwoman is the female author's double and that the ultimate meaning of any woman's text is feminist rage. The criticism is certainly justified; but Gilbert and Gubar's approach remains useful if

---

[94] Gilbert, Sandra M., and Susan Gubar, *The Madwoman in the Attic: The Woman Writer and the Nineteenth-Century Literary Imagination*, New Haven: Yale University Press, 1979, p. 28.

[95] Moi, Toril, *Sexual/Textual Politics: Feminist Literary Theory. New Accents*. London, Routledge, 1985, pp. 61-62.

modified to the effect that an identification of author and character is not necessary for interpreting madness as rebellion, and that such an interpretation need not be defined as the only "true" one. With this proviso, we can regard Torquil as personifying rage at marginalization as well as the margin's desire for self-expression. It is significant in this context that Torquil's mother Minerva is said to be the carrier of his disease. She has given up the urban life she loved to accommodate her ailing husband. From one point of view, Torquil thus gives expression to Minerva's frustration; and when he has killed her, he finds he has nothing left to live for himself. From another point of view, the way in which Torquil attempts to assert himself is of course doomed to failure, because in its irrationality it replicates the patterns of dominant (metropolitan/patriarchal) discourse, the very discourse which has marginalized him.

Another stereotype of femininity is passivity. On a physical level, Sir Peter Stornaway in *The Toll-Gate*, set in Derbyshire, is almost unable to move after a stroke. Aubrey Lanyon in *Venetia* and Lord Lynton in *A Civil Contract* are both lame—in other words, doomed to a certain degree of physical passivity; the former lives in Yorkshire, the latter finds happiness as a farmer on his country estate. As for more general patterns of behavior, Sir Peregrine Taverner again provides an excellent example: in *Regency Buck*, he is the passive victim of murder plots laid by his London cousin, and has to be rescued by his London guardian; in *An Infamous Army*, he is captivated by a *femme fatale* and proves incapable of extricating himself unaided. In *The Corinthian*, young Piers Luttrell, who lives in rural Somerset, shows a pronounced tendency towards passivity: he is used as a cover by an acquaintance involved in a robbery; and he reacts with helpless despondency to his father's disapproval of the girl he loves. It is left to the London hero and heroine to disentangle the robbery case and send Piers and his beloved off to Gretna Green. *Venetia* presents a variation on the theme of country passivity: whereas in most other Heyer romances, passivity is a fixed attribute of certain characters, in Venetia it depends on their actually being in the country. At the beginning of the story, the eponymous heroine lives in Yorkshire, waiting for things to happen. A notorious rake soon arrives and shocks her with a kiss.  However, as he settles down in Yorkshire, he gradually loses his initiative, and he and Venetia passively drift into loving each other.  The idyll lasts until Venetia's uncle arrives from London to separate them.  He succeeds at first: the rake (reformed by now) promises to give Venetia up, and she accompanies her uncle to London.  There, however, she unexpectedly gains the ability to make decisions and to act.  She returns home, and with her new-found energy is able to overcome her love's scruples and get engaged to him.

Other feminine stereotypes, such as an association with nature, could be employed to analyse Heyer's romances.  However, the examples discussed should suffice to illustrate my point—that Heyer tends to feminize "non-London" in accordance with traditional images of women. By way of relativizing my framework, I shall now briefly look at a phenomenon which at first sight seems to invalidate it: that of narcissism in London men.  Narcissism has often been considered more typical of women than of men (witness Freud, for example); but Heyer's London dandies are certainly nothing if not in love with their own physical appearance.  Are they feminine, then?  Consider the following description of Sir Richard Wyndham, the eponymous hero of *The Corinthian*:

> From his windswept hair (most difficult of all styles to achieve) to the toes of his gleaming Hessians, he might have posed as an advertisement for the Man of Fashion.  His fine shoulders set off a coat of superfine cloth to perfection; his cravat [...] had been arranged by the hands of a master; his waistcoat was chosen with a nice eye; his biscuit-coloured pantaloons showed not one crease [...].  A quizzing-glass on a black ribbon hung round his neck; a fob at his waist; and in one hand he carried a Sèvres snuff-box.[96]

---

[96] Mandarin ed., 1992, p. 9.

Many of Heyer's heroes dress carefully and well; but while emphasizing this, the narrator as a rule is also at pains to point out that they are very handy with swords, pistols, or fists, and excellent judges and drivers of horses—masculine, in fact. About Sir Richard Wyndham, for example, the narrator reveals that "no tailoring, no amount of studied nonchalance, could conceal the muscle in his thighs, or the strength of his shoulders" (9) and that "[h]e was marked down by every cut-throat and robber [...] as dangerous, one who carried pistols, and could draw and fire with a speed and a deadly accuracy which made him a most undesirable man to molest" (122). Moreover, a clear line is usually drawn between the well-dressed hero and the showy wearers of a "profusion of rings, pins, fobs, chains, and seals"[97]; and the heroes on occasion ironically distance themselves from the very fashion they embody—for instance, Robert Beaumaris in *Arabella*, called the Nonpareil:

> "Remember when the Nonpareil wore a dandelion in his buttonhole three days running?" [Mr. Warkworth] said darkly. "Remember the kick-up there was, with every sap-head in town running round to all the flower-women for dandelions, which they hadn't got, of course. Stands to reason you don't buy dandelions! [...] but of course the Nonpareil was only hoaxing us! Once he had the whole lot of us decked out with them, he never wore one again, and a precious set of gudgeons we looked! [...]" (214)

Minor dandy characters with no aptitude for sport are usually portrayed as either ridiculous (Crosby Drelincourt in *The Convenient Marriage*, Sir Nugent Fotherby in *Sylvester*, Claud Darracott in *The Unknown Ajax*) or sinister (the suave murderer Basil Lavenham in *The Talisman Ring*, ruthless Francis Cheviot in *The Reluctant Widow*). A man's preoccupation with clothes thus proves acceptable only if offset by

---

[97] *Arabella*, Mandarin ed., 1991, p. 104.

physical prowess.

To turn from characterization to narrative devices, Pam Morris shows in *Literature and Feminism*[98] that both plot structure and point of view can serve to reinforce the representation of woman as Other. In Heyer's romances, the same is true of the representation of "non-London" as Other. As for plot structure, *Powder and Patch*, for example, centres on the transformation of a young man from a respectable rustic oaf into a fashionable gentleman with easy social manners, the point being that the latter guise enables him to win the woman he loves—an achievement which, we may assume, is tantamount to fulfilling his destiny. In *The Corinthian*, the heroine transfers her affection from a squire's son to Sir Richard Wyndham, the dandy described above. In *The Quiet Gentleman*, the urbane hero, Lord St. Erth, visits the country seat which he has inherited on his father's death (his father's dislike of him having previously kept him away). Several of its residents make life difficult for him: most notably his younger brother, by his open hostility, and his cousin by covert assassination attempts. By overcoming his brother's jealousy and disposing of his cousin, he establishes his mastery over the place. In those romances which focus on the relationship between a "London" hero and a "non-London" heroine, an eventual dominance by the hero obviously implies a dominance by "London": thus when Freddy Standen appears as a *deus ex machina* at the end of *Cotillion* to save a situation bungled by Kitty Charing through her lack of worldly experience, this demonstrates not only his superiority over the heroine, but also that of "London" over "non-London." Briefly, one of Heyer's most persistent plot patterns is the self-assertion of "London" as personified by male protagonists.

With regard to point of view, Morris argues that the judging consciousness in literature, with which readers are invited to identify, has traditionally been masculine rather than feminine. For reasons of space, I can only give a few short examples of a comparable principle at work in Heyer's treatment of place. First, an extract from *Arabella* (as mentioned

---

[98] Morris, Pam, *Literature and Feminism: An Introduction*, Oxford: Blackwell, 1993, pp. 27-33.

above, this romance brings together a Yorkshire heroine and a London hero):

> [Arabella] decided, in a wave of remorse, that [Mr. Beaumaris] was the greatest gentleman of her acquaintance, with the best manners, the most delicate forbearance, and quite the kindest disposition. It was at this point that the moment for which Mr. Beaumaris had been waiting arrived. All at once Arabella wondered how soon after the wedding-ceremony she could break the news to him that she required him not only to forgive her brother's debt to him, but also to bestow a hundred pounds on him for the settlement of all his other liabilities; and what words she could find with which most unexceptionably to express this urgent necessity. There were no such words, as a very little cudgelling of her brain sufficed to convince her. (302)

The focus is mainly on Arabella's thoughts; but the phrase "the moment for which Mr. Beaumaris had been waiting" clearly signals to the reader that he or she should enjoy the heroine's dilemma, together with the superior hero, rather than suffer with her. In this example, the "London"/"non-London" opposition is paralleled by the man/woman one; but this is not a prerequisite for the "London" point of view. In the following extract from *The Corinthian*, Sir Richard Wyndham, after presenting a slightly angled report of a murder to a Somerset magistrate, ends the conversation by saying:

> "[...] You, as a man of the world, will, I am assured, appreciate the need of the exercise of—ah— the most delicate discretion in handling this affair."
> Mr. Philips, who had once spent three weeks in London, was flattered to think that the imprint of that short sojourn was pronounced enough to be

discernable to such a personage as Beau Wyndham,
and swelled with pride. (147)

Since the magistrate has up to this point shown himself both credulous
and rather inarticulate ("Your disclosures, Sir Richard, open up—are in
fact, of such a nature as to—Upon my word, I never thought—But the
murder!" [146]), the narrator's elevated style appears to be a case of
irony at his expense, an expression of complicity with Sir Richard.

Finally, the "London" perspective can be doubled, as in *The
Nonesuch*. A minor character, the aspiring dandy Laurence Calver,
creates a stir when he visits Yorkshire:

> Laurence [...] was secretly as much exhilarated as
> surprised by his sudden and unexpected rise to
> importance. In London, amongst men of more
> natural parts and longer purses than his, it was almost
> impossible to make a hit: particularly (as he had
> often and resentfully thought) if one had the
> misfortune to be overshadowed by so magnificent a
> cousin as the Nonesuch [...]. He would have
> repudiated with scorn any suggestion that he should
> seek fame [sic] a rural district remote from the hub of
> fashion; but having been compelled by circumstance
> to visit his cousin he did not find it at all disagreeable
> to have become a star in this lesser firmament. [...]
> His appearance at the Colebatches' ball
> transcended all expectations, and quite eclipsed the
> local smarts. The beautiful arrangement of his
> pomaded locks, the height of his shirt-points, the
> intricacies of his neckcloth, the starched frill which
> protruded between the lapels of his tightly-fitted coat,
> with its short front and its extravagantly cutaway
> tails, the fobs and the seals which hung from his
> waist, and even the rosettes on his dancing-pumps,
> proclaimed him to be a Tulip of the first stare. His

> bow was much admired; if he was not precisely
> handsome, he was generally held to be goodlooking;
> and [...] even the most hostile of his critics
> acknowledged him to be a most accomplished
> dancer.[99]

The first paragraph quoted (and indeed the portrayal of Laurence Calver
in general) ironically colours the second, making it evident that the
admiration of the Yorkshire notables is misguided. However, the
narrator does not identify with Laurence here; a phrase such as "amongst
men of more natural parts," extremely unlikely to come from self-
absorbed Laurence, invites readers to gaze at both the "Tulip" and the
locals from a certain distance—in other words, to assume a position close
to that of the eponymous hero, who provides the yardstick by which
other characters are measured and judged. Thus, "London" as a whole
marginalizes Yorkshire; and the "London" of Sir Waldo Hawkridge, the
impeccable Nonesuch, marginalizes that of Laurence Calver. "London"
is not a monolith (and neither is "non-London," of course).

In examining Georgette Heyer's topography, I have ignored the
historical context of her work (or rather the two historical contexts: the
twentieth-century one and the Regency or pre-Regency one)—not
because I consider it irrelevant to an analysis of her romances in general,
but because taking it into account would have produced a different paper
altogether. My purpose has been to show that place in Heyer is a
gendered category. To conclude, I shall attempt to link my findings to
the overall conference theme of communication in Europe. What have
aspects of Heyer's work such as the frequent association of a "London"
hero with a "non-London" heroine, the presence of feminine stereotypes
in the portrayal of "non-London" men, and the marginalization of "non-
London" by means of narrative devices to do with linguistic and cultural
barriers in Europe? To begin with, they demonstrate—if any
demonstration is needed—that patterns of femininity can be found far
beyond the confines of (real or imaginary) womanhood, forming part of

---

[99] Pan ed., 1975, pp. 169-170.

more general patterns of Otherness. This is certainly relevant to cross-cultural communication insofar as any contact with another culture in principle involves the temptation to define its Otherness—and to define it using the pervasive stereotypes supplied by what Malcolm Chapman calls "the common grammar of European thought."[100] Bringing out the gender dimension of such stereotypes, and of other means of marginalization, is one way of drawing attention to their discursive character, of foregrounding and thereby (possibly) defusing them. More generally speaking, it is also one way of incorporating women's studies into the debate on region and nation, and vice versa; and the cross-fertilization made possible by this interpenetration of research fields can safely be expected to enhance our understanding of the question of identity, and consequently to refine on our perception, or rather our construction, of cultural difference.

**Sheri Cobb South, "What Color Is Your Heroine's Dress (and Why Should You Care?)," in *Romance Writer's Report*, September 1997, p. 20:**

. . . A color's message may change with its shade. Our lady in red might find seduction a bit trickier if she'd worn pale pink. Likewise, warm apricot creates a very different impression than hunter's fluorescent orange. And do you remember the notorious purple gown in Georgette Heyer's 1948 Regency, *The Foundling*? While a delicate lilac would have been perfectly acceptable for a young girl, beautiful but brainless Belinda has her heart set on a purple satin gown, and will gladly follow any man who promises to provide her with one. Belinda's ignorance of the color language of her day suggests that she is equally ignorant of the price her gentleman provider would require in exchange for the garish garment. . . .

---

[100] Chapman, Malcolm, *The Gaelic Vision in Scottish Culture*, London: Croom Helm, 1978, p. 165.

**Barbara Bywaters, "Decentering the Romance: Jane Austen, Georgette Heyer, and Popular Romance Fiction" (1999, unpublished essay based on Bywaters' 1989 dissertation "Re-Reading Jane: Jane Austen's Legacy to Twentieth Century Women Writers [Pym, Heyer, Gibbons, Brookner]"):**

> She said, closing the volume: "Surely the writer of that must possess a most lively mind? I am determined to take this book. It seems all to be written about ordinary people, and, do you know, I am quite tired of Sicilians and Italian Counts who behave in such a very odd way. *Sense and Sensibility*! Well, after *Midnight Bells* and *Horrid Mysteries* that has a pleasant ring, don't you agree?"

> —Judith Taverner in Georgette Heyer's
> *Regency Buck*

"Another Jane Austen" has become one of the most common marketing phrases in twentieth-century publishing. It has been applied to writers who range from Barbara Pym to Barbara Cartland. The writer who has most consistently been described as Austen-like, however, is Georgette Heyer, the best-selling British author labeled the "queen" or "mistress" of the modern romance form.

Heyer began publishing her novels in 1921 at the age of nineteen and proceeded to produce fifty-five more novels and one book of short stories which regularly made the best seller list until her death in 1974. Her reputation has developed around her use of the historical novel and romance forms. Thirty-three of Heyer's novels qualify as historical romance in which the romance encounter takes precedence over the historical detail.

Despite the popular forms she utilized in her work, Heyer viewed her writing as a craft rather than as a business. Much to her chagrin, though, she has been perceived by some throughout her fifty-year writing career as a "purveyor of romantic froth." A closer examination of Heyer's

493

novels reveals neither formulaic fiction nor "romantic froth." Her works can best be described as social comedy or comedy of manners much in the style of Jane Austen rather than as "romance fiction."

If there truly is "another Jane Austen" in 20th century literature, then Georgette Heyer can make a strong claim for the title. The connection between Jane Austen and Georgette Heyer is perhaps less marketing ploy than it at first seems. Heyer herself consciously connected her writing with Austen's in such a way that she literally "looks forward into the past" to Austen. She expressed her distaste for the twentieth century by declaring, "Christ, why did I have to be born into this *filthy* age!" and set the majority of her novels in a period not her own. After experimenting for the first ten years of writing with a variety of historical settings, from the eighteenth century to the middle ages, she settled by the mid-1930s on the early nineteenth century, particularly the second decade, as the setting for the majority of her historical novels. The age Heyer *chose* to live in through her fiction was the period of the Regency in England (1811-1820), when George IV was Prince Regent. Significantly, this is the period in which Jane Austen lived most of her adult life and in which all of her novels were published, beginning in 1811 with *Sense and Sensibility* and ending with the posthumously published *Persuasion* and *Northanger Abbey* in 1818.

Not only did Heyer choose to write novels set in the period in which Austen lived, but she also named Austen as one of her favorite authors, one whom she frequently reread. Several of Heyer's heroines are also readers of Austen. In one of Heyer's best works, *A Civil Contract*, the atypical heroine stammers to the hero that she prefers novels like those by the author of *Sense and Sensibility* to Byron's dramatic poetry, even though her rival, like Charlotte Brontë, complains that Austen's work is "too humdrum." As with her heroine, Heyer discovered in Austen the standards and codes of behavior that corresponded to her own view of the role of romance, and it becomes clear that Austen exercises considerable influence over Heyer's treatment of the romance form.

Romance as Center and Romance Decentered

Jane Austen's critical view of passion and sentimental love plays a key role in her fiction, and her anti-romantic stance has been widely acknowledged. Georgette Heyer's view of romance is less discernible, clouded by her categorization as "the queen of romance" who wrote novels of "moonlight and roses." Despite this classification, Heyer's novels, like those by Austen, present a vision of romance and marriage that challenges the standard conventions of romance fiction. Indeed Heyer herself described her view on love relationships in terms as unequivocal as Austen's. Heyer once emphatically declared, "Romantic I am not."

Although Heyer was attracted to romantic writing like that of the Brontë sisters, Heyer's novels diverge in crucial ways from the romance formula. As anti-romantics, both Heyer and Austen *center* their fiction on the romantic relationship, then proceed to *decenter* it by treating it in a comic-ironic fashion. In their novels, the portrayal of love as passionate and sentimental is repeatedly parodied, and the romance relationship is exposed to a form of psychological realism. Following Austen's lead, Heyer plays with the convention of character, plot and theme, deflating and distorting the elements which compose the romance form by her use of satire. The infusion of comedy into the romance structure is a large part of that which distinguishes Austen's and Heyer's fiction from other popular romance novels and which ultimately leads these writers to challenge the romance form itself.

## Romantic Heroes and Heroines

According to the "ideal romance" formula, the standard heroine exhibits the following characteristics: intelligence, independence, a sense of humor, and a kind of "femininity" which is expressed in a display of sympathy and vulnerability—the ability to be hurt, particularly by the hero. Because innocence and inexperience are key features of the romantic heroine, her age is typically between seventeen and twenty. Even though she is beautiful, she must be totally unselfconscious of her attractions which have a sensual effect on the hero. It is the combination of sensuality and feminine nurturing that softens the hero and makes him receptive to love.

The standard hero must also display intelligence and a sense of humor, but above all spectacular masculinity. He must be strong and forceful, sexually experienced and successful in a man's world, which usually means he is wealthy, aristocratic and powerful. In order to turn him into the fully caring male that he must be at the end of the novel, most romances introduce the hero as strong, but with some feature of vulnerability which will justify his transformation. In most standard romances, the hero turns from an arrogant sparring partner to protector and lover without adequate motivation or process being revealed.

A comparison of Heyer's protagonists to the characters of the "ideal romance" reveals some similarities between the two, but there are also specific differences in both the characters and the love relationship which place Heyer on the periphery of the circle of traditional romance writers. Heyer creates a number of atypical heroes and heroines who fail to adhere to the romance stereotypes. Her novels present a wide range of female and male characters unusual in romance fiction. The heroines include young girls, society beauties, impecunious older women, and unattractive females. Her heroes are represented by types such as the virile and savage male (*à la* Charlotte Brontë's Rochester), the fashionably debonair gentleman, and even the quiet, untried youth. Her male characters are not all strong and virile, and her female characters are sometimes plain, dowdy, and painfully inarticulate.

In her early fiction, Heyer presented spirited love stories that helped in part to formulate the romance conventions and types she would later parody. An early work such as *These Old Shades* (1926), for example, centers on the romance between the powerful and experienced Duke of Avon, nicknamed Satanas, and Léonie, a penniless girl disguised as a boy who is twenty years younger. Léonie succeeds in bringing out a more tender, "human" side of the Duke's personality, becoming in the end "his salvation." The traditionalism of the male and female roles in the romance relationship is clear: the male is protector, and patriarch, and the female is the nurturer of the gentler passions.

As Heyer's fiction developed, however, she gradually turned away from this form of hierarchical male-female relationship. Heyer's 1944

*Friday's Child*, for example, develops the romantic relationship between two very unromantic characters, Lord Sheringham, a spoiled nobleman, and Hero Wantage, an impoverished dependent. Lord Sheringham, in particular, departs from the romantic ideal: he has mistresses; he gambles and drinks too much; and he is selfish and irresponsible. Besides being impetuous and very prosaic, he has one quality never found in a romantic hero: he is often stupid. Heyer's comic treatment of him serves to undercut much of the romantic surface of the novel.

## Conventions of the Romance Plot

In the standard romance plot the hero and the heroine initially clash, undergo a protracted period of forced peace, and then declare their love when endangered. Georgette Heyer encorporates these elements of the romance plot into her novels in much the same manner that she uses the conventions of characterization. Instead of telling a simple story of romance, she twists features of the romance plot to expose the myth behind the story. Many of her novels emphasize the female or male protagonist's gradual recognition of the inadequacy of the romantic ideal and his or her acceptance of an unconventional partner as an object of romantic love.

As with Austen's novels, the majority of Heyer's historical romances fail to follow the standard romance pattern of the initial antipathy between hero and heroine and a later, gradual reconciliation. Instead, a number of novels such as *Sprig Muslin* (1956) and *Charity Girl* (1970) center on the story of old friends who, through a series of circumstances, reassess their relationship and discover their mutual love, much in the manner of Austen's *Emma* and *Mansfield Park*. Using a similar storyline, Heyer fashions some of her most comic fiction on another major concern in Austen's fiction: the ability to discern the most suitable marriage partner. In novels such as *Devil's Cub* (1936), *The Quiet Gentleman* (1951) and *Frederica* (1965), male and female protagonists learn to distinguish between shallow and mature love. Unlike the conventional romance plot, many of Heyer's narratives deal with the main characters' progress toward attaining the same rational approach to romance that Heyer expressed herself.

In the novels in which Heyer does adopt the standard plot of the romance form, she undermines its force by her comic treatment. In *Sylvester; or, The Wicked Uncle* (1957), for example, the narrative begins with a variation of Austen's *Pride and Prejudice*, which stands as one of the prototypes for the romantic plot formula. The male protagonist, the proud Duke of Salford, angers the unconventional heroine, Phoebe Marlow, by slighting her at a ball, just as Darcy insulted Elizabeth Bennet in Austen's work. Pressing the conventional plot to its extreme, Heyer constructs a fitting method of revenge for her heroine, as Phoebe writes a novel lampooning the haughty Duke, making him a laughingstock throughout society. This action sets off a series of farcical events which conclude with the Duke's declaration of love and proposal of marriage. Like Darcy's first proposal to Elizabeth in *Pride and Prejudice*, the Duke's proposal is regarded by Phoebe as the ultimate insult. Although the two are reconciled at the conclusion of the novel, Heyer pushes the classic repulsion-attraction plot to its most extreme limit and in the process deflates it.

## Plot Devices in the Romance Narrative

Devices such as the marriage proposal convention play a significant role in the development of the plot in the romance form. Love-at-first-sight, the suffering of lovers, and the purity and idealism of love are among the devices that have been part of the Western literary tradition since the twelfth century. Other conventions such as elopement and abduction became standard features in the novel form of the eighteenth century. By the end of the eighteenth century, they were standard features in the popular sentimental and gothic novels of the period. Given Austen's unromantic and ironic vision, these elements of the romance plot were ripe for parody when Austen began writing.

The device of love-at-first-sight is one which Austen treats with great comic energy. As early as *Love and Freindship* [Austen's original spelling] (1790), she carried the convention to such absurd lengths that the young girl Laura falls deeply in love with a man before he even speaks. As her writing developed, however, Austen began to use ironic techniques rather than exaggeration and farce to undercut the romance plot. In *Sense and Sensibility*, for example, Marianne Dashwood is inspired with a great passion for her rescuer Willoughby. She is able to discern that Willoughby is very like the "hero of a favorite story," even though in her distress she has been unable to see him clearly. Heyer reveals that from the very beginning of her writing she too was consciously manipulating the conventions of the romance plot that she inherited. Beginning with farce, as did Austen in her juvenilia, Heyer utilized more sophisticated comic treatments as her writing developed. In Heyer's early novels, her parody of conventions relies primarily on broad physical humor. But by the middle of her career, she had evolved a comic style that was based on situation and characterization and was therefore more intrinsically ironical such as that found in Austen's fiction. In this way, both authors sought to challenge the components of the romance form even as they used them.

Heyer uses a variety of the standard romance conventions such as the abduction, the elopement and the flight from the arranged marriage as devices to advance the plot. In several novels, she opens with one of these conventions, but most frequently she utilizes the abduction or the elopement sequence to bring the right lovers together at the close of the novels. For Heyer, elopements, abductions and flight most often occur among the minor characters, but when she uses these devices most skillfully, she is capable of weaving together a sophisticated structure which utilizes several of these elements to advance the plot and produce a comic effect. In a novel like *Friday's Child*, for example, the narrative begins with a hasty elopement between the main characters and concludes with an abduction and a second elopement, followed by a double rescue which brings the right lovers together. Almost two-thirds of Heyer's historical romances include abductions, elopements or flights from arranged marriages.

Heyer's mature fiction exhibits an ironic style closer in technique to Austen's. At the middle of their careers, both authors could skillfully deflate the elements of the romance plot with a controlled, ironic touch rather than with the physical comedy of the early fiction. Heyer's 1950 novel *The Grand Sophy* compares favorably in this way with Austen's *Emma*. Sophy, like Emma, is a strong woman character who controls the action of the novel. Tall, striking and forceful, she manages the lives of the other characters. Her father, Sir Horace, is no Mr. Woodhouse, but his casual parenting is similar to Mr. Woodhouse's in that it produces the same results. Both daughters are independent and accustomed to having their own way. Each is twenty years old and unmarried, but an ardent match-maker for others. Both novels are lively and full of wit and energy, largely due to the formidable heroines who drive the narrative. Both women finally discover love with men inside their family circle—Sophy ends mated with her cousin, Charles Rivenhall, and Emma with an older brother-in-law.

Sophy follows the model set by Emma Woodhouse in many respects, but there are significant differences. The force of Austen's novel comes from the power of Emma's personality and the painful discovery of her own fallibility. Emma plays games with romance and eventually realizes that she is not above the courtship process herself. Without question Emma changes in the work, and it is the humbling of the powerful--and the possibility that Emma will bounce back again--which makes *Emma* such a compelling novel.

The major difference between Heyer's work and Austen's is that Sophy, unlike her counterpart Emma Woodhouse, remains a static character. She rearranges people's lives, but she is never fallible: her matches always work out for the best, and she enters the novel in the same high-spirited and high-handed manner as she departs. She is a comic character to the last.

## Romances Without the Romance

The romance formula presents an idealized relationship between the male and female: the standard romance novel always ends happily, frequently with either a declaration of love or actual marriage. As the primary criterion of the romance form, the happy ending is considered an "indispensable" feature. Marriage becomes the goal, the conclusion of the romantic process toward which the romance plot is driven. Thus personal feelings are placed before wealth, social advancement or the common good. In particular, the romance narrative which concludes in marriage underscores the importance of the woman in the story. It is her feelings and her existence which become paramount in the romance formula. A central feature of the standard romance is the softening effect that the heroine has on the hero. The hero's declaration of love and proposal of marriage at the conclusion of the romance illustrates that the heroine has taught him the highly valued female art of loving.

All of Austen's novels close with the marriage of the hero and heroine and the sense of social and emotional union. Most of Heyer's historical romances conclude in a similar way, with the betrothal of the protagonists and frequently the pairing off of secondary couples as well. Austen's and Heyer's fiction generally follows the movement of the narrative structure toward marriage, although four of Heyer's novels begin with the marriage of the hero and heroine and explore romance within the institution of marriage. The portrait of the institution of marriage which they present in their novels, however, is largely unromanticized. Their view of love and marriage stands at odds with the passionate sentimentality that permeated the romance writing of the nineteenth century and became formalized in the mass-market romances of the twentieth century.

An examination of Austen's principal male characters reveals that most of male protagonists view marriage as an economic and social action or as a union based on mutual attraction. Wealthy landowners such as Mr. Darcy in *Pride and Prejudice* and Mr. Knightley in *Emma* perceive marriage as the "proper" course for a gentleman, the fulfilling of one's social obligation. Austen's other main male characters seek more than social and economic equality in marriage. These male protagonists desire women who exhibit an attractiveness born of charm, vivacity and prettiness, and in the process, overlook women who are quieter, more intelligent and compassionate.

In Austen's novels, marriage takes on greater complexity and significance for the women characters. Because marriage defined a woman's economic, social, and personal positions in the patriarchal society of the nineteenth century, the choice of mate became the single

501

most important decision a woman could make in her life.  Austen's female protagonists, Elizabeth Bennet, Fanny Price, Emma Woodhouse and Anne Elliot, all engage in romantic relationships, but their relationships function on a variety of levels.   Each relationship encompasses more than a woman and man falling in love and marrying. For Austen's main female characters, the courtship process includes psychological and moral dimensions.

While Heyer's depiction of the romance relationship lacks the profound analysis that Austen brings to  her portrayal of courtship and marriage, following Austen's lead, Heyer *does* present a more developed and less idealistic picture of the romance relationship in her novels than that which has evolved in the popular romance formula.  In Heyer's mature fiction, she consistently satirizes romance based on passion and sentimental love.  The love between the hero and heroine is based on the recognition of common personality traits, a mutual acceptance of one another's limitations, and a sense of comfort and stability culled from sharing everyday experiences.

All the participants in the main courtship in Heyer's novels exhibit certain qualities that will insure a successful union.  Male and female characters show a compassion and an intelligence which involves a mutual realization of the foibles of others and the hypocrisies inherent in the social structure.  The most important quality in both partners is a sense of humor, an ability to laugh which symbolizes a deeper understanding of human nature, an acceptance of human frailty, and an ability to love.

Comparing several of Austen's novels to three of Heyer's strongest works illustrates the dichotomy between the idealistic and realistic views of romance that permeates their fiction.  Of all of Heyer's novels, *A Civil Contract* best conveys the sense of disappointment and disillusionment that comes from an overly idealistic, passionate view of romance.  In *Bath Tangle* and *Black Sheep*, Heyer further examines the role of courtship and marriage, questioning like her heroines what is the ideal and what is the real.

### *A Civil Contract*

More somber and realistic than Heyer's other fiction, *A Civil Contract* (1961) remains within the marriage framework to act out the opposing perspectives to romance as defined in Austen's equally somber and realistic *Sense and Sensibility*. *A Civil Contract* charts the course of an ordinary young man's marriage to Jenny Chawleigh (Sense), rather than Julia Oversley (Sensibility), and the slowly developing love between the two incongruous characters. The novel covers a seventeen-month period, opening in 1814 with the male protagonist's return home from the Peninsular Army to inherit his title and face bankruptcy. Unable to provide for his dependent sisters and in love with the beautiful Julia Oversley, the hero Adam Deveril is persuaded to marry an heiress of the mercantile class, Jenny Chawleigh, in order to save the family estate. Adam is a handsome, charming and sensitive hero, while Jenny, on the other hand, is that one species very seldom—if ever—found in the romance novel. She is an unattractive heroine. Plump and squat, with a short neck, a small mouth and button nose, Jenny is a direct contrast to the lovely Miss Julia Oversley, her rival.

Sense versus sensibility is the key. Julia Oversley with her swooning fits, frail nerves and her narcissistic, idealistic view of love is Austen's Marianne Dashwood. In many ways, Jenny is a less attractive Elinor Dashwood, viewing marriage in a very prosaic, highly anti-romantic way. Jenny vows to make Adam "comfortable," to provide companionship and support for him instead of passion. Her sensible approach to romance indicates not a lack of feeling but a more critical and thoughtful evaluation of sensibility. Throughout the novel, hers is a love based on reality, not dreams.

As the hero, it is Adam who most embraces an idealistic vision of marriage and love and who must change as the novel progresses. His own innate kindness and Jenny's "reasoned love" bring him to the realization that there is a significant difference between reality and dreams. Jenny's "prosaic attitude" carries them through the many difficult moments of their marriage including the intimacies of the honeymoon and the birth of their first child.

503

Eventually, Adam and Jenny achieve a relationship based not on passion but on shared experience and compatibility. Adam learns to "respect and esteem" Jenny, and he gradually becomes disillusioned with the beautiful Julia Oversley. At the conclusion of the novel, he tells Jenny, "You are a part of my life. Julia was never that—only a boy's impractical dream!" Jenny must accept then too that she will never be loved by Adam in the manner in which he adored Julia. She becomes reconciled to a different kind of loving that is more profound and enduring.

## Bath Tangle

Georgette Heyer's *Bath Tangle* (1955) seems at first a standard re-telling of Shakespeare's comic *Taming of the Shrew*, with another high-spirited, beautiful heroine, Lady Serena, matched against the virile and masterful Marquis of Rotherham. But Heyer's portrayal of their relationship, and the secondary romance that complements it, reflects a deeper examination of the romantic relationship from an Austen point of view. As in many of her novels, Heyer uses a secondary courtship as a foil for the primary romance, which in this novel is more unconventional than the main relationship.

The novel opens with the unexpected death of Lady Serena's father, the Earl of Spenborough, in a hunting accident. Left to grieve his death are Lady Serena and his second wife, Fanny, whom he married in order to provide an heir. Fanny's circumstances are particularly difficult. Because her parents are members of the impoverished nobility and have a large family, Fanny found herself coerced into marriage at nineteen to the forty-seven-year-old Earl. Their marriage is described as an "unnatural tie," and clearly Fanny's intimate relationship with a man older than her father has had an adverse effect on her.

The social and economic constraints placed upon women in the nineteenth century are seriously considered through Heyer's portrayal of their marriage. Although Fanny is more passive and vulnerable than the novel's heroine, Lady Serena, Heyer portrays Fanny's situation with sensitivity and imbues her with a degree of dignity and thoughtfulness not previously associated in Heyer's fiction with the weak woman figure. Fanny's concern for duty and her genuine belief in the system of propriety which regulates a woman's behavior makes her sound very much like Austen's Fanny Price in *Mansfield Park*, another timid, obedient heroine.

The relationship between the main characters, Lady Serena and the Earl of Rotherham, is also treated with more perception than in Heyer's earlier fiction. Lady Serena and the Earl come together again after a romantic encounter in their youth which failed. At the beginning of the novel, the two have settled into a comfortable form of friendship which Serena describes as one based on the "sort of fondness one has for an old acquaintance, who shares many of one's ideas and tastes." Complications occur in the lives of Serena and Fanny when Serena encounters a Major Kirby, an old love whom her father persuaded her not to marry when she was nineteen. The two renew their engagement, but as Lady Serena recognizes, she and the Major are completely mismatched. Serena declares to Fanny, "He does not know me." Gradually Serena realizes that their relationship is based on a romantic idealism that has no foundation in reality.

By the conclusion of the novel, the couples sort themselves out. Major Kirby who wants to protect his wife falls in love with the gentle Fanny who needs to be cherished after her painful first marriage. On the other hand, Serena and the Earl have been forced to examine themselves and the pain they cause others and themselves. At the conclusion of the novel, their mutual vow, "we will do better this time," is full of more humility and self-knowledge than the standard lovers' vows.

## Black Sheep

Heyer's female protagonist who most closely resembles Austen's Anne Elliot is Abigail Wendover of *Black Sheep* (1967). Twenty-eight, unmarried, and her prettiness faded, Abigail represents another mature heroine who views love and marriage not with the passion of youth, but with the wisdom gained from experience. Set in Bath, *Black Sheep* deals with Abigail's attempt to keep her young niece from succumbing to the charming fortune hunter, Stacy Calverleigh. Meanwhile, Abigail herself fights her attraction to Stacy's uncle, Miles Calverleigh. Miles Calverleigh is another antithesis of the romantic hero. He is not handsome, and he dresses carelessly. Sent to India for his indiscretions, he makes a fortune and returns to England a cynical, self-made man, immune to the social conventions and restrictions of the society into which he was born. Abigail views him as immoral, but Miles Calverleigh is actually amoral, a modern individualist.

The initial attraction between the main characters is based on a shared sense of humor. The existence of a sense of humor indicates more than just an appreciation of life's absurdities in Heyer's novels; it also represents a shared understanding. Abigail in *Black Sheep* discerns a deeper compatibility between Miles and herself that is underscored by the similarity in their sense of the ridiculous. As a younger woman, Abby had fallen in love with a "handsome countenance, and had endowed its owner with every imaginable virtue." Older and more mature, she accepts Miles's faults and can even overlook his harsh features.

In spite of her love for him, Abby refrains from accepting Miles's proposal of marriage which is made two-thirds of the way into the novel. Her own sense of independence and her reluctance to place her own happiness before the concerns of her family cause her to realistically reassess the role of marriage in her life. Like Austen's protagonist Emma Woodhouse, Abby is financially secure and therefore marriage for her is not an economic necessity as it is for some of Heyer's and Austen's other heroines. Instead, the question of marriage becomes a personal decision [as] Abby is confronted with the choice of placing her personal feelings before the fulfillment of her social and familial duties. Because of Miles Calverleigh's disreputable past, Abby's marriage to him would cause considerable discomfort to her very proper family. As Abby recognizes, "in consulting only her own ardent desire, she would be subjecting every member of her family to varying degrees of shock, dismay, and even, where Selina and Mary [her sisters] were concerned, to grave distress."

In *Black Sheep*, Heyer reflects Austen's profound use of the courtship theme: individual happiness is pitted against the dominating social

506

structure. Abby must decide whether to marry for personal fulfillment or to consider the larger social implications of the marriage act as well. Her detailed reasoning of the romantic relationship with Miles Calverleigh questions the role of romance as personal and social. Abby finally rejects Miles' offer for the good of her family and in accordance with the social code. As the amoral agent in the novel, it is Miles, however, who overrides Abby's decision at the conclusion of the novel. He steals her away from her family, clearly choosing the happiness of the individual over duty.

## Austen, Heyer and the Romance Formula

A quick reading of any of Georgette Heyer's novels will make it abundantly clear that Georgette Heyer is not a Jane Austen. Austen's fiction is eminently superior. Heyer mimicked those elements of Austen's art which were easiest to comprehend: the form of the comedy of manners; the comic-ironic style; the anti-romantic stance; even the social and historical period in which Austen lived and wrote. Heyer's novels, however, lack the subtle characterization and the psychological insight that mark Austen's works. The styles of the two authors differ in fundamental ways as well: Heyer's is more light-hearted and comic; Austen adroitly exposes human weakness and folly with skillful irony. Austen examines courtship and marriage in such a way that what is merely romance in a lesser writer takes on the seriousness of moral and personal choice in her novels.

Yet Heyer and Austen do come together on the continuum of the female literary tradition in the context of the development of the romance formula. Heyer functions as an interim figure in the development of the popular romance form. Her fiction mediates between that of Austen's, which uses courtship and marriage to examine the larger concerns of the society and the individual, and that of mass-produced romance fiction which, at its very worst as in a Barbara Cartland work, reduces the male-female relationship to a lifeless formula. From Austen, to Heyer, to popular romance fiction, we encounter a gradual shift from the complex to the simple, from the consciously ironic vision to an unquestioning acceptance. In this process, Austen herself finally becomes codified into the romance formula as Cartland illustrates in her novels when a heroine enters a library and by accident pulls a novel by Jane Austen off of the shelf. This casual reference to Austen becomes part of a necessary obligatory acknowledgement in popular romance of Austen's influence on the form. In the most formulaic popular romance fiction, Austen's name is all that survives of her complex legacy. But with her comic-ironic vision, and with her unromantic stance fashioned on that of her mighty foremother, Georgette Heyer merges the forces of high art and the appeal of popular fiction in her mastery of the elements of the romance formula.

**Helen Hughes, "Georgette Heyer and the Changing Face of Historical Romance" (1999, unpublished essay based on Hughes's 1988 dissertation, "Changes in Historical Romance, 1890s to the 1980s: The Development of the Genre from Stanley Weyman to Georgette Heyer and Her Successors"):**

Georgette Heyer's early novels were published by Mills & Boon, and they still claim her as one of "their" authors. As well as being a historical novelist who took great pains to fill her work with accurate historical detail, she can be considered a writer of quintessential women's romantic fiction. Even though most of her later output was published by Heinemann, Heyer remains in a sense a Mills & Boon author since the formula she developed—almost by accident at first in writing *These Old Shades* (1926), intended originally as a kind of sequel to an earlier novel—was the one which was to become characteristic of the traditional Mills & Boon romance.

The roles of hero and heroine in the genre have been seen as providing a model for relationships which maintain male dominance and female subservience in a patriarchal society. In many ways they do; but at the same time, the presentation of these fictions offers the woman reader an opportunity to experience a cathartic female anger at the inequalities of power in such a society. An examination of the ways in

508

which Heyer constructed her heroes and heroines can throw light on this subtext, but in order to appreciate her innovations, it is useful to look back beyond Heyer's work to the traditional historical romances like those with which she began her career, and which her later work displaced.

In an article in *The Times Literary Supplement* of 21 September 1984, Gillian Avery bewailed the loss of the historical adventure story which she had enjoyed as a girl, its place having been taken by historical romance of the kind associated with Heyer. At the end of the nineteenth century and the beginning of the twentieth, such historical adventure stories, written by authors such as A. E. W. Mason, Baroness Orczy, Raphael Sabatini, and, above all, Stanley Weyman, dominated the popular book market.

In their books the young Gillian Avery would not have found any very inspiring role models among the heroines. In these stories, adventures were primarily for males: females might function as assistants, but they were essentially passive adjuncts of the hero, and at times actually a hindrance to the adventurous life. In A. E. W. Mason's *Lawrence Clavering*, for example, the heroine nearly brings the hero and herself to disaster as they run for their life across the Cumbrian fells because, through feminine vanity, she insists on wearing fashionable high-heeled shoes. This is presented as a lovably absurd female trait.

The image of a heroine as a kind of annoying but delightful pet is, of course, one of the stereotypical images of women familiar from nineteenth century novels, particularly those written by male authors. The other major stereotypes are those of the pure heroine whose virtue inspires the hero and keeps *him* virtuous—Agnes Wicksteed as opposed to Dora Copperfield—and the ultimate aim, perhaps, of all heroines, the mother of the family, the centre of the home and ruler in her own sphere. At the turn of the century such stereotypes were particularly apropos, since this was a period when middle class women, at least, were beginning to enter the labour market, for example, as part of the growing army of clerks and secretaries, to demand professional careers and the right to vote. Philip Dodd has suggested (Colls and Dodd, eds., *Englishness: Politics and Culture 1880-1920* [1986]) that at this time a positive valuation of "manliness" associated with an image of what "Englishness" represented was reconstituted "in order," as he wrote, "to incorporate and neuter various social groups"—including women—who threatened the social order." "Incorporation" implied that the image of womanliness formed in response to that of manliness and based on the "Angel in the House" stereotype, though limiting in the role it offered, was a flattering one, promising a kind of power and status attainable easily by just existing.

At the turn of the century historical romance of the swashbuckling adventurous type mourned by Gillian Avery was the dominant popular genre, and within the genre the best-selling author was Stanley Weyman. His heroines illustrate the acceptable image of womanliness well, as can be seen from a romance such as *The Abbess of Vlaye.* The gender roles in this novel are not, as a matter of fact, straightforward pictures of womanliness and manliness. Rather, there is a continuum which ranges from the excessively masculine to the extremely feminine, and which includes two characters who are close to androgynous: a more feminine male character and a strong, masculine female—the "Abbess" of the title. It is this variety which makes the book an interesting case, but the presentation of the characters leaves the reader in no doubt that the more strongly gendered characters are morally preferable.

*The Abbess of Vlaye* is set in the reign of Henri IV, a king who particularly interested Weyman. The hero, des Ageaux, is the king's Lieutenant-Governor in Perigord, and, like a number of Weyman heroes, could be described as serviceable rather than exciting. He is dull and unromantic, indifferent to "the favour of the ladies," but passing among men as "a man more useful than most." He is a brave and competent soldier who reveals an uncomplicated pride in doing his duty for his country and a love of justice which is described as "part of his nature, part of his passion."

He is matched with a heroine, Bonne, who typifies the domestic virtues. Sent by the king to put down a rebellion in Perigord, des Ageaux visits one of his castles in disguise. The castle is a poor place, the castellan having fallen upon hard times and living mainly in the past, and his son having left home to join the rebels. Bonne, the daughter of the

510

house, tries to keep some semblance of comfort about the place, contriving to find food for the rest of the family—even if she herself must go short—when otherwise the household must have starved, and helping with the work in the fields. Throughout her trials she remains cheerful and patient. In her worn clothes and shabby surroundings, she has a strong resemblance to Tennyson's Enid, presented as an ideal of womanliness in the *Idylls of the King*. Neither Bonne nor des Ageaux is a charismatic character. Far more memorable are the other two major characters, Bonne's sister Odette de Villeneuve (the "Abbess" of the title) and the Duke of Joyeuse, who swings between extreme religiosity and every kind of dissolute behavior. Joyeuse is glamorous and brave, following des Ageaux into danger on his own and in disguise, but his whims and passions endanger the whole enterprise, while as for Odette, the cool politician who tries to use men to her own advantage, her intelligence and courage are counterbalanced by a selfishness and pride which makes her ultimately unattractive. It is, in fact, the caring and unselfish Bonne who is allowed to achieve happiness in the end. Curiously enough, she is also allowed the most heroic action in the story; when she and des Ageaux are kidnapped and bound to the backs of their horses by the rebels, it is Bonne who manages to free her hand, take des Ageaux's knife from his sheath, and cut his bonds so that he is able to free both of them. She is heroic on behalf of the man she loves, of course, and her courage is balanced by weakness: once the two reach safety, she faints.

The qualities which make Bonne admirable—self-sacrifice, care for her family, loyalty to her man—are repeated in other heroines of Weyman, though some have to learn them in circumstances of danger and difficulty. Henrietta, for instance, in *Starvecrow Farm*, is something of a rebel at the start of the story. She has eloped with Walterson, a man she hardly knows, and whose only recommendation is that he is the only person she has ever met who has been moderately kind to her. Walterson, in reality a member of the Cato Street conspiracy who is trying to escape from justice in disguise, abandons her but kidnaps the son of Captain Clyne, the man to whom Henrietta has been betrothed by her heartless relatives.

Henrietta's rebellion goes no further than to accompany Walterson to an inn near Windermere, where she immediately puts herself under the protection of the landlady. This does not prevent her relatives and Clyne from casting her off, or Weyman from suggesting that she is blameworthy and foolish. Clyne is particularly brutal. He tries to bully her into telling him Walterson's whereabouts. Henrietta, curiously, is roused and excited by his violence rather than frightened, though she feels humiliated and angry at the same time; when Clyne seizes her by the wrist, she feels it to be a "humiliation." It is apparent when they talk later, however, that she has pleasurable memories of the episode.

Germaine Greer (*The Female Eunuch* [1971]) has suggested that in enjoying reading about the typical brutal hero of romance, women are "cherishing the chains of their bondage." Henrietta's capitulation certainly seems to conform to Tania Modleski's description of the heroine's progress in a typical Harlequin romance: "The heroines rebel against the male authority figure. . . but then comes the constant reminder of the impossibility of winning. . . if you can't lick them, you might as well love them" (*Loving With a Vengeance: Mass-Produced Fantasies for Women* [1982]).

No doubt had this been a romance written for women, this would have been sufficient to provide the "turn" of the story. Since this is Weyman, however, there has to be a character change from silly, rebellious girl to potential mother and mistress of a household. Clyne's unkindness conquers Henrietta: partly, no doubt, because of a new feeling for Clyne aroused by his action, but partly also by her realisation of Clyne's love for his son, which arouses her latent motherly feelings; as a result, she is haunted by pity for the little boy, and later puts herself in danger to rescue him.

In Weyman's work, therefore, there is little sympathy for women's aspiration for independence and power. The destiny which a woman *should* look forward to was that of mistress in her own home, the centre of the household, with no existence beyond its bounds, and her own status dependent upon her husband. No matter that the husband was totally lacking in charisma; all that was necessary to be a Weyman hero was bravery and the ability to be "useful" when military action was required. The Weyman hero was a man's man and the woman had in the end to come to love him as he was. If any change of character was required, it had to be hers.

Heyer's main innovation was to change this relationship so that female rebellion became the centre of the story, which was to turn on the hero's growing love for *her*, and the creation of heroes who were not to be approved by men, but by women. It was enough to establish a new kind of historical romance as primarily a woman's genre. Between Weyman's career and Heyer's, it is true, new kinds of hero had been created by writers of historical fiction: Raphael Sabatini's Captain Blood, for example, always polite, calm, and witty, or, even more strikingly, Baroness Orczy's Scarlet Pimpernel. Whatever the changes, however, these remained heroes of adventure stories and essentially the power relationship between hero and heroine remained the same as it had been in the novels of Weyman. For all Marguerite Blakeney's acting talent in *The Scarlet Pimpernel*, for instance, she sacrifices her career happily to marry Percy, and the novel shows her to be looking for a hero to look up to rather than a partner. Her attempts to warn Sir Percy of his danger are as useless as the activities of an A. E. W. Mason heroine in supporting the hero, and end in her own capture by Chauvelin, leaving Percy in more danger than before.

It was a hero and heroine of this type that Heyer used for her first novel, *The Black Moth*, and the story is similar, too. Jane Aiken Hodge, in her biography of Heyer (*The Private World of Georgette Heyer* [1984]) mentions Orczy and Sabatini as important influences. It is a "cloak-and-dagger" adventure story, centred round a disgraced hero who makes his living as a highwayman, and the attempts of the villain to abduct the heroine. There are duels and hair's-breadth escapes, and the climax is a nerve-tingling ride across country for the hero as he goes to rescue the heroine from the villain. The novel was originally written for her ailing brother, and might be supposed to be the kind of story a boy would enjoy. The hero has charm, but his leading characteristic is an exaggerated sense of school-boy honour, while the heroine has the same kind of role as Marguerite Blakeney in *The Scarlet Pimpernel*: indeed, in some ways she can be linked with the older tradition of Weyman and

Mason, since a large part of her function is to look after the hero when he is wounded, as happens in Weyman's *A Gentleman of France* or Mason's *Lawrence Clavering*.

*The Black Moth* brought Heyer some success, but though she maintained this, she felt it was not growing. In 1925, she attempted to develop her work by writing a kind of sequel to *The Black Moth*: a novel which used the same characters, but with changed names and a changed situation. The result was *These Old Shades*, and it became a best-seller. Thereafter, Heyer's reputation was assured, but it was as a writer for a female readership. Her solution to her problem had been essentially a simple one. The hero of *These Old Shades* is not based on Jack, the highwayman hero of the earlier book, but on Tracy, its villain. Justin Alastair, Duke of Avon, has some of Jack's characteristics, such as a fondness for dressing in colours rather than the black which Tracy affects—though Justin's purple coat, with its imperial connotations, suggests a power which is missing from Jack's pale lilac silk. In other ways, Justin and Tracy are alike. Both are callous and unscrupulous, and Justin is revengeful as well.

Such heroes were, of course, to become almost the hallmark of women's romance, and have attracted attention from feminist critics because of the image of male power as opposed to female submission which they reproduce for women readers. Not all such criticism is damning. Though many would support the view of Germaine Greer quoted above, Tania Modleski believes that, first, women did not, as Greer had suggested, "invent" masculine characters who "assert masculine superiority in the same ways men often do in real life" and, second, that the pleasure of a romantic text comes for women in large part "from the elements of a revenge fantasy, from our conviction that the woman is bringing the man to his knees." In such a view, the power of a figure like Avon is his pre-eminent characteristic, since the revenge fantasy becomes more satisfying in proportion to the potency of the male figure.

It seems difficult, however, to believe that ultimately revenge is a sufficient satisfaction. Janice Radway (*Reading the Romance*, 1991) may have been nearer the mark when she suggested that romances which featured heroes like Avon were chiefly about "transformation": the hero is "feminised," developing qualities of "motherly" tenderness and care already latent in his nature. This model would certainly fit the relationships in *These Old Shades*. The relationship between hero and heroine has much in common with that between caregiver and child, even if its quality is only gradually revealed to the reader. The callous Avon is balanced by a heroine whose leading characteristic is naivete—though at the same time Leonie offers a more positive role model to a feminist critic since, in contrast to earlier heroines, she is capable, shrewd, and active—even, despite her essential innocence, worldly wise.

Heyer was able to give her such apparently contradictory qualities by hiding her female identity at the beginning of the novel, so that until about halfway through, she is Leon, ex-street-urchin, and now a page. Having lived as a boy for four years, she has had time to unlearn much of her feminine identity. She has a turn of speed which can easily outdistance her foster-brother and can "hurl" herself at Avon in boyish fashion. Her wildness contrasts with Avon's "mincing" gait. When she relaxes, she squats or sits with her feet tucked under her—a freedom of which no earlier heroine would have been capable. She has a bravery based on a stoical endurance of hardship in her earlier life, and is capable enough to escape without help when, as with less capable heroines, she is kidnapped.

Her "Puck-like quality of old and young wisdom" appeals to Avon, and transforms him, so that he tolerates "impertinence" from her which no one else would dare to offer. His friends hear a note "of. . . faith, of tenderness" in his voice, and believe that Justin will cherish Leonie. If not exactly Radway's mother figure, at least he offers Leonie the kind of non-judgmental acceptance which can give her a stable background and allow her personality to flower.

At the same time, it must be admitted that Leonie remains childlike, and Avon's role is more that of a loving parent than of a lover. It was a way of solving the problem of making sure the heroine remained as innocent as her Victorian ancestor, while gaining more personal freedom to appeal to a new generation—suggesting that perhaps attitudes had not, despite the upheavals of war and the efforts of the suffragettes, changed very much in the 1920s.

Later heroines of Heyer usually had more spirit. A woman such as Judith Taverner in *Regency Buck* felt the restrictions which hedged her to protect her "virtue" were unfair because of what Rosalind Brunt in her article "A Career in Love" (C. Pawling, *Popular Fiction and Social Change* [1984]) has called "the double standard iniquities of 'innocence' for her and 'experience' for him." One incident provides an illustration. Judith, out walking near Grantham on the day of a race meeting, and having stopped to shake a stone from her shoe, is accosted and kissed by the Earl of Worth; later, as her guardian, he warns her against such immodest behavior (as showing a naked foot!) which could lead to sexual harassment. The heroine is indignant both at the way she, the victim, is made into the guilty party, *and* at the assumption of superiority on the part of the transgressor. This kind of reaction was frequent in Heyer's heroines: the motif established the idea of restrictions on *women* by both men and women which were imposed for *male* purposes and made necessary by *male* behavior—and this was clearly presented as unfair.

Nevertheless, Heyer's heroines were less independent than their sense of justice might suggest. They might be aware of the inequality of a patriarchal society, but were none the less represented as pure and innocent as much as heroines of earlier romance. This was probably because Heyer's readers accepted the stereotype and could not sympathise with a heroine they felt to be immoral—and Heyer shared this attitude.

Heyer had to solve the problem of creating a heroine who was aware of the inequalities of a patriarchal society and capable of resenting them, while at the same time showing her as conforming to the feminine stereotype which belonged to such a society. One way in which she solved this can be seen in *Regency Buck*. In this novel, the climax is a curricle race involving Judith and one of her (male) admirers. The Earl of Worth, who allows himself such latitude of behavior with chance-met girls in Grantham, confronts her as she waits for a change of horses at an inn and upbraids her for her immodesty. Judith experiences a moment of moral illumination in which she understands clearly how right Worth is in his criticism: it is presented as the kind of illumination that Jane Austen's heroines experience in novels such as *Pride and Prejudice* and *Emma*. The use of Austen as a model helped to validate the morality, which may have been presented as an attitude of Regency England, but which also had a seductive attraction in the twentieth century.

However much Worth may have humiliated her, Judith wins the sexual contest between herself and Worth in a way. When she needs help because her family is in danger, Worth rushes to provide it because he realises her value to him—finally, in a sense, brought to his knees. In *Loving With a Vengeance*, Tanya Modleski saw this kind of outcome in a romance as a revenge fantasy: the woman may be subordinate, and indeed brutally treated by the hero, but in the final analysis he needs her. Heyer's novels suggest that this point of view contains some justification; her heroines are presented as victims in an unfair society, but at the same time possessing a special kind of power.

Heyer's characters and situations did produce reading attractive to women. Modleski pointed out that her formula of hero and heroine could be found in earlier novels (she instanced Darcy and Elizabeth in *Pride and Prejudice* and Rochester and Jane in *Jane Eyre*) but it was Heyer who made the relationship into a formula. She was in fact largely forced into doing so, because whenever she tried to write a different kind of novel she lost sales so drastically that she was no longer able to pay her tax bills.

Hence other writers followed suit—and this is especially true of those who wrote for Mills & Boon. Today the publishing house has developed different lines, including ones which are much more explicit than traditional romances in depicting female sexual behavior. But a brief glance at *The Briar Rose*, by Dinah Dean, published in 1986, shows a familiar situation. Kate, the heroine, is shown as discontented with the narrowness of her life, spent in looking after her father who is the bailiff of Waltham Abbey. Nonetheless, when the hero comes to inspect and close the monastery by Thomas Cromwell's orders, she resents his power to disrupt her life. Her sharpness to him earns her the name of "briar rose." But when he is ambushed by an enemy and she saves his life, he comes to value her. In turn, she comes to love him when he is wounded

517

and she has to look after him. The love which grows between a wounded hero and the girl who cares for him is one of the commonest in romance. It is there in Tennyson's *The Princess*, and it is common in Weyman's novels—the flighty court lady who is such a trial to *A Gentleman of France*, for instance, changes altogether when she has to nurse the hero through an attack of the plague. It is a motif which, in Ian Fleming's work, Tony Bennett and Janet Woollacott have noted as symbolic of a kind of phallic castration of the hero (*Bond and Beyond: The Political Career of a Popular Hero* [1987]). The heroine retains her femininity in her caring role, but gains a kind of power because the hero realises how necessary she is to him—Modleski's view of the attraction of romance again. The caring role is shown as an instinctive reaction in an independent heroine: a reassurance, surely, that women may claim the freedom and status which is their right without forfeiting their "natural" function. The feminine stereotype is adapted to a new age: *The Briar Rose* ends with Kate content, returned to her home, which the hero has been granted by Cromwell as a reward for his services, still as its mistress, but subject to a new male. The relationships of traditional historical romance still have their attractive power, it seems.

It is an adaptation which can be seen as beginning with the novels of Georgette Heyer. Only a few years after Virginia Woolf had begun to promote the virtues of "androgyny," one can see in the hero and heroine of *These Old Shades*—Leonie the masculine child-woman and Avon the "motherly" roue hero—a kind of androgyny adapted for romance. It turns out to be only a dream, and female subservience is firmly reinforced. The denouement is flattering enough to women readers to offer its own pleasure. Nonetheless, the more critical subtext remains to be read, for those who care to read it.

# VI. *Dramatizations, Including Reviews*

## *Merely Murder*

A comedy in three acts by A. E. Thomas, based on Georgette Heyer's novel of the same name. Settings by Watson Barratt; staged by Miriam Doyle; produced by Laurence Rivers, Inc. (Rowland Stebbins), at the Playhouse, New York, November 1937.

[According to one source, a typescript of the play may be found in the Billy Rose Collection at the Library of Performing Arts at Lincoln Center.]

### Cast:

Kenneth Vereker. . . . . . . . . . . .Rex O'Malley
Violet Williams. . . . . . . . . Muriel Hutchison
Rudolph Mesurier. . . . . . . . Stiano Braggiotti
Murgatroyd. . . . . . . . . Jessamine Newcombe
Leslie Rivers. . . . . . . . . . . . . . .Betty Jenckes
Tony (Antonia) Vereker. . . . . Claudia Morgan
Inspector Hannasyde. . . . . . . Edward Fielding
Giles Carrington. . . . . . . . . .George Macready
Harry Chippendale. . . . . . . Lawrence Fletcher
Sergeant Armstrong. . . . . . . Charles Campbell

519

**Review:**

**Brooks Atkinson, a review of the play *Merely Murder*, in *The New York Times*, 4 December 1937, p. 21:**

People who can read say that *Merely Murder* was a gay little homicide in Georgette Heyer's crime novel. People who go to the theatre are likely to find it politely debilitating in the comedy written by A. E. Thomas that was presented at the Playhouse last evening. For it is a difficult thing to spin three acts of silken dialogue out of the mere rumor of a murder without driving the audience farther and farther down in its seats. Probably the nimble-tongued characters in this Scotland Yard hocus-pocus are not too phlegmatic to contemplate at one long sitting. But for some reason, which cannot be the actors' fault exclusively, they seem so, and they also fatigue a body remarkably.

The idea is to take a murder with an Oscar Wilde show of verbal pyrotechnics. Although Kenneth Vereker, artist, and his sister, tramp, are both under suspicion of having murdered a step-brother and moved into a fabulous inheritance, they match Scotland Yard's wits with their own witticisms, annoying the police considerably without pleasing the audience very much. When another step-brother is murdered they become a little more serious, even quoting from *Hamlet* when the culprit is unmasked. But the whole business has a feeling of dramatic insecurity and aimlessness. When a murder is to be discussed in the theatre it is a good thing to have a look at the corpse either before or after he got that way.

Probably Booth and Duse could not have played the leading parts without causing some unrest in the audience. Rex O'Malley and Claudia Morgan are not much better. Their associate actors have even less sparkle to work with, and Miriam Doyle has not sheltered them behind inventive direction. Although Watson Barratt has provided an attractive scene design in which some fun might be had on a more ebullient occasion, *Merely Murder* carries the supercilious manner to the verge of nothingness. It all goes to show that one should learn to read and stay home with a clever crime book occasionally.

## *The Reluctant Widow*

**Screenplay by Gordon Wellesley and J. B. Boothroyd; directed by Bernard Knowles; score by Allan Gray; produced by Mr. Wellesley for Two Cities Films; released by Fine Arts Films, Inc., September 1951; running time, 86 min.**

### Cast:

| | |
|---|---|
| Elinor. . . . . . . . . . . . . . . . . . | .Jean Kent |
| Lord Carlyon. . . . . . . . . . . . . | .Guy Rolfe |
| Mme. de Chevreaux. . . . | Kathleen Byron |
| Louis Nivelle. . . . . . . . . . . . | .Paul Dupuis |
| Becky. . . . . . . . . . . . . . . . . | Lana Morris |
| Francis Cheviot. . . . . . . . . | Julian Dallas |
| Nicky. . . . . . . . . . . . . | Anthony Tancred |
| Eustace Cheviot. . . . . . . | Peter Hammond |
| Mrs. Barrows. . . . . . . . . . . . | Jean Cadell |
| Lord Bedlington. . . . | Andrew Cruikshank |

### Reviews:

**Bosley Crowther in *The New York Times*, 8 September 1951, p. 8:**

There is, indeed, a justification for the frankly proclaimed attitude of the leading lady in *The Reluctant Widow*, which came to the Trans-Lux Sixtieth Street yesterday. The lady is in a pickle—as well as in a very poor film, which happens to have been made in Britain with a generally unfamiliar cast.

The pickle in which the young lady finds herself is this: she is plopped into the middle of an eighteenth century spy plot through the odd chance of marrying a strange and dying man. All sorts of in-law relations come flapping and fluttering around, foremost of whom is the handsome cousin of her late departed spouse. And before the plot is unthickened and the stolen dispatches for the Duke of Wellington have been found, the lady has been married to this cousin and everyone—including the audience—has been confused.

There is no point in even beginning to try to unravel the plot. It is a wholly unfathomable tangle of family bickerings, boudoir blandishments and duels, all in a painfully pompous and slumberously static vein. Jean Kent plays the baffled widow as though she were ill most of the time, and Guy Rolfe, Paul Dupuis and Julian Dallas circulate ponderously.

Except for the rather fine surroundings and some nice eighteenth century costumes, there is no more in *The Reluctant Widow* than a genteel invitation to doze.

**Herm. in *Variety*, 5 September 1951, "*The Reluctant Widow*: Minor British-made espionage meller with poor b.o. potential."**

*The Reluctant Widow*, a British-made costumed espionage meller set in the Napoleonic era, is a poor item with weak prospects in the U.S. market. Initially handicapped by a minor troupe of thespers unknown in this country, pic is completely floored by a confusing yarn made even more confusing by a choppy editing job.

Pic was apparently intended as a farce, but the script fails to sustain any comic mood. The film quickly gets lost in a maze of complications amateurishly strung together and lacking real point.

Yarn revolves around a young British governess who accidentally falls heir to a home which is a hangout for French spies and British traitors. They are looking for a plan of Wellington's military strategy, but the gal foils them by finding the papers first.

Performances are fair. Jean Kent, as the heroine, plays competently, while Guy Rolfe, as the hero, is a bit wooden. Film's standout is Julian Dallas who, as the dandified British traitor, plays with suave finesse. (Dallas is currently under contract to Warner Bros. under the name of Scott Forbes). Kathleen Byron, as a French femme fatale, is badly miscast and wholly unconvincing. Rest of the minor roles, however, are adequately filled.

# The Talisman Ring

**Adapted by Christina Calvit; directed by Dorothy Milne; presented by Lifeline Theatre, Chicago, IL; opening night, June 12, 1996.**

### Cast:

Tristram. . . . . . . . . . . . . Peter Greenberg
Eustacie. . . . . . . . . . . . . . . .Krista Lally
Basil/Peabody. . . . . . . . . . . . . .Ric Kraus
Ludovic. . . . . . . . . . . . . . . .Ned Mochel
Sarah. . . . . . . . . . . . . .Elizabeth Laidlaw
Nye/Gregg/Stranger. . . . . . . . . Paul Myers
Sylvester/Hugh/Abel. . . . . . . John Neisler
Stubbs/Butlers/Exciseman. .Patrick Blashill

### Reviews:

**Mary Houlihan-Skilton, "*Talisman* brims with wit, heart," (in "Arts & Show," *Chicago Sun-Times*, 25 July 1996).**

Historical romances are more often than not dismissed as "trash." But this enduring genre, awash with an aura of mystery and adventure, embodies harmless escapism in its finest form.

Lifeline Theatre's production of *The Talisman Ring*, based on an out-of-print novel by romance maven Georgette Heyer, also prompts the possibility of being dismissed as "trash" theater. That would be a mistake.

Lifeline gives surprising new heart to the genre with its witty and lively rendition of Heyer's swashbuckling story. Don't get me wrong. *The Talisman Ring* is still lofty escapism, but in the process, the audience gets to enjoy two hours of great fun.

The setting is 18th century England, and sparks are in the air as wide-eyed, sometimes silly Eustacie makes plans to fulfill her romantic visions of adventure. An opinionated French maid, she is betrothed to the stalwart and righteous Tristram, whose biggest problem, as far as

Eustacie is concerned, is his "lack of sensibility and romance." (Luckily, neither takes the marriage situation very seriously, and each is allowed a refreshing sense of humor about the future.)

The mystery arrives in the form of their cousin, Ludovic, who has been on the run since he was accused of killing a man two years earlier. Now he has returned in hopes of clearing his name and inheriting his late father's estate, which is about to go to his conniving brother, Basil.

Foppish in fussy brocades and sumptuous velvets, Basil has plans of his own—plans that involve Eustacie and anyone trifling with *his* inheritance.

As Eustacie and Tristram plot to clear Ludovic, two travelers staying at the local inn, Sarah and her brother Hugh, are drawn into the fun. In the clever and observant Sarah (a character right out of Jane Austen), Eustacie finds a confidante and Tristram finds his match and a reawakened sense of romance.

In the end, the whodunit plot and romantic esccapades are predictable, but thanks to the talents of adapter Christina Calvit and director Dorothy Milne, *The Talisman Ring* is enlivened by slyly humorous (and sometimes biting) dialogue and the actors' comedic timing.

Casting just the right tone are Peter Greenberg as Tristram, Krista Lally as Eustacie, Ric Kraus as Basil, Ned Mochel as Ludovic and Elizabeth Laidlaw as Sarah. As Basil's flamboyant co-conspirator, Paul Myers steals every scene he glides into.

Set designer Alan Donahue's splendid job of styling the tight space with mahogany paneling, brocade drapes and a clever moveable staircase skillfully adds to the story's momentum. Donna M. Kress' lovely and sumptuous costumes fit each character's disposition perfectly.

**Jack Helbig, *The Talisman Ring* (in "Stage," *New City*, Vol. 11, No. 421 [27 June 1996]):**

Other theatre companies and artists may get more press for their adaptations, but few Chicago theatres have produced as many good-to-great ones over the years as Lifeline. And this seasoning shows in the masterful way Lifeline artistic associate Christina Calvit adapted Georgette Heyer's witty 1936 tongue-in-cheek gothic novel, *The Talisman Ring*. Calvit's spot-on script embodies all of the strengths of her fine version of Austen's *Pride and Prejudice* and avoids all the excesses of her less-successful version of Thackeray's *Vanity Fair*. Director Dorothy Milne—another Lifeline veteran—deserves lots of credit for her sensitive, intelligent translation of Calvit's words to the stage. Her casting is flawless—Krista Lally in particular makes a wonderful if somewhat whiny romantic heroine—and her pacing of this sometimes funny, sometimes suspenseful story—about a man wrongly accused of murder—is perfect. Best of all, Milne's cast of Chicago stalwarts handles Heyer's comedy deftly with just the right amount of restraint—not so much that the fun is spoiled, and not so little that the humor is lost in all the over-the-top nonsense. At a time when so many shows feel too long—even the one-acts—it's a real treat to catch a full-length play that leaves an audience wanting more.

**Mary Shen Barnidge, *The Talisman Ring* (in "Theater," *Chicago Reader*, 5 July 1996):**

Georgette Heyer has been called the "20th-century Jane Austen," her intelligent humor and unsentimentality distinguishing her popular novels from those of the many copycat authors of Regency romances. Adapting *The Talisman Ring*'s intricate plot, larger-than-life characters, and lofty language would be a daunting task even without hordes of Heyer devotees prepared to pounce on the slightest page-to-stage distortion. But Christina Calvit pulls it off, making Heyer's frivolous tale of two ladies bent on adventure, no matter how many innocent bystanders must be enlisted, an effervescent romp from beginning to end.

The cast—led by Elizabeth Laidlaw and Krista Lally as the resourceful heroines, Peter Greenberg and Ned Mochel as their reluctant swains, and Ric Kraus as the sinister (and atrociously attired) villain—leap from poker-faced formality to madcap impetuosity, while immersing themselves so completely in the play's period that a pair of lovers sharing an innocent kiss seems downright shocking.

## *Cotillion*

**Adapted by Christina Calvit; directed by Dorothy Milne; presented by Lifeline Theatre in Chicago, IL, opening in July, 1998.**

**Cast:**

Dolphinton. . . . . . . . . . . . . . . . . . . . . Peter Greenberg
Mr. Penicuik/Sir Henry Gosform. . . . . . . Shelton Key
Reverend Hugh Rattray/Camille/Finglass. . . Steve Key
Miss Fishguard/Olivia. . . . . . . . . . . . . . . Krista Lally
Freddy Standen. . . . . . . . . . . . . . . . . . . .John Neisler
Lady Ledgerwood/Mrs. Broughty/Hannah Plymstock
. . . . . . . . . . . .Katharine Spellman
Lord Biddenden/Lord Ledgerwood. . .Danne W. Taylor
Meg/Lady Buckhaven. . . . . . . . . . . . . . Kendra Thulin
Kitty Charing. . . . . . . . . . . . . . . . . . . . . Jenifer Tyler
Jack Westruther/Pluckley. . . . . . . . . . .Kelly Van Kirk

**Reviews:**

**Lawrence Bommer, "*Cotillion*" (in *Chicago Reader*, 26 June 1998):**

Playwright Christina Calvit again adapts historical-romance writer Georgette Heyer for the stage; Calvit dramatized *The Talisman Ring* in 1996. Set in Regency England, *Cotillion* is a likable Austen clone celebrating the pluck and resourcefulness of Kitty Charing. The poor ward of a mean guardian who will disinherit her if she doesn't marry one of her cousins, she induces her good-hearted cousin Freddy to proffer a pretend proposal, thereby exchanging her country captivity for a month in the capital. Under Freddy's increasingly sensible guidance, Kitty embarks on various matchmaking adventures, learning to distinguish Mr.

526

Right from Lord Wrong. Amid the swirl of cotillions and soirees, she encounters unexpected worth and hard-earned swinishness. Fortunately, the outcome is not predictable: Kitty's true love, proven by adversity, arrives with none of the inevitability of romance.

Particularly in the potboiling second act, Calvit can't quite tame the novel's prolix plot. But she does provide intriguing situations and colorful characters, depicted broadly if not deeply in Dorothy Milne's knowing staging and garbed in Regency elegance by Kim Fencl Rak. Jennifer Tyler's wary Kitty is a study in demure determination, steering a courageous course through the gauntlet of cousins. The other characters are broad-brush caricatures by contrast; notable are John Neisler's kindly twit, Steve Key's French adventurer, Kelly Van Kirk's rotten rake, Kendra Thulin's merry minx, and Krista Lally's charming chatterbox.

## Anne Libera, for *The Roy Leonard Show*, 21 June 1998:

*Cotillion*, now playing at the Lifeline Theatre on Chicago's north side, is an adaptation of a novel by Georgette Heyer, queen of the Regency romance. The plot of *Cotillion* concerns young Kitty, an orphan forced to choose one of her adoptive cousins as husband or be left penniless. She hatches a scheme to hold the suitors at bay for a while which takes her to London where scheme and plan piles on top of scheme and plan until the glorious and complicated resolution in which the evil are vanquished and the good get married to the right person at last.

While there is no denying that *Cotillion* is a frothy piece of escapism, it is also really terrific storytelling. I can't remember the last time I walked out of a theatre at intermission so excited to find out what happens next. In addition, the acting is fine across the boards and the staging, by Dorothy Milne makes good use of a number of curtains and a few inventive stage pieces to create locations all over London and the surrounding countryside.

With inexpensive tickets available for students and seniors, *Cotillion* makes an ideal night out with a romantic teenager or your great aunt who takes her tea with a little lemon.

527

**Lucia Mauro, "*Cotillion*" (in "Showcase: Reviews," *Chicago Sun-Times*, 19 June 1998):**

Recommended.

An air of pastel-colored whimsy may pervade Georgette Heyer's novel, *Cotillion*, as her characters traipse through parties and devise matchmaking schemes in early 19th century English society. Yet the contemporary British author could never be accused of concocting fluff.

Frequently compared to Jane Austen, the late Heyer knew how to balance ridiculous situations against firmly grounded heroines who resolve to inspire others to become better human beings.

Christina Calvit's adaptation of *Cotillion* for Lifeline Theatre preserves Heyer's preposterous witticisms without undermining her characters. In Lifeline's fanciful staging, directed by Dorothy Milne, heartfelt truths emerge from the farcical goings-on.

When Kitty Charing's cranky adoptive father alters his will so that she must marry one of her cousins or be left destitute, the bright girl determines a way to escape her predicament. Kitty thinks she is in love with her rakish cousin, Jack, who refuses to propose to her. So she persuades her slightly daffy cousin, Freddy, to agree to a false engagement so that she might travel with him to London, where Jack lives.

Once in London, Kitty finds herself caught up in other couples' desperate affairs. She tries to save her dim-witted cousin, Dolphinton, from his domineering mother by uniting him with the commoner he loves. She also rescues her friend Olivia from marrying a wealthy old man by introducing her to the passionate Camille. Through her good-spirited meddling, Kitty discovers that Jack is really a deceitful cad, while Freddy remains loyal and true.

Although parts of the second act tend to move along clumsily, overall Lifeline pulls off Heyer's dry satire with aplomb. Milne may play up the script's caricaturized tone, but she never succumbs to hysterics.

The cast offers playful and frank portrayals. Jenifer Tyler as Kitty totters delightfully between resourceful rancor and befuddled innocence. John Neisler's foppish Freddy grows into a decisive force.

Steve Key convinces in outrageously disparate roles. Audiences will joyously sympathize with the honesty Peter Greenberg brings to the mentally challenged Dolphinton. Only Shelton Key as Kitty's curmudgeonly father delivers a tentative portrayal.

**Mary Shen Barnidge, "Regency Romp" (in *Windy City Times*, 9 July 1998):**

The period covered in the Regency Romance is a remarkably narrow one chronologically (the invalid George III's frivolous son reigned as Prince Regent from 1811 to 1820, only), geographically (characters are mostly English, with an occasional European introduced for a touch of exoticism) and socially (plots invariably revolve around the fashionable nobility, with serious matters—the recent revolution in France, for example, or Napoleon's subsequent attempts to conquer the world—existing only as domestic inconveniences). What inspired such an extensive body of popular literature, however, was the giddy flush of freedom engendered by a suddenly unstable universe in which it seemed Anything Could Happen and All Things Were Possible.

Georgette Heyer's attention to historical detail and sensitivity to her milieu's psychological profile places her nearer the genre's founder, Jane Austen, than to the hundreds of imitators who clutter the bookstore shelves. And Christina Calvit's adaptation of *Cotillion* retains not only the novel's motifs—fashionable clothes, fast carriages and much forbidden flirting—but hints of more substantial matters in its tale of three pairs of lovers thwarted in their happiness by families clinging to rigid rules of conduct with all the stubbornness of elitists who sense their imminent extinction. Kitty Charing's guardian demands that she marry one of his good-for-nothing nephews or be disinherited. The dominating mother of Foster, Earl of Dolphinton, threatens him to have him declared insane if he marries the commoner he loves. And Olivia Broughty's social-climbing mama would rather have her offspring be mistress to a titled playboy than the wife of a bourgeois businessman. How all these obstacles are circumvented provides not only screwball comedy in abundance, but firm reaffirmation of Love's triumph over the false orderliness of a superficial universe.

The cast assembled for this Lifeline production—all but three of whom play multiple roles—spring through their costume and identity changes with finely-honed agility (though Steve Key, playing the stuffy Reverend Hugh Rattray and the dashing Monsieur Camille, slips a bit during the fast-and-furious finish).

In the role of Kitty, Jenifer Tyler's agent provocateur duties keep her too busy to develop much of a personality for her character, but John Neisler and Peter Greenberg—as Freddy Standen and Lord Dolphinton, respectively, two wimpish men spurred by Cupid to discover unsuspected resources within themselves—surround her with sufficient activity to make this negligible. Likewise sprightly performances are forthcoming from Krista Lally as the impetuous Olivia, Kelly Van Kirk as the cynical Jack Westruther and Katherine Spellman as the nannyish Hanna Plymstock. Under the nimbly-paced direction of Dorothy Milne, assisted by Kim Fencl Rak's luscious wardrobe and Rebecca Hamlin's protean set (which includes a delightfully ingenious carriage-and-four), *Cotillion* generates a merry dance to please the most scholarly Heyer devotee.

**Kathleen Tobin, *"Cotillion"* (in "Chicago Alive," *The Beverly Review*, 19 August 1998):**

Georgette Heyer—a prolific, 20th-century English novelist (she had 51 titles in print)—romanticized the social mores of 19th-century England with historical accuracy, much attention to detail and a great deal of humor. Though not as well known as Jane Austen, Heyer has often been called her 20th-century clone.

Lifeline Theatre, celebrating its 15th anniversary, is staging one of Heyer's popular works, *Cotillion*, with a cleverly concocted adaptation by Christina Calvit. It is a delightful production, charmingly realized under Dorothy Milne's deft direction.

Calvit received a Jeff Award for the 1996 adaptation of another Heyer gem, *The Talisman Ring*, at Lifeline with Milne also in the director's chair.  And the two have scored another richly textured tapestry with *Cotillion*.  In it, Heyer's heady witticisms lose none of their punch, and her characters remain true to the author's insightful balance of satiric farce with genuine emotion.

It is 1810.  The heroine, Kitty Charing, is a poor ward of an eccentric uncle who keeps her secluded on his country estate.

Charing has just learned that she will be disinherited unless she chooses a husband from among the uncle's four eligible nephews.  The choices are the dim-witted Dolph, the squeamish preacher Hugh, the foppish Freddy and the rakish Jack.

She has always been fond of the dashing Jack, but his narcissistic attitude doesn't allow him to leave his London haunts for the country to propose to Kitty.  In desperation, the quick-witted girl convinces the kind-hearted Freddy to fake an engagement.

Freddy's mother lives in London, and she will provide the excuse for Kitty to spend a month there.  Her protective uncle will be placated, and Kitty will be free to sow some of her own oats among London society.

She pairs up with Meg, Freddy's sister, and enters into the cosmopolitan whirl of London cotillions and soirees.  She plays matchmaker for the mother-dominated Dolph and the sincere commoner who would marry him.

She rescues Olivia, a young lady she takes a liking to, from her mother's plans for Olivia to marry a rich old man.  She saves her from Jack's dishonorable intentions and arranges for her to elope with Camille, her French cousin, who comes to London to find a rich wife but finds instead Olivia, his true love.

As for Kitty, her own true love comes from an unexpected source!  But that's for you to discover.  A strong cast and gorgeous period costumes make *Cotillion* a fulfilling delight.

Jenifer Tyler as Kitty changes beautifully from the plain country girl to a society lady.  Peter Greenberg is a richly earnest Dolph.

Steve Kay is comic extravagance as Hugh and Camille.  John Neisler steps right out P. G. Wodehouse's "Jeeves" caricatures with a priceless Freddy.  Kendra Thulin shines as Meg/Lady Buckhaven, with Krista Lally as the pretty Olivia.

**Rob Thomas, "Spry romance. Lifeline ends season with light, witty show" (in "Sidetracks," *The Northwest Herald*, 10 July 1998):**

After some fairly heady productions drawing from classic Russian literature and contemporary Native American life, Chicago's Lifeline Theatre is closing out the season on a lighter note.

The latest offering, *Cotillion,* is a spry romance whose comedic tone and elegant staging make it a welcome antidote for a hot summer night.

Set in England's Regency period, *Cotillion* is a comedy of manners sure to appeal to the Jane Austen set. The 20th century novel by Georgette Meyer [sic] has been adapted to the stage by Christina Calvit and director Dorothy Milne.

Like an Austen novel, *Cotillion* requires its young heroine to use her wits and charm to navigate a labyrinth of social mores until she finds real love.

Kitty (Jenifer Tyler) is told by her adopted father that she must marry one of her four cousins, or be cut out of her inheritance. The reason behind this demand is not clear, except that her father is a real jerk.

For varying reasons, none of her four cousins suits her. So Kitty schemes with cousin Freddy (John Neisler) to pretend to be engaged to her, so that she may keep her father's money and spend the month in London.

That engagement catches the eye of womanizer Jack (Kelly Van Kirk), for whom Kitty has always had a unexpressed crush. Before the play is over, Kitty and several other characters will end up with the right partners.

One of the pleasures of the play is watching how seemingly stock characters display unexpected shadings and humanity. This is especially true of Freddy, who comes across initially as something of a superficial dandy.

But Freddy becomes a remarkably likable and even heroic character by the end of the play, thanks especially to Neisler's funny, nuanced performance. Neisler's jutting chin alone qualifies him for the role, but the actor behind the chin is terrific at light comedy.

As Kitty, Tyler balances coquettish charm with fierce independence.

And as Jack, Van Kirk displays a wolfish, silken charm that reminded me of Ralph Fiennes.

A couple of the show's back-benchers don't meet the same standards as the main characters. Luckily, one of three central figures is in almost every scene, and their presence alone keeps the tone light and the pacing tight. . . .

# *Appendix A:*
# *Her books, chronologically*

The Black Moth (1921)
The Great Roxhythe (1922)
Instead of the Thorn (1923)
The Transformation of Philip
Jettan (1923, pseud. Stella Martin;
    (1930 as **Powder and Patch** under her
    own name)
Simon the Coldheart (1925)
These Old Shades (1926)
Helen (1928)
The Masqueraders (1928)
Beauvallet (1929)
Pastel (1929)
Barren Corn (1930)
The Conqueror (1931)
Devil's Cub (1932)
Footsteps in the Dark (1932)
Why Shoot a Butler? (1933)
The Unfinished Clue (1934)
The Convenient Marriage (1934)
Death in the Stocks (1935;
    **Merely Murder** in the U. S.)
Regency Buck (1935)
Behold, Here's Poison! (1936)
The Talisman Ring (1936)
They Found Him Dead (1937)
An Infamous Army (1937)
A Blunt Instrument (1938)
Royal Escape (1938)
No Wind of Blame (1939)
The Spanish Bride (1940)
The Corinthian (1940; **Beau
    Wyndham** in the U. S., 1941)
Envious Casca (1941)
Faro's Daughter (1941)
Penhallow (1942)
Friday's Child (1944)
The Reluctant Widow (1946)
The Foundling (1948)

Arabella (1949)
The Grand Sophy (1950)
Duplicate Death (1951)
The Quiet Gentleman (1951)
Cotillion (1953)
Detection Unlimited (1953)
The Toll-Gate (1954)
Bath Tangle (1955)
Sprig Muslin (1956)
April Lady (1957)
Sylvester; or, The Wicked Uncle
    (1957)
Venetia (1958)
The Unknown Ajax (1959)
Pistols for Two and Other Stories
    (1960)
A Civil Contract (1961)
The Nonesuch (1962)
False Colours (1963)
Frederica (1965)
Black Sheep (1966)
Cousin Kate (1968)
Charity Girl (1970)
Lady of Quality (1972)
My Lord John (1975, posth.)

## Appendix B:
### Her books, alphabetically

April Lady (1957)
Arabella (1949)
Barren Corn (1930)
Bath Tangle (1955)
Beauvallet (1929)
Behold Here's Poison (1936)
The Black Moth (1921)
Black Sheep (1966)
A Blunt Instrument (1938)
Charity Girl (1970)
A Civil Contract (1961)
The Conqueror (1931)
The Convenient Marriage (1934)
The Corinthian (1940; **Beau Wyndham** in the U.S., 1941)
Cotillion (1953)
Cousin Kate (1968)
Death in the Stocks (1935; **Merely Murder** in the U.S.)
Detection Unlimited (1953)
Devil's Cub (1932)
Duplicate Death (1951)
Envious Casca (1941)
False Colours (1963)
Faro's Daughter (1941)
Footsteps in the Dark (1932)
The Foundling (1948)
Frederica (1965)
Friday's Child (1944)
The Grand Sophy (1950)
The Great Roxhythe (1922)
Helen (1928)
An Infamous Army (1937)
Instead of the Thorn (1923)
Lady of Quality (1972)
The Masqueraders (1928)
My Lord John (1975, posth.)
No Wind of Blame (1939)
The Nonesuch (1962)

Pistols for Two and Other Stories (1960)
Powder and Patch (1923 [as The Transformation of Philip Jettan]; 1930)
The Quiet Gentleman (1951)
Regency Buck (1935)
The Reluctant Widow (1946)
Royal Escape (1938)
Simon the Coldheart (1925)
The Spanish Bride (1940)
Sprig Muslin (1956)
Sylvester; or The Wicked Uncle (1957)
The Talisman Ring (1936)
These Old Shades (1928)
They Found Him Dead (1937)
The Toll-Gate (1954)
The Unfinished Clue (1934)
The Unknown Ajax (1959)
Venetia (1958)
Why Shoot a Butler? (1933)

# *Index*

543